Organizations and Organizing

Rational, Natural, and Open System Perspectives

W. Richard Scott
Stanford University

Gerald F. Davis
University of Michigan

Upper Saddle River, New Jersey 07458

Library of Congress Cataloging-in-Publication Data

Scott, W. Richard.
  Organizations and organizing : rational, natural, and open systems
perspectives / W. Richard Scott, Gerald F. Davis.—1st ed.
     p. cm.
  Rev. of: Organizations / W. Richard Scott. 5th ed. 2003.
  Includes bibliographical references and index.
  ISBN 0-13-195893-3
  1. Organizational sociology.   I. Davis, Gerald F. (Gerald Fredrick), 1961–
II. Scott, W. Richard. Organizations.   III. Title.
  HM786.S3846 2007
  302.3'5—dc22

                                                                 2006025219

Editorial Director: Leah Jewell
Executive Editor: Jennifer Gilliland
Editorial Assistant: Lee Peterson
Executive Marketing Manager:
  Marissa Feliberty
Marketing Assistant: Irene Fraga
Production Liaison:
  Marianne Peters-Riordan
Manufacturing Buyer: Brian Mackey
Cover Art Director: Jayne Conte
Cover Design: Indigo Studio
Cover Illustration/Photo:
  Photodisc/Getty Images, Inc

Director, Image Resource Center:
  Melinda Patelli
Manager, Rights and Permissions:
  Zina Arabia
Manager, Visual Research: Beth Brenzel
Manager, Cover Visual Research &
  Permissions: Karen Sanatar
Composition/Full-Service Project
  Management: Nisha Jatin/Integra
  Software Services
Printer/Binder: R.R. Donnelley & Sons

Credits and acknowledgments borrowed from other sources and reproduced, with
permission, in this textbook appear on appropriate page within text.

Pearson Education LTD.
Pearson Education Singapore, Pte. Ltd
Pearson Education, Canada, Ltd
Pearson Education–Japan
Pearson Education Australia
  PTY, Limited

Pearson Education North Asia Ltd
Pearson Educación de Mexico,
  S.A. de C.V.
Pearson Education Malaysia, Pte. Ltd
Pearson Education, Upper Saddle
  River, New Jersey

10 9 8 7 6 5 4 3 2 1

ISBN 0-13-195893-3

Again, for
Jennifer, Elliot, and Sydney
And now for
Ben and Gracie

Contents

Preface

This volume is intended as a successor to Scott's earlier text, *Organizations: Rational, Natural and Open Systems,* first published in 1981 and undergoing four revisions—the fifth and last appearing in 2003. As the time approached to consider yet another edition, Scott approached Jerry Davis, a younger colleague but established scholar, to join him in the effort.

As we planned the work, we agreed it was important to retain the book's historical grounding as well as some sense of the progressive evolution of the field over time. The field of organization studies displays a distinctive pattern of past theoretical arguments and research approaches and findings that continues to frame current scholarship. In particular, we agreed that the original scaffolding, emphasizing the interrelation of three somewhat separate strands of work—rational, natural, and open system perspectives—retained its salience and relevance as an organizing device. Thus, the three foundation chapters—Chapters 2, 3, and 4—draw heavily from previous editions of the Scott text.

However, as we proceeded to examine developments in the field in the past decade, we found ourselves involved in extensive revisions, deleting large chunks of previous material and adding a substantial amount of new. The more we rethought, revised, and rewrote, the more we realized that, rather than simply update an existing text, we were engaged in producing a substantially new book—a book which incorporates the themes of its predecessor volume but takes them in new and different directions. The title *Organizations and Organizing* reflects this new emphasis on flexible forms of coordinated action taking place within, around, and among formal organizations.

Before noting these new directions, let us comment on the continuing features that, we believe, distinguish our own approach from other efforts to comprehend the field of organization studies. Some of these features follow.

- The book continues to be "introductory" without being "elementary." That is, we assume that readers do not necessarily have previous knowledge of this specific field, but that they are serious about their inquiry into the fundamentals of the study of organizations.
- We endeavor, to the extent possible, to provide a judicious and even-handed introduction to the multiple perspectives and modes of work that comprise the field. Critical commentaries are provided, but we try to offer these in an even-handed and constructive manner.
- We devote roughly equal time to describing changes in the "real world" of organizations and to changes in theories of organizations, emphasizing, wherever possible, their connections.
- Although we endeavor to be inclusive and interdisciplinary in our coverage, our bias continues to favor sociological and institutional approaches, and, with the addition of Davis, economic sociology network approaches, and managerial theory and research.
- And, while both of us deplore the micro–macro division that permeates our field, we devote most of our own efforts to reviewing the more macro developments.
- We recognize the benefits but also point to the problems posed for all who live in an organizational society. Organizations are not just about efficiency and productivity but also often exhibit pathology and produce inequity.
- Finally, we strive to include the full range of organizations, including voluntary and public as well as private firms, and to recognize the valid interests of the full range of affected parties, not simply managers and shareholders, but rank-and-file participants and publics.

Along with these continuities, the present volume offers a number of new features:

- In addition to surveying how organizations engage with their environments, we devote much attention to the many ways that environments of organizations are themselves becoming more highly organized—in organizational populations, fields, and networks.
- We emphasize the emergence of networks within, across, and among organizations, and describe both measures and methods of network analysis as well as recent research on network organizations.
- After describing the predominant paradigms for studying organizations, we survey how these are used to understand the links among strategy, structure, and organizational performance.
- We offer a broad survey of the changing modes of structuring organizations, from medieval guilds and early industrial organizations to contemporary postindustrial forms.
- In tandem with changes in organizational forms, theoretical conceptions of organizations and approaches to their study have also moved to encompass more attention to flexibility and process—*organizing vs. organizations*—and the use of dynamic relational models rather than to those portraying stable entities. Our final chapter assays new directions in organization studies that build on these shifts.

ACKNOWLEDGMENTS

Both of us are veterans in the field of organization studies, a field that is sufficiently new and relatively intimate that we count as friends or acquaintances most of the scholars on whose work we have relied. We indeed inhabit a "small world" with only one or two degrees of separation in our network of colleagues. Thus, it seems pointless for us to attempt to single out particular individuals to thank. However, we acknowledge the assistance of Amanda Sharkey, doctoral student at Stanford, who helped us in updating data for several chapters.

We also wish to recognize the contributions made to our work and the quality of our intellectual lives by the faculty and graduate students of the two university communities within which we have labored throughout the past years. Both Stanford University and the University of Michigan are blest with an abundance of insightful and productive organizational scholars who have come together in collegial communities to share ideas and insights. For many years, at Stanford, this community was coordinated by a Research Training Program on Organizations under the auspices of the National Institute of Mental Health (NIMH). During the 1990s, the Stanford Center for Organizations Research (SCOR) provided both support and leadership for this effort. At Michigan, the Interdisciplinary Committee on Organizational Studies (ICOS) has performed, and continues to carry on, a similar role. These organizations have helped to overcome some of the centrifugal forces at work to undermine the unity of our field.

The senior (in age) author asserts the privilege of publicly thanking his coauthor. As an experienced collaborator across many research and writing projects, I knew that this augmentation of staff would not reduce the workload involved—indeed, if anything, it was increased. However, the costs of coordination were more than repaid in the fun and intellectual excitement of working with Jerry. More important, his contributions have, I believe, brought about a substantial increase in the quality of the product.

Finally, I acknowledge once again the love and forbearance offered by my wife, Joy, who allows me to disappear into my office for hours at a time emerging only to refill my coffee cup. Our own collaboration passed its fiftieth anniversary milestone last year.

The junior author also thanks his wise senior colleague for inviting him to join in this endeavor. Twenty years after taking Dick's class at Stanford and poring over the first edition of *Organizations,* I felt like a window washer at the cathedral at Chartres in working on its successor volume. It's been a fun adventure, and I hope the rose window is still intact. I want to thank the Ross School of Business at the University of Michigan for sabbatical support to write this. I also thank Christie Brown for all the other forms of support that made this work both possible and thrilling.

CHAPTER 1

The Subject Is Organizations; The Verb is Organizing

> The recurrent problem in sociology is to conceive of corporate organization, and to study it, in ways that do not anthropomorphize it and do not reduce it to the behavior of individuals or of human aggregates.
>
> GUY E. SWANSON (1976)

Organizations play a leading role in our modern world. Their presence affects—some would insist that the proper term is *infects*—virtually every sector of contemporary social life. This book is about organizations—what they are and what they do, how they have changed, and how people have thought about them and studied them.

One theme of the book is commonality. Organizations share certain features that differentiate them from other social forms. Students of this field believe that we can understand much about a specific organization from knowing about other organizations. Understanding how a factory functions can illuminate the workings of a hospital; and knowledge of a software company can help us understand the workings of a prison. A second theme is diversity. Although organizations may possess common, generic characteristics, they exhibit staggering variety—in size, in structure, and in operating processes. What kinds of organizations exist also varies over time. Just as organizations vary, so do those who study them. Students of organizations bring to their task varying interests, tools, and intellectual preconceptions. Some study individuals and groups in organizational contexts, while others examine organizations as basic units in themselves. Still others see the character of a nation's organizations as providing insights into its overall social structure. And some scholars focus primarily on the structural attributes of organizations, whereas others emphasize the processes that reproduce and change them.

In this chapter we introduce three influential perspectives as competing definitions of organizations. We have our first encounter with rational, natural, and open system conceptions. The subsequent three chapters are devoted to an intensive examination of these perspectives, which have shaped and continue to govern our understanding of organizations.

THE IMPORTANCE OF ORGANIZATIONS

Ubiquity

Organizations are perhaps the dominant characteristic of modern societies. Organizations were present in older civilizations—Chinese, Greek, Indian—but only in modern industrialized societies do we find large numbers of organizations performing virtually every task a society needs in order to function. To the ancient organizational assignments of soldiering, public administration, and tax collection have been added such varied tasks as discovery (research organizations); child and adult socialization (schools and universities); resocialization (mental hospitals and prisons); production and distribution of goods (industrial firms, wholesale and retail establishments); provision of services (organizations dispensing assistance ranging from laundry and shoe repair to medical care and investment counseling); protection of personal and financial security (police departments, insurance firms, banking and trust companies); preservation of culture (museums, art galleries, universities, libraries); communication (radio and television studios, telephone companies, the U.S. Postal Service); and recreation (bowling alleys, pool halls, the National Park Service, professional football teams).

How many organizations are there, exactly? Until very recently, even highly "organized" societies such as the United States did not keep accurate records on organizations per se. We kept close watch of the numbers of individuals and the flow of dollars but gave less scrutiny to organizations. It was not until the 1980s that the U.S. Bureau of the Census launched a Standard Statistical Establishment List for all businesses, distinguishing between an *establishment*—an economic unit at a single location—and a *firm* or company—a business organization consisting of one or more domestic establishments under common ownership. In 2002, the U.S. Census Bureau reported the existence of 7.2 million establishments, comprising nearly 5.7 million firms. Impressive as these numbers are, they do not include public agencies or voluntary associations, which may be almost as numerous. Tax records suggest there are perhaps two million tax-exempt nonprofit organizations, of which upwards of 400,000 are sizable nonreligious organizations required to file with the IRS, including charities, foundations, political organizations, and other nongovernmental organizations (NGOs).

The first attempt to create a representative national survey of all employment settings in the United States was carried out during the early 1990s by a team of organizational researchers (Kalleberg et al., 1996). To conduct this "national organizations study," Kalleberg and associates developed an ingenious design to generate their sample. Because no complete census of organizations existed, they began by drawing a random sample of adults in the United States who were asked to identify their principal employers. As a second step, data were gathered by telephone, from informants in the organizations named as employers, regarding selected features of each of these employment settings, in particular, human resources practices. This procedure resulted in a random sample of employment organizations (establishments), weighted by size of organization (Kalleberg et al., 1996). Their results indicate that, as of 1991, 61 percent of respondents were employed in private sector establishments, 27 percent in the public sector, and 7 percent in the nonprofit sector (1996: 47).

Even though organizations are now ubiquitous, their development has been sufficiently gradual and uncontroversial so they have emerged during the past few centuries almost unnoticed. The spread of public bureaucracies into every arena and the displacement of the family business by the corporation "constitutes a revolution" in social structure, but one little remarked until recently.

> Never much agitated, never even much resisted, a revolution for which no flags were raised, it transformed our lives during those very decades in which, unmindful of what was happening, Americans and Europeans debated instead such issues as socialism, populism, free silver, clericalism, chartism, and colonialism. It now stands as a monument to discrepancy between what men think they are designing and the world they are in fact building. (Lindblom, 1977: 95)

Organizations in the form that we know them emerged during the seventeenth to eighteenth centuries in Europe and America, during the period of political and economic expansion occasioned by the Enlightenment period. Not only did organizations rapidly increase in number and range of applications, but they also underwent a transformation of structure as formerly "communal" forms based on the bonds of kinship and personal ties gave way to "associative" forms based on contractual arrangements among individuals having no ties other than a willingness to pursue shared interests or ends (Starr, 1982: 148).

Source of Social Ills?

The increasing prevalence of organizations in every arena of social life is one indicator of their importance. Another, rather different index of their significance is the increasing frequency with which organizations are singled out as the source of many of the ills besetting contemporary society. Thus, writing in 1956, C. Wright Mills pointed with alarm to the emergence of a "power elite" whose members occupied the top positions in three overlapping organizational hierarchies: the state bureaucracy, the military, and the larger corporations. At about the same time, Ralf Dahrendorf (1959 trans.) in Germany was engaged in revising and updating Marxist theory by insisting that the basis of the class structure was no longer the ownership of the means of production, but the occupancy of positions that allowed the wielding of organizational authority. Such views, which remain controversial, focus on the effects of organizations on societal stratification systems, taking account of the changing bases of power and prestige occasioned by the growth in number and size of organizations.

A related criticism concerns the seemingly inexorable growth in the power of public-sector organizations. The great German sociologists Max Weber (1968 trans.) and Robert Michels (1949 trans.) were among the first to insist that a central political issue confronting all modern societies was the enormous influence exercised by the (nonelected) public officials—the bureaucracy—over the ostensible political leaders. An administrative staff presumably designed to assist leaders in their governance functions too often becomes an independent branch with its own distinctive interests (Skocpol, 1985).

Other criticisms point to the negative consequences of the growth of organizations in virtually *every* area of social existence. Borrowing from and enlarging on a theme pervading the thought of Weber, these critics decry the rationalization of modern life—in Weber's phrase, the "disenchantment of the world" (1946 trans.: 51). Organizations are viewed as the primary vehicle by which, systematically, the areas of our lives are rationalized—planned, articulated, scientized, made more efficient and orderly, and managed by "experts." (See, for example, Mannheim, 1950 trans.; Ellul, 1964 trans.; Goodman, 1968; Galbraith, 1967; Ritzer, 1993; Schlosser, 2001).

A prosaic but powerful example is provided by the worldwide success of fast-food chains—the "McDonaldization of Society" (Ritzer, 1993)—which has rationalized food preparation, depersonalized employee–customer relations, and stimulated the growth of mass production techniques in agribusiness:

> The basic thinking behind fast food has become the operating system of today's retail economy, wiping out small businesses, obliterating regional differences, and spreading identical stores througout the country like a self-replicating code. America's main streets and malls now boast the same Pizza Huts and Taco Bells, Gaps and Banana Republics, Starbucks and Jiffy-Lubes, Foot Lockers, Snip N' Clips, Sunglass Huts, and Hobbytown USAs. Almost every facet of American life has now been franchised or chained. From the maternity ward at a Columbia/HCA hospital to an embalming room owned by Service Corporation International . . . a person can now go from the cradle to the grave without spending a nickel at an independently owned business. (Schlosser, 2001: 5)

These critics thus add their voices to others who have called attention to the ways in which organizational structures damage the personalities and psyches of their participants. Alienation, overconformity, and stunting of normal personality development are among the consequences attributed, not to such special cases as prisons and concentration camps, but to everyday, garden-variety organizations (see Argyris, 1957; Maslow, 1954; Whyte, 1956). And with the predominance of the service economy has come the increasing "commercialization of human feeling" in jobs such as flight attendant or salesperson, which require projecting a happy face regardless of one's true feelings (Hochschild, 1983)—or simulated hostility, in the case of bill collectors and criminal interrogators (Rafaeli and Sutton, 1991).

Large organizations have long been subject to criticism, either because they are alleged to be rule bound, cumbersome, and inefficient (Mises, 1944; Parkinson, 1957) or because they are believed to take advantage of their size and resulting power to exploit others. Perrow (1991) asserts that large organizations increasingly "absorb" society, internalizing functions better performed by communities and civic society. And critics such as Korten (2001) point with alarm to the increasing power of the multinational corporations as they search for cheap labor, despoil the environment, and disrupt the continuity of stable communities.

We attempt to evaluate such criticisms of organizations at appropriate points throughout this volume. Here we simply note that these wide-ranging accusations and concerns regarding the pervasive negative consequences of organizations provide further testimony to their importance in the modern world.

As Media

In addition to their being mechanisms for accomplishing a great variety of objectives and, perhaps as a necessary consequence, the source of many of our current difficulties, organizations have yet another important effect on our collective lives. This effect is more subtle and less widely recognized, but it may be the most profound in its implications. It is perhaps best introduced by an analogy: "The medium is the message." This twentieth-century aphorism was coined by Marshall McLuhan to focus attention on the characteristics of the mass media themselves—print, radio, movies, television—in contrast to the content transmitted by these media. McLuhan defines media very broadly as "any extension of ourselves"; elaborating his thesis, he notes, "The message of any medium is the change in scale or pace or pattern that it introduces into human affairs" (1964: 23, 24).

McLuhan's thesis appears to be more clearly applicable to our subject—organizations—than to any specific media of communication. First, like media, organizations represent extensions of ourselves. Organizations can achieve goals that are quite beyond the reach of any individual—from building skyscrapers and dams to putting a person on the moon. But to focus on what organizations do may conceal from us the more basic and far-reaching effects that occur because organizations are the mechanisms—the media—by which those goals are pursued. A few examples suggest some of these unanticipated and, often, unrecognized organizational effects.

- The Federal Aviation Administration (FAA) and the North American Aerospace Defense Command (NORAD) had developed protocols for working together in the case of a hijacking but failed to take into account a scenario in which the hijacked aircraft would not be readily identifiable, would not allow time to utilize appropriate chains of command within the two agencies, and would not take the traditional form of taking hostages to an alternative destination but convert the aircraft into a guided missile. (National Commission on Terrorist Attacks Upon the United States, 2003) The events of 9/11, 2001, provided a catastrophic exception.

- Although we seek "health" when we visit the clinic or the hospital, what we get is "medical care." Clients are encouraged to view these outputs as synonymous, although there may be no relation between them. In some cases, the relation can even be negative; more care can result in poorer health (Illich, 1976).

- While most of us believe schools are designed to increase the knowledge and skills of student participants, their major function may well be the indirect effects they have in preparing students to assume a compliant role in the organizational society: to learn how to be dependable employees (Bowles and Gintis, 1977).

- Organizations may exert only weak effects on the activities of their participants but still exert influence in situations because they embody and exemplify purposeful and responsible action. They depict rationality, enabling providers to offer an acceptable account of how resources were used and policies pursued (Meyer and Rowan, 1977).

To suggest that our organizational tools shape the products and services they produce in unanticipated ways and, in some cases, substitute "accounts" for outcomes indicates the quite substantial impact that organizations have on individual activity. However, even this expanded view does not reveal the full significance of these forms.

As Collective Actors

Organizations are not only contexts influencing the activities of individuals—they are actors in their own right. As *collective* actors, they can take actions, use resources, enter into contracts, and own property. Coleman (1974) describes how these rights have gradually developed since the Middle Ages to the point where now it is accurate to speak of two kinds of persons— *natural* persons (such as you and me) and *collective* or juristic persons (such as the Red Cross and General Motors).[1] In the United States, although the corporation is regarded as a legal fiction, it has many of the same rights as

---

[1]These developments were associated with and facilitated by changes in legal categories and codes (see Coleman 1974). Lawyers' practices also reflect the distinction in a revealing way, as described by Heinz and Laumann (1982). They point that that much of the variation in current legal practice is accounted for by

> one fundamental distinction—the distinction between lawyers who represent large organizations (corporations, labor unions, or government) and those who represent individuals. The two kinds of law practice are the two hemispheres of the profession. Most lawyers reside exclusively in one hemisphere or the other and seldom, if ever, cross over the equator. (1982: 379)

It is also instructive that layers who represent collective actors rather than natural persons are the more powerful, prosperous, and prestigious segment.

nonfictional human beings, including free speech and, in some cases, the right to bear arms. The social structure of the modern society can no longer be described accurately as consisting only of relations among natural persons; our understanding must be stretched to include as well those relations between natural and collective actors, and between two or more collective actors. In short, we must come to "the recognition that the society has changed over the past few centuries in the very structural elements of which it is composed" (Coleman, 1974: 13).

Theoretical Significance

To this point, we have assembled a variety of evidence and arguments to support the case that organizations merit attention. All of these claims relate to their social significance: their ubiquity, their impact on power and status, their effects on personality and performance. A different kind of rationale for justifying the study of organizations points to their sociological significance: the contribution their study can make to our understanding of the social world. Organizations provide the setting for a wide variety of basic social processes, such as socialization, communication, ranking, the formation of norms, the exercise of power, and goal setting and attainment. If these generic social processes operate in organizations, then we can add as much to our knowledge of the principles that govern their behavior by studying organizations as by studying any other specific type of social system. In general, all processes—communication, socialization, decision making— are more highly formalized in organizations. It is our belief that the study of organizations can contribute to basic sociological knowledge by increasing our understanding of how generic social processes operate within distinctive social structures.

Moreover, as detailed below, organizations themselves exist only as a complex set of social processes, some of which reproduce existing modes of behavior and others that serve to challenge, undermine, contradict, and transform current routines. Individual actors are constrained by, make use of, and modify existing structures. In *The Sociological Imagination,* C. Wright Mills (1959) described the role of the social scientist as making sense of the intersection of biography and history in social structure. When organizations are the characteristic structures in society, understanding how they operate can shed much light on the biographies of their participants. Consider social stratification—how equal (or unequal) is the distribution of wealth and income in society. The hiring, pay, and promotion policies of organizations can explain why some are paid tens of millions of dollars per year while others are unemployed, why some have health insurance and child care while others do not, why some achieve high executive positions while others hit a "glass ceiling." The Great Migration of African Americans from the rural South to the industrial North, beginning around the time of the First World War, was encouraged by the hiring policies of automakers and other manufacturers in

Detroit, Chicago, and elsewhere. The Civil Rights Movement and federal enforcement of equal employment opportunity statutes beginning in the 1960s facilitated advancement of people of color into higher level positions in business. And the presence of African Americans at top levels in organizations shapes those organizations' employment practices and their degree of engagement with social issues, such as the AIDS pandemic. Put another way, one cannot understand how social mobility happens in contemporary society *without* understanding the employment practices of organizations.

More broadly, contemporary history plays itself out in and through organizations. Economic development occurs through a combination of governmental policies (public organizations) and the actions of those that create and run private organizations. Multinational corporations and international nongovernmental organizations (INGOs), ranging from the World Bank to Friends of the River, increasingly determine the ways in which economic development and societal modernization is pursued. While historians continue to tell history through the biographies of so called great men and women, it may perhaps be more appropriate today to tell history through stories of interactions among its great (and not-so-great) organizations.

ORGANIZATIONS AS AN AREA OF STUDY

Emergence of the Area

The study of organizations is both a specialized field of inquiry within the discipline of sociology and an increasingly recognized focus of multidisciplinary research and training. It is impossible to determine with precision the moment of its appearance, but it is safe to conclude that until the late 1940s, organizations did not exist as a distinct field of social inquiry. Precursors may be identified, but each lacked some critical feature. Thus, there was some empirical research on organizations by criminologists who studied prisons (Clemmer, 1940), political analysts who examined party structures (Gosnell, 1937), and industrial sociologists who studied factories and labor unions (Whyte, 1946). But these investigators rarely attempted to generalize beyond the specific organizational forms they were studying. The subject was prisons or parties or factories or unions—not organizations. Similarly, in the neighboring disciplines, political scientists were examining the functioning of legislative bodies or public agencies, and economists were developing their theory of the firm, but they were not attempting to generalize beyond these specific forms.

Industrial psychologists did pursue such general problems as low morale, fatigue, and turnover within several types of organizational settings, but they did not attempt to determine systematically how the varying characteristics of different organizational contexts influenced these worker reactions. And although, from early in this century, administrative and management theorists such as Taylor (1911), Fayol (1949 trans.), and Gulick and Urwick (1937) concentrated on the development of general principles concerning administrative arrangements, their approach was more often prescriptive than empirical. That is, they were interested in determining what the proper form "should be" in the interests of maximizing efficiency and effectiveness rather than in examining and explaining organizational arrangements as they existed. They also focused primary attention on managerial activities and functions rather than on the wider subjects of organizations and organizing (Guillén, 1994).

It is possible to identify two important strands of work that came together to provide the foundations for organizational studies. Engineers played a central role early in attempting to rationalize approaches to work, attending to the design of both technical and administrative systems (Shenhav, 1999). This work stimulated a reactive response from a diverse collection of "human relations" scholars, principally social psychologists and sociologists, who emphasized the human and social features of organizations. Organization studies were founded on the "cleft rock" provided by joint consideration of technical, instrumental, rational emphases on the one hand and human, social, natural system emphases on the other (Scott 2004b; see also Chapters 2 and 3).

Within sociology, the emergence of the field of organizations may be roughly dated from the translation into English of Weber's (1946 trans.; 1947 trans.) and, to a lesser extent, Michels's (1949 trans.) analyses of bureaucracy. Shortly after these classic statements became accessible to American sociologists, Robert K. Merton and his students at Columbia University attempted to outline the boundaries of this new field of inquiry by compiling theoretical and empirical materials dealing with various aspects of organizations (Merton et al., 1952). Equally important, a series of pathbreaking and influential case studies of diverse types of organizations was launched under Merton's influence, including an examination of a federal agency—the Tennessee Valley Authority (Selznick, 1949)—a gypsum mine and factory (Gouldner, 1954), a state employment agency and a federal law-enforcement agency (Blau, 1955), and a union (Lipset, Trow, and Coleman, 1956). For the first time, sociologists were engaged in the development and empirical testing of generalizations dealing with the structure and functioning of organizations viewed as organizations.

At about the same time, an important interdisciplinary development was under way at the Carnegie Institute of Technology (now Carnegie Mellon University). Herbert Simon, a public administration scholar, became head of the Department of Industrial Management in 1949; assembled an eclectic group of political scientists, economists, engineers, and psychologists; and encouraged them to focus their energies on building a behaviorally oriented science of administration. Following Simon's lead, emphasis was placed on decision making and choice within organizations (Simon, 1997). The unrealistic assumption of a single, towering entrepreneur, rational and all-knowing, that dominated economic models of the firm was replaced first by the view of intendedly rational but cognitively limited actors (March and Simon, 1958), and subsequently by models emphasizing the multiple and competing objectives of participants in organizations (Cyert and March, 1963). Economic models of administrative behavior were modified and enriched by the insights of psychologists and political scientists.

These central and other related efforts gave rise to the identification of a new area of study—organizations, an area defined at a level of *theoretical abstraction* sufficiently general to call attention to similarities in form and function across different arenas of activity, and a subject matter that exhibited sufficient diversity and complexity to encourage and reward *empirical investigation*. The key elements for creating a new arena of scientific study were in place. As Alfred North Whitehead, the astute philosopher of science, observes:

> All the world over and at all times there have been practical men, absorbed in "irreducible and stubborn facts": all the world over and at all times there have been men of a philosophical temperament who have been absorbed in the weaving of general principles. It is this union of passionate interest in the detailed facts with equal devotion to abstract generalization which form the novelty of our present society. (1925: 3–4)

Accompanying the creation of the new subject area was a search for appropriate intellectual ancestors to provide respectability and legitimacy—Machiavelli, St. Simon, Marx, and Weber were obvious candidates. And more recent forebears, such as Taylor, Barnard, Mayo, and Follett, were rediscovered and reprinted. Also included were Lillian and Frank Gilbreth, who collaborated to find ways to improve work efficiency in factories (Gilbreth and Gilbreth, 1917) but also employed similar techniques at home, celebrated in the book and movie *Cheaper by the Dozen*.

After about a decade of empirical research and theory development, three textbook treatises—by March and Simon (1958), Etzioni (1961), and Blau and Scott (1962)—provided needed integration and heightened interest in the field. Also, a new journal, *Administrative Science Quarterly*, beginning publication in 1956 under the editorship of James D. Thompson, emphasized the interdisciplinary character of the field.[2]

---

[2]Other brief histories of the development of organizations as an identifiable field of inquiry are offered by March (1965: ix–xvi) and Pfeffer (1982: 23–33). An entertaining, if jaundiced, view of the evolution of organization theory is provided by Perrow (1973). Summaries of the contributions of major organizational theorists together with brief biographical information have been assembled by Pugh and Hickson (1996); and Augier and colleagues (Augier, March, and Sullivan, 2005) provide a useful discussion of the rise of organization studies and its migration into professional schools of management.

COMMON AND DIVERGENT INTERESTS

Common Features

What features do all organizations exhibit in common? What are the general organizational issues analysts began to perceive among the great diversity of specific goals and structural arrangements? Most analysts have conceived of organizations as *social structures created by individuals to support the collaborative pursuit of specified goals.* Given this conception, all organizations confront a number of common problems: all must define (and redefine) their objectives; all must induce participants to contribute services; all must control and coordinate these contributions; resources must be garnered from the environment and products or services dispensed; participants must be selected, trained, and replaced; and some sort of working accommodation with the neighbors must be achieved.

In addition to these common operational requirements, some analysts have also emphasized that all organizations are beset by a common curse. All resources cannot be devoted directly to goal attainment; some—in some cases a high proportion—of the resources utilized by any organization must be expended to maintain the organization itself. Although organizations are viewed as means to accomplish ends, the means themselves absorb much energy and, in the extreme (but perhaps not rare) case, become ends in themselves. And, organizations must find ways of combining and harmonizing features associated with the work flow—technologies, equipment, skills, know-how, communication of task information—with features associated with the human/social features—motivation, dealing with differing interests, authority and status matters, equity and distribution issues.

There is a convergence of interest around these common features, but we must not overlook the many bases of divergence. These include differences among the organizations themselves as objects of study, differences in the interests and backgrounds of those who study organizations, and differences in the level of analysis at which inquiry is pitched.

Divergent Features

Diverse organizations. Organizations come in a bewildering variety of sizes and shapes. The largest of them are immense. Although the exact numbers depend on how the boundaries are defined, the largest organizational units found in modern society are often the military services. The People's Liberation Army of China employs 2.3 million persons, and the U.S. Department of Defense employs roughly 1.4 million. The largest of the U.S. military services, the Army, employed approximately 733,000 employees in 2004—500,000 active duty military personnel and 233,000 civilians. An additional 320,000 served in the U.S. Army Reserve. Large organizations also exist within the civilian world. The state railroad of India, Indian Railways, employs 1.6 million people to transport 5 billion passengers per year. The

British National Health System employs 1.3 million. And in 2005 the largest U.S. corporate employer, Wal-Mart Stores, employed 1.7 million. The largest manufacturer, General Motors, was substantially smaller at 325,000. Indeed, of the ten largest U.S. corporate employers in 2005, six were in sales and services, while four were in manufacturing, and two of these—GE and IBM—derived most of their revenues from services. This reflects broader trends in the composition of the labor force as the United States has moved from a manufacturing to a service or postindustrial economy (see Figure 1–1). In 1990, employment in retail surpassed that in manufacturing, while manufacturing dipped below state and local government in 2002. Yet the United States still accounted for 23.8 percent of the world's value-added in manufacturing in 2004—about the same as its share twenty years earlier. Employment in manufacturing is declining worldwide due in large part to productivity gains, just as agricultural employment shrank in previous decades. Indeed, while the number of manufacturing jobs in the United States saw a large decline from 1995 to 2002, China lost proportionally even more.

Most workers in this country are employees of someone else, while about 7.5 percent of the workforce is self-employed. And more workers are employed by fewer and larger companies than in the past. In 1900, 42 percent of the workforce was spread among 5.7 million farms. By 2002, about half the workforce was employed by firms with 500 or more employees, and Wal-Mart Stores alone now has more paid employees than all U.S. farms combined.

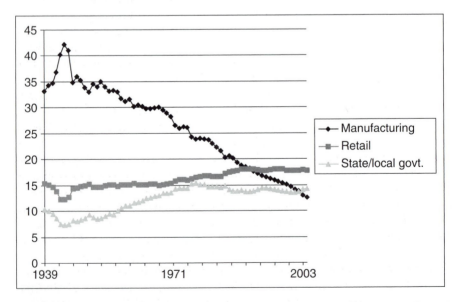

FIGURE 1–1   Proportion of the Nonfarm Labor Force Employed in Manufacturing, Retail, and Local Government, 1939–2003.
Source: U.S. Bureau of Labor Statistics.

Size, however, should not be equated with success. Perhaps for a time in the industrial age size, as measured by employees or productive capacity, was instrumental to success (survival, profitability), but such an association is ill-suited to the postindustrial era. Recent years have seen efforts to restructure and downsize many of the corporate giants. Among them, AT&T, GM, and Ford employed over 2 million people in 1980, a number that shrank to roughly 700,000 (and falling) in 2005. Conversely, one of the largest corporate enterprises in the United States is Manpower, a temporary services firm, which reported placing 2 million employees in temporary assignments in 2004. Still, most productive and innovative businesses are often small or intermediate in size.

In an age when giant organizations seem to dominate the landscape, it is important to emphasize that small organizations are actually in the majority: in 2002, 88 percent of all employing organizations in the United States employed nineteen or fewer individuals. And the predominant ownership form remains the sole proprietorship, with more than 13.8 million such organizations reporting income in 2002, compared to 1.3 million partnerships and 2.8 million corporations. Of course, the corporation far outstrips the other forms in assets, employees, and earnings. These employment organizations also vary greatly in the types of goods and services provided: from coal mining to computers, from fortune telling to futures forecasting.

Large numbers of people are employed in the public sector. In 2002, in the United States, over 21 million individuals—about one out of every six nonfarm workers—were employed in federal, state, and local governments. The number of units or agencies involved is difficult to determine because of the nested character of governmental forms. *The United States Government Manual* (U.S. Office of the Federal Register, 2006) provides organizational charts and brief descriptions of the principal agencies. It currently numbers almost 700 pages! Federal employees make up only about 13 percent of all governmental officials, the vast majority of whom are employed at the state (5 million) and local levels (13.6 million), where there exists great variation in organizational arrangements (Littman, 1998).

The gender composition of the workforce has also changed greatly in a relatively short period. In the 1940s women made up only about 20 percent of the workforce. By 2004, over 46 percent—nearly half—of all workers were women. Put another way, the proportion of women aged 25–44 in the paid labor force increased from 18 percent to 76 percent between the beginning and end of the twentieth century. Moreover, by 1997 women owned 26 percent of U.S. firms.

While for-profit forms provide the lion's share of employment in the United States, nonprofit charitable organizations provide an important alternative mode of organizing. In 2004, nearly 825,000 public charities and 103,000 private foundations were in existence. Roughly 12.5 million individuals, or 9.5 percent of all workers, were employed in nonprofit organizations as of 2001.

An important trend visible during the past three decades in the United States is a reduction in the attachment of workers to specific employers.

The proportion of workers employed by the same organization for more than ten years has dropped to roughly 30 percent, and the proportion of workers in "nonstandard" work arrangements—for example, independent contractors, part-time employees, workers affiliated with temporary help agencies—approached 31 percent of female workers and 23 percent of male workers in 2001 (Mishel, Bernstein, and Allegretto, 2005). While many workers appreciate the new flexibility afforded by these changes, others suffer from increased insecurity and the absence of regular job benefits. (see Chapter 7.)

Employing organizations do not exhaust the list of organizational forms. Robert Putnam (2000: 59) reports that just under 70 percent of Americans claimed membership in at least one voluntary organization in the early 1990s. The number and variety of such forms is large and includes labor unions, political parties, professional societies, business and trade associations, fraternities and sororities, civic service associations, reform and activist groups, and neighborhood organizations. Two "slices" into this world suggest how diverse it is. A vertical slice, extracting only one occupational group, doctors of medicine, reveals over 380 specialty associations listed in the Directory of Medical Specialists. A horizontal slice, an attempt to compile a detailed list of all voluntary associations in Birmingham, England, reported 4,264 such organizations (Newton, 1975).

In addition to size and sector, organizations vary greatly in structural characteristics. The relatively flat authority and control structure found in many voluntary associations and software design companies stands in sharp contrast with the multilayer hierarchy of a military unit or a civil service bureaucracy. And both seem relatively clean and simple in comparison with the project team or matrix structures found in research and development units of high-tech companies. Much attention has recently been directed to "network" or alliance forms: cooperative connections among formally independent organizations that enable them to enjoy simultaneously the benefits associated with being small, such as rapid response, and with those of being large, such as economies of scale (see Chapter 11).

Some organizations are capital intensive, placing most of their resources in machinery and automated equipment. Others invest heavily in the "human capital" of their workforce, selecting highly qualified personnel, underwriting their further, specialized training, and then struggling to keep them from carrying off their expertise to some other company. Some organizations directly employ most of the personnel who carry on the activities of the enterprise; others contract out much of their work, even the functions of general management.

Organizations also vary greatly because they relate to and draw on different surrounding environments. Public agencies differ from private firms, even when they carry on the same kinds of work, because they function in different institutional contexts. It matters considerably whether you operate to satisfy the demands of many decentralized customers or one centralized oversight bureau or multiple political constituencies. Much of what we know about organizations is drawn from organizations operating in the second half of the twentieth century in capitalist, democratic societies—and in one such society in particular, the United States. Only recently have there been extensive efforts to examine the structure and operation of organizations in different times, using historical documents, and in different kinds of societies (see Chapter 13).

Large-scale organizations devoted to the pursuit of specialized goals developed in the United States during the middle of the nineteenth century. Many of the characteristics we associate with modern organizations—the specialized equipment, the sizable administrative hierarchy, the collection of specialists—first appeared in association with the development of the railroads. The "managerial revolution" occurred in response to the problems of scale and scope, of distance and tight scheduling posed by railroads (Chandler, 1977). Organizations developing at this time were different in structure from those arriving later. The unified structures soon gave way to diversified and conglomerate forms, which in turn are being replaced by more flexible, network arrangements (see Chapter 13). More generally, as Stinchcombe (1965) first observed, organizational forms exhibit distinctive structures that reflect the times in which they were created. Thus, at any given time, much of the diversity exhibited by a collection of organizations is due to the varying conditions present at the time of their birth (see Chapter 13).

Although researchers have often portrayed the organizations of their home country—often the United States—as somehow "typical," the globalization of the organizational research enterprise has documented the wide variety of forms that have flourished around the world. Different cultural, legal, and historical patterns have produced quite varied configurations of national institutions, and with them divergent forms of organizations, from the *keiretsu* networks of Japan to the postsocialist forms of Hungary and China to the bank-centered capitalism of Germany. Comparisons of the economic trajectories of the United States, China, Germany, and Japan make clear that many different approaches to organizing are consistent with economic vibrancy. Moreover, these forms do not sit still: the system of lifetime employment came under increasing stress in Japan in the postbubble years of the 1990s, while banks increasingly unwound their corporate ownership positions in Germany during the same period. Among all of the other sources of variation, we must not overlook temporal, regional, and cultural factors.

Diverse research interests and settings. Another basis for divergence in work on organizations resides in the interests, training, and employment settings of those who study organizations. As already noted, researchers from different disciplines vary to some extent in the kinds of organizations they choose to study. Political scientists primarily focus on political parties and state administrative structures, economists on business firms, sociologists on voluntary associations and on nonprofit agencies engaged in social welfare and social-control functions, and anthropologists on comparative administration in non-Western, colonial, and developing societies. Disciplinary differences remain even when a single type of organization is selected for study: specialists tend to look not only at different objects but also at different aspects of the same object. Thus, the political scientist will be likely to emphasize power processes and decision making within the organization; the economist will examine the acquisition and allocation of scarce resources within the organization and will attend to such issues as productivity and efficiency; the sociologist has quite varied interests, but if there is a focus it will likely be on status orderings, on the effect of norms and sentiments on behavior, and on organizational legitimacy; the psychologist will be interested in variations in perception, cognition, and motivation among participants; and the anthropologist will call attention to the effects of diverse cultural values on the functioning of the system and its members. The study of organizations embraces all these interests, and students of organizations work to develop conceptual frameworks within which all of these topics and their interrelations may be examined. And organizational analysts attempt to specify what is distinctive about power or status or motivation or cultural processes because they occur within the context of organizations.

A more general basis of divergence among those who study organizations is between those with a practice orientation—studying organizations in order to improve their performance—and those who treat organizations as objects of interest in their own right. This distinction dates from the very origins of the study of organizations and their management. Frederick Taylor (1911) took a bottom-up, engineering approach, seeking to rationalize work systems by dividing them into the smallest tasks, organizing the sequencing of tasks to maximize throughput, and combining tasks into jobs and jobs into departments. This approach lives on to this day—consider, for instance, the methods of "business process re-engineering." Henri Fayol (1919/1949) took a top-down, managerial approach to dividing and coordinating complex work systems. In both cases, the aim was prescriptive, to advise management. Subsequent social scientists, particularly those in the "human relations" tradition as exemplified by the famous Hawthorne Studies, sought to humanize the workplace and encouraged attending to employees as human beings with complex needs beyond just a paycheck. But again, the organization was viewed as a context in which work got done, an instrument to achieve particular ends, rather than a distinct social system of its own.

Other theorists, starting with Barnard (1938) and Selznick (1948), focused on the organization itself as an adaptive social system. Research in this tradition is driven more by theory than by a quest to provide immediately useful advice. This approach is evident in its choice of problems and of variables. Particular concepts—authority, legitimacy, institutionalization—are of interest because of their place in theoretical arguments, not because of their practical significance. Such basic research is more likely to focus on the independent variables—on understanding the effects of certain concepts of interest—than on the dependent variables and to be aimed at testing particular arguments. Conversely, practical research is driven by an interest in solving some identified problem—low morale or productivity, high turnover—and is willing to incorporate any and all kinds of variables, whether economic, psychological, or cultural, that may shed light on it.

Since Vannevar Bush coined the terms "basic research" and "applied research" in 1944, they have been viewed as distinct poles of science—Bush even went as far as to say that "applied research invariably drives out pure." But Stokes (1997) argues that this dichotomy is inaccurate. Rather, basic and applied represent two distinct dimensions, forming a two-by-two matrix. In Bohr's quadrant, research seeks fundamental understanding, with no consideration for practical applications (that is, high on basic, low on application). In Edison's quadrant, research is oriented strictly toward practical applications for individuals, groups, or society, with no concern for fundamental knowledge (high application, low basic). Pasteur's quadrant is high on both dimensions—it is a quest for fundamental knowledge inspired by use. (Research with neither knowledge nor practical use in mind would include laboratory training for students.) Louis Pasteur's research in the mid-1800s documented that the transfer of microorganisms, rather than spontaneous generation, caused infectious diseases, and his work created both a revolution in basic medicine and in health practices (including, of course, pasteurization). Stokes argues that such a quest for knowledge inspired by use—that is, Pasteur's quadrant—has generated some of the most significant advances in science since the Second World War, and thus that basic and applied are not only compatible, but also complementary. Problem-driven work, in short, can produce good science.

In organization studies, problem-driven research is research that takes its cue from questions in the world and answers them using organizational paradigms, rather than pursuing questions arising strictly out of the paradigms themselves. One reason for the productivity of problem-driven research is that it is much more likely to be interdisciplinary: real-world problems do not respect disciplinary boundaries. Organizational problems can implicate psychology, sociology, political science, economics, and anthropology, and thus organization theory stands at the crossroads of these disciplines, to the mutual benefit of all of them. On the other hand, as organizational research increasingly moved into professional schools—particularly business schools—beginning in the 1970s, the contexts of study have become increasingly narrowed to for-profit settings, a development that reduces variance among the types of organizations studied and, we believe, impedes examination of the full range of forms available for organizing.

Diverse levels of analysis. Apart from the variety of conceptual schemes and orientations that guide inquiry and differences in research settings, investigators differ in the level of analysis at which they choose to work (Blau, 1957). For present purposes, the level of analysis is determined by the nature of the dependent variable, the object of theoretical analysis—that is, by whether primary attention is given to the behavior of individuals, of organizations, or of systems of organizations. Thus, the basic levels are

- The *social psychological* level, focusing on the behavior of individuals or interpersonal relations involving individual participants within organizations. At this level, organizational characteristics are viewed as context or environment, and the investigator attempts to explore their impact on the attitudes or behavior of individuals. Such a perspective is exemplified by the work of Katz and Kahn (1978) and of Weick (1969; 1995).
- The *organizational* level, focusing on the structural features or processes that characterize organizations. Here, the major concern is to explain the structural features and social processes that characterize organizations and their subdivisions. The investigator working at this level may focus on the various subunits that make up the organization (for example, work groups, departments, authority ranks) or may examine various analytical components (for example, specialization, communication networks, hierarchy) that characterize the structural features or operational routines of organizations, or examine the behavior of the organization itself as a collective actor. Researchers working at this level include Blau and Schoenherr (1971), and Pfeffer and Salancik 1978).
- The *ecological* level, focusing on the characteristics or actions of the organization viewed as a collective entity operating in a larger system of relations. At this level, the analyst may choose either to examine the relation between a specific organization or class of organizations and the environment (e.g., Hannan and Freeman 1989; Pugh and Hickson, 1976) or to examine the relations that develop among a number of organizations viewed as an interdependent system (e.g., DiMaggio and Powell 1983; Laumann and Knoke, 1987).

Admittedly, distinguishing among these three levels of analysis is somewhat arbitrary.[3] Many more refined levels of analytical complexity can be identified as one moves from organizational-individual to societal-organizational relations. Nevertheless, if only to remind us of the complexity of the subject matter and the variety of aims and interests with which analysts approach it, the three levels are helpful in providing a rough gauge for distinguishing among broad categories of studies.

Early research on organizations was conducted almost exclusively at the social psychological level. The structural level of analysis became prominent in the early 1960s and continues to be heavily utilized by sociologists. The ecological level was the last to develop, emerging in the late 1960s, but it is at this level that much of the intellectual excitement and energy that characterizes the field during the past four decades has transpired.[4]

Yet another base of divergence among those who study organizations is the *theoretical perspective* employed by the analyst. However, this is, in our view, such

[3]The most commonly employed levels distinction is that between "micro" and "macro" organizational studies. The former is equivalent to the social psychological level; the latter encompasses both the structural and the ecological levels.

[4]Our "ecological" level is meant to broadly encompass all approaches in which the organization is viewed as an actor in a larger system of related actors and systems. As we discuss in Chapter 5, it include both "dyadic" models of organization-environment relations as well as more systemic models in which the environment itself is seen to be organizations, for example into populations or fields of organizations.

a fundamental difference that it provides the basic themes around which we have organized this volume. Whether the analyst employs a *rational, natural,* or *open system* perspective, or some combination, is viewed as central to interpreting the work. Chapters 2, 3, and 4 are devoted to reviewing these perspectives, while later chapters explicate the ways in which they have subsequently been developed and combined.

Because so much of our attention in succeeding chapters will be devoted to emphasizing divergent perspectives, it is prudent in the next section to return to explicate the theme that all organizations share some basic characteristics.

THE ELEMENTS OF ORGANIZATIONS

If asked to draw a map of their organization, many people will draw an organization chart, as shown in Figure 1–2.

Organization charts are enormously useful but convey only a small part of what we mean by "organizations." There have been many models that render the diversity and complexity of organizations manageable by focusing on a few central dimensions—somewhere between an organization chart and an actual organization. For our initial discussion, we use Figure 1–3 adapted from Nadler and Tushman's "congruence framework" (1997). Let us briefly consider each element.

The Essential Ingredients

Environment. Every organization exists in a specific physical, technological, cultural, and social environment to which it must adapt. No organization is self-sufficient; all depend for survival on the types of relations they establish with the larger systems of which they are a part. Environments are all those significant elements outside the organization that influence its ability to survive and achieve its ends. The environment can be seen as a store of resources as well as a source of opportunities and constraints, demands and

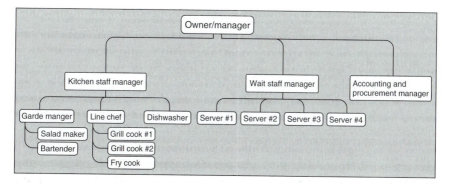

FIGURE 1–2   Generic organizational chart.

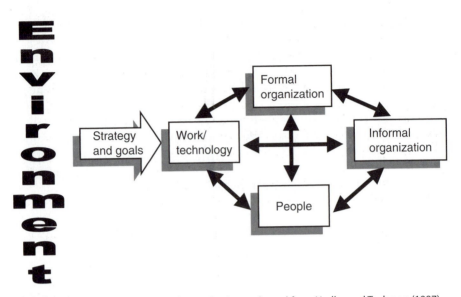

FIGURE 1–3   Congruence Model of Organizations, adapted from Nadler and Tushman (1997).

threats. It includes the clients, constituents, or customers that the organization serves and the providers of resources it requires to do so.

Students of corporate strategy have developed a framework for analyzing resource environments using the tools of industrial economics. Porter's (1980) "five forces" framework, which we describe in Chapter 12, describes the factors that make industries more or less attractive. These forces include the bargaining power of buyers or clients (which is high to the extent that they are few in number and/or well organized), the bargaining power of suppliers, the barriers to entry by new competitors that seek to serve the same customers, the existence of substitute products that serve the same function as the focal organization's products, and the intensity of rivalry among existing competitors. All of these elements combine to influence how profitable (or, conversely, how competitive) an industry is. Similarly, resource dependence theory, which we describe in Chapter 9, analyzes how resource exchanges with the environment create power/dependence relations among organizations, and how organizations respond to their situation of power or dependence (Pfeffer and Salancik, 1978). And network analysts such as Burt (1980) provide means to measure these power/dependence relations explicitly; network approaches are described in Chapter 11.

To these elements we would add several more. Governmental bodies can create both opportunities and constraints through regulation, through their ability to enhance or stifle demand for the organization's outputs, and in myriad other ways. The broader cultural milieu, including institutional arrangements, shapes both the ends and the means of organizations, a theme taken up in Chapter 10. And all of these elements can change over time: organizational environments are dynamic as discussed in Chapter 12.

Strategy and Goals. Strategy describes the choices organizations make about which markets or clients the organization intends to serve, the basis on which it competes in its domain (that is, the distinctive way it seeks to provide its outputs), the specific tactics the organization employs, and the output goals it sets for itself. Organizations do not simply pop up in an environment—their creators often choose which domains they will operate in, based on how attractive those domains might be. This will not always be the case, of course: public school systems usually have only limited control over which students and which geographic areas they will serve, and what level of financial resources they will have available. Within these constraints, however, organizations determine a particular way to do what they do. One typology distinguishes among three broad strategic types: *prospectors* focus on creating innovative products and services in order to shape their domain; *defenders* focus less on innovation and more on developing efficiencies in their internal processes; and *analyzers* combine these approaches by maintaining a combination of established products/services while also regularly updating with new offerings (Miles and Snow, 1994). An alternative typology distinguishes between a *low-cost* approach, focused on high volume and efficient production; *differentiation*, or providing products/services recognized as being unique; and *focus*, oriented toward serving a particular geographic or customer segment particularly well (Porter, 1980). We describe organizational strategies and how they link to the environment in Chapter 12.

Given a broad strategy, organizations have particular tactics that they use to pursue that strategy, which might be seen as intermediate or ground-level goals and approaches. And finally, organizations often set particular output objectives for themselves, such as "Increase students' average scores on standardized tests by 10 points within three years" or "Lower employee turnover to 10 percent per year" or "Increase earnings by 15 percent per year." Chapter 8 describes how goals, power, and control interact within organizations, while Chapter 12 discusses organizational performance.

Work and Technology. In order to pursue particular strategies, organizations have to perform particular critical tasks effectively to transform the organization's goals into realities. What is required to provide personalized and effective service to clients is different from what is required to produce the highest volume at the lowest cost. *Work* describes the tasks that the organization needs to accomplish given the goals it has set for itself. It includes the character of the work flows and the level of interedependence among the parts of the organization, which is a theme we take up in Chapter 6; the types of skills and knowledge required of participants; and the constraints that the work imposes on the organization, such as particular quality or timing requirements.

We include in this component *technology*, broadly construed. To focus on the technology of an organization is to view the organization as a place where energy is applied to the transformation of materials, as a mechanism for transforming inputs into outputs. The connotations of the term *technology* are narrow and hard, but we will insist that every organization does work and possesses a technology for doing that work. Some organizations process material inputs and fabricate new equipment and hardware. Others "process" people, their products consisting of more knowledgeable individuals, in the case of effective school systems, or healthier individuals, in the case of effective medical clinics. Still others process primarily symbolic materials, such as information or music. The technology of an organization is often partially embedded in machines and mechanical equipment but also comprises the technical knowledge and skills of participants.

All organizations possess technologies, but organizations vary in the extent to which these techniques are understood, routinized, or efficacious. Some of the most interesting theoretical and empirical work has focused on the relation between the characteristics of technology and the structural features of organizations. This work is described and evaluated in Chapter 6.

Formal Organization. Organizations codify more or less explicitly how they do their work and how their parts relate to each other. We label this the formal organization and include elements such as human resource practices (including hiring and compensation policies), the design of jobs, and the overall organization structure. We define the concept of formalization in the next section and discuss its implications for organizing in Chapter 2.

Human resource practices describe how participants are recruited, what kinds of rewards they receive, and what kinds of careers they have once inside the organization, including the promotion ladders offered (if any). Recruiting and retaining members is a central task for any kind of organization, as is getting them to contribute once they have showed up. Some organizations have elaborate methods of socialization and training to bring members up to speed, and equally elaborate structures to retain them for extended periods, including health insurance, pensions, and other benefits. Other organizations treat employment as, in effect, a day-to-day agreement. We describe these alternative arrangements and their rationale in Chapter 7.

Job design describes what tasks are done as part of a single job. Adam Smith famously argued for the advantages of highly divided labor by describing a pin factory, which—by dividing the tasks of creating a pin into eighteen different discrete operations—vastly increased the daily output of finished pins. Frederick Taylor (1911) systematized this insight with his method of "scientific management" in the early part of the twentieth century, and Henry Ford brought it to fruition at the Highland Park assembly line that made Model Ts in Detroit. An unfortunate side effect, of course, was that the highly divided tasks were mind-numbingly repetitive and boring, a fact that was not lost on subsequent commentators, who lamented the seemingly inevitable trade-off between meaningful work and productivity. Organizational psychologists working in the 1960s and 1970s argued that intrinsically motivating work led to more productivity and that jobs could be enlarged and enriched in ways that produced both intrinsic interest and high productivity (e.g., Hackman and Oldham, 1980).

Organization structure groups together jobs into larger units, such as teams and departments, and analyzes authority relations and patterns of formal communication among participants and units. These choices are summarized and depicted in the familiar organization chart that we began this section with. Prominent organization designs include the *functional form*, in which jobs are grouped into departments or "functions" (e.g., engineering, manufacturing, sales); the *multidivisional form*, in which different geographic areas, products, or services each have a separate functional form whose managers in turn report to a corporate headquarters unit; and a *matrix form*, in which the organization has a simultaneous hierarchy by function and by project or program. We discuss these and other forms in more detail in Chapter 6.

Informal Organization. Not all aspects of the organization are captured by the organization chart, of course. The informal organization refers to the emergent characteristics of the organization that affect how the organization operates. This includes the organization's culture, norms, and values; social networks inside and outside the organization; power and politics; and the actions of leaders.

Culture describes the pattern of values, beliefs, and expectations more or less shared by the organization's members. Schein (1992) analyzes culture in terms of underlying assumptions about the organization's relationship to its environment (that is, what business are we in, and why); the nature of reality and truth (how do we decide which interpretations of information and events are correct, and how do we make decisions); the nature of human nature (are people basically lazy or industrious, fixed or malleable); the nature of human activity (what are the "right" things to do, and what is the best way to influence human action); and the nature of human relationships (should people relate as competitors or cooperators, individualists or collaborators). These components hang together as a more-or-less coherent theory that guides the organization's more formalized policies and strategies. Of course, the extent to which these elements are "shared" or even coherent within a culture is likely to be highly contentious (see Martin, 2002)—there can be subcultures and even countercultures within an organization. These issues are discussed in Chapter 8.

Social networks are the informal connections among individuals that often arise out of work patterns but can have a large influence beyond them. As individuals seek others out for advice, or to have lunch, or to look for information or favors, their person-to-person ties evolve into a social structure that can be quite consequential for things ranging from individual career advancement to the creation of innovative products or services. Chapter 11 describes the origins and influence of networks in and around organizations.

Because organizations involve exchanges of resources, sharing information, and trading favors, they become "markets for influence and control," as

Pfeffer and Salancik (1978) put it. *Power and politics* arise more or less spontaneously in organizations as individuals and subunits pursue agendas and as the resource environment around the organization changes. As Chapter 8 describes, power can both enable organizations to get things done, and hinder useful changes. Thus, it is an important dimension to consider when analyzing organizations.

People. Organizational participants make contributions to the organization in return for a variety of inducements, as Barnard (1938) and Simon (1997) emphasize. All individuals participate in more than one organization (recall that, by definition, organizations are specialized in their purposes), and the extent and intensiveness of their involvement may vary greatly; the decision as to who is to be regarded as a participant is thus often a difficult one and may legitimately vary with the issue at hand. For example, a single individual may simultaneously be an employee of an industrial firm, a member of a union, a church member, a member of a fraternal lodge or sorority, a "member" of a political party, a citizen of the state, a client of a group medical practice, a stockholder in one or more companies, and a customer in numerous retail and service organizations.

Several characteristics of the individuals comprising an organization are relevant. These include their knowledge and skills and how they fit with the tasks they perform; their needs and preferences; and the broader background they bring with them to the organization. The demographic characteristics of participants—for example, their age, gender, and ethnic distributions—also have important consequences for many aspects of organizational structure and functioning. We explore these implications in Chapter 7.

Finally, *leaders* and their actions can have an important influence on organizations—although as Khurana (2002) points out in *Searching for a Corporate Savior: The Irrational Quest for Charismatic CEOs*, this influence is often less than observers imagine! Both initial strategies and structures, and the composition of the organization's management team, often reflect the experiences, preferences, and even whims of founding leaders, and such individuals have an ongoing influence on how organizations operate—for better or worse—as we describe in Chapter 12.

Each of these organizational elements—environment, strategy and goals, work and technology, formal organization, informal organization, and people—represents an important component of all organizations. Indeed, each element has been regarded as being of surpassing importance by one or another analyst of organizations. However, the chief value of the congruence model is as a graphic reminder that no one element is so dominant as to be safely considered in isolation from the others. Organizations are, first and foremost, *systems* of elements, each of which affects and is affected by the others. Strategies are not the key to understanding the nature and functioning of organizations, no more than are the people, the formal structure, or the technology. And no organization can be understood in isolation from the larger environment. We will miss the essence of organization if we insist on focusing on any single feature to the exclusion of all others.

A Corrective Argument; From Structure to Process

While, as noted, we will discuss throughout this volume the various ingredients of organization just introduced, we also want to point out two important limitations to this approach and begin to introduce an alternative formulation. First, the Nadler and Tushman model, as well as related approaches, tends to perpetuate the dualism that distinguishes structure, whether formal or informal, from people and their actions. Second, the entire model is highly static, privileging elements and structures over actions and processes. The social theorist Anthony Giddens (1979; 1984) has proposed an alternative theoretical model that seeks to overcome both of these limitations in his theory of *structuration*. This argument reminds us that social structures only exist to the extent that people act in ways to reproduce ongoing patterns of action.[5] Social structures are comprised of rules or schema (models for behavior) and resources (both material and human) which acquire their meaning and value from the schema applicable to them. Actions always take place within an existing structure of rules and resources: these structures provide the context for action. On the other hand, actions work to reproduce as well as to alter existing structures: structures are the product of human action. As Giddens elaborates:

> Every process of action is a production of something new, a fresh act; but at the same time all action exists in continuity with the past, which supplies the means of its initiation. Structure thus is not to be conceptualized as a barrier to action, but as essentially involved in its production, even in the most radical processes of social change. (1979: 70)

This conception of the "duality" of structure helps to overcome the age-old debates between freedom and order. More specifically, it works to correct sociological arguments, which are overly determinist, assuming that individual actors have little choice or autonomy, but also challenges psychological (and economic) assumptions that actors are free to make any choice that suits them or to act in unconstrained ways.

Giddens's formulation also reinforces the need to take a more dynamic view of social structure and behavior. Rather than focusing on a stable, static, cross-sectional view of an organizational structure, it reminds us to consider the ways in which moment by moment, day by day, and year by year, structures are undergoing transformation, thereby providing new and different opportunities

---

[5]It is not only social structures that are subject to these processes but also social objects such as technologies. See Chapter 6.

for individuals making choices and taking action. These ideas will be revisited throughout this volume, but especially in Chapters 10, 13, and 14.

The Capacities of Organizations

The foregoing discussion represents an opening attempt to identify some of the key elements or ingredients of organizations: to specify their building blocks (and wheels). However, such an approach does not go far in explaining why organizations are so prevalent. What are their distinctive capacities? We briefly address this question here but will return to it again throughout the volume.

Hannan and Carroll (1995) identify a number of features that help to explain why organizations are much in demand as vehicles for conducting the myriad activities associated with modern social life.

1. More so that many other types of social structures, organizations are *durable*: they are designed in such a way as to persist over time, routinely and continuously supporting efforts to carry on a set of specified activities. More so than other types of social structures, they are expected to operate as long-distance runners. Attaining stability over time and in spite of shifting participants is one of the major functions of formalization, as we emphasize in Chapter 2. Durability does not necessarily imply effectiveness; organizations often persist that are deemed by many to be inept (Meyer and Zucker, 1989). And durability should not to be equated with rigidity. Some of the newer forms of organizations are designed to combine great flexibility with the maintenance of an organizational core that persists across changing combinations of personnel, structure, and even goals.

2. Another capacity of organizations is their *reliability* (Hannan and Carroll, 1995: 20). Organizations are good at doing the same things in the same way, over and over, and for many types of activities there are many advantages associated with this characteristic. In later chapters we will describe all the numerous mechanisms of control utilized in organizations, including formalization, authority structures, elaborate rules and routines, strong cultures, and the use of specialized machinery. All of these factors are designed in part to increase the reliability of the work activities being performed. Reliability of performance is not, of course, an unmixed blessing. To the extent that conditions change and new activities are called for, the very factors associated with effective performance may suddenly prevent an organization from changing its rules and procedures quickly enough to develop new ways of behaving. Still, for many types of activities and many situations, there are great advantages associated with the ability to produce goods and services reliably.

3. Organizations exhibit the trait of being *accountable* (Hannan and Carroll, 1995: 21; see also Meyer and Rowan, 1977). Behavior takes place within a framework of rules that provides both guidelines and justifications for decisions and activities. They establish a scaffolding of rationality that allows participants to give an accounting of their past behaviors (Scott and Lyman, 1968). In most industrial societies, this framework is connected to and supported by legal codes that define the powers and limits of organizations. Records are kept and a "paper trail" created so that, if necessary, the bases for past actions can be reviewed. The hierarchy of authority is expected, at least in part, to ensure that rules are being followed and work is performed in

accordance with agreed-on standards and procedures. Of course, not all organizations measure up to these standards: there is much evidence of both incompetence and corruption. More important, as we will learn, the type of rationality involved—formal rationality—is itself a limited and flawed basis for ensuring reasonable, let alone moral, conduct. Nevertheless, in an imperfect world, a system in which individuals attempt to operate within an explicit framework of rules nested in wider legal systems to which they are accountable, has much to recommend it.

DEFINING THE CONCEPT OF ORGANIZATION

How we define "organization" shapes how we think about the phenomenon—what we see as essential, and what we ignore as irrelevant. Few of us have difficulty viewing Toyota or Amnesty International as organizations. Stanford University or the *New York Times* are slightly more problematic. But what about the "global justice" movement, which stages protests at meetings of the World Trade Organization and other supranational entities? Or Freedom Wireless—a corporation consisting of four employees and six patents, whose primary source of revenue comes from suing cellphone companies for infringing on their patents? Or corporations set up in Montana by elderly couples purchasing recreational vehicles to avoid sales taxes and registration fees in their home states? Scientific theories are often sparked by analogies. Merton notes that

> Gilbert begins with the relatively simple idea that the earth may be conceived as a magnet; Boyle, with the simple idea that the atmosphere may be conceived as a 'sea of air'; Darwin, with the idea that one can conceive of atolls as upward and outward growths of coral over islands that had long since subsided into the sea. Each of these theories provides an image that gives rise to inferences. To take but one case: if the atmosphere is thought of as a sea of air, then, as Pascal inferred, there should be less air pressure on a mountain top than at its base. The initial idea thus suggests specific hypotheses which are tested by seeing whether the inferences from them are empirically confirmed. (1968: 40)

By the same token, those that theorize about organizations often start from an image—an organization as a machine for accomplishing goals, or as a small society with a social structure and culture, or as an organism making its way through a resource environment (Morgan, 1986). Each highlights different aspects of organizations and encourages us to see different patterns of relationships. Differing analogies give rise to varying paradigms for examining organizations.

Consistent with the objectives of this volume, not one but three definitions of organizations will be presented. These definitions pave the way for our description and evaluation, in the next three chapters, of three major perspectives developed over the course of the twentieth century to understand organizations. We leave to later chapters the considerable task of spelling out the implications of these differing definitions. Special attention is accorded here to the first definition because it continues to be the dominant perspective in the field, not only in guiding the work of the majority of organizational scholars but also by being embraced at least implicitly by most real-world managers and other practitioners. Moreover, this definition served to establish organizations as a distinctive field of study. The first definition underpins the *rational system* perspective on organization. Two other definitions—one associated with the *natural system* perspective and the other with the *open system* perspective—will be briefly described here and examined more fully in later chapters.

A Rational System Definition

Because a primary function of a definition is to help us to distinguish one phenomenon from another, most definitions of organizations emphasize the distinctive features of organizations—those that distinguish them from related social forms. Many analysts have attempted to formulate such definitions, and their views appear to be similar, as illustrated by the following three influential definitions.

According to Barnard,

> formal organization is that kind of cooperation among men that is conscious, deliberate, purposeful. (1938: 4)

According to March and Simon,

> Organizations are assemblages of interacting human beings and they are the largest assemblages in our society that have anything resembling a central coordinative system. . . . The high specificity of structure and coordination within organizations—as contrasted with the diffuse and variable relations among organizations and among unorganized individuals—marks off the individual organization as a sociological unit comparable in significance to the individual organism in biology. (1958: 4)

And according to Blau and Scott,

> Since the distinctive characteristic of . . . organizations is that they have been formally established for the explicit purpose of achieving certain goals, the term "formal organizations" is used to designate them. (1962: 5)

All of these early definitions point to the existence of two structural features that distinguish organizations from other types of collectivities.

1. Organizations are collectivities oriented to the pursuit of relatively specific goals. They are "purposeful" in the sense that the activities and interactions of participants are coordinated to achieve specified goals. Goals are *specific* to the extent that they are explicit, are clearly defined, and provide unambiguous criteria for selecting among alternative activities.

2. Organizations are collectivities that exhibit a relatively high degree of formalization. The cooperation among participants is "conscious" and "deliberate"; the structure of relations is made explicit. A structure is *formalized* to the extent that the rules governing behavior are precisely and explicitly formulated and to the extent that roles and role relations are prescribed independently of the personal attributes and relations of individuals occupying positions in the structure.

It is the combination of relatively high goal specificity and relatively high formalization that distinguishes organizations from other types of collectivities. Note that both goal specificity and formalization are viewed as variables: organizations vary along both dimensions. Nevertheless, as a structural type, organizations are expected to exhibit higher levels of formalization and goal specificity than are other types of collectivities, such as primary groups, families, communities, and social movements. In general—exceptions certainly exist—families and kinship structures tend to rank relatively high on formalization but low on goal specificity (Litwak and Meyer, 1966); social movements tend to exhibit low levels of formalization combined with higher levels of goal specificity[6], although the specificity of goals varies greatly from movement to movement and from time to time (Gusfield, 1968); and communities are characterized by low levels of both goal specificity and formalization (Hillery, 1968: 145–52).

We arrive, then, at the first definition, associated with the rational system perspective: *organizations are collectivities oriented to the pursuit of relatively specific goals and exhibiting relatively highly formalized social structures.* Note that this definition focuses not only on the distinctive characteristics of organizations, but also on their normative structure. In Chapter 2 we consider the development and significance of this perspective on organizations.

A Natural System Definition

Gouldner (1959) reminds us that the distinguishing features of a phenomenon are not its only characteristics and, indeed, may not be the most important ones. Although organizations often espouse specific goals, the behavior of participants is frequently not guided by them, nor can they be safely used to predict organizational actions. Similarly, formal role definitions and written rules may have been developed, but all too frequently they exhibit little or no influence on the behavior of members.

---

[6]Beginning in the 1980s, analysts of movements began to place more emphasis on their organizational features—for example, the extent to which they are guided by a full-time, paid staff and have regularized mechanisms for obtaining resources and recruits and for setting goals. Like many other phenomena in modern society, social movements, if they endure, morph into social movement organizations (Zald and McCarthy, 1987).

Thus, if the behavioral structure is attended to, rather than the normative structure—if we focus on what participants actually do rather than on what they are supposed to do—the first definition of organizations can be quite misleading.

Focusing attention on the behavioral structure produces a view of organizations quite different from that proffered by the rational system theorists. The goals pursued become more complex, diffuse, differentiated, and subject to change; participants appear as motivated by their own interests and seek to impose these on the organization. It is recognized that the organization itself is a major asset, a valuable resource to be captured. Rather than being only a means, an instrument to pursuing other ends, the maintenance and strengthening of the organization becomes an end in itself. Informal and interpersonal structures are seen to be of greater importance than are formal structures, which often serve only as a decorative facade concealing the "real" agenda and structure. And power is recognized as stemming from many sources other than occupancy of a formal position.

Hence, a second definition of organizations, useful for viewing them as natural systems, is suggested: *organizations are collectivities whose participants are pursuing multiple interests, both disparate and common, but who recognize the value of perpetuating the organization as an important resource.*

The natural system view emphasizes the common attributes that organizations share with all social collectivities. And because organizations are not set apart from other social systems, they are viewed as subject to forces affecting all such systems. In particular, we find replicated in this perspective the two contrasting versions of the bases of social order in the sociological literature at large: one emphasizing social consensus, the other, social conflict. The first, *social consensus*, version emphasizes a view of collectivities as comprised of individuals sharing primarily common objectives. The assumption underlying this conception is that social order (of any type) is a reflection of underlying consensus among the participants; that organizational stability and continuity reflect the existence of cooperative behavior and shared norms and values. This widely held and influential view of the basis of social order is generated in the writings of Durkheim (1961 trans.) and Parsons (1951), among others, and reflected in the organizational theories of Barnard (1938) and Mayo (1945), among others. The contrasting *social conflict* version views social order as resulting from the suppression of some interests by others. Order results not from consensus, but from coercion, the dominance of weaker by more powerful groups. And analytic attention is devoted not to the appearance of consensus, but to the reality of underlying conflicts, which provide a basis for understanding instability and change. The sociological progenitors of this view include Marx (1954 trans.) and Coser (1956). Applications to organizations are provided by such theorists as Gouldner (1954), Bendix (1956), and Collins (1975).

In Chapter 3 we review the development of the basic assumptions of the natural system perspective and examine the competing consensus and conflict models.

An Open System Definition

The previous definitions tend to view the organization as a closed system, separate from its environment and encompassing a set of stable and easily identified participants. However, organizations are not closed systems, sealed off from their environments, but are open to and dependent on flows of personnel, resources, and information from outside. From an open system perspective, environments shape, support, and infiltrate organizations. Connections with "external" elements can be more critical than those among "internal" components; indeed, for many functions the distinction between organization and environment is revealed to be shifting, ambiguous, and arbitrary.

All three perspectives agree that if an organization is to survive, it must induce a variety of participants to contribute their time and energy to it. However, open system theorists emphasize that individuals have multiple loyalties and identities. They join and leave or engage in ongoing exchanges with the organization depending on the bargains they can strike—the relative advantage to be had from maintaining or ending the relation. Viewed from this perspective, participants cannot be assumed to hold common goals or even to routinely seek the survival of the organization. Thus, much of the work of organizing entails hard bargaining and "horse training"—as well as creating affective ties and common interpretive systems—as participants attempt to form and re-form transitory coalitions.

An open system perspective is less concerned with distinguishing formal from informal structures; instead, organizations are viewed as a system of interdependent activities. Some of these activities are tightly connected; others are loosely coupled. All must be continuously motivated—produced and reproduced—if the organization is to persist. The arrival of this perspective triggered the elaboration and elevation of levels of analysis. No longer was the single organization the privileged unit of analysis. Rather, analysts recognize that many organizational phenomena are better understood and explained by viewing individual organizations as representatives of a given type of structure, or by viewing organizations as components in larger systems of relations. The open system perspective is associated with the development of studies aimed at understanding organizational sets, populations, and fields—topics we pursue in subsequent chapters.

Also, the open system perspective stresses the importance of cultural-cognitive elements in the construction of organizations. Nothing is more portable than ideas—conceptions, models, schemas, and scripts. Organizations swim in this cultural soup and continuously adopt and adapt these templates, intendedly and inadvertently.

We arrive, then, at a third definition, useful for viewing organizations as open systems: *organizations are congeries of interdependent flows and activities linking shifting coalitions of participants embedded in wider material-resource and institutional environments.*

The open system perspective is explicated in Chapter 4.

Why Three Perspectives?

It is no doubt unsettling to be confronted so early with three such diverse views of organizations. But better to know the worst at the outset! The definitions are quite different in that they not only encompass somewhat divergent types of collectivities but also emphasize different facets of a given organization. But this is precisely why they are useful. Definitions are neither true nor false but are only more or less helpful in calling attention to certain aspects of the phenomenon under study. With the assistance of these definitions, and the more general perspectives with which they are associated, we can expect to see and learn more about organizations than would be possible were we to employ a single point of view. As we proceed, we will call attention to the remarkably varied portraits painted by theorists embracing each of the conceptions. Each has its own charms as well as its own blemishes; and each carries its own truth as well as its own biases.

We describe rational, natural, and open systems as *perspectives* or *paradigms* because in each case we are dealing not with a single, unified model of organizational structure, but rather with a number of varying approaches that bear a strong family resemblance. Thus, our concern will be with three types of approaches or three schools of thought, the notion of perspective serving as a conceptual umbrella under which we gather the related views. To add further to the complexity, the three perspectives partially conflict, partially overlap, and partially complement one another.

An understanding of these perspectives is valuable for several reasons. It is very difficult to comprehend or to fruitfully utilize the large literature on organizations without knowledge of the differing perspectives underlying this work. Why do some investigators assume that organizational goals are central and obvious whereas others presume that goals are dispensable and cannot be taken at face value? Why does one analyst assert that organizations have great difficulty in changing their structures while another assumes that change is easy and continuous? These are the kinds of issues that cannot be understood without knowledge of the underlying perspectives that frame the work. Also, we should expect to receive help not only in making sense out of past studies but also in examining contemporary efforts of organizational analysts. For although these perspectives emerged at different times, later perspectives have not succeeded in supplanting earlier ones. The perspectives continue to guide and inform work in the field.

The perspectives should be understood in two senses. On the one hand, they are historical products—systems of ideas and practice that developed and held sway in specific times and circumstances. To completely divorce them from their context would be a mistake, since much of their meaning is historically situated. But at the same time, the perspectives selected are not just of historical interest. Each has shown great resilience and has been invented and reinvented over time so that each has persisted as an identifiable, analytic model. In our discussion, we try to do justice to both moments: the historically specific versions and the underlying analytically enduring features. In their pure form, the perspectives share many of the features of paradigms as described by Kuhn in his influential essay on scientific revolutions. Kuhn describes *paradigms* as "models from which spring particular coherent traditions of scientific research" (1962: 10). Rational, natural, and open system perspectives are, in this sense, organizational paradigms.

SUMMARY

Organizations are important objects of study and concern for many reasons. They are vital mechanisms for pursuing collective goals in modern societies. They are not neutral tools because they affect what they produce; they function as collective actors that independently possess certain rights and powers. Both as instruments and as actors, organizations are alleged to be the source of some of contemporary society's most serious problems. Organizations encompass generic social processes but carry them out by means of distinctive structural arrangements.

Although an interest in organizational forms and processes may be traced far back in history, an institutionalized field of scholarly inquiry focusing on the creation and empirical testing of generalized knowledge concerning organizations did not emerge until after 1950. This development was fashioned primarily on a foundation that recognized both the technical and rational features of organizations as well as their human and social aspects. Hence from the beginning the field of organizational studies has been highly interdisciplinary.

Organizations are studied for many purposes and from many points of view. Important bases of divergence include variation among types of organizations, differences in disciplinary background of the investigators, whether research is addressed to more immediate and applied problems or seeks longer-term basic understanding, and level of analysis selected. Three levels of analysis are identified: social psychological, organizational structural, and ecological. It is possible to identify a set of ingredients common to all organizations as well as to identify some of their distinctive capacities as one type of social structure.

Three contrasting definitions of organizations have arisen, each associated with one of three perspectives on organizations: the rational, natural, and open system. The first definition views organizations as highly formalized collectivities oriented to the pursuit of specific goals. The second definition views organizations as social systems, forged by consensus or conflict, seeking to survive. And the third definition views organizations as activities involving coalitions of participants with varying interests embedded in wider environments. The three definitions frame analytically useful, if partial, views of organizations based on differing ontological conceptions. And all three perspectives, albeit in varying combinations, continue to guide and influence the ways we think about organizations and organizing.

CHAPTER 2

Organizations as Rational Systems

A well-designed machine is an instance of total organization, that is, a series of interrelated means contrived to achieve a single end. The machine consists always of particular parts that have no meaning and no function separate from the organized entity to which they contribute. A machine consists of a coherent bringing together of all parts toward the highest possible efficiency of the functioning whole, or interrelationships marshalled wholly toward a given result. In the ideal machine, there can be no extraneous part, no extraneous movement; all is set, part for part, motion for motion, toward the functioning of the whole. The machine is, then, a perfect instance of total rationalization of a field of action and of total organization. This is perhaps even more quickly evident in that larger machine, the assembly line.

JOHN WILLIAM WARD (1964)

From the rational system perspective, organizations are instruments designed to attain specified goals. How blunt or fine an instrument they are depends on many factors that are summarized by the concept of rationality of structure. The term *rationality* in this context is used in the narrow sense of technical or functional rationality (Mannheim, 1950 trans.: 53) and refers to the extent to which a series of actions is organized in such a way as to lead to predetermined goals with maximum efficiency. Thus, rationality refers not to the selection of goals but to their implementation. Indeed, it is perfectly possible to pursue irrational or foolish goals by rational means. Captain Ahab in Melville's classic *Moby Dick* chases the white whale across the seven seas musing; "All my means are sane, my motive and my object mad." Nazi Germany provides a more terrible, nonfiction example. Adolf Hitler's insane objective of eradicating Europe's Jewish population was efficiently pursued by hosts of functionaries like Adolph Eichmann. He took the goal as given and worked faithfully to rationally bring it about, illustrating in Arendt's (1963) phrase, "the banality of evil." It is essential to keep in mind the restricted definition of rationality used within the rational system perspective.

THE DEFINING CHARACTERISTICS

From the standpoint of the rational system perspective, the behavior of organizations and their participants is viewed as actions performed by purposeful and coordinated agents. The language employed connotes this image of rational calculation; terms such as information, knowledge, efficiency, optimization, implementation, and design occur frequently. But other, somewhat different terms also occur, including authority, control, coordination, rules, directives, and performance programs. These terms suggest the cognitive and motivational limitations of individuals and the constraints imposed upon their choices and actions within organizations. They imply that rational behavior within organizations takes place within—some analysts would argue, because of—clearly specified limits.

It is no accident that the key features of organizations emphasized by rational system theorists are the very characteristics identified as distinguishing organizations from other types of collectivities. Rational system theorists stress goal specificity and formalization because each of these elements makes an important contribution to the rationality of organizational action.

Goal Specificity

Goals are conceptions of desired ends. These conceptions vary in the precision and specificity of their criteria of desirability. Specific goals provide unambiguous criteria for selecting among alternative activities. As viewed by economists or by decision theorists, goals are translated into a set of preference or utility functions that represent the value of alternative sets of consequences. Without clear preference orderings among alternatives, rational assessment and choice are not possible.

Specific goals not only supply criteria for choosing among alternative activities; they also guide decisions about how the organization structure itself is to be designed. They specify what tasks are to be performed, what kinds of personnel are to be hired, and how resources are to be allocated among participants. The more general or diffuse the goals, the more difficult it is to design a structure to pursue them.

It is important to note that some organizations espouse quite vague and general goals, but in their actual daily operation are guided by relatively specific goals that do provide criteria for choosing among alternative activities and for designing the organization structure itself. Consider the case of education. Although both educators and lay people will argue endlessly about the true function of education and about the virtues of liberal arts versus more practical types of programs, within a given school there will be considerable agreement on such matters as what disciplines should be represented among the faculty, what courses will count toward graduation (or, at least, who has the right to make these decisions), and how many units are required for a student to graduate. With agreement on such matters as these, administrators can safely allow the faculty occasionally to debate the ultimate aims of education. Similarly, although physicians cannot agree on abstract definitions of health or illness, they do successfully organize their work around such proximate outcomes as relieving pain and prolonging life.

Vague goals do not provide a solid basis for formal organizations. Either the goals become more specific and limited over time, as often happens, or the structures developed are likely to be unstable and amorphous (see Chapter 8). Collective movements such as radical political sects or protest groups may temporarily succeed in mobilizing resources and participants around vague concepts such as human liberation or environmental protection. Indeed, the generality of the goals may broaden their appeal and enlist the support of diverse groups. But such generalized movements are usually sustained and their energy focused by the definition of more specific and limited objectives that can provide the basis for particular organizing efforts. Organizations such as the Sierra Club and Greenpeace gain legitimacy from the broader environmental movement but carve out limited goals around which to mobilize attention and resources.

The most precise description of the manner in which specific goals support rational behavior in organizations is that developed by Herbert Simon, whose classic *Administrative Behavior,* first appeared in 1945 (see Simon, 1997). His ideas on this subject are summarized later in this chapter as an example of one of the major contributions to the rational system perspective.

Formalization

All rational system theorists assume the existence and presume the importance of a formalized structure, but few make explicit the contributions that formalization makes to rationality of behavior in organizations. Let us attempt to do so.

Recall that a structure is formalized to the extent that the rules governing behavior are precisely and explicitly formulated and to the extent that roles and role relations are prescribed independently of the personal attributes and relations of individuals occupying positions in the structure. Formalization may be viewed as an attempt to make behavior more predictable by standardizing and regulating it. This, in turn, permits "stable expectations to be formed by each member of the group as to the behavior of the other members under specified conditions. Such stable expectations are an essential precondition to a rational consideration of the consequences of action in a social group" (Simon, 1997: 110).[1]

Formalization entails a system of abstraction which, to be of value, should be cognitively adequate—sufficiently accurate and complete to guide action—communicable—transmissible to and transparent to users—and contain an improvement trajectory that enables correction over time (Stinchcombe, 2001). Formality may be viewed as "abstraction plus government" (p. 41).

Formalization may also be seen as an attempt to make more explicit and visible the structure of relationships among a set of roles and the principles that govern behavior in the system. It enables participants or observers to diagram the social structures and the work flows, allowing them to depict these relationships and processes with the possibility of consciously manipulating them—designing and redesigning the division of responsibilities, the flow of information or materials, or the ways in which participants report to one another. As Gouldner notes,

> Fundamentally, the rational model implies a "mechanical" model, in that it views the organization as a structure of manipulable parts, each of which is separately modifiable with a view to enhancing the efficiency of the whole. Individual organizational elements are seen as subject to successful and planned modification, enactable by deliberate decision. (1959: 405)

Thus, in a fundamental sense, the organizational structure is viewed as a means, as an instrument, which can be modified as necessary to improve performance. Organizational designers and managers draw and redraw the organizational chart; coaches attempt to improve performance by diagramming plays and giving chalk talks; and consultants are employed to recommend better arrangements for achieving business goals. Over the last several decades, highly technical managerial systems, such as management by objectives (MBO), planning, programming, and budgeting systems (PPBS), program evaluation review techniques (PERT), and international standardization for quality (ISO 9000)—all designed to provide greater visibility and, hence, greater accountability for the critical work flows—have been developed and widely adopted to facilitate rational decision making within complex organizational systems (Drucker, 1976; see ISO, 1998; Odione, 1965; Wildavsky, 1979: 26–40).

Formalization can contribute to rationality in other, less obvious ways. In addition to making behavior more available for conscious design, the structuring of expectations prior to interaction carries with it another distinct advantage. Laboratory research by Bales (1953) documents the strains and tensions generated when a status structure begins to emerge among individuals who entered the situation as presumed status equals. These status battles and their associated interpersonal tensions are reduced by the prestructuring of differentiated role

---

[1]Simon's basic work, *Administrative Behavior*, first appeared in 1945. However, all our references are to the fourth edition of this work, published in 1997, which contains an extensive new introduction and commentaries on original chapters.

expectations in which an individual is assigned a role prior to his or her participation. Thus, in an experimental study, Carter and his colleagues (1953) found that group leaders who had been appointed to their position by the experimenter spent less time attempting to assert their power and defend their position and encountered less resistance to their leadership efforts than leaders who emerged through interaction processes (see also Verba, 1961: 161–72).

Formalization also serves to "objectify" the structure—to make the definitions of roles and relationships appear to be both objective and external to the participating actors. These qualities contribute substantially to the efficacy of these systems in controlling behavior. A series of experiments conducted by Zucker (1977) demonstrate this effect. Subjects placed in an ambiguous situation were much more likely to accept influence from another when that person was defined as holding a specified organizational position (not, by the way, a position of authority but simply a named office) than when the person was described simply as "another person." Formalization, hence, works to legitimate inequalities in hierarchies.

The social cement that binds and regulates activities and interactions in informal groups is the *sociometric* structure—the patterning of affective ties among participants (Moreno, 1953). The creation of a formal structure constitutes an important functional alternative to the sociometric structure. With formalization, the smooth functioning of the organization is to some degree made independent of the feelings—negative or positive—that particular members have for one another. As Merton notes, "formality facilitates the interaction of the occupants of offices despite their (possibly hostile) private attitudes toward one another" (1957: 195). Indeed, many organizations even discourage the development of positive sentiments among their members for fear that such emotional ties will undermine discipline and judgment and interfere with attempts to deploy participants rationally.

Formalization makes allowances for the finitude and inconstancy of human actors. The process of *succession*—the movement of individuals into and out of offices—can be routinized and regularized so that one appropriately trained person can replace another with minimal disturbance to the functioning of the organization. In this sense, organizations can—although few actually do—achieve a kind of immortality. The Roman Catholic Church provides a notable example.

Formalized structures are thus rendered independent of the participation of any particular individual. A related consequence is that it becomes less essential to recruit unusually gifted individuals for the key positions. The power and influence of leaders can be determined in part by the definition of their offices and not made to depend on their personal qualities—their charisma. In his discussion of political structures, MacIver notes,

> The man who commands may be no wiser, no abler, may be, in some sense no better than the average of his fellows; sometimes, by any intrinsic standard, he is inferior to them. Here is the magic of government. (1947: 13)

More generally, here is the magic of formalization! To explain more clearly the alchemy of this process, Wolin draws an analogy between the formalization of structure and scientific method:

> Method, like organization, is the salvation of puny men, the compensatory device for individual foibles, the gadget which allows mediocrity to transcend its limitations. . . . Organization, by simplifying and routinizing procedures, eliminates the need for surpassing talent. It is predicated on "average human beings." (1960: 383)

In the highly formalized organization, the innovating entrepreneur is supplanted by a corps of administrators and technical specialists. Leadership, even innovation, is routinized and regularized by being incorporated into the formal structure (Galbraith, 1967; Schumpeter, 1947).

All of this may be hard to accept by today's sophisticated and increasingly cynical observers of organizations, most of whom are likely to stress the inadequacies of formalization—its rigidity, its ineptness, its tendency to elevate form over substance. Many observers, including sociologists, have concluded that "formality is all a fraud" (Stinchcombe, 2001: 1). However, rational system theorists insist that, while formal routines do not always work and may sometimes be corrupted, they represent a powerful tool to improving rationality of action. Stinchcombe argues,

> The unpopularity of formality in social life is due to the fact that it has been understood by its pathologies. When it works properly it achieves the ends it was built for, the substantive ends that people have decided to pursue. When formality pursues ends alien to us, it is in general because those are the ends of others. It is not the formality that is at fault, but the politics that delivers formal powers to others. (2001: 17)

Note that in describing the contributions of formalization to rational functioning of the organization, emphasis has been placed simply on formalization per se—on the existence of role specifications—without attention to content, to the particular rules prescribing preferred behaviors. Most rational system theorists, examples of which are described in the following section, assume the importance of formalization and devote their energies to developing precise, concrete guidelines to govern participants' activities. They attempt to describe or to prescribe principles that will be conducive to supporting rational organizational behavior in particular times and places.

SELECTED SCHOOLS

The preceding discussion represents an effort to distill the central elements characterizing the rational system perspective. As noted, this perspective does not reflect a unitary theory but encompasses a set of generically related but distinctive approaches. Four such approaches will be briefly described: Taylor's scientific management; administrative theory as developed by Fayol and others; Weber's theory of bureaucracy; and Simon's discussion of administrative behavior.

Taylor's Scientific Management

The scientific management approach received its primary impetus from the work of Frederick W. Taylor (1911) in the late nineteenth and early twentieth centuries but was carried forward by the contributions of others, such as Frank and Lillian Gilbreth, Henry Gantt, and Charles Bedeaux. Taylor may be viewed as the culmination of a series of developments occurring in the United States between 1880 and 1920 in which engineers took the lead in endeavoring to rationalize industrial organizations (Shenhav, 1995; 1999). With the maturation of the industrial revolution, engineers, particularly mechanical engineers, began to promote rationalization of practice through standardization of, first, "fittings, screws, nuts, [and] bolts" and, subsequently, "the human element in production" (Calvert, 1967: 178; see also Noble, 1977: 83). The extension of standardization principles to workers was associated with an increase in industrial unrest during the period 1900–1920 (Shenhav, 1995), whether as cause or effect is less clear. Unlike similar developments in Europe, the drive toward "systematization" in the United States appeared to be largely a professional project rather than one championed by the state (Guillén, 1994).

Taylor and his followers insisted that it was possible to scientifically analyze tasks performed by individual workers in order to discover those procedures that would produce the maximum output with the minimum input of energies and resources. Efforts were concentrated on analyzing individual tasks, but attempts to rationalize labor at the level of the individual worker inevitably led to changes in the entire structure of work arrangements. Ward describes the sequence of changes that resulted from Taylor's efforts to improve the efficiency of performing such menial tasks as shoveling coal and iron ore in a steel mill:

> First, a variety of kinds of shovels had to be designed to handle different kinds of materials. That also meant building shovel rooms in the various parts of the yard, so that a gang would have the proper tools at hand. To eliminate the waste motion of wandering about so large a yard, it meant, as Taylor said, "organizing and planning work at least a day in advance," so that when men checked in, they would be at that day's work. This meant, Taylor reported, building a labor office for a planning staff—a bureaucracy, as we would say. Large maps of the yard were then necessary to show at a glance the location of different kinds of work and the location of men. Furthermore, the installation of a telephone network was essential for more effective interior communication. Once the yard was mapped so that one could see at a glance the relationships in time and sequence between different jobs, it led, naturally enough, to the reorganization of the yard itself, so that materials could be delivered or dumped in a more logical sequence.

One can see readily enough what happened. Taylor's attempt to make the crudest physical act of labor efficient led inexorably to a further organization of every aspect of the production process. (Ward, 1964: 64–65)

It was not only, or even primarily, the lot of workers that was to be altered by the introduction of scientific management: the role of management was also to be transformed. Taylor aspired to replace the arbitrary and capricious activities of managers with analytical, scientific procedures:

Under scientific management arbitrary power, arbitrary dictation, ceases; and every single subject, large and small, becomes the question for scientific investigation, for reduction to law. . . .

The man at the head of the business under scientific management is governed by rules and laws which have been developed through hundreds of experiments just as much as the workman is, and the standards which have been developed are equitable. (Taylor, 1947: 211, 189)

The activities of both managers and workers were to be rationalized; both were equally subject to the regimen of science.

Taylor believed that the adoption of scientific management principles by industrial concerns would usher in a new era of industrial peace. The interests of labor and management would be rendered compatible. Workers could be scientifically selected to perform those tasks for which they were best suited. Scientifically determined procedures would allow them to work at peak efficiency, in return for which they would receive top wages.

Once work was scientifically plotted, Taylor felt, there could be no disputes about how hard one should work or the pay one should receive for labor. "As reasonably might we insist on bargaining about the time and place of the rising and setting sun," he once said. (Bell, 1960: 228)

Managers would cooperate with workers in devising appropriate work arrangements and pay scales and enjoy the fruits of maximum profits.

Many of the elements that Taylor pioneered were employed to provide the basis for the mass production technologies—known after their most famous exemplar, Henry Ford, as "Fordism"—which represented the high-water mark of the Industrial Revolution. To Taylor's meticulous time-motion studies and perfection of each worker's movement, Ford added the specialized machines, interchangeable parts, simplified modes of assembly, and conveyor belts that greatly enhanced the productivity of workers turning out standardized products for mass markets (Womack, Jones, and Roos, 1991: 26–38). Zuboff summarizes the key elements of Fordism:

This formula has dominated the design of mass-production techniques throughout the twentieth century. Effort is simplified (though its pace is frequently intensified) while skill demands are reduced by new methods of task organization and new forms of machinery. (1988: 47)

Taylor was also a leader in formulating the elements of what Cole (1994) has termed the "traditional quality paradigm." This approach stressed the "importance of identifying work tasks and then making that method the standard," together with an emphasis on inspection, involving elaborate designs to ensure that the inspectors' activities were themselves subject to careful review. In contrast to the contemporary emphasis on total quality management (TQM), which we discuss in Chapter 6, the traditional approach devised by Taylor and others viewed quality as a specialized staff function and embraced "an inspection-oriented rather than a prevention-oriented approach" (Cole, 1994: 69; see also, Cole, 1999).

The underlying spirit of Taylor's approach—an amalgam of the Protestant ethic, social Darwinism, and a faith in technical expertise—struck an important nerve that continues to reverberate up to the present time.

> Taylor bequeathed a clockwork world of tasks timed to the hundredth of a minute, of standardized factories, machines, women, and men. He helped instill in us the fierce, unholy obsession with time, order, productivity, and efficiency that marks our age. (Kanigel, 1997: 7)

Taylor's methods were by no means restricted to manufacturing plants but rapidly spread to the organization of schools, fast-food restaurants, and even amusement parks like Disneyland (Callahan, 1962; Ritzer, 1993; Van Maanen, 1991).

Still, he and his methods were anathema to workers and to many managers. Workers and their unions resisted time-study procedures and attempts to standardize every aspect of their performance. They rejected incentive systems requiring them to perform continuously at a peak level of efficiency. Managers, for their part, increasingly were disquieted by Taylor's vision of their role.

> After all, Taylor had questioned their good judgment and superior ability which had been the subject of public celebration for many years. Hence, many employers regarded his methods as an unwarranted interference with managerial prerogatives. (Bendix, 1956: 280)

Given the increasing resistance of both managers and workers, scientific management has persisted more in the guise of a set of technical procedures than as an overarching managerial ideology (Guillén, 1994: 48–58).[2]

---

[2]Perhaps the most useful statement of Taylor's conception is contained in his testimony before the Special House Committee to Investigate the Taylor and Other Systems of Shop Management in 1912. This testimony is reprinted in Taylor (1947). Summaries of and commentaries on his contribution will be found in Bell (1960: 222–37), Bendix (1956: 274–81), and Guillén (1994: 30–58). Kanigel (1997) provides a detailed biography and an assessment of the wider impact of Taylor's work. A severe critique of Taylor's approach from a Marxist perspective is provided by Braverman (1974: 85–138).

Fayol's Administrative Theory

A second approach, developing concurrently with scientific management, emphasized management functions and attempted to generate broad administrative principles that would serve as guidelines for the rationalization of organizational activities. Whereas Taylor and his fellow engineers proposed to rationalize the organization from the "bottom up"—changes in the performance of individual tasks affecting the larger structure of work relations—the administrative management theorists worked to rationalize the organization from the "top down." Henri Fayol, a French industrialist writing in the early part of the twentieth century, was one of the earliest exponents of this approach, but his ideas did not become widely available in this country until 1949, when his major work was translated. Influential participants in this movement in the United States included two General Motors executives, Mooney and Reiley (1939), whose treatise on management principles gained a wide following, and Gulick and Urwick, who in 1937 collaborated to edit the volume *Papers on the Science of Administration.*

The various contributors to this perspective did not reach agreement as to the number of principles required or the precise formulation of many specific principles, but there was considerable consensus on the importance of two types of activities: cordination and specialization (Massie, 1965).

- The major principles developed to guide *coordination* activities include the scalar principle, which emphasizes the hierarchical organizational form in which all participants are linked into a single pyramidal structure of control relations; the unity-of-command principle, specifying that no organizational participants should receive orders from more than one superior; the span-of-control principle, which emphasizes that no superior should have more subordinates than can be effectively overseen (theorists were unable to agree on the precise number of subordinates who could be supervised); and the exception principle, which proposes that all routine matters be handled by subordinates leaving superiors free to deal with exceptional situations to which existing rules are inapplicable.

- *Specialization* issues include decisions both about how various activities are to be distributed among organizational positions and about how such positions can most effectively be grouped into work units or departments. Among the principles espoused to guide these types of decisions is the departmentalization principle, which maintains that activities should be grouped so as to combine homogeneous or related activities within the same organizational unit. Homogeneity might be based on similarity of purpose (activities contributing to the same subgoal—for example, marketing); process (activities requiring similar operations—for example, computer programming); clientele (activities performed on the same set of recipients—for example, a medical team organized around the care of a specific group of patients); or place (for example, services provided to individuals in a given geographical territory). Also proposed is the line–staff principle in which "line" activities, those directly concerned with achieving organizational goals, are distinguished from "staff" activities, consisting of advice, service, or support. Staff units are to be segregated from the scalar organization of power and made responsible and subordinate to appropriate line units.

Note the heavy emphasis on formalization implicit in these principles. Careful specification of work activities and concern for their grouping and coordination are the hallmark of the formalized structure. Mooney makes explicit this call for formalization by distinguishing between jobs (positions) and the person on the job:

> In every organization there is a collective job to be done, consisting always of the sum of many individual jobs, and the task of administration, operating through management, is the co-ordination of all the human effort necessary to this end. Such co-ordination, however, always presupposes the jobs to be coordinated. The job as such is therefore antecedent to the man on the job, and the sound co-ordination of these jobs, considered simply as jobs, must be the first and necessary condition in the effective co-ordination of the human factor. (1937: 92)

The more astute administrative theorists recognized that their managerial principles furnished at best only broad guidelines for decision making. Thus, Fayol reminds practitioners:

> The soundness and good working order of the body corporate depends on a certain number of conditions termed indiscriminately principles, laws, rules. For preference I shall adopt the term principles whilst dissociating it from any suggestion of rigidity, for there is nothing rigid or absolute in management affairs, it is all a question of proportion. Seldom do we have to apply the same principle twice in identical conditions; allowance must be made for different changing circumstances. (1949 trans.: 19)

And Gulick cautions:

> Students of administration have long sought a single principle of effective departmentalization just as alchemists sought the philosopher's stone. But they have sought in vain. There is apparently no one most effective system of departmentalism. (Gulick and Urwick, 1937: 31)

In spite of such disclaimers, the managerial principles enunciated by the administrative theorists drew considerable criticism. Much of this criticism came from natural system proponents (see Chapter 3), but a good deal of the fire came from other rational system theorists on the ground that the so-called principles were mere truisms or common-sense pronouncements (Massie, 1965: 406). No doubt the most devastating critique was provided by Herbert Simon whose classic, *Administrative Behavior*, commenced with "an indictment of much current writing about administrative matters" (1997: 43). He examines one principle after another, observing that many occur in pairs that are, on close inspection, contradictory; others lack specificity or reveal "a deceptive simplicity—a simplicity that conceals fundamental ambiguities" (p. 30).

Without gainsaying any of these criticisms, we can admire what the administrative theorists attempted to do. They were pioneers in identifying the fundamental features of formal organizational structure, audaciously clinging to the view that all organizations contain certain common structural characteristics. They raised the level of analysis to focus not on individual behavior, but on organization structure. With the improved vision of hindsight, it is now apparent that their search for general principles was confounded in part by their failure to develop conditional generalizations—statements that specify the limits of their applicability to particular situations or types of organizations. Indeed, this is the major insight that underlies the contingency theory of organizations, described in Chapters 4–6.

Weber's Theory of Bureaucracy

Our consideration of Weber's work must begin with an important disclaimer. Although Weber's writings had a profound influence on the development of organization theory in the United States from the time when they were first translated into English, because his arguments were available in disconnected fragments, they were taken out of context and incorrectly interpreted. As Collins has observed,

> there is nothing better known in the field of organizations, perhaps in all of sociology, than Weber's model of bureaucracy. It also happens that there is no more complete misunderstanding of a major sociological theory than the way Weber's organizational theory was treated in American sociology. (1986: 286)

Early interpretations of Weber's work were flawed in two major respects. First, his famous depiction of the central features of rational-legal "bureaucratic" structures was decontextualized, taken out of historical context, and treated as a kind of caricature of modern administration forms. Second, most of his arguments were interpreted as belonging within the framework of a conventional technical rationality, whereas his conception was more complex, paving the way to an alternative conception of rationality. We begin our review by attempting to place Weber's work back in its proper historical context.

Bureaucracy and Rational-legal Authority. Max Weber, the influential German sociologist/political economist was a contemporary of Taylor and Fayol but working along quite different lines. Weber's analysis of administrative structures was only a limited segment of his much larger interest in accounting for the unique features of Western civilization (see Bendix, 1960; Swedberg, 1998). In his view, what was distinctive was the growth of rationality in the West, and his active mind roamed across legal, religious, political, and economic systems, as well as administrative structures, as he searched for materials to test and extend his notions by comparing and contrasting differing cultures and historical periods. Weber's analysis of administrative systems can be fully appreciated only if it is seen in this larger context, since his listing of the structural characteristics of bureaucracy was generated in an attempt to differentiate this more rational system from earlier forms.

In his justly famous typology, Weber distinguishes three types of authority:

- *Traditional* authority—resting on an established belief in the sanctity of immemorial traditions and the legitimacy of those exercising authority under them
- *Rational-legal* authority—resting on a belief in the "legality" of patterns of normative rules and the right of those elevated to authority under such rules to issue commands
- *Charismatic* authority—resting on devotion to the specific and exceptional sanctity, heroism or exemplary character of an individual person, and of the normative patterns or order revealed or ordained by him or her (1968 trans.; Vol. 1: 212–301).

For Weber, differences in authority were based on differences in the beliefs by which legitimacy is attributed to an authority relation (see the discussion of power and authority in Chapter 8). Each authority type is associated with a distinctive administrative structure. Traditional authority gives rise to the particularistic and diffuse structures exemplified by patrimonial systems, including gerontocracy, patriarchalism, and feudalism (see Dibble, 1965; Swedberg, 1998: 62–70).[3] The simplest way to visualize a patrimonial system is as a household writ large: an estate or production organization governed by a ruler-owner who in managing the enterprise relies for assistance on a variety of dependents, ranging from slaves to serfs to sons. Rational-legal authority provides the basis for the more impersonal specific and formal structures of which the most highly developed form is the modern bureaucracy. And charismatic authority is associated with the "strictly personal" relations linking an impressive leader with his or her devoted coterie of followers or disciples.

In Weber's view, only traditional and rational-legal authority relations are sufficiently stable to provide a foundation for permanent administrative structures. And, during recent centuries, particularly in Western societies, traditional structures are viewed as gradually giving way to rational-legal structures, most notably in "the modern state" and in "the most advanced institutions of capitalism," due to their "purely technical superiority over any other form of organization" (Weber, 1946 trans.: 196, 214).

Charismatic forms arise in periods of instability and crisis when extraordinary measures are called for and seemingly offered by individuals perceived as possessing uncommon gifts of mind and spirit. Lenin, Hitler, Gandhi, Mao, and Martin Luther King Jr. are only a few recent examples of such charismatic leaders, illustrating their diversity and their power to inspire the fanatical devotion of others around their personal vision of "reform." However, for such movements to persist, they must move in the direction of one or the other stable forms, by establishing "new" traditional structures or new bureaucratic structures.[4]

---

[3]Such traditional structures are not simply of historical interest. Many contemporary societies contain various traditional and "neo-traditional" elements in their political and economic organizations. For example, Walder (1986) provides an interesting account of such arrangements in Maoist China.

[4]The art of "inventing" traditions is described by Hobsbawm and Ranger (1983).

Charisma becomes routinized: the circle of adherents expands to include larger numbers of, but less committed, participants; systematic sources of support replace voluntary and heartfelt, but irregular, contributions; personal ties between leader and followers are replaced by more orderly but impersonal arrangements; and rules of succession are developed in recognition of the truth that no one lives forever–not even a superhuman leader.[5]

Weber's typology of authority is of interest not only because it underlies his conception of basic changes occurring in administrative systems over time. In addition, the distinction between traditional and rational-legal forms serves as the basis for his influential conception of the characteristics of bureaucratic structures. Before describing Weber's conception, however, it is necessary to briefly comment on the concept of bureaucracy because this term is used in so many ways. For many, bureaucracy is employed as an epithet, signifying rule-encumbered inefficiency or mindless overconformity (see for example, Mises, 1944; Parkinson, 1957). While acknowledging that this description fits all too many organizations, we define bureaucracy in a more neutral manner, following the lead of Bendix. He observes: "Seen historically, bureaucratization may be interpreted as the increasing subdivision of the functions which the owner-managers of the early enterprises had performed personally in the course of their daily routine" (1956: 211–12). Such functions include supervision, personnel selection, accounting and financial management, record keeping, job design, and planning. This definition excludes the head of the organization—whether president, dictator, or owner—as well as those who carry out the direct work of the organization: the production personnel. A useful way of thinking about a bureaucracy is that it consists of those positions or activities whose function is to service and maintain the organization itself. In short, we define *bureaucracy* as the existence of a specialized administrative staff. Like formalization and goal specificity, bureaucracy should be viewed as a variable; organizations vary in terms of the proportion of personnel they devote to administrative as compared to production and service.

Weber's definition of bureaucracy differs from our own. In his conception, bureaucracy refers to a particular type of administrative structure, developed in association with the rational-legal mode of authority. In many discussions of Weber's work, his model of bureaucracy is depicted as a simple list of administrative characteristics present in bureaucratic forms, characteristics such as

- fixed division of labor among participants
- hierarchy of offices
- set of general rules that govern performance
- separation of personal from official property and rights

---

[5]Modern political structures typically incorporate charismatically based authority systems at their core. The personal staff of contemporary political leaders—presidents, governors, senators—exhibit many of the features associated with the leader-disciple model (Hamilton and Biggart, 1984: 15–54).

- selection of personnel on the basis of technical qualifications
- employment viewed as a career by participants

However, his contribution can be better appreciated if these bureaucratic elements are described in relation to the traditional features they supplanted. Thus, according to Weber, bureaucratic systems are distinguished from traditional administrative forms by features such as the following:

- Jurisdictional areas are clearly specified: the regular activities required of personnel are distributed in a fixed way as official duties (in contrast with the traditional arrangement, in which the division of labor is not firm or regular but depends on assignments made by the leader, which can be changed at any time).
- The organization of offices follows the principle of hierarchy: each lower office is controlled and supervised by a higher one. However, the scope of authority of superiors over subordinates is circumscribed, and lower offices enjoy a right of appeal (in contrast with traditional forms, where authority relations are more diffuse, being based on personal loyalty, and are not ordered into clear hierarchies).
- An intentionally established system of abstract rules governs official decisions and actions. These rules are relatively stable and exhaustive and can be learned. Decisions are recorded in permanent files. (In traditional systems, general rules of administration either do not exist or are vaguely stated, ill-defined, and subject to change at the whim of the leader. No attempt is made to keep permanent records of transactions.)
- The "means of production or administration"—for example, tools and equipment or rights and privileges—belong to the office, not the officeholder, and may not be appropriated. Personal property is clearly separated from official property, and working space from living quarters. (Such distinctions are not maintained in traditional administrative systems since there is no separation of the ruler's personal household business from the larger "public" business under his direction.)
- Officials are personally free, selected on the basis of technical qualifications, appointed to office (not elected), and compensated by salary. (In more traditional administrative systems, officials are often selected from among those who are personally dependent on the leader—for example, slaves, serfs, relatives. Selection is governed by particularistic criteria, and compensation often takes the form of benefices—rights granted to individuals that, for example, allow them access to the stores of the ruler or give them grants of land from which they can appropriate the fees or taxes. Benefices, like fiefs in feudalistic systems, may become hereditary and sometimes are bought and sold.)
- Employment by the organization constitutes a career for officials. An official is a full-time employee and anticipates a lifelong career in the agency. After a trial period he or she gains tenure of position and is protected against arbitrary dismissal. (In traditional systems, officials serve at the pleasure of the leader and so lack clear expectations about the future and security of tenure.) (Weber, 1968 trans.: Vol. 3: 956–1005)

When we thus juxtapose Weber's list of bureaucratic characteristics and the related aspects of traditional systems, a clearer view emerges of Weber's central message. He viewed each bureaucratic element as a solution to a problem or defect contained within the earlier administrative systems.[6] Further, each element operates not in isolation but as part of a system of elements that, in combination, is expected to provide more effective and efficient administration. To capture both the notions of distinctive elements and their interrelation, Weber employed what is termed an "ideal-type" construct. This approach attempts to isolate those elements regarded as most characteristic of the phenomenon to be explored. The term *ideal-type* is somewhat misleading, since it does not refer to a normatively preferred type, but to the construction of a simplified model that focuses attention on the most salient or distinctive features of some phenomenon.

Even though Weber's model of administrative systems emphasized that they were composed of many interrelated factors, in his own analysis he focused primarily on organizations as systems of power or domination in which the leader exercises control over and through a hierarchy of officials who both receive and give orders. It is administration based on discipline, and discipline is "nothing but the consistently rationalized, methodically prepared and exact execution of the received order" (Weber, 1968 trans.: 1149).

In contrasting the rational-legal with the other two (nonrational) types, Weber stressed two seemingly contradictory points. First, the rational-legal form provides the basis for a more stable and predictable administrative structure for both superiors and subordinates. The behavior of subordinates is rendered more reliable by the specificity of their role obligations, the clarity of hierarchical connections, and their continuing dependence on the hierarchy in the short run for income and in the longer term for career progression. And superiors are prevented from behaving arbitrarily or capriciously in their demands made on subordinates.

But, second, the rational-legal structure permits subordinates to exercise "relatively greater independence and discretion" than is possible in the other types of administrative systems (Smith and Ross, 1978). Because obedience is owed not to a person—whether a traditional chief or a charismatic leader—but to a set of impersonal principles, subordinates in bureaucratic systems have firmer grounds for independent action, guided by their interpretation of the principles. They also have a clear basis for questioning the directives of superiors, whose actions are presumably constrained by the same impersonal framework of rules. By supporting increased independence and discretion among lower administrative officials constrained by general administrative policies and specified procedures, bureaucratic systems are capable of handling more complex administrative tasks than traditional systems.

---

[6]For a revealing description of the gradual replacement of a patrimonial by a bureaucratic structure, see Rosenberg's (1958) account of the emergence of the Prussian state during the eighteenth century. This "German" case was, of course, well known to Weber, whose father was a municipal official in Berlin and subsequently a member of both the regional and imperial parliament (see Weber, 1975 trans.).

Critics and Admirers. Weber's analysis of bureaucratic structure, while influential, has also been controversial, and his ideas have been subject to continuing disputation and varied interpretation. Some critics challenged Weber's views on authority which, as we have suggested, play a central role in his analysis of administration systems. Parsons and Gouldner have suggested that Weber tended to conflate two analytically distinguishable bases of authority. On the one hand, in his discussion of the administrative hierarchy of bureaucracies, Weber asserts that authority rests on "incumbency in a legally defined office." On the other hand, in his discussion of criteria for recruitment and advancement, Weber argues that authority is based on "technical competence" (Parsons, 1947: 58–60). Indeed, at one point Weber states, "Bureaucratic administration means fundamentally the exercise of control on the basis of knowledge" (1947 trans.: 339). Gouldner underlines the contradiction:

> Weber, then, thought of bureaucracy as a Janus-faced organization, looking two ways at once. On the one side, it was administration based on discipline. In the first emphasis, obedience is invoked as a means to an end; an individual obeys because the rule or order is felt to be the best known method of realizing some goal.
>
> In his second conception, Weber held that bureaucracy was a mode of administration in which obedience was an end in itself. The individual obeys the order, setting aside judgments either of its rationality or morality, primarily because of the position occupied by the person commanding. The content of the order is not examinable. (1954: 22–23)

One might defend Weber by insisting that there is likely to be a strong positive correlation between a person's position in the hierarchy and his or her degree of technical competence. Such may have been the case in Weber's day, when on-the-job experience was a major source of technical competence but seems far off the mark in today's world of minute specialization supported by prolonged and esoteric training in institutions separated from the work setting. Thompson convincingly portrays the ever-widening gap between ability and authority in modern organizations, asserting that

> Authority is centralized, but ability is inherently decentralized because it comes from practice and training rather than from definition. Whereas the boss retains his full rights to make all decisions, he has less and less ability to do so because of the advance of science and technology. (1961: 47)

Staff–line arrangements, in which the positional authority of the line administrator is distinguished from the technical expertise of the staff specialist, appear to be not so much a solution to the difficulty (see studies by Dalton [1950; 1959] of staff–line conflict) as a structural recognition of the distinctiveness of the two sources of authority sloughed over in Weber's analysis.

As previewed at the beginning of our discussion, a number of recent commentators have suggested that early generations of organizational analysts, especially Americans, misread Weber's work and distorted his views (see Collins, 1975; McNeil, 1978; Thompson, 1980). In particular, contemporary Weberian scholars point out that Weber identified a number of types of rationality that his early readers tended to conflate or confuse (see Albrow, 1970; Kalberg, 1980). Early influential interpreters such as Blau (1956) and J. D. Thompson (1967) assumed that Weber equated bureaucratic rationality with efficiency. A closer reading, however, makes it clear that Weber distinguished between technical rationality—emphasizing instrumental means-ends efficiency—and formal rationality, and that he defined bureaucracy as rational primarily in the latter sense. *Formal rationality* refers to the orientation of action to formal rules and laws (Kalberg, 1980: 1158).

> At the heart of Weber's idea of formal rationality was the idea of correct calculation, in either numerical terms, as with the accountant, or in logical terms, as with the lawyer. . . . Each of the propositions involved in his pure type of bureaucracy referred to a procedure where either legal norms or monetary calculation were involved, and where impersonality and expert knowledge were necessary. Any such procedure was for Weber intrinsically rational, irrespective of its relation to organizational objectives. In short, he was not offering a theory of efficiency, but a statement of the formal procedures which were prevalent in modern administration. (Albrow, 1970: 65)

Employing this conception of formal rationality, Weber recognized the potential for conflict between the abstract formalism of legal certainty on the one hand and objective accomplishments on the other. He understood the difference between, for example, the perfection of legal procedures and the attainment of justice. He realized the possibility that formalization can degenerate into formalism. Most important, he recognized in his work alternative meanings of rationality and, in so doing, anticipated truths that contemporary institutional theorists have rediscovered and amplified (see Meyer, 1990). We pursue these insights in Chapter 10.

Early readers of Weber also failed to recognize his strong ambivalence about the developments he charted: his recognition that bureaucratic forms were capable of growing with an inexorable logic of their own, concentrating great power in the hands of their masters, reducing individual participants to the status of "cog in an ever-moving mechanism," and having the potential to imprison humanity in an "iron cage" (Weber, 1946 trans.: 228; 1958 trans.: 181). These concerns continue to be voiced by bureaucracy's many critics.

Finally, early conveyers of Weber's work decontextualized it, extracting Weber's ideal-type characterization of bureaucratic structure from its historical context. Rather, as we will see, Weber was ahead of his time in recognizing the importance of the wider social context on the form and functioning of organizations.

In sum, Weber was clearly a rational system theorist even though early interpreters misconstrued and oversimplified the type of rationality Weber had in mind. While there remains controversy over some aspects of Weber's conceptions and arguments, there is virtually universal agreement that he was the premier analyst of organizations, an intellectual giant whose conceptions continue to shape and enrich our understandings of how and why organizations arose, and the ways in which their operation affects the wider social structure.[7]

Simon's Theory of Administrative Behavior

Herbert Simon, both in his early work on administration and in his later collaborative work with March, clarified the processes by which goal specificity and formalization contribute to rational behavior in organizations (March and Simon, 1958; Simon, 1997). We earlier observed that Simon was critical of the platitudes developed by Fayol and others searching for management principles. He also criticized the assumptions made by Taylor and other early theorists about the actors in organizations. For the "economic man" motivated by self-interest and completely informed about all available alternatives, Simon proposed to substitute a more human "administrative man." The latter seeks to pursue his or her self-interests but does not always know what they are, is aware of only a few of all the possible alternatives, and is willing to settle for an adequate solution ("satisfice") rather than attempting to optimize.

Following the lead of Barnard (1938), whose contributions are described in Chapter 3, Simon distinguishes between (1) an individual's decisions to join and to continue to participate in an organization and (2) the decisions an individual is asked to make as a participant in the organization. Only the latter set of decisions is of interest in the present context. A scientifically relevant description of an organization, according to Simon, details what decisions individuals make as organizational participants and the influences to which they are subject in making these decisions. In general, in Simon's view, organizations both simplify decisions and support participants in the decisions they need to make.

A primary way in which organizations *simplify* participants' decisions is to restrict the ends toward which activity is directed. Simon points out that goals affect behavior only as they enter into decisions about how to behave. Goals supply the value premises that underlie decisions. *Value premises* are assumptions about what ends are preferred or desirable. They are combined in decisions with *factual premises*—assumptions about the observable world and the way in which it operates. The more precise and specific the value premises, the greater their impact on the resulting decisions, since specific goals clearly distinguish acceptable from unacceptable (or more from less acceptable) alternatives. Typically, participants higher in the hierarchy make decisions with a larger value component, whereas lower participants are more apt to make decisions having a larger factual component. Those closer to the top make decisions about what the organization is going to do; those in lower positions are more likely to be allowed to make choices as to how the organization can best carry

---

[7]The secondary literature examining Weber's work is immense, but the discussions of Alexander (1983, vol. 3), Collins (1986), and Swedberg (1998) are particularly insightful.

out its tasks. Simon (1997: 55–67) insists that quite different criteria of correctness underlie these two classes of decisions: choice of ends can be validated only by fiat or consensus; choice of means can be validated empirically.

Ultimate goals served by organizations are frequently somewhat vague and imprecise. Some organizations exist to develop and transmit knowledge, others to maintain public order, and others to care for and cure patients. Such general goals in themselves provide few cues for guiding the behavior of participants. However, as March and Simon argue, they can serve as the starting point for the construction of *means-ends chains* that involve

> (1) starting with the general goal to be achieved, (2) discovering a set of means, very generally specified, for accomplishing this goal, (3) taking each of these means, in turn, as a new subgoal and discovering a set of more detailed means for achieving it, etc. (1958: 191)

In this manner, a hierarchy of goals is established in which each level is

> considered as an end relative to the levels below it and as a means relative to the levels above it. Through the hierarchical structure of ends, behavior attains integration and consistency, for each member of a set of behavior alternatives is then weighted in terms of a comprehensive scale of values—the "ultimate" ends. (Simon, 1997: 74)

For example, in a manufacturing organization, an assignment to an individual worker to construct a specific component of a piece of equipment such as an engine provides that worker with an end toward which to direct his or her activities. This end, viewed from the level of his or her supervisor, is only a means toward the creation of the engine. The supervisor's end is to ensure that all parts are available when needed and are correctly assembled to produce the engine. However, this objective, when viewed from the next higher level, is only a means to the end of completing the final product, such as a lawn mower, containing the engine. The completion of all parts and assembly operations required to produce the lawn mower, while an end for the manufacturing division, is only a means at a higher level to the ultimate end of selling the lawn mower for profit to retail outlets. Viewed from the bottom up, the rationality of individual decisions and activities can be evaluated only as they relate to higher-order decisions; each subgoal can be assessed only in terms of its consistency or congruency with more general goals. Viewed from the top down, the factoring of general purposes into specific subgoals that can then be assigned to organizational subunits (individuals or departments) enhances the possibility of rational behavior by specifying value premises and hence simplifying the required decisions at every level. From this perspective, then, an organization's hierarchy can be viewed as a congealed set of means-ends chains promoting consistency of decisions and activities throughout the organization. Or, as Collins suggests, March and Simon describe organizational structure "as a nested set of plans for action" (1975: 316).

The ultimate goals—making a profit, achieving growth, prolonging life—are those that, by definition, are not viewed as means to ends, but as ends in themselves. They may be determined by consensus or by decree. In either case, any challenge to these ultimate objectives is likely to be met with strong resistance. Physicians, for example, are reluctant to consider the merits of euthanasia, and capitalists react with righteous indignation to any questions concerning their right to profits. Apart from any considerations of self-interest, such emotional reactions stem from the half-conscious realization that any challenge to the ultimate objectives calls into question the premises around which the entire enterprise is structured.

In addition to simplifying decisions for participants in all these ways, organizations also *support* participants in the decisions they are expected to make. A formalized structure supports rational decision making not only by parceling out responsibilities among participants but also by providing them with the necessary means to handle them: resources, information, equipment. Specialized roles and rules, information channels, training programs, standard operating procedures—all may be viewed as mechanisms both for restricting the range of decisions each participant makes and for assisting the participant in making appropriate decisions within that range. As Perrow (1986: 128–131) notes, Simon's model of organizational influence stresses "unobtrusive" control of participants: training and channeling of information and attention play a larger role in producing dependable behavior than do commands or sanctions.

Underlying Simon's model of organizational decision making is a conception of cognitive limits on individual decision makers.[8] Simon stresses that

> It is impossible for the behavior of a single, isolated individual to reach any high degree of rationality. The number of alternatives he must explore is too great, the information he would need to evaluate them so vast that even an approximation to objective rationality is hard to conceive. Individual choice takes place in an environment of "givens"—premises that are accepted by the subject as bases for his choice; and behavior is adaptive only within the limits set by these "givens." (1997: 92)

By providing integrated subgoals, stable expectations, appropriate information, necessary facilities, routine performance programs and, in general, a set of constraints within which required decisions can be made, organizations supply these "givens" to individual participants. This is the sense in which March and Simon (1958: 169–71) propose the concept *bounded rationality*—a

---

[8]Simon and the Carnegie School led the way in recognizing the relevance of the "new" cognitive psychology with its emphasis on heuristics and organizational routines as a means of responding to complexity and uncertainty. Rationality does not always entail thoughtful choice, but often the following of rules. Later studies by cognitive psychologists pursued in detail the specific types of biases underlying judgment and decision making by individuals (see Bazerman, 2002; Kahneman, Slovic, and Tversky, 1982; Nisbett and Ross, 1980). Organizational routines are, in part, designed to overcome such limitations, as evolutionary economics has emphasized (Nelson and Winter, 1982).

concept that both summarizes and integrates the two key elements of the rational system perspective: goal specificity and formalization.[9]

Also, in his later collaboration with March, Simon gave substantial emphasis to the importance of rules and routines in supporting rational behavior within organizations. As DiMaggio and Powell stress, "March and Simon (1958) taught us that organizational behavior, particularly decision making, involves rule following more than the calculation of consequences" (1991: 19). Thus, Simon, like Weber, was among those who began to identify formal rationality as distinct from technical rationality.

The model developed by Simon also can be used to explain how the very structures developed to promote rationality can, under some conditions, have the opposite effect: subgoals can become disconnected from the wider goals they were intended to serve.

SUMMARY AND TENTATIVE CONCLUSIONS

Any conclusions reached at this point must be tentative; it is difficult to appraise the strengths and limitations of any one perspective in isolation from the others. Nevertheless, a few general observations on the rational system approach can be made at this juncture.

From the rational system perspective, structural arrangements within organizations are conceived as tools deliberately designed to achieve the efficient realization of ends or, from Weber's perspective, the disciplined performance of participants. As Gouldner notes, "the focus is, therefore, on the legally prescribed structures—i.e., the formally 'blue-printed' patterns—since these are more largely subject to deliberate inspection and rational manipulation" (1959: 404–05). Hence, all theorists utilizing this perspective focus primary attention on the normative structure of organizations: on the specificity of goals and the formalization of rules and roles. There are, however, important differences among the various schools in their approach to the normative structure.

Taylor was highly *pragmatic* in his approach, placing his faith in a method by which, beginning with individual jobs, superior work procedures could be developed and appropriate arrangements devised for articulating the myriad tasks to be performed. Work planning was distinguished from work performance, the former becoming the responsibility of management, especially engineering. Taylor was concerned primarily with devising methods for the planning of work and working arrangements. The administrative theory group exemplified by Fayol was less pragmatic and more *prescriptive* in its approach. They believed that general principles of management could be devised to guide managers as they

---

[9]A useful overview of Simon's contributions to the analysis of decision making in organizations is provided by Taylor (1965). An interesting critique of Simon's work is provided by Krupp (1961), and applications and extensions of Simon's framework have been carried out by Allison (1971) and Steinbruner (1974).

designed their organizations, and so they busied themselves constructing lists of "do's and dont's" as guides to managerial decision making. Weber was less concerned with discovering ways—whether pragmatic or prescriptive—for improving organizations than with attempting to develop a parsimonious *descriptive* portrait of the characteristics of the newly emerging bureaucratic structures. Like Weber, Simon was also descriptive in his approach, examining the effect of structural features on individual decision makers within the organization. Simon's conception, in particular, enables us to understand better how thousands and even hundreds of thousands of individual decisions and actions can be integrated in the service of complex goals. Such integrated, purposeful collective behavior requires the support of an organizational framework.

The four theorists also differ in the level of analysis at which they work. Taylor and Simon operate primarily at the social psychological level, focusing on individual participants as they perform tasks or make decisions; they treat structural features as contexts affecting these behaviors. By contrast, Fayol and Weber work at the structural level, attempting to conceptualize and analyze the characteristics of organizational forms.

J. D. Thompson provides a simple summary of the general argument underlying the rational system perspective: "structure is a fundamental vehicle by which organizations achieve bounded rationality" (1967: 54). The specification of positions, role requirements, procedural rules and regulations, value and factual inputs that guide decision making—all function to canalize behavior in the service of predetermined goals. Individuals can behave rationally because their alternatives are limited and their choices circumscribed.

In a larger sense, however, rationality resides in the structure itself, not in the individual participants—in rules that assure participants will behave in ways calculated to achieve desired objectives, in cognitive decision-premises that guide individual decision making, in control arrangements that evaluate performance and detect deviance, in reward systems that motivate participants to carry out prescribed tasks, and in the set of criteria by which participants are selected, replaced, and promoted. As Taylor concluded:

> no great man can . . . hope to compete with a number of ordinary men who have been property organized so as to efficiently cooperate. In the past the man has been first, in the future the system must be first. (1947: 7)

Because of its emphasis on the characteristics of structure rather than the characteristics of participants, Bennis has dubbed the rational system perspective as depicting "organizations without people" (1959: 263).[10]

---

[10]Consistent with this conclusion, Boguslaw has observed that whereas the classical utopians strove to achieve their end of the rational social system by "populating their social systems with perfect human beings," the "new utopians"—systems engineers and control-systems experts—have become impatient with human imperfections, so that "the theoretical and practical solutions they seek call increasingly for decreases in the number and in the scope of responsibility of human beings within the operating structures of their new machines systems. . . . the new utopians are concerned with nonpeople and with people-substitutes" (1965: 2).

Let us not forget, however, that the conception of rationality employed by this perspective is limited. At the top of the organization, the value premises that govern the entire structure of decision making are excluded from rational assessment: as long as they are specific enough to provide clear criteria for choice, these premises can support a "rational" structure no matter how monstrous or perverted their content. And, at the bottom of the organization, "rational" behavior often involves turning off one's mind and one's critical intellectual judgment and blindly conforming to the performance program specified by the job description (see Veblen, 1904).

We have also noted the great emphasis the rational system perspective places on control—the determination of the behavior of one subset of participants by another, by either unobtrusive or more obvious measures. Most rational system theorists justify these arrangements as serving rationality: control is the means of channeling and coordinating behavior to achieve specified goals. Few recognize the possibility that interpersonal control may be an end in itself—that one function of elaborate hierarchies, centrally determined decision premises, and an extensive division of labor is to allow (and justify) arrangements in which some participants control others. The critical or Marxist perspective calling attention to these possibilities is examined in Chapter 3.

With the important exception of Weber, early rational system theorists did not take much notice of the effect of the larger social, cultural, and technological context on organization structure or performance. Attention was concentrated on the internal features of organizations.

By concentrating on the normative structure, these rational system analysts accorded scant attention to the behavioral structure of organizations. We learn much from them about plans and programs and premises, about roles and rules and regulations, but little about the actual behavior of organizational participants. Normative structure is celebrated; the behavioral, ignored.

This chapter has identified the primary features and charted the early development of the rational system perspective from the early decades of the twentieth century up to roughly 1960. This is, however, by no means, the end of the story. We consider more recent developments (beginning in Chapter 5) after reviewing the history of two related, competing perspectives. The natural system perspective, the second perspective to be considered, developed in response to the perceived inadequacies and limitations of the rational system perspective.

CHAPTER 3

Organizations as Natural Systems

To administer a social organization according to purely technical criteria of rationality is irrational, because it ignores the nonrational aspects of social conduct.

PETER M. BLAU (1956)

Although the natural system perspective developed in large measure from
critical reactions to the inadequacies of the rational system model, it should not
be seen as merely providing a critique of another perspective. Rather, it defines a
novel and interesting view of organizations that deserves to be considered and
evaluated in its own right. As in our discussion of the rational system approach,
we begin by identifying those more general or basic ideas common to natural system advocates and then briefly examine selected schools within this perspective.

BASIC VERSUS DISTINCTIVE CHARACTERISTICS

Whereas the rational system theorists conceive of organizations as collectivities
deliberately constructed to seek specific goals, natural system advocates emphasize that organizations are, first and foremost, collectivities. While the rational
system perspective stresses those features of organizations that distinguish them
from other types of social groups, the natural system theorists remind us that
these distinguishing characteristics are not their only characteristics (Gouldner,
1959: 406). Indeed, they are not the most important characteristics.

We have already seen that much is made by rational system theorists of goal
specificity and formalization as characteristics differentiating organizations from

other types of collectivities. Natural system theorists generally acknowledge the existence of these attributes but argue that other characteristics—characteristics shared with all social groups—are of greater significance. Take first the matter of organizational goals and goal specificity.

Goal Complexity

Organizational goals and their relation to the behavior of participants are much more problematic for the natural than the rational system theorist. This is largely because natural system analysts pay more attention to behavior and hence worry more about the complex interconnections between the normative and the behavioral structures of organizations. Two general themes characterize their views of organizational goals. First, there is frequently a disparity between the stated and the "real" goals pursued by organizations—between the professed or official goals that are announced and the actual or operative goals that can be observed to govern the activities of participants. Second, natural system analysts emphasize that even when the stated goals are actually being pursued, they are never the only goals governing participants' behavior. They point out that all organizations must pursue *support* or "maintenance" goals in addition to their output goals (Gross, 1968; Perrow, 1970: 135). No organization can devote its full resources to producing products or services; each must expend energies maintaining itself.

These distinctions, though useful, do not go quite far enough. They do not capture the most profound difference between these two perspectives on organizational goals. The major thrust of the natural system view is that organizations are more than instruments for attaining defined goals; they are, fundamentally, social groups attempting to adapt and survive in their particular circumstances. Preserving the organization becomes an end in itself. Gouldner emphasizes this implication of the natural system perspective:

> The organization, according to this model, strives to survive and to maintain its equilibrium, and this striving may persist even after its explicitly held goals have been successfully attained. This strain toward survival may even on occasion lead to the neglect or distortion of the organization's goals. (1959: 405)

A dramatic example of this tendency is provided by the National Foundation for Infantile Paralysis which suffered the misfortune of selecting a disease for which a cure was found, forcing it to shift its focus to other diseases and change its name (Sills, 1957). Under many conditions, organizations have been observed to modify their goals so as to achieve a more favorable adjustment. In their longitudinal study of a sample of several hundred charitable nonprofit organizations in Minneapolis studied between 1980 and 1994 Galaskiewicz and Bielefeld (1998) observed that during an economic downturn although some organizations stayed true to their mission and employed retrenchment tactics as necessary—some even closing their doors—many others opted to change their mix of products and services and seek alternative sources of funding. It is because of such tendencies that organizations are not to be viewed simply as means for achieving specified ends, but as ends in themselves.

Two types of explanations have been proposed to account for the survival instincts of organizations. The first, and more elaborate, argues that the organizations are social systems characterized by a number of needs that must be satisfied if they are to survive. This view is linked to a broader theoretical framework known as *functional analysis*, a dominant perspective in sociology during the 1940s and 1950s. The approach has many variants but, as Stinchcombe notes: a functional explanation "is one in which the *consequences* of some behavior or social arrangements are essential elements in the *causes* of that behavior" (1968: 80). Just as the human body requires a continuing flow of oxygen, a need met by the lungs and circulation of blood, social systems "need" mechanisms, for example, to gather and circulate information to relevant participants. All functional explanations assume that the ends or consequences attained are "homeostatic" variables: the system remains viable as long as certain conditions are maintained.[1]

Other theorists reject such assumptions as being anthropomorphic at worst and unnecessary at best. They suggest instead that one does not have to posit a survival need for the collectivity itself. It is sufficient to assume that some participants have a vested interest in the survival of the organization. Because it is a source of power, or resources, or prestige, or pleasure, they wish to see it preserved and include among their own goals that the organization itself be protected and, if possible, strengthened. This view is developed by the conflict and strategic contingency theorists (see below and Chapter 8).

One of the earliest and most influential analyses of how some participants seek to preserve an organization even at the sacrifice of the goals for which it was originally established is that provided by Robert Michels (1949 trans.), a contemporary of Weber's writing in pre–World War I Germany. His analysis of the changes that occurred in the largest socialist party in Europe, Germany's Social Democratic party, is rightly regarded as a classic. This work is most famous for its formulation of "the iron law of oligarchy," which equates the processes by which complex administrative work is carried out in an organization with the transfer of power from rank-and-file members to a small coterie of leaders. "Who says organization says oligarchy." However, of particular interest for present purposes are Michels's views on the consequences of these oligarchical tendencies for the professed goals of the organization. The leaders of the party continued to give lip service to its revolutionary objectives but over time became increasingly conservative, reluctant to risk the gains

---

[1]Functional explanations have come under attack because many analysts employ them in a rather casual manner. To be a valid functional explanation, it is not sufficient simply to show that a given practice is associated with the desired consequence. In addition, the analyst must identify the causal feedback loop by which the forces maintaining the structure are themselves activated by forces threatening the equilibrium (Stinchcombe, 1968: 88). As Elster (1983) notes, most functionalists are content to argue "as if" rather than to "demonstrate that" such forces are at work.

they had achieved or to endanger the party, which was their source of strength. Michels gloomily concludes:

> Thus, from a means, organization becomes an end. To the institutions and qualities which at the outset were destined simply to ensure the good working of the party machine (subordination, the harmonious cooperation of individual members, hierarchical relationships, discretion, propriety of conduct), a greater importance comes ultimately to be attached than to the productivity of the machine. Henceforward the sole preoccupation is to avoid anything which may clog the machinery. (1949 trans.: 390)

Michels's analysis points to the importance of power and conflict processes in organizations: if the interests of the rank-and-file members diverge from those of the leaders, the former are likely to be sacrificed.

Another way of viewing differences in the uses of goals by rational and natural system analysts is suggested by Brunsson (1985). He argues that the rational system decision-making model is in fact rational only if attention is focused on the decision itself as outcome. If instead we attend to actions (goal implementation) as outcome, then a more "irrational" decision process can produce better results. Irrational decision processes speedily remove alternative possibilities and overestimate probabilities of success attached to the chosen alternative in order to structure participants' expectations, eliminate conflicts, and mold commitment to the selected course of action. Rational system theorists emphasize the normative structure and so focus on decisions—designs or proposals for action—as if they were the principal outcomes. Natural system theorists stress the behavioral structure and are more interested in examining what is done rather than what is decided or planned. Commitment and motivation loom as more salient variables than search and choice if action rather than "talk" (a decision) is the focus.

Informal Structure

Just as the ends that organizations are designed to serve are not pure and simple and specific in the view of the natural system analysts, neither are the structures that exist to attain them. The natural system theorists do not deny the existence of highly formalized structures within organizations, but they do question their importance, in particular, their impact on the behavior of participants. Formal structures purposefully designed to regulate behavior in the service of specific goals are greatly affected—supplemented, eroded, transformed—by the emergence of *informal* structures. As first discussed in Chapter 1, we equate formal structures with those norms and behavior patterns that are designed to operate independently of the characteristics of the individual actors. Informal structures are those based on the personal characteristics and relations of the specific participants. Thus, for example, formal authority refers to a collection of control rights that are available to and exercised by all incumbents of a given position, such as supervisor or teacher; whereas informal authority would indicate those rights that are acquired by a particular supervisor or teacher because of his or her special qualities or interpersonal ties. Obviously, one of the clearest ways to distinguish empirically between the formal and the informal elements in a given situation is to observe what happens to beliefs and behaviors when there is a change in personnel.

Natural system analysts emphasize that there is more to organizational structure than the prescribed rules, the job descriptions, and the associated regularities in the behavior of participants. Individuals are never merely "hired hands" but bring along their heads and hearts: they enter the organization with individually shaped ideas, expectations, and agendas, and they bring with them distinctive values, interests, sentiments, and abilities.

Expressed through interaction, these factors come together to create a reasonably stable informal structure. One of the most important insights of the natural system perspective is that the social structure of an organization does not consist of the formal structure plus the idiosyncratic beliefs and behaviors of individual participants, but rather of a formal structure *and* an informal structure: informal life is itself structured and orderly. Participants within formal organizations generate informal norms and behavior patterns: status and power systems, communication networks, sociometric structures—patterns of attraction and conflicts—and working arrangements.

In the early studies exploring informal structures, it was presumed that these "irrational" relations characterized only the lower strata of the organization; managers and executives were thought to be immune to such developments. But empirical studies by Dalton (1959) and others dispelled such class-based stereotypes. Also, early studies emphasized the dysfunctional consequences of the informal structures, viewing them as reflecting private and irrational concerns that impeded the implementation of the rational formal design. Thus, Roethlisberger and Dickson equated the formal structure with the "logic of cost and efficiency" (devised by management) while the informal structure expressed the "logic of sentiments" (created by workers) (1939: 562–64). Later analysts emphasized the positive functions performed by informal structures—in increasing the ease of communication, facilitating trust, and correcting for the inadequacies of the formal systems (Gross, 1953).

Greater appreciation for the functions of informal systems was coupled with increasing skepticism that formalization was conducive to rationality. Natural system analysts emphasize that formalization places heavy and often intolerable burdens on those responsible for the design and management of an organization. No planners are so foresighted or omniscient as to be able to anticipate all the possible contingencies that might confront each position in the organization. Attempts to program in advance the behavior of participants are often misguided, if not foolhardy. Such programming can easily become maladaptive and lead to behaviors both ineffective and inefficient, giving rise to the "trained incapacity" that Veblen (1904) called attention to long ago and for which some organizations have become notorious (Merton, 1957: 197–200).

Further, formal arrangements that curtail individual problem solving and the use of discretion undermine participants' initiative and self-confidence, causing them to become alienated and apathetic. Such restrictive arrangements not only damage participants' self-esteem and mental health but also prevent them from effectively contributing their talents and energies to the larger enterprise (Argyris, 1957; McGregor, 1960). In sum, natural system analysts insist that highly centralized and formalized structures are doomed to be ineffective and irrational in that they waste the organization's most precious resource: the intelligence and initiative of its participants.

SELECTED SCHOOLS

As with the rational system perspective, the natural system perspective constitutes an umbrella under which a number of rather diverse approaches can be gathered. While they share certain generic features, they differ in important particulars. We discuss briefly four influential variants of the *social consensus* subtype—Mayo's human relations school, Barnard's conception of cooperative systems, Selznick's institutional approach, and Parsons's AGIL model. Then we briefly describe work associated with the *social conflict* model.

Mayo and the Human Relations School

Hawthorne Studies. It is not possible to recount in detail the famous series of studies and experiments conducted at the Hawthorne plant of the Western Electric Company outside Chicago during the late 1920s and early 1930s. This research is meticulously described by Roethlisberger and Dickson (1939) and given its most influential interpretation by Elton Mayo (1945; see also Homans, 1950). Mayo, along with Roethlisberger, was a member of the Harvard Business School faculty. He was trained as an industrial psychologist and his early work grew out of the scientific management tradition established by Taylor. Like Taylor, Mayo studied individual factors affecting work but focused on physical and psychological factors such as fatigue and stress, in an attempt to determine the optimum length and spacing of rest periods for maximizing productivity. The early research in the Hawthorne plant followed the scientific management approach: the researchers set about to determine the optimal level of illumination for the assembly of telephone relay equipment. Mayo summarizes the surprising results:

> The conditions of scientific experiment had apparently been fulfilled— experimental room, control room; changes introduced one at a time; all other conditions held steady. And the results were perplexing. . . . Lighting improved in the experimental room, production went up; but it rose also in the control room. The opposite of this: lighting diminished from 10- to 3-foot-candles in the experimental room and the production again went up; simultaneously in the control room, with illumination constant, production also rose (1945: 69).

The researchers were in confusion. Other conditions were run with similar inexplicable results. In desperation, they decided to ask the workers themselves what was going on and learned that the workers were so pleased to be singled out for special attention that they had tried to do the best they could for the researchers and for the company. The "Hawthorne effect" was discovered. Although this effect has been variously interpreted, a summary translation of its lessons might be stated: change is interesting; attention is gratifying!

Additional studies carried out by the Harvard group—the second relay-assembly group, the mica-splitting test room, the bank-wiring observation room—all served to call into question the simple motivational assumptions on which the prevailing rational models rested. Individual workers do not behave as "rational" economic actors, but as complex beings with multiple motives and values; they are driven as much by feelings and sentiments as by facts and interests. They do not behave as individual, isolated actors, but as members of social groups exhibiting commitments and loyalties to colleagues stronger than their individualistic self-interests. Thus, in the bank-wiring observation room, workers were observed to collectively set and conform to daily work quotas—group norms restricting production—at the expense of their own higher earnings. And informal status hierarchies and leadership patterns developed that challenged the formal systems designed by managers (see Homans, 1950: 48–155; Roethlisberger and Dickson, 1939: 379–447). At the social psychological level, the Hawthorne studies pointed to a more complex model of worker motivation based on a social psychological rather than an economic conception of man.[2] At the structural level, the studies discovered and demonstrated the importance of informal organization.

In drawing general conclusions from this work, Mayo adopted a reactionary intellectual stance: he emphasized the evils of industrialism and nostalgically longed for the stability and socially cohesive ways of the preindustrial past (see Guillén 1994; Trahair, 1984). Later researchers discarded this metaphysical pathos but pursued the insights of Mayo and associates regarding the complexity of human motivation and the importance of informal structure.

The Hawthorne trunk gave rise to a rich assortment of research and reform offshoots, each of which has produced many individual branches. The major research issues pursued include studies of work groups, leadership behavior, and the impact of worker background and personality on organizational behavior. Reform measures include the use of personnel

---

[2]After inspecting the results of the bank-wiring observation room study at the Hawthorne plant, Mayo concluded: "It is unfortunate for economic theory that it applies chiefly to persons of less, rather than greater, normality of social relationships. Must we conclude that economics is a study of human behavior in non-normal situations, or alternatively, a study of non-normal human behavior in ordinary situations?" (1945: 43).

counselors, leadership training, job redefinition, and participation in decision making. Each of these interests merits a brief description; all of them are still flourishing.

Research Offshoots

Small-group behavior. The discovery of informal group processes in organizational settings both stimulated and received impetus from the study of small-group behavior carried on by social psychologists and sociologists. Among the former, Likert (1961) and Katz (Katz, Maccoby, and Morse, 1950), together with their colleagues at the Institute for Social Research, University of Michigan, were particularly influential; among the latter, Homans (1950) and Whyte (1951; 1959) were leaders in analyzing group processes in organizational settings. A few analysts, such as Sayles (1958), attempted to understand how organizational factors affected the number, types, and tactics of groups that emerged, but most focused not on the determinants, but the consequences of group membership—for example, the impact of group cohesiveness on individual conformity to production norms (Roy, 1952; Seashore, 1954).

Leadership. From the human relations perspective, leadership is conceived primarily as a mechanism for influencing the behavior of individual subordinates. Early studies sought a set of leadership traits that would stimulate individual performance in the service of organizational goals. Thus, studies by White and Lippitt (1953) reported that participants in experimental task groups performed more effectively under "democratic" than "laissez-faire" or "authoritarian" leaders. Other research stressed the relational aspects of leadership. For example, a series of studies conducted at the Ohio State Leadership Studies Center (Stogdill and Coons, 1957) isolated two basic dimensions of leadership behavior: *consideration*, the extent to which trust, friendship, and respect mark the relation between the supervisor and his or her workers, and *initiating structure*, the degree to which the supervisor is a good organizer who can "get the work out." These dimensions were observed to vary independently, and in general, the more effective leaders—that is, the leaders whose subordinates performed better and had higher morale—were those who scored high on both dimensions.

Later efforts emphasized that leadership characteristics vary with the nature of the situation (Fiedler, 1964; 1971) and the specific needs or motivations of the individual subordinates (Cartwright, 1965). Studies by Pelz (1952) suggested that a supervisor's relation to his or her own superior—specifically, the extent of his or her influence upward—is a powerful determinant of the supervisor's influence over his or her own subordinates. Likert (1961) built on this finding to create his model of the supervisor's critical function as a "linking pin" relating lower to higher levels of the hierarchy. Most of these leadership studies ignored the effects of incumbency in a formal office on an individual's influence, either by overlooking this aspect of the situation or by deliberately holding it constant—for example, by studying differences in leadership behavior among all first-line supervisors in a given office or factory situation (Katz and Kahn, 1952).[3]

Individual differences. From the very beginning, human relations analysts have emphasized the great variability of individual characteristics and behaviors and have insisted on the relevance of these differences in understanding organizational behavior. Early research demonstrated that such officially irrelevant differences as race (Collins, 1946), class (Warner and Low, 1947), and cultural background (Dalton, 1950) had strong effects on allocation to work roles and organizational behavior. These studies are important forerunners of the more recent interest in the relation between stratification and organizations, which we discuss in Chapter 7.

Many of the lessons learned by the human relations researchers were codified by Douglas McGregor in his influential book *The Human Side of Enterprise* (1960). McGregor emphasized that the most significant differences between classical (rational system) management theory, which he labeled "Theory *X*," and the human relations approach, termed "Theory *Y*," was the nature of the assumptions made about human actors. Principal assumptions underlying Theory *X* were

- Individuals dislike work and will seek to avoid it (p. 33).
- Therefore, "most people must be coerced, controlled, directed, threatened with punishment to get them to put forth adequate effort toward the achievement of individual objectives" (p. 34).
- "The average human being prefers to be directed, wishes to avoid responsibility, has relatively little ambition, wants security above all" (p. 34).

By contrast, human relations theory was constructed on the assumption that

- Most individuals do not "inherently dislike work . . . the expenditure of physical and mental effort in work is as natural as play or rest" (p. 47).
- "External control and threat of punishment are not the only means for bringing about effort toward organizational objectives" (p. 47).
- The most significant rewards are those associated with "the satisfaction of ego and self-actualization needs" (p. 47–48).

One constructs very different kinds of organizational structures depending on which set of assumptions is embraced.

Reform Efforts. The human relations school has also given rise to much activity directed at changing organizations—modifying and improving them

---

[3]Blau has pointed out that "although managerial authority in organizations contains important leadership elements, its distinctive characteristic, which differentiates it from informal leadership, is that it is rooted in the formal powers and sanctions the organization bestows upon managers" (1964: 210). It is in keeping with the natural system perspective to ignore this distinctive component of leadership in formal organizations. (We examine it in Chapter 8.)

as social environments. The original Hawthorne researchers were themselves interested in pursuing practical applications of their findings. Stressing the positive relation in their studies between worker satisfaction and productivity, they sought techniques to improve the adjustment and morale of individual workers. One approach involved the introduction of a set of *personnel counselors*, distinct from the line hierarchy, whose task it was to listen sympathetically to workers' complaints (Roethlisberger and Dickson, 1939: 189–376, 590–604). The interviewing techniques devised for this program contributed to the development of nondirective counseling techniques now in wide use.

Another change strategy devised by the human relations school stressed the importance of *supervisory skills* in promoting worker morale. Supervisors required special training if they were to become more sensitive to the psychological and social needs of their subordinates. Mayo (1945), influenced in part by Barnard, stressed the important role to be performed by supervisors and managers whose social function it was to elicit cooperation among workers—cooperation that could not be assumed to be automatic (Bendix and Fisher, 1949). Thus, the human relations approach helped to spawn many diverse efforts in leadership training, from simple attitude-change efforts to more intensive Bethel-type sensitivity or T-group training. (See, e.g., Blake and Mouton, 1964; National Training Laboratories, 1953.)

Yet another reform approach focused on the need to redefine and enlarge the role definitions specified for workers. Contrary to the assumptions of the rational system model, the human relations group stressed the dangers of excessive formalization with its emphasis on extreme functional specialization. *Job enlargement* or, at least, job rotation, was advocated as a method of reducing the alienation and increasing the commitment and satisfaction of workers performing routine work (Herzberg, 1966).

Still other reformers stressed the importance of worker *participation in decision making* within the organization, particularly in decisions directly affecting them. Although the notion of linking participation to motivation and commitment was given encouragement by the Hawthorne studies, more direct support came from the experimental and theoretical work of Lewin (1948) and his colleagues (e.g., Coch and French, 1948). From the outset and continuing to the present, however, attempts to encourage participation by workers in organizational decisions received more attention and support in Europe than in the United States (Blumberg, 1968; Jaques, 1951).

Critics. Virtually all of these applications of the human relations movement have come under severe criticism on both ideological and empirical grounds. Paradoxically, the human relations movement, ostensibly developed to humanize the cold and calculating rationality of the factory and shop, rapidly came under attack on the grounds that it represented simply a more subtle and refined form of exploitation. Critics charged that workers' legitimate economic interests were being inappropriately deemphasized; that actual conflicts of interest were denied and "therapeutically" managed; and that the roles attributed to managers represented a new brand of elitism. The entire movement was branded as "cow sociology": just as contented cows were alleged to produce more milk, satisfied workers were expected to produce more output (see Bell, 1960: 238–44; Bendix, 1956: 308–40; Braverman, 1974: 139–51; Landsberger, 1958).

It is argued that in spite of the label "human" relations, humanizing the workplace was viewed not as an end in itself, but primarily as a means to increasing productivity. It was not until well into the 1960s that employee well-being came to be recognized as a valid objective of organization design, and even then and up to the present time, this emphasis has been stronger in European than in U.S. organizations and organization theories (Kahn, 1990).

The ideological criticisms were the first to erupt, but reservations raised by researchers on the basis of empirical evidence may in the long run prove to be more devastating. Several decades of research have demonstrated no clear relation between worker satisfaction and productivity (see Brayfield and Crockett, 1955; Schwab and Cummings, 1970); no clear relation between supervisory behavior or leadership style and worker productivity (see Hollander and Julian, 1969); no clear relation between job enlargement and worker satisfaction or productivity (see Hulin and Blood, 1968); and no clear relation between participation in decision making and satisfaction or productivity (see Cotton, 1993; Seibold and Shea, 2001). Where positive relations among these variables are observed, the causal direction may be opposite to that predicted: productivity producing satisfaction (Porter and Lawler, 1968) or productivity influencing supervisory style (Lowin and Craig, 1968), rather than vice versa. Even the original Hawthorne results have been reanalyzed and challenged (Carey, 1967; Franke and Kaul, 1978; Jones, 1990; 1992).

Our brief survey of the human relations school cannot do justice to the variety of theoretical implications, empirical studies, and practical reform efforts it has generated. Guillén (1994) argues that there is evidence to show that the human relations programs and techniques had a substantial impact both in reducing conflict and increasing productivity in U.S. industrial firms between 1930 and 1960, in part because they were adopted and promoted by the rapidly developing personnel profession. In terms of intellectual impact, it is only a small exaggeration to suggest that the academic field of industrial sociology first saw the light of day at the Hawthorne plant, with Mayo serving as midwife. Moreover, sociological work on organizations well into the 1960s was shaped primarily by the human relations model—whether it was attempting to verify and elaborate the model or attacking its shortcomings and biases. And all of the thousands of studies concerned with motivation, morale, and leadership either have been directly stimulated by or are indirectly beholden to a tiny group of workers who kept increasing their output even though the lights were growing dimmer.[4]

---

[4]For a more extensive summary of the human relations work, see Katz and Kahn (1978) and Waring (1991). Perrow (1986: 79–114) provides a review and highly critical assessment.

Barnard's Cooperative System

At the same time that Mayo and his associates were conducting their studies and extrapolating from them to underline the importance of interpersonal processes and informal structures, Chester I. Bernard was developing his own views of the nature of organizations. Barnard was not an academic, but an executive who served as president of New Jersey Bell Telephone Company. Although Barnard's major book *The Functions of the Executive* (1938)[5] was a very personal work reflecting his rather distinctive views and concerns, he was in regular contact with the human relations group at Harvard, including Mayo and Roethlisberger. Barnard's influence on the field has been great, in part because his treatise was one of the first systematic attempts to outline a theory of organization available to U.S. readers, since Weber's work had not yet been translated. Barnard's ideas contributed to human relations approaches and provided a foundation for both Selznick's institutionalist views (discussed below) and for Simon's theory of decision making (see Chapter 2). The institutional economist Oliver Williamson (1990: 4) regards Barnard as a key figure in generating "the new science of organization."

Inducing Cooperation. Barnard stressed that organizations are essentially cooperative systems, integrating the contributions of their individual participants. As noted in our review of organizational definitions in Chapter 1, Barnard defined a formal organization as "that kind of coöperation among men that is conscious, deliberate, purposeful" (p. 4). Like many other natural system analysts, Barnard defined organizations so as to emphasize their rational system features—their distinguishing characteristics—but then concentrated on other, more generic aspects in his analysis. Political scientists such as Simon and March and economists such as Arrow and Williamson embraced and elaborated Barnard's view of organizations as arising from the limitations of individuals—physical, but more important, cognitive constraints—organizations serving to both inform and channel decision making (see Chapter 2).

Barnard also emphasized that organizations rely on the willingness of participants to make contributions. Participants must be induced to make contributions—a variety of incentives can be used to motivate them to do so, including material rewards, opportunities for distinction, prestige, and power—and make them in sufficient quantities, or the organization cannot survive.[6]

Thus, Barnard attempts to combine and reconcile two somewhat contradictory ideas: goals are imposed from the top down while their attainment depends on willing compliance from the bottom up (see Etzioni, 1964: 41). This view of accepted direction is developed most fully in Barnard's conception

---

[5]Unless otherwise indicated, all references in this section are to this work.

[6]Note that this "contributions-inducements" schema, later elaborated by March and Simon (1958), is an attempt to frame an answer to how participants deal with Simon's first type of decision: whether or not to join and continue to participate in an organization (see Chapter 2).

of authority. He argues that it is a "fiction that authority comes down from above" (p. 170), noting the many situations in which leaders claim authority but fail to win compliance. This is because authority depends ultimately on its validation from the response of those subject to it: "the decision as to whether an order has authority or not lies with the persons to whom it is addressed, and does not reside in 'persons of authority' or those who issue these orders" (p. 163). Still, some types of orders have a greater "potentiality of assent of those to whom they are sent" (p. 173). These are orders that are products of a well-designed and integrated communications system that links all contributions in a purposeful cooperative framework.

> At first thought it may seem that the element of communication in organization is only in part related to authority; but more thorough consideration leads to the understanding that communication, authority, specialization, and purpose are all aspects comprehended in coördination. All communication relates to the formulation of purpose and the transmission of coördinating prescriptions for action and so rests upon the ability to communicate with those willing to coöperate. (p. 184)

This conception of an organization as a purposefully coordinated system of communications linking all participants in such a manner that the purposes of superiors are accepted as the basis for the actions of subordinates became the foundation for Simon's theory of decision making, as described in Chapter 2.

Barnard's views thus contain many ideas that are consistent with a rational system conception of organizations. What sets them apart is his insistence on the nonmaterial, informal, interpersonal, and, indeed, moral basis of cooperation. Material rewards are viewed as "weak incentives" that must be buttressed by other types of psychological and social motivations if cooperative effort is to be sustained. As for informal organization, Barnard argued that "formal organizations arise out of and are necessary to informal organization, but when formal organizations come into operation, they create and require informal organizations" (p. 120). Informal structures facilitate communication, maintain cohesiveness, and undergird "the willingness to serve and the stability of objective authority" (p. 122). Interpersonal ties at their best create a "condition of communion": "the opportunity for commandership, for mutual support" forming the "basis of informal organization that is essential to the operation of every formal organization" (p. 148).

Distinctive Function of the Leader. But, for Barnard, the most critical ingredient to successful organization is the formation of a collective purpose that becomes morally binding on participants. Developing and imparting a mission is the distinctive "function of the executive."

> The distinguishing mark of the executive responsibility is that it requires not merely conformance to a complex code of morals but also the creation of moral codes for others. The most generally recognized aspect of this function is called

securing, creating, inspiring of "morale" in an organization. This is the process of inculcating points of view, fundamental attitudes, loyalties, to the organization or coöperative system, and to the system of objective authority, that will result in subordinating individual interest and the minor dictates of personal codes to the good of the coöperative whole. (p. 279)

On the one hand such views sound quaint and hopelessly old-fashioned; they have been subjected to scathing attack by critics such as Perrow (1986: 62–68), who scoff at Barnard's moral imperialism and point out the duplicity inherent in "willing" cooperation that is managed from above. But other scholars, such as Selznick, built on Barnard's recognition of the motivating power of purpose and the ways in which organizational structures and procedures themselves become infused with value (see below). In addition, many of the themes initiated by Barnard have become highly fashionable in recent decades as students of organizations rediscover the importance of *organizational cultures* shaped by zealous managers supplying strongly held values to their members. Barnard is the godfather of contemporary business gurus, such as Tom Peters (Peters and Austin, 1985; Peters and Waterman, 1982), who advocate the cultivation of "strong cultures." We discuss these neo-Barnardian deveopments in Chapter 8.[7]

More so than his contemporaries, Barnard did give some attention to the environment. His conception of organizations as systems of consciously coordinated *activities* rather than persons allows him to recognize that individuals "stand outside all organizations and have multiple relations with them" (p. 100). And, more generally, he recognizes that many organizations are "incomplete, subordinate, and dependent" (p. 98), thus acknowledging the power of external ties and forces. However, unlike the open system theorists, he did not systematically pursue these insights (Scott, 1990).

Consistent with the natural system framework, however, Barnard recognized the existence of organizational forces even more powerful than purpose:

Finally it should be noted that, once established, organizations change their unifying purposes. They tend to perpetuate themselves; and in the effort to survive may change the reasons for existence. (p. 89)

The necessity of survival can override the morality of purpose.

Selznick's Institutional Approach

The Institutionalization of Organizations. Philip Selznick, a student of bureaucracy under Merton at Columbia, but an intellectual descendant of Michels and Barnard, developed his own unique natural system model, one that has recently been refurbished and elaborated to constitute an influential

---

[7]A collection of essays edited by Williamson (1990) celebrates the fiftieth anniversary of the publication of *The Functions of the Executive* as a number of organizational scholars appraise Barnard's intellectual legacy and continuing influence.

approach to the analysis of organizations known as institutional theory (see Chapter 10). We restrict attention here, however, to Selznick's seminal early contributions and to the related work of his immediate intellectual followers. Unlike Barnard, Selznick did not present his approach in one single, unified statement but scattered his ideas through several books and articles. We attempt to piece together a short, but coherent sketch of his framework.

For Selznick, "the most important thing about organizations is that, though they are tools, each nevertheless has a life of its own" (1949: 10). He agrees with the rational system analyst that the distinguishing characteristic of formal organizations is that they are rationally ordered instruments designed to attain goals. However, these formal structures can "never succeed in conquering the nonrational dimensions of organizational behavior" (1948: 25). The sources of these nonrational features are (1) individuals, who participate in the organization as "wholes" rather than acting merely in terms of their formal roles; and (2) organizational structures that include the formal aspects but also the complex informal systems that link participants with one another and with others external to the official boundaries. Organizational rationality is constrained by "the recalcitrance of the tools of action": persons bring certain characteristics to the organization and develop other commitments as members that restrict their capacity for rational action; organizational procedures become valued as ends in themselves; the organization strikes bargains with its environment that compromise present objectives and limit future possibilities (1949: 253–59).

Although Selznick's earlier work emphasized the constraints imposed by individual and environmental commitments, his later work increasingly recognized that these same processes can be a source of strength. In some cases, participants come to share a common set of commitments and a unity of purpose that can create a formidable weapon (Selznick, 1952). The underlying theme stresses the importance of *institutionalization*: the processes by which an organization "takes on a special character" and "achieves a distinctive competence or, perhaps, a trained or built-in incapacity" (Selznick 1996). Thus, institutionalization refers to a morally neutral process: "the emergence of orderly, stable, socially integrating patterns out of unstable, loosely organized, or narrowly technical activities" (Broom and Selznick 1955: 238). Selznick argued that the most significant aspect of institutionalization is the process by which structures or activities become "infused with value beyond the technical requirements at hand" (Selznick 1957: 17).

Selznick views organizational structure as an adaptive organism shaped in reaction to the characteristics and commitments of participants as well as to influences from the external environment. He explicitly embraces a functional form of analysis, explaining,

> This means that a given empirical system is deemed to have basic needs, essentially related to self-maintenance; the system develops repetitive means of self-defense; and day-to-day activity is interpreted in terms of the function served by that activity for the maintenance and defense of the system. (1948: 29)

Insisting that the overriding need of all systems "is the maintenance of the integrity and continuity of the system itself," Selznick attempts to spell out certain more specific "derived imperatives," including the security of the organization as a whole in relation to its environment, the stability of lines of authority and communication, the stability of informal relations within the organization, and a homogeneity of outlook toward the meaning and role of the organization. However, he does not develop a general framework or catalog of such needs.

Institutional commitments develop over time as the organization confronts external constraints and pressures from its environment as well as changes in the composition of its personnel, their interests, and their informal relations. No organization is completely immune from these external and internal pressures, although the extent of institutionalization varies from one organization to another. To examine these processes Selznick proposes that, rather than following the lead of experimental psychologists who study routine psychological processes, we should imitate the clinical psychologists who examine the dynamic adaptation of the organism over time. Instead of focusing on the day-to-day decisions made in organizations, we should concentrate on those critical decisions that, once made, result in a change in the structure itself. The pattern of these critical decisions, viewed over time, results in the development of a distinctive character structure for each organization, just as an individual's critical decisions and typical mode of coping with problems give rise to the development of a distinctive personality (Selznick, 1957).

Following Barnard, Selznick believes that leadership can play a central role in this evolutionary process. Leaders, unlike mere managers, are those who define the mission of the enterprise. It is their responsibility to choose and to protect its distinctive values and "to create a social structure which embodies them" (1957: 60). Among the critical decisions confronting any enterprise are the selection of a social base—what clientele or market to serve; the selection of central personnel; and the determination of the nature and timing of critical strategic decisions. Selznick thus invites us to observe the process by which an organization develops its distinctive structures, capacities, and liabilities; he proposes, in sum, that we carry out a "natural history" of organizations.

Empirical Studies. If we examine some of the empirical work stimulated by Selznick's institutional model, we will obtain a clearer picture of both the strengths and weaknesses of the proposed approach. Selznick's most famous study is of the Tennessee Valley Authority (TVA), a decentralized government agency created during the depression to improve the economic status of the entire Tennessee Valley, a chronically depressed, flood-ravaged region. Massive federal funds—at least by the standards of the 1930s—were provided to support a broad-gauged attack on the problems of the area. Flood control, hydroelectric power, and soil conservation were to be provided in an integrated manner. Top agency officials were located at the site, not in far-off

Washington, so that officials would be less inclined to impose solutions from above but would work in a democratic fashion with the local inhabitants and community agencies in developing acceptable projects (Lilienthal, 1944).

As we would expect, Selznick (1949) focuses on the "internal relevance"—the consequences for the agency—of these policies. He points out that the democratic ideology not only served to recruit and motivate talented participants but also enabled the New Deal agency to gain access to a suspicious and conservative area. Agency officials employed co-optation as a strategy to gain legitimacy and political support. *Cooptation* is a mechanism by which external elements are incorporated into the decision-making structures of an organization: in the case of the TVA, local leaders were recruited to participate in the agency's decision-making and advisory bodies. This tactic ensured that the agency would enjoy local political support for its programs, but such support always comes at a price: local leaders exchanged support for influence on the agency's programs and goals. As a consequence, some public interest goals were subverted to serve private interests. For example, improved land values surrounding water projects that were supposed to benefit the public often fell into private hands, and reforested land intended as watershed was taken over by lumber interests.[8]

Selznick's analysis set the pattern for a number of similar studies that examined the ways in which the original goals of an organization can be displaced or undermined. Thus, Clark's (1956) study of an adult education program in Los Angeles argues that its professed goals of providing cultural and intellectual programs could not be realized because of its marginal organizational and institutional status. Because the program lacked full legitimacy, only those parts of it that could attract large numbers of students were retained, with other academically valuable but less popular offerings losing out to an "enrollment economy." And Zald and Denton (1963) describe the transformation of the YMCA from a religious organization performing rehabilitative and welfare services for the urban poor into a social and recreational center for suburban and middle-class young people.

These and related studies exhibit several common features. The analyst focuses on the administrative history of the organization: the structural features and programs of the organization are viewed as changing over time in response to changing conditions. The methodology employed tends to be that of the case study, and heavy reliance is placed on the analysis of organizational documents and interviews with informants knowledgeable about the organization's history. Given this approach, most of the organizations selected for study have been relatively recently founded. Selznick insists that he is interested not in recounting the history of any given organization for its own sake but in seeking "to discover the characteristic ways in which types of

---

[8]A reanalysis of the data concerning the early development of the TVA by Colignon (1996) utilizes a conflict model to provide a somewhat divergent interpretation of the agency's formative years.

institutions respond to types of circumstances" (1957: 142). However, this interest in generalization is somewhat at odds with the intensive case-study approach. As Cohen points out: "As the desire to explain more and more aspects of a single study, situation, or phenomenon increases, the possibility of using this explanation outside the situation for which it was created approaches the vanishing point" (1972: 402).

Exposés and Exemplars. Thus, in these earlier uses of the institutional approach, a rather consistent pattern emerges. Fundamentally, analysts sought to explain changes in the goals of the organization—not the professed goals, but the ends actually pursued, the operative goals. The general mode of explanation is similar to that offered by Michels: to increase their own influence or security, organizational participants modify controversial goals in the face of hostile environments. As Perrow notes, the literature spawned by the approach—to which Perrow himself had contributed (see Perrow, 1961)—takes on an "exposé" character: "The major message is that the organization has sold out its goals in order to survive or grow" (1986: 163). This early work stimulated by Selznick's conception appears to go out of its way to inspect the seamy side of organizational life, although in doing so it perhaps served as a useful antidote to the paean to organizational rationality being sung during this era by some overexuberant rational system theorists.

However, with time, this negative emphasis has been tempered by more constructive concerns about the ways in which precarious values can be protected. Selznick himself, as we have noted, began to emphasize that leaders could and should act to defend and, if necessary, reinterpret and renew the mission of their organization (1957). And Clark (1970; 1972) turned his attention from weak community colleges to examining how such "distinctive" and successful colleges as Antioch, Reed, and Swarthmore managed to survive and to preserve their special character. This broadened research agenda has gained a number of adherents. Not only is Selznick's work recognized as providing important underpinnings for the institutionalist perspective, which has garnered much attention in the most recent decades, but also his concern for the role of leaders in making critical decisions and in defining institutional values has contributed to the current interest in strategic decision making and the creation of organizational cultures. We consider these developments in later chapters, especially Chapters 8 and 12.

Parsons's AGIL Schema

System Imperatives. Working in the grand theory tradition, in a long and productive career of scholarship, Harvard scholar Talcott Parsons attempted to revive, build on, and synthesize works by the leading European sociological theorists (see Alexander, 1983, vol. 4). One of his projects involved perfecting a general analytic model suitable for the analysis for all types of social systems—from small, primary groups to entire societies (see Parsons, 1951; Parsons, 1966; Parsons, Bales, and Shils, 1953). He first applied the model to formal organizations in two papers published in the late 1950s and collected in his book on societies (1960). More so than other analysts working within the natural system tradition, Parsons developed a very explicit model detailing the needs that must be met if a social system is to survive. The model is identified by the acronym AGIL, from the first initial of each of the four basic needs:

Adaptation: the problem of acquiring sufficient resources.

Goal attainment: the problem of setting and implementing goals.

Integration: the problem of maintaining solidarity or coordination among the subunits of the system.

Latency: the problem of creating, preserving, and transmitting the system's distinctive culture and values.

In addition to being applicable to all types of social systems, the schema may be applied at more than one level in analyzing a given type of system. Thus, Parsons applies his model to organizations at the ecological, the structural, and the social psychological levels. Linkages across these levels are also stressed.

Multiple Levels. First, at the ecological level, Parsons relates organizations to the functioning of the larger society. Applying AGIL at the societal level, Parsons suggests that subordinate social units such as organizations can be classified according to their social function (see Table 3–1). For example, economic organizations such as firms function to meet the adaptive needs of the larger society. As Parsons points out:

What from the point of view of the organization is its specified goal is, from the point of view of the larger system of which it is a differentiated part or subsystem, a specialized or differentiated function. (1960: 19)

TABLE 3–1   Parsons's Typology Based on Societal Functions

Societal Function	*Organizational Type*	*Examples*
Adaptation	Organizations oriented to economic production	Business firms
Goal attainment	Organizations oriented to political goals	Government agencies Other organizations that allocate power, such as banks
Integration	Integrative organizations	Courts and the legal profession Political parties Social-control agencies
Latency	Pattern-maintenance organizations	Cultural organizations, such as museums Educational organizations Religious organizations

Because of this functional linkage, the place or role of the subsystem is legitimated within the value system of the overarching social order, and it may expect to receive societal approval and resources in accordance with the relative value placed in the society on the particular functions it performs.

Shifting down to the structural level of analysis, Parsons notes that each formal organization may also be analyzed as a social system in its own right, and each must develop its own differentiated subsystems to satisfy the four basic needs. Thus, each organization must develop structures that enable it to adapt to its environment and must mobilize resources needed for its continued operation. Arrangements are also needed to enable the organization to set and implement its goals. To solve its integrative problems, an organization must find ways to command the loyalties of its members, enlist their effort, and coordinate the operations of its various sectors. And mechanisms must be developed to cope with latency problems, to promote consensus on the values that define and legitimate the organization's output and system goals.

While Parsons does not insist that a specific structural unit will develop to manage each of these functional needs, he does argue that structural differentiation will tend to occur along these divisions. Functional imperatives generate the fault lines along which a social structure becomes differentiated. The explanation for this linkage between functional requirements and structural arrangements is simply that the various functional needs are somewhat in conflict, so that efforts directed at solving one functional problem interfere with efforts directed toward the others.[9] Differentiation reduces social frictions. Specifically, energies devoted to adapting the organization to its environment partially conflict with efforts toward goal attainment—a problem emphasized by Selznick and his colleagues—and efforts directed toward integration—a tension emphasized by Bales (1953)—and so on. A structural "solution" to these tensions is to create roles and subsystems focused on each problem area. For example, Bales and his colleagues argue that in informal groups the inherent tensions involved in goal attainment (for example, winning the game) versus integration (for example, providing satisfaction for all participants) is partially resolved by the emergence of a "task" leader, who specializes in directing and controlling goal attainment activities, and a "socio-emotional" leader, who specializes in motivating members and reducing tensions (Bales, 1953; Slater, 1955). And in formal organizations, specialized departments and roles—supervisors, maintenance workers, personnel counselors, inspectors—emerge to carry out the multiple, and somewhat conflicting, functions.

[9]Parsons's reasoning at this point is assisted by knowledge of the intellectual origins of the AGIL schema. His conception of these system problems grew out of his work on the "pattern variables"—basic value dichotomies representing the dimensions along which structures can be analytically described. The pairs of opposing values—universalism-particularism, affectivity-affective neutrality, ascription-achievement, and specificity-diffuseness—were cross-classified, producing the four system needs. For example, values identified as most appropriate for solving the problem of adaptation are universalism, affective neutrality, specificity, and achievement. At the opposite extreme, values appropriate for improving integration are particularism, affectivity, diffuseness, and ascription (see Parsons, 1951; Parsons, Bales, and Shils, 1953).

This solution only simplifies the definitions of individual roles and sub-systems and does not, of course, eliminate the incompatibilities: these are merely pushed to a higher level of the system for resolution. For example, at the level of the informal group, Bales (1953) argues that the differentiated leader roles provide a stable basis for group functioning only if the two leaders form a coalition of mutual support. At the organizational level, Lawrence and Lorsch (1967) have argued that organizations characterized by a higher level of structural differentiation are in greater need of integrative and conflict-resolution mechanisms (see Chapter 4).

Moving toward a more micro or social psychological level, Parsons again employs the AGIL schema, arguing that each subsystem within the organization itself comprises finer subdivisions that can be distinguished in terms of the functional requirements. However, as these applications become excessively complex and esoteric, we will not pursue them here.

Like many other natural system models, Parsons's framework emphasizes a set of functional needs that all social systems must satisfy in order to survive. As noted, this approach emphasizes the similarities between organizations and other types of social systems. But unlike other natural system models, Parsons's formulation also provides a clear basis for distinguishing between organizations and other social systems. Parsons states, "As a formal analytical point of reference, primacy of orientation to the attainment of a specific goal is used as the defining characteristic of an organization which distinguishes it from other types of social systems" (1960: 17). Within the Parsonian framework, this definition implies more than the widely shared view that organizations tend to pursue specific goals. Parsons calls attention to the relative importance placed on the goal-attainment subsystem in organizations. That is, organizations are social systems that place greater priority—and accordingly higher status and power—to those processes and functionaries by means of which goals are set and resources are mobilized for goal attainment than is the case in other social systems.

Parsons's theoretical model has been employed by some, but not many, researchers to guide their empirical studies of organizations. Georgopoulos (1972) has adapted it in his analysis of hospitals, and Lyden (1975) makes use of it in his study of public organizations. Of course, Parsons's generalized social system paradigm has had considerable impact on the work of sociologists (see Alexander, 1983, vol. 4) and many of his specific concepts and ideas have influenced work in the area of organizations, as we will document in later chapters.

We restrict ourselves to only a few general comments in assessing Parsons's contributions. On the positive side, his work aims at developing and perfecting a limited set of abstract concepts that can then be adapted for use in examining the structure and functioning of diverse social groupings. Using the same generic concepts helps us to see similarities in social structure and process across systems that appear to be quite different (Scott, 1970). Also, more than those of other natural system theorists, Parsons's framework is quite comprehensive, encompassing the formal and rational aspects of organizations as well as the informal. Further, Parsons is more explicit than other functional theorists in identifying the system needs that must be served for survival. Finally, Parsons, emphasized the importance for organizations of their connections to wider societal frameworks of norms and values. In this manner, he anticipated the interests of contemporary institutional theorists (Scott, 2001a: 25–27; see also Chapter 10).

Problems with the Parsonian approach are numerous, but perhaps its most important limitation is that his formulation tends to be more of a highly abstract conceptual framework than a substantive theory. We are provided with numerous concepts that suggest but are not clearly related to empirical indicators and are given relatively few testable propositions. The functional paradigm underlying the approach does provide some implicit hypotheses—such as, structural differentiation will occur along the lines separating differing functions—but such predictions are difficult to test.[10]

Early Exemplars of the Social Conflict Model

As previewed in Chapter 1, the natural system perspective exhibits two subtypes: the social consensus and the social conflict variants. Both have their adherents although the consensus version has always had more support among U.S. scholars while the social conflict version enjoys greater receptivity in Europe. Both are grounded in general sociological theory with applications made to organizations, the conflict version developing later than the consensus model.

Conflict theory traces its origins most directly to the writings of Marx (1954 trans.; 1963 trans.), although a number of conflict scholars claim Weber and Michels as early progenitors because of their recognition that organizations are systems of domination serving the interests of those holding power. This school emphasizes the extent to which participants' interests diverge and values of stakeholders conflict. Change is seen to be as natural and common as is stability, and much of the stability of social order results from the dominance of one group or coalition of interests over others, not to be mistaken for unity or harmony of interests. A fully developed Marxist theory of organizations did not emerge until the 1970s following the appearance of open systems models (we review this later work in Chapter 7), but conflict models appeared much earlier. We briefly comment on four influential examples of this early work.

Managerial Conflict. As already noted, Dalton (1950; 1959) was among the first to extend the concept of informal organization beyond the study of workers to include managers. His work is based on extended participant

---

[10]Alexander (1983) provides an overview of Parson's overall contributions to social theory, while Landsberger (1961) offers an useful description and critique of Parsons's model as it applies to organizations.

observation—"the aim is to get as close as possible to the world of managers" (1959: 1) and, as a consequence, we learn much more about the behavioral than the normative structure, the unofficial world of power struggles rather than the official realm of rules and organizational charts. He studied four organizations over a ten-year period—three factories and a department store. Dalton concludes: "If our cases are typical, then conflict is typical." Conflict is not depicted as abnormal or pathological. "Conflict fluctuates around some balance of the constructive and disruptive" (p. 263). Rather than adopting "bureaucratic theory" that assumes that members of the organization are relatively inert and ready to follow the intent of rules, he recognizes the "active seeking nature of man, his ancient and obvious tendency to twist the world to his interests" (p. 165). Dalton depicts in elaborate detail the multiple bases of conflict arising within organizations: between departments, between higher and lower ranks of line officials, between staff and line officers, between cliques, and between personalities.

Who Benefits from Rules? As a member of Columbia University's pioneering cohort of organizational students, Gouldner (1954) attempted to uncover some of the tensions in Weber's theory of bureaucracy. Picking up on Weber's statement that "any given legal norm may be established by agreement or by imposition" (1947 trans.: 329), Gouldner insisted that these two processes would lead to quite different consequences. In his study of a gypsum factory, he identified several classes of rules varying in degree of consensus or conflict and examined the implications of these differences for the managers and workers involved. Gouldner also raised other questions about Weber's schema:

> First, to whom did the rules have to be useful, if bureaucratic authority was to be effective? Secondly, in terms of whose goals were the rules a rational device? Whose end did they have to realize to operate effectively? . . . Had he [Weber] focused on the factory bureaucracy with its more evident tensions between supervisor and supervised, as this study shall, he would have been immediately aware that a given rule could be rational or expedient for achieving the ends of one stratum, say management, but might be neither rational nor expedient for the workers. (1954: 20–21)

To assume that organizations are rational instruments for the pursuit of goals ignores the question of whose goals are being served. It assumes that there is consensus rather than conflict over goals. More generally, to adopt an approach that posits the existence of "organizational goals" masks the reality that the goals served by organizations are selected by individuals and may favor the interests of some parties over those of others (see Chapter 8).

Managerial Ideologies. One of the most important early comparative studies in organizations, conducted by Bendix (1956), examined the variable nature—across time and space—of managerial ideologies. Building on the insights of both Marx and Weber, Bendix contrasted social class—"the universal tendency of men who are similarly situated socially and economically to develop common ideas and to engage in collective action"—with bureaucracy—"the universal tendency of men who are employed in hierarchical organizations to obey directives and to identify their own interests and ideas with the organization" (p. xx). How is this possible? Bendix argues:

> Employers, entrepreneurs, and managers typically act in such a way as to combine these tendencies. To safeguard and advance their interests they will join with others like them in the collective actions of a social class. But within each of their separate economic enterprises they will use their authority to have the workers identify their ideas and interests with the enterprise rather than with each other. Ideologies of management are attempts by leaders of enterprises to justify the privilege of voluntary action and association for themselves, while imposing upon all subordinates the duty of obedience and the obligation to serve their employers to the best of their ability. (1956: xxi)

Different ideologies are developed to fit varying circumstances. Bendix contrasts the ideologies developed by managerial elites during the time of industrialization in England and in imperial Russia, contrasting these with the twentieth-century ideologies utilized in the United States and the Soviet Union. Among the ideologies justifying managerial control examined in the United States are scientific management and human relations (Bendix, 1956: 274–340).[11]

Changing Bases of Power. The most explicit early application of Marxist theory to organizations was provided by the German theorist Dahrendorf (1959) who, as noted in Chapter 1, attempted to revise Marx's arguments by insisting that the basis of power in modern society was no longer ownership of the means of production, which was increasingly in the hands of widely dispersed stockholders, but occupancy of managerial and executive positions within organizations. In explicit contrast to Taylor, Parsons and others emphasizing "social integration," Dahrendorf elaborated a theory of organizations built on an assumption of the existence of socially structured conflicts of interest.

Scholars proposing a social conflict model of organizations were a distinct minority, particularly among students of organizations in the United States, and they remain so to this day. Nevertheless, the concerns they addressed are real: conflict and change are a part of organizational life no less than consensus and stability. Interest in these issues developed rapidly in the 1970s and has been reactivated recently by feminist and critical theorists. We consider these developments later, particularly in Chapters 7 and 8.

---

[11]Bendix's classic book has recently been reissued with additional material and a helpful introductory essay by Guillén (see Bendix, 2001).

SUMMARY AND TENTATIVE CONCLUSIONS

Divergent Views. Whereas the rational system model focuses on features of organizations that distinguish them from other social groupings, the natural system model emphasizes commonalities among organizations and other systems. The natural system theorists do not deny that organizations have distinctive features, but they argue that these are overshadowed by the more generic systems and processes shared by all social collectivities. Thus, the specific output goals of organizations are often undermined or distorted by energies devoted to the pursuit of system goals, chief among which is the concern to survive. The formal aspects of organizational structure that receive so much attention from the rational system analysts are treated as faded backdrops for the "real" informal structures, imbued with human frailties and agency. More generally, whereas the rational system model stresses the normative structure of organizations, the natural system model places great emphasis on the behavioral structure. And where the rational system perspective stresses the importance of organizational structure over individual interests and capabilities, the natural system perspective reverses these priorities—so much so that Bennis labels this orientation as one portraying "people without organizations" (1959: 266).

Most of the early theorists who shaped the natural system perspective embrace a functional model of analysis, although they vary considerably in how explicitly and how fully they pursue its development. The human relations analysts tend to be less overt and less consistent in their use of this model than Barnard, Selznick, or Parsons. All schools within the consensus branch of the natural system framework presume the existence of certain needs that must be met if the system is to survive, and all direct attention to discovering the mechanisms by which these needs are satisfied. This is less so with the conflict models, although some versions emphasize the "functions" of social conflict for attaining and preserving social order (Coser, 1956).

Varying views of the environment appear to be associated with the natural system theorists. Most of the human relations analysts simply overlook it as a factor. Like the early rational system theorists, they concentrate on the internal organizational arrangements and their effects on participants, treating the organization, in effect, as a closed system. This neglect is especially striking in the case of the Hawthorne studies, conducted during the 1930s, in the depths of the Great Depression. In the bank-wiring observation room study, for example, the workers' efforts to restrict production were viewed as irrational conformity to group norms. Given the larger economic situation, however, these activities appear to be a perfectly rational response to the threat of being laid off (see Blau and Scott, 1962: 92–93; Landsberger, 1958: 58). Indeed, during the period of the research, many layoffs occurred at the Hawthorne plant; in fact, the bank-wiring room study had to be discontinued because so many workers were let go! (Roethlisberger and Dickson, 1939: 395).

Barnard takes more account of the environment than the human relations group (see Scott, 1990). He shows awareness that organizations must attract participants by providing them with inducements, indeed, that they must compete with other organizations attempting to attract their services and loyalties. Moreover, he recognizes that a given individual participates in many cooperative groups simultaneously, so that his or her involvement in any single organization is both partial and intermittent. It is undoubtedly such insights that cause Barnard to emphasize the importance of obtaining contributions and inspiring commitment. However, Barnard does not explicitly conceptualize the environment or examine the extent to which organizations vary in their environment locations. Selznick and his students, by contrast, do explicitly consider the environment in their analyses of organizations. However, their view is a highly selective one: the environment is perceived primarily as an enemy, as a source of pressures and problems. In most of the pioneering studies in this tradition, the organization is viewed as confronting a hostile environment. Organizing occurs against the environment. In the work of Parsons we begin to have a more balanced view of the environment. Parsons recognized the importance of the organization-environment relation, the organization being viewed as a subsystem within a more comprehensive societal unit, and the environment seen more as a stabilizing element sustaining and legitimating the organization in its special mission than as a source of resistance. In these ways, Parsons anticipates the view of the open systems theorists.

Natural system theorists working out of the social conflict tradition emphasized the extent to which organizational structures and the rules and ideologies that support them work to suppress and conceal the conflicts of interests among participants and constituencies. They insist that organizational systems are, fundamentally, systems of domination, systems for "rationally" exploiting the weak to serve the interests of the powerful.

As with the rational system theorists discussed in Chapter 2, our discussion of natural system theorists in the current chapter follows the story only up to the early 1960s. We will see the concerns of natural system theorists reflected in the work of many contemporary analysts, in particular, organizational ecologists and evolutionary theorists (Aldrich, 1999).

Accounting for the Differences. Two quite different perspectives on organizations—the rational and natural system perspective—have now been described. How could two such different viewpoints have arisen? Several explanations have been proposed.

Lawrence and Lorsch (1967: 163–84) propose that some of the differences in perspective were produced by variations in the experience and background of the analysts themselves. They point out that among the rational system or "classical" theorists, as they label them, Fayol, Mooney, and Urwick were all practical men with managerial experience. Taylor's training was as an industrial engineer. By contrast, among the natural systems theorists, Mayo, Roethlisberger, Selznick, McGregor, Parsons, Bendix, Dalton,

Gouldner, and Dahrendorf were all from academic backgrounds, with experience largely in the university. (Exceptions to this division were, on the one side, Weber, who was a university professor [although, in terms of lifestyle and experience he is more accurately described as a recluse scholar] and Gulick, who was also an academic. On the other side, of course, was Barnard, a company executive.) Lawrence and Lorsch argue that divergent backgrounds shaped the reactions of these analysts to organizations. Coming from the relatively nonhierarchical arrangements of a university, the natural system analysts were prone to react negatively to the formalism of an industrial plant and inclined to attribute their own needs for autonomy to workers.

A second explanation offered is that the two types of analysts concentrated on different types of organizations. The rational system analysts were more likely to investigate industrial firms and state bureaucracies, while the natural system analysts tended to focus on service and professional organizations—schools, hospitals, and voluntary organizations, such as the YMCA. Since the degree of formalization and of goal specificity varies greatly across the spectrum of organizations, it is quite possible that rational system analysts concentrated on the more highly structured end of the continuum and the natural system analysts, the less structured. We examine other explanations for the existence and continuation of these contrasting models in Chapter 5.

Deeper Differences. Although differences in the analysts' backgrounds or in the particular organization on which they chose to focus may account for some of the variance in the two perspectives, it is our view that these points of view represent more fundamental divisions than are suggested by these explanations. Underlying the perspectives are quite basic divergences in moral and philosophical views and assumptions.

Natural and rational system theorists base their approaches on differing assumptions about human nature: the interests that guide and the factors that motivate behavior in organizations. Natural system theorists posit a more expansive, social, and motivationally complex actor than do rational system analysts. Also, theorists from the two schools hold differing conceptions of the actual and the proper relation of individual participants to organizations. Rational system theorists argue that only selected aspects of behaviors of participants are relevant to the organization. Natural system theorists expand the definition of organizationally relevant behavior to include a broader range of an individual's activities and attitudes. They do so on two grounds: (1) such behaviors have an impact on the task behavior of participants, and hence are empirically relevant to an understanding of organizational behavior, and (2) organizations as social contexts affect the participants' well-being, a situation that has normative significance to anyone concerned with bettering the human condition. Many natural system theorists point to the dysfunctions arising from the partial inclusion of participants and argue, partly on moral grounds, that organizations should take more responsibility for the well-being of the "whole person." These arguments are not without merit, but all of the morality is not on one side. Rational system theorists insist that rational-legal structures developed in part out of efforts to place limits on the demands superiors could make on their subordinates. The development of formal role definitions—definitions of the limits of a participant's obligations—was an important step in increasing and protecting the freedom of individuals. Whether the organization's purview should incorporate more or fewer facets of the lives of its participants is a basic philosophical difference separating the two perspectives.

Further, the two approaches are characterized by quite divergent views of the fundamental nature of social systems. These differences are reflected in the contrasting imagery and metaphors employed by the two schools (Morgan 1980). For the mechanistic model of structure employed in the rational system perspective, the natural system substitutes an organic model. Rational systems are designed, but natural systems evolve; the former develop by conscious design, the latter by natural growth; rational systems are characterized by calculation, natural systems by spontaneity. Lest we regard these images of social structure as being of recent vintage, Wolin (1960: 352–434) reminds us that they have a long history in political and social thought. The view of organizations as economic, technological, efficient instruments is associated with the work of such social theorists as Hobbes, Saint-Simon, and Lenin—the precursors of Taylor, Weber, Fayol, and Simon. The view of organizations as communitarian, natural, nonrational, organic systems may be traced back to the social theories of Rousseau, Proudhon, Marx, Burke, and Durkheim, the intellectual ancestors of Mayo, Barnard, Selznick, Parsons, Gouldner, and Bendix. With such lengthy and distinguished pedigrees, it is unlikely that either of these two lines of thought will soon end, or that their differences will quickly be resolved.

CHAPTER 4

Organizations as Open Systems

That a system is open means, not simply that it engages in interchanges with the environment, but that this interchange is an essential factor underlying the system's viability.

WALTER BUCKLEY (1967)

The open system perspective emerged as a part of the intellectual ferment following World War II, although its roots are much older. This general movement created new areas of study, such as cybernetics and information theory; stimulated new applications, such as systems engineering and operations research; transformed existing disciplines, including the study of organizations; and proposed closer linkages among scientific disciplines. The latter interest was fostered especially by general system theory. Its founder, biologist Ludwig von Bertalanffy, was concerned about the growing compartmentalization of science:

> The physicist, the biologist, the psychologist and the social scientist are, so to speak, encapsulated in a private universe, and it is difficult to get word from one cocoon to another. (Bertalanffy, 1956: 1)

Bertalanffy and his associates argued that key concepts could have relevance across a broad spectrum of disciplines.[1] In particular, they pointed out that many of the most important entities studied by scientists—nuclear particles, atoms, molecules, cells, organs, organisms, ecological communities, groups,

---

[1]In a similar fashion, a half-century later, another biologist, Edward O. Wilson (1998), has proposed that all knowledge is intrinsically unified, that behind disciplines as diverse as physics and sociology lie a small number of natural laws, stemming largely from biological principles.

organizations, societies, solar systems—are all subsumable under the general rubric of *system.*[2]

SYSTEM LEVELS

All systems are characterized by an assemblage or combination of parts whose relations make them interdependent. While these features underlie the similarities exhibited by all systems, they also suggest bases for differences among them. The parts of which all systems are composed vary from simple to complex, from stable to variable, and from nonreactive to reactive to the changes in the system to which they belong. As we move from mechanical through organic to social systems, the parts of which systems are composed become more complex and variable. In addition, relations among the parts varies from one type of system to another. In this connection, Norbert Wiener, the founder of cybernetics, notes; "Organization we must consider as something in which there is an interdependence between the several organized parts but in which this interdependence has degrees" (1956: 322). In mechanistic systems, the interdependence among parts is such that their behavior is highly constrained and limited. The structure is relatively rigid, and the system of relations determinant. In organic systems, the connections among the interdependent parts are somewhat less constrained, allowing for more flexibility of response. In social systems, such as groups and organizations, the connections among the interacting parts are relatively loose: less constraint is placed on the behavior of one element by the condition of the others. Social organizations, in contrast with physical or mechanical structures, are *complex* and *loosely coupled* systems (see Ashby, 1968; Buckley, 1967: 82–83).

Also, as we progress from simple to complex and from tightly to loosely coupled systems, the nature and relative importance of the various flows among the system elements and between the system and its environment change. The major types of system flows are those of materials, energy, and information. And, as Buckley notes:

> Whereas the relations among components of mechanical systems are a function primarily of spatial and temporal considerations and the transmission of energy from one component to another, the interrelations characterizing higher levels come to depend more and more on the transmission of information. (1967: 47)

The notion of types or levels of systems that vary both in the complexity of their parts and in the nature of the relations among the parts has been usefully elaborated by Boulding, who devised a classification of systems by their level of complexity. Boulding identifies nine system types (see Table 4–1).

---

[2]In his monumental book *Living Systems*, Miller (1978) identifies seven basic levels: the cell, the organ, the organism, the group, the organization, the society, and the supranational system.

TABLE 4–1   Boulding's System Types

1. *Frameworks:* systems comprising static structures, such as the arrangements of atoms in a crystal or the anatomy of an animal.

2. *Clockworks:* simple dynamic systems with predetermined motions, such as the clock and the solar system.

3. *Cybernetic systems:* systems capable of self-regulation in terms of some externally pre-scribed target or criterion, such as a thermostat.

4. *Open systems:* systems capable of self-maintenance based on a throughput of resources from their environment, such as a living cell.

5. *Blueprinted-growth systems:* systems that reproduce not by duplication but by the production of seeds or eggs containing preprogrammed instructions for development, such as the acorn-oak system or the egg-chicken system.

6. *Internal-image systems:* systems capable of a detailed awareness of the environment in which information is received and organized into an image or knowledge structure of the environment as a whole, a level at which animals function.

7. *Symbol-processing systems:* systems that possess self-consciousness and so are capable of using language. Humans function at this level.

8. *Social systems:* multicephalous systems comprising actors functioning at level 7 who share a common social order and culture. Social organizations operate at this level.

9. *Transcendental systems:* systems composed of the "absolutes and the inescapable unknowables."

Source: Adapted from Boulding (1956: 200–207).

Boulding's typology is illuminating in several respects. It quickly persuades us of the great range and variety of systems present in the world. Levels 1 to 3 encompass the physical systems, levels 4 to 6 the biological systems, and levels 7 and 8 the human and social systems. Progressing from level 1 to 8, each successive system becomes progressively more complex, more loosely coupled, more dependent on information flows, more capable of self-maintenance and renewal, more able to grow and change, and more open to the environment. Boulding adds level 9 so that the schema will not be closed, but open to new possibilities not yet envisioned.

Although the nine levels can be distinctly identified and associated with specific existing systems, they are not meant to be mutually exclusive. Indeed, each higher-level system incorporates basic features of those below it. For example, it is possible to analyze a social organization as a framework, a clockwork, a cybernetic system, and so on up to level 8, the level that captures the most complex, the higher-level, processes occurring in organizations. Boulding argues that because each level incorporates those below it, "much valuable information and insights can be obtained by applying low-level systems to high-level subject matter." At the same time, he reminds us that "most of the theoretical schemes of the social sciences are still at level 2, just rising now to 3, although the subject matter clearly involves level 8" (1956: 208).

In 1980, Daft reviewed all of the theoretical and empirical papers published between 1959–1979 in *Administrative Science Quarterly*, the leading outlet for organizational studies during that period. Classifying articles by the "level of complexity" at which organizational systems were treated using Boulding's typology, Daft (1980) noted that it was not until after 1969 that articles began to drift toward greater complexity, although no articles published during that period reached Boulding's higher levels. This suggests that Boulding's conclusion continued to be applicable for many years and constitutes an important criticism of reigning theoretical models of organizations throughout this period.

The most systematic introduction of open systems concepts and models into organization theory was provided by Katz and Kahn (1978) in the first edition (1966) of their influential text. Buckley (1967) also served as a useful guide for many sociologists.

SPECIAL EMPHASES AND INSIGHTS

Enormous benefits have been realized by students of organizations simply in elevating their conceptual level from 1 and 2, frameworks and clockworks, up to level 3, where organizations are viewed as cybernetic systems, and to level 4, where they are viewed as open systems. Along with our consideration of organizations as cybernetic and open systems, we take note of two other concepts associated with this perspective: organizations as loosely coupled systems and organizations as hierarchical systems.

Organizations as Cybernetic Systems

Systems functioning at Boulding's level 3 are capable of self-regulation. This important feat is attained through the development of specialized parts or subsystems related by certain processes or flows. Consider the mechanical example of the thermostat related to a source of heat. As Figure 4–1 illustrates, the system contains differentiated parts: a component for converting inputs into outputs—in this case, a heater that converts fuel and oxygen into heat; and a component for comparing the actual and desired temperatures—the thermostat. The parts are interrelated: the heater produces changes in temperatures detected by the thermostat; the thermostat controls a switch on the heater turning it on or off based on information provided by comparing the actual and desired temperatures.

The key mechanism that effects the control process, that renders the system capable of self-regulation, however, is the *program*. Beniger provides an illuminating discussion of programs which he defines as "any prearranged information that guides subsequent behavior" (1986: 39). He continues:

> Programs control by determining decisions. . . . the process of control involves comparison of new information (inputs) to stored patterns and instructions (programming) to decide among a predetermined set of contingent behaviors (possible outputs). (p. 48)

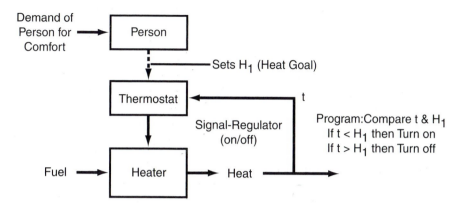

FIGURE 4–1   Illustration of a Cybernetic System: The Thermostat and the Heater. *Source:* Adapted from Swinth (1974: Figure 2–1, p. 18).

The identification of programs that exercise control through information processing and decision making circumvents the problem of teleology: the attempt to explain present activities by reference to their future consequences.[3] Programs "must exist prior to the phenomena they explain"; "their effects precede rather than follow their causes" (Beniger, 1986: 40).

Figure 4–1 also depicts a person who sets the standards in terms of which the cybernetic system functions. The person is capable of altering the system by reprogramming it, that is, by changing the desired temperature level. However, the person is not a component in the basic cybernetic system, which is, in its simplest manifestation a closed system consisting, in the current example, of simply an existing program governing the thermostat, the heater, and their interconnections.[4] If the standard-setting and programming functions are included as a part of the system, then the model is transformed into a powerful, general model of control, depicted in Figure 4–2, a type of control that is widely employed in organizational settings.

To view an organization as a cybernetic system is to emphasize the importance of the operations, control, and policy centers, and the flows among them (Swinth, 1974). The policy center sets the goals for the system. This activity occurs in response to demands or preferences from the environment (flow 1 in Figure 4–2), some of the environmental demands take the form of orders (flow 2) from, for example, customers or from a higher-level organizational system. Note that the setting of goals is based on

[3]Functional arguments, described in Chapter 3, suffer from the difficulties of teleological explanation.

[4]Not too surprisingly, the founder of cybernetics, Norbert Wiener, insists that the subject is broader in scope than indicated by Boulding. Wiener defines cybernetics as the "study of messages and the communication facilities that belong to it . . . [including] messages between man and machines, machines and man, and between machines and machines" (1954: 16).

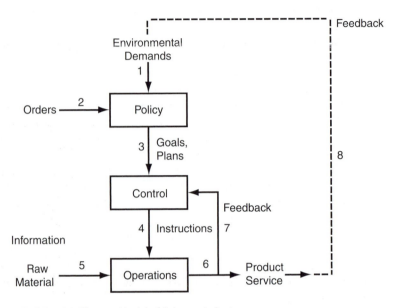

FIGURE 4–2 Abstract Model of Cybernetic System.
Source: Adapted from Swinth (1974: Figure 2–4, p. 23).

information received from the environment so that favorable exchanges between the environment and organization can occur. The policy center transmits goals or performance standards (flow 3) to the control center. This unit applies its program(s) to the operations level (flow 4), where raw materials are transformed into products and services (flows 5 and 6). It is also the task of the control center to monitor the outputs, comparing their quality and/or quantity with the standards set by the policy center (flow 7). Discrepancies are the occasion for corrective actions as prescribed by the program. The figure also displays a second feedback loop (flow 8) to illustrate the possibility that reactions to the system's outputs by those outside the system, for example, customers, may lead the organization to revise its goals. Ashby (1952) points out that in such double feedback systems, the primary loop handles disturbances in "degree," applying existing decision rules, while the secondary loop handles disturbances in "kind," determining whether it is necessary to redefine the rules controlling the operating levels. Argyris (1982) labels such adaptive behaviors that result not simply in different activities but in different rules for choosing activities "double-loop learning." Monitoring environmental feedback on the system's past performance—for example, a company reviewing records on sales by product lines—is an important mechanism of adaptation for any open system, although many organizations do not avail themselves of such occasions for learning.

Buckley stresses that cybernetic systems result in behavior that is "goal-*directed*, and not merely goal-*oriented*, since it is the deviations from the goal-state itself that direct the behavior of the system, rather than some pre-determined internal mechanism that aims blindly" (1967: 53). Further, a feedback mechanism detects departures from the established goals no matter what their cause, an important control characteristic as systems become so complex that all the potential sources of disturbance cannot be identified in advance (see Beer, 1964: 29–30).

The cybernetic model places great emphasis on the operational level of the organization—the level at which the production processes of the system are carried out. The analysis of these technical flows—inputs, throughputs, and outputs—is regarded as vital to an understanding of the system; indeed, the control and policy centers are examined chiefly in terms of their impact on these technical flows. In keeping with this de-emphasis on formal structure and attention to how the organization actually does its work, Mintzberg and Van der Heyden (1999) propose that organizations would be well advised to discard their organization charts and replace them with "organigraphs." These diagrams, composed of "sets" (items such as materials or machines), "chains" (linear connections among sets), "hubs" (coordination centers), and "webs" (networks), emphasize flows and other relations among the component parts of organizations.

The cybernetic framework can be applied to the organization as a whole or to any of its subsystems. It can be used, for example, to analyze the operation of a company's personnel subsystem, which must meet the demands of other subsystems for trained employees and must control the recruitment and training of new workers and monitor their turnover (Carzo and Yanouzas, 1967: 345–47). Or it can be used to examine the working of an entire organization, for example, a company producing, distributing, and exercising quality control over its products and attempting to monitor past sales and customer preferences so as to keep abreast of a changing marketplace.

Organizations as Loosely Coupled Systems

The cybernetic model gives the impression of a taut system—an arrangement of parts such that each is highly responsive to changes in the others. Such system relations are certainly found within organizations, but we should guard against overgeneralization. One of the main contributions of the open systems perspective is the recognition that many systems—especially social systems—contain elements that are only weakly connected to others and capable of fairly autonomous actions (Ashby, 1968; Glassman, 1973; Weick, 1976).

This insight can be applied to many different components or elements of organizations and their participants. Thus, we have seen that from the standpoint of the natural system analysts, the normative structure of an organization is only loosely coupled with its behavioral structure. Rules do not always govern actions: a rule may change without affecting behavior, and vice versa. At the social psychology level, analysts have noted that an individual's goals or intentions may be only weakly linked to his or her actions (March and

Olsen, 1976). Often there is, at best, a weak connection between "talk" and "action" in organizations (Brunsson, 1989). Executives and managers may talk convincingly about the total quality management (TQM) programs in their organizations, but researchers may find little or no evidence of such activities in production and service departments (Cole and Scott, 2000). Pfeffer and Sutton (2000) provide much evidence of this sort of "knowing-doing" gap in organizations. The concept of loose coupling can also be applied to the relationship among structural units such as work groups or departments. Some may be tightly coupled while others are, at best, loosely connected, and still others, virtually independent. Inspection of official organizational charts can convey the impression that these units are all highly interrelated and closely coordinated, whereas observation of their actual behavior may reveal that they are only slightly or occasionally connected.

A particularly important application of the loose coupling image is that proposed by Cyert and March (1963) and adopted by Pfeffer and Salancik (1978). As noted in Chapter 1 in describing the open system definition of the concept of organization, these theorists propose to view the key participants in organizations not as a unitary hierarchy or as an organic entity, but as a loosely linked coalition of shifting interest groups. According to Pfeffer and Salancik:

> The organization is a coalition of groups and interests, each attempting to obtain something from the collectivity by interacting with others, and each with its own preferences and objectives. (1978: 36)

Rather than being rigidly oriented to the pursuit of consistent, common objectives, these coalitions change

> their purpose and domains to accommodate new interests, sloughing off parts of themselves to avoid some interests, and when necessary become involved in activities far afield from their stated purposes. (1978: 24)

The relation between dominant coalitions and goal setting is further discussed in Chapter 8.

Another important application of the loose-coupling concept is the argument that formal administrative structures within organizations are often de-coupled from production systems. We discuss this argument, developed by institutional scholars, in Chapter 10.

Contrary to first impressions and to rational system assumptions, open system theorists insist that loose coupling in structural arrangements can be highly adaptive for the system as a whole (see Orton and Weick, 1990; Weick, 1976). It appears that loose coupling need not signify either low moral or low managerial standards.

On the other hand, the loose coupling of organizational elements no doubt contributes to what has been termed, the "productivity paradox," the

situation in which a great many organizations have made enormous investments in information-processing technologies without appreciable effects on
the overall rate of productivity growth in this country (see Harris, 1994).
Enhancement in the productivity of individual workers does not quickly or
easily translate into gains in productivity assessed at the departmental or firm
level, let alone that of the industry.

The Characteristics of Open Systems

Organizations may be analyzed as cybernetic systems, but they also function at higher levels of complexity (review Table 4–1). They operate as open
systems. *Open systems* are capable of self-maintenance on the basis of throughput of resources from the environment. As Buckley (1967: 50) observes, this
throughput is essential to the system's viability. Note that the heating unit, one
of the components in our example of a cybernetic system, is not an open system as we have defined the concept. Although the heater receives inputs such
as fuel from its environment and emits heat and various waste products to the
environment, it is not capable of using the fuel to replace or repair its own elements. It cannot transform its inputs in such a way as to prolong its own survival or self-maintenance. Organic systems, including plants and animals, have
this capacity, as do human and social systems.

Some analysts have mistakenly characterized an open system as having
the capacity for self-maintenance *despite* the presence of throughput
from the environment. Their assumption is that because organizations are
open, they must defend themselves against the assaults of the environment.
This view is misguided and misleading, since interaction with the environment is essential for open system functioning. As Pondy and Mitroff argue,
rather than suggesting that organizational systems be protected "against
environmental complexity," we should realize that "it is precisely the
throughput of nonuniformity that preserves the differential structure of an
open system" (1979: 7).

This is not to say that open systems do not have boundaries. They do,
of course, and must expend energy in boundary maintenance. But it is of
equal importance that energies be devoted to activities that span and, more
recently, redraw boundaries. Because of the openness of organizations,
determining their boundaries is always difficult and sometimes appears to
be a quite arbitrary decision. Does a university include within its boundary
its students? Its alumni? Faculty during the summer? The spouses of students in university housing? Pfeffer and Salancik (1978: 30) propose to
resolve this type of problem by reminding us that individual persons are not
enclosed within the boundaries of organizations, only certain of their activities and behaviors. Although this interpretation helps, we all know that
many actions have relevance for more than one system simultaneously. For
example, a sale from the standpoint of one system is a purchase when
viewed from another, and an act of conformity for one system can be an act

of deviance for another. (Boundaries are considered in more detail in Chapters 7, 9, 11, and 14.)

Moreover, as will be emphasized, all systems are made up of subsystems and are themselves subsumed in larger systems—an arrangement that creates linkages across systems and confounds the attempt to erect clear boundaries around them. Ultimately, our determination of whether a system is open is itself a matter of how the boundaries of the system are defined. As Hall and Fagen note:

> whether a given system is open or closed depends on how much of the universe is included in the system and how much in the environment. By adjoining to the system the part of the environment with which an exchange takes place, the system becomes closed. (1956: 23)

General systems theorists elaborate the distinction between closed and open systems by employing the concept of *entropy*: energy that cannot be turned into work. According to the second law of thermodynamics, all systems spontaneously move toward a state of increasing entropy—a random arrangement of their elements, a dissolution of their differentiated structures, a state of maximum disorder. But open systems, because they are capable of importing energy from their environment, can experience negative entropy, or "negentropy." By acquiring inputs of greater complexity than their outputs, open systems restore their energy, repair breakdowns in their organization, and may improve their structures and routines. Bertalanffy concludes, "such systems can maintain themselves at a high level, and even evolve toward an increase of order and complexity" (1962: 7).[5]

To emphasize these twin properties of open systems, Buckley (1967: 58–62) distinguishes between two basic sets of system processes: morphostasis and morphogenesis. The term *morphostasis* refers to those processes that tend to preserve or maintain a system's given form, structure, or state. Morphostatic processes in biological systems would include circulation and respiration; in

---

[5]Information theorists posit a close relation between the concepts of organization and entropy: they are viewed, in effect, as opposite states. If entropy is a state of randomness, or zero organization, it is also the state that provides maximum variety, maximum information, to someone observing a set of elements. As organization develops, constraints and limitations grow, restricting the number of states that may be present among the elements. Miller elaborates this point:

> A well-organized system is predictable—you know what it is going to do before it happens. When a well-organized system does something, you learn little that you didn't already know—you acquire little information. A perfectly organized system is completely predictable and its behavior provides no information at all. The more disorganized and unpredictable a system is, the more information you get by watching it. (1953: 3)

Based on such reasoning, information theorists Shannon and Weaver (1963) have proposed a measure of information, H, which assesses the amount of entropy present in a set of elements—their variation, their relative frequency of occurrence, and their interdependence. The higher the H level, the more information and the less organization are present (see also Buckley, 1967: 82–89).

social systems, socialization and control activities. *Morphogenesis* refers to processes that elaborate or change the system—for example, growth, learning, and differentiation. In adapting to the external environment, open systems typically become more differentiated in form, more elaborate in structure. Thus, in biological systems, organs whose sensitivities to external stimuli are coarse and broad are succeeded, over time, by more specialized receptors capable of responding to a wider range and finer gradations of stimuli. Biological organisms move toward greater complexity through the process of evolution: individual organisms are little affected, but over time, as mutations occur and are selected for their survival value, species are gradually transformed. Social organizations, more variable and loosely coupled than biological systems, can and do fundamentally change their structural characteristics over time. The General Motors of today bears little structural resemblance to the company of the same name fifty years ago. Indeed, social organizations exhibit such an amazing capacity to change their basic structural features that researchers who study organizations over time have difficulty determining when the units they are studying are the same organizations with reorganized structures and when they represent the birth of new organizations (see Chapters 10 and 13).

To repeat, the source of system maintenance, diversity, and variety is the environment. From an open system point of view, there is a close connection between the condition of the environment and the characteristics of the systems within it: a complex system cannot maintain its complexity in a simple environment. Open systems are subject to what is termed the *law of limited variety*: "A system will exhibit no more variety than the variety to which it has been exposed in its environment" (Pondy and Mitroff, 1979: 7). Great universities do not arise in deserts or other sparsely inhabited areas. Although the processes by which such "laws" operate are not clearly understood, most of this volume is devoted to explicating and illustrating the interdependence of organizations and environments.

Organizations as Hierarchical Systems

General systems theorists also stress that hierarchy is a fundamental feature of complex systems—not hierarchy in the sense of status or power differences, but hierarchy as a mechanism of clustering. Systems are composed of multiple subsystems, and systems are themselves contained within larger systems. This is such a common feature of virtually all complex systems that it is easily overlooked. Books like this one are made up of letters, words, sentences, paragraphs, sections and chapters. The U.S. political system is constituted of precincts, special districts, counties, and states, all contained within the nation-state. And organizations are made up of roles clustered into work groups, departments, and divisions. Many organizations are themselves subsystems of larger systems, of corporate structures, associations, or a branch of government. And an increasing number of organizations are connected into wider collaborative networks and alliances with other organizations (see Chapter 11).

Combining the notion of hierarchy with that of loose coupling, we grasp an important feature of complex systems. The connections and interdependencies within a system component are apt to be tighter and of greater density than those between system components. In a well-written book, for example, the ideas expressed in a single paragraph are more closely interrelated than those expressed in different paragraphs. Similarly, interactions within a given academic department of a university are likely to be more frequent and more intense than those occurring between departments. Indeed, as will be discussed in Chapter 6, this generalization provides the basis for an important principle of organizational design.

When subsystems take the form of "stable subassemblies"—units capable of retaining their form without constant attention from superior units—then hierarchical forms have a significant survival advantage over other systems (Simon, 1962). Many seemingly complex organizational systems are made up of, and depend for their stability on, units that are highly similar and capable of relatively autonomous functioning—for example, work teams, departments, franchise units, or chain stores. From this perspective, the apparent complexity of many systems is significantly reduced. Everything is *not* connected to everything else; connections are loose or missing, and many components of systems are identical or nearly so (see Aldrich, 1979: 75–80).

To this point, we have emphasized that all systems are composed of subsystems. Of equal significance is the observation that all systems are subsumed by other, more encompassing systems. This suggests that to understand the operation of a system, it may be as important to look outside the system of interest to examine its context as to look inside the system at its component units. Schwab (1960) has termed this perspective "rationalism," the opposite of reductionism. In rationalism, explanation entails looking outside an entity to the environment or a higher system in which it is embedded (see also McKelvey, 1982: 5). In these many ways, the open systems perspective points to the significance of the wider environment.

SELECTED SCHOOLS

As with our discussion of the previous perspectives, we consider several schools that exemplify the open systems approach. We briefly describe the systems design approach; contingency theory (closely related to systems design), and Weick's social psychological model of organizing. Although open systems approaches to organizations were the last of the three perspectives to emerge, they have spread very rapidly and have had an enormous effect on organization theory. We discuss in this section only selected early developments; in Chapter 5 and later chapters we consider other approaches embodying open systems assumptions and insights.

Systems Design

A large and growing number of organization theorists look to general systems theory as a source of ideas to improve the design of organizations—determining proper work flows, control systems, information processing, planning mechanisms, knowledge transfer, and their interrelations (see Burton and Obel, 2004; Carzo and Yanouzas, 1967; Huber and Glick, 1993; Khandwalla, 1977; Mintzberg, 1979; Nissen, 2006; Sternman, 1994). Unlike some schools devoted to the study of organizations, the orientation of this group is pragmatic and applied: design theorists seek to change and improve organizations as viewed from a managerial perspective, not simply to describe and understand them.

Levels of System Complexity. Many of the analysts applying systems ideas to organizations are aware both of the great complexity of organizations as one type of system and of the danger of misapplying or overextending analogies based on the operation of other, less complex systems. Beer (1964) proposes a classification of systems ranging from those that are both simple and deterministic (e.g., the behavior of a block and tackle system) to those that are complex and probabilistic (e.g., the operation of an assembly line in a factory), to those that are "exceedingly complex" and probabilistic (e.g., an entire organization such as GM). Complex probabilistic systems, whose behavior can be generally described and predicted with statistical procedures, are the province of operations research. Efforts to understand exceedingly complex probabilistic systems have given rise to the fields of cybernetics and systems design (Beer, 1964: 18). Because of their great complexity, the latter systems currently defy conventional mathematical modeling approaches. Instead, the most widely employed analytic technique is to simulate the operation of the system. "Here, all the variables and relationships of interest are linked as understood into a model and then the manager-analyst-researcher manipulates certain ones and observes how others change as the simulation of the system plays itself out" (Swinth, 1974: 11). This approach emphasizes the importance of treating the system as a system—as more than the sum of its component elements.

Recent branches of systems theory, termed "complexity" and "chaos" theory, currently pursued with most vigor by scientists at the Santa Fe Institute for Study of Complexity in New Mexico, examine the behavior of nonlinear dynamic systems. These theories were developed to account for the behavior of the flow of fluids or the behavior of mental balls suspended over two or more magnets in which "a single set of deterministic relationships can produce patterned yet unpredictable outcomes" (Levy, 1994: 168). Scholars have explored the applicability of such models to the study of highly complex, probabilistic, nonlinear social systems, such as the economy or the behavior of a firm. Chaos theorists insist that much "order emerges naturally because of unpredictable interaction" and that far from "being meaningless void, chaos is the source of creativity and construction in nature and in social dynamics" (Marion, 1999: xi–xii). Nonlinear dynamics systems can reach three types of equilibrium: systems governed by negative feedback loops such that after a time, the system returns to its initial state; systems driven by positive feedback loops which amplify the initial disturbances so that small changes over time lead to explosive outcomes; and complex systems in which the interaction of positive and negative feedback loops gives rise to unpredictable but patterned outcomes (Thietart and Forgues, 1995). Since organizations are systems that combine elements that suppress variation (e.g., control systems) and elements that create and amplify variation (e.g., diversity of personnel, R&D units), they appear to be likely candidates for chaos and complexity models.

No complex system can be understood by an analysis that attempts to decompose the system into its individual parts so as to examine each part and relationship in turn. This approach, according to Ashby, one of the founders of the general systems movement,

> gives us only a vast number of separate parts or items of information, the results of whose interactions no one can predict. If we take such a system to pieces, we find that we cannot reassemble it! (1956: 36)

Simulation techniques are popular with systems analysts because they are consistent with this "wholistic" image of a unit whose behavior can be understood only as the resultant of complex and probabilistic interactions among its parts. They also support the systems view that to understand organizations it is essential to focus on the operational level of the organization. Thus, a systems design analyst would be more interested in obtaining diagrams depicting the flows of information, energy, and materials throughout the organization than in inspecting the formal table of organization. In examining a football team, for example, such an analyst would seek out the play books—the programs— governing the activities of the various players during the course of a game rather than the formal authority arrangements among the players, coaches, managers, and owners of the club. Current investigators are successful in simulating actions and interactions among actors performing interdependent tasks, including processes of attention, capacity allocation, and communication. Outputs assessed include project duration, costs, and coordination quality and costs (e.g., Levitt et al., 1994). These results can then be compared and contrasted with similar "real-world" situations. Similations are also used as learning exercises, as microworlds are created that "simulate the real world with sufficient fidelity that decisions and actions within the simulation produce the same kinds of results and consequences that would be expected in the real world" (Nissen, 2006: 62).

It is consistent with the holistic emphasis of the systems analyst that the approach can incorporate parts of systems whose detailed structure and operation are unknown. These parts are treated as so-called "black boxes" (Haberstroh, 1965: 1174). For the purposes of systems analysis, all the information that is required is a description of the inputs to and the outputs from each of these parts (or the relation between the inputs and the outputs). It is not necessary to know the internal working of these system components to understand or simulate the workings of the larger system.

Normal Accidents versus Reliable Organizations. An important characteristic of exceedingly complex, probabilistic systems is that the whole is more than the sum of its parts in the pragmatic sense that given the properties of the parts and the laws of their interaction, it is not a trivial matter to infer the behavior of the larger system. As a consequence, it is virtually impossible to predict and protect against all the ways in which such systems can fail—for example, move rapidly toward an explosive state. When the systems are characterized by high levels of interactive complexity and tight coupling—for example, nuclear power plants—then, as Perrow argues, many of the accidents that occur should be regarded as "normal." The odd term *normal accident* is meant to signal that, given the system characteristics, multiple and unexpected interactions of failures are inevitable (1984: 5). From an in-depth analysis of the near-disaster at the Three Mile Island nuclear plant in Pennsylvania, Perrow acknowledges the role of such ever-present problems of design and equipment failures and operator error but emphasizes the effects of "negative synergy."

> "Synergy" is a buzz word in business management circles, indicating that the whole is more than the sum of its parts, or in their congenial familiarity, two plus two equals five. But minus two plus minus two can equal minus five thousand in tightly-coupled, complex, high risk military and industrial systems . . . where complex, unanticipated, unperceived and incomprehensible interactions of off-standard components (equipment, design, and operator actions) threaten disaster. (Perrow, 1982: 18)

Gall identifies concisely the dilemma posed by these systems: "When a fail-safe system fails, it fails by failing to fail safe" (1978: 97).

A lively debate has developed between analysts adopting the normal accidents view and others who insist that it is possible to develop "high reliability" organizations. Both camps agree the hallmark of these systems is the combination of interactive complexity and tight coupling, but the latter insist that high reliability can be achieved by constructing redundant systems, relying on extensive training and simulation of crisis situations, and creating a "culture of safety" (LaPorte 1982; Roberts, 1990; Weick, 1987). Those insisting that accidents cannot be completely avoided point to our inability to anticipate all the ways in which complex systems can fail and noting that excessive concern for perfection can cause lower-level personnel to cover up inevitable lapses and shortcomings, so that safety is undermined by procedures designed to insure its attainment (Sagan, 1993; Vaughan, 1996). More recently, the terrorist incident of September 11, 2001, and the natural disaster of Hurricane Katrina on the Gulf coast in September 2005, indicate that major system failures are difficult to predict, to prepare for, and to deal with the aftermath.

Information Flows. Among the various flows connecting system elements, the flow of information is the most critical. The gathering, transmission, storage, and retrieval of information are among the most fateful activities of organizations, and design theorists devote much attention to them (Burton and Obel, 2004). We described in Chapter 2 Simon's views on the cognitive limits of decision makers. From the perspective of systems design, Simon is calling attention to the limitations of individuals as information processors. Viewing individuals in this manner, Haberstroh asserts that they exhibit "low channel capacity, lack of reliability, and poor computational ability." On the other hand, individuals possess some desirable features: "The strong points of a human element are its large memory capacity, its large repertory of responses, its flexibility in relating these responses to information inputs, and its ability to react creatively when the unexpected is encountered" (Haberstroh, 1965: 1176). The challenge facing the system designers is how to create structures that will overcome the limitations and exploit the strengths of each system component, including the individual participants.

Recent developments in information and community technologies (ICT) have transformed many aspects of the workplace, as we describe in Chapter 6 and elsewhere. Observers like Burton and Obel assert that "these new media for information exchange may be viewed as a new phase of automation similar in importance as the industrial revolution in the beginning of the 20th century" (2004: 5). Although in many organizational sectors, such a conclusion sounds greatly exaggerated, there is no doubt that these developments have spawned a whole new assemblage of networked organizational forms, as discussed in Chapter 11.

Of course, not all environments place the same demands on organizations and their participants for information processing. Since individual participants are limited in their capacity to process complex information, organization designers endeavor to construct structures capable of assisting participants to deal with these shortcomings. Recognition of these variable information-processing demands has given rise to a special perspective known as contingency theory, which we briefly summarize next.[6]

---

[6]Some economists, especially Arrow (1974) and Williamson (1975; 1985), also place great emphasis on the cognitive inadequacies of individuals confronted by complex situations. They view these conditions, however, not simply as posing special problems for organizational designers, but also as a general explanation for the existence of organizations. Their arguments are considered in Chapter 9.

Contingency Theory

As a branch of systems design, contingency theory emphasizes that design decisions depend—are contingent—on environmental conditions. Contingency theory is guided by the general orienting hypothesis that organizations whose internal features match the demands of their environments will achieve the best adaptation. The challenge facing those who embrace this orientation is to be clear about what is meant by "the organization's internal features," "the demands of their environments," "best adaptation," and, most difficult of all, "best fit." Details of attempted answers to these questions will be postponed to later chapters, but the general arguments developed by Lawrence and Lorsch are briefly described to illustrate the directions pursued within this theoretical tradition.

Paul Lawrence and Jay Lorsch (1967), who coined the label "contingency theory," argue that different environments place differing requirements on organizations. Specifically, environments characterized by uncertainty and rapid rates of change in market conditions or technologies present different challenges—both constraints and opportunities—to organizations than do placid and stable environments (see also, Burns and Stalker, 1961). They conducted empirical studies of organizations in the plastics manufacturing, food processing, and standardized container industries to assess the relation between these environments—ranging from high to low uncertainty—and the internal features of each type of organization. They also suggest that different subunits within a given type of organization may confront different external demands. Thus, within plastics manufacturing companies, the research and development units face a more uncertain and rapidly changing environment than do the production departments. To cope with these various challenges, organizations create specialized subunits with differing structural features. For example, some subunits may exhibit higher levels of formalization, be more centralized in decision making, or be oriented to longer planning horizons than others. The more varied the types of environments confronted by an organization, the more differentiated its internal structure needs to be. Moreover, the more differentiated the organizational structure, the more difficult it will be to coordinate the activities of the various subunits and the more bases for conflict will exist among participants. Hence, more resources and effort must be devoted to coordinating the various activities and to resolving conflicts among members if the organization is to perform effectively.

In sum, Lawrence and Lorsch propose that the match or coalignment of an organization with its environment occurs on at least two levels: (1) the structural features of each organizational subunit should be suited to the specific environment to which it relates; and (2) the differentiation and mode of integration characterizing the larger organization should be suited to the overall complexity in the environment in which the organization must operate (see Chapter 6).

Over time, contingency theory has become greatly elaborated, partly as analysts discover more and more factors on which the design of organizations is, or should be, contingent. In a recent review article, Lawrence (1993) provides a partial list of factors that one or another theorist has considered important. They include size or scale, technology, geography, uncertainty, individual predispositions of participants, resource dependency, national or cultural differences, scope, and organizational life cycle. Such an elaboration of the conditions on which structural design is dependent indicates both the broadening interests of scholars as well as the looseness of many versions of contingency theory. In spite or, perhaps, because of this expansion of concerns, contingency theory remains "the dominant approach to organization design" (Lawrence 1993: 9) as well as the most widely utilized contemporary theoretical approach to the study of organizations (see Donaldson 1985; 1996). We revisit this approach in succeeding chapters, particularly Chapters 5 and 6.

Weick's Model of Organizing

Weick defines *organizing* as "the resolving of equivocality in an enacted environment by means of interlocked behaviors embedded in conditionally related process" (1969: 91). Let us attempt to unpack this dense definition. Weick argues that organizing is directed toward information processing generally and, in particular, toward removing its equivocality. He explains that

> The basic raw materials on which organizations operate are informational inputs that are ambiguous, uncertain, equivocal. Whether the information is embedded in tangible raw materials, recalcitrant customers, assigned tasks, or union demands, there are many possibilities, or sets of outcomes that might occur. Organizing serves to narrow the range of possibilities, to reduce the number of "might occurs." The activities of organizing are directed toward the establishment of a workable level of certainty. (1969: 40)

In short, Weick asserts that "human beings organize primarily to help them reduce the information uncertainty they face in their lives" (Kreps, 1986: 111).

Organizational activities become structured as sets of "interlocked behaviors"—repetitive, reciprocal, contingent behaviors that develop and are maintained between two or more actors" (Weick, 1969: 91). The activities involved in organizing are carried on in three stages: enactment, selection, and retention.[7] *Enactment* is the active process by which individuals, in interaction, construct a picture of their world, their environment, their situation. Weick argues that

---

[7]It is instructive to note that these three stages are Weick's translation of the three phases of evolution—variation, selection, and retention—as formulated by Campbell (1969b; see also Chapter 5). Weick is one of the earlier theorists to employ evolutionary arguments; others are considered in subsequent chapters. Weick substitutes the term "enactment" for Campbell's label of "variation" for the first stage to emphasize the active role played by individuals—and organizational participants—in defining the environments they confront.

> Since human beings actively create the world around them through perception, organization members do not merely react to an objectively accepted physical environment but enact their environment through information and the creation of meaning. (Kreps, 1987: 116)

The concept of enactment emphasizes the role of perception but also recognizes that organizational members not only selectively perceive but also directly influence the state of their environments through the cognitive frames they utilize as well as by their own actions, which can alter the state of the environment.

"The activities of organizing are directed toward the establishment of a workable level of certainty" (Weick, 1969: 40). Participants selectively attend to their environments and then, in interaction, make collective sense of what is happening. "Making sense" entails not only developing a common interpretation or set of common meanings, but also developing one or more agreed-upon responses that are *selected* from among the many possibilities. Among responses that are selected, some are more useful and robust than others and it is these which are *retained* in the form of rules or routines. In this manner communal sense making gives rise to a repertory of repeated routines and patterns of interaction—which constitute the process of organizing. As an example, Weick discusses the gradual emergence among physicians of the construction of a "battered child syndrome," to account for the otherwise inexplicable incidents of injuries to children appearing in medical clinics. Lacking this construct, physicians were unable to "make sense" of what they were seeing; with the aid of the new model, explanations, routines, and counteractive remedies could be crafted (Weick, 1995).

Although the objective of the entire process is to reduce equivocality, some ambiguity does and must remain if the organization is to be able to survive into a new and different future. In other words, "organizations continue to exist only if they maintain a balance between flexibility and stability" (Weick, 1979: 215). The information received and selected by the organization must be both credited (retained) and discredited or questioned if the organization is to safely face a future that may resemble, but must inevitably differ from, its past.

Weick's major concern is to spell out the implications of the open systems perspective when applied at the social psychology level—to the behavior of individual participants and the relationships among them. The semiautonomy of the individual actors is stressed: the looseness and conditionality of the relationships linking them is emphasized. Attention and interpretative processes are highlighted. And whereas conventional wisdom asserts that goals precede activities, that intention precedes action, Weick (1969: 37) insists that behavior often occurs first and then is interpreted—given meaning. Rationality is often retrospective. In these and related ways, Weick attempts to "open up" our conception of organizational structure and behavior. More generally, Weick was the first organization theorist to substitute a process- for a structure-based conception of organizations. In this sense, he anticipated later developments in the evolution of organization theory.

Many other theories emerging after the 1960s have expanded the range of insights and implications based on the open systems perspective, but we reserve discussion of them to later chapters.

SUMMARY AND TENTATIVE CONCLUSIONS

The open systems perspective developed later than the rational and natural system views, but it has gained adherents rapidly and profoundly altered our conception of organizations and their central features and processes. The open systems view of organizational structure stresses the complexity and variability of the parts—both individual participants and subgroups—as well as the looseness of connections among them. Parts are viewed as capable of semiautonomous action; many parts are viewed as, at best, loosely coupled to other parts. Further, in human organizations, as Boulding emphasizes, the system is "multi-cephalous": many heads are present to receive information, make decisions, direct action. Individuals and subgroups form and leave coalitions. Coordination and control become problematic. Also, system boundaries are seen as amorphous and transitory; the assignment of actors or actions to either the organization or the environment often seems arbitrary and varies depending on what aspect of systemic functioning is under consideration.

Open system scholars emphasis process over structure. Also, evolutionary theory is introduced to support studies of change, as new elements are introduced, selected or rejected, and retained. The cultural and cognitive dimensions of social life loom large in the open systems perspective. Great attention is devoted to information flows and sense-making activities. Organizations create, but also, appropriate knowledge, know-how, and meaning from their environments.

In this and other ways, the interdependence of the organization and its environment receives primary attention in the open systems perspective. Rather than overlooking the environment, as tends to be true of most early rational and natural system theories, or viewing it as alien and hostile, as is true of some early theories, the open systems perspective stresses the reciprocal ties that bind and relate the organization with those elements and flows that surround and penetrate it. The environment is perceived to be the ultimate source of materials, energy, and information, all of which are vital to the continuation of the system. Indeed, the environment is seen to be the source of order itself.

With the arrival of open system arguments in the 1960s, it quickly became clear that, to the extent that previous perspectives were grounded on closed systems views of organizations, they would need to be radically revised. To remain credible, all subsequent theories have had to take into account the openness of organizations to their environments. So did these developments signal the end of rational and natural system models? Have these early perspectives been consigned to the dustbins of history? Hardly! As discussed in the next chapter, they have continued to flourish as viable perspectives, by moving into the halls of open systems.

CHAPTER 5

Combining Perspectives, Expanding Levels

A paradigm is a fundamental image of the subject matter within a science. It serves to define what should be studied, what questions should be asked, how they should be asked, and what rules should be followed in interpreting the answers obtained. The paradigm is the broadest unit of consensus within a science and serves to differentiate one scientific community (or subcommunity) from another.

GEORGE RITZER (2005).

The three preceding chapters have described and illustrated three perspectives, or paradigms, on organizations as they emerged and developed from the early part of this century up to the early 1960s. Our intent was to present these theoretical frameworks succinctly but fairly, discussing examples of the work of influential theorists who have contributed to them, and to assess their strengths and limitations. We sought to avoid treating these viewpoints as caricatures or as approaches having only historical interest. We believe that each perspective is valuable. Each identifies a set of significant and enduring features of organizations.

We begin in this chapter to examine the ways in which open system views have transformed the field of organization studies. Indeed, in an important sense, the exploration and elaboration of the nature and significance of the open system perspective for the study of organizations is the topic of the remainder of this book. But, the ascendance of open system perspectives has not meant the disappearance of earlier rational or natural system views. Rather, these perspectives have been updated, elaborated, and *combined* with open systems approaches in multiple ways to create a wide variety of new theories varying in emphasis and in level of analysis.

ATTEMPTS AT INTEGRATION

Lawrence and Lorsch's Contingency Model

We have already described Lawrence and Lorsch's proposals for reconciling the rational and natural system perspectives (in Chapter 3) and introduced their contingency model of organizations (in Chapter 4). We briefly review these ideas at this point to emphasize that they may be interpreted as providing a general framework within which all three perspectives can be reconciled.

In essence, Lawrence and Lorsch (1967) argue that if an open system perspective is taken—so that any given organization is viewed not in isolation but in relation to its specific environment—then the rational and the natural system perspectives serve to identify different organizational types which vary because they have adapted to different types of environments. The rational and natural system perspectives are at variance because each focuses on a different end of a single continuum representing the range of organizational forms. At one extreme, some organizations are highly formalized, centralized, and pursue clearly specified goals; at the other extreme, other organizations are less formalized, rely greatly on the personal qualities and initiative of participants, and pursue less clear and sometimes conflicting goals. The two extreme types depicted by the rational and the natural systems models are not viewed as differing aspects of the same organizations—as theorists such as Etzioni (1964) proposed—but rather as different kinds of organizations. And, as emphasized by the open system perspective, the nature of the form is determined by the type of environment to which the organization must relate. Specifically, the more homogeneous and stable the environment, the more prevalent will be the formalized and hierarchical form. And the more diverse and changing the task environment, the more appropriate will be the less formalized and more organic form (see also Burns and Stalker, 1961).

Thus we arrive at the central contingency theory argument: there is no one best organizational form but many, and their suitability is determined by the goodness of fit between organizational form and the diverse environments to which they relate. The argument is framed at the ecological level of analysis (employing the tripartite classification described in Chapter 1); it rests on the assumption that different systems are more or less well adapted to differing environments. Environmental conditions determine which systems survive and thrive: those best adapted are most likely to prosper. By this argument, Lawrence and Lorsch attempt to account both for the different forms of organizations as well as for the different theoretical perspectives that have developed to characterize them. They propose:

> In simplified terms, the classical [rational system] theory tends to hold in more stable environments, while the human relations [natural system] theory is more appropriate to dynamic situations. (1967: 183)

Note that this view can also explain why the rational system perspective preceded in time the natural system perspective if it is assumed, as most open system analysts would contend, that the environments of organizations were more stable in the past and have become progressively more volatile (see Terryberry, 1968).

The open systems perspective is viewed by Lawrence and Lorsch as the more comprehensive framework within which the rational and natural system perspectives are housed, each dealing with a subset of organizational forms.

Thompson's Levels Model

Simultaneously with the emergence of Lawrence and Lorsch's contingency model, James D. Thompson (1967; 2003) developed a somewhat different basis for reconciling the three perspectives. In his influential work *Organizations in Action*, Thompson argues that analysts should be mentally flexible enough to admit the possibility that all three perspectives are essentially correct and applicable to a single organization. They do not, however, apply with equal force to all organizational locations. Thompson adopts a set of distinctions developed by Parsons (1960: 60–65), who differentiated among three levels within organizations:

- The *technical* level: that part of the organization carrying on the production functions that transform inputs into outputs (e.g., shop floors, laboratories, classrooms).
- The *managerial* level: that part of the organization responsible for designing and controlling the production system, for procuring inputs and disposing of outputs, and for securing and allocating personnel to units and functions (e.g., engineering, marketing and personnel departments).
- The *institutional* level: that part of the organization that relates the organization to its wider environment, determines its domain, establishes its boundaries, and secures its legitimacy (e.g., the board of directors, public relations and legal departments).

Thompson proposes that each of the three perspectives is suitable to a different level of the organization: the rational system perspective to the technical level, the natural to the managerial, and the open to the institutional level.

Thompson's thesis in a nutshell is that organizations strive to be rational although they are natural and open systems. It is in the interest of administrators—those who design and manage organizations—that the work of the organization be carried out as effectively and efficiently as possible. Since technical rationality presumes a closed system, Thompson (1967: 10–13) argues that organizations will attempt to "seal off" their technical level, protecting it from external uncertainties to the extent possible. Thus, it is at the level of the core technology—the assembly line in the automobile factory, the operating and treatment rooms in the hospital—that we would expect the rational system perspective to apply with the most force. At the opposite extreme, if it is to perform its functions, the institutional level must be open to the environment. It is at this level, where the environment is enacted and adaptation is managed, that the open system perspective is most relevant. Between the upper and lower levels is the managerial level, which must mediate between the relatively open institutional and the artificially closed technical levels. To do so effectively requires the flexibility that is associated with the less formalized and more political activities depicted by the natural system theorists. It is also the managers—whose power and status are most intimately linked to the fate of the organization—who have the greatest stake in and are more likely to seek to secure the survival of the organization as a system.

There is much to be said for, and learned from, these efforts to reconcile the three perspectives. Lawrence and Lorsch are correct that some types of organizations exhibit higher levels of formalization and goal specificity than do others and that these differences are related to the environments in which they operate. And Thompson is correct that some components or levels of organization are more protected from, while others are more open to, environmental influences. And, as a consequence, some components are more strongly governed by rational system concerns while others are more subject to natural system influences. These combinations and applications of the three general perspectives serve to illuminate the multiple facets of organizations, and in this way, the utility of the perspectives has been reinforced for a new generation of students of organizations.

Whereas Thompson's and Lawrence and Lorsch's arguments addressed themselves to the characteristics of organizations—as they related to organizational theories—Scott's approach reverses the telescope, centering attention on organizational theories—as they relate to our understanding of organizations.

Scott's Layered Model

Our discussion of the perspectives in earlier chapters implied that they fell into a neat time order with the rational perspective preceding the natural system view, and the open system perspective developing most recently. However, we know that the natural system views did not supplant rational system formulations. Moreover, with the arrival of open systems models, as they invaded organization studies they were in turn rapidly combined with either rational or natural system assumptions and arguments. Hence, acknowledging that it involves considerable oversimplification, Scott (1978) proposed that theoretical models of organizations underwent a major shift about 1960 at the time when open systems perspectives supplanted closed system models. Analyses focusing primarily on the internal characteristics of organizations gave way at approximately that date to approaches emphasizing the importance for the organization of events and processes external to it. After 1960, the environments of organizations, whether conceived in terms of economic, technological, relational, political, or cultural elements, figure prominently in all efforts to explain organizational structure and behavior. Viewed retrospectively, then, early rational and natural systems models can be seen to be either closed-rational or closed-natural system models.

On both sides of the watershed representing the transition from closed to open system models, a second trend can be identified: a shift from rational to natural system models of analysis. It appears that this shift has occurred twice! It occurred for the closed system models in the late 1930s and early 1940s, as already described in Chapters 2 and 3—the rational system formulations exemplified by Weber's bureaucratic theory, Taylor's scientific management, and Simon's decision theory were challenged by the cooperative systems views of Barnard, the human relations work of Mayo, and the conflict models of Gouldner and others. And a parallel shift occurred again during the late 1970s as the neorational approaches of contingency theorists such as Lawrence and Lorsch and Thompson and the transaction cost approach of Williamson that arose to confront the advent of open system models were, in turn, challenged by such neonatural theories as resource dependence (Pfeffer and Salancik, 1978), population ecology (Hannan and Freeman, 1977), and institutional theory (Meyer and Rowan, 1977)—theories still be discussed.

This layered model proposes, in sum, that the rational and natural systems models developed prior to the 1960s shared in common the fact of being layered under closed system assumptions. The open system models that developed in the 1960s did not supplant either the rational or the natural systems arguments but strongly challenged and eventually displaced the (often implicit) closed system assumptions underlying earlier formulations. When the open systems models appeared, they in turn were quickly combined with, first, rational system and, later, natural system perspectives.

Table 5–1 displays major representative theories/theorists for each of the four periods: closed-rational; closed-natural; open-rational; and open-natural. The theories tend to fall into an orderly sequence with closed-rational models dominating during the period 1900–1930; closed-natural models during the period 1930–1960; open-rational models during the period 1960–1975; and open-natural models dominant after 1975. In addition to changing theories and passing time, we note, on the vertical axis, differences in levels of analysis. The theories and theorists included in Table 5–1 are by no means exhaustive of all of the important contributions and contributors to our understanding of organizations during the past century. However, they serve as placeholders for the paradigms dominant during each period throughout the twentieth century.

The typology presented in Table 5–1 serves as a rough guide to the structure of this book: closed-rational and natural-system perspectives have been the primary subject of Chapters 2 and 3. Open-rational and open-natural system perspectives will be the focus of Chapters 6 through 12. Moreover, from this point on, chapters move from more micro to more macro levels of analysis. Chapter 13 provides an overview of the changing nature of organizations—and organization theory—over time, and Chapter 14 considers current trends and new directions in organization studies.

TABLE 5-1 Dominant Theoretical Models and Representative Theorists: A Layered Model

| Levels of Analysis | Closed System Models | | Open System Models | |
	1900–1930 Rational Models	1930–1960 Natural Models	1960–1970 Rational Models	1970– Natural Models
Social Psychological	Scientific Management Taylor (1911) Decision Making Simon (1945)	Human Relations Whyte (1959)	Bounded Rationally March and Simon (1958)	Organizing Weick (1969)
Structural	Bureaucratic Theory Weber (1968 trans.) Administrative Theory Fayol (1919)	Cooperative Systems Barnard(1938) Human Relations Mayo (1945) Conflict Models Gouldner (1954)	Contingency Theory Lawrence and Lorsch (1967) Comparative Structure Woodward (1965) Pugh et al. (1969) Blau (1970)	Sociotechnical Systems Miller and Rice (1967)
Ecological			Transaction Cost Williamson (1975) Knowledge-based Nonaka and Takeuchi (1995)	Organizational Ecology Hannan and Freeman (1977) Resource Dependence Pfeffer and Salancik (1978) Institutional Theory Selznick (1949) Meyer and Rowan (1977) DiMaggio and Powell (1983)

GLANCING BACK AND LOOKING FORWARD

Closed-Rational and Natural-System Models

The entries in the left-hand portion of Table 5–1 merit brief comment. Theorists listed as representative of closed system models should look familiar by this time. Taylor, Weber, Fayol, and Simon are old friends (see Chapter 2). Taylor, with his focus on the rationalization of mechanical work, concentrated primarily on the social psychological level, as did Simon in his early work. Fayol and Weber worked primarily at the structural level. As previously discussed, we again insist that Weber is (mis)classified as a closed system theorist; he appears in this company because of the way his work was read and interpreted by scholars during this period. Simon is a transitional figure: his earlier work (1945) fits into the closed system tradition; his later work with March (March and Simon, 1958) is an important early statement of an open-rational model, as discussed below.

Our prime candidate for natural system theorists working primarily within a closed system conception is the human relations school. Their attention to the details of work groups and worker-manager relations added greater complexity and nuance to our understanding of organization structure and process but kept the spotlight clearly within organizational boundaries. Barnard's (1938) model of cooperative systems also concentrated on internal structure but, as noted, accorded some attention to the wider environment (see Chapter 3). Early conflict theorists, such as Dalton (1959) and Gouldner (1954) concentrated on conflict processes within organizations, although later scholars such as Braverman (1974) and Edwards (1979) attended to broader community and societal forces. Other natural system theorists, such as Selznick and Parsons, were "ahead of their time" in the attention they gave to organization-environment connections.

Open-Rational and Natural-System Models: New Levels

As we move into the era of open system models, we encounter not only new theories, but also new levels of analysis. Prior to 1960, theorists were operating primarily at either the social psychological or the structural level of analysis (see Chapter 1).

Social Psychological Level. Simon has continued to work primarily at the social psychological level, but, as noted, in his fruitful collaboration with March, he advanced from a primarily closed-rational system to an open-rational system view (March and Simon, 1958). In their formulation of "bounded rationality," Simon continues his concern with the cognitive limits of individual decision makers and the ways in which structures can help to support improved decisions, but more recognition is given to the variety of challenges posed by tasks and environments. Organizations and their decision makers are viewed as more open to their environment. March and Simon identify "performance programs" that guide the decisions of individuals, but whereas some of these programs can be routinized, others must be problem-solving responses, requiring the decision maker to exercise more discretion in the face of greater uncertainty (p. 139). Moreover, it is recognized that some organizations face such volatile environments they must institutionalize innovation, devising metaprograms for changing existing performance programs, often rapidly (p. 186).

March and Simon suggest a number of additional ways in which decision making is simplified within organizations. Organizations encourage participants to "satisfice"—to settle for acceptable as opposed to optimal solutions, to attend to problems sequentially rather than simultaneously, and to utilize existing repertories of performance programs whenever possible rather than developing novel responses for each situation. There is a stronger sense in this later work that organizations face environments of varying complexity, that they must adjust their internal decision-making apparatus to take these variations into account, and that some environments pose levels of complexity that organizations cannot manage unless they introduce simplifying restrictions on the information processed. Many of these insights are folded into the later work of contingency theorists.

Weick, in his work on organizing, described in Chapter 4, also operates primarily at the social psychological level, but his arguments combine open with natural system perspectives. Rather than presuming rationality, Weick views the cognitive processes of organizational participants as operating in an evolutionary fashion involving trial and error, change, superstitious learning, and retrospective sense making. And rather than seeing evolution as tended toward improvement, he points out that successful patterns of organizing "can occur without any necessary increase in the productivity or viability of the system" (Weick, 1979: 179).

Structural Level. The early efforts of Fayol and Weber to examine the structural features of organizations early in the twentieth century were pursued into 1960s and 1970s by *comparative structural* analysts, who embraced an open system approach. Among the leading figures in the area were Udy (1959; 1970), Woodward (1958), the "Aston group"—Pugh, Hickson, and associates (Pugh and Hickson, 1976; Pugh et al., 1968)—and Blau and colleagues (Blau, 1970; Blau and Schoenherr, 1971). These were the first analysts to collect systematic data on large samples of organizations rather than on individual participants or organizational subunits. In this work, formal structure is viewed as the dependent variable, its characteristics to be measured and explained. A large variety of explanatory (independent) variables were examined—with most attention concentrated on size, technology, and uncertainty—but most studies focused on characteristics of the environment in which the organization is located. In short, organizations are treated as open systems. At the same time, however, most of these studies assumed that organizations are striving to develop effective and efficient structures, embracing a rational system perspective.[1]

A good exemplar of an open-natural system framework developed at the structural level is represented by sociotechnical systems (Trist, 1981). The approach attempts to give equal attention to the technical and social components of organizations in the design of work systems. This work is reviewed in Chapter 7.

Ecological Level. As more attention was accorded to the environment, more theories began to be formulated at the ecological level. The open system revolution in organization theory stimulated much new theorizing and research in which organizations themselves are seen as actors in, or components of, wider systems. In remarkably rapid succession a raft of new theories—including contingency, transaction cost, resource dependence, population ecology, institutional, and network—tumbled forth during the decades of the 1970s and 1980s. These theories are briefly introduced after we describe new sublevels within the ecological level.

EXPANDED LEVELS OF ANALYSIS

Over the past three decades, the arena of organizational studies has expanded both "up" and "out": up to include higher and wider levels of analysis and out to encompass more kinds of factors or forces shaping organizations. Analysts have also increasingly come to recognize that the causal arrows point in both directions: environments influence organizations, but organizations also affect environments. All of the newer theories to be examined in this and subsequent chapters are located within the ecological level. We distinguish three sublevels within the ecological level.

Organizational Sets

An important level of analysis is that of the organization set (Blau and Scott, 1962; 2003: 195–99; Evan, 1966). Blau, Scott, and Evan acknowledge that the concept of organization set was developed by analogy from Merton's (1957: 368–80) concept of role set. Merton noted that a single position such as "mother" is associated with not one, but a cluster of different roles depending on the identity of the counterpositions. Thus, a mother has specific role obligations toward her children, others toward the father, still others toward the child's teachers, and so on. Similarly, a given organization participates in a variety of relations depending on the identity of its specific

---

[1]Interest in these types of studies has waned, but important insights were gained from these studies. For a review of findings see Donaldson (2001: chap. 3); Hall (1999: chap. 3); and Scott (2003: chap. 10).

partners and competitors. For example, a small grocery store will relate in one manner with its suppliers, another with its customers, yet another with city officials, and so on. The fundamental idea is a simple one, but its implications are quite rich. One is led to ask questions regarding, for example, the relative size of the organization set, the extent to which one group of role partners is aware of the demands made by another, and the extent to which expectations held by partners coincide.

One of the more useful concepts to emerge at the analytical level of the organization set is that of organizational domain (Levine and White, 1961; Thompson, 1967). An organization's *domain* consists of the range of products or services it provides and the types of clients or consumers served. Producing goods and providing services necessarily relate each organization to a number of other organizations—suppliers, customers, competitors—that affect its behavior and outcomes. Some organizations, for example diversified corporations, operate in multiple domains. In such cases, an important consideration is the degree of overlap or extent of synergies between them (Chandler, 1977; Ghoshal and Westney, 1993).

A crucial, defining characteristic of the concept of organization set is that it views the environment from the standpoint of a specific (*focal*) organization. In this sense, it is a *dyadic* conception of the environment (see Chapter 9). Relations or connections between other (counter) members of the set are not of concern unless they affect the activities or interests of the focal organization. It is from this level that the interests, the resources, the dependencies of a given organization are best examined and its survival tactics probed. Hence, the organization-set level is frequently utilized by students of organizational strategy.

While the organization-set level of analysis has proved to be extremely useful in directing attention to the impact of information and resource flows and relations on a select organization, it does so at the expense of detracting attention from the nature of the larger system of relations in which the focal organization is but one player among many. Other approaches attempt to correct this shortcoming.

Organizational Populations

A second level identified by analysts is that of the population of organizations. This concept is used to identify aggregates of organizations that are alike in some respect—for example, colleges or newspapers or automobile assembly plants. Although the specific concept of population is borrowed from demography, most of the theoretical insights associated with this level are derived from biology. Organizational populations are equivalent, in many respects, to biological species. From a population perspective, for any given actor, whether ant or multinational corporation, the most relevant occupants of the environment are other actors of the same kind. Actors similar to oneself provide the most direct competition for scarce resources: they provide the main source of competitive pressure. At the same time, actors of the same kind share similar interests and may, under appropriate circumstances, band together to protect them, for example, in unions or trade associations. Moreover, actors of the same kind look to each other for ideas about how to look—what to wear, what structures to erect—and how to act—what dishes to eat, which technologies to adopt. As if this weren't enough, populations of actors exhibit their own structures and dynamics. They possess characteristics such as size or density and carry on processes such as births or founding rates. Of course, viewed as populations, organizations do display some distinctive features—they are different from ants or individual persons. We consider these issues, both similarities and differences, in detail in Chapter 10.

In a population approach, primary attention is given to the analysis of an aggregate of organizations exhibiting a similar form, to varying strategies of competition, and to the selective effects of changes in environments. The level of analysis shifts from the individual organization to the population itself, as analysts examine the differential birth and death rates and modes of adaptation that shape the population over time. Although this level of analysis clearly identifies an important set of questions and has attracted great interest, it directs attention away from connections among organizations—both similar and dissimilar—in particular those organizations whose relations are more symbiotic and cooperative than commensalistic and competitive. To examine these connections, we need other models that encompass both similar and dissimilar organizations.

Organizational Fields

This level of analysis focuses attention on a collection of diverse types of organizations engaged in competitive and cooperative relations. The concept of field resembles an earlier concept, the *interorganizational community,* which emerged out of the work of urban ecologists (Baum, 1996: 91–94; Hawley, 1950; Warren, 1967), who focused on a geographically bounded collection of organizations rendered interdependent because of functional ties or shared locality. Notably, Hawley insisted that communities of organizations could develop structures that were collectively beneficial, improving adaptation to the environment for all its members. Hawley asserts: "That the community is the essential adaptive mechanism may be taken as the distinctive hypothesis of ecology" (1950: 31). As elaborated by Astley and Van de Ven:

> Rather than view organizations as pitched in a competitive battle for survival through a direct confrontation with the natural, or exogenous, environment, [community ecology theorists] emphasize collective survival, which is achieved by collaboration between organizations through the construction of a regulated and controlled social environment that mediates the effects of the natural environment. (1983: 250–51)

Early students of interorganizational communities tended to focus more on colocation than on functional interdependence. A more important limitation was a tendency to ignore important connections and exchanges among organizations taking place outside the spatial boundaries of the community of interest. For example, connections between schools and businesses might be considered, but not those between local school districts and state educational agencies or between the local bank and its corporate headquarters. This is a serious problem when the population is one of organizations since many significant organizational ties are not "horizontal"—linking organizations at the same level—but vertical—connecting systems organized in hierarchies—and not local, but distant (Scott and Meyer, 1991a: 111).

With the emergence of the institutional perspective, theorists developed the concept of organizational field to bound a collection of interdependent organizations operating with common rules, norms, and meaning systems. As defined by DiMaggio and Powell, an *organizational field* consists of

> those organizations that, in the aggregate, constitute a recognized area of institutional life: key suppliers, resource and produce consumers, regulatory agencies, and other organizations that produce similar services and products. (1983: 143)

Scott elaborates: "The notion of field connotes the existence of organizations that partake of a common meaning system and whose participants interact more frequently and fatefully with one another than with actors outside of the field" (1994: 207–08). Closely related concepts include Hirsch's (1985) concept of "industry system," Scott and Meyer's (1991a) concept of "societal sector," and Aldrich's concept of "organizational community," defined as "a set of coevolving organizational populations joined by ties of commensalism and symbiosis through their orientation to a common technology, normative order, or legal-regulatory regime" (1999: 301). Such a definition appears to be virtually interchangable with that of organizational field.

The organization field isolates for analysis a system of organizations operating in the same realm as defined by both relational linkages and shared cultural rules and meaning systems. Local as well as distant connections are included as are both horizontal and vertical ties and linkages between similar and dissimilar organizations. The field concept also calls attention to organizations that may not be linked by direct connections but, because they are operating under similar conditions, exhibit similar structural characteristics and types of relationships—a condition referred to as "structural equivalence" or "isomorphism" (see DiMaggio, 1986). Figure 5–1 diagrams the major types of players in the U.S. health care field. Major types of governance structures are identified as are principal types of providers, purchasers, and fiscal "intermediaries" developed to pool resources and risks.

The community or field level represents a significant shift in focus from that of the individual organization, the organization set, or the population. Organizations are treated as members of larger, overarching systems exhibiting, to varying degrees, structure and coherence. A number of advantages are associated with this level of analysis. First, as Aldrich's definition emphasizes, we can examine the interdependence and coevolution of organizations of differing

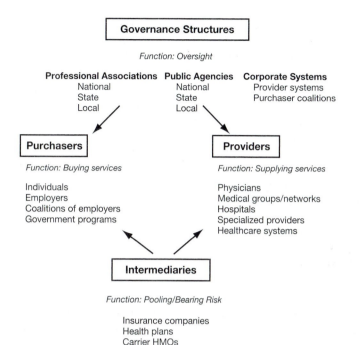

FIGURE 5–1 The Healthcare Field: Principal Social Actors and Functions.
Source: Scott et al., (2000).

types. Organizations both compete and cooperate with similar and diverse organizations. A community hospital, for example may compete with other health care providers, such as other hospitals or home health agencies but can also merge into broader systems or develop strategic alliances with these forms (see Scott et al., 2000). Second, a community or field-level perspective allows us to observe not only the waxing and waning of a particular type of organization, but also the disappearance of some types and the emergence of new forms (Astley, 1985). Third, the organization field can be viewed as encompassing the other levels: the individual organization, the organization set, and organizational populations. In this sense, it provides a basis for integrating previous approaches and supports efforts to examine not only the effects of wider structures and processes on populations, sets, and organizations, but also the ways in which individual organizations and their participants can influence their environments (Scott, 1993; Scott et al., 2000).

Finally, organizational fields provide an important intermediate unit connecting the study of individual organizational structure and performance with broader social structures and processes. As DiMaggio observes: "the organizational field has emerged as a critical unit bridging the organization and societal levels in the study of social and community change" (1986: 337).

For example, federal and state regulations directed at individual organizations, such as pollution controls, seldom directly impact single organizations but are typically mediated by field-level structures and processes such as trade associations. Indeed, a major, largely unnoticed effect of such policies is the changes they induce in the structure of organizational fields.

THEORIES AT THE ECOLOGICAL LEVEL

Theories at the ecological level gained prominence in organization studies with the open systems movement. The preceding section has identified three sublevels within the broader ecological zone. The organization-set level has given rise to a number of "dyadic" models of the environment (Davis and Powell, 1992). Among the most influential theories operating at this level are *contingency theory* as proposed by Lawrence and Lorsch (1967) and by Thompson (1967); *transaction cost theory* developed by Williamson (1975), and *resource dependence theory* developed by Pfeffer and Salancik (1978: 2003).

A related theory complex at this level, which we will not pursue in depth, are *knowledge-based theories*. Beginning as early as 1959 with the seminal work of Edith Penrose, theorists have examined how variations in an organization's access to key resources or in its "know-how" might lead to differences in performance. Recent years have witnessed a groundswell of interest in organizational differences in "core competence" (Pralahad and Hamel, 1990), "dynamic capabilities" (Teece and Pisano, 1994), and "knowledge" (Nonaka and Takeuchi, 1995). All of these approaches call attention to the competitive advantages that result from idiosyncratic combinations of resources—"financial, human, intangible, organizational, physical, technological"—that are not readily assembled in markets or coordinated by the price system but can be mobilized within a specific organization (Dobbin and Baum, 2000: 9).

While early work focused on more tangible resources such as financial capital and location, more recent approaches emphasize the central importance of knowledge. As Brown and Duguid conclude:

> While knowledge is often thought to be the property of individuals, a great deal of knowledge is both produced and held collectively. Such knowledge is readily generated when people work together in the tightly know groups known as "communities of practice." As such work and such communities are a common feature of organizations, organizational knowledge is inevitably heavily social in character . . . The hard work of organizing knowledge is a critical aspect of what firms and other organizations do. (1998: 91)

Most analysts employing knowledge-based approaches follow the lead of Polanyi, who pointed out, "We know more than we can tell" (1967: 4), stressing the importance of the distinction between tacit and explicit or codified knowledge. *Tacit knowledge* is "sticky," "slippery," "elusive," less observable, and less teachable than is explicit knowledge. Tacit knowledge is embedded in the skills of workers and in work routines and shared understandings that, in combination, comprise an organization's distinctive capabilities (Nelson and Winter, 1982).

Knowledge-based approaches exhibit crucial elements of rational-open perspectives but also include features of natural-open system perspectives. Behavioral economics with its emphasis on purposive but boundedly rational behavior is combined with a recognition that organizations function at levels 7 and 8 of Boulding's typology (see Table 4–1) as symbol-processing, sense-making social systems.

Common to all of these approaches—contingency, transaction cost, resource dependence, knowledge-based—is the centrality of the focal organization. Organizations are assumed to devise structures that better enable them to adapt to the specific environments in which they operate. Hence, attention is concentrated on a given organization and the characteristics of its environment. The theories vary in what aspects of environments are of interest. Contingency theorists focus on the degree of certainty-uncertainty in the organization's task environment—factors affecting the predictability of the flow of inputs from and outputs to the exchange partners. Transaction cost theorists share an interest in these flows but attend more to the costs involved in negotiating and monitoring these exchanges. Resource dependence theorists emphasize the importance of the political processes accompanying exchange processes. Technical exchanges both give rise to and may be settled by power and influence processes. Chapter 6 is devoted to explicating contingency theories and attendant research. Chapter 9 reviews transaction costs and resource dependence theories and related studies.

Population ecologists typically select the organizational population as the level of analysis while *community ecologists* and *institutional theorists* operate primarily at the organizational field level. Rather than considering an organization and its environment, these approaches shift our attention to a more "systemic" level: the organization *of* the environment.

Ecological theory can be utilized at the organization, population, or community level (Carroll, 1987), but most work to date has concentrated at the population level. Network theories are applicable at any level of analysis, from the individual to the ecological, but we concentrate attention on work at the latter level, examining networks of organizations. These theories concentrate on somewhat different facets of the structure of environments. Population ecologists concentrate on the patterns arising from competition among similar organizations for scarce resources. Institutional theorists examine the role of symbolic forces—rules, norms, and beliefs—in shaping organization and field-level structures. And network theorists examine the determinants and consequences of relational systems—the multiplex ties that link organizations in varied networks. Ecological and institutional theories are reviewed in Chapter 10, network theories, in Chapter 11.

CONCLUDING COMMENT

The rational-, natural-, and open-system perspectives for analyzing organizations provide contrasting paradigms. In spite of the varying assumptions that underlie these perspectives, several theorists have attempted to reconcile the three perspectives by combining them into more complex models of organizations. Lawrence and Lorsch propose that all organizations are open systems, and that rational and natural forms emerge as varying adaptive structures in response to different environmental forces. Thompson suggests that the three perspectives are differentially applicable to various levels of an organization's structure, the open system being most suited to the institutional level, the natural system to the managerial level, and the rational system to the technical level.

Following Scott, we offer an alternative framework for combining the perspectives, suggesting that they have appeared in varying combinations over time and that they are applicable to differing levels of analysis. The "layered model" emphasizes four axes: (1) the extent to which organizations are means—disposable, deliberately designed instruments for goal attainment—or value-impregnated ends in themselves; (2) whether organizations are self-sufficient, relatively self-acting, insulated forms or are highly context-dependent, substantially constituted, influenced, and penetrated by their environment; (3) the level of analysis employed, whether organizations are themselves viewed as contexts for individual actors, collective actors in their own right, or components in broader organized systems; and (4) time—when a given conception was dominant. Applying this framework to classify organizational theories suggests that the earliest models, dominant between 1900 and 1930, were closed-rational system models. Some of these were developed at the social psychological level—for example, Taylor's scientific management approach—while others were advanced at the structural level—for instance, Weber's model of bureaucracy and Fayol's administrative theory. From the 1930s through the 1950s, a new set of perspectives developed that combined closed with natural system assumptions. Again, some of these approaches were developed primarily at the social psychological level—such as the human relations models of Roy and Dalton—and others at the structural level—for example, Barnard's theory of cooperative systems and Mayo's version of human relations.

Beginning in the early 1960s, open system models largely replaced closed system assumptions, and analyses at the ecological level began to appear. At the same time, rational and natural system models persisted, providing competing theoretical explanations for organizational structure and behavior. During the 1960s, open-rational system models were dominant, represented by the work of March and Simon at the social psychological level and by contingency theory and comparative analyses at the structural level. Transaction cost analysis was added to these approaches in the 1970s. These open-rational system models were joined and challenged by open-natural system models that emerged in the 1970s and have developed up to the present time. These rapidly proliferating approaches range from the work of Weick at the social psychological level, through the sociotechnical approach developed at the structural level, to the organization ecology, resource dependence, and institutional theories at the ecological level.

Many new and competing theories concerning organizations now occupy the landscape. We have reviewed some of the most influential of these and will add more in subsequent chapters as we consider their contributions to understanding some of the important processes and problems posed by organizations.

CHAPTER 6

Technology and Structure

Every organized human activity—from the making of pots to the placing of a man on the moon—gives rise to two fundamental and opposing requirements: the division of labor into various tasks to be performed, and the coordination of these tasks to accomplish the activity. The structure of an organization can be defined simply as the sum total of the ways in which it divides its labor into distinct tasks and then achieves coordination among them.

HENRY MINTZBERG (1979)

This chapter examines the ways in which the nature of the work being carried on affects the organizational structure that is constructed to support it. The arguments reviewed largely rely on dyadic models—those that locate a given organization as the center of analysis and construct the environment from its vantage point. Theories based on such models were the first to emerge after the open systems revolution and were extremely popular during the 1960s and 1970s. They include contingency theory— a family of approaches that is arguably still the most widely used theory in organization studies (see Donaldson, 2001)—resource dependence and transaction cost economics.

In this chapter we focus primarily on contingency theory and related work in organization design that emphasize the ways in which organizational structures are shaped by technology and by the wider task environment. In an important sense, this is a continuation but updating of Taylor's thesis that job design should reflect the nature of the tasks performed (see Chapter 2). In the approaches to be reviewed here, attention is shifted to the organizational level: How can organizational structures be constructed to reflect the overall level of complexity or uncertainty of the technology employed? Arguments exploring these connections have been generated by both rational and natural system analysts, the former emphasizing effects on formal structure, the latter on informal structure. Both are examined.

ORGANIZATIONS AS TECHNICAL ADAPTIVE SYSTEMS

Several major theories appearing during the 1960s stressed the interdependence of organizational structures with the technical environment, and a number of these embrace a contingency perspective: the assumption that how an organization is structured depends on the nature of the environment to which it relates. As discussed in Chapter 5, Lawrence and Lorsch (1967) proposed to view *all* organizations as open systems, arguing that different organizational types—rational or natural—exist because they have adapted to different types of environments. Simultaneously with the emergence of Lawrence and Lorsch's contingency model, Thompson (1967; 2003) developed a somewhat different basis for reconciling the three perspectives (also discussed in Chapter 5). His "levels" approach emphasized that variations in the environment gave rise to structural differentiation *within* organizations.

To pursue the insights associated with contingency theory, we consider the nature of technology and task environments in order to examine their relation to organizational structure.

Technology

As previewed in Chapter 1, *technology* refers to the work performed by an organization. This concept can be narrowed to include only the hardware—"the equipment, machines and instruments"—individuals use in productive activities (Orlikowski, 1992: 399). However, most organization theorists embrace the broader view that technology includes not only the hardware used in performing work, but also the skills and knowledge of workers, and even the characteristics of the objects on which work is performed. Given the importance of this area, a variety of related concepts have arisen, among which we distinguish four that we find useful. *Environment* is the more inclusive term and incorporates technological, political, and institutional aspects of the organizational context. *Task environment* emphasizes those features of the environment relevant to its supply of inputs and its disposition of outputs but also includes the power-dependence relations within which the organization conducts its exchanges. *Technology* refers to "the physical combined with the intellectual or knowledge processes by which materials in some form are transformed into outputs" (Hulin and Roznowski, 1985: 47). Finally, *technical system* refers to "a specific combination of machines and methods employed to produce a desired outcome" (Sproull and Goodman, 1990: 255). The distinction between technology and technical system calls attention to the difference between the general state of knowledge in some domain and the particular manner in which this knowledge is deployed and embedded in a given work situation. Technology informs and constrains but does not dictate the precise configuration of machines and methods that make up a specific technical system (see Weick, 1990).

We emphasize the extent to which an organization's technology—in many respects an "internal" element—links the organization to its environment. The environment is not only the source of inputs and the recipient of outputs, but also the major source of technical knowledge, work techniques and tools, and trained personnel employed by the organization. Most organizations do not themselves invent their technologies but import them from the environment.

Early students of industrial and organizational sociology noted the impact of technical and production features of the work process on worker behavior and work group structure (for example, Sayles, 1958; Trist and Bamforth, 1951; Walker and Guest, 1952; Whyte, 1948). But it was the empirical research of Woodward (1958; 1965) and a theoretical article by Thompson and Bates (1957) that first called attention to technology as a general determinant of organizational structure. In her study of a large sample of industrial organizations, Woodward (1958) distinguished between mass production, small batch, and process models of production, noting that each was associated with differing levels of skill and structural arrangements. Her typology was broadened and generalized by Thompson (Thompson, 1967; Thompson and Bates, 1957), Litwak (1961), and Perrow (1967; 1970) to be applicable to all types of organizations.

Literally dozens of specific indicators have been developed by students of technology to capture its salient dimensions—for example, uniformity of inputs, automaticity of machinery, customization of outputs, among others.[1] Although a great many specific measures of technology have been generated, we believe that three general underlying dimensions encompass most of the more specific measures and, more to the point, isolate the most critical variables needed to predict structural features of organizations. These three dimensions are complexity or diversity, uncertainty or unpredictability, and interdependence.

- *Complexity or diversity.* This dimension refers to the number of different items or elements that must be dealt with simultaneously by the performer. Specific measures such as variety of inputs and multiplicity and customization of outputs tap this dimension.
- *Uncertainty or unpredictability.* This dimension refers to the variability of the items or elements upon which work is performed or the extent to which it is possible to predict their behavior in advance. Specific measures of uncertainty include uniformity or variability of inputs, the number of exceptions encountered in the work process, and the number of major product changes.
- *Interdependence.* This dimension refers to the extent to which the items or elements upon which work is performed or the work processes themselves are

---

[1]A summary classification of these and other measures may be found in Scott (1992: 229, Table 9–1). The two dimensions underlying the classification are (1) facets of technology—materials, operations, or knowledge; and (2) stage of processing—inputs, throughputs, or outputs.

interrelated so that changes in the state of one element affect the state of the others. Thompson (1967: 54–55) usefully identifies three levels:

1. *Pooled* interdependence, in which the work performed is interrelated only in that each element or process contributes to the overall goal (for example, in a hospital, the interdependence between the activities of physicians and housekeeping staff).
2. *Sequential* interdependence, when some activities must be performed before others (for example, surgical prep work and surgery).
3. *Reciprocal* interdependence, which is present to the degree that elements or activities relate to each other as both inputs and outputs (for example, interactions among members of a surgical team performing an operation).

These three levels of interdependence form a Guttman-type scale, in that elements or processes that are reciprocally interdependent also exhibit sequential and pooled interdependence, and processes that are sequentially interdependent also exhibit pooled interdependence.

Structure: Rational System Approaches

Jay Galbraith states succinctly two assumptions underlying contingency theory: "There is no one best way to organize; however, any way of organizing is not equally effective" (1973: 2).

The first assumption challenges the conventional wisdom of those administrative theorists who sought to develop general principles applicable to organizations in all times and places (see Chapter 2). Such a quest not only overlooks the vast diversity of existing organizational forms but also fails to recognize the great variety of tasks undertaken by organizations. The second assumption challenges the view, held by early economists developing the theory of the firm, that organizational structure is irrelevant to organizational performance. As James Q. Wilson wryly observes: "Only two groups of people deny that organization matters: economists and everybody else. . . . The most frequent remark I hear from people in all walks of life with respect to organizations is that it's not the organization that's important, it's the people in it" (1989: 23–24).[2]

A third assumption can be formulated to represent the position of the contingency theorist:

• The best way to organize depends on the nature of the task environment to which the organization relates.

As an offshoot of systems design, contingency theory emphasizes that design decisions depend—are contingent—on environmental conditions.

The structural features of organizations that are of primary interest are those designed to reduce uncertainty, to deal with complexity, and to coordinate interdependent tasks. Since matters can rapidly become

---

[2]This critique is less relevant today since a growing number of institutional economists have begun to take seriously the importance of structural differences in organizations.

complicated, we state at the outset the major linkages that are expected to exist between an organization's technology and its structure. In noting these main effects, we recognize that the interaction effects—the effects produced by two or more of the variables in combination—are more powerful and frequently of greater interest than the effects of a given variable. The predictions are as follows.

- The greater the technical uncertainty, the more likely organizations will devise structures to buffer their technical core.
- The greater the technical uncertainty, the less formalization and centralization.
- The greater the technical complexity, the greater the structural complexity—including occupational and role specialization, departmentalization and divisionalization. The structural response to technical diversity is organizational differentiation.
- The greater the technical interdependence, the more resources must be devoted to coordination.

Buffering the Core. To the extent possible, organizations attempt to seal off their technical core from environmental disturbances. This central proposition proposed by Thompson (1967: 20) helps to account for the defensive behavior of many types of organizations. They seek in a variety of ways to *buffer* their technical core from the effects of environmental uncertainty. Some of the specific tactics utilized by organizations to suppress or restrict external perturbations include

- *Coding*—the classifying of inputs before they are inserted in the technical core (e.g., the sorting and refinement of raw materials or the categorization of client problems)
- *Stockpiling*—the accumulation of scarce inputs or valued outputs in order to control the timing of their insertion into the technical core or release on the market (e.g., the storage of fuels or the holding of better films until the onset of the "Oscar season")
- *Leveling*—attempts to reduce the variance in supply or demand (e.g., by advertising or conducting special sales)
- *Forecasting*—attempting to predict variance in supply and demand (e.g., by taking account of regular environmental fluctuations or by keeping records on past experience)

Although these and similar activities may reduce the uncertainty confronted by the technical core, they also result in increased structural complexity as new types of staff roles and even departments are added to perform these functions.

But what if the buffers are inadequate and uncertainty penetrates the technical core? In many ways, the tactic of sealing off the organization from uncertainty seems dated—outmoded and ill-advised—for today's organizations that, in order to survive, need to attend more closely to what the customers want and what their competitors are doing. As organizations take on more complex and customized tasks, it is no longer reasonable to assume that all traces of uncertainty will be buffered out of the core. How can the structure of the technical core be modified to accommodate more demanding tasks and more uncertain prospects?

Restructuring the Core. Galbraith (1973; 1977) has usefully argued that one way in which the varying demands of technologies on structures can be summarized is to ask: How much information must be processed during the execution of a task sequence? He argues that information requirements increase as a function of increasing complexity, uncertainty, and interdependence of work flows, and that these factors interact such that the effects of complexity are much greater if, for example, it is accompanied by uncertainty. Thus,

$$\text{Complexity} \times \text{Uncertainty} \times \text{Interdependence} = \text{Task Information Requirements}$$

Using this simple formula to gauge information-processing demands, a number of contingency and design theorists have identified a series of structural modifications organizations can make in their technical core as a means of adapting to increased demands for the processing of information.

Coordination Principles and Mechanisms

- *rules and programs*—often embedded in routines and forms
- *schedules*—adding instructions about "when" to information concerning "what" and "how"
- *departmentalization*—determining who sits with whom
- *hierarchy*—determining who reports to whom

Recall, as suggested by open system theorists (Chapter 4), that hierarchy is not just about status and power, but, like departmentalization, reflects decisions about how to cluster tasks. According to Thompson,

> It is unfortunate that [hierarchy] has come to stand almost exclusively for degrees of highness or lowness, for this tends to hide the basic significance of hierarchy for complex organizations. Each level is not simply higher than the one below, but is a more inclusive clustering, or combination of interdependent groups, to handle those aspects of coordination which are beyond the scope of any of its components. (1967: 59)

A number of different rationales can guide the grouping of activities and workers. Nadler and Tushman (1988) identify four different bases of "strategic grouping" or departmentalization:

- *Grouping by activity*—bringing together individuals who perform the same functions, share the same disciplines, employ similar work processes.
- *Grouping by output*—bringing together individuals who provide the same service or contribute to the same product.

- *Grouping by user*—bringing together individuals who serve the same customers or markets.
- *Grouping by multiple foci*—the simultaneous use of two or more of these criteria. Multifocus grouping creates some type of multiplex structure (see below).

Each mode of grouping is associated with a set of trade-offs. Grouping by activity (process) makes better use of resources and the sharing of skill-sets but impedes interunit coordination. Grouping by output or user (product) improves coordination but leads to duplication of resources and loss of economies of scale. Employing multiple foci supports attention to diverse objectives but increases conflict amd coordination costs (Nadler and Tushman, 1988: 75).

Decisions regarding departmentalization affect who communicates with whom and how frequently and frictionlessly such exchanges occur. Conventional hierarchies can also be augmented by structural innovations to support increased information flows. Structural modifications include

- *Staff roles*—specialized administrative personnel charged with gathering and summarizing information needed for decision making. These officials report to and augment the information-processing capacity of a line (authority) position.[3]
- *Liaison roles*—specialized positions or units created to facilitate interchange between two or more interdependent departments. They are similar to staff but relate to two or more managers.
- *Task forces*—temporary groups given specific assignments to carry out delimited tasks. Members are selected for their expertise and stature in their own departments, relieved of regular assignments, and work intensively for short periods to solve critical problems.[4]
- *Project teams*—groupings of personnel representing various functions or departments who are allocated a specific product or outcome to achieve. Both task forces and project teams combine specialists across departments to work on common objectives.

Basic Organizational Forms

In response to greater amounts of task complexity, uncertainty, and interdependence, organizational forms are likely to exhibit increasing differentiation and structural flexibility. Contingency and design analysts have identified a number of basic organizational forms that represent structural arrangements capable of coping with increased information-processing

---

[3]Although the line–staff distinction may preserve the appearance of a unified command system, studies show that a good deal of power passes from line to staff officers (Dalton, 1959; Goldner, 1970; Hamilton and Biggart, 1984).

[4]A particularly interesting and dramatic example is provided by President John Kennedy's creation of a task force—the Excom, composed of trusted advisers and associates—to make recommendations to him on the course of action to be pursued during the Cuban missile crisis of 1962. The best account of this group's structure and deliberations is provided by the president's brother, Robert Kennedy (1969).

demands (Burton and Obel, 2004; Mintzberg, 1979; Nadler and Tushman, 1988). The labels vary, but there is considerable consensus on the importance of the following forms.

- *Simple structure*—associated with small organizations, involving minimal division of labor and management by direct supervision (see Figure 1–2).
- *Bureaucracy*—characterized by highly routinized tasks, high levels of formalization, and centralized authority.
- *Functional or unitary*—based on departmentalization around varying specialized activities contributing to overall goals, including "line" departments, involved in activities directly related to producing or distributing goods or services, and staff departments, involved in support matters such as accounting, finance, or personnel (see Figure 6–1).
- *Multidivisional*—based on groupings by products or markets overlaid on functional forms. Divisional units operate in a relatively autonomous manner from each other, and each contains departments typically organized along function lines. A superordinate "corporate" level oversees divisional performance and allocates resources accordingly (see Figure 6–2).
- *Matrix*—a dual-hierarchical form that organizes work simultaneously by functional and project criteria. Workers associated with diverse functional departments are regularly assigned to project teams organized to produce particular products or services (see Figure 6–3).
- *Adhocracy*—structures characterized by low formalization and centralization, relying heavily on highly trained, independent, self-organizing individuals who move in and out of project teams.
- *Network*—structures allowing integration of activities across formal boundaries, both within and across organizations (Baker, 1992; see Chapter 11).

These organization forms or archetypes cross a major watershed—the distinction between unified and more multiplex modes of organizing. The first three forms—simple, bureaucracy, and functional—presume singularity of purpose and unity of command. The latter forms—divisional, matrix, adhocracies, and networks—accommodate multiple objectives and divided authority. The various forms also represent a shift from a reliance primarily on *buffering* tactics—sealing out or suppressing uncertainty and variety from the core—to the use of *bridging* tactics—expanding boundaries to incorporate uncertainty within the core (see Chapters 9 and 11).

Functional or *unitary forms* embrace the key organizing logic of "centrally coordinated specialization" (Miles and Snow, 1994: 38). As the complexity of work conducted increases, organizations operating under norms of rationality are likely to evolve from simple arrangements involving an owner-manager and a few employees to a functionally differentiated structure that fosters attention to interrelated subgoals such as design, manufacture, and distribution (see Figure 6–1). Chandler (1977) provides a detailed historical account of the development of functionally organized departments with appropriate specialized managers principally associated with the development of railroads during the nineteenth century in the United States. We addressed the principle features of bureaucracy in Chapter 2.

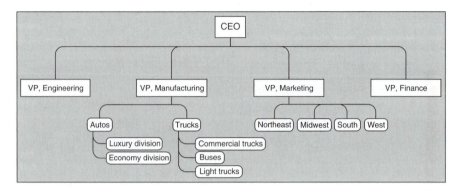

FIGURE 6–1   Functional or Unitary Form.

Multiplex forms are a family of organizational structures supporting simultaneous attention to diverse goals. Multidivisional forms first appeared in the United States during the 1920s as a means of managing organizations that were expanding not only in scale (size), but also in scope (range of products or services); (Chandler, 1962; see also Chapters 12 and 13). In a divisional form, a new level of hierarchy is created. Lower levels (divisions) typically retain their functional structures and concentrate on the design, manufacture, and distribution of a specific line of products or services (see Figure 6–2). For example, the firm depicted in Figure 6–2 contains a number of related divisions, including explosives, films, and plastics, each of which incorporates a variety of functional units, for example, purchasing, production, and sales departments. To oversee these divisions a general corporate office is created that contains staff departments, such as finance and accounting, and corporate officers in charge of deciding which businesses to enter, to leave, or to expand. In a divisional form, operational decisions reside within divisions while strategic decisions are allocated to corporate headquarters. The organizational logic involved is that of "the coupling of divisional autonomy with centrally controlled performance evaluation and resource allocation" (Miles and Snow, 1994: 39).

Matrix systems allow simultaneous attention to functional or process considerations and product or program demands: vertical and lateral channels of information and authority operate simultaneously (see Figure 6–3). The ancient and sacred principle of unity-of-command is set aside, and competing bases of authority are allowed to jointly govern the work flow. The vertical controls are typically those exercised by functional departments that operate as "home bases" for all participants; the lateral lines represent project groups or geographical arenas, whose managers combine and coordinate the services of the functional specialists around particular projects or service areas (Davis and Lawrence, 1977; Hill and White, 1979).

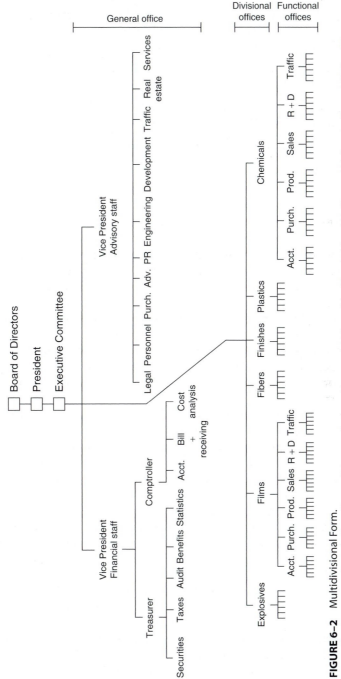

FIGURE 6–2 Multidivisional Form.

Source: See Figure 1–2 in A. D. Chandler and Herman Daems, *Managerial Hierarchies* [Cambridge, MA: Harvard University Press, 1980], p. 33.

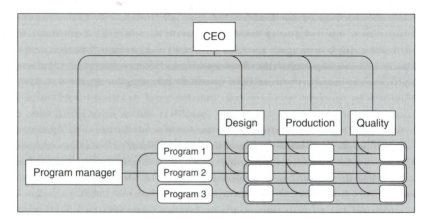

FIGURE 6–3 Matrix Form.

The constituent units of matrix structures may be relatively permanent or shifting (Sayles, 1976). A permanent matrix structure is illustrated by the rocket division of a space agency in which it is essential to attend simultaneously to technical standards and integration across functional groups, such as design, manufacturing, and testing. A shifting matrix structure employs a fairly stable set of specialists but allocates them across a changing mix of project teams. Examples are organizations such as RAND that perform research under contract to clients whose interests vary greatly—from assessing an experimental health care system to designing an airport complex for a developing nation. Each project requires a unique mix of expertise.

The conflicts between function and product that exist in at least a latent form in most organizations are elevated by the matrix organization into two competing structural principles. Although institutionalization of conflict does not resolve it, it does ensure that both functional and product interests are viewed as legitimate and have managerial representatives who continually define and defend them. Moreover, assigning specific roles the responsibility for defending particular values gives them higher visibility and makes trade-offs or compromises more evident: conflicts between decision makers are more visible than (role) conflicts within a single decision maker. Still, much ambiguity must be tolerated and competing claims accommodated for the matrix to function. For many participants, matrix structures are high-demand, high-stress work environments (Davis and Lawrence, 1977; Larson and Gobeli, 1987).

In some organizations, work is organized so that project teams become the primary basis for the organization of work, replacing functional departments and even standardized jobs. Rather than relying on an elaborate fixed division of labor, organizations institute flexible teams composed of individuals with diverse training, but not fixed responsibilities, who are assigned targets or goals that are subject to modification based on experience and learning (Hackman, 1987; Powell, 2001). A formal structure remains intact, but its units are teams rather than departments. In some arenas, project groups become more salient than host organizations causing Barley and Kunda (2001) to raise the question of "whether a theory of postindustrial organizing might usefully reconceptualize firms as contexts for projects."

Some contingency theorists are prone to overemphasize the role of internal organizational forces in explaining why organizations develop more lateral structures. However, a major incentive for many organizations to develop a project management structure came not from within as a rational response to information-processing demands or internal power considerations, but from outside the organization. Beginning as early as the 1950s, for example, the Department of Defense *required* its vendors to employ this structural arrangement as a condition for bidding on defense contracts (Wieland and Ullrich, 1976: 39). Government contract officers were tired of getting the runaround from functional department heads, each of whom had only partial control over any given project. The insistence of a project management format gave these officers someone they could identify and hold responsible for the successful and timely completion of the project.

Adhocracies and network forms, which include both internal and external types, are discussed in Chapters 8 and 11.

Organization Slack. Galbraith (1973) notes that an organization can reduce its information-processing demands simply by reducing the required level of performance. Higher performance standards increase the need for coordination: lowered standards create *organizational slack*—unused resources—that provides some ease in the system. For example, if delivery deadlines are not set so as to challenge the production units, then the need for information processing is reduced. If there are few constraints on inventory levels, then rapid response to changes in supply and demand messages is less essential. And, to use a nonmanufacturing example, if every third-grade teacher uses the first several weeks of the school year to reteach the basic lessons and skills of the second grade, then the sequential interdependence between second- and third-grade teachers is reduced, resulting in less need for coordinating their efforts.

Some slack in the handling of resources, including information, is not only inevitable, but also essential to smooth operations. All operations require a margin of error—an allowance for mistakes, waste, spoilage, and similar unavoidable accompaniments of work. Starbuck and Milliken (1988) argue that some of the failures in complex military and space systems are due to excessive "fine-tuning." The question, then, is not whether there is to be slack, but how much slack is to be permitted. Excessive slack resources increase costs for the organization that are likely to be passed on to the consumer. Since creating slack resources is a relatively easy and painless solution available to organizations, the extent to which it is employed is likely to be determined by the amount of competition confronting an organization.[5]

While Galbraith emphasizes that slack resources reduce information-processing requirements by lowering standards, it is equally important to recognize that they reduce the need for information processing by reducing interdependence. Conventional organizational routines of mass and batch production assume pooled or, at most, sequential interdependence. Functional forms are employed in which design engineers are buffered by departmental boundaries from production workers who, in turn, are separated from marketing personnel. Designs are "tossed over the wall" to production workers who have little say in the design and are expected to produce products for salespersons who often have little say in what is being produced. These functionally specialized and insulated departments— "chimney" structures—are considered by most contemporary students of organizations to be hopelessly old-fashioned and noncompetitive. Multiplex forms are attempts to address these shortcomings.

The Effects of Information and Communication Technologies. Information and communication technologies (ICTs) are often subsumed under the general concept of technology, but we agree with Burton and Obel (2004: 262) that they are more appropriately treated as a "dimension of structural design"—a means for communication and coordination. The new ICT systems—variously combining microelectronics, computer systems, and telecommunications—affect not only the gathering and transmission of information, but also its use in decision making. Huber (1990) suggests that such technologies support the more rapid and accurate identification of problems and opportunities, increase the availability of relevant and timely information and, in this way, improve both the speed and quality of decision making.

In earlier times, and at the present time for many functions, information-processing capacity was increased by adding staff specialists—analysts, accountants, and clerks. More recently, these functions have been taken over by increasingly sophisticated electronic monitoring, transmission, and data-reduction systems. The creation of ICT systems that permit the rapid transmission of relevant, "on-line" information through feedback loops to appropriate decision centers is one of the major aims and achievements of the modern systems-design movement (Burton and Obel, 2004; Schilling, 2002). Huber (1990) argues that the employment of advanced ICT increases the number of information sources but reduces the number of intermediate human actors

---

[5]March and colleagues have pointed out that organizational slack is also a critical resource supporting organizational experimentation and learning (Cyert and March, 1963; Levitt and March, 1988). March notes that search activities motivated by slack—rather than by immediate problem-solving pressures—are "less likely to solve immediate problems, more likely to be directed to subunit or individual objectives, and more likely to discover distinctively new alternatives" (1988: 4).

involved in its transmission. ICT increases the ability to record, store, analyze, and transmit information in ways that permit greater flexibility, timeliness, and the overcoming of distance barriers (Zuboff, 1985). But, it does not enhance participants' ability to interpret and to create shared meanings from the information received (Santos, 2003). Information does not in itself constitute knowledge to support action (Nissen, 2006). Various social sense-making functions (Weick, 1995) become even more critical as ICT spreads.

Many of the most recent innovations in ICT and in production processes—CAD (computer-aided design), CAM (computer-aided manufacturing), JIT (just-in-time inventory controls)—do not simply entail the use of new computer technologies but also involve significant structural changes as buffers between departments are reduced and interdependence increased (Adler, 1990; Susman and Chase, 1986). Designers are expected to interact with production personnel workers as they take into account the "manufacturability" of the product; and marketing personnel—who best know their customer's needs—exercise increased influence in both the design and production process (Chase and Tansik, 1983). Encouraging such interaction among workers across departments escalates interdependence from pooled to sequential to reciprocal.

Empirical Evidence. Donaldson (2001) provides a comprehensive review of empirical studies of contingency arguments. He discusses research around three types of issues: (1) the association between contingency and organizational structure—for example, the relation between size and structure (Blau and Schoenherr, 1971) or between technology and structure (Child and Mansfield, 1972; Van de Ven and Ferry, 1980); (2) ways in which changes in contingencies cause modifications in organizational structure—for example, changes in strategy leading to structural modifications (Chandler, 1962; Rumelt, 1986) or changes in tasks leading to changes in coordination modes (Van de Ven, Delbecq, and Koenig, 1976); (3) tests of how fit affects performance—the better the fit between environmental and organizational features, the better the organization's performance (Khandwalla, 1974).

However, the evidence for these associations is often relatively weak or conflicting, in part because of the wide variety of measures employed, differences in the level of units studied (individuals, teams, departments, organizations), and vagueness over the form of the predicted relation (linear, curvilinear, threshold effects) (Comstock and Scott, 1977; Pennings, 1973; Schoonhoven, 1981).

TECHNOLOGY AND STRUCTURE: NATURAL SYSTEM FORMULATIONS

The critiques of rational system approaches and the alternatives proposed by natural system theorists can, somewhat crudely, be organized around three themes: (1) social and cultural factors shaping the relation between technology and structure; (2) substituting informal for formal structure; and (3) the importance of tacit knowledge, under the control of performers, in contrast to explicit performance programs designed by officials. We consider each and conclude with a discussion of professional organizations.

Social and Cultural Factors Shaping Technology

Cross-cultural Studies. A number of cross-cultural studies have been conducted to determine whether contingency arguments are "culture-free." Three sets of studies are of particular interest. The first, carried out by the Laboratory for the Economic and Sociological Study of Work in Aix-en-Provence, France, under the leadership of Maurice, examined the organization of work in nine factories, three each in Great Britain, France, and Germany, matched for technology using Woodward's (1958) categories. Consistent with a natural system perspective, these researchers emphasized more qualitative comparisons which recognize "that organizational features have to be seen as socially constructed in different ways, rather than measured along a standardized dimension" (Maurice, Sorge, and Warner, 1980: 72). They report relatively large and consistent differences by country in the organization of work. German firms, regardless of technological complexity, exhibited higher levels of worker expertise, flexibility, and autonomy; British firms were intermediate, while French firms concentrated expertise and decision making in top managers and technical specialists. Maurice and colleagues interpret such differences as reflecting broad variations in the wider societies in educational institutions and industrial relations practice (see Maurice, 1979; Rose, 1985; see also Dore, 1973).

The second set of studies, conducted by Lincoln and colleagues (Lincoln and Kalleberg, 1990; Lincoln, Hanada, and McBride, 1986), contrasts a sample of fifty-five American and fifty-one Japanese manufacturing plants. This research reports differences between firms in the two countries, with Japan exhibiting less specialization and taller hierarchies than the United States regardless of technology, and also some differences in the effects of technology, with Japan exhibiting weaker relations between work-flow rigidity and centralization measures.[6] The important conclusion is drawn that "the impact of technology on structuring is stronger among U.S. organizations" than Japanese organizations of the same type, suggesting that in the Japanese context "the design of the organization becomes detached to some degree from the technology process and more attuned to the needs of the human workforce" (Lincoln, Hanada, and McBride, 1986: 358, 362).

---

[6]Two different kinds of cultural effects are distinguished: (1) variable level effects, for example, the assertion that Japanese organizations exhibit lower levels of specialization than their U.S. counterparts; and (2) variable causal effects, for example, the assertion that task complexity is associated with different degrees of centralization in Japan than in the United States (see Przeworski and Teune, 1970; Lammers and Hickson, 1979).

A final group of studies is based on the use of a set of scales devised by Hofstede (1984; 1991) for assessing cross-cultural differences across nations, pursuing earlier work by Inkeles and Levinson (1969). Hofstede regards culture as "mental programs"—"patterns of thinking, feeling, and acting" (1991: 4). In survey studies of employees of the IBM Corporation working in over fifty countries, Hofstede identified a number of value dimensions along which national cultures appeared to vary, including differences in power distance (inequality of power) among individuals, preferences for collectivism versus individualism, orientation to femininity or masculinity, and ways of dealing with uncertainty (Hofstede, 1984). This and subsequent studies demonstrated the existence of substantial relative differences in modal cultural values across nations. Some of the dimensions, for example, power distance and individualism-collectivism, were correlated with broader national or geographical variables. Thus, power distance was higher in larger countries, lower in wealthier countries and in those farther from the equator. Individualism was higher in wealthier, more urbanized and industrialized countries. However, other dimensions, such as femininity-masculinity and uncertainty avoidance showed no clear relation to such geographic or economic differences (Hofstede, 1991). A study with Bond (Hofstede and Bond, 1988) including a larger sample of Asian subjects identified a fifth dimension—short- versus long-term time orientation—the latter "Confucian" value being more characteristic of Asian cultures.

Hofstede argues that national cultural differences lead to different preferred modes of organizing, the French preferring a more hierarchial model, the British a more "village market" model, and the Asian countries a more extended family model (1991: chap. 6). He has also employed his scales to examine differences between national and organizational cultures. In a study of employees within a diverse sample of organizations within two similar countries (Denmark and the Netherlands) he reports that whereas national cultures tend to vary considerably in values but engage in rather similar practices, he

> found the roles of values versus practices to be exactly reversed with respect to the national level. Comparing otherwise similar people in different organizations showed considerable differences in practices but much smaller differences in values. (1991: 181–82)

House and colleagues (2004) have employed Hofstede's scales in their collaborative study of organizations in sixty-two societies to examine the modes of leadership best suited to deal with cultural differences.

Social and Political Factors. These and other cross-cultural studies contribute to the growing evidence that technology-structure relations are influenced by the broader social context. The thrust of these studies is a critique of early work based on the contingency framework, arguing that this approach embraced what Orlikowski (1992: 400) has labeled the "technological imperative" model: a view that technology "exerts unidirectional, causal influences over humans and organizations." Natural system theorists challenge this conception.

We reserve for later discussion how technical innovations are themselves shaped by social processes (see Chapter 10) and consider here the ways in which organizational factors affect what technologies are adopted and how they are implemented by organizations. To do so, we employ a broader lens than that used in conventional studies of technological innovation. Thomas (1994) points out that too many studies of "the social impact of technology" focus attention on the consequences attendant to the introduction of new tools or machines, overlooking earlier, critical phases of the process:

> I argue that the analysis cannot be limited to the final moments of change, that is, to implementation only. Rather, we must include the full range of activities associated with the introduction of new technology, including the *identification* of problems to be solved and solutions to be attached to problems; the *selection* among alternative technologies and, within a given technology, among alternative configuration; and finally, the *implementation* of a chosen technology. (1994: 13; emphasis in original)

Pursuing this agenda through a series of case studies, Thomas concludes that

> the choice between technological possibilities involves three screens: (1) a *technical* screen (e.g., does it physically do what we need it to do?); (2) an *economic* screen (e.g., will it achieve a recognizable or organizationally acceptable payoff?); and (3) a *political* or interest-based screen (e.g., does it express my/our vision of the proper way to accomplish the task? what will it do to my/our role in the organization? and, what does it say about me/us?). (1994: 83; emphasis in original)

Such accounts emphasize the role played by organizational politics, by vested interests, and by institutional arrangements in shaping and selecting the technical system employed by a specific organization. These views suggest that technology is itself a socially shaped if not a socially constructed reality. The causal arrows are shifted by these scholars to examine how social structures shape technology rather than how technology shapes structure.

Strategic Choice and Strategic Contingency

Theorists such as Child (1972) insist that the state of technology and other environmental conditions pose, at most, only broad and general constraints on structural design. Many contingency theorists place too much weight on external constraints, giving insufficient attention to actors and their capacity for choice. This line of argument, labeled *strategic choice,* emphasizes that a given set of circumstances can support many alternative adaptive strategies and responses. Actors can exercise agency: a range of choices is possible.

Strategic choice theorists also remind us that the division of labor and the differential contacts of participants with others inside and outside the organizations create divergent perspectives and interests as well as new sources of power that can be used to pursue these interests (Greenwood and Hinings, 1996; Hickson et al., 1971; Pfeffer, 1981). The recognition of multiple interests within organizations gave rise to the model of organizations as coalitions (Cyert and March, 1963; see also Chapter 8). In this conception, organizations are viewed not as unified actors, but as shifting combinations of varying interest groups moving in and out of the organization and up and down in relative power. Power can be employed to select those technologies that advance the interests of the dominant players, as Thomas (1994) has demonstrated.

When we shift from the selection of technology to the design of a technical system, the opportunity for social and political forces to operate is greatly enlarged. The complexity and uncertainty of work are strongly influenced by the specific systems that are created to conduct it—for example, on the extent to which work is divided and routinized or delegated to trained personnel. Similarly, interdependence is not only a function of the technical processes per se but also greatly affected by the ways in which the work is distributed among workers. Through role differentiation, complex tasks can be subdivided, made simpler, and more interdependent. Alternatively, by emphasizing a craft approach or through professionalization, complex tasks can be left intact, delegated to individual performers, and interdependence among participants reduced. Differentiation, deskilling, and interdependence (simplifying evaluation, increasing the need for coordination) are more likely to occur when managers exercise power; the recognition of craft expertise, the need for judgment, and skill enhancement (rendering external control more difficult, justifying increasing autonomy) occur when performers exercise power (Dornbusch and Scott, 1975). Such arguments are not limited to, but are clearly consistent with, those developed by Marxist theorists, who point to the continuing struggle for discretion and control occurring in the work place (see Chapter 7).

The emphasis that strategic contingency theorists place on the flexibility of connections—loose coupling—between technology and structure and on the role of power in shaping these connections is echoed by analysts examining effects associated with the introduction of new information technologies. Zuboff (1988) argues that ICT has two effects on work processes: first, it enhances *automation*, carrying forward the logic of nineteenth-century machine systems that "enables the same processes to be performed with more continuity and control." Second, however, the new technologies differ fundamentally from earlier machines because of their capacity to *informate* work processes by simultaneously generating information about the underlying productive and administrative processes through which an organization accomplishes its work. It provides a deeper level of transparency to activities that had been either partially or completely opaque. (1988: 9)

More specifically,

The intelligence of the microprocessor that resides at the base of virtually every application not only applies instructions to equipment but can convert the current state of product or process into information (Zuboff, 1985: 105).

Recalling Galbraith's insight that technologies affect structures by determining how much information must be processed during the task sequence, it is possible to see that some aspects of new technologies act to *absorb* information: such technologies as automation and robotics eliminate the need for the information-processing capacities of social structures. By contrast, other aspects of the new technologies *create* new information: they are able to not only "apply programmed instructions to equipment but also convert the current state of equipment, product, or process into data" (Zuboff, 1988: 9). However, whether this new information is employed primarily to exercise greater managerial control over the work process or to provide the basis for increased innovation and autonomy among performers is not determined by the technology, but by choices made by those exercising influence in these work sites. Those responsible for designing organizations must determine whether or not, and in what manner, work systems are to be "transformed" to exploit the new opportunities (Morton, 1992: 272). Again we see that while technology affects structure, structure (and participants) also affects the choice and use of technology.

The Duality of Technology

Rather than being forced to choose between the relative importance of technology versus structure, a superior formulation has been proposed by both Barley and Orlinkowski. They adapt Gidden's (1984) conception of the "duality" of social structure (see Chapter 1), applying it to the relation of technology and structure. Orlinkowski summarizes the conception as containing two premises. First, technology exhibits duality: it is both product and object:

Technology is the product of human action, while it also assumes structural properties. That is, technology is physically constructed by actors working in a given social context, and technology is socially constructed by actors through the different meanings they attach to it . . . However, it is also the case that once developed and deployed, technology tends to become reified and institutionalized, losing its connection with the human agents that constructed it or gave it meaning, and it appears to be part of the objective, structural properties of the organization. (1992: 406)

But, second, even through undergoing reification, technologies vary in their "interpretive flexibility" (Pinch and Bjiker, 1987):

> [There are] differences among technologies in the degree to which users can effect redesign. While we can expect a greater engagement of human agents during the initial development of a technology, this does not discount the ongoing potential for users to change it (physically and socially) throughout their interaction with it. (Orlinkowski, 1992: 408)

Both premises are persuasively illustrated in a study by Barley (1986) of changes occurring in the social order of two radiology departments in hospitals at the time when computer tomography (CAT) scanners were first introduced. Far from viewing it as determinant in its effects, Barley regards the introduction of the new technology as providing "an occasion" for restructuring the technical system. "The scanners occasioned change because they became social objects whose meanings were defined by the context of their use" (p. 106). He documents how the interaction patterns exhibited by radiologists and technicians changed over time by isolating "scripts" that define identifiable sequences of interactive behavior. Because of differences in the surrounding contexts, the varying expertise and experience of personnel, and the specific course of interactions, identical technologies gave rise to different structural outcomes in the two departments. Although "each department changed in similar directions, one department became far more decentralized" (p. 105), as measured by departmental decision making.

Barley's study provides support for both contingency and strategic choice theory. As predicted by contingency theory, the increased complexity and uncertainty associated with the new technology were associated with increased decentralization (in both situations). And, as predicted by strategic choice theorists, the reactions of participants were constrained, not determined, by technological parameters. Decentralization was greater in one hospital department than the other, and the trajectory of interactions varied between hospitals. The resulting social structures reflected the varied reactions, diversity of interests, and power differences among participants.

Reliance on Informal Structure

Contingency theory approaches to structural design, like all other rational system models, stress the benefits of formalization. The rational system response to increasing task demands is to shorten and strengthen the leash: provide superiors with more timely information so they can more rapidly change the instructions to performers. The mental/manual distinction pervades the menu of choices. Some of the modifications move in the direction of decentralization: power and authority are more widely dispersed as hierarchies are augmented and, particularly, as lateral connections are added. But formalization is, if anything, increased in these systems.[7] New types of roles are created and new linkages specified that increase the complexity, flexibility, and capacity for change in the structure. But the flexibility involved is designed, not spontaneous, and the formulas endeavor to create a capacity to shift rapidly from one set of formal rules and roles to another.

These assumptions and approaches are, as we know, challenged by natural system theorists, who stress the advantages of informal structures, particularly in the face of task uncertainty. These alternative approaches, which have received much recent attention, rely primarily on enlarged roles, internalized and peer controls, and informal structures to confront high levels of uncertainty and complexity. Rather than augmenting hierarchies, they minimize vertical distinctions and flatten hierarchies, and rather than creating new, specialized lateral roles and relations, they encourage more direct, open, face-to-face communications among any or all participants as required. Decision making becomes more decentralized, and organizational roles less formalized. Several bodies of theory and research emphasize the value of informal structures in a work organization. (A development that embodies many of these features of expanded roles and increased autonomy for workers, high-performance work teams, is described in Chapter 7.)

Sociotechnical Systems. Following World War II, the Tavistock Institute of Human Relations in England concentrated on the study of work systems. From the beginning, the preferred approach was one of "action" (applied) research, the investigators working with management and labor to introduce change into a work setting and then attempt to learn from its results (Jaques, 1951). A central premise of Tavistock's approach is that work involves a combination of social and technical requisites and that the object of design is to "jointly optimize" both components—not sacrifice one for the other. By contrast, a rational system approach privileges an engineering solution with technical systems being designed and human workers "fitted in" to their requirements.

If human as well as technical requirements are to be served, then it is necessary to determine what kinds of work situations motivate and satisfy workers. The Tavistock group emphasizes both individual task features as well as organizational, particularly work-group, features. At the task level, repetitive, undemanding, isolated jobs were viewed as undermining commitment and weakening performance motivation. Organizations may thrive on certainty, but individuals do not! This counterassumption originating in the sociotechnical school has given rise to a large body of theory

---

[7]The relation between formalization and decentralization is discussed in Chapter 2.

and research pursued primarily at the social psychological level of the individual worker.[8]

The sociotechnical approach has placed greater emphasis on the social organization of work groups—together with the necessary support features at higher organizational levels—than on the narrower matter of the design of individual jobs. Work groups, properly structured, can provide workers with an ongoing source of incentives, error correction, assistance, learning opportunities, and social support that no amount of attention to individual job design can hope to match. Tavistock researchers worked with companies to successfully create semiautonomous work groups for British coal mines (Trist and Bamforth, 1951). A similar solution was developed by Volvo of Sweden when it decided to replace the traditional conveyor line for assembling its automobiles with movable automobile carriers that would permit more task variety and worker discretion embedded within a system empowering work groups as the central work elements (Gyllenhammar, 1977). And Cole (1979) has described how, on the other side of the globe, Toyota Auto Body of Japan reorganized its work process to enrich worker skills, enlarge worker discretion, and activate work-group incentives and controls in the now-famous "quality circles." These work groups are ordinarily organized around a particular type of job and are granted primary responsibility for such matters as safety and quality control. They become involved with "almost every other kind of problem, including improvement of productivity, the speed and way of stopping the conveyor belt, job procedures, job training, and human relations problems" (1979: 161; see also, Womack, Jones, and Roos, 1990).[9] General Motors adopted and adapted many of these approaches in its Saturn division (Rubinstein and Kochan, 2001).

When the organizational environment becomes more turbulent and the work demands more uncertain, a sociotechnical design suggests that redundancy of function is superior to redundancy of parts (Emery and Trist, 1965). Pugh, Hickson, and Hinings summarize the critical difference between these two emphases:

> The traditional technocratic bureaucracy is based on redundancy of parts. The parts are broken down so that the ultimate elements are as simple as possible; thus an unskilled worker in a narrow job who is cheap to replace and who takes little time to train would be regarded as an ideal job design. But this approach also requires reliable control systems—often cumbersome and costly.

---

[8]The most influential of these is *job characteristics theory* and its elaboration in work design and individual needs approaches (see Hackman and Oldham, 1980; Turner and Lawrence, 1965).

[9]In a later study, Cole (1989) contrasts efforts to establish worker participation structures in Japan, Sweden, and the United States. They are more widely diffused in Japan than in Sweden and in Sweden than in the United States. His analysis shows that they are much more highly institutionalized in Japan and Sweden, receiving support from industry groups and the state.

An alternative design, based on the redundancy of functions, is appropriate to turbulent environments. In this approach individuals and units have wide repertoires of activities to cope with change, and they are self-regulating. For the individual they create roles rather than mere jobs; for the organization, they bring into being a variety-increasing system rather than the traditional control by variety reduction. . . . Autonomous working groups, collaboration rather than competition (between organizations as well as within them) and reduction of hierarchical emphasis, are some of the requirements for operating effectively in modern turbulence. (1985: 89)

Organizational Routines and Tacit Knowledge. From the insights of March and Simon (1958), if not long before (note Adam Smith's vivid description of pin making in Chapter 7), students of organizations have recognized the importance of "performance programs"—sets of activities that are conducted in a predictable way to carry out the work of the organization. Rational system theorists emphasize that these programs can and should be rationalized: engineers and technical staff must analyze the work requirements and design the necessary operations so as to minimize time and resource use. This orientation is best exemplified by Taylor's scientific management approach (see Chapter 2) but remains a widely utilized approach.

Natural system theorists also recognize the importance of these patterned activities or routines but see them as more often the accomplishment of the ingenuity of workers than the expertise of the designer. Natural system views have been reinforced by the arguments of evolutionary economists, organization learning, and knowledge-based theorists who stress the importance of encouraging variation (variety), experiential learning, gradual accumulation of experience, and tacit knowledge. Much of the knowledge on which the organization relies is contained in the skills and tacit knowledge of its workforce—such routines are the "genes" of the organization (Nelson and Winter, 1982), rather than such knowledge being

represented in the firm in a form that makes alternative ways of doing things accessible to an effective survey, leading to a choice founded on economic criteria . . . organizational capabilities are fragmented, distributed, and embedded in organizational routines. No individual knows how the organization accomplishes what it actually does, much less what alternatives are available. (Winter, 1990: 99)

The recent movement aimed at improving organizational performance known as "total quality management" (TQM), recognizes the importance of these routines and the wisdom they contain but seeks to capture tacit knowledge and make it accessible to all through discovering "best practices" which can then be codified and widely disseminated. Innovations such as quality circles and team problem solving are attempts to provide occasions for making explicit what some performers "know" but may not recognize that they know (Cole and Scott, 2000). While TQM offers more autonomy to teams for collective problem solving, it tends to resort to more conventional, top-down approaches, as Hackman and Wageman point out:

> Once such practices are identified and documented, they are diffused throughout the organization and standardized, with the result that work-unit members may wind up with very little discretion about how they perform their tasks. The potential for overspecification of work procedures is so great that one is reminded of industrial engineering during the heyday of scientific management . . . The motivational costs of this approach are well documented. (1995: 326–27)

So, the old battles between rational and natural systems views of organizations continue under new labels.

Professional Organizations

There is an organizational form that constitutes a hybrid model, combining aspects of rational and natural system approaches to dealing with complex tasks. In earlier and simpler times, professionals worked independently. They underwent long training and socialization to acquire both the skills and the understanding to apply general principles to complex cases. To the extent that they entered into organizations—for example, physicians in community hospitals—it was on their own terms: they retained their autonomy and were subject to, at most, collegial controls (Freidson, 1970). But as organizations proliferated, professionals increasingly became dependent on their equipment and resources. Today the great majority of professionals—doctors, teachers, lawyers, scientists—are either employees of organizations or are subordinated to them in their everyday working life.

We began the discussion of technology and structure by stating four general principles relating characteristics of technology and of structure (see p. 00). We now call attention to an important exception to the first principle. Technical complexity does not invariably give rise to greater complexity of structure; it may give rise instead to increased "complexity" of the performer. That is, one way to manage greater task complexity is not to divide the work and parcel it out among differentiated workers or work groups, but to confront the complexity with more highly qualified and flexible performers—with professionals (Scott, 1966; Stinchcombe, 1990). This response is particularly effective when (1) the work is both complex and uncertain, a condition that militates against preplanning and subdivision; and (2) the work—or at least, substantial portions of it—can be carried out by a single performer, reducing levels of interdependence among workers. As an example of the latter condition, teaching by faculty members in universities, work of lawyers in law firms, and practice of physicians in out-patient clinics as customarily performed tend to involve relatively little interdependence. Whether complexity and uncertainty of work give rise to complex organizations or to complex performers is determined partly by the characteristics of the work itself, but it is also influenced by the political and social power of the performer group, as we argued earlier in this chapter (see also Dornbusch and Scott, 1975; Larson, 1977; Abbott, 1988).

However, as levels of complexity, uncertainty, and interdependence increase, "independent" professionals are likely to move their work into organizational structures, thus becoming components of a wider division of labor and increasingly subject to more formalized coordination mechanisms. In this sense, professional organizations incorporate two layers of response to task complexity: complex performers enter into and are supported and constrained by complex organizational structures.

Historically, professionals have performed the core tasks of the organization under two general types of arrangements. The first, labeled the *heteronomous* professional organization, is one in which "professional employees are clearly subordinated to an administrative framework," and the amount of autonomy granted them is relatively small (Scott, 1965: 67). Employees in these settings are subject to administrative controls, and their discretion is clearly circumscribed. Professional employees are subject to routine supervision, often by nonprofessionals. This type of professional organization is exemplified by many public agencies—libraries, secondary schools, social welfare agencies—as well as some private organizations, such as small religious colleges, engineering companies, applied research firms, and public accounting firms (see Bidwell, 1965; Brock, Powell, and Hinings, 1999; Etzioni, 1969; Kornhauser, 1962; 1968; Scott, 1982).

The structure of heteronomous professional organizations is in many respects similar to the arrangements already described in which organizations handle tasks of moderate complexity and uncertainty by *delegation*. The work of the professionals takes place within a structure of general rules and hierarchical supervision, but individual performers are given considerable discretion over task decisions, particularly those concerning means or techniques. Thus, individual teachers make choices regarding instructional techniques, and individual engineers make decisions concerning design or construction strategies. For some kinds of tasks, short-term task forces or project teams are assembled.

A second arrangement, termed the *autonomous* professional organization, exists to the extent that "organizational officials delegate to the group of professional employees considerable responsibility for defining and implementing the goals, for setting performance standards, and for seeing to it that standards are maintained" (Scott, 1965: 66). The professional performers organize themselves—as a "staff" in hospitals or clinics, as an "academic council" in universities—to assume these responsibilities. Ideally, a fairly well demarcated boundary is established between those tasks for which the professional group assumes responsibility and those over which managers have jurisdiction. Examples of types of professional organizations likely to conform to the autonomous pattern include general hospitals, therapeutic psychiatric hospitals, medical clinics, elite colleges and universities, and scientific institutes oriented to basic research (see Clark, 1963; Freidson, 1975; Galanter and Palay, 1991; Robinson, 1999; Smigel, 1964).

Current developments in professional services in the United States suggest that the choice among these structural arrangements, as for any type of structure, is not simply a matter of rational design. For example, physicians have lost power and legitimacy during recent decades for many reasons— fragmentation of specialties, increased competition as the numbers of physicians have grown, inability to curtail treatment costs, the rise of the consumer movement—and as a consequence, are more subordinated to corporate structures and managers (Brock, Powell, and Hinings, 1999; Robinson, 1999; Salmon, 1994; Scott et al., 2000). Leicht and Fennell (2001) argue that such developments are part of a broader trend. Managerial work is itself becoming increasingly professionalized in that we observe

> (1) the growing definition of a distinctive domain of action that is the exclusive prerogative of business managers, (2) the defense and furtherance of freedom of action (autonomy) in that domain, and (3) a defense of that domain against encroachment by competing occupational groups and stakeholders. (2001: 10)

And, although professionals work within a wide variety of organizational settings, all are more subject to managerial and financial controls than was earlier the case. Under what Leicht and Fennell (2001: 21) label the "neoentrepreneurial" form, formerly autonomous professional organizations are being "captured" by managerial forms that treat the professional services group as simply another service unit to which work can be subcontracted. Increasing specialization among professional workers and the relative success of the managers' drive to themselves professionalize have resulted in the decline of those distinctive forms of organizations long associated with traditional professional work.

SUMMARY

Most efforts to explain the structural complexity within the technical core of an organization focus on the characteristics of the work being performed— on the technology. While many specific measures of technology have been proposed, it appears that the most important dimensions to represent in relating technology to structure are complexity, uncertainty, and interdependence. In general, we expect technical complexity to be associated with structural complexity and/or performer complexity (professionalization); technical uncertainty, with lower formalization and decentralization of decision making; and interdependence, with higher levels of coordination. Complexity, uncertainty, and interdependence are alike in at least one respect: each increases the amount of information that must be processed during the course of a task performance. Thus, as complexity, uncertainty, and interdependence increase, structural modifications need to be made to increase the capacity of the information-processing system.

because the criteria can vary from time to time and from location to location in the organization. We have already described, in Chapter 6, some of the mechanisms employed by organizations to protect ("buffer") their technical work, and in Chapter 9 we consider the question of how organizations determine where to place their technical boundaries. Here, we concern ourselves with the social boundaries of organizations, examining the various indicators used to mark those boundaries and the criteria employed by organizations in determining whom to admit or reject and how to regard their "external" characteristics.

Determining Organizational Boundaries

In Chapter 1, we considered the various elements that come together to comprise an organization and, in discussing varying definitions, we quietly slipped in the notion of *collectivity*. This concept adds a new element: the idea of boundary. A collectivity is a specific instance of social organization—an identifiable "chunk" of the social order. As noted, the criteria for the existence of a collectivity are (1) a *delimited* social structure—that is, a *bounded* network of social relations—and (2) a normative order and cultural-cognitive framework *applicable to the participants* linked by the network. All collectivities—including informal groups, communities, organizations, and entire societies—possess, by definition, boundaries that distinguish them from other systems. With organizations in particular, however, as we discuss throughout this volume, the issue of boundaries has become ever more problematic and controversial.

Accepting the view that organizations, as a type of collectivity, possess boundaries is one thing, but determining how to define them and what indicators to employ in assessing them present a challenge. Establishing the boundaries of an organization is a difficult business, raising both theoretical and empirical problems.

To embrace the notion of organizations as open systems is to acknowledge that organizations are penetrated by their environments in ways that blur and confound any simple criterion for distinguishing the one from the other. How are we to regard customers, clients, suppliers, or stockholders, to list only a few categories of players? A second difficulty is presented by the growing number of organizations that are subsumed under broader structures—for example, schools within districts, local banks that operate as branches of larger financial enterprises, and establishments that are components of multidivisional corporations. Such connections may strongly influence many aspects of the structure and performance of the local units, so that treating them as independent may create serious errors. Third, contemporary organizations are more likely to regularly collaborate with other "independent" units so that even "core tasks" may not be performed within the formal boundaries of the organization. Finally, organizational boundaries are very likely to fluctuate over time, always over long, but sometimes over short periods (Freeman, 1978).

Laumann, Marsden, and Prensky (1983) identify two approaches and, within each, three substantive foci frequently used to define boundaries. The two approaches are the realist and the nominalist. In the *realist* approach, the investigator adopts the "vantage point of the actors themselves in defining the boundaries" of the system, assuming that this view will importantly influence their behavior. Under the *nominalist* strategy, the "analyst self-consciously imposes a conceptual framework constructed to serve his own analytic purposes" (p. 21). Regardless of the approach selected, the investigator must determine what features of the situation to emphasize as the criterion for determining boundaries. Laumann and associates distinguish among three alternatives—the characteristics of the actors, their relations, and their activities. The actors may be individuals or organizations.

Many investigators define the boundaries of an organization by focusing on its *actors*—for example, attempting to determine who is and who is not regarded as a member. Members also are likely to share other attributes—such as interests, training, age, or ethnicity, in the case of individuals, or goals, strategies, or structures, in the case of organizations. Laumann and Knoke (1987), for example, show how a shared interest in specific issues, such as mental health or medical education, creates linkages among organizations involved in health policy-setting domains.

A second approach—favored by network analysts—is to establish the boundaries of the system by noting which actors are involved in *social relations* of a specified type. Network analysts prefer measures of relations to measures of actor's attributes, arguing that the former provides a better indicator of social structure. A widely used behavioral indicator of relatedness is frequency of interaction. Although no social unit is completely separated from its environment on the basis of this criterion, Homans suggests that it is possible to locate the system boundaries where the web of interaction shows "certain thin places" (1950: 85).[1] The structure of an organizational system is frequently mapped using graph theoretical approaches that assess proximity and distance among network actors. "The social distance between actors is measured by 'paths,' the smallest number of directed communication links necessary to connect a pair" (Laumann and Knoke, 1987: 218; see also Marsden, 1990). Burt (1990) has proposed that ties between actors vary along the dimension of strength, frequency of contact, and role relations (for example, distinguishing between workplace and kinship ties).

A third possibility is to focus on the nature of the *activities* performed. We would expect to observe a change in the activities performed by individuals as

[1]It is not only social scientists who wrestle with the question of how to bound a system under study. Other observers of the social scene, such as novelists, confront a similar problem. The strategy proposed by Henry James is not dissimilar to that adopted by scientific investigators:

> Really, universally, relations stop nowhere, and the exquisite problem of the artist is eternally but to draw, by a geometry of his own, the circle within which they shall happily appear to do so. (1907: vii)

they cross a system boundary.[2] Pfeffer and Salancik favor this criterion, arguing that organizational boundaries are coterminous with activity control:

> When it is recognized that it is behaviors, rather than individuals, that are included in structures of coordinated behavior, then it is possible to define the extent to which any given person is or is not a member of the organization. . . . The organization is the total set of interstructured activities in which it is engaged at any one time and over which it has discretion to initiate, maintain, or end behaviors. . . . The organization ends where its discretion ends and another's begins. (1978: 32)

A focus on relationships or activities emphasizes behavioral criteria for defining the limits of organizations. Since both interactions and activities require time and space, two useful indicators of significant boundaries are an organization's spatial barriers and their guardians (e.g., fences, walls, doors, guards, receptionists) and the temporal systems (e.g., working hours and activity schedules) it creates to contain them. A focus on the characteristics of actors emphasizes normative criteria for defining the significant characteristics of membership. In many of the newly emerging work systems, such as the "boundaryless" office and the virtual organization, spatial and temporal markers no longer bound organizational activities.[3] Normative boundaries may also be weakened by the use of temporary or contract workers. In such situations, what boundaries exist reside in the heads of the participants— cognitive understandings shared by participants—and in the terms of legal contracts. The boundaries are not gone but have been reenvisioned and involve different mechanisms.

The concept of *organizational identity* focuses attention on the shared beliefs and self-conceptions held by organizational participants. Defined by Albert and Whetten as the "central, enduring, and distinctive" set of beliefs and values "that distinguish the organization from others with which it might be compared" (1985: 265), these cognitive understandings have been demonstrated to influence participants' behavior and their relation to "outsiders" (Dutton and Dukerich, 1991; Whetten and Godfrey, 1998). Studies have also been conducted documenting the importance of "collective cognition" in constructing boundaries at the organizational field or industry level. Researchers have examined the role played by managers' conceptions of field boundaries, asking, for example, what business they are in or who their primary competitors are (e.g., Lant and Baum, 1995; Porac, Thomas, and Badden-Fuller, 1989). Such studies illustrate the role that microprocesses, such

---

[2]Barnard took the position that activities, not participants, are the basic elements of organizations. Thus, he defined an organization as "a system of cooperative activities of two or more persons" (1938: 75).

[3]An article in *Newsweek* (August 6, 2001) reports that 40 percent of working Americans were in daily contact with their office during their vacations.

as perception and cognition, play in creating macro-level phenomena, such as organization and industry boundaries (Abrahamson and Fombrun, 1994).

Membership, interaction, activity, and cognitive boundaries often do not coincide. The operational systems—as revealed by studies of patterns of interaction and of interdependent activities—through which organizations actually accomplish their tasks may cross-cut formal or membership boundaries in ways to be detailed later. Nevertheless, most groups, and particularly organizations, carefully differentiate members from nonmembers and develop explicit criteria for recruiting and selecting the former. Why is this true? What is the importance of membership boundaries for the functioning of organizations?

Recruitment Criteria

Rational system theorists are quite certain that they understand the functions of organizational boundaries: boundaries contribute to organizational rationality. Several of the characteristics Weber (1968 trans.) identified as defining rational-legal systems may be viewed as bounding or insulating the organization from its social context. For example, his stipulation that officials be appointed by free contract according to their technical qualifications is intended to ensure that selection criteria are organizationally relevant and that the selection process will be relatively free from the influence of other social affiliations, whether religious, economic, political, or familial (Udy, 1962; for a discussion, see Scott, 1998: 185–90).

Organizationally controlled recruitment criteria are but one important mechanism fostering insulation of the organization from its social environment; Weber (1968 trans.) pointed to the need for others. His insistence that officials, once recruited, should regard the office as their sole, or at least their primary, occupation indicates his recognition that other occupational affiliations of members may affect their performance within organizations. And it is not only other occupational demands that may create claims on participants that may conflict with those of the focal organization. Kinship and family roles may become the basis of conflicting expectations and behavior patterns. Indeed, Martin and Knopoff (1997) argue that, while Weber's criteria appear to be objective and gender-neutral, the emphasis on full time commitment discriminates against women, who historically have borne disproportionate family responsibilities. And other bases of social identity, such as age, sex, ethnicity, and social class have been shown to intrude on "rational" decision making in organizations (see Bielby and Baron, 1986; Cox, Nkomo, and Welch, 2000; Dalton, 1959; England and Folbre, 2005; Hughes, 1958: 102–15; Kanter, 1977b).

The extra-organizational identities of individual participants play a relatively small and perverse role in rational system views of organization: they are viewed primarily as a problem to be managed by appropriate recruitment criteria, differentiation and segregation, and control mechanisms. By contrast, the many faces of participants are of great interest to natural system analysts.

To begin, from a natural system perspective, it is impossible for any organization to eliminate completely these sources of "disturbance": social identities—externally validated roles, qualities, interests—are among the most portable of baggage. Some extreme types of organizations do attempt to eliminate the external status connections of a subset of their participants. This is the case for such *total institutions* as prisons, early mental hospitals, monasteries, and army barracks. As Goffman explains,

> The barrier that total institutions place between the inmate and the wider world marks the first curtailment of self. In civil life, the sequential scheduling of the individual's roles, both in the life cycle and in the repeated daily round, ensures that no one role he plays will block his performance and ties in another. In total institutions, in contrast, membership automatically disrupts role scheduling, since the inmate's separation from the wider world lasts around the clock and may continue for years. Role dispossession therefore occurs. (1961: 14)

In addition to imposing these time and physical barriers, many such institutions forbid all contact with outsiders, strip the inmate of personal possessions, segregate sex or age groups, issue institutional garb, and restrict interaction among inmates (see also McEwen, 1980). It is possible to view these measures as a set of mechanisms for ensuring that organizations will be buffered from the disturbing effects of the external roles occupied by participants. But surely they serve better to remind us how difficult it is for any organization to eliminate the influence on its participants of their nonorganizational identities. Total institutions are best viewed as a limiting case—as defining one extreme on a continuum in which most organizations are located near the middle.[4]

Later work by the "Chicago school" of sociology expands Goffman's insights to examine the ways in which individuals in mainstream organizations find ways to subvert, undercut, or resist organizational pressures for conformity. For example, in their study of the socialization of medical students in a state university, Becker and colleagues (Becker et al., 1961) describe the conflicting perspectives of faculty and students as students find ways to survive in an overly demanding context. This and related studies "focus on the microprocesses by which individuals attempt to limit the power of institutions" (Fine and Ducharme, 1995: 125).

Most organizations do not erect excessive barriers or engage in elaborate stripping tactics; hence, we should expect most organizations to be composed of participants who possess multiple identities and behave accordingly. Certainly, natural system analysts embrace this view. We have already noted (in Chapter 3) the interest of human relations investigators in the effects of sex, class, and ethnicity on the allocation of workers to roles and on worker behavior (Bean and Stevens, 2003; Miller, 1986). Far from stressing the disruptive and constraining

---

[4]The other end of this continuum is one in which an organization loses its distinctive structure and influence over participants and dissolves into the broader social structure, becoming socially "engulfed" (Scott, 1998: 188–90).

effects of participants' other roles; natural system theorists insist that these characteristics often constitute a vital resource for the organization. Even within a rational-system, performance-oriented context, natural system analysts point out that most organizations do not themselves train their members to talk, to think, or to use specialized tools: these fundamental skills are typically acquired in different settings and imported into the organization. And, from the natural system perspective where goal-attainment considerations are secondary to survival, it becomes apparent that many participants are recruited precisely because they possess extra-organizational characteristics viewed as valuable to this end. For most organizations—and especially for those operating in more elaborated institutionalized environments—it is important to recruit the "right" kinds of participants, for symbolic as well as technical considerations. Schools need to hire credentialed teachers; nursing homes, licensed administrators; universities, faculty members with Ph.D.s; and financial organizations, certified public accountants. Incorporating such externally acquired and validated social identities enhances organizational legitimacy (see Chapter 10).

Organizations also conform to the expectations of their social environments by maintaining some consistency between their own status systems and the stratification criteria used in the larger society (Anderson et al., 1966). For example, from the beginning of their entry into paid employment, women have gone into predominantly female occupations. Occupations remain heavily sex-segregated up to the present time; for example, 58 percent of men or women would need to change jobs in order for there to be equal numbers across occupations—down from 68 percent in 1970 (England and Folbre, 2005), And, it remains the case up to the present time that women are rarely appointed to high managerial positions in U.S. corporations, partly because their social identities are viewed by their male colleagues as introducing additional sources of uncertainty into transactions requiring high trust (Kanter, 1977a), but also because organizations wish to inspire confidence in outsiders with whom they conduct business, and so try not to violate widely shared community norms. Further, for certain types of boundary-spanning roles, such as being a member of a board of directors, an individual's selection may depend entirely on his or her external roles and connections. Thus, a banker may be asked to serve on the board of directors of a hospital because of ties with the financial community.

Conflict theorists within the natural systems perspective observe that participants enter organizations with different and often conflicting interests, and that organizational resources are often deflected to serve personal ends (Bamberger and Sonnenstuhl, 1998; Perrow, 1986). Worker interests can differ from those of managers or directors; human resource professionals may prefer longer-term and more diffuse employment systems which build employee loyalty while financial specialists emphasize the advantages of narrow and short-term contracts and externalization of work. At more macro levels, Marxist theorists note appointments to the board of directors may serve the interests of the elite class rather than those of the individual organization (see Chapter 11).

Feminist theorists, in particular, stress the hidden agenda underlying attempts to distinguish formal roles from other informal or "private" roles. The distinction both delegitimates and diminishes other nonorganizational sources of power (abilities, resources, connections) and at the same time shores-up and formalizes existing organizationally based inequalities (Acker, 1990; Martin, 1990). For example, much less attention is given by the public-at-large or by social scientists to unpaid work—performed primarily by women in the home—than to market-based work (England and Folbre, 2005). There is also much current discussion, fueled by feminist concerns, of modifying work arrangements to better accommodate family requirements (see Hochschild, 1989; Presser 2003; Roman and Blum, 2000). Some organizations are experimenting with flextime hours, work sharing, and off-site work locations, and providing family-oriented benefits, including maternity/paternity leave and day-care services. But critics point out that progress is slow, that the United States lags behind Europe, and that these services continue to be unavailable to most American workers.

An interesting instance of combining multiple roles—business and personal—is represented by direct sales organizations, which currently employ about 5 percent of the U.S. labor force, and a disproportionate number of women. In her study of such organizations as Tupperware, Amway, and Mary Kay, Nicole Biggart observes that

> Whereas bureaucratic firms seek to exclude nonwork social relations in order to control workers, the direct selling industry pursues profit in the opposite way: by making social networks serve business ends. (1989: 8)

Direct sales organizations encourage the inclusion of family members, relatives, and friends in the business organization; they combine business and personal relationships as well as business and social occasions; and they reverse the process, "making the economic ties of sponsorship the basis for family-like social relations." The combination of economic and affective ties creates "a double-stranded bond far stronger than either one alone" (p. 85).

These types of organizational arrangements support the contention of the natural system theorists that the external identities and connections of participants—far from being disruptive and restrictive—are, under many conditions, a primary resource for the organization, providing skills, legitimacy, and valued connections with the larger social environment.

DIVISION OF LABOR

The Rationalization of Work

It is widely assumed that the reorganization of work associated with the industrial revolution was essential to the emergence of the modern productive enterprise. The classic statement of the rational system version of this argument was provided by Adam Smith in 1776 in his celebrated account of the manufacture of pins. Smith observed that whereas an untrained worker without the proper machinery could "scarce, perhaps, with his utmost industry, make one pin in a day," vastly different results obtain when the work is properly divided into a number of branches.

> One man draws out the wire, another straights it, a third cuts it, a fourth points it, a fifth grinds it at the top for receiving the head; to make the head requires two or three distinct operations; to put it on is a peculiar business, to whiten the pins is another; it is even a trade by itself to put them into the paper; and the important business of making a pin is, in this manner, divided into about eighteen distinct operations. (Smith, 1957 ed.: 2)

So arranged, ten persons "could make among them upwards of forty-eight thousand pins a day."

This miracle of productivity is accomplished primarily by the application of technology to the work process. As Galbraith (1967) explains, "technology means the systematic application of scientific or other organized knowledge to practical tasks." This is possible only when the tasks are subdivided into their components in such a manner that they become "coterminous with some established area of scientific or engineering knowledge" (1967: 24). In addition to this prime benefit, specialization within the workforce allows the organization to take advantage of particular skills possessed by a member and also fosters the development of such skills through repetition and learning. And to the extent that the various skills required are of differential complexity, variable pay scales may be introduced, so that further economies are realized through task subdivision (Braverman, 1974: 79).

A related process, "agglomeration"—the gathering of workers together in a common location—was encouraged by the use of common energy sources, first water power, later steam and electric engines (Rosenberg and Birdzell, 1986). This, in turn, results in a more efficient and effective use of energy, centralized locations for shipping and receiving of raw materials and products, and economies of scale. Moreover, concentration of workers allows increased supervision and control, including the imposition of specified work hours and schedules (E. P. Thompson, 1967).

It is not only production organizations that benefit from work subdivision and specialization. As discussed in Chapter 2, Weber advanced similar arguments for the transformation of systems of political (and corporate) administration. His ideal-type conception of bureaucracy—the form of rational administration emerging at the end of the nineteenth century—places great emphasis on technical expertise and a fixed division of labor among officials. Weber contended that this form replaced earlier, more traditional social structures because of its greater efficiency.

> Experience tends universally to show that the purely bureaucratic type of administrative organization . . . is, from a purely technical point of view, capable of attaining the highest degree of efficiency and is in this sense formally the most

rational known means of exercising authority over human beings. It is superior to any other form in precision, in stability, in the stringency of its discipline, and in its reliability. (Weber, 1947 trans.: 337)

Giddens notes the extent to which Weber's conception draws on technical and mechanical imagery:

> Weber's talk of "precision," "stability" and "reliability" points to the direct connection between bureaucracy and mechanisation that he sometimes makes quite explicit. Bureaucracy, he says, is a "human machine": the formal rationality of technique applies with equal relevance to human social organisation as to the control of the material world. (1983: 202)

On the other hand, work division entails sizable overhead costs. Someone must design the work segments, oversee, and coordinate the divided work. A horizontal division of labor is usually accompanied by a vertical hierarchy providing oversight—a separation of production from administrative work. Also, the technologies associated with high levels of specialization are likely to be special-purpose machinery of a sort that is dedicated to producing a particular product or service. Such machines increase the rigidity of production, so that long-term productivity requires the continuing expansion of markets for uniform goods (Piore and Sable, 1984: 26–28).

According to these well-known arguments, the division of labor supports the application of technology and rationalized procedures to work, increases the scale of work organizations and their markets, and gives rise to a managerial hierarchy (Chandler 1977). These developments unfold because they are associated with increasing productivity, heightened efficiency of operations, and greater profitability for owners. Rational system analysts assert that these processes are fundamental to the appearance and growth of organizations. As the administrative theorist Luther Gulick concludes, "work division is the foundation of organization; indeed, the reason for organization" (Gulick and Urwick, 1937: 3).

The Subordination of Workers

These benign efficiency-based views of the division of labor were challenged during the 1970s by critical theorists, who drew on and elaborated Marxist critiques of industrial organization. Of the two giants of European social thought, the influence of one of them, Max Weber, on organizational theory was apparent from the beginning—indeed, in many ways, it was the beginning! The effect of the second, Karl Marx, though widely felt in many areas of inquiry, did not seriously begin to make waves in work on organizations until much later.[5] Organization theorists such as Albrow (1970),

---

[5]For lucid reviews connecting Marx's insights to more recent organizational work, see Burrell and Morgan (1979: 279–392) and Tilly and Tilly (1998: 2–35).

Burawoy (1982), Clegg and Dunkerley (1977) and, especially, Collins (1975) combined Weberian and Marxian themes and connected the latter with other work on social conflict to arrive at a general critical theory of organizations.

Consistent with the origins of the natural system perspective, the Marxist approach began essentially as a critique of the dominant rationalist views, and of the mainstream natural system models as well, particularly those developed by Barnard and the human relations school. Marxists argue that organizational structures are not, as they claim to be, rational systems for performing work in the most efficient manner; rather, they are power systems designed to maximize control and profits. Work is divided and sub-divided not to improve efficiency but to "deskill" workers, to displace discretion from workers to managers, and to create artificial divisions among the work force (Braverman, 1974; Hardy and Clegg, 1996). While recognizing that all social structures involve role differentiation, Marxists argue that the minute division of labor that developed in the early days of industrialization was aimed more at maximizing managerial control than at achieving productive efficiency. In their famous tract, Marx and Engels (1955 trans.: 65) describe how in the factories of capitalist systems, the worker "becomes an appendage of the machine, and it is only the most simple, most monotonous and most easily acquired knack, that is required of him." Marx argued that the type of work division developed in these organizations destroyed the craft skills of workers:

> Hence, in the place of the hierarchy of specialized workmen that characterizes manufacture, there steps, in the automatic factory, a tendency to equalize and reduce to one and the same level every kind of work that has to be done by the minders of the machines. (Marx, 1954 trans.: 420)

Braverman and Marglin amplify Marx's position. The dissection of work separates workers from their products; deskills workers, turning artisans into operatives; increases the potential pool of workers, thereby weakening the job security of each; and segments workers, fragmenting their common experience and undermining their class consciousness (Braverman, 1974). Not only does the division of labor reduce the power of workers, it also increases and legitimates the power of managers. Returning to Adam Smith's pin factory, Marglin insists that

> Without specialization, the capitalist had no essential role to play in the production process. . . . Separating the tasks assigned to each workman was the sole means by which the capitalist could, in the days preceding costly machinery, ensure that he would remain essential to the production process as integrator of these separate operations into a product for which a wide market existed. (1974: 38)

Indeed, dividing work creates and justifies many managerial and technical roles: not only that of integrator but also those of designer of the work process, recruiter, trainer, inspector, troubleshooter, procurer of supplies, securer of markets, and so forth. In short, work division leads to the bureaucratization of organizations (Edwards, 1979).

Hierarchy develops not as a rational means of coordination but as an instrument of control and a means of accumulating capital through the appropriation of surplus value (Edwards, 1979; Marglin, 1974). Human relations and an emphasis on cooperative systems are misguided because they do not challenge the fundamental exploitative nature of organizations. Indeed, they help to shore it up by assuming a congruence of goals and by providing managers with new psychological tools for controlling workers and with new arguments justifying this control (Bendix, 1956; Braverman, 1974). As Alvesson and Deetz point out:

> To a large extent studies of the "human" side of organizations (climate, job enrichment, quality of work life, worker participation programs, and culture) have been transformed from alternative ends into new means to be brought under technical control for extending the dominant group interests of the corporation. (1996: 200)

From the perspective of critical theorists, *rationality is an ideology*—the use of ideas to legitimate existing arrangements and to deflect criticism of those with excessive power by depersonalizing the system of relations (see Zey-Ferrell and Aiken, 1981).

In addition to arguing that discretion was removed from workers and transferred to managers (and their growing technical staff), Marx insisted that the surplus value created by productive labor was stripped from workers and grasped by manager-capitalists. Although Marx and many other critical analysts have condemned this practice, Marglin acknowledges that this form of "enforced savings" created the surplus capital that led to the subsequent technological revolution. He argues that "the social function of hierarchical work organization is not technical efficiency, but accumulation" (1974: 34).

On the one hand, Marx argued that the concentration of workers in factories would increased their class consciousness and the will and ability to collectively organize to protect their interests, while, on the other hand as noted, the specialization of workers undermined solidarity. The differentiation of work leads to the segmentation of interests (Gordon, Edwards, and Reich, 1982). Critical theorists point out that workers are disadvantaged in their struggle with management in advanced capitalist societies because workers have no alternative to working in the capitalist market; they are hampered by unemployment that creates a reserve army of competitors for jobs; and the power of capital is backed by the authority of the state (Tilly and Tilly, 1998: 9).

But a division of interests is not restricted to workers. Both Stark and Burawoy suggest that Marx and Braverman have overstated the cohesion and unity of managers under capitalism and understated those of workers. Stark emphasizes the resourcefulness of workers who have found ways to counter-act and undermine the effectiveness of the new control systems. Some changes introduced to improve managerial control have actually increased the power of workers:

> Assembly line production, for example, decreases the degree of direct coopera-tion among workers, but the objective interdependence of workers also increases their ability to disrupt production either through individual acts of sabotage, collective activity, or the more passive form of simply not showing up for work. (Stark, 1980: 93)

And, as we noted in our discussion of scientific management in Chapter 2, these attempts to rationalize the work process were resisted not only by work-ers but also by managers who did not want to see their powers usurped by engineers. As Burawoy points out, control over the labor process emerges as a result, "not only of struggle between capital and labour, but also of struggle among the different agents of capital . . . one cannot assume the existence of a cohesive managerial and capitalist class that automatically recognizes its true interests" (1985: 46).

We also need to take into account the effects of the specific social circumstances within which interests develop and struggles take place. This more contextualized approach is stressed by Granovetter and Tilly:

> Differences in bargaining power among the actors . . . depend on the resources each actor brings to the bargaining and on the interpersonal networks in which the actors are embedded. Workers' success in strikes depends, for example, not only on their ability to hold out without wages, but also on their capacity to keep out strikebreakers and to enlist the support of third parties, including government officials. (1988:181; see also, Tilly and Tilly 1998)

Wider political contexts, such as the posture and policies of the state, are also relevant, as Burawoy (1985) and Sabel (1982) emphasize. It is also argued that more general social values, like the great importance placed in the United States on individualism, has undermined the power of unions in this country compared to those advocating more social democratic values.

In short, while it is important to recognize the power aspects of the emergence of hierarchical organizations—as well as their effects on the divi-sion of labor or the structuring of work processes—it is an oversimplification to view all of the power advantages as being on any one side, or even to pre-sume that there are only two sides. The work setting is indeed a "contested terrain," as Edwards (1979) has argued, with various parties vying for control and for a greater share of the value created there. In contemporary organ-izations, it is not only workers, but also managers who find their jobs are no longer secure.

LABOR MARKETS AND ORGANIZATIONAL BOUNDARIES

Internal Labor Markets

Private Companies. The changing saga of how firms and agencies structure their relations with employees illustrates the complex nature of the social boundaries of organizations. During the greater part of the twentieth century, organizations in the United States were involved in developing more formalized and bureaucratized approaches to labor relations. As technologies became more complex, companies were more adversely affected by labor turnover and unrest. Henry Ford was among the first (in 1913) to reduce the arbitrary power of foremen, centralize hiring and firing in an employment department, and raise wages for workers with at least six months seniority (Cappelli, 2000). Rational production-oriented factors led employers to develop stronger ties to their workers. But, as Jacoby (1985) points out,

> The historical record indicates that the employment reforms introduced during World War I and after 1933 were attributable not so much to competitive market forces as to the growing power of the unions and the ascendance of the personnel department over other branches of management. (p. 277)

Improvements for workers resulted from their increased organizational power—both within and external to firms and agencies (and, of course, the two were related).

Gradually during this period, the classical economic view of the employment relation as mediated by simple market processes began to give way to a view that labor was a unique type of commodity—supplied by "human beings endowed with economic, physical, psychological and social needs, who participate as citizens in a democratic society"—deserving of special protections from the state (Kochan, Katz, and McKersie, 1994: 23). This view was consolidated by a series of laws during the 1930s giving rise to what Kochen and colleagues term the "the New Deal industrial relations system." Under pressure from the increasing power of unions, a growing personnel bureaucracy provided improved job security, medical and retirement benefits, training and promotion opportunities. Jobs were highly formalized with explicit rules and classification of task activities. Core production and management jobs were incorporated into *internal labor markets* (ILMs), defined as "an administrative unit, such as a manufacturing plant, within which the pricing and allocation of labor is governed by a set of administrative rules and procedures" rather than market forces (Doeringer and Piore, 1971: 1). ILMs are characterized by a cluster of jobs that are hierarchically structured into one or more job ladders representing a progression of knowledge or skills. New employees enter only at lower rungs while upper positions are filled primarily by internal promotion. "The typical employment contract protected a firm's long-term white- and blue-collar employees against competition from outside job applications for the better paid and more responsible positions" (Knoke 2001: 169). Such employees enjoyed high job security and were expected to exhibit loyalty to the company.[6]

Improved protections and benefits for workers during the early decades of the twentieth century grew largely in response to the increase in union power, which at its peak (as measured by numbers of members) in 1945 represented over 35 percent of workers in the private sector labor force. However, the power of unions extended far beyond unionized companies. Personnel policies in nonunion firms paid wages and provided benefits in line with unionized firms partly because of a "threat effect"—to forestall unionizing activities—and partly because union models established industry-wide normative standards of fair wages and working conditions (Jacoby, 1985: 250; Osterman, 1999: 30). And, due to mobilization efforts during World War II the federal government, acting through such agencies as the War Production Board and the War Manpower Commission to stabilize employment in key industries, fueled the growth of bureaucratic personnel systems and employment protections.

> Federal activities during the war fostered bureaucratization of employment in two ways. First, early employment-stabilization plans . . . provided models of employment practices that often extended to entire industries . . . thereby encouraging isomorphism among firms. Second, . . . the government-led movement to reduce turnover provided strong incentives for firms to establish or extend personnel departments that could analyze and justify labor needs and institute bureaucratic mechanisms to reduce turnover. (Baron, Dobbin, and Jennings, 1986: 373)

A final factor stimulating the growth of bureaucratic employment systems within the private sector was the professionalization of personnel managers, who sought to strengthen their position within the organization and gain increased legitimacy in management circles. Baron and colleagues (1986: 373–77) assemble data showing that the numbers and influence of personnel managers and departments grew rapidly after the war and well into the 1970s.

Public Agencies. We have focused on the development of ILMs within the private sector, but it is important to recognize that parallel developments were occurring in the public sector. Throughout the nineteenth century, the "spoils system," by which winning politicians appointed their friends and cronies to public office, came increasingly under attack. As the size of the public sector grew and the administrative structure began to require not just

---

[6]Note that in this conception it is not necessarily the case that all jobs in a given firm are organized in ILMs (Althauser, 1989). Estimates based on data collected on a representative sample of employees in the United States suggest that approximately half of the establishments in which these employees worked, in 1991, met minimal criteria as ILM for their "core" occupations (Kalleberg et al., 1996: 94).

secretaries and clerks, but also specialists and managers, serious reform efforts commenced in the 1870s under Ulysses Grant, but it was not until the assassination of President Garfield in 1881 by a disgruntled job seeker that a serious effort began to end the corrupt and inefficient system. The resulting Civil Service System began by focusing efforts on recruitment, relying primarily on examinations; later reforms stressed the creation of job ladders and promotion from within (DiPrete, 1989). The system gradually expanded throughout the end of the nineteenth and beginning of the twentieth centuries, and under the impetus of the Progressive movement, elaborate job classifications with linkages to work qualifications were introduced. The creation of a union in 1917 afforded employees a strong role in setting wages and securing more equitable job assignments. Throughout the twentieth century, civil service rules covered an increasing number of positions; and other public bodies, first states and then cities, gradually adopted similar forms in their own administrative units (DePrete, 1989; Tolbert and Zucker, 1983). Still, the line between the political and the administrative remains a tortured and contested one, as in the top echelons, political appointees work side by side with "supergrade" civil service executives, types of positions are regularly reclassified, and political appointees are frequently blanketed into formerly civil service jobs in the closing days of a president's term (Heclo, 1977). The battle between impartiality and merit on the one hand and responsiveness to political leadership continues unabated.

Explaining ILMs. As this brief history illustrates, various forces operated to create and diffuse employment systems during the past century in the United States. (Similar movements produced even more significant protections for labor in Western Europe due to the presence of a stronger social democratic movement in these countries [Esping-Andersen, 1985].) As we elaborate in Chapter 9, Williamson's (1975; 1981) transaction costs framework—a rational-open system perspective—argues that the most important influence on what type of labor market is created is the *specificity of human assets*. The "human assets" of an organization are, of course, the skills and knowledge of its personnel. Specificity refers not simply to the extent of specialization of knowledge and skills, but also to the degree to which these skills are transferable across employers. The deeper and more specialized employee' skills are in the view of a specific employer, the more dependent is the employer on the employee, and vice versa, so that it is in the interests of both to create a "protective governance structure, lest productive values be sacrificed if the employment relation is unwittingly severed" (p. 563). An ILM serves the employee's interests by providing the prospects of secure employment and upward mobility through a regularized career of advancement, with increased earnings accompanying progression in skills. And the employer's interests are served because valuable workers in whom investments in training have been made are less likely to desert to a competitor.

In a related discussion, Williamson and Ouchi distinguish between "hard" and "soft" contracting:

> Under hard contracting, the parties remain relatively autonomous, each is expected to press his or her interests vigorously, and contracting is relatively complete. Soft contracting, by contrast, presumes much closer identity of interests between the parties, and formal contracts are much less complete. (1981: 361)

Soft contracting is characteristic of internal labor markets. It assumes a more elaborate governance structure (the personnel bureaucracy with its extensive rules and systems) and a higher level of investment and trust on the part of both employers and employees. In this sense, ILMs may be viewed as mechanisms for bringing employees more fully and firmly within the boundaries of an organization than is the case with external labor markets, in which the "hard" bargaining between employers and employees more closely resembles that occurring between two independent contractors.

The existence of ILMs is explained in a rather different manner by natural-open system theorists. Marxist theorists such as Edwards (1979) argue that internal labor markets are more likely to arise in "core" segments of the economy—in large and powerful firms that have obtained an oligopoly, or near monopoly, in their industries (Averitt, 1968). As these firms grow in size and complexity, they shift from simple hierarchical to technical to bureaucratic control systems. Edwards explains:

> *Bureaucratic* control, like technical control, differs from the simple forms of control in that it grows out of the formal structure of the firm, rather than simply emanating from the personal relationships between workers and bosses. But while *technical* control is embedded in the physical and technological aspects of production and is built into the design of machines and the industrial architecture of the plant, bureaucratic control is embedded in the social and organizational structure of the firm and is built into job categories, work rules, promotion procedures, discipline, wage scales, definitions of responsibilities, and the like. Bureaucratic control establishes the impersonal force of "company rules" or "company policy" as the basis for control. (1979: 131; emphasis added)

Because they rely on social definitions rather than technical distinctions, bureaucratic control structures can be elaborated with ease: the number of offices, levels, titles, and salary levels can be multiplied without limit. Moreover, incentives can be added to reward not simply effort and productivity, but also such qualities as dependability, loyalty, and commitment to the organization.

Marxists view ILMs as reflecting the greater power of some classes of workers to wrest economic advantages from employers, but they also view these structures as undermining the power of labor more generally by creating

> graded hierarchies that foster a docile "status" orientation and dissuade workers from utilizing the power implicit in their skills. Internal labor markets also

institutionalize cleavages among workers along racial, sexual, and ethnic lines, thereby reducing the likelihood of working-class cohesion. (Baron, 1984: 40)

Pfeffer and Cohen (1984) employed data from a sample of about 300 large organizations in the San Francisco Bay area to test alternative explanations of ILMs. Skill specificity, as measured by extensiveness of employer training, was positively associated with ILMs, providing support for the transaction cost arguments. However, extent of unionization and being located in a core industry were also associated with ILMs, providing support for both resource dependence and Marxist interpretations. In addition, Pfeffer and Cohen report that the development of ILMs was associated with the existence of a personnel department, a finding that supports an institutional interpretation of the spread of this structural form. These results are largely corroborated by Kalleberg and colleagues (1996) in their study of a nationally representative sample of organizations. They found that ILMs were more likely to occur in organizations that were larger, more bureaucratic, unionized, faced with asset specificity problems, and whose personnel decisions were made by a centralized personnel office.

Institutional theories are particularly useful in accounting for the diffusion of organizational structures and practices (see Chapter 10). In particular, the regulatory power of the nation-state and the normative influence of professional associations have played an important role in the spread of personnel departments and standardized employment practices (see Baron, Dobbin, and Jennings, 1986; Dobbin and Sutton, 1998; Dobbin et al., 1993; Scott, 2001a: 126–32).

Market-Mediated Employment

All of this theoretical and empirical attention to internal labor markets, their causes and consequences, may seem rather dated given recent developments in U.S. employment systems. Beginning during the mid-1980s and continuing up to the present time, many large corporations have engaged in extensive "downsizing" efforts that affect not only blue-collar and lower-level employers, but also white-collar workers and middle- and upper-level managers. Between 1979 and 1993, employment totals of the *Fortune* 500—the 500 largest corporate organizations in the United States—declined annually from 16.2 million employees in 1979 to 11.5 million in 1993 (Baumol, Blinder, and Wolff, 2003; Useem, 1996). As a consequence, there is much speculation in the popular and academic press about whether the "implicit contract" between management and workers—which promised promotion and job security to faithful and productive workers—has been repealed (see Blair and Kochan, 2000; Bluestone and Bluestone, 1992; Cappelli,1999; 2001; Kochan, Katz, and McKersie, 1994; Osterman, 1999). Informed observers report that conventional career paths through corporations no longer work: the rules for success in organizations have changed (see Arthur and Rousseau, 1996; Cappelli, 1999; Kotter, 1995). Multiple indicators suggest the breadth of changes that have occurred. Although median job tenure for workers twenty-five years and older eroded only slightly between 1983 and 2004, tenure decreased dramatically for some groups of workers. For example, the number of years on average that men between the ages of fifty-five and sixty-four had been with the same employer dropped from fifteen to ten years during this period (U.S. Bureau of Labor Statistics, 2004). On the other hand, during these years, the proportion of contingent or temporary workers in the workforce has increased from the 1970s up to the present, although the number of temporary workers still remains relatively small, roughly 10 percent of the workforce (Carré et al., 2000; Finegold, Levenson, and Van Buren, 2003; Mishel, Bernstein, and Schmitt, 1999).

Increasingly, firms have discovered the benefits of various forms of *externalization* of the workforce. Pfeffer and Baron (1988) identify three ways in which the attachment between firms and workers may be decreased: locational, temporal, and administrative.

- Reduced *locational* attachment is exemplified by the increasing number of workers who perform their activities off-site, for example, "home work" or "flexiplace" arrangements. Such arrangements are encouraged by developments in computers that support home work not only through rapid information transfer but also by increasing the ease with which work can be monitored from a distance.
- Reduction in *temporal* attachment refers to the increasing tendency for organizations to employ part-time or short-term workers, who often lack job benefits and job security.
- In addition, increasing numbers of workers are *administratively* detached from the employment setting in the sense that they are hired on specific short-term contracts or are employed on another firm's payroll—for example, a temporary staffing agency.

Temporary employment organizations have grown rapidly during the past two decades as have contracting-out arrangements. In 2002, the personnel services industry, which is comprised primarily of temporary help agencies, employed 3.2 million workers, up from 247,000 in 1973 (Mishel, Bernstein, and Allegretto, 2005). Three of the five largest private employers in the United States are temporary agencies; Manpower, a temporary employment agency, now ranks as the largest company in the United States. Barley and Kunda report that "between 70 and 80 percent of companies in the United Sates use some type of contingent labor, including part-time workers" (2004: 37).

Organizations pursue externalization strategies for numerous reasons: to evade restrictions on hiring (public sector organizations often circumvent hiring restrictions by contracting-out), to better focus attention and resources on the firm's distinctive competence, to pay reduced salaries and eliminate benefits, as a screening device for hiring, and to increase flexibility, both with respect to number of employees and mix of skills. Pfeffer and Baron comment:

> Ironically, then, because externalization enhances flexibility and focus, it may actually be an essential concomitant of human resource policies that emphasize long-term employment, commitment of the permanent workforce, and a shared vision or distinctive competence. In order to adapt to changes in the environment, firms need to have some way of changing staffing levels and work assignments and to do so without reneging on the implicit contracts held with the permanent workforce. Thus, the very elements of bureaucratic control and clan control that promise careers and continuity in return for loyalty and commitment may require a buffer work force to absorb fluctuations in environmental demand. (1988: 274)

Economic "dualism" may not only be an important characteristic of the economy—that is, the differentiation of industries into "core" and "periphery" components; it may also become an increasingly important feature of many individual firms. These trends are accompanied by problems for workers and firms, which we discuss below.

The downsizing and outsourcing by corporations of work and workers is also occurring in response to the growing power of stockholders who provide the necessary capital and who increasingly embrace a financial conception of the firm. Short-term financial gains can be garnered by firms that reduce workers or sell off parts of the company, although such steps may not serve the long-range interest of the firm or of the society in which it operates (Baumol, Blinder, and Wolff, 2003).

All of these trends—reduction in the prospect of lifetime employment, reliance on external rather than internal labor markets, use of temporary and contract employees—are characterized by Cappelli (1999; 2000) as "market-mediated" employment strategies. His historical survey wryly notes that such "modern" approaches to managing labor return us "back to the future"—to practices that prevailed in the early stages of capitalism at the turn of the nineteenth century, when workers had little job security and large portions of production tasks were contracted out to independent units. The new employment relations are "less like marriage or dating than serial monogamy—several long-term relationships that either party can end unilaterally, each shaped by possibilities" (1999: 35). Clearly, old arrangements between employees and employers are undergoing significant revision.

HIGH-PERFORMANCE WORK ORGANIZATIONS

In a pioneering early study, Burns and Stalker (1961) studied a rather diverse group of about twenty industrial firms in Great Britain. Their sample included rather traditional textile companies, engineering firms, and a number of firms attempting to move into the rapidly growing market of electronics.

Early in their field research, the investigators were struck by the presence of two quite distinct management styles—which they labeled the *mechanistic* and the *organic*. They noted that the two approaches tended to be associated with differing industries, or, more accurately, with differing types of industrial environments. The mechanistic firms were to be found in relatively stable environments, the organic in more rapidly changing environments. Burns and Stalker describe these two organizational systems as follows:

> In mechanistic systems the problems and tasks facing the concern as a whole are broken down into specialisms. Each individual pursues his task as something distinct from the real tasks of the concern as a whole, as if it were the subject of a subcontract. "Somebody at the top" is responsible for seeing to its relevance. The technical methods, duties, and powers attached to each functional role are precisely designed. Interaction within management tends to be vertical . . .
>
> Organic systems are adapted to unstable conditions, when problems and requirements for action arise which cannot be broken down and distributed among specialist roles within a clearly defined hierarchy. Individuals have to perform their special tasks in the light of their knowledge of the tasks of the firm as a whole. Jobs lose much of their formal definition in terms of methods, duties and powers, which have to be redefined continually by interaction with others participating in a task. Interaction runs laterally as much as vertically. Communication between people of different ranks tends to resemble lateral consultation rather than vertical command. (1961: 5–6)

Organic systems, in response to conditions of high complexity and uncertainty, represent instances "where organization becomes an invertebrate process rather than a structure" (Grandori, 1987: 93).

Based on his analysis of Japanese organizational structure, Ouchi (1980; 1981) elaborated these arguments, identifying what he termed a *clan* system of organization as particularly suited to handling complex and interdependent tasks. Although clan systems are distinguished from formalized bureaucracies by a number of elements—including nonspecialized roles and career paths, implicit and internalized control mechanisms, holistic rather than segmented concerns, and slow and diffuse evaluation—Ouchi argues that their most important feature is the long-term, often lifetime, employment offered to participants. This characteristic was identified quite early as a distinctive feature of Japanese organizations (Abegglen, 1958; Dore, 1973). Ouchi proposes it as a defining characteristic of all clan organizations—which include not only Japanese organizations, but also many others including some of the more progressive U.S. firms, such as Hewlett-Packard, IBM, and Eastman Kodak (Ouchi, 1981). However, under increased pressures posed for firms by globalization for cost cutting, long-term commitments to workers are being curtailed if not eliminated (Ahmadjian and Robinson, 2001).

Clan systems are one of several modes of what are termed "high-performance work organizations" (HPWOs). Among the models that have been included within this emerging category are the "sociotechical systems" as previously described, "lean production" systems, as exemplified by Toyota (Womack, Jones, and Roos, 1990), "flexible specialization," as reflected in Italian industrial districts (Brusco, 1982), and diversified quality production systems, such as those operating in Germany (Streeck, 1991). While these systems differ in important respects (see Appelbaum and Batt,1994) all emphasize (1) a dismantling of the Fordist strait-jacket of narrowly designed, specialized jobs in favor of broader, more flexible work roles; (2) reduction of the gap in decision-making authority separating managers and workers to afford greater discretion to workers; (3) replacement of isolated, individuated work roles with work teams whose members collectively assume some of the functions formerly reserved to managers, and (4) design of governance structures that support and sustain the conduct of work across conventional organizational boundaries.

How widespread are such HPWOs? Utilizing data from a representative survey of U.S. establishments at two points in time, Paul Osterman (1999) examined changes occurring between 1992 and 1997 in the adoption of selected HPWO practices, such as quality circles, job rotation, and self-managed work teams. Survey results indicate a rather substantial increase in the use of HPWO practices during this period, to the point where almost 40 percent of the firms had adopted three or more such practices by the end of the study period.[7] Do firms adopting HPWO approaches also utilize more temporary and contingent workers than other firms, as Pfeffer and Baron suggested? It appears not. Osterman's results suggest that establishments that are more advanced in the use of HPWO practices tend to rely less on contingent and outsourcing strategies; and they also have lower ratios of managers than more conventional forms. However, contrary to the arguments of Ouchi and most labor relations scholars, HPWOs were more likely than conventional organizations to lay off workers and, although HPWO practices have been shown to be associated with productivity gains, these gains were not reflected in improved earnings for HPWO workers. Osterman concludes:

> It is more than a little surprising that employers have been so successful in spreading HPWOs even in the face of restructuring and layoffs. Recall that at the core of these new work systems is that employees are more forthcoming with their ideas about production and service and are more focused than before on the success of the firm and its relationship with its customers. That this higher level of employee commitment should exist, and even grow, in the face of reduced commitment on the part of the firm to its workforce is striking. On the one hand it reinforces the notion that employees find these new systems attractive. It also suggests that fear and insecurity have deep and broad consequences, influence a wide range of behavior, and have fundamentally shifted the terms of trade in the labor market. (1999: 114–15)

---

[7]Because these are survey data based on the reports of managers, they probably somewhat overstate the actual amount of various innovative practices. Such exaggeration is a common manifestation of the "learning-doing" gap (Pfeffer and Sutton, 2000).

PROBLEMS FOR PARTICIPANTS

Although organizations provide many important opportunities and benefits for their participants, it is important that we take note of some of the problems they pose for many of their members. We briefly consider three types of frequently cited difficulties: problems of alienation, inequity, and insecurity.

Alienation

Much time and attention have been devoted over the years to the impact of organizations on the personal characteristics of their participants. There are many claims and considerable evidence regarding these effects—and most of them are conflicting! At least since the time of Marx and down to the present, observers have pointed to the debilitating consequences of organizational involvement, and in particular, employment, for individual participants. These destructive processes are often summarized under the concept of alienation—a concept with enough facets and varied interpretations to serve as an adequate umbrella under which to gather a quite varied set of criticisms.

Even Marx, who more than any other theorist called attention to the importance of alienation of workers, identified several possible forms of alienation (Faunce, 1968; Marx, 1963 trans.). Workers may be alienated from the *product* of their labor. Labor gives value to the objects it creates, but as a worker loses control over his product, it comes to exist "independently, outside himself, and alien to him and . . . stands opposed to him as an autonomous power" (Marx, 1963 trans.: 122–23). Workers can also be alienated from the *process* of production. This occurs to the extent that

> the work is external to the worker, that it is not part of his nature, and that, consequently, he does not fulfill himself in his work but denies himself, has a feeling of misery rather than well-being, does not develop freely his mental and physical energies but is physically exhausted and mentally debased. . . . His work is not voluntary but imposed, forced labor. (Marx, 1963 trans.: 124–25)

As a consequence of the first two processes, workers become alienated from both self and others in the work setting. Marx explains:

> The alien being to whom labour and the product of labour belong, to whose service labour is devoted, and to whose enjoyment the product of labour goes, can only be man himself. If the product of labour does not belong to the worker, but confronts him as an alien power, this can only be because it belongs to a man other than the worker. (1963 trans.: 130)

Enter the capitalist and the argument that it is not work that alienates, but exploitation of workers by the misuse of power.

Marx's arguments and insights have been elaborated by Seeman and Israel. Like Marx, Seeman (1959; 1975) views alienation as a multifaceted concept. He identifies six varieties:

1. *Powerlessness*—the sense of little control over events
2. *Meaninglessness*—the sense of incomprehensibility of personal and social affairs
3. *Normlessness*—use of socially unapproved means for the achievement of goals
4. *Cultural estrangement*—rejection of commonly held values and standards
5. *Self-estrangement*—engagement in activities that are not intrinsically rewarding
6. *Social isolation*—the sense of exclusion or rejection

Seeman argues that powerlessness and self-estrangement are the two types of alienation that have most salience in the workplace, and these seem most consistent with Marx's distinctions. Numerous measures, including several multiple-item scales, have been developed to empirically assess each of these dimensions (see Seeman, 1975).

The survey approach to measuring alienation tends to regard these conditions as subjective, social psychological states. Israel (1971) takes strong exception to this conception, insisting that alienation is more accurately and usefully viewed as an objective condition of the social structure, not a subjective attitude or disposition. Because of psychological manipulation or false consciousness, individuals are not always able to recognize that they are alienated. Sentiments may not accurately reflect circumstances.

In spite of Israel's concerns, most empirical studies on alienation rely on data obtained from individual respondents who report their feeling or attitudes—for example, work satisfaction and dissatisfaction, levels of interest or commitment—or their behavior—for example, turnover, absenteeism, physical and mental health symptoms. Most surveys conducted in this country over the past half century report (1) generally high levels of worker satisfaction and morale, but (2) large variation in satisfaction and symptoms across differing occupational strata and work situations. These surveys also show that higher satisfaction tends to be associated with such factors as intrinsic interest of the work, extent of worker control, level of pay and economic security, and opportunities for social interaction (see Blauner, 1964; Rousseau, 1977; Special Task Force, 1973).

Whereas much of this earlier work was based on a relatively passive model of worker behavior, later studies embraced the view that workers respond more "proactively" to their environments (J. Scott, 1985). A quantitative analysis of a large number of ethnographic studies of worker responses to a variety of workplace conditions by Hodson (1996) suggests that while workers respond more positively to organizations supporting worker participation in decision making than to more bureaucratic or assembly-line systems, craft organizations continued to evoke the highest levels of worker satisfaction and pride.

The most impressive body of research relating characteristics of work to personality measures is that conducted by Kohn and associates (see Kohn and

Schooler, 1983; for a summary and assessment, see Spenner, 1988). Variables employed to measure jobs included complexity of work and closeness of supervision, job pressures, risks and rewards, and location in the hierarchy. Personality dimensions include intellectual flexibility, self-directedness, and sense of well-being or distress. The nature of the data (longitudinal) and analysis techniques (structural equations) allowed the investigators to distinguish effects in both directions. Their results suggest that more of the effects of job on personality were contemporaneous whereas more of the effects of personality on (reports of) job conditions were lagged, that is, only apparent after several years. The strongest effects were associated with work complexity. Spenner summarizes the results:

> Considering all the effects, components of occupational self-direction are most important, particularly substantive complexity. . . . men [sic] in self-directed jobs become less authoritarian, less self-deprecatory, less fatalistic, and less conformist in their ideas while becoming more self-confident and more responsible to standards of morality. (1988: 74–75)

These and related studies provide convincing evidence that the nature of work and working conditions can have significant effects on personality.

As the number and variety of service occupations expand in contemporary society, an interesting new variant of self-estrangement has arisen that requires workers to simulate emotions they do not feel. Workers such as flight attendants, retail clerks, and food servers perform "emotional labor" in that they are required to "induce or suppress feeling in order to sustain the outward countenance that produces the proper state of mind in others" whom they serve (Hochchild, 1983: 7). The manipulation of emotion exacts its costs on the performer, who is subject to "burnout" and to feelings of insincerity and inauthenticity; and their audiences may come to discount such "phony" commercialized feelings. Hochchild estimates that about one-third of all U.S. workers currently have jobs that require them to engage in some emotional labor; however, more than half of all women workers hold such jobs (p. 11).

A number of analysts have claimed that the impact of organizations on their participants extends far beyond the walls of the organization itself. Argyris (1957; 1973) summarizes several studies that indicate that workers who experience "constraint and isolation" on the job carry these attitudes into their free time: such workers are less involved in organized leisure, community, or political activities. Kanter (1977b) reviewed a number of studies that suggest that both men's and women's occupational experiences have important implications for their family roles. She asserts that these studies contradict the "myth of separate worlds" perpetuated by companies that do not wish to assume responsibility for the effects of their policies and practices on the "personal" lives of their employees. The "myth" is also sustained by social scientists who tend to specialize in studying organizations or families but not their interdependence (see also, Ferber, O'Farrell, and Allen, 1991;

Gerstel and Gross, 1987). Similarly, Ouchi argues that organizations have a vested interest in failing to recognize their psychological casualties:

> The costs of psychological failure are not borne entirely by the firm, but rather are externalized to the society generally. That is, employees who reach the point of emotional disability, who become unsatisfactory workers, are the first to be laid off during depressions or, in extreme cases, are fired. The firm which has "used up" people emotionally does not have to face the cost of restoring them. In much the same manner that firms were able until recently to pollute the air and the water without paying the costs of using up these resources, they continue to be able to pollute our mental health with impunity. (1979: 36–37)

Kanter argued in the late 1970s that "a major social welfare issue of the decades to come" is likely to be focused on the question, "Can organizations more fully and responsibly take into account their inevitable interface with the personal lives of their participants?" (1977b: 89), but more than three decades later, most observers would conclude that little has changed.

Social critics correctly accuse many organizations of generating alienation among their participants that spills over into the wider social structure. While such problems require attention and correction, a long line of social analysts from Saint-Simon (1952 trans.) through Barnard (1938) to Ouchi (1981) and Peters and Waterman (1982) have gone to the opposite extreme, looking to organizations to provide the primary source of social integration, personal identity, and meaning in modern society. Wolin calls attention to the underlying anxiety and elitist stance that nurtures this point of view:

> The fondness for large scale organization displayed by contemporary writers largely stems from anxieties provoked by the emergence of the mass. They see organizations as mediating institutions, shaping disoriented individuals to socially useful behavior and endowing them with a desperately needed sense of values. These large entities supply the stabilizing centers, which not only integrate and structure the amorphous masses, but control them as well. (1960: 427)

On the one hand, we embrace the concern that organizations all too frequently serve as a source of alienation and estrangement to their participants, but, on the other hand, we cannot accept the view that employment organizations should become the principal centers of meaning and of moral and social integration in contemporary society. As indicated in Chapter 13, we see the development of special-purpose organizations as being closely associated with the emergence of the ideology of individualism, including the doctrine of natural rights and the value of individual freedom. The development of the rational-legal mode replacing traditional forms, to use Weber's terms, signals the emergence of norms and other institutional arrangements that place restrictions on the extent and scope of power exercised by any particular organization in relation to the individual. The healthy participant is one who is "partially involved" in many diverse and competing organizations as well as in the wider institutions comprising a civil society (Bellah et al., 1991).

Inequity

Formal organizations are expected to be fair in their treatment of personnel. Universalistic criteria of hiring, promotion, and pay are purported to operate, and achievement is supposed to replace ascription as the basis for distributing rewards. There is no question that in the United States there is long-term evidence that more universalistic, equalitarian standards of employment are being utilized, with improvements in occupational status attainment for both women and minorities (Farley, 1984; Featherman and Hauser, 1978). These trends continue into the recent period as shown by an examination of data from the General Social Survey for the period 1972 to 1987. Analyses conducted by DiPrete and Grusky (1990) show that ascriptive processes continue to recede; however, there is also evidence of a gradual slowdown in the rate of change. The timing of this slowdown coincides with the onset of more conservative federal policies during the 1980s, when many of the earlier equal opportunity initiatives were either weakened or eliminated. Moreover, since the 1970s earnings inequality between lower and higher ranks of employees has steadily increased in most Western countries, but especially the United States (Tilly and Tilly 1998: 213). Particularly dramatic are changes occurring in recent decades in executive compensation in the United States. In 2004, the average chief executive officer (CEO) of a *Fortune* 500 company—the largest corporations in the United States—received a total compensation of $10.2 million. In 1963, CEOs made 24 times as much as workers; in 2003 they made 185 times as much (Mishel, Bernstein, and Allegretto, 2005: 214). While apologists point to the need for incentives to encourage risk taking, studies suggest that there is not a strong correlation between executive compensation and company performance (see Jensen and Murphy, 1990).

In spite of advances throughout the twentieth century, a substantial disparity remains between the advancement and earnings of men in comparison to women and whites in comparison to nonwhites. Race and gender characteristics of employees continue to be important factors affecting their opportunities and outcomes (Cox, Nkomo, and Welch, 2000). In the United States, African American men steadily increased their earnings throughout the middle of the twentieth century, moving from average earnings of 43 percent of their white counterparts in 1940 to 73 percent in 1980. However, "the trend toward a black-white convergence in earnings ceased in the mid-1970s as industrial restructuring took hold" (Farley, 1996: 248). Similarly, in the United States during the 1980s, women earned only about 70 percent of the wage rate of men, and these differences have changed little between 1920 and 1980 (Marini, 1989). Nevertheless, because of the loss of blue-collar jobs in the manufacturing sector, women have fared better than men in recent decades. On average, employed men in 2003 earned less than men did in the early 1970s, but employed women earned more (Mishel, Bernstein, and Allegretto, 2005).

Sociological analyses of labor markets emphasize that, in order to understand the distribution of social and economic rewards to workers, we must not only examine the "supply side" characteristics of the individual workers—their aspirations and human capital—but also the "demand side" characteristics of jobs, their numbers, variety, and linkages. And, as emphasized in our earlier discussion of labor markets, most jobs are defined by and embedded in organizations (Baron and Bielby, 1980; Tilly and Tilly 1998).

The conventional assumption is that jobs exist independently of their occupants, but research by Baron, Bielby, and others suggests that the more powerful and advantaged groups (e.g., white males) are able to develop more elaborate and differentiated job positions and titles than less privileged groups. Jobs remain highly segregated by gender. At the beginning of the twenty-first century, in the United States, the sex segregation index for occupations was 0.52, meaning that roughly half of the employed women (or men) would need to change occupations in order to achieve an equal gender distribution (see Padavic and Reskin, 2002: 67). At the organizational level, gender segregation of jobs is even more pronounced. Research conducted in a diverse sample of organizations within California by Bielby and Baron shows that even within seemingly integrated occupations:

> Work done by both men and women is often done in distinct organizational settings, and when enterprises employ both sexes in the same occupation, they typically assign them different job titles. Once established, sex labels of job titles acquire tremendous inertia, even when similar work is done by the opposite sex elsewhere in the same establishment or in other settings. (1986: 787)

Research comparing the occupations dominated by men or women shows that "women's jobs are not usually *less* skilled than men's, but women's and men's jobs generally require *different kinds* of skills" (England, 1992). These are the types of findings that fuel efforts to ensure comparable pay for comparable work.

Feminist theorists carry the critique of modern organizations well beyond the accusation that qualified women do not receive equal treatment or compensation. Recall Martin and Knopoff's (1997) arguments that universalistic criteria that appear to be gender-neutral can disadvantage women who may be unable to make full-time work commitments or lack access to training opportunities. Conventional discussions that ignore the interdependence of work and family responsibilities, that treat the former as public and masculine and the latter as private and feminine, distort reality in a manner that disadvantages women (see Bose, Feldberg, and Sokoloff, 1987; Martin, 1990; Parcel, 1999).

A different kind of inequity has arisen among organizations in their treatment of employees during the last two decades. The downsizing activities of many organizations during the past decade has removed large numbers of regular, secure positions and increasingly substituted the use of part-time, temporary, low-wage employees. In addition to giving organizations greater flexibility, the use of contract and temporary workers also enables companies to secure major savings because they are not obligated to provide employees benefits, such as health insurance and contributions to pension funds. The share of people below the poverty line who hold full-time, year-round jobs has been on the rise over the last quarter of a century. In 2003, 10.9 percent of the poor in the United States were working full-time, year-round, compared to 7.7 percent in 1978 (Stawser, 2005: 62). Harrison (1994) regards these trends toward increasing polarization in earnings as "the dark side of flexible production": corporate flexibility is purchased at the cost of decreased job security and reduced benefits for millions of workers (see also Shulman, 2003).

Insecurity

Earlier in this chapter we described the apparent termination of the "implicit contract," as increasing numbers of workers can no longer count on long-term employment from a given company. Many kinds of change have occurred to reduce the economic security of workers.

Downsizing has occurred on a large scale beginning during the early 1990s and the process continues up to the present time. *Downsizing* refers to the elimination of "permanent" jobs from the workforce of an organization, including middle- and upper-managerial positions. Data compiled by the *Economist* (2000) and by Challenger, Gray & Christmas, the global outplacement firm that tracks firm's announcements of layoffs, indicate that despite eight years of economic growth throughout the 1990s, the number of regular jobs eliminated in U.S. companies on an annual basis increased from 100,000 in 1989 to nearly one million in 2004 (CNN Web site, 2005). Numerous causes for these reductions in staff are cited including advances in production and information technologies and a general move to reduce labor costs under the pressure of global competition (Gowing, Kraft, and Quick, 1998). The types of positions being eliminated include those that formerly carried the greatest safeguards. Jobs nested in internal labor markets offering job security and regular career advancement have not been exempt from downsizing strategies. While earlier job cuts were mainly directed at blue-collar workers in manufacturing companies, as technical advances and automation reduced the need for skilled workers, more recent reductions have targeted white-collar employees, including middle managers in a wide range of sectors. An American Management Association survey reported that in 1992, for the first time in the survey's seven-year history, a majority of the jobs eliminated by its member corporations belonged not to hourly workers, but to supervisors, middle managers, and technicians or professionals. This trend continued throughout the decade (Baumol, Blinder, and Wolff, 2003: 47–48).

Many of these upper-level jobs as well as other, more routinized kinds of work have disappeared from manufacturing and service organizations through a variety of routes: downsizing, vertical deintegration, outsourcing, and the formation of network companies. Some of the functions lost through downsizing have been replaced by temporary or contingent workers, whose numbers have increased dramatically in recent decades. In addition to giving organizations greater flexibility, the use of contract, temporary, and part-time workers enables companies to secure major saving because they are not obligated to provide employee benefits, such as health insurance and contributions to pension funds. While some highly skilled workers choose to operate as independent contractors, most do so out of necessity.

Vertical deintegration—the selling off of corporate divisions or departments—outsourcing—the decision to buy products or services rather than produce them in-house—and the formation of network linkages all serve to externalize work and workers formerly operating within a given company. While such "focusing" may allow all parties to concentrate on their "core competence," it also means that a larger proportion of the workforce is employed in peripheral, "second-tier" firms less likely to provide employment security or benefits. Indeed, many of the manufacturing components of large U.S. corporations are now located in overseas locations, removed from U.S. legal protections and regulatory oversight.

Harrison (1994) regards these developments as ushering in a "new dualism" in employment systems. The "core" operations of a company are placed in one location, whose workers—albeit reduced in numbers—continue to enjoy secure employment and benefits. Related activities occur at other, often foreign sites, where cheap labor is more readily available and regulatory controls are weak or nonexistent.

Another kind of insecurity is produced by the increasing use of flexible pay arrangements as more organizations replace guaranteed salaries with performance-related payment schemes. Nonsalary compensation now accounts for more than 10 percent of the pay for U.S. workers (Eisenberg, 2001). The use of bonuses, profit sharing, stock options, commission payments, and overtime pay has grown rapidly during the past decade and, while such arrangements benefit workers in good times, they can dramatically reduce earnings during slowdowns and recessions.

Some observers celebrate these developments as providing new opportunities for self-realization as individuals are released from the confines of restricted internal labor markets and encouraged to maximize their opportunities by moving across organizations. Hall (1996), for example, announces the onset of the "protean career":

> The career of the twenty-first century will be protean, a career that is driven by the person, not the organization, and that will be reinvented by the person from time to time, as the person and the environment change. (This term is derived from the Greek god Proteus, who could change shape at will.) (p. 4)

Such a vision seems overly utopian and, at best, would characterize a minority of high-end careers. Barley and Kunda (2001; 2004) describe such a case in their examination of skilled technical contractors in Silicon Valley. Many of these workers are free agents by choice, viewing their careers as "a sequence of projects" and "firms as mediators who broker information and match individuals to positions" (2001: 80). But such careers require, and have given rise to, a set of new intermediary institutions including staffing firms, user groups, and online resumé services, which in turn are "overlaid and laced together by multiple loose networks of contracts organized around technical specialties" (p. 80). It appears that even Proteus needs some tangible social supports!

And much more support will be required if the presumption of a permanent job is no longer a fixture of occupational social structure. In the United States, jobs have been linked to many wider social programs, ranging from health insurance and pension funds to eligibility for unemployment insurance and access to various legal protections regarding racial and gender discrimination (Kochan, Katz, and McKersie, 1994). Many of our central Social Security and social welfare institutions will have to be redesigned should current trends toward weakening employment relations continue.

CONCLUDING COMMENTS

Organizations require the participation of human participants to carry on activities related to goal attainment. However, who, how many, and what kind of relations tie participants to organizations vary across organizations and over time. Since organizations are open systems, the delimitation of their social boundaries is necessarily a complex question which has, increasingly, become more problematic.

The question of how to regard the "external" connections of organizational participants evokes different responses from rational and natural system proponents. Those of the rational persuasion generally seek to ignore and/or suppress the external identities of organization participants; natural system views emphasize the benefits to be realized by their recognition and exploitation.

During the greater part of the twentieth century, organizing processes favored higher and tighter boundaries. Mainstream organizations in core economic sectors constructed elaborated internal labor markets to segregate and tightly bind critical employees to a given firm or agency. Both employers and employees invested in improving the "specific assets" of employees. More recently, however, employers attend more to the benefits resulting from reduced commitments and limited contracts for both production workers and middle-management employees. The volatility of markets and increasing global competition undermines the advantages of dedicated specialists and stresses the virtues of flexibility.

The resulting "new" world of employment is one in which workers appear to be experiencing increased levels of alienation, inequity of returns, and insecurity. The dissolution of the "New Deal industrial relations system" is far advanced. However, newer systems such as "high-performance work organizations" suggest that some firms continue to recognize the value of those members responsible for performing the work.

CHAPTER 8

Goals, Power, and Control

Group decision-making extends deeply into the business enterprise. Effective participation is not closely related to rank in the formal hierarchy of the organization. This takes an effort of mind to grasp. Everyone is influenced by the stereotyped organization chart of the business enterprise. . . . Power is assumed to pass down from the pinnacle. Those at the top give orders; those below relay them on or respond.

This happens, but only in very simple organizations—the peacetime drill of the National Guard or a troop of Boy Scouts moving out on Saturday maneuvers. Elsewhere the decision will require information. Some power will then pass on to the person or persons who have this information. If this knowledge is highly particular to themselves then their power becomes very great.

JOHN KENNETH GALBRAITH (1967)

The subjects of goals, power, and control have recurred frequently enough throughout the preceding chapters of this volume so that their importance must now be established. Although we have touched on these topics in many places—and have skirted them in others—we have not yet confronted them directly. We begin by discussing the concept of organizational goals, indicating some of the reasons it has proved so obstreperous. We will find that it is helpful to change the questions, What are goals? and Do organizations have goals? to the question, Who sets the goals in organizations? It is in addressing this query that the topics of goals and power come together. It is also instructive to ask whether some organizations lack goals, and, if so, what effect this has on their structure and functioning.

We also examine control systems in organizations. What are the sources of power, and how does power become authority? Some organizations substitute internal for external control systems, relying heavily on shared cultural beliefs. These types of controls are also examined.

GOAL SETTING IN ORGANIZATIONS

Problems in Conceptualizing Organizational Goals

The Varying Uses of Goals. The concept of organizational goals is among the most slippery and treacherous of all those employed by organizational analysts. Many factors contribute to the confusion in this area. A brief description of them may not resolve all of the questions but at least will clarify some of them. One source of difficulty is that statements of organizational goals are used in a number of ways by those who discuss organizations. We consider five alternative uses: cognitive, cathectic, symbolic, justificatory, and evaluative.

Rational system analysts emphasize the *cognitive* functions of goals. Goals provide criteria for generating and selecting among alternative courses of action (Simon, 1964; 1997); they provide directions for and constraints on decision making and action. Natural system analysts, such as Barnard (1938), Clark and Wilson (1961), and Whetten and Godfrey (1998), emphasize the *cathectic* (motivational) properties of goals. Goals serve as a source of identification and motivation for participants. For example, Selznick (1949) notes that goals may be employed as ideological weapons with which to overcome opposition and garner resources from the environment. Note that a goal statement that is satisfactory for analysts concerned with the cathectic properties of goals may be ill-suited for those interested in their cognitive contributions. Vague and general goals may suffice for motivational purposes—indeed, they may be especially suited to this function—but be unsatisfactory for cognitive guidance. For example, colleges may be able to attract students or funds with the claim that they are "preparing tomorrow's leaders," but such goal statements provide meager guidance to those designing the curriculum or hiring the faculty.

Institutional analysts stress the *symbolic* functions of goals. Whereas the cognitive and cathectic properties of goals emphasize their effects on organizational participants, the symbolic aspect of goals points to their significance for organizational audiences: publics, clients, taxpayers, regulators. The goals an organization espouses, claims to serve, or are perceived to represent— these symbolic goals have important effects on the organization's ability to acquire legitimacy, allies, resources, and personnel.

Some analysts challenge the conventional view of behavior in which goals precede actions. Weick points out that goals often serve to provide *justification* for actions already taken. Following the work of Festinger (1957), who developed dissonance theory to account for our tendency to selectively focus on evidence that confirms the correctness of our judgments, Weick argues that:

> Rationality seems better understood as a postdecision rather than a predecision occurrence. Rationality makes sense of what has been, not what will be. It is a process of justification in which past deeds are made to appear sensible to the actor himself and to those other persons to whom he feels accountable. (Weick, 1969: 38)

In short, behavior can precede rather than stem from goals, the goals devised to provide an acceptable account of past actions (see also, Scott and Lyman, 1968; Staw, 1980).

Finally, goals serve as a basis for *evaluating* the behavior of participants or of entire organizations (Dornbusch and Scutt, 1975; Scott, 1977). They provide criteria for identifying and appraising selected aspects of organizational functioning. The criteria used to evaluate performance may or may not be the same as those employed to direct it. We examine goals used as evaluation criteria applied to organizational performance in Chapter 12.

The various functions of goals—guiding, motivating, symbolizing, justifying, and evaluating behavior—do not coincide because they not only serve different purposes but also emanate from different sources. Symbolic goals are likely to be promulgated at the institutional level of the organization, which seeks to legitimate organizational purposes by stressing their larger social functions. Upper-level managers are likely to stress cathectic goals as a way of developing commitment among their participants. From Barnard (1938) to Selznick (1957) to Peters and Waterman (1982) the "functions of the executive" are to articulate and inculcate commitment to corporate values. Middle-level managers, in concert with their technical staff, are expected to translate general aspirations into specific products and services and so are expected to emphasize the cognitive aspects of goals. Workers who carry out daily activities are particularly likely to employ goals to help them justify past actions when asked to supply an accounting. And, evaluators at all levels, external and internal, employ goals as a basis for evaluating past performance—but not necessarily the same goals.

Goals receive less explicit attention from contemporary organizational scholars, not because they are unimportant but because they have been subsumed under somewhat more general concepts, in particular "strategies" (in connection with firms) and "policies" (referring to public agencies). However, strategy and policy discussions lead in somewhat different directions—for example, the relation of strategy to structure or policy to implementation—than those that concern us here, so are addressed later, in Chapter 12.

Individual and Organizational Goals

Simon (1964; 1997) has most forcefully urged the distinction between individual goals that govern a participant's decision to join or remain in an organization, and organizational goals that are expected to govern decisions of individuals as participants (see Chapter 2). Simon proposes that for the sake of clarity such individual goals be labeled *motives*. However, this rational system conception of a relatively clear distinction between individual motives and organizational goals is challenged by the natural system perspective, which insists that individuals are not completely contained within their roles but introduce their own preferences into the choices that confront them as participants. Simon (1964) does not deny the operation of such processes but insists that the distinction retains value. He notes, for example, that many requirements organizations impose on their participants are orthogonal to their motives—for example, it is often a matter of indifference to employees what particular products they manufacture or sell. More generally, one would need to deny the existence of social roles and their impact on individual behavior to assert that organizational goals are indistinguishable from individual motives. The separation of these concepts is also aided by Clark and Wilson's (1961) discussion of incentive systems. Their typology reminds us that in only a limited set of organizations—which they label *purposive*—do individual motives and organizational goals coincide. In most organizations the goals toward which participants direct their behavior are different from the goals that motivate them to participate in the organization.[1]

One implication of these considerations is that it would make no sense to survey individual participants and then aggregate their individual objectives to serve as a description of the organization's goals. In escaping from this reductionist fallacy, however, we must not go to the opposite extreme and posit the existence of some type of metaphysical corporate mind in which collective goals are formulated. To do so is inappropriately to reify the organization, granting it anthropomorphic properties it does not possess. We can avoid both reductionism and reification by reformulating the question. Instead of asking, Do organizations have goals? we will ask, Who sets organizational goals? and How are organizational goals set?

The Dominant Coalition

The most satisfactory basis for addressing the question of who sets organizational goals is provided by Cyert and March (1963). They note that the classic economist's response to this question is to point to the goals of the entrepreneur and to equate the organization's goals with this person's objectives: the firm is seen as the shadow of one powerful actor. A second proposed solution is to presume that goals are consensually defined: all participants share equally in goal setting. Both of these models of goal setting are rejected as exceptional patterns found only rarely in nature. Cyert and March (1963: 27–32) propose the alternative conception of organizational goals being set by a negotiation process that occurs among members of the *dominant coalition*.

Organizations are viewed as composed of coalitions—groups of individuals pursuing similar interests. Each group attempts to impose its preferences (goals) on the larger system, but in the typical case, no single

---

[1]Their typology distinguishes among organizations relying on (1) utilitarian, (2) solidary, (3) and purposive incentives. The first employ material incentives, for example, money or other valuable commodities, to motivate participation; the second, prestige or social ties, for example, elite social clubs or fraternal associations; and the third, intrinsic interest in the organization's goals, for example, environmental or political groups.

group will be able to determine completely the goals to be pursued. Group members seek out as allies other groups whose interests are compatible, and they negotiate and bargain with those groups whose interests are divergent, but whose participation is necessary. One group can make a "side payment" to another to secure its cooperation. For example, a management group, to secure its goal of continued growth, will agree to provide a given level of return on investment to its stockholders and to pay a specified level of wages to its employees. Note, however, that what is a goal for one group is viewed as a side payment by another group, and vice versa. Each group whose interests must be taken into account helps to define the goals of the organization.

All such groups are, by definition, members of the dominant coalition. Each negotiated agreement provides guidance to the organization and places constraints on what may be regarded as an acceptable course of action. And the goals themselves are complex preference statements that summarize the multiple conditions any acceptable choice must satisfy. Simon amplifies this point:

> In the decision-making situations of real life, a course of action, to be acceptable, must satisfy a whole set of requirements, or constraints. Sometimes one of these requirements is singled out and referred to as the goal of the action. But the choice of one of the constraints, from many, is to a large extent arbitrary. For many purposes it is more meaningful to refer to the whole set of requirements as the (complex) goal of the action. (1964: 7)

The conception of the dominant coalition, though certainly not the last word on the subject of who sets organizational goals, avoids many problems that have plagued earlier explanations. We embrace this conception because

- The problem of reification is avoided: individuals and groups have interests, and the process by which these preferences come to be imposed on the organization is specified.
- It is recognized that although individuals and groups specify the goals of the organization, there is no presumption that they do so on an equal footing.
- It is recognized that although individuals and groups impose goals on the organization, in most cases no single individual or group is powerful enough to determine completely the organization's goals; hence, the organization's goals are distinct from those of any of its participants.
- Allowance is made for differences in interests among participants. Some, but not all, of these differences may be resolved by negotiation, so at any time, conflicting goals may be present.
- It is recognized that the size and composition of the dominant coalition differ from one organization to another and vary within the same organization over time.

All of these represent useful insights into the goal-setting process. We suggest two amendments or additions to this list:

- While interests are seated in specific individuals and groups, it is an oversimplification to assume that organizational goals represent simply a negotiation among and an aggregation of existing interests, because new interests continually emerge in the course of interaction (Wallace 1975: 127).
- It is essential to emphasize that the dominant coalition may include and represent interests of constituencies or "stakeholders" outside of the formal boundaries of the organization.

As Ancona and colleagues (1996) point out:

> *Stakeholders* are the social actors (meaning groups of individuals or other organizations) who play a role in the survival and success of the organization and who are affected by the organization's activities . . . The stakeholder model of the organizational environment extends the political perspective's focus on power, interests, influence, coalition-building and negotiation beyond the formal boundaries of the organization to provide a way to assess the environment's influence—and potential influence—on the organization. (module 9, p. 11)

Oftentimes, coalitions connect organizational participants to stakeholders in ways that transcend conventional conceptions of who is empowered to decide what. One's most important allies, or enemies, may reside outside the organization's boundaries.

What Factors Affect the Size and Composition of the Dominant Coalition?

Participants and Stakeholders

Owners and Managers. Those who own property, whether in the form of capital, land, machinery, or disposable goods, have "a socially defensible right to make a decision on how to use" these resources (Stinchcombe, 1983: 131). *Ownership* is an important basis of power in most economic systems. However,

> Usually the person or group that has a socially and legally defensible right to make a decision on the use of the resource does not do so directly. . . . Instead, the fund of resources is entrusted to an administrative apparatus, of which the property-owning group (the board of directors) is the formal head. . . . The property rights are . . . used to make the activities of an administrative apparatus controlling the resources legitimate. (Stinchcombe, 1983: 135–36)

Owners delegate control over resources to *managers* who are expected to act on their behalf—to serve as their agents. But, as numerous analysts, from Berle and Means (1932) and Galbraith (1967) to agency theorists such as

Pratt and Zeckhauser (1985), have noted, the interests of owners and managers may diverge. Managers develop their own power base to the extent that owners become dependent on their expertise and detailed knowledge of the administration of the enterprise.

Throughout most of the twentieth century, managerial power increased relative to that of other organizational participants. The joint-stock company allowed for the dispersion of ownership rights, sometimes among thousands of otherwise disconnected individuals, and managers were more than willing to move into the power vacuum created. However, managerial power, both within the firm and at wider field and societal levels, is being challenged in the United States in recent decades. Managerial interests seemed to be ascendant at the beginning of the 1980s with the election of the business-friendly administration of Ronald Reagan and the passage of much-sought-after deregulation statutes.

> Ironically, however, de-regulation extended to the "market" for hostile takeovers, in which outsiders seek to buy control of a corporation directly from its owners against the wishes of its managers. This produced a wave of takeovers that threatened over one-fourth of the largest American corporations and undermined the very basis of the managerial class by reducing the gap between ownership and control. (Davis, 1994: 217)

This effort to create a "market for corporate control" (Herman, 1981) can be viewed at least in part as an "attempt to reestablish the link between ownership and control that the managerial revolution allegedly severed" (Davis, 1990). Managers fought back and have been largely successful in securing the adoption (and the legal sanction through state laws) of a variety of mechanisms—for example, "poison pills," "shark repellents," and related measures—that reduce the desirability of and, hence, the likelihood of hostile takeover (Davis and Thompson, 1994). But they have been much less effective in adjusting to the declining power of banks (with whom they could align themselves with the use of interlocks) and the rise of large-scale institutional investors and other new brokers of capital such as financial analysts (Useem, 1993). It appears that ownership has recently enjoyed a renaissance at the expense of management (see Chapters 11 and 12).

Labor. Organizations also depend on the energies and skills of workers who carry out the work of transforming resources. Although as individuals they may exercise relatively little power, collectively workers are often able to acquire considerable power by engaging in or threatening strikes, slowdowns, or sabotage and expressing their demands through collective bargaining or other forms of negotiation. However, the power of organized labor in the United States has declined substantially, as exemplified by a drop in the number of union members from a high point of 36 percent of the labor force in 1945 to 13 percent in 2004—8 percent for private sector workers and 36 percent in the private sector (U.S. Bureau of Labor Statistics, 2005). As Lipset (1986: 421) observed, the United States "has, in proportionate numerical terms, the weakest labor movement in the industrial world." Even though union power is at an all-time low, it is still the case that workers, acting both individually and collectively, exercise considerable power within their organizations. In part, simply the threat of unionization helps them in their negotiations with employers, who provide benefits and procedural safeguards to employees in order to forestall unionization (Jacoby, 1985; Sutton et al., 1994).

Moreover, perspectives, such as evolutionary economics, the knowledge-based view of the firm, and total quality management, stress the strategic value to the organization of the tacit know-how and intelligence embedded in the skilled, technical, and professional workforce (Nelson and Winter, 1982; Pfeffer, 1994; Teece, 1998). This source of value is gaining increased attention in business circles and has the potential to increase labor's power.

Boundary Roles. Power also accrues to those who occupy critical *boundary roles* in the organization. Individuals and work groups that connect with important resource suppliers, mediate the demands of critical regulatory agencies, or embody the concerns of institutional actors obtain power within the organizations they serve. Hickson and collegues (1971) usefully argue that individuals and subunits that (1) are relatively central to the work flow, (2) do not have readily available substitutes, and (3) successfully cope with important sources of uncertainty are more likely to garner power.[2] Coping with uncertainty is one of the major functions of boundary-spanning units. These are the units responsible for building and maintaining the "bridges" discussed in Chapter 9.

What sources of uncertainty are confronted and their relative importance shift over time. Whereas labor was a major source of uncertainty for many organizations earlier in the twentieth century—increasing the power of industrial relations departments (Goldner, 1970)—financial markets have become both more volatile and more important in recent years. As expected, those boundary roles within the firm that can deal with shareholders and their intermediaries—financial analysts—have become increasingly powerful. Most corporations now have an office for dealing with "investor relations," and these units are exploring new ways to manage this source of uncertainty (Useem, 1996). Empirical research examining the sources of subunit power carried out in seven organizations

---

[2]The strategic contingency arguments of Hickson and colleagues build directly on Emerson's formulation of power, discussed in Chapter 9 and later in this chapter. Also, Crozier's (1964) intensive case study of a tobacco company in France focused interest on the connection between "coping with uncertainty" and power.

(twenty-eight subunits) provided support for the arguments of Hickson and colleagues (Hinings et al., 1974).

To supplement these technical arguments, we need to add the institutionalist perspective. As Meyer points out:

> Organizations and their internal units derive legitimacy, power, and authority from their status in social environments. . . . The social validity of a given unit—a professional group, a technical procedure, or a departmentalized function—is often defined more importantly in the environment than by internal technical efficacy. (1978: 357)

Such units have power—based on their external connections and supports—that is *independent* of their contributions to internal operations.

External Actors. Power over organizations is not restricted to those within its formal boundaries (see Mintzberg, 1983). From the early study by Selznick (1949) of the TVA, the power of external constituencies to shape organizational objectives has been clear (see Chapter 3). Zald's (1970) "political economy" perspective provides a systematic framework for examining both internal and external sources of power affecting organizations. Regulative agencies, employee associations—both trade unions and profession—business associations, tax authorities, planning commissions, and organized interests within host communities—these and many other "stakeholders" exert varying levels of influence over organizational decision making. There is considerable controversy over the legitimacy of these multiple interest groups and which among the multiple stakeholders has priority (see Chapter 12).

Social movement scholars have long considered the conditions under which excluded individuals and interests mobilize to seek entrée into the circles of power. As discussed (see Chapter 1), movement scholars have increasingly attended to the importance of organizational considerations to the success and longevity of social movements (see McAdam, McCarthy, and Zald, 1996a; Zald and McCarthy, 1987). For their part, organizational analysts have begun to examine the ways in which movement processes enter into and influence organizational structures, as power processes oscillate between the "transgressive contention" of challengers and the institutionalized power of incumbents. The actors may be formally external to the organization but able to exert sufficient pressure to change public policies having a significant effect on organizations (Davis et al., 2005).

Moreover, there is a connection between external conditions and the internal distribution of power (Greenwood and Hinings 1996). Which interests are in control change as environmental conditions vary. Fligstein (1987; 1990) has shown that as the environments confronting large U.S. corporations have changed over this century, the composition of the dominant coalition has also varied. Using as an indicator the power shifts of the departmental origin of the chief executive officer (CEO), Fligstein observed how modal origins changed between 1919 and 1979 in his sample of 216 major corporations. He reports that whereas entrepreneurs—those who founded the company—dominated during the period 1880–1920, CEOs tended to come from manufacturing departments between 1920–1940, from sales departments between 1940–1960, and from finance departments after 1960. He argues that these shifts mirror the changing challenges confronting corporations: production problems dominated in the 1920–1930s, distributional problems in the 1940–1950s, and financial problems after 1960. In a similar vein, research by Thornton and Ocasio (1999) shows that executives in publishing companies are increasingly drawn from business and marketing backgrounds rather than having had experience with books, reflecting changing institutional logics in this field.

Modes of Capital. The power of owners resides in *financial capital*: property ownership, cash, investments, creditworthiness. That of managers and workers is based on *human capital*: their personal attributes and skills, education and experience. Also, to varying degrees, the power of managers and, particularly, that of those occupying boundary roles, rests on their social capital. Putnam defines *social capital* as "those features of social organization, such as networks, norms, and trust that facilitate coordination and cooperation for mutual benefit. Social capital enhances the benefits of investment in physical and human capital" (1993: 36; see also Coleman, 1990: chap. 12) Social capital is embedded in social relationships, although such networks can both constrain and empower (Granovetter, 1985). Some analysts view networks as conduits, helping one person to access the resources and information of others. Others insist that "networks themselves are a form of social capital" (Burt, 1992b: 12). "Social capital is at once the structure of contacts in a nework and the resources they each hold" (Burt, 1992a: 61). Features of networks giving rise to power are discussed in Chapter 11.

Yet another mode of power is that based on *cultural capital*. Based on the work of Bourdieu (1986; Bourdieu and Passeron, 1977), this concept focuses on power associated with social groups who create prestigious knowledge and who cultivate distinctive tastes and modes of discourse. The concept has been seized upon and amplified by institutional theorists, such as DiMaggio (1991) and Meyer (1994; Meyer and Jepperson 2000), who point to the influence of scientific, professional and other elite groups who create new forms of knowledge, new distinctions and associated organizational models—for example, high culture and art museums—and new goals and standards. Many "external" actors exercise power over organizations by virtue of their cultural capital and the more successful of these succeed in persuading organizations to incorporate representatives of their interests.

Size of Coalition. Rather than highly centralized hierarchies in which one or a few persons exercise most of the power and make most of the decisions, most contemporary organizations exhibit power and decision-making structures that include a substantial number of individuals. Galbraith (1967) argues that one of the most fundamental changes in the organization of the modern corporation has been the shift from an entrepreneurial mode in which a single powerful person dominates the enterprise to a flatter structure in which power is more widely diffused.

Thompson (1967: 127–36) clarifies the reason for the increasing size of the organization's power structure. Consistent with the views of Crozier and Hickson, Thompson argues that the number of positions of power within the organization, and hence the size of the dominant coalition, is affected both by the nature of the organization's technology and by its task and institutional environments. The more uncertain the technology and the greater the number of sources of uncertainty in the organization's environment, the more bases for and modes of power there are within the organization and the larger will be the dominant coalition. When organizations embrace more uncertain technologies and when sources of uncertainty increase in the environment of the organization, we should expect both those who represent and those who cope with these problems to demand a voice in the decision-making councils of the organization.

Uses of Power. What difference, if any, does it make when power shifts from one group to another or is shared with a wider range of individuals and groups? The difference should be reflected, of course, in the goals pursued by the organization. Admission to the dominant coalition is an empty victory if the new partners cannot affect the definition of the goals to be served.[3] The shift in control from trustee to physician to managerial and financial control of health care organizations has been accompanied by a change in orientation from community service to clinical medicine to efficiency and cost-containment (Perrow, 1961; Scott et al., 2000).

In his study of major U.S. corporations just referenced, Fligstein (1987; 1990) documents changes in goals associated with changes in the composition of the dominant coalition. He asserts that associated with changes in the origins of CEOs are basic changes in the goals of these organizations—in the types of strategies being pursued. Founding entrepreneurs pursued strategies of horizontal merger as they attempted to control the market. As the scale of production increased, coordination and resource problems came to the fore and manufacturing officials became dominant, pursuing strategies of vertical

---

[3]Power can used appropriately to determine which of several possible goals should guide the organization. It can also be misused to divert organizational resources to serve personal ends, as discussed below.

integration. Functional (unitary) forms were constructed to support these strategies. However,

> Once production is routinized, power shifts to sales and marketing personnel as the key issue for the organization becomes growth. . . . A sales and marketing strategy focuses on attempting to broaden the firm's markets by expanding across regions and countries. (Fligstein, 1985: 380)

This strategy is supported by the creation of multidivisional forms to support production and product-related distribution systems. Then, because of constraints imposed by regulatory agencies, corporations were forced to abandon attempts to increase market share and began to pursue growth through multiple, unrelated product lines. Financial experts were in the best position to devise these strategies, and the conglomerate form was best suited to their support. Environmental changes, shifting power-dependency relations, changing goals and strategies, and new structural forms—while the temporal sequence and the causal ordering of these elements are not clear, and will often be difficult to establish, there are strong interdependencies among them.

In more differentiated and loosely coupled systems, such as universities, power differences among subunits may be reflected not so much in direct attempts to redefine the goals of the larger system, but in efforts to lay claim to a disproportionate share of the organization's resources. This process is well illustrated in a study by Pfeffer and Salancik (1974), who examined the allocation of university resources among twenty-nine academic departments over a thirteen-year period. These researchers convincingly show that the greater the power of individual departments, as measured by indicators such as perceived influence and representation on powerful university committees, the greater the proportion of general university funds received. Also, departments with higher amounts of research funding or other types of external support were better able to leverage other university resources (Pfeffer, 1992). Even more important, the powerful departments were better able than their weaker counterparts to influence the criteria employed to determine the allocation of resources. Pfeffer regards this as an instance of the "new golden rule: the person with the gold makes the rules" (1992: 83). Although such budgetary decisions may appear remote from the general goals of the university, they are in reality highly relevant. The allocation of scarce resources among diverse programs is one of the clearest indicators available as to the "real" goals of the organization (Wildavsky, 1988).

Misuses of Power

Crime. A useful distinction differentiates criminal acts in organizations into "occupational" and "corporate" crimes (Clinard and Quinney, 1973). *Occupational crimes* are committed by individual employees against their employers for their own gain while *corporate crimes* are committed by individual employees acting on behalf of the corporation itself. The former crimes—which involve the pursuit of personal (illegal) motives—include workplace theft, sabotage, fraud, and embezzlement (see Bamberger and Sonnenstuhl, 1998; Ermann and Lundman, 1982; Sutherland, 1949). The latter—the pursuit of illegal organizational goals—may also involve fraud, but on a large scale, such as when officials in the Revco drug store chains developed a computer-generated double billing scheme to defraud Medicaid (Vaughan, 1983). Sometimes officials from more than one organization collude to commit fraud, creating "interorganizational corporate crime networks" (Zey, 1998). Zey (1993) describes the complex arrangements underlying the illegal actions of Michael Milken and others involved in securities fraud in connection with leveraged buyouts of companies. All too often, organizations respond to regulatory controls and other governmental requirements not simply by buffering and bridging tactics, as described in Chapters 6 and 9, but by deception and bribery.

Corruption. The useful distinction between occupational and corporate crimes becomes blurred when a breakdown of governance structures—both public and corporate—occurs and crime becomes a way of life for large numbers. Such appears to be the case in many developing countries where bribery is a routine cost of doing business (Klitgaard, 1991). In states such as China and Russia undergoing rapid economic transformation, observers report the widespread looting of the assets of firms as organizations formerly owned and managed by a centralized state undergo privatization in the absence of effective oversight structures. In China, public funds budgeted for one purpose are often diverted to different ones, as officials create multiple "backyard" enterprises whose profits benefit, individually and collectively, the state functionaries in the sponsoring agencies (Lin, 2001). In Russia, in addition to widespread corruption in the handling and selling of public assets, criminal "mafiya" organizations have multiplied, each demanding protection money from legitimate businesses (Lowther, 1997).

Responding to these issues, an international nongovernmental organization, Transparency International, devised a "corruption perceptions index" (CPI) based on a variety of international surveys on perceptions by both the public and by "elites" of the extent of corruption—for example, the misuse of public power for private benefit—in a specific country (Lambsdorff, 1999b). Such data have been compiled for over 100 countries.[4] Using such indices, research shows that countries that exhibit lower levels of competition, higher levels of inequality, freedom of the press, merit-based recruitment of public officials, and higher degrees of distance between

---

[4]A related measure, the "opacity index," was developed by PricewaterhouseCoopers in 2001 for thirty-five countries. McKinsey & Company and Credit Lyonnais have devised other indices restricted to the assessment of the quality of corporate governance across a number of countries (Wu, 2005).

superiors and subordinates ("power-distance") are more likely to exhibit lower levels of corruption (Lamsbsdorff, 1999a; Rose-Ackerman, 1999).

However, corruption is by no means limited to developing societies, or societies in transition to a differing mode of governance (Clinard, 1990; Cressey, 1969). The recent scandals evidenced by U.S. corporations such as Enron and Worldcom have reminded us that corruption on a large scale is possible even in a modern economy with fairly transparent governance systems. Even though securities acts dating from the mid-1930s were designed to ensure that the public received accurate information on which to base investment decisions, corporate fraud—for example, the creation of sham partnerships selling the same products back and forth—and collusion—with "independent" accounting agencies—occurred on a massive scale, providing misleading information about the financial status of the company (McLean and Elkind, 2003). Governmental reforms—principally, the Sarbanes-Oxley Act—have created a new board to oversee accounting firms and require that the chief executive officers of the company assume responsible for the accuracy of financial reporting (Bratton, 2003).

It is not only corporations, but also the federal government itself that may be the site of corruption. Scandals involving the administration of the "superfund" cleanup of toxic sites have been ongoing since the 1990s, and, more recently, Congress has passed a variety of laws that allow corporations to renege on their commitment to workers with respect to provisions ranging from pensions to health care. In 2006, Jack Abramoff became the poster boy of Washington lobbyists, notorious for buying votes for corporate special interests from elected political officials.

ANARCHIES, ADHOCRACIES, AND LEARNING

Both the bureaucratic-administrative model of the rational system perspective and the coalitional-bargaining model of the natural and open system perspectives provide for the development of a set of goals by which organizational decisions can be made. Both allow for the construction of relatively clear criteria or preference orderings in terms of which priorities can be set and selections made among alternative courses of action. But there are classes of organizations—and, more important, classes of decision situations within many organizations—in which no clear preference orderings have been determined. Organizations pursuing ill-defined goals are on the fringe if not beyond the pale of those collectivities included within the conventional definitions and theories of organizations (see Chapter 1). Yet they present both interesting and instructive lessons.

Decisions and Structures

Thompson and Tuden (1959) focus on these situations by constructing a typology that combines two dimensions: (1) how much agreement there is among organizational participants about the goals or preferred outcomes of the system, and (2) how much agreement there is about the means or the causal processes by which these outcomes can be realized. The cross-classification of this simple ends-and-means distinction produces four types of decision contexts, each of which is calls for a different decision strategy:

Beliefs About Causation	*Preferences About Outcomes*	
	Agreement	Disagreement
Agreement	*Computation* [bureaucracy]	*Compromise* [legislature]
Disagreement	*Judgment* [collegium]	*Inspiration* [charismatic leader]

Our current focus is on the right-hand column—situations in which participants lack consensus on goals, but let us briefly consider the simpler and more familiar situations in which such agreement is present (the left-hand column).

Thompson and Tuden use the term *computation* to denote those decisions most suited to the typical bureaucratic decision-making structure, which, as we have often noted, are situations in which goals are clearly defined and the technology relatively certain. The term *judgment* is employed to refer to the strategies required when agreement on goals exists, but the means of achieving them is uncertain. This situation is best handled by a structure allowing for extensive discussion and the use of expert judgment, termed a "collegium," illustrated by the structure of a court or tribunal, or autonomous professional organizations, as described in Chapter 6.

Turning to the column of interest, Thompson and Tuden argue that there are sometimes situations in which participants agree about how to accomplish some objective or about what the expected consequences of available alternatives are but disagree over which alternative is preferable. Such situations call for *compromise*. A mild version of this situation is provided by the coalitional view of decision making—which, as we have described, is resolved by negotiation, bargaining, and sequential attention to goals. More extreme instances of disagreement and conflict can sometimes be resolved through the creation of representative bodies that allow for the expression of differences and the engineering of compromises. Most such forums—for example, the United Nations and the United States Congress—presume the existence of substantive differences in preferences but rely on procedural agreements—such as Robert's Rules of Order—for resolving them.

The fourth and final decision situation is characterized by the absence of agreement about either ends or means. Thompson and Tuden suggest these anomic and ill-structured situations, if they are not to result in complete system disintegration, call for *inspiration*. This is consistent with Weber's arguments, described in Chapter 2, that charismatic leaders are more likely to emerge in crisis situations—times when conventional goals are being challenged and established procedures are not working. And, like Weber, Thompson and Tuden expect such leadership to give rise over time to a computational (bureaucratic) structure based on a new definition of goals and accepted procedures, as charisma becomes routinized.

Organized Anarchies.   March and his colleagues (Cohen and March, 1976; Cohen, March, and Olsen, 1972; 1976; March, 1988; March and Olsen, 1976; 1989) have devoted much effort to examining decision making under conditions of "inconsistent and ill-defined preferences," "unclear technologies," and "fluid participation"—the shifting involvement of members in decision situations (Cohen, March, and Olsen, 1972: 1). They label these conditions *organized anarchies*. But unlike Thompson and Tuden, March and associates suggest that these circumstances are not always crises or transitory states. Rather, they insist that they have been "identified often in studies of organizations," "are characteristic of any organization in part," and "are particularly conspicuous in public, educational, and illegitimate organizations" (Cohen, March, and Olsen, 1976: 25).

The portrait of organized anarchies is set within a more general framework that stresses the prevalence of ambiguity in decision making. March and Olsen comment on their approach:

> We remain in the tradition of viewing organizational participants as problem-solvers and decision-makers. However, we assume that individuals find themselves in a more complex, less stable, and less understood world than that described by standard theories of organizational choice; they are placed in a world over which they often have only modest control. (1976: 21)

The organizational world depicted here is similar to that described by Weick (1969; 1995; see also Chapter 4): individual decision makers have cognitive and attention limits; external conditions constrain alternatives and affect outcomes but often go unnoticed; and choices by individuals in decision-making positions may not result in organizational action. Under such conditions, all choices are somewhat ambiguous.

> Although organizations can often be viewed conveniently as vehicles for solving well-defined problems or structures within which conflict is resolved through bargaining, they also provide sets of procedures through which participants arrive at an interpretation of what they are doing and what they have done while in the process of doing it. From this point of view, an organization is a collection of choices looking for problems, issues and feelings looking for decision situations in which they might be aired, solutions looking for issues to which they might be the answer, and decision makers looking for work. (Cohen, March, and Olsen, 1972: 2)

Under conditions of organized anarchy, the ambiguity of choice present in all decision-making situations reaches its apex. Here problems, solutions, participants, and choice opportunities are viewed as flows that move relatively independently into and out of the decision arena— metaphorically labeled a "garbage can." Which solutions get attached to which problems is partly determined by chance—by which participants with what goals happened to be on the scene, by when the solutions or the problems entered, and so on. Although the system described seems bizarre and even pathological when compared with the conventional model of rational decision making, it does produce decisions under conditions of high uncertainty: that is, some solutions do get attached by some participants to some problems.

Cohen, March, and Olsen (1972) have developed and examined some of the implications of their garbage-can model under varying assumptions by using computer-simulation techniques.[5] However, this model of decision making was originally suggested to them on the basis of observations of decision-making processes in colleges and universities:

> Opportunities for choice in higher education can easily become complex "garbage cans" into which a striking variety of problems, solutions, and participants may be dumped. Debate over the hiring of a football coach can become connected to concerns about the essence of a liberal education, the relations of the school to ethnic minorities, or the philosophy of talent. (Cohen and March, 1976: 175)

Perhaps it is due specifically to the characteristics of universities, or perhaps they intend their comments to apply more generally to all organized anarchies, but unlike Thompson and Tuden, Cohen and March (1974: 1976) do not look for a charismatic leader to ride in on horseback bringing inspiration for new goals. Rather, they perceive the role of leaders—for example, university presidents—in such situations in much more problematic and pessimistic terms. They suggest that leaders can improve their performance if they take into account the unusual nature of decision-making situations in these organizations. By carefully timing issue creation, being sensitive to shifting interests and involvement of participants, recognizing the status and power implications of choice situations, abandoning initiatives that have become hopelessly entangled with other, originally unrelated problems, realizing that the planning function is largely symbolic and chiefly provides excuses for interaction, leaders in organized anarchies can maintain their sanity and, sometimes, make a difference in the decision made.

Turbulent Environments. A major factor often accounting for the absence of clearly specified goals is the unstable nature of some organizational environments. If environments are turbulent, then it is difficult to establish clear and

---

[5]Bendor and colleagues (Bendor, Moe, and Shotts, 2001) provide a strong critique of both the theoretical arguments and the simulation model underlying the garbage-can model. Olsen (2001) has supplied a spirited defense of the work.

specific objectives around which to design a structure and orient participant activities. Under unsettled conditions, tents may be preferable to palaces:

> In constant surroundings, one could confidently assemble an intricate, rigid structure combining elegant and refined components—an organizational palace. . . . However, systematic procedures offer weak protection against unpredictability, just as increased rigidity does not effectively prepare a building for earthquakes. . . . Residents of changing environments need a tent. An organizational tent places greater emphasis on flexibility, creativity, immediacy, and initiative than on authority, clarity, decisiveness, or responsiveness; and an organizational tent neither asks for harmony between the activities of different organizational components, nor asks that today's behavior resemble yesterday's or tomorrow's. Why behave more consistently than one's world does? (Hedberg, Nystrom, and Starbuck, 1976: 44–45)

Unstable environments undermine clear and consistent goals, just as they unsettle rigid formalized structures. This theme is reflected in much of the advice provided by contemporary business consultants and popular business writers to organizational managers on "liberation management" and "coping with chaos." It also explains the intense attention given by organizational scholars to some of the newer "network forms" that enable managers to devise reconfigurable free-standing components that can be assembled into temporary structures, to be dis- and reassembled to fit changing conditions (see Child, 2005; and Chapter 11).

Still, some elements of consistency can be found in the goal structures of organizations operating under unstable conditions. If, following Mintzberg and McHugh (1985), strategies are defined as "a pattern in a stream of decisions or actions," then it may be possible to retrospectively identify underlying motifs. Not all intended strategies are realized, and those that are realized may be emergent rather than deliberate. In their case study of the National Film Board (NFB) of Canada from its inception in 1939, Mintzberg and McHugh were able to discern a number of patterns in its products and approach that although unplanned, nevertheless provided a fabric with discernible designs. The film makers provided the warp, but the environment furnished the woof.

> The NFB had an ironic relationship with its environment. In one sense, it was highly responsive—to social trends, new fashions, new media, social turmoil. Ultimately, the NFB found its purpose—when it did—in the world around it, not in itself: it truly was a mirror for its society. . . . Yet in another sense, this was truly an organization that "did its own thing." Except during the war years, the NFB as a whole catered largely to its own needs, for the most part selecting those parts of the environment to which it cared to respond. . . .
>
> The essence of adhocracy, in contrast to machine bureaucracies that seek to control their environments in order to support their standardized systems of mass production, would seem to be rapid and continuous responsiveness to the environment, with minimal organizational momentum. (Mintzberg and McHugh, 1985: 191)

Organizations such as the NFB that rely less on long-term strategic planning and more on ad hoc, emergent strategies may also be said to replace conventional rational decision-making techniques with *experiential learning* (Hedberg, 1981; March 1988). Whereas rational system models assume that goals are stable, learning models assume that they are subject to change, that many choices are not guided by pre-established intentions and can result in the discovery of new purposes. And whereas rational system models propose that technologies are known, learning models stress that they must be continuously invented, shaped, and modified in the light of feedback from the environment. Learning approaches embrace the open system conception of organizations:

> Learning in open, cognitive systems takes the form of positive feedback which changes the systems or their knowledge, whereas learning in closed, natural systems is the function of negative feedback which aims at maintaining the genotype unchanged. (Hedberg, 1981: 5)

Learning that "changes the system," that results not simply in new decisions but also in new rules and methods for deciding, and even in new preferences, is what Argyris (1982) terms "double-loop" learning, as discussed in Chapter 4. It requires the "unlearning" of the old ways as well as the acquisition of new ones.

March (1991) contrasts two types of adaptive processes in organizations: exploitation and exploration. *Exploitation* involves taking advantage of what one already knows: cashing in on the investments made in existing machinery and skills. By contrast, *exploration* involves a search for new knowledge and skills, learning new ways of thinking and working. Organizations must adjudicate the proper balance between these modes, deciding how much effort to invest in turning out goods and services and how much to invest in developing future products. Exploration is, by definition, always risky. There is no guarantee of returns on investments made. But, under conditions of even modest change, some investment in exploration—for example, research and development, travel to conferences—is essential to ensure long-term survival. In general, the longer the time horizon used, the more "rational" it is to tilt the balance from exploitation to exploration.

We should not underestimate, however, how difficult it is for organizational systems to learn anything useful—and how easy it is to derive the wrong lessons ("superstitious learning")—given a rapidly changing environment, selective attention and inattention processes, cognitive limits, the changing behavior of competitors, and the ambiguity of feedback.

Conceptions of Goals and Theoretical Models

Grandori (1987) argues that there is a close relation between an analyst's conception of organizational goals and the choice of a theoretical model for explaining organization structure. She takes contingency theory as the base-line model, a model that assumes that organizations are pursuing single or consistent objectives and that they are capable of rationally adapting their structure to fit changing circumstances. To the extent that analysts are aware that there are multiple, conflicting objectives that are associated with varying types of participants, the theoretical model adopted tends to be that of resource dependence. Resource dependence theorists also assume that organizations do not simply adapt to their environments but are capable of influencing or choosing among them. Population ecologists and many institutional theorists question the assumption of both contingency and resource dependence theorists that organizations adapt or react to their environments, emphasizing instead the inertia of organizational structure. Finally, theorists who relax the assumption that organizations have fixed objectives—whether unified or conflicting—embrace models of anarchy and learning. Actors in such organizations are viewed as lacking a priori preferences but instead discover what their goals are in the course of acting.

Note that the theoretical models differ in their views concerning how goals affect behavior but also in the extent to which rationality of action is posited. Organizations vary—and so do the perspectives we employ to understand them.

CONTROL SYSTEMS

It is one thing to set goals; it is another to see that energies are directed toward their accomplishment. To this end, control must be exercised. Of course, all collectivities control their members. As we have previously argued in defining them, if collectivities do not show evidence of a distinctive normative and cognitive structure and some regular patterns of participant behavior, we cannot even establish their existence. But, as Etzioni has argued, the problems of control in organizations are especially acute:

> The artificial quality of organizations, their high concern with performance, their tendency to be far more complex than natural units, all make informal control inadequate and reliance on identification with the job impossible. Most organizations most of the time cannot rely on most of their participants to internalize their obligations to carry out their assignments voluntarily, without additional incentives. Hence, organizations require formally structured distribution of rewards and sanctions to support compliance with their norms, regulations, and orders. (1964: 59)

Perhaps this explains why so many of the topics discussed in connection with organizations relate more or less directly to the subject of control. Consider the following list: administration, authority, automation, boundaries, bureaucratization, centralization, contracts, coordination, culture, decision premises, discipline, evaluation, formalization, hierarchy, incentives, integration, internalization, performance programs, power, procedures, routinization, rules, sanctions, socialization, supervision—these are some of the many specific manifestations and instruments of control.

We begin this section by discussing the interpersonal control system—the structure of power and authority in organizations. Then we consider how these arrangements are supplemented and, in some measure, replaced by various impersonal control mechanisms. Finally, we discuss culture as a mode of control present in all but dominant in some types of organizations.

Power

Much ambiguity and ambivalence attend the discussion of power in organizations. As Pfeffer observes, "Power has a bad name in social science research and is most often conspicuous by its absence from the literature" (1997: 137). On the other hand, particularly in the sociological literature, a great many pages have been filled with discussions of power, and many definitions of this important concept have been proposed (see Cartwright, 1965; Hardy and Clegg, 1996). One of the simplest and most satisfactory approaches to this topic is that proposed by Emerson:

> It would appear that the power to control or influence the other resides in control over the things he values, which may range all the way from oil resources to ego-support, depending upon the relation in question. In short, power resides implicitly in the other's dependence. (1962: 32)

To unpack this conception, it appears that Emerson views power as *relational, situational,* and at least potentially *reciprocal.*[6] Thus, his approach emphasizes that power is to be viewed as relational, not as a characteristic of an individual but rather as a property of a social relation. To say that a given person has power is meaningless unless we specify over whom he or she has power. We must take into account the characteristics of both the superordinate and the subordinate individual in examining a power relation. The power of superordinates is based on their ability and willingness to sanction others—to provide or withhold rewards and penalties—but we must recognize that what constitutes a reward or a penalty is ultimately determined by the goals or values of subordinates in the relation. To use two extreme examples, a gunman has no power over the individual who does not value his or her life, nor does a person with money have power over another who does not value money or the things it will buy. Emerson's formulation also provides a means of determining the degree of power in a relation. He argues that A's power over B is (1) directly proportional to the importance B places on the

---

[6]An important strength of Emerson's approach is that it is applicable to relations among varying types of units, including individuals, groups, and organizations. Here, it is applied to relations among individuals; in Chapter 9 it is applied, by Pfeffer and others, to examine relations among organizations.

goals mediated by A, and (2) inversely proportional to the availability of these goals to B outside the A–B relation (1962: 329).

It is consistent with this approach that power can have many bases: it is situational. An individual's power is based on all the resources—money, skills, knowledge, strength, sex appeal—that he or she can employ to help or hinder another in the attainment of desired goals. What types of resources function as sanctions will vary from individual to individual and situation to situation. Thus, if workers in an office value the quality of their technical decisions, then expertise becomes an important resource that can be used as a sanction (Blau, 1955); and if managers in the company wish to keep production machines running, then mechanics who can repair breakdowns will acquire power (Crozier, 1964). Recall also that power can reside in relational ties (social capital) and in cultural resources, as discussed above.

Emerson's formulation also allows for the possibility of mutual dependency—reciprocal power: power relations can cut in both ways. I may depend on you for expertise, but you may depend on me for access to those you seek to influence. Just as the degree of individual dependence may vary by situation, so may the degree of mutual dependence, or interdependence.

We define interpersonal *power* as the potential for influence that is based on one person's ability and willingness to sanction another person by manipulating rewards and punishments important to the other person. That is, power has its origin in the dependency of one person on resources controlled by another, but power itself is best defined as a potential for influence.

Power in Informal Groups. During the late 1950s a large number of studies examined the operation of power in informal groups and, in particular, the emergence of power differences in previously undifferentiated task groups. These processes were examined in field studies (e.g., Sherif and Sherif, 1953) as well as in the laboratory (e.g., Bales, 1952). These studies describe how personal qualities and social relations that differ among members become the basis for differences in sanctioning ability. As analyzed by Homans (1961) and Blau (1964), the process of differentiation occurs through a series of exchanges among group participants. Over time, some members emerge who are both more willing and more able to make important contributions to goal attainment, whether to the goals of individual members or to those of the group as a whole. As Blau notes, "a person who commands services others need, and who is independent of any at their command, attains power over others by making the satisfaction of their need contingent on their compliance" (1964: 22). Both Blau and Homans see the origin of power structures as a product of unequal exchange relations that occur when some individuals become increasingly dependent on others for services required in reaching their objectives. A person lacking resources to repay the other for these services, who is unwilling to forgo them and unable to find them in other relations, has but one alternative: "he must subordinate himself to the other and comply with his wishes, thereby rewarding the other with power over himself as an inducement for furnishing the needed help" (Blau, 1964: 21–22). In this manner, exchange processes that involve asymmetries give rise to a differentiated power structure.

Pfeffer (1992) reviews a number of individual attributes which research has shown to be the source of power. These include energy and physical stamina, an ability to focus one's interests and energies, sensitivity to others, their interests and needs, flexibility as conditions change, an ability to tolerate conflict, and to submerge one's ego in the interest of building coalitions and alliances (see also Cialdini, 2001). In addition to these exchange views of power, Tyler (1993) has proposed a social identification model suggesting that individuals conform primarily because of their interest in their social standing in the group. This work stresses the importance of affective as against more instrumental types of rewards as sources of control. Network-based conceptions stress the importance of social relations—social capital—rather than individual attributes: who has access to whom. Not only the number of ties but also the structure of the network (including the diversity of relations (Granovetter, 1973) and whether or not the ties are redundant (Burt, 1992b), greatly affect the value to be gained from a relation and, hence, power.

Power in Formal Organizations. Power in informal groups is based on the characteristics of individuals—individual differences that can function as resources allowing some to reward and punish others. By contrast, power in formal organizations is determined at least in part by design: sanctioning powers are attached to positions, available to any individual who occupies one, regardless of his or her personal qualities. Power is not personal but structural (Brass, 2002).

Rational system theorists emphasize the importance of formal power structures in the functioning of organizations. They argue that it is possible to design power structures in such a manner that sanctioning power may be made commensurate with responsibilities and distributed so as to facilitate the organization's requirements for coordination and control of participants' contributions. They also note that although the theoretical range of subordinates' values and, hence, of power bases is quite broad, the actual range is quite narrow: certain values are widely shared, so that it is possible to identify resources, such as money and status, that will function as sanctions for most participants most of the time. They further note the quite palpable advantages associated with the formalization process itself, which results in the "domestication" of power. Thus, tensions associated with the generation of power differences are avoided; the organization is freed from the necessity of finding "superior" individuals to fill superior positions; and power is more readily transferred from one person to another as position occupants come and go (see Chapter 2). Formalization is one of the important ways in which the "personal" element is removed from interpersonal control systems.

Natural systems theorists insist, on the other hand, that no organization ever succeeds in completely controlling all sources of power or in rationally allocating power among its positions. There are two reasons for this. First, positions are filled by persons, who possess diverse attributes and enter into various relations. Such differences can serve as resources that sometimes supplement and sometimes contradict and erode the formal distribution of power. Second, in the organization's allocation of resources to positions, some participants inevitably obtain access to resources that can be used in ways not intended by the organizational designers (Mechanic, 1962). For example, access to information is an important resource that can become the basis for sanctioning and controlling others. Boundary roles or staff positions allow occupants access to sensitive information that they can use to enhance their own power and influence. Moreover, some individuals in organizations play the role of "tempered radical" (Meyerson, 2001). Because of their social identity or philosophical differences, these individuals find themselves at odds with prevailing beliefs or practices. Employing a range of tactics—from quiet resistance to negotiation, to active organization for collective action—such individuals are able to achieve "small wins" as well as major victories.

Research by Tannenbaum and associates (Tannenbaum, 1968; Tannenbaum et al., 1974) supplies evidence for the general expectation that the amount of control or influence is positively associated with position in the formal hierarchy. If individuals are asked to describe how much influence is associated with each type of position in the organization, then it is possible to construct a "control graph" that depicts how centralized or decentralized is the distribution of power in the organization (see Figure 8–1). The centralization of power varies from organization to organization, largely as a function of differences task complexity (see Chapter 6) or in ideology that directly affects the formal definitions of how power is to be distributed. For example, power was more evenly distributed in the League of Women Voters, a voluntary agency emphasizing member participation, and in European companies emphasizing worker participation than in more traditional U.S. business and industrial concerns. (However, as Tannenbaum emphasizes, power was centralized in all of these organizations, ideology and preferences notwithstanding.)

Of more interest is Tannenbaum's demonstration that aside from its distribution, the *total amount* of control exercised varies from one organization to another. (Contrast line A with line X in Figure 8–1.) In some organizations all or more positions are perceived by members as exercising more influence over others. This condition may result from (1) differences in the amount of exchange involving compliance; (2) differences in the extent to which members are "partially" or more fully involved in the organization; and (3) differences in the extent to which lower level participants are allowed to participate in decision making and other venues for exercising power. Organizations with higher total control levels—higher levels of

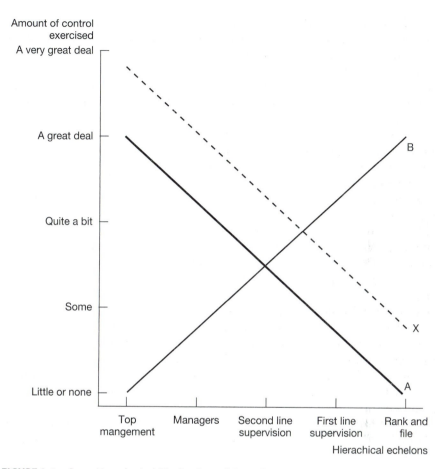

FIGURE 8-1 Some Hypothetical Distributions of Control.
Source: Tannenbaum (1968: Figure 2, p.13).

interdependence and mutual influence—were found to be more effective in pursuit of their goals than organizations with lower levels (Tannenbaum, 1968). Tannenbaum's diagram also gives a graphic portrayal of what it means to have a revolution in a control system—simply rotate the control graph from position A to position B!

Authority

Weber has pointed out that in his experience no organization

voluntarily limits itself to the appeal to material or affectual motives as a basis for guaranteeing its continuance. In addition, every such system attempts to establish and to cultivate the belief in its "legitimacy." (Weber, 1947 trans.: 325)

In other words, no organization is likely to be content with establishing a power structure; in addition, it will attempt to create an authority structure. Most social scientists define *authority* as legitimate power.

> *Legitimacy* is a generalized perception or assumption that the actions of an entity are desirable, proper, or appropriate within some socially constructed system of norms, values, beliefs and definitions. (Suchman 1995b: 574)

Thus, to speak of legitimate power is to indicate (1) a set of persons or positions linked by power relations and (2) a set of norms or rules governing the distribution and exercise of power and the response to it.

In the case of informal groups, we refer to the exercise of power as legitimate to the extent that there emerges a set of norms and beliefs among the members subordinate to the power wielder that the distribution and exercise of power is acceptable to them and is regarded as appropriate. The emergence of such norms significantly alters the control structure, as Blau and Scott have argued:

> Given the development of social norms that certain orders of superiors ought to be obeyed, the members of the group will enforce compliance with these orders as part of their enforcement of conformity to group norms. The group's demand that orders of the superior be obeyed makes obedience partly independent of his coercive power or persuasive influence over individual subordinates and thus transforms these other kinds of social control into authority. (Blau and Scott, 1962: 29)

In this manner, a set of dyadic power relations between the superior and each subordinate is transformed by the emergence of legitimacy norms into a multiperson control structure in which each subordinate now participates in the control of each of his or her colleagues. Peer-group controls are harnessed in the support of the power structure. Further, the emergence of legitimacy norms helps to render power relations more impersonal and reduces the tensions associated with the exercise of interpersonal power. As Thibaut and Kelley suggest, in an authority structure, in contrast with a power structure,

> Nonadherence is met with the use of power to attempt to produce conformity, but the influence appeal is to a supra-individual value ("Do it for the group" or "Do it because it's good") rather than to personal interests ("Do it for me" or "Do it and I'll do something for you"). (1959: 129)

The emergence of legitimacy norms deflects the actors' attention from their personal preferences to the requirements of the system and of their roles within it. In this sense, as Kelman and Hamilton emphasize:

> the person acts as if he were in a nonchoice situation. . . . when a person is presented with a demand in a situation that has all the earmarks of legitimacy, he does not usually ask himself what he would like to do. The central question

he confronts is what he must do or should do—his obligations rather than his preferences. (1989: 90)

Rules and role requirements replace preferences and choice.

For all of these reasons—involvement of subordinate participants in the control system, development of differentiated expectations among participants, depersonalization of power processes with consequent reduction of interpersonal tensions, elevation of role requirements over personal preferences—authority structures tend to be much more stable and effective control systems than power structures. Like formalization, authority cloaks personal power in impersonal garb.

There is, however, another equally important consequence of the legitimation process. The emergence of social norms not only allows a greater measure of control of subordinates by the power wielder but also regulates and circumscribes his or her exercise of power. Emerson (1962) points out that the emergence of legitimacy norms among subordinates allows them to act as a coalition vis-à-vis the power wielder, defining the arena within which he or she can appropriately exercise power. Subordinates are individually weaker, but collectively stronger than the superior, allowing them to place some limits on his or her power. Legitimacy norms specify the orders to which subordinates are expected to comply—and hence support the exercise of power—but also identify demands that the power wielder cannot appropriately make of subordinates—and hence limit the exercise of power. In sum, legitimacy norms cut both ways: they permit greater and more reliable control of subordinates within certain limits defined as appropriate areas of control—Barnard (1938) referred to these areas as the "zone of indifference"—and they restrict the exercise of power to these areas. We conclude that *authority is legitimate power* and that *legitimate power is normatively regulated power.*

Two Types of Authority: Endorsed and Authorized power. Dornbusch and Scott (1975) raised a question that had not been explicitly asked by previous students of authority. Having decided that social norms that regulate power relations provide the basis for legitimate control structures, they sought to determine who—what group of participants—defines and enforces these norms. In most informal groups, there is only one possible source: the set of participants who are subject to the exercise of power and hence are subordinates of the power wielder. We have noted how, by acting as a coalition, this subordinate group can limit and regulate the exercise of power over them by a superordinate. Dornbusch and Scott label this type of situation *endorsed power*, or authority by endorsement. A number of theorists—in particular, Barnard (1938)—view the enforcement of norms by subordinates, or endorsement, as the basic mechanism underlying authority in formal organizations. While this process operates in organizations, it is secondary to another process.

An important characteristic of formal organizations is the presence of persons superordinate to as well as persons subordinate to a given power wielder. Most hierarchies are multilevel, so that norms may be developed and enforced by persons superior to the power wielder. Indeed, this is one of the primary features of a hierarchy of offices. As Weber states:

> The principles of office hierarchy and of levels of graded authority mean a firmly ordered system of super- and subordination in which there is a supervision of the lower offices by the higher ones. (Weber, 1946 trans.: 197)

A familiar safeguard built into most hierarchies is the principle of appeal, by which subordinates who feel that their immediate superior is making unfair or unreasonable demands on them, may turn to their superior's boss with the expectation that he or she will enforce authority norms that curb the superior's power. Dornbusch and Scott label a situation in which power is regulated by those superior to the power wielder *authorized power*, or authority by authorization.[7]

For authorization to operate as a source of normative control, there must be a level of the hierarchy above that of the person or position whose exercise of power is at issue. What happens at the very top of the hierarchy, where there is no superordinate level to regulate the exercise of power? In the usual case, as Parsons (1960) has pointed out, the managerial hierarchy ends with its top position being responsible to a different type of office: institutional representations, exemplified by the board of directors or board of trustees. These offices are defined as being legitimated by—normatively regulated by—some different, nonhierarchical principle, often by some type of electoral process.

A principle function of the institutional level—one noted several times throughout this volume—is to secure the legitimation of the organization's hierarchy. This is accomplished by linking the norms and values supporting the hierarchy to broader institutionalized normative systems, demonstrating their congruence and consistency (Parsons, 1960). Weber's famous typology of authority systems, described in Chapter 2, is based on differences in the types of norms that legitimate power systems. Recall that he distinguished between traditional, charismatic, and bureaucratic systems, each of which justifies and regulates an existing structure of power on a different basis. Scholars from Weber (1968 trans.) to Bendix (1956) to Guillén (1994) have examined how these broadly accepted normative beliefs change over time, causing and reflecting changes in power arrangements within specific administrative

---

[7]Another possible source of the creation and enforcement of norms in organization is the colleagues or peers of the power wielder—those occupying the same formal position in the organization. This source is expected to be of particular importance in professional organizations and can be labeled *collegial power.*

systems. For example, the legitimacy of the nation-state is no longer likely to be justified by the doctrine of the divine right of kings but is instead supported by beliefs in its consistency with constitutional documents or the "people's will." Similarly, the authority systems of more limited organizations are justified by beliefs in property rights, or procedural correctness, or the legitimacy of specialized expertise.

It is equally important to recognize that in most situations there exist multiple, competing sets of norms and beliefs supporting alternative authority regimes. Such divided authority is especially associated with the Judeo-Christian tradition, which early insisted on the differentiation of the ecclesiastical realm from the secular polity. As Berman notes, "Perhaps the most distinctive characteristic of the Western legal tradition is the coexistence and competition within the same community of diverse jurisdictions and diverse legal systems" (1983: 10). Such legal pluralism is especially prevalent in the Western democracies, which take great pains to create divided and counterbalancing authorities. One of the most important strategic choices confronting all organizations, although it is seldom recognized as a conscious choice, is the selection of the set of authority norms with which to become aligned. The existence of competing regimes also enables individual participants to engage in "principled disobedience" (Kelman and Hamilton, 1989) when confronted by commands they believe to be illegitimate.

Returning to our basic distinction, it is possible for some control attempts to be authorized—that is, supported by superiors of the power wielder—but not endorsed—that is, not supported by subordinates of the power wielder—or vice versa. Consider, for example, the authority exercised by a police officer in an urban neighborhood whose residents are suspicious or hostile toward police activities. It is also possible for control attempts to be both authorized and endorsed, for example, the supervisor who is also a natural leader in a work group. Authority that is both authorized and endorsed enjoys greater legitimacy and is expected to be more effective and more stable than that which receives support from only one source (Dornbusch and Scott, 1975: 56–64; see also Zelditch and Walker, 1984).

Structural Control. Authority and power are usually thought to be personal or interpersonal control systems, but as we have noted, in moving from informal to formalized power and from power to authority, more impersonal supports are introduced. Formal power is attached to positions rather than persons, and authority is power justified—authorized or endorsed—by normative beliefs.

As Edwards (1979) has pointed out, simple and more personal power systems tend to give way over time to more complex and impersonal forms—to technical and bureaucratic structures (see Chapter 7). Controls are built into technical production systems in the form of machine pacing or, in the case of continuous-flow systems, in the layout and speed of the assembly line. These more impersonal controls reduce the need for personal direction and in this manner change the role of supervisors from overseer to troubleshooter (see Blau and Scott, 1962: 176–83; Walker and Guest, 1952). The new communication and information technologies can both inform and support work as well as monitor and regulate it. From electronic surveillance to the monitoring of phone calls to the feedback on quality and quantity measurements built into the equipment used to perform the work, the actions of employees are increasingly subject to surveillance. These controls are so effective that they enable many types of work to be performed off-site, isolated from the typical, multiple controls in place in all organized work settings (see Cornfield, Campbell, and McCammon, 2001; Morton, 1991; Zuboff, 1988).

Even more elaborate and less visible controls are embedded in the organization structure itself—in the layout of offices, functions, rules, and policies. Edwards emphasizes that the force of these bureaucratic arrangements resides in their seemingly impersonal character.

> Above all else, bureaucratic control institutionalized the exercise of capitalist power, making power appear to emanate from the formal organization itself. Hierarchical relations were transformed from relations between (unequally powerful) people to relations between jobholders or relations between jobs themselves, abstracted from the specific people or the concrete work tasks involved. "Rule of law"—the firm's law—replaced rule by supervisor command. And indeed, the replacement was not illusory. To the extent that firms were successful in imposing bureaucratic control, the method, extent, and intensity of sanctions imposed on recalcitrant workers were specified by organizational rules. (1979: 145–46)

Technical and bureaucratic control structures thus represent important instances of *structural* controls. Differences in power are built into the design of the technologies or into the definition of relations among positions, and these power differences are normatively justified. There are two major advantages to power wielders in gaining structural control. The first is that one's power advantages are partially concealed: all participants—both those with greater power and those with lesser power—appear to be commonly subordinated to a normative framework exercising control over all. The second advantage is that those with structural power do not need to mobilize in order to have their interests taken into account. It is automatically assumed that they are "entitled" to be represented in any matter affecting their interests. By contrast, interests that are not structured have to become mobilized if they are to be heard. It is in this sense that power functions less as a "wild card" and more like a "trump suit" in the game of politics within organizations (see Heilbroner, 1980: 146).

Culture

Some types of organizations, as described in Chapter 7, rely less on formalized control systems than on the development of a set of common beliefs and norms that participants employ to orient and govern their contributions. These types of controls denote the existence of a *corporate culture*. Pointing to culture as one basis of control should come as no surprise, since anthropologists have long believed most of the orderliness and patterning found in social life is accounted for by cultural systems, but such views have only recently been employed by students of organizations.[8]

Smircich points out that the concept of culture is used in two quite different ways by organizational analysts: "as a critical variable and as a root metaphor" (1983: 339). In the first usage, culture is something that an organization *has*; in the second, it is something an organization *is*. We restrict attention here to the first meaning and consider the second in the following section. Viewed as a variable (or set of variables),

> The term "culture" describes an attribute or quality internal to a group. We refer to an organizational culture or subculture. In this sense culture is a possession— a fairly stable set of taken-for-granted assumptions, shared beliefs, meanings, and values that form a kind of backdrop for action. (Smircich, 1985: 58)

Culture so defined may be employed either as an external variable that may infuse the organization—for example, organizations in France are molded by a distinctive set of cultural beliefs unique to that society (Crozier, 1964)—or as an internal variable that characterizes the values or style of a particular organization.

Most of the analysts focusing on culture as a variable embrace a functionalist perspective and focus on the contributions which cultural elements make to "organizational unification and control." (Smircich and Calás, 1987: 238; see also, O'Reilly and Chapman, 1996) Schein, for example, suggests that the concept of culture should be reserved for the "deeper level of basic assumptions and beliefs that are shared by members of an organization" and embraces the functionalist assumption that: "These assumptions and beliefs are learned responses to a group's problems of survival in its external environment and its problems of internal integration" (1992: 6).

Trice and Beyer distinguish between the substance and the forms of cultures. They suggest that cultural substance consists of the "shared, emotionally charged belief systems we call ideologies," whereas cultural forms are the "observable entities, including actions, through which members of a culture express, affirm, and communicate the substance of their culture to one another" (1993: 2).

Every organization necessarily has a culture, but cultures vary in their attributes. Much attention has been devoted in the popular organizations

---

[8]Recall, however, the precursor arguments of theorists such as Barnard (1938) and Selznick (1957), who emphasized the importance of symbolic controls, including common missions and ideologies (see Chapter 3).

literature to the competitive advantages for organizations of creating "strong" cultures—belief systems that define a general mission sustaining commitment to something larger than self, provide guidelines so that participants can choose appropriate activities, and create sources of meaning and identification such that participants not only know what they are expected to do for the good of the organization but also want to do it. Such beliefs are inculcated and reinforced by rituals and ceremonies that provide collective occasions for expressing solidarity and commitment; by the raising up of heroes that personify common goals; and by the creation of slogans and symbols that signify shared values (Deal and Kennedy, 1982; Peters and Waterman, 1982). Precisely how such strong cultures are created and maintained is the subject of much current study (see Ashkanasy, Wilderom, and Peterson, 2000; Cameron and Quinn, 1996; Frost et al., 1985; Jelinek, Smircich, and Hirsch, 1983; Martin, 2002).

A major concern raised by the cultural controls in organizations is their potential development into an authoritarian system that is subject to abuse precisely because its controls are internalized and individual participants are unconstrained in the demands that they place on themselves and their colleagues. Peters and Waterman describe this darker side of cultural controls in the corporate setting:

> So strong is the need for meaning . . . that most people will yield a fair degree of latitude or freedom to institutions that give it to them. The excellent companies are marked by very strong cultures, so strong that you either buy into their norms or get out. (1982: 77)

This high level of commitment to special-purpose organizations is of concern in a society based on pluralism and committed to democratic institutions. We regard this kind of commitment as a potential source of pathology and comment further on its implications in the next chapter. On the other hand, based on his case study of a technology firm, Kunda (1992) argues that individual employees are not "cultural dopes." While, on the one hand, they can experience and respond to direct and overt cultural pressures they, on the other hand, are usually aware that they are being manipulated and "cognitively distance" themselves from the prevailing ideologies.

Other students of organizational culture emphasize its diversity and variety. Martin (1992; 2002), for example, contrasts dominant approaches which stress the unity of cultural beliefs within an organization with others that stress the extent of differentiation—subcultures—or still others that acknowledge the absence of a shared, integrated set of values—a fragmented culture. Martin treats these differences as paradigms—analytic models applicable to any organization—but also recognizes that the cultures of specific organizations may be better characterized by one rather than another perspective.

CRITICAL AND POSTMODERN CONCEPTIONS OF POWER

Our decision to discuss organizational goals in the same chapter that considers power and control processes was not an arbitrary one. As noted earlier, the concept of a dominant coalition as the agent by which organizational goals are selected and imposed highlights the linkage of power and goal setting. Critical theory and postmodern views of organizations emphasize the significance of this association and point to alternative models. Since our own discussion of power and control in organizations has remained within the mainstream boundaries of organization theory, it is important to call attention to alternative conceptions that challenge the validity of the conventional, "modernist" account. Since the Enlightenment period in Europe, which celebrated the emergence of an autonomous subject who could be emancipated from the bonds of tradition by knowledge informed by scientific methods, Western societies have favored models based on reason and positivism over those rooted in myth and tradition. This view is deeply entrenched in most accounts of organizations and management. The prevailing consensus is challenged by two differing, but related, critiques: critical and postmodern theory.

Critical Theory

Critical theory incorporates the central concerns and issues embodied in the views of conflict theorists. Whereas mainstream organizational theory views existing arrangements, as "structures not of domination but of formal, legitimate, functional authority" (Hardy and Clegg, 1996: 626), critical theorists view organizations as systems of domination in which one class of actors exploits others, and differences in interests, far from being negotiated and reconciled, are typically resolved by the more powerful suppressing the weaker. As discussed in Chapter 7, Marx emphasized the ways in which managerial ideologies developed to justify and "naturalize" arrangements that were arbitrary and inequitable.

> Through obscuring the construction process, institutional arrangements are no longer seen as choices but as natural and self-evident. The illusion that organizations and their processes are "natural" objects and functional responses to "needs" protects them from examination as produced under specific historical conditions (which are potentially passing) and out of specific power relations. In organization studies, organismic and mechanistic metaphors dominate, thereby leading research away from considering the legitimacy of control and political relations in organizations. (Alvesson and Deetz, 1996: 199)

Studies by Burawoy (1979) and Kunda (1992) among others illuminate the ways in which employees sometimes embrace and embroider these ideologies, so that workers achieve marginal gains but co-produce their own subordination. In modern organizations, technical rationality becomes elevated to be the exclusive basis for decision making, rendering marginal alternative forms of reason (Habermas, 1984/1987). From Taylor and Weber, to Thompson and Williamson, the quest is for heightened control of work processes in the service of efficiency. Intrinsic work qualities, such as creativity, variation, learning and personal development, and satisfaction, are subordinated to instrumental values (Alvesson, 1987). Individuals, the natural environment, human relationships become commodified: not ends of intrinsic value, but means to be appropriated and exploited. Genuine differences in interests are not allowed to surface as political issues but reframed as technical problems to be resolved by professional managers. In the view of critical theorists, modernism—which arose to combat the myths of traditional values—has itself become a myth, having "acquired an arbitrary authority, subordinated social life to technological rationality and protected a new dominant group's interests" (Alvesson and Deetz, 1996: 194).

Postmodernism

Postmodernism is a recent intellectual movement and still a work in progress. During the past quarter-century, a steady stream of loosely related ideas and critiques, primarily generated by European social and cultural theorists, has begun to challenge many of the central assumptions underlying contemporary social science, including views of organizations. This work shares much in common with other natural open system perspectives. Like resource dependence theory, it emphasizes the central role of power in shaping social institutions; like Marxist and critical theory, it does not accept at face value the rationalist claims of organizational designers and officials; and, like institutional theory, it stresses the overriding importance of cultural beliefs and symbolic processes. But its critique is more far-reaching than any of these. The principal architects of this approach include Foucault (1977) and Lyotard (1984); Nietzsche was the early guiding spirit.[9]

Postmodernists stress the importance of the symbolic, cultural elements of the social world. Our social world is socially constructed, and what we "see" or believe depends on the social situation and our location in it. Emphasis shifts from seeking explanations to providing interpretations, a development that signifies a number of important changes. First, as Agger observes, "postmodernism rejects the view that science can be spoken in a singular, universal voice" (1991: 121). Rather, "every knowledge is contextualized by its historical and cultural nature." Different truths are associated with differing social or temporal locations. "Social science becomes an accounting of social experience from these multiple perspectives of discourse/practice, rather than a larger cumulative enterprise committed to the inference of general principles of social structure

---

[9]Related perspectives include, in addition to critical theory, poststructuralism, for example, Derrida (1976), and some modes of feminist theory, for example, Moi (1985). For a thoughtful review of the relation between postmodernism and social science, see Rosenau (1992).

and organization" (p. 117). A related difference: all knowledge is self-referential or reflexive; that is, we as interpreting subjects understand events in the world not only in their relation to one another, but also to ourselves.

> Culture—the shared meanings, practices, and symbols that constitute the human world—does not present itself neutrally or with one voice. It is always multivocal and overdetermined, and both the observer and the observed are always enmeshed in it; that is our situation. There is no privileged position, no absolute perspective, no final recounting. (Rabinow and Sullivan, 1987: 7–8)

And there is a power/knowledge connection in that "the impossibilities in separating power from knowledge are assumed and knowledge loses a sense of innocence and neutrality" (Alvesson and Deetz, 1996: 205).

The more open one's conception of organization, the more vague and permeated its boundaries, the more varied its constituent elements, the more diverse the actors and their interests, the more discordant their conceptions and cognitive frames, the less possible it is to embrace a single, simple view of organization as rational system. Rationalities become multiple, interests and purposes are differentiated and contextualized. All organizations, being composed of multiple different individuals, each with his or her own unique history and constellation of interests and affiliations, are open systems, but they vary greatly in the extent to which these differences are recognized, legitimated, and taken into account in the organizing process. A "modernist" mentality seeks to impose order on the chaos, to resolve or suppress the contradictions, to integrate the competing interests and agendas so that a single, harmonious vision guides decisions and a consistent set of premises governs the conduct of participants. Clearly, in doing so, power will need to be invoked, conflicts resolved by negotiation or by recourse to authority, some participants excluded from decisions, or even from continued involvement in the organization. These are the instruments by which a uniform rationality is forged.

A postmodernist view emphasizes the diversity of elements that make up organizations. If uniformity exists, it is because diversity has been suppressed; if consistency dominates, it has been arbitrarily imposed. At the present time, postmodernism exists more as a critique of conventional understandings of organization than as an alternative model of organizing. As an approach to examining organizations, it resonates with the work of those theorists who insist that organizations *are* cultures: that their essence is to be found in their symbolic order. This order is constructed in and through social interactions of particular individuals in a particular setting (Smircich and Calás, 1987). One mode of analysis is, therefore, to "deconstruct" (Derrida, 1976) this order, to show that "meaning and understanding are not naturally intrinsic to the world and that they have to be constructed" (Cooper and Burrell, 1988). Postmodernists also do not privilege the formal structure but insist that this version of what is necessary or "rational" must be set alongside the various informal systems that represent attempts to resist any such single vision of order. The task of the analyst is to understand "what is 'going on' in a situation," recognizing that there is no one correct version, including that developed by the analyst. Truth is recognized to have many aspects and to speak with many voices.

As noted, it is less clear what a "postmodern" organization might look like. Presumably, its culture would support diversity, pluralism, and ambiguity (see Martin, 1992). Such a model would also push in the direction of de-differentiation, as Lash (1988) argues. This process would occur both internally, as specialized roles are eschewed and formalized hierarchies disestablished, but also externally, as organizational boundaries are disregarded, and actors allowed to mobilize support and pursue interests across lines seen to be artificial and arbitrary. Under such circumstances, organizational boundaries operate less and less to contain and support individual behavior. Perhaps the organic forms described in Chapter 7 or the "network" forms discussed in Chapter 11 provide evidence of steps toward postmodernist organizations (see also Clegg, 1990; Alvesson and Deetz, 1996).

Alternatively, it may be that the major contribution of postmodernist work will not be to serve as a guide for designing new forms of organizations, but to undermine or challenge the hegemony of existing modernist discourse that permeates most contemporary treatments of organization.

SUMMARY

Goals are put to many uses by organizational participants. They serve cognitive functions, guiding the selection of alternative courses of action. They have cathectic properties, serving as a source of identification and commitment for participants and as symbolic properties appealing to external constituencies. They provide present justifications for actions taken in the past and they provide criteria for the evaluation of performances, participants, and programs of action.

The concept of a dominant coalition that determines goals in organizations solves some of the mysteries of goal setting. It helps to avoid reification of the organization as a single purposeful actor but at the same time allows the organization's goals or preference structures to differ from those of all its human agents. The concept allows for the possibility that groups and individual participants have different interests and agendas and indicates how, through negotiation and the making of side payments, bargains are struck and a basis for common action developed. The concept of dominant coalitions also reminds us that individual participants do not have equal power in decision making and that the preferences and interests of some will receive more attention than those of others. Although individuals and groups bring preferences and interests with them into the organization, organizations are more than a setting where existing interests come together: they are places where new interests are created.

The size and shape of the dominant coalition changes over time in response to the changing external conditions to which the organization must adapt. Multiple sources of power exist in organizations, variably based in ownership, managerial and work skills, and boundary roles. As new sources of uncertainty and challenge develop in its environment, the organization creates offices to deal with them. Those who can successfully cope with such problems may be expected to acquire power within the organization, since others are dependent on them for critical services. As environments become more complex and turbulent, the dominant coalition grows and its shape changes to incorporate more and different specialists capable of managing one or another boundary problem. And as the composition of the membership of the dominant coalition changes, the goals of the organization also change, reflecting these shifts in power.

Some organizations lack clear goals or efficacious technologies. Such conditions are not hospitable to the formation and maintenance of organizations, but when they exist several alternative strategies are possible. Organizations may suffer and hope for inspiration, awaiting the appearance of a charismatic leader who will clarify ends and supply means. They may attune themselves to high levels of ambiguity, recognizing that almost-random connections among streams of problems, participants, and solutions will produce some decisions. Or they may engage in experiential learning, interpreting environmental cues in order to improvise changing strategies.

All collectivities control their members, but some distinctive control arrangements are to be found in organizations. Power is the potential for influence based on sanctioning ability, and authority is normatively regulated power. In informal groups authority tends to exist as endorsed power—power constrained by norms enforced by subordinates—but in formal organizations authority exists primarily as authorized power—power circumscribed and supported by norms enforced by officers superior to the power wielder. In some types of organizations, control may reside more in organizational cultures—that is, in shared, internalized beliefs and norms that provide meaning and guidance to individual members engaged in collective action.

Modernist views of organizations see them as structures for coordinating activities in the pursuit of specialized goals. Critical theories assert that such structures can only be created by power used to suppress diverse interests, and postmodernist theorists argue that unified goals can only arise when dominant actors delegitimate alternative interpretations and rationalities.

CHAPTER 9

The Dyadic Environment of the Organization

[T]he economic institutions of capitalism have the main purpose and effect of economizing on transaction costs.

OLIVER WILLIAMSON (1985)

[T]he fundamental concept in social science is Power, in the same sense in which Energy is the fundamental concept in physics.

BERTRAND RUSSELL (1938)

From the perspective of an organization, the world outside consists mainly of other organizations. A typical business might compete with other organizations in the same industry, buy inputs from suppliers, sell outputs to distributors, receive financing from banks or institutional investors, and partner with neighboring firms to support the local non-profit sector, which consists of yet more organizations. Their activities are regulated by governmental organizations such as the Occupational Safety and Health Administration, and when they want to influence these entities, they typically do so by retaining lobbying organizations. Blau and Scott (1962) called this environment the "organization set," a concept developed further by Evan (1966) that we have visited in prior chapters. In this chapter, we examine the array of tactics organizations use to manage their relations within their organization set.

Our discussion is organized around two broad questions: First, where do organizations place their boundaries? That is, why do organizations buy some inputs from suppliers outside the organization, while making others inside the organization's boundary? Why do they maintain close relationships with some "partners" and keep others at arm's-length? And why do they treat some employees as their most important asset, while treating others as relatively disposable "temps"? Second, what tactics do organizations use to navigate the power dynamics that arise through their exchange relations? How do organizations get the resources they need to survive while maintaining their maneuverability and avoiding dependence on powerful outsiders?

Transaction cost economics (TCE) addresses the first question by conceiving organizations as structures for governing exchange relations. The animating question of the transaction cost approach follows from the Nobel Prize–winning work of Ronald Coase (1937). Coase asked: Why are there firms at all? Why aren't all exchanges among the different parts of an organization left to the market? After all, hierarchical organizations are expensive—why pay for costly buildings filled with layers of bosses who don't produce anything if markets are good at coordinating activities without them? And if firms are so useful, why is there not just one big firm to coordinate the entire economy? The broad answer to Coase's question, elaborated below, involves comparative costs: sometimes it is cheaper to coordinate transactions through the market, and sometimes it is cheaper to have an organization oversee particularly vulnerable transactions. Transaction cost analysis has been the most influential import of economic thinking into organization theory, and the influence has been mutual. As Oliver Williamson, the most important theorist of TCE, concludes: "Economics should both speak and listen to organization theory" (1985: 402).

Resource dependence theory addresses the second set of questions by highlighting the give-and-take of interorganizational relations. Some exchanges create power imbalances: a potato processor that sells all its products to a single fast-food restaurant is highly vulnerable to the demands of that restaurant. This situation creates just the sort of uncertainty that open systems theorists highlighted, and that contingency theorists found so noxious to rational organizing. But the people who manage organizations are not stuck with the hand they are dealt—they have a large bag of tricks to manage their organization set, from cultivating alternative sources of supplies, to co-opting powerful outsiders by placing them in insider positions in the organization, to buying troublesome suppliers outright (Pfeffer and Salancik 1978). Resource dependence theory describes an array of tactics organizations use to manage their exchange relations so as to balance the need to minimize dependence and uncertainty while also maintaining managerial autonomy.

WHY ARE THERE ORGANIZATIONS, AND WHERE DO THEY PLACE THEIR BOUNDARIES?

TRANSACTION COSTS AND THE ORIGINS OF FIRMS

Markets and Organizations

In 1937 Ronald Coase, then an assistant lecturer at the London School of Economics, asked: Why, in a specialized exchange economy such as ours, are there firms? And even more basically, What *is* a firm? The second question was a bit easier: a firm is "the system of specialized relationships which comes into existence when the direction of resources is dependent on an entrepreneur" rather than on the price mechanism (Coase, 1937: 393). Instead of agreeing to exchange specified performances for specified payment, factors "inside" the firm simply agree to obey the entrepreneur's directions (within limits) in exchange for remuneration. But why are such agreements—which, after all, involve the suppression of the price mechanism—so widespread? Why does so much economic activity take place *inside* organizations rather than *between* them? The answer is that even "free" markets are not costless—the process of transacting creates its own costs. Formal contracts often require lawyers, and sometimes courts; negotiating them takes time and effort; and making sure that the counterparty (the person on the other side of the contract) does what they say they are going to do may be costly. In some circumstances, it is cheaper to just hire an input and specify the details later, rather than putting the effort and expense into writing a detailed contract. And it is just these circumstances, according to Coase, that determine which things are done inside firms, and how big a firm gets: "a firm will tend to expand until the costs of organizing an extra transaction within the firm become equal to the costs of carrying out the same transaction by means of an exchange on the open market or the costs of organizing in another firm" (Coase, 1937: 395).

Of course, we could just as well ask, "Why start with markets first and then ask about organizations?" Herbert Simon notes that

> A mythical visitor from Mars, not having been apprised of the centrality of markets and contracts, might find the new institutional economics rather astonishing . . . [Viewing through a telescope that showed organizations as solid areas of green and market transactions as red connecting lines], the greater part of the space below it would be within green areas, for almost all of the inhabitants would be employees, hence inside the firm boundaries. Organizations would be the dominant feature of the landscape . . . Our visitor . . . might be surprised to hear the structure called a market economy. 'Wouldn't "organizational economy" be the more appropriate term? (Simon, 1991: 27–28)

Drawing Boundaries

But we are still left with the question of where the boundaries come from. And to think about this question, it is useful to consider the larger flow of goods and services through the economy, as they are transformed from raw materials to final consumption.

The goods we buy at the store can be seen as final steps in a series that economists call the *value-added chain* (or just "value chain"). A box of corn flakes, for example, started as seeds sold by an agribusiness to a seed distributor. The seed distributor sold them to a farmer, who planted them, watered them, harvested the corn, and sold it to a processor. The processor shucked and processed the corn and sold it to a mill. The mill ground the corn and sold it to a cereal company. The cereal company processed the corn into flakes, packaged it, and sold it to a distributor. The distributor put the box of flakes on a truck that brought it to a grocery store. You took it from there.

At each step along the chain, *value* is added. "Value" in this sense is not a moral judgment, but an operational definition. It simply means that someone paid more for the goods (say, the processed corn) after the step than the cost of the labor and materials that went into that step. (If value is *not* added, then whoever performed that step is not likely to stay in business for long.) The economy can be seen as a nearly endless series of value chains linking organizations and industries into a network of transactions. A chain that leads to a final product is an *input-output system*, "a collection of activities that lead to the production of marketable outputs" (Harrison, 1994: 142). As Harrison points out, input-output systems are usefully seen as units of competition. That is, the choices of consumers at the end of these chains determine the fate of all the organizations along the way, from seed company to grocery. *Vertical integration* concerns the question of whether any two steps along this chain take place in one organization or two. Does the cereal company do its own milling, or pay someone else to do it? This is known as the "make or buy" question and applies both backward (milling the corn) and forward (distributing the boxes of cereal directly or selling to a distributor) along the supply chain.

There are many alternative ways of organizing input-output systems across organizational and national boundaries, and different formats have been prevalent at different times, places, and industries. In the United States, "The factory of 1880 remained a congeries of craftsmen's shops rather than an integrated plant" (Nelson, 1975: 4). But with the advent of mass production, vertically integrated manufacturing became the norm, particularly in North America. Ford Motor Company, widely regarded as the most significant pioneer of mass production, reached perhaps an apex of vertical integration with its famous River Rouge plant. During the 1930s, Ford made the steel and glass on-site that went into the Model A cars assembled there, and Ford owned the iron mines and lumber yards in Michigan, coal mines in Kentucky, and rubber plantations in Brazil that provided the raw materials, which were often transported on Ford-owned railroads and ships.

More recent experiments in automotive production have produced a mirror image of the organizational structure of the River Rouge plant. The Volkswagen light-truck and bus plant in Resende, Brazil opened in 1997 as a "modular consortium" of multinational suppliers that included Eisenmann from Germany, Delga from Brazil, and Cummins Engine from the United States.

> At the start of the Resende assembly line, workers from IochpeMaxion (a Brazilian manufacturer) put together a vehicle's chassis. Just across the first yellow line, a team from Rockwell International Inc. adds the axles and suspension. As the emerging vehicle proceeds down the spotless assembly line, passing one yellow line and then another, workers from Cummins Engine Co., Bridgestone/Firestone Inc. and other American, Brazilian, German, and Japanese firms add their respective pieces. What emerges less than 10 hours later on the other end of the line is a Volkswagen truck or bus chassis built with the help of just one Volkswagen employee—a master craftsman assigned to track the vehicle and solve problems on the spot. (*Chicago Tribune*, 4/13/97)

Clothes manufacturing offers a similar range of organizational forms. Those who stroll down 7th Avenue in New York City's garment district might be puzzled by the racks of partially completed clothing that are regularly rolled down the street. The garment district is a virtual version of the Resende plant: high-end fashion clothes are commonly produced by teams that consist of dozens of small, hyperspecialized firms located cheek-by-jowl in perhaps the last major manufacturing industry left in Manhattan, with separate firms doing tasks as specialized as sewing button holes and pleating skirts. Teams of firms are disbanded, and new ones organized, five times per year in anticipation of each new fashion "season," with the finished products going out under the name of a designer who most likely had nothing to do with either the design or the production of the garments bearing their moniker (Uzzi, 1997). At the other end of the fashion scale, the humble T-shirt is typically made from cotton grown in Texas, spun and woven in China, and printed in local shops in the United States—to be resold in markets in low-income countries in Africa or elsewhere when they are no longer fashionable to their wearers in the United States (Rivoli, 2005).

It is easy to document the great diversity of ways to organize production across organizational and national boundaries, from hyperintegrated forms like the River Rouge plant to the hyperdisintegrated forms that manufacture garments. But the relevant question from an economic perspective is: Which of these ways of organizing can survive competition with other ways, by providing goods for a price that consumers will pay and that allow participants to cover costs? The answer, according to transaction cost theorists, turns on the transaction costs of organizing in one way or another. Indeed, Oliver Williamson goes even further to claim that "the economic institutions of capitalism have the main purpose and effect of economizing on transaction costs" (Williamson, 1985: 17).

Defining Transaction Cost

A transaction occurs "when a good or service is transferred across a technologically separable interface" (Williamson, 1981: 552). This definition aims to identify the "atom" of production, the smallest element that could, in principle, be a freestanding unit. In the Resende plant, for instance, assembling the chassis and attaching the axles and suspension system are technologically separable and thus might each be done by separate units (indeed, by different firms), but painting the cab cannot be divided any further. These basic elements are like the Lego blocks from which the organization is built. Transactions can be analyzed in terms of *contracts*—voluntary agreements between actors for some kind of performance (completing a particular piece of work, delivering a good, and so on). Although using the terminology of contracts may sound like a symptom of our litigious society, it has a venerable history dating back to political theorists such as Hobbes, who referred to the "social contract" among citizens and government. The contract metaphor is a useful way to analyze voluntary transactions among actors, whether formally spelled out in a document or informally understood. Contract thus "provides a framework for well-nigh every type of group organization and for well nigh every type of passing or permanent relation between individuals and groups" (Llewellyn, quoted in Williamson, 1985: 5).

Transaction costs, then, are the costs of contracting, taken broadly. They include the costs of planning, adapting, and monitoring task completion and are "the economic equivalent of friction in physical systems" (Williamson 1985: 19). *Ex ante* costs include the expenses (in time and funds) of drafting, negotiating, and safeguarding contracts. A home buyer, for example, incurs the expense of a real estate agent to show her around available houses, the back-and-forth of making an offer and coming to an agreement, the lawyer who drafts the agreement, the earnest money placed in escrow, and the inspector who examines how well the house was built and maintained. *Ex post* transaction costs include maladaptation, haggling, setup and running costs, and bonding costs. Thus, our home buyer and seller might disagree about how clean is clean enough, whether the bookshelves are "built in" or not, or whether the pets buried in the back-yard are "material" to the contract.

Dimensions of Transactions. According to Williamson, "any issue that can be formulated as a contracting problem can be investigated to advantage in transaction cost economizing terms. Every exchange relation qualifies" (Williamson, 1985: 17). The kinds of contracts one needs vary by the kinds of transactions or relationships they are meant to govern. Williamson (1975; 1985) analyzes these dimensions in some detail. Transactions vary in their level of *uncertainty*, that is, the extent to which one can confidently map out all future contingencies. Transactions also vary in *frequency*. The greater the uncertainty and frequency, the greater the transaction costs are likely to be. But even highly uncertain and frequent transactions do not necessarily justify bringing a transaction within an orga-nization's boundaries. The key, Williamson argues, is the degree of *asset specificity* invested in the relationship between the two parties. Asset specificity is high when assets invested in a particular exchange relationship are much less valuable in other relationships (that is, the extent to which they are not "redeployable"). Examples of asset specificity include site specificity (e.g., a supplier opening a factory next door to its customer), physical asset specificity (e.g., buying specialized equipment or facilities to serve a parti-cular client), and human asset specificity (such as specialized training or learning-by-doing). In each case, one or both of the parties have devoted resources to the relationship that are much less valuable elsewhere. This leaves them vulnerable, and their vulnerability is likely to lead them to require safeguards before making relationship-specific investments. This is where organizations come in: organizations are a particularly effective kind of mechanism for protecting economically vulnerable relationships.

The problem could easily be solved if people were hyperrational, or were always perfect angels. If humans were boundlessly rational, then contracts could spell out all possibilities in advance. Or if they were perfect angels, then contracts could specify that, if circumstances changed, the parties would simply do the honorable thing. But people are boundedly rational (that is, "intendedly rational, but only limitedly so," as Simon put it), and they are sometimes opportunistic—indeed, when given a chance, some people lie, cheat, and steal! As a result, there is a limit to what written contracts can do, which in turn limits the willingness of parties to invest in specific assets.

The dilemma is that asset specificity often lowers downstream costs. Locating a supplier plant next door to a customer, for instance, makes delivery faster and cheaper, which in turn lowers the cost to the final consumer, which is potentially good for everyone along the value chain. But this situation of "bilateral supply," in which both buyer and supplier are particularly invested in each other, creates a prisoner's dilemma. Each has an incentive to cooperate for mutual benefit, but each also has an incentive to exploit the other. Consider the (apocryphal) story of General Motors (GM) and Fisher Body. In 1919, GM agreed to buy all of its closed auto bodies from Fisher, an outside supplier, for ten years. Auto bodies are, of course, made with highly specific dies—Fisher could not sell Chevrolet auto bodies to Ford. When GM's requirement for Fisher bodies unexpectedly rose dramatically, the Fisher brothers—who had negotiated a cost-plus contract—were in a position to "hold up" GM through using costly labor practices and refusing to open plants nearby (which would have reduced the cost base for GM). To avoid such hold up in the future, GM ended up acquiring the 40 percent of Fisher Body that it did not already own in 1926, making it a division of General Motors. (This case is described in Klein, Crawford, and Alchian [1978] and more carefully dissected in Freeland [2000].) Of course, one can also find many stories where GM, as the sole buyer, has sought to renegotiate with suppliers in midstream, which is its version of a hold-up problem. The point is that exchange relationships involving high asset specificity can be highly fraught.

How Organizations Solve the Bilateral Supply Problem. The dilemma introduced by asset specificity is this: investing in relationship-specific assets (e.g., locating a Fisher Body factory next to the GM/Buick assembly plant) can lower costs, which in turn lowers prices for final consumers and thus benefits the entire supply chain. But without some kind of contractual protection that assures each that they won't be the victim of opportunism, contracting parties will avoid investing in relationship-specific assets even if both would benefit. The cost of this contractual protection is, of course, a transaction cost. This is the kind of problem that formal organizations are uniquely able to solve, according to Williamson. Because organizations own both parties, the incentive to focus on one unit's best interests at the expense of the other (to "suboptimize") is lessened. It makes little sense for one unit of GM to overcharge another (e.g., after Fisher Body became a division of GM), as they all contribute to the same bottom line. Organizations can also invoke "fiat" (authority) to resolve disputes quickly, rather than threatening to go to court, as happens outside the organization. And organizations have better access to information to resolve disputes among units. Thus, vertical integration, although costly, can resolve the hold-up problem.

Yet this does not mean that organizations should vertically integrate all the way up the value chain (which Ford came close to doing at the River Rouge plant). Building auto bodies might be specialized enough to merit being brought within the organization's boundaries, but wheels and tires are relatively standardized, and thus there is little reason to bring them in-house: if one supplier is troublesome, then it can be replaced by another. Hierarchies are costly to build and maintain and therefore should be seen as the choice of last resort, when the potential costs resulting from asset specificity are particularly high. Between market (arm's-length exchange) and hierarchy (vertical integration) lie a range of alternative means of governing exchanges that may be less costly, including hierarchical contracting—where buyers might require the ability to inspect the operations of suppliers, and even leave employees on-site (Stinchcombe, 1985)—joint operating agreements, or other hybrid forms (covered in more detail in Chapter 11).

Empirical Applications

There have been dozens of studies arising out of transaction cost reasoning, from domains such as economics and organization theory, to corporate strategy, to marketing and operations management. In a review of many of these studies, David and Han summarize six main testable ideas from TCE:

1. As asset specificity increases, the transaction costs associated with market governance increase.
2. As asset specificity increases, hybrids and hierarchies become preferred over markets; at high levels of asset specificity, hierarchy becomes the preferred governance form.
3. When asset specificity is present to a nontrivial degree, uncertainty raises the transaction costs associated with market governance.
4. When asset specificity is present to a nontrivial degree, increasing uncertainty renders markets preferable to hybrids, and hierarchies preferable to both hybrids and markets.
5. When both asset specificity and uncertainty are high, hierarchy is the most cost-effective governance mode.
6. Governance modes that are aligned with transaction characteristics should display performance advantages over other modes; for example, when both asset specificity and uncertainty are high, hierarchy should display performance advantages over markets and hybrids. (2004: 41–42)

We highlight several of these below.

Make-or-buy decisions. Most early tests of TCE investigated specific make-or-buy decisions, and several of them examined the American auto industry, which is evidently the seedbed of TCE. The basic hypothesis is that the greater the asset specificity involved in producing a particular part or supply, the more likely that part is to be made inside the organization rather than by an outside supplier. Monteverde and Teece (1982) studied 133 components used by Ford and GM in 1976 and, using expert ratings of engineering cost (as a measure of asset specificity), found that the greater the engineering effort, the more likely the component was made primarily (80 percent or more) in-house. A subsequent study by Walker and Weber (1984) of sixty make-or-buy decisions by a division of an automaker also found a link between the level of market competition for suppliers (as a measure of asset specificity) and the decision to make or buy. They also found, however, that "in general, the effect of transaction costs on make-or-buy decisions was substantially over-shadowed by comparative *production* costs (Walker and Weber, 1984: 387). Masten (1984) found that complex and specialized inputs were much more likely to be sourced in-house than externally in a complex aerospace system.

One of the difficulties with cross-sectional studies is that we can't tell if asset specificity is a cause or an effect of vertical integration. In other words, it is possible that the higher asset specificity of internally produced parts *results from* being "inside" (and thus nearer to the design and manufacturing process). Walker and Poppo (1991) addressed this problem in a study of an assembly division of a large manufacturer by explicitly measuring transaction costs (the difficulty of reaching agreements with suppliers on cost allocation) and asset specificity (survey measures of the uniqueness of skills and equipment needed for the part) for both "made" and "bought" components. They found that, as TCE predicts, specialized assets generate lower transaction costs from internal suppliers than from sole-source external suppliers. And in a study of buyer-supplier relations in Japan, Lincoln and associates (1992) found that these relationships were often vouchsafed with shared directors or equity ownership ties rather than either being brought within a single organizational boundary or governed by hierarchical contracts. That is, sharing a director, or having ownership stakes in each other, can also shelter a potentially fraught relationship, substituting tighter ties for vertical integration.

Finally, in a particularly well done recent study, Nickerson and Silverman (2003) examined companies in the trucking industry and the nature of their contracts with drivers. Much as chain restaurants often have a combination of franchises (operated by independent owners) and corporate-owned outlets, trucking firms can draw on a combination of company drivers (who are employees of the firm, analogous to the "make" decision) and owner-operators (who are self-employed and own their own cab, analogous to "buying" an input). The appropriate mix of company drivers and owner-operators depends on the kind of business the trucking firm does (weight, distance, full-load or less-than-full load, and other factors), which can vary over time. Nickerson and Silverman found that firms' profitability was affected by the extent to which they used company drivers in the appropriate proportion to the kin̄ business they were doing, as TCE would predict. Moreover, the more ṃis-aligned the mix of drivers was, the faster the firm moved toward alignment, although the speed with which they did so varied among firms; unionized firms, for instance, were slower to adjust than nonunionized firms.

The M-form. In addition to discrete make-or-buy decisions, TCE proposes that some particular organizational forms are better than others for their task. Williamson (1975: chap. 8) argued for the benefits of the multidivisional form (or M-form) in large enterprises. In the functional organizational form (which Williamson calls the unitary form, or U-form), the organization is divided into departments such as manufacturing, sales, finance, and engineering. But at some level of size, these different parts become like informational silos, pursuing agendas that are best for their own interests but that may not be best for the firm overall. Management at the top doesn't get all the information it needs, and the information it does get overwhelms its ability to make decisions. In the ideal typical M-form, on the other hand, each division has the characteristics of a free-standing U-form organization, with its own manufacturing, sales, and other departments, as well as its own profit-and-loss responsibility. (GM, for instance, had separate divisions for Chevrolet, Pontiac, Buick, Oldsmobile, and Cadillac, each of which had its own dealer network.) Corporate headquarters acts as an internal capital market, determining which divisions get how much funding but stays out of the local operational details. Williamson states the "M-form hypothesis" elegantly: "The organization and operation of the large enterprise along the lines of the M-form favors goal pursuit and least-cost behavior more nearly associated with the neoclassical profit maximization hypothesis than does the U-form organizational alternative" (1975: 150). Or, big firms do better with an M-form than a U-form.

Evidence for the performance benefits of the M-form came from a study by Armour and Teece (1978) of twenty-eight petroleum firms among the 500 largest manufacturers in 1975. They found that large petroleum firms with an M-form increased their return on equity by an impressive 2 percentage points during the 1955–1968 period compared to firms with a functional form. Yet by the 1969–1973 period, the effect had disappeared—perhaps because by that point all the organizations that would benefit from the M-form had already adopted one. Fligstein (1985) found mixed evidence for the idea that size, or growth in size, prompted the adoption of the M-form in decade-by-decade analyses of large U.S. firms from 1919–1979. On the other hand, Palmer, Jennings, and Zhou (1993) found that large manufacturers that did not have an M-form in 1962 were more likely to adopt one subsequently to the extent that they were industrially diverse, geographically dispersed, and were expanding via acquisitions, each broadly consistent with the M-form hypothesis.

The employment relation. A third main area of research in TCE has examined the employment relation, using the same reasoning that applied to the make-or-buy decision for suppliers. The basic proposition is that the strength of connection between firms and employees (from day-to-day temp to lifetime employee bound by an internal labor market) depends on the level of *human asset specificity* that the employee has with respect to the organization. Note that asset specificity and skill are not the same thing: executives and physicians may have high levels of skill that are completely transferable from one organization to another. Rather, asset specificity entails skills that are idiosyncratic to one particular employer—knowing the unique database system, or having a network of colleagues and other contacts that allows one to get things done. In describing the "modern enterprise" of his day, Kaysen stated that "The whole labor force of the modern corporation is, insofar as possible, turned into a corps of lifetime employees, with great emphasis on stability of employment" (1957: 312). By today's standards, this seems inconceivable. Moreover, from a TCE perspective, it doesn't make economic sense: organizations ought to offer long-term employment (and related perquisites) only to those employees with highly specific human assets. Other employees could ideally be hired on a day-to-day, as-needed basis. The empirical implication of this reasoning is that employment contracts should be more binding (and perhaps more generous) the more firm-specific human assets an employee has (see Pfeffer and Baron, 1988). Tests of this idea are considerably more ambiguous, and indeed Goldberg (1980) argues that even the most avowedly un-specific jobs—such as on Ford's assembly line, where training was virtually instantaneous—can merit protection when it supports greater productivity.

Anomalies and extensions. Several studies have explicitly addressed some of the limitations of transaction cost analysis. Stinchcombe (1985) describes contracts that combine some of the "arm's-length" characteristics of conventional contracts with other control features usually associated with authority exercised within organizational boundaries. He observes that these augmented contracts are employed as the principal control mechanisms even under conditions of extraordinary complexity and uncertainty—for example, in relations between defense agencies and supplier firms or between nation-states and offshore oil companies—where we would expect, under transaction cost arguments, to find reliance on internal organizational controls. The contracts developed to manage such interdependence involve a variety of conditional clauses evoking hierarchical mechanisms to handle possible contingencies and to resolve disputes. For example, defense contractors may allow the purchaser to inspect compliance to requirements and progress toward objectives as necessary; to change requirements or specifications as the work proceeds; and to renegotiate the allocation of costs and benefits depending on what outcomes occur. Such hierarchical rights undermine the autonomy of the independent contractors and constitute a step in the direction of creating a joint venture between the contracting parties—except that the "venture" is a specific project rather than a continuing program of cooperative activity. Such admittedly complex contracting arrangements are widely employed in high-cost–high-gain (and high-risk) situations, such as large-scale construction and defense and space technology.

Another theme that arises in more recent work is that the diversity of "survivable" forms may be too great to be explained by the simple mechanics of transaction costs. Lazerson (1995) finds that the knitwear industry in Modena, Italy is organized much as it might have been prior to the industrial revolution, with the work done by individual household microfirms (a system known as "putting out"). Such a system would be seen by TCE as archaic and riddled with transaction costs compared to a centralized factory, according to Lazerson, yet it manages to thrive when embedded in the right close-knit (so to speak) social context. Larson (1992) also argues for the importance of social rather than legal control in a very different context—dyadic ties among entrepreneurial firms. And Zhou and colleagues (2003) examine contractual relations among private and state-owned firms in China's transitional economy, finding that formal contracts were very widely used, but that social interactions also served as a sort of contractual support, increasing with the level of risk. In each case, the language of formal contracts would seem to obscure the importance of social embeddedness that allows some kinds of exchange relations (Granovetter, 1985), a concern we take up in the next section.

Criticisms and Responses

Transaction cost analysis has provoked a vigorous dialogue in organization theory, and criticisms of the approach range from the theoretical (it represents "Panglossian functionalism"—Granovetter [1985] to the highly practical (it is "bad for practice" and its cynical view of human nature becomes a corrosive self-fulfilling prophecy—Ghoshal and Moran [1996]. The first critique has received the most attention from scholars. As Mark Granovetter (1985) describes it, TCE suffers from several difficulties. First, its view of human nature is "undersocialized," portraying people as if they were social atoms unsentimentally pursuing their pecuniary interests with little regard for the social connections around them—which, in any case, are mostly a source of friction. As we saw above, however, social relations are a central part of several contemporary input-output systems, from knitwear in Modena to interfirm relations in China to high-tech alliances in Silicon Valley. Far from being a source of friction, they are an essential element in the structure of business.

Williamson would agree: social structures and culture really do matter, in that they shape the kinds of contracts that can be created and enforced. If family connections reduce the cost of enforcing contracts, and this enables family-based business networks to thrive, then so much the better for TCE! Moreover, Williamson argues, finding occasional anomalies is hardly enough to falsify the theory—it is more theoretically fruitful to focus on the main case, and not the "bump on the pickle" or "tosh" (Williamson, 1994).

Perhaps more importantly, Granovetter argues, TCE pursues a flawed approach to explanation by working backwards from the kinds of organizations we see today to the economic purpose or "function" they must serve. This is analogous to the "just-so" stories told by Rudyard Kipling—fanciful children's tales such as "How the Leopard Got His Spots." The problem with this approach (known in sociology as "functionalism"—see Chapter 3) is that current structures are often compatible with any number of alternative explanations. An economist might claim that, in a competitive economic system, only the strong organizations survive, while the weak are quickly selected out; thus, the organizations we see today are the "fit" ones. But Granovetter states, "The operation of alleged selection pressures is here neither an object of study nor even a falsifiable proposition but rather an article of faith" (1985: 493).

Again, Williamson responds that he is not like Dr. Pangloss—we do not (necessarily) live in the "best of all possible organizational worlds." But business people (and others) are pretty good at choosing, if not the best, then the better of the available options among organizational structures. People with reasonable foresight, and with at least a modest level of self-interest, can choose better from worse without being omniscient—this is simply "plausible foresightedness" (Williamson, 1994: 88). Over time, as other business people see that some forms work better than others, they are prone to gravitating toward those forms. On the other hand, what it is that business people "see" when they observe organizational forms may well be flawed—Freeland (1996) argues that the idealized M-form at GM described by Williamson bore little resemblance to how the organization really worked, and that following Williamson's blueprint for an M-form would have been disastrous for the company! (Similarly, executives at AT&T in the late 1990s were fired for failing to achieve the profitability of their rivals at WorldCom—profitability that later turned out to be fabricated!)

A final kind of criticism of TCE comes from other economists, who argue that the very idea of a "make or buy" decision might be a misstatement—firms, in essence, "buy" everything, so there is nothing special about one kind of contract or another. Jensen and Meckling state, "it makes little or no sense to try to distinguish those things that are 'inside' the firm (or any other organization) from those things that are 'outside' of it. There is in a very real sense only a multitude of complex relationships (i.e., contracts) between the legal fiction (the firm) and the owners of labor, material and capital inputs and the consumers of output" (1976: 311). The implications of this are troubling not just for TCE, but for *any* theory that takes seriously organizational boundaries. But Williamson (1994) points out that this kind of criticism is simply misleading: for example, courts might decide a legal case between Fisher Body and GM as separate companies, but they would not adjudicate a dispute between two divisions of the same company. Similarly, full-time employees have different legal rights from independent contractors and temps, even when they are performing the same kind of work. Organization boundaries, in short, do matter—at least in the eyes of the law.

By this point, many of the essential insights of TCE are largely taken for granted within organization theory, and thus the most vibrant research on transaction costs today is in research on franchising and supply chain management, rather than organization studies. But as we will see, examination of network organizations, and of the influence of information and communication technologies on organizational forms, still owes a great debt to TCE.

HOW DO ORGANIZATIONS MANAGE THEIR RELATIONS WITH OTHER ORGANIZATIONS?

RESOURCE DEPENDENCE AND THE NEGOTIATED ENVIRONMENT

Transaction cost analysis gives a useful set of tools for analyzing the question of organizational boundaries, but there is a range of tactics beyond make or buy that organizations use to manage their organization set. Moreover, organization theorists are often dissatisfied with economic explanations that focus on the efficiency benefits of particular organizational actions. Any observer of the U.S. economy during the late 1990s Internet bubble and the corporate scandals of the early 2000s might have a hard time believing that a search for economic efficiency was behind these events—baser motivations like greed, fear, and a quest for power might seem more like it! And it is from this perspective that resource dependence theory arose. In contrast to the rational systems approach of TCE, resource dependence offers a natural system perspective that highlights the organizational politics behind choices such as the make-or-buy decision. As Pfeffer recalled, "Resource dependence was originally developed to provide an alternative perspective to economics theories of mergers and board interlocks, and to understand precisely the type of interorganizational relations that have played such a large role in recent 'market failures'" (2003: xxv).

Resource dependence draws on three core ideas to explain how organizations manage their relationships with other organizations. First, social context matters: while observers often attribute great potency to organizational leaders, even to the point of hero worship, much of what organizations do is in response to the world of other organizations that they find themselves in, as open systems theorists emphasized. Second, organizations can draw on varied strategies to enhance their autonomy and pursue their interests. This idea is familiar from Cyert and March's (1963) description of "the negotiated environment" and Thompson's (1967) bridging strategies. Third, and most distinctively, power—not just rationality or efficiency—is important for understanding what goes on inside organizations and what external actions they take. The emphasis on power, and the careful analysis of the repertoires available to firms to pursue it, is the distinctive hallmark of resource dependence theory.

Virtually all of the formulations of power and exchange relations among organizations, including resource dependence theory, build on the conception of power developed by Richard Emerson (1962), as discussed in Chapter 8. But whereas Emerson applied his power-dependence formulation to individual actors, Pfeffer shifted the level of analysis to organizations.

Emerson's formulation is useful for several reasons when applied to a given organization and the set of organizations to which it relates (see Thompson, 1967). Power is not viewed as some generalized capacity, but as a function of specific needs and resources that can vary from one exchange partner to another. Thus, it is possible for an organization to have relatively little power in relation to its suppliers, but considerable power in relation to its buyers. Further, we would expect each supplier's power to vary with the importance of the resources it supplies and the extent to which alternative suppliers are available. This approach avoids a zero-sum view of power, in which it is assumed that when one actor gains power, another must lose it. Rather, it becomes possible for two actors both to hold power over each other—through an increase in their interdependence. This theory of exchange-based power also allows the use of sophisticated network measures, such as those developed by Ronald Burt (1983). Knowing how much organizations exchange with each other, and the extent to which they have alternatives, allows a fairly precise rendering of the power-dependence relations between any two organizations.

How is this different from transaction cost analysis? After all, the central theme of TCE is the friction between two organizations that arises when they are mutually dependent. The story of Fisher Body and GM sounds like just the sort of thing that Emerson's theory of power would predict. The difference is that resource dependence argues that organizational actions are often taken "regardless of considerations of profit or efficiency" (Pfeffer, 1987: 27). Whereas TCE assumes that selection pressures will, sooner or later, select out the weak and allow the strong to survive due to their greater efficiency in the marketplace, resource dependence assumes there is a lot more slippage out there, and that organizations—particularly large ones—have a great deal of discretion to manage their environment. And because it does not rely on arguments about market selection, it is arguably more general: "Thus, the resource dependence approach readily encompasses the explanation of behavior from organizations of any type" (Pfeffer, 1987: 30), covering businesses, nonprofits, or governmental organizations. In short, anywhere there is power, resource dependence will have something to say.

Organizational Responses to Interdependence

The core argument of resource dependence is quite similar to what we saw with the contingency theory of organizational design, namely, that organizations should choose the least constraining approach to coordinate relations with other organizations and to reduce the dependence that their exchanges create. One of the simplest approaches is to grow big: larger size, particularly relative to one's competitors, is typically associated with increased power. Larger firms are better able to set prices, control how much they produce, and influence the decisions of related organizations, including regulators. Pfeffer and Salancik summarize the advantages of size:

> Organizations that are large have more power and leverage over their environ- ments. They are more able to resist immediate pressures for change and, moreover, have more time in which to recognize external threats and adapt to meet them. Growth enhances the organization's survival value, then, by providing a cushion, or slack, against organizational failure. (1978: 139)

A second approach is to keep one's options open by finding and main- taining alternatives. Rather than relying entirely on Fisher Body for its auto bodies, GM might instead have cultivated a set of alternative suppliers to reduce Fisher's power position. Of course, for the reasons described in the previous section, it is often difficult to do this because the resource might be too specialized.

Bridging Mechanisms. The other major strategies all involve some kind of bridging mechanisms: efforts to control or in some manner coordinate one's actions with those of formally independent entities. One important bridging tactic is cooptation.

Cooptation. As defined in Chapter 3, *cooptation* is the incorporation of representatives of external groups into the decision-making or advisory structure of an organization. The significance of this practice in linking organizations with their environments was first described by Selznick (1949), who also noted its daunting costs. Selznick argued that by coopting representatives of external groups, organizations are, in effect, trading sovereignty for support.

Most studies of cooptation have focused on boards of directors, investigating the extent of interlocking ties (directors serving on more than one board) among various types of organizations. It is argued that allowing representatives of other organizations to participate in decision making in the focal organization is an effort by the linked organizations to coordinate their activities. Such representatives may range from strong, controlling directors imposed by one organization on another to common messengers transmitting information of mutual interest. Not all board members are environmental representatives: some are there to provide specialized expertise, to oversee and augment the administrative skills of management (Mizruchi, 1996). To the extent that directorate ties function as a coopta- tion tactic for dealing with the interdependence of organizations, we would expect board appointments to vary with the amount and type of resource needs and flows confronting the focal organization. For instance, GM might invite an executive of Fisher Body to serve on its board, in the hopes of gaining a sympathetic ear. This idea has been widely studied. Indeed, "The structure of corporate boards and, in particular, the use of interlocks to manage resource dependence has probably been the most empirically examined form of intercorporate relation" (Pfeffer, 1987: 42).

How widely used is this tactic? The answer varies by sector, and the popularity of cooptation via board ties has probably waned. Pfeffer and Salancik (1978) find two kinds of evidence. First, the extent to which firms share directors within a broadly defined industry sector is highest at an intermediate level of industry concentration. At high levels of concentration, they argue, firms in an industry can simply observe each other's actions to coordinate, while in highly competitive industries, ties to other industry members are unlikely to help much. At moderate levels of concentration, sharing directors might help firms to avoid damaging (for the firms) price competition. Second, the extent to which directors are shared *across* industries is positively related to the volume of exchange among these industries. Similarly, Burt (1983) finds that the prevalence of interindustry interlocks maps onto levels of interindustry constraint, consistent with the cooptation hypothesis. On the other hand, evidence at the firm level is much less compelling. Palmer (1983) found that "broken" ties (ties between companies that are lost when the shared director retires or dies) were rarely reconstituted during the 1960s, and the level of resource constraint between two firms did not affect reconstitution (Palmer, Friedland and Singh, 1986). (Ties to financial institutions, however, follow a different pattern from other interlocks—see Stearns and Mizruchi [1986].) More recent work suggests that ties within the same industry almost *never* happen—in the United States, they have been illegal since the 1914 Clayton Act (Zajac, 1988). Moreover, very few firms invite executives of powerful customers or suppliers to serve on their boards for the simple reason that it would place them at a severe disadvantage when it came to negotiating prices and terms; thus, fewer than 5 percent of large corporations in the 1990s had executives of major buyers or suppliers on the board (Davis, 1996).

In the nonprofit sector, cooptation takes on a slightly different cast. With the coming of more conservative policies in the 1980s, including the reduction in the federal role and in funding for community services, cooptation shifted from being a primarily vertical tactic to being a horizontal tactic. Community agencies employ numerous cooptation mechanisms— joint board memberships, liaison roles, interorganizational brokers—as a way to increase resources, reduce uncertainty, and increase legitimacy (Galaskiewicz and Bielefeld, 1998). Indeed, federal and state programs currently place great emphasis on coordination among community agencies, often as a condition of eligibility for funding. Whereas federal regulations discourage or proscribe cooptation among competing organizations in the for-profit sector, they encourage or mandate it as a means of coordination among public and nonprofit agencies.

Alliances. Another approach to dealing with interdependence is to form alliances or joint ventures. Alliances involve agreements between two or more organizations to pursue joint objectives through a coordination of activities or sharing of knowledge or resources. A joint venture occurs when two or more firms create a new organization to pursue some common purpose. From a resource dependence perspective, both of these are potentially useful tools for managing interdependence. Pfeffer and Salancik (1978: 152–61) find that joint ventures are most common in industries at intermediate levels of concentration, as was true of interlocks. We go into further details on alliances in Chapter 11.

Mergers and acquisitions. Yet another, and the most resource-intensive means of managing interdependence, is the one emphasized by TCE, namely, to merge or acquire. Three major types of mergers have been identified:

1. *Vertical integration* occurs when organizations at adjacent stages in the value chain merge with one another. Vertical integration, of course, takes place between actual or potential exchange partners. For example, furniture manufacturers may merge (backward) with lumber companies or (forward) with furniture distributors or showrooms.

2. *Horizontal mergers* occur when organizations performing similar functions merge to increase the scale of their operation. For example, two or more hospitals may merge, forming a hospital "chain." Economies of scale are often realized, such as in housekeeping, laundries, or specialized therapeutic or managerial services.

3. *Diversification* involves one organization acquiring one or more other organizations that are neither exchange partners nor competitors, but organizations operating in different domains. For example, in the 1960s ITT, an electronics-manufacturing company, acquired a rent-a-car company, a major hotel chain, a home-building company, a baking company, a producer of glass and sand, a consumer-lending firm, and a data-processing organization. The product of extreme diversification is the *conglomerate.*

Pfeffer and Salancik argue that

> vertical integration represents a method of extending organizational control over exchanges vital to its operation; that horizontal expansion represents a method for attaining dominance to increase the organization's power in exchange relationships and to reduce uncertainty generated from competition; and that diversification represents a method for decreasing the organization's dependence on other, dominant organizations. (1978: 114)

Each type, in short, represents a method of managing organizational interdependence.

Most of the evidence on resource dependence theory comes from the study of mergers and acquisitions. This is a particularly useful context because the predictions arising out of TCE and resource dependence are to some extent in conflict: TCE emphasizes the efficiency benefits of "appropriate" vertical integration, while resource dependence argues that merger "is undertaken to accomplish a restructuring of the organization's interdependence and to achieve stability in the organization's environment, rather than for reasons of profitability or efficiency" (Pfeffer and Salancik, 1978: 114). On the face of it, the weight of evidence would seem to favor resource dependence, as most acquisitions either do not increase organizational performance, or actually decrease it—share prices of acquiring firms frequently decline upon the announcements of acquisitions (Morck, Shleifer, and Vishny, 1990), suggesting that the stock market generally views them as a bad idea. The verdict on diversifying mergers is especially negative: "The evidence that corporate diversification reduces company value is consistent and collectively damning" (Black, 1992: 903), and Porter (1987) finds that firms that diversified ended up disposing of three-quarters of their acquisitions. But what about the causes of mergers?

Early evidence on merger activity came from industry-level studies of the link between exchange relations and the propensity of mergers. As with interlocks, the expectation is that the greater the exchanges between industries, the more likely are mergers between members of those industries. There was indeed a link between the volume of interindustry exchange (at the level of highly aggregated industries) and the tendency to merge. Evidence on horizontal mergers is similar to the findings on interlocks: firms in an industry were most likely to merge when the industry was at an intermediate level of concentration. The evidence on diversification was rather indirect, suggesting that firms in industries that did more business with the government (i.e., those with greater exchange-based dependence on one customer) were more likely to diversify into other industries that were not as constrained.

Collective Action. While the tactics we have described thus far involve dyadic ties with particular members of the organization set, organizations can also engage in collective action to help manage their environment. We consider two options.

Associations. These are arrangements that allow collections of organizations to work in concert to pursue mutually desired objectives. They operate under many names, including trade associations, cartels, leagues, coordinating councils, and coalitions. Both similar and dissimilar organizations enter into associations at the community or local level. We find many associations of similar organizations—for example, hospital councils and associations of retail merchants—as well as associations of diverse organizations—such as the Community Chest and Chamber of Commerce. Individual organizations join associations in order, variously, to garner resources, secure information, exercise influence, or obtain legitimacy and acceptance. The structure and strength of associations vary greatly: some are informal and weak, others are formally structured and exercise great power over their members. (Warren [1967] provides a useful typology.)

The trade association is an important form operating at the field or industry, national, and even international level. It is "a coalition of firms or business persons who come together in a formal organization to cope with forces and demands to which they are similarly exposed" (Staber and Aldrich, 1983: 163). There is evidence that trade associations are more likely to form in less highly concentrated sectors where too many firms are present to permit more tacit coordination (Pfeffer and Salancik, 1978: 179). The power of trade associations varies markedly from society to society. Trade associations in the United States are more numerous, more specialized, and much less influential than those in most Western European countries, Japan, and Korea (Gerlach and Lincoln, 1992; Granovetter, 1994). Most trade associations in the United States are not sufficiently strong or organized to serve as vehicles for centralizing and representing the interests of industries, as do trade associations in more corporatist states (see Berger, 1981; Streeck and Schmitter, 1985). Institutional theorists attend to these structures as important examples of governance systems at the organizational field level (see Campbell, Hollingsworth, and Lindberg, 1991; Scott, 2001a).

Turning to the state. A final approach to managing interdependence is to draw on the powers of the state to change the profile of dependencies. Lindblom has pointed out that "an easy way to acknowledge the special character of government as an organization is simply to say that governments exercise authority over other organizations" (1977: 21). Governments set the rules of the game that shape what organizations can do, and even what will count as an "organization" (as opposed to another kind of actor). Different governmental bodies in China have different standards for what counts as a firm, and thus the simple question "How do we know when an enterprise exists?" cannot be answered definitively (Clarke, 2003). In the United States, the Sherman Act of 1890 was created to limit the ability of organizations to form cartels (or "trusts," hence the name "antitrust"), which encouraged competitors to merge instead, forming large national enterprises such as US Steel and General Electric (GE). The Clayton Act of 1914 was intended to limit collusion, including by banning interlocks among firms in the same industry. The Celler-Kefauver Act of 1950 limited both vertical and horizontal mergers, which encouraged firms seeking to grow through acquisition to pursue strategies of diversification. But organizations are not simply passive recipients of laws handed down from above: they have resources of their own to shape governmental policies. Through political contributions, lobbying, cooptation, and the exchange of personnel with government agencies such as regulators, organizations can shape their political environment in ways that reduce their constraint. Mizruchi (1992) argues that the ability of companies to coordinate their political actions, and thus to be more effective, hinges on some of the same factors identified by resource dependence theory, namely, that firms with substantial exchange relations—particularly those connected by shared directors or ownership ties—are more prone to cooperate, for example, giving to the same political candidates via their political action committees (PACs—which are legally separate from the company itself). Moreover, sometimes these tactics work: Vogus and Davis (2005) find that states in which locally headquartered companies were densely tied by shared directors were quick to adopt laws regulating hostile takeovers, which the executives of those companies favored.

Choosing Among Tactics

How do those who run organizations decide which of these tactics to pursue in order to manage their interdependence? Organizations face a dilemma: "On the one hand, future adaptation requires the ability to change and the discretion to modify actions. On the other hand, the requirements for certainty and stability necessitate the development of interorganizational structures of coordinated behaviors—interorganizational organizations. The price for inclusion in any collective structure is the loss of discretion and control over one's activities" (Pfeffer and Salancik, 1978: 261). This suggests that each strategy implies a trade-off between autonomy and adaptability, on one hand, and stability and certainty on the other. Mergers are both costly and constraining, and at some times legally proscribed, so merger is likely to be a strategy of last resort. When merger is either illegal or too costly in terms of resources and potential lost autonomy, organizations will seek to use cooptation, such as by appointing outsiders to the board or engaging in associations (Pfeffer and Salancik, 1978: 167). The array of strategies can thus be seen as a kind of continuum from maintaining alternatives and seeking to hold outside actors at arm's length, to cooptation through board ties, alliances, or associations, to outright acquisition (see Figure 9–1).

Recent Empirical Applications

The early evidence reported in Pfeffer and Salancik (1978) was highly appealing but often relied on relatively underdeveloped empirical methods. Finkelstein (1997) replicated the studies on mergers using a longer time frame and more precise measures of interindustry resource constraint, examining acquisitions by fifty-one manufacturing industries from 1947 to 1982 at five-year intervals, finding evidence that the effects were substantially larger in the late 1970s and 1980s (i.e., after the original studies). This suggests that when firms make acquisitions, they have a preference for

Symbiotic	*Commensalistic*
⌐ Vertical mergers	⌐ Horizontal mergers
├ "Symbiotic" joint ventures	├ Cooperative joint ventures
├ Hierarchical contracts	├ Trade associations
├ Contracting	├ Cooptation/collusion
Markets	Markets

FIGURE 9–1 Symbiotic and Commensalistic Bridging Strategies.
Source: Adapted from Davis, Kahn, and Zald (1990: Figures 2.1 and 2.2, pp. 34–35).

buying constraining suppliers rather than unrelated firms. Notably, the effect was weaker when "industry" was defined more finely (at a four-digit SIC level rather than a two-digit level, as in the original study). Finkelstein notes that this may reflect the difficulty of testing a firm-level theory using industry-level data. Indeed, this is an important point: the research evidence on mergers, interlocks, and joint ventures was all at the industry level, but the theory is about organizations, not industries. This is an instance of the "ecological fallacy" described by Robinson (1950).[1]

More recent studies have examined organization-level power relations and found important links between an organization's power position and its tactics for maneuvering in its environment. Baker (1990) examined the decline in the traditional system of ties between companies and their investment banks and found that the effect was more pronounced among powerful firms: such firms were able to weaken ties to their main investment banks and cultivate a set of alternative "suppliers," as resource dependence would advise, whereas weaker companies were compelled to maintain strong primary ties to particular banks. Conversely, large commercial banks, which traditionally recruited "celebrity" directors such as major CEOs and former government officials to serve on their board, have substantially retrenched as their traditional business of lending to corporations has faced increased competition from markets (Davis and Mizruchi, 1999). The result is that banks' level of network centrality has declined substantially from their previous glory days. By the same token, interorganizational alliances, which grew substantially during the 1980s and particularly the 1990s, tend to follow patterns of resource interdependence (Gulati and Gargiulo, 1999). Pfeffer (2003) quotes Christensen and Bower (1996: 212): "a firm's scope for strategic change is strongly bounded by the interests of external entities (customers, in this case) who provide the resources a firm needs to survive." Power, in short, seems to have continuing value in explaining why organizations do what they do.

Challenges

Resource dependence has been a widely influential theory of organizations, providing a parsimonious yet provocative power-based explanation of organizational actions such as why organizations make the acquisitions they do, and whom they recruit for their boards of directors. It also provided

---

[1]This fallacy involves taking statistical relationships at the group level (industry) and treating them as if they applied at the individual level (organization). Robinson famously showed that on a state-by-state level, there was a very high positive correlation between the rate of literacy and the percentage of the state's population that was foreign-born, yet on an individual-by-individual level the true relationship between literacy and being foreign-born was negative, as one might expect. Interested readers can read how this happens mathematically in Robinson's original article (1950). Similar examples are rife: states with higher average incomes tended to go for Kerry in the 2004 presidential election, while the link between individual-level income and voting for Kerry was much more complicated.

substantive questions that prompted the development of network analyses of organizational relations, such as Burt's (1983) work specifying how networks of exchange relations among industries produce either autonomy or constraint for firms in those industries. One of the theory's great strengths, however—its focus on highly topical strategies such as mergers and interlocks—has also posed some limitations, as the prevalence of these different forms has changed substantially since the 1970s along with broader economic shifts. Indeed, the kinds of firms that followed the prescriptions of resource dependence theory in the 1970s, by diversifying into unrelated industries in order to avoid dependence on any one, were highly likely to be taken over and "busted up" during the 1980s de-conglomeration wave. About one-third of the largest manufacturers in the United States were acquired or merged during the 1980s, usually through a "hostile takeover" in which outsiders buy the company's stock against the wishes of the company's board of directors and then installs its own management team. Most diversified companies were broken back up into more "focused" parts, and often resold to competitors in those same industries. By the second half of the decade, almost all firms had abandoned the tactic of diversification, and very few did vertical acquisitions; rather, freed from antitrust concerns by the Reagan-era Justice Department, most mergers were with competitors large and small (Davis, Diekmann, and Tinsley, 1994).

By the 1990s, the manufacturing conglomerate had largely disappeared in the United States (with a few exceptions, such as GE), and firms increasingly sought greater flexibility by selling off parts of their operations and laying off permanent employees in favor of contingent workers ("downsizing"). Sara Lee, formerly a diversified manufacturer of foods (such as Ball Park Franks) and clothing (Champion, Hanes), announced plans in 1997 to sell off most of its manufacturing capability (regrettably labeled "de-verticalization") in order to focus on design and marketing. This followed a model pioneered by Nike, which does almost none of its own manufacturing but rather subcontracts to firms in East Asia. Where size had been a primal source of power in resource dependence theory, being "lean" was more valued in the 1990s, and the measure of size that mattered most was market capitalization (that is, the value of the company's outstanding shares on the stock market). And vertical integration, once a way to stabilize exchange relations, had become a source of constraint, a topic we take up in more detail in Chapter 11.

As we have already described, the use of board interlocks as tools of cooptation also lost favor during the 1980s and 1990s. Board ties among competitors had been illegal since 1914, so to the extent that interlocks mapped onto industry concentration, it was only at a very highly aggregated level. And by 1994, the number of firms that invited executives of firms in major buyer or supplier industries to serve on their boards had reached a minimal level: an examination of 786 firms that included members of the *Fortune* 500 largest manufacturers, 100 largest banks, 50 largest service firms, 50 largest diversified financials, 50 largest retailers, and 50 largest transportation firms revealed that no more than 4 percent of manufacturers had a significant buyer or supplier executive on their board, and only one in twelve had an executive from one of the 100 largest banks (Davis, 1996). Surveys of directors revealed great hesitancy at the prospect of having a supplier on the board, with the exception of the company's law firm. The cost of cooptation, it seems, is too great for most firms to bear.

Changing economic times and regulatory regimes, in short, lead to changes in the repertoires that organizations use to mange their interdependence. While achieving greater size and stabilizing dependencies through mergers may have been the preferred tactic of the 1960s and 1970s, business organizations now draw on a different set of tools. These include legal tactics such as re-incorporation and housing subsidiaries in tax havens, changing industries and identities, and using ties to financial institutions to exercise power and achieve legitimacy in the eyes of the institutional investors that now own the preponderance of corporate America. We explore some of these newer tactics in Chapter 13.

Our two theories, transaction cost economics and resource dependence theory, have described alternative means of assessing which dyadic relations are especially important and varying sets of tactics organizations can use to manage their relations with their organization set. They point to different sources of change—TCE, as a rational systems approach, highlights the economic functions served by different organizational structure, while resource dependence focuses on the power dynamics behind much organizational action. But in combination, they provide a rich language and set of tools for analyzing the changing nature of interorganizational relations.

SUMMARY

A primary task facing organizations is to manage their relationships with other organizations. First, organizations face the problem of which tasks to do inside their own boundary, and which to leave to outside suppliers. Transaction cost analysts describe this as the "make-or-buy" question and argue that understanding this choice is essential to understanding why there are firms at all, and how they come to look the way they do. Goods and services pass through a series of steps—from raw material to final consumption—known as the value chain. By describing the relations among the separate steps of production in terms of more-or-less costly contracts, transaction cost economics provides tools for analyzing where the boundaries around organizations arise. When two adjacent steps have relationship-specific assets—that is, the two are more valuable to each other than they are to other partners—their relationship is vulnerable and therefore more likely to justify the expense of protecting it within an organization or other, intermediate structure (such as a hierarchical contract). Critics argue that transaction cost reasoning fails to take culture and social structure into account and focuses too much on "economic" factors, but the theory has shown itself to be a useful starting point for understanding organizational boundaries.

A second problem organizations face is how to manage relations with those organizations that remain outside their boundaries. Exchanges of resources create power/dependence relations that can leave organizations vulnerable to the demands of resource providers. Resource dependence theory describes the tactics that organizations use to manage this inter-dependence, from developing and maintaining alternatives, to coopting representatives of outside groups by placing them in positions of power (e.g., on the board of directors), to forming joint ventures and alliances, to pooling their influence via associations, to outright merger intended to bring the problematic dependencies inside the organization's boundary. Broadly speaking, organizations adopt the least constraining structures from among this set sufficient to maintain autonomy and ensure access to critical resources. By focusing on generic resource exchange relations, this approach seeks to provide a general theory applicable to all kinds of organizations, including businesses, non-profits, and government agencies.

CHAPTER 10

Organization of the Environment

The ecology of organizations seeks to understand how social conditions affect the rates at which new organizations and new organizational forms arise, the rates at this organizations change forms, and the rates at which organizations and forms die out. In addition to focusing on the effects of social, economic, and political systems on these rates, an ecology of organizations also emphasizes the dynamics that take place *within* organizational populations.

MICHAEL T. HANNAN AND JOHN FREEMAN (1989)

Although other theoretical perspectives . . . acknowledge the importance of the environment, the institutional approach calls attention to a wider range of environmental influences. Organizations are recognized to exist in wider fields that can include influences not only in the near vicinity but also operating at distant locations. Organizations are recognized as being affected not only by present influences and pressures and also by past circumstances. Organizations are seen to exist not just as technical systems, exchanging resources, inputs, and outputs, but also as social systems, incorporating actors and relationships. Organizations are seen as being constructed and shaped by cultural systems embodying symbolically mediated meanings. In short, the institutional perspective highlights, in particular, nonlocal, historical, relational, and cultural forces as factors shaping organizations.

W. RICHARD SCOTT AND SØREN CHRISTENSEN (1995a)

In this and the following chapter we raise the level of analysis, shifting from an examination of the environment as experienced by a given organization, a dyadic view, to consider ways in which the organizational environment—the environment for a given, individual organization—is itself organized, a systemic view. As previewed in Chapter 5, we widen our conceptual lens from examining the organization and the organization set levels to consider the organizational population and the organizational field (or community) levels. Here we examine the insights associated with ecological and institutional theoretical perspectives; Chapter 11 reviews the contribution of network theorists.

Ecologists and institutionalists challenge the assumption underlying contingency and transaction cost analysts that organizations can readily change their basic structural features. Rather, they suggest that organizations are relatively inertial structures, difficult to change. Change is viewed as hard, rare, and, indeed, dangerous to the viability of organizations. Rather than being planned or internally induced, the sources of change are often located in the wider environment—in the dynamics of population-level demographic processes or in political demands and normative pressures stemming from, for example, the nation-state or the professions. To understand these processes, we need to ask questions such as: How are organizations, and new types of organizations created? Why do they increase or decrease in numbers? Why do they fail? How do wider political, social and cultural factors shape the structure and fate of organizations? How do collections of diverse organizations engaged in related activities interact, seek stability, and undergo significant change?

We begin by reviewing some of the insights associated with ecological theory and then introduce the arguments of institutional scholars. These two approaches have different roots and displayed differing early trajectories of development but, during the late 1980s, began to interact and develop complementary formulations in several arenas. Also, in a similar manner, institutional and resource dependence theories connected during the early 1990s. These developments are considered in this chapter.

HOW DO NEW ORGANIZATIONS AND NEW POPULATIONS OF ORGANIZATIONS ARISE, AND WHY DO THEY FAIL? : ECOLOGICAL PERSPECTIVES

As briefly described in Chapter 5, ecological perspectives on organizations have their origins in the natural selection theories originating in biology with the work of Charles Darwin. Although the application of these ideas to social systems has a long and checkered history (see Hofstadter, 1945), more recent and promising efforts have been stimulated by the work of Hawley (1950) and Campbell (1969b). Applications of these general ideas to organizations by Hannan and Freeman (1977; 1989) and by Aldrich (1979; 1999), among others, have led to a rapidly growing body of research and theory. Carroll and Hannan (2000) have recently proposed that the organizational ecology framework be broadened to incorporate what they term *corporate demography*. Just as much scientific effort has been expended in understanding the vital rates and varying life chances of populations of individuals, they call for comparable efforts to understand populations of organizations, ranging from single-site establishments to multi-unit firms such as global corporations.

Ecologists analyze organization birth, change, and death as the most informative dependent variables. Although differences exist in how much attention is paid to "external" conditions, such as political or institutional factors, there appears to be widespread agreement among ecologists on two methodological precepts: (1) study all members of the population. To focus only on a subset—the survivors, the most effective, the *Fortune* 500—leads to bias in understanding the full range of organizations; (2) study processes that take place over time rather than relations among variables at a single point in time. Dynamic approaches focusing on processes uncover different connections than static or cross-sectional studies.

Evolutionary models may be applied all levels, from social psychological to ecological. For example, evolutionary arguments have been applied to social learning—what ideas survive—(Weick, 1979); organizational processes such as rules and routines (Levitt and March, 1988; Miner, 1994); entire organizations as explanation for their differential survival (Carroll, 1984); and to larger systems of organizations, such as populations or fields, that exhibit adaptation and learning (Astley, 1985; Miner and Haunschild, 1995). But the great bulk of studies has been concentrated at the population level. *Organizational populations* are comprised of all organizations sharing the same general form (see below). A principal concern has been to explain organizational diversity—to answer the question, Why are there so many—or so few—organizational forms? While diversity occurs partly because individual organizations change their characteristics through *adaptation* over time, ecologists have devoted attention primarily to *selection* processes: "change in the composition of a set of organizations from differential replacement of one form by another" (Hannan and Carroll, 1995: 23). Organizations are formed and die at varying rates. For example, an ecologist might examine factors associated with the decline of teachers' colleges and the growth in the numbers of community colleges over recent decades in the United States.

It is central to the natural selection thesis that environments differentially select organizations for survival on the basis of fit between organizational forms and environmental characteristics. Three processes are emphasized in evolutionary analysis: the creation of variety, the selection of some forms over others, and the retention and diffusion of those forms (Aldrich, 1999; Campbell, 1969b). In the first stage, variety is created by some process, planned or unplanned. In the second, some forms of organization are differentially selected for survival. And in stage three, the selected forms are preserved in some fashion, by reproduction or duplication. Positively selected variations survive and reproduce similar others, which then form the starting point for a new round of selection as mutants appear (Aldrich and Pfeffer, 1976). In the founding work primary emphasis was placed on selection as the prime process by which change occurs in organizations, but more recent work has recognized the part played by adaptation of exiting forms (Singh, Tucker, and House, 1986).

The ecological approach has created much interest among students of organizations: it employs a well-known and highly regarded intellectual (Darwinian) framework and has been able to adapt for use quite sophisticated concepts and dynamic models from the work of population biologists. Also, by emphasizing the population level of analysis, it has focused on a new set of issues largely ignored by earlier theorists. In particular, it asserts that most change that occurs in the realm of organizations is the result, not of adaptation or change on the part of existing organizations, but of the replacement of one type of organization with another.

The ecological conception is firmly grounded in an open system model: the importance of the environment can hardly be more strongly underlined than it is in the population ecology framework. It is also clearly a natural system approach. The bottom line is survival (not effectiveness). And although based on an evolutionary framework, in its contemporary usage, "evolution is no longer equated with progress, but simply with change over time" (Carroll, 1984: 72). The ability to perpetuate one's form is the hallmark of successful adaptation.[1]

Creating New Organizations

While the concept of *entrepreneurship* conjures up a number of meanings, one of the more important is its association with the founding of a new organization (Aldrich, 2005). The act of organizational creation conjures up the image of the towering, independent risk taker celebrated in American pop fiction. Survey research by Reynolds and White (1997) reports that during the late 1990s, about one person in twenty-five in the United States was engaged in trying to start a new firm, a higher rate than observed during earlier periods. Of course, what it means to "try" to found a firm is hard to pin down, the responses varying greatly from planning a new business, buying facilities or equipment, to hiring employees. To account for organization creation, earlier research focused on the disposition or traits of entrepreneurs, psychologists examining such variables as "need for achievement" and "risk-taking propensity" (McClelland, 1961). Interest in the attributes of founders is ongoing. For example, Bruderl and colleagues (1992) found that businesses founded by more educated and experienced individuals were less likely to fail.

However, most recent work by economists and sociologists has focused on the importance of context and the relational network of founders. The playing field is not level: important differences exist in opportunity structures as well as in the capacity of individuals to take advantage of them. Aldrich and Ruef (2006: chap. 4) note the relevance of three facets of context: networks, knowledge, and resources. Social networks vary greatly, but the diversity of one's ties is especially critical since it increases access to a wider range of information. Also important is having a combination of strong and weak ties: strong ties, with close friends, to facilitate trust and emotional support; weak ties, with more distant acquaintances, to insure heterogeneity of ideas and

---

[1]Useful summaries and general statements of the ecological and evolutionary approach to organizations are provided by Aldrich and Ruef (2006), Baum (1996), Baum and Amburgey (2002), Baum and Singh (1994), and Hannan and Freeman (1989). In related work, Nelson and Winter (1982) developed an evolutionary economics approach to organizations that focuses on the selective survival of internal features of organizations, in particular, organizational routines.

interests (Granovetter, 1973). Knowledge is both an individual and a social variable, affected by one's intelligence and work experience but also by access to education, expertise, and the general level of technical and organizational knowledge available. Access to resources, including labor, capital, and land, varies greatly among individuals and over time.

Moreover, it is not only individuals that start organization. About half of all efforts to start a new business involve teams of two or more people. Employing a nationally representative sample, Ruef, Aldrich, and Carter (2003) report that such founding teams were likely to exhibit homophily—similar characteristics such as gender and ethnicity—and to involve strong—for example, romantic or family connections—rather than weak ties. Also, increasingly, existing organizations initiate new organizations. About one-quarter of the individuals surveyed by Reynolds and White (1997) who reported being involved in developing start-ups were sponsored by their employers. Indeed, many corporations, organized as multidivisional companies (see Chapter 6), develop new venture divisions specifically designed to create new products and services that can be "spun off" into new companies. Such "corporate entrepreneurship" (Burgelman and Sayles, 1986) has become a standard component of many corporations. Venture capital firms, specifically devoted to providing financing to new (and therefore risky) ventures, have existed since the mid-1930s, but during the decade of the 1990s grew rapidly to become an important player in nurturing fledgling organizations. It appears that, either as mothers or midwives, existing organizations are increasingly involved in the creation of new organizations (Schoonhoven and Romenelli, 2001; Thornton, 1999).

How novel ways of organizing arise and are transmitted from one organization to another is a subject of much current interest and research. While many scholars stress the role of genius and leadership, more macro and evolutionary versions stress the role of randomness, chance variations, trial and error, good timing, and luck. Evolutionary and learning theorists emphasize that most new ideas are wrong or flawed and lead to failure. There are many false starts and dead-ends; setbacks occur frequently (Van de Ven et al., 1999). More often than not, other firms exploit and benefit from the innovative work of first-movers (Miner and Haunschild, 1995).

Creating New Organizational Populations

Most entrepreneurs establish what Aldrich terms "reproducer" rather than "innovator" organizations.

Reproducer organizations are defined as those organizations started in an established population whose routines and competencies vary only minimally, if at all, from those of existing organizations. They bring little or no incremental knowledge to the populations they enter, organizing their activities in the same way as their predecessors. *Innovative organizations,* by contrast, are those organizations started by entrepreneurs whose routines and competencies vary significantly from those of existing organizations. (1999: 80)

The former increase the density of existing populations of organizations; the latter, if they are successful in reproducing themselves, give rise to new populations of organizations. So, how are we to understand what is meant by an organizational population?

Defining Organizational Population. This concept of *organizational population* is used to identify aggregates of organizations that are alike in some respect—for example, institutions of higher education or newspapers (see Chapter 9). Those concerned with studying populations have to wrestle with the question of what it means to be "alike in some respect." How are populations identified? When one studies "colleges," for example, what sorts of organizations are included—private as well as public schools? universities? community colleges? technical institutes? computer-based "virtual" schools? Organizational ecologists borrow or adapt biological language and ideas in working on this problem. Hannan and Freeman in their early formulation noted that biologic species are defined in terms of genetic structure and proposed that the appropriate analogue for organizations is to define them in terms of their "blueprint for organizational action, for transforming inputs into outputs" (1977: 935). McKelvey (1982) adopts a similar stance, suggesting that all organizations in the same population contain "elements of dominant competence," or "comps," drawn from the same "compool," or collection of elements. By dominant competence McKelvey refers essentially to the technical core of the organization—that is, the activities that transform "inputs into those outputs critical to a population's survival" (p. 174). Both of these definitions of the boundaries of populations are conceptually clear, but neither is easy to operationalize. Blueprints and comps are hard to measure.

Over time, Hannan and Carroll have amended their stance to conclude that the basic key to identifying a population is the possession of a common organizational form.[2]

> Form serves as the organizational ecologist's analogue to the biological ecologist's species. Form summarizes the core properties that make a set of organizations ecologically similar. . . . *Organizational populations* are specific time-and-space instances of organizational forms. (Hannan and Carroll, 1995: 29)

Forms are viewed as "a recognizable pattern that takes on rule-like standing" (Carroll and Hannan, 2000: 67). They consist of cultural-cognitive patterns that have "imperative standing"—that is, are supported by normative codes. Forms may be viewed "as a kind of externally-enforced identity" (p. 68).

---

[2]Ecologists define populations as organizations exhibiting the same structural form while economists define industries as including all organizations serving the same demand or function, which could include quite diverse types of providers of substitutable services.

Closely related formulations have been developed by Greenwood and Hinings (1993), who speak of organizational *archetypes*; and by Suchman (forthcoming), who views organizational forms as shaped by the "constitutive value of cultural information—the scripts, definitions and models that determine organization structure." (These kinds of arguments recognize that organizational forms rest on an institutional foundation, an argument that we elaborate later in this chapter.) Of course, there is a hierarchy of structural elements: some structural elements are more fundamental, representing the "core" properties while others are more peripheral. Returning to the education example, to the extent that community colleges and universities exhibit different structural forms—and they clearly do in important respects—then they would be considered to be different populations operating within the general field (or industry) of higher education.

While the concept of population obviously rests on analogs from biological organisms, including humans, and gains resonance from these associations, there remain fundamental differences between organizations and organisms. Carroll and Hannan identify eight differences:

1. The greater variety of types of events that define organizational births and deaths.
2. The potential immortality of formal organizations.
3. The lack of clear parentage for organizations.
4. The absence of genetic transmission of information in the organizational world.
5. The multilayered, partly decomposable structure of formal organizations.
6. The great heterogeneity found within organizational populations.
7. The ability of organizations to transform themselves and change populations.
8. The potentially high levels of endogeneity in the environments of organizations (that is, an organization's capacity to shape its own environments) (2000: 40).

Each of these differences poses a challenge for those studying organizational populations.

When it comes to empirical research, several approaches have addressed the problem of defining organizational populations. First, one can use "native" common-sense categories—for example, hospitals, universities, newspapers—or researchers can employ more abstract, theory-based classification schemas, such as those proposed by Parsons (1960; see also Chapter 3) or McKelvey (1982). Alternatively, more empirically derived classifications can be developed based on statistical techniques that detect the existence of similar combinations of characteristics (see, e.g., McPherson, 1983; Mohr and Guerra-Pearson, forthcoming). Yet another approach involves the recognition that the boundaries that define organizational forms are dynamic, changing over time. Some organizational populations are more sharply demarcated than are others (Hannan and Freeman, 1989). We see yet again that boundary defining processes are among the more important subjects confronting organizational theorists.

Most of the empirical studies of organizational populations have relied on fairly common-sense definitions of a population and have employed geographical criteria for bounding it. A wide range of populations has been studied by organizational ecologists, ranging from cement producers (Tushman and Anderson, 1986) and thrift associations (Haveman and Rao, 1997) to child care centers (Singh, Tucker, and House, 1986) and semiconductor firms (Freeman, 1990). In an ambitious cross-societal comparative study, Hannan and colleagues (Hannan et al., 1995) investigated the evolution of the automobile manufacturing industry as it developed in five European countries in a multinational context.[3]

Imprinting. New organizational forms must perforce draw on an existing stock of resources, knowledge, and supporting structures and so are always constrained by the conditions present in the environment at the time of their founding (Romanelli, 1991). Stinchcombe calls attention to the remarkable pattern exhibited by the founding of organizations of a given type:

> An examination of the history of almost any type of organization shows that there are great spurts of foundation of organizations of the type, followed by periods of relatively slower growth, perhaps to be followed by new spurts, generally of a fundamentally different kind of organization in the same field. (1965: 154)

Stinchcombe cites numerous U.S. examples: the founding of savings banks and the first manufacturing companies, textiles, in the 1830s; the development of railroads and steel companies in the 1850s and 1870s; the founding of universities and labor unions from the 1870s to the 1900s; the development of department stores in the 1850s and mail-order houses in the 1870s; the growth of the oil, rubber, and automobile industries in the 1920s; the emergence of the airline manufacturing and transportation companies during and after World War II; and the development of data processing and electronic equipment after the 1960s (1965: 154–55). In related work, Aldrich and Mueller (1982) note that differing organizational forms—prefactory to factory production and competitive to monopoly capitalism—were associated with broad changes in the U.S. economy during the nineteenth and twentieth centuries.

Because they confront similar circumstances, organizational cohorts arising during a given period tend to exhibit similar structural features. What is more remarkable is that, once established, an organization of a given type tends to retain the basic characteristics present at its founding. Organizational forms are *imprinted*, and because of their inertial properties, they are likely to retain the features acquired at their origin. Ecologists regard *inertia*—resistance to change—as a normal state for organizations. It is the product of such internal

---

[3]For general reviews of population studies, see Baum (1996), Baum and Amburgey (2002), Carroll and Hannan (2000), and Singh and Lumsden (1990).

forces as sunk costs, vested interests, and habitualized behaviors as well as such external forces as contractual obligations and regulatory constraints (Hannan and Freeman, 1984; 1989).

Both open-rational and open-natural system explanations help account for this association between organizational characteristics and time of founding. The characteristics may provide a competitive advantage over alternative arrangements (a rational system argument); alternatively, they may be preserved by a set of "traditionalizing forces," including the internal and external forces just described. In addition, as organizations age, they are likely to become increasingly institutionalized, their structures and routines "infused with value" and legitimacy, resisting change (a natural system explanation). Whatever the case, it is notable that the form organizations acquire at their founding is likely to shape the structure they retain over their life. The mix of initial resources out of which an organizational structure is created has lasting effects.

Technological Change. Whereas changes in organizations and populations normally follow an incremental model of slow, gradual evolution, theorists argue that new populations are most likely to arise in periods of rapid and discontinuous change—referred to as a "punctuated equilibrium" model (see Astley, 1985; Gould and Eldredge, 1977). The great institutional economist Joseph Schumpeter (1961 ed.) characterized such times as unleashing "the gales of creative destruction." He held that the creation of new technologies was largely responsible for the development of new kinds of organizations and industries. Later researchers have refined this insight to distinguish between two types of technical innovations—those that enhance the competence of existing participants and those that "destroy" their competence in the sense that old ways of doing the work are not augmented but displaced by the new techniques or materials. Destructive innovations are more likely to be associated with the creation of new types of organizations and new industries (Tushman and Anderson, 1986). Indeed, because of organizational inertia and sunk costs, existing forms confront formidable obstacles in adapting to major convulsions since they must "unlearn" hard-won competencies before they can adapt. Large and powerful electronics companies, for example, were not able to change quickly enough to capture the new technologies underpinning the computer revolution.

Other Population Processes. Baum (1996) proposes that ecological theory and research have attended to three broad categories of factors that affect the dynamics of organizational populations: demographic processes, ecological processes, and environmental processes. It is not possible to reproduce here the complexities and nuances of the arguments developed and evidence examined, but we can outline their major contours.

Demographic Processes. The principal organizational attributes that enter into ecological arguments are organizational age and size. Whereas conventional biological arguments would assume that advancing age is associated with failure and death, organizational ecologists make the opposite argument. In his influential 1965 essay, Stinchcombe pointed to the "liability of newness": the increased likelihood that younger organizations, especially if they are new types of organizations, are more likely to fail. Young organizations often lack established role structures or trained personnel; they lack stable relations both among personnel and with external stakeholders; and they often lack sufficient slack resources to weather lean times. At the other end of the life cycle, because organizations are more open than biological systems, they have a greater capacity to delay death—to incorporate replacement resources into the maintenance and repair of their structures. Empirical evidence strongly supports the negative relation between organizational age and death. Carroll (1983) reviewed models of death rates across fifty-two data sets involving populations of retail stores, manufacturing firms, and craft and service organizations, finding that death rates declined with age in most of these populations (for other reviews, see Baum, 1996: Table 2; Baum and Amburgey, 2002).

A related argument suggests that organizations may also suffer from a "liability of smallness." Age is often confounded with size. Indeed, size may be a better proxy measure of slack (excess) resources than age. Baum reviews a large number of studies across diverse populations to show that "after controlling for contemporaneous organizational size, failure rates do not decline with age" (1996: 79). The argument has become more refined over time to consider intermediate stages (for example, "the liability of adolescence" (Fichman and Levinthal, 1991), but the general argument remains that the composition of a population—the distribution of newer and/or smaller organizations—affects its viability.

Ecological Processes

Niche-width. Ecologists differentiate between two organizational strategies for survival: "specialist," exhibiting a limited range of tolerance to environmental variation versus "generalist," with the capacity to thrive and reproduce under diverse environmental conditions. A population's "niche-width" is defined by "its tolerance for changing levels of resources" (Freeman and Hannan, 1983). In their seminal article, Hannan and Freeman (1977) suggest that environmental niches vary along two dimensions: variability over time and "grain"—whether these variations are frequent and small ("fine-grained") or less frequent and prolonged ("coarse-grained"). They argue that specialist organizations, which tend to be smaller and leaner, are more likely to be successful in fine-grained environments whereas generalist organizations are better able to cope with coarse-grained, uncertain environments, having the capacity to "ride out" the environmental fluctuations.

In a related approach, Carroll (1985) suggests that these alternative strategies may be interrelated. Under some conditions, which he labels "resource partitioning," the strategies pursued by successful generalist organizations create conditions under which specialist organizations can coexist. Generalist firms tend to compete by moving to the center of the market, appealing to conventional demands, which opens up niches on the margins for specialist players catering to more selective tastes. Thus, for example, large middle-of-the road newspapers service the majority of subscribers but open up opportunities for specialist papers that target smaller audiences, such as ethnic or political minorities (Carroll, 1985). Similarly, generic American beer companies catering to mainstream tastes have been unable to please connoisseurs, who supported the rise of a variety of select microbreweries (Carroll and Swaminathan, 2000).

Competitive processes are often determined by niche location. For example, Baum and Mezias (1992) found that Manhattan hotels competed most strongly with those in the same price range and neighborhood within the city. And Lomi (1995) reports that the founding rates of rural coop banks in Italy were shaped by the density of organizations at the local geographic level. Oftentimes, niche is defined more by technology than by geography. Thus, Podolny, Stuart, and Hannan (1996) found that competition among firms in the semiconductor industry was defined primarily by a shared technological arena, defined by patents.

Density Dependence. An important continuing assumption guiding ecological studies is that "density"—the number of prior foundings and failures in a population—is an important factor affecting future population dynamics. Thus, on the one hand, prior foundings suggest available resources that act to encourage additional births; on the other hand, increased failure rates signal depleted resources that may operate to discourage new entrants. Changing density levels signal both resource munificence as well as the extent of competition for its use. Hannan and Freeman employ the concept of *density dependence* to account for the routinely observed trajectory of populations of organizations that characteristically exhibit a period of growth, the rate of which gradually increases up to some point (the carrying capacity of the environment) at which a leveling-off occurs to be followed by a gradual decline (Carroll, 1984; Hannan and Freeman, 1989). This pattern is illustrated in Figure 10–1 displaying data on U.S. labor unions. In the very early stages of the development of a population, founding rates tend to be low. There is no easy way to obtain relevant experience, and organizations suffer, as noted, from a "liability of newness." Not only are experienced participants lacking, but also the organizational form itself is being developed. It lacks both reliability and legitimacy. Thus, Barron and colleagues (Barron, 1999; Barron et al., 1994) found a U-curve relation between density and failure rates in New York City credit unions, while Ranger-Moore, Banaszak-Holl, and Hannan (1991) reported an inverse U-curve relation for founding rates of Manhattan banks and insurance companies. While early studies (e.g., Carroll and Delacroix, 1982; Delacroix and Carroll, 1983) pursued a straightforward argument highlighting relative competition for scarce resources, later interpretations connected ecological to institutional processes. We return to this productive theoretical junction later.

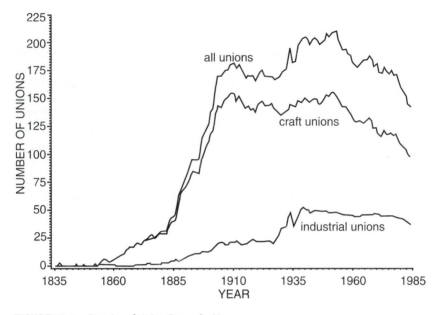

FIGURE 10–1   Density of Union Forms by Year.
Source: Hannan and Freeman (1987: Figure 3, p. 927).

Environmental Processes. From the earliest ecological studies, it was recognized that ecological processes work within and are affected by broader social, political, and economic processes. Stinchcombe (1965), in particular, was attentive to the role of general societal processes in shaping the fate of varying types of organizations. For example, in explaining the emergence of organizations, he stressed the causal influence of factors such as the breakup of traditional power structures that released free-floating resources for mobilization, increasing literacy, a money economy, and competing centers of power (see also Scott, 2003: 153–54). And, in a wide-ranging essay, Carroll, Delacroix, and Goodstein (1988) attempt to reconnect the ecological agenda with relevant political factors, ranging from political turmoil and revolution and wars to the political structure of the state and its regulative processes. For example, the sharp increase in the density of industrial unions after 1932, visible in Figure 10–1, indicates the effect of the passage of the Wagner Act in 1935, which granted legal protections to unions and to union-organizing processes.

State actions—both subsidies and regulations—have been shown to affect organizational foundings. For example, Dobbin and Dowd (1997) report that public capitalization and policies favoring cartels increased the founding rates of railroads in Massachusetts, while antitrust policies decreased foundings. And Russo (2001) demonstrates that state-level regulations, such as formally defining cost structures, influenced the founding rates of independent power producers across the states in the United States in the wake of a shift in federal energy policy.

But it is not only the behavior of public agencies that influence organizing prospects; private associations and corporate systems can also affect population processes. Thus, Ingram and Inman (1996) found that membership in a broader association decreased the failure rates of Israeli worker coops (Kibbutzim), although this effect was attenuated after the state of Israel was created. Similarly, ties to hotel chains generally enhanced survival chances for Manhattan hotels, depending on the characteristics of the chain (Ingram and Baum, 1997). These and related arguments can more readily be developed after we introduce the institutional perspective, which has productively interacted with ecological arguments in accounting for population processes.

Critique

The arrival of organizational ecology has productively opened up new levels of analysis, motivated the creation of new archival data sets, and developed new theoretical explanations for a range of organizational phenomena. Although in its early period it borrowed too heavily from existing biological models, both methodological and theoretical, the maturation of the field has worked to better accommodate methods and assumptions to social forms and processes.

Although there have been many calls for and some movement from a population to a community-based approach, most of the work to date continues to focus attention on a single organizational population, albeit, in some cases, with attention to competing subpopulations. The prime focus continues to be on the operation of competitive processes, with relatively little attention given to cooperation and mutualistic processes. Also, theoretical models have not been devised to readily accommodate the simultaneous consideration of selection and adaptation processes. The capacity of social organizations to adapt to environmental challenges, including movement into new environments, has not received sufficient attention.

Moreover, as Davis and Powell (1992) point out, ecologists assume that the dynamic processes which they model operate in the same way across diverse populations of organizations.

> It is assumed that American labor unions, semiconductor firms, early telephone companies, newspapers, and breweries in various areas of the world and voluntary social service organizations in Toronto all share timeless causal regularities by dint of the fact that we can refer to them as organizations. (1992: 353)

But in a world where some organizational forms are subject to takeover or buyout attempts and others, because of deregulation or global competition, suddenly find themselves confronted with completely new types of competitors or forms of competition, such assumptions seem naïve.

HOW ARE ORGANIZATIONS SHAPED BY BROADER SOCIAL-POLITICAL-CULTURAL PROCESSES?: INSTITUTIONAL PERSPECTIVES

Institutions and Institutional Elements

Whereas ecological theorists recognized the role of general social processes stemming from competition for scarce economic resources as factors affecting the fate of organizations and larger classes of organizations, institutional theorists broadened the framework to comprehend the role of regulative, normative, and cultural forces working to constrain and constitute organizations, organizational populations, and organizational fields.

Institutional concerns have a long and illustrious history in the social sciences but did not become a central focus in the study of organizations until the 1970s. (For a review, see Scott, 2001a) Early work by political scientists such as Burgess (1902), by economists such as Commons (1924), and by sociologists such as Cooley (1956 ed.) and Weber (1968 trans.) recognized the extent to which organizations were shaped by political and legal frameworks, the rules governing market behavior, and general belief systems (recall Weber's typology of authority). Close examination of this work, however, reveals that while there is substantial overlap in themes and interests, these and subsequent theorists singled out somewhat different aspects of institutions as the focus of attention. Three somewhat distinctive approaches can be identified, summarized and, we believe, encompassed, within the following omnibus definition:

> *Institutions* are composed of cultural-cognitive, normative, and regulative elements that, together with associated activities and resources, provide stability and meaning to social life. (Scott, 2001a: 48)

In any fully developed institutional system, all three of these forces or elements are present and interact to promote and sustain orderly behavior. Nevertheless, over the years and up the present, theorists vary in the extent to which they focus analytic attention on one or another of these elements. Generally speaking, economists and political scientists stress regulatory factors, sociologists, normative factors, and anthropologists and organizational theorists, cultural-cognitive factors. Not only the focus, but also the arguments and assumptions made by each camp tend to vary systematically and substantially, as suggested by Table 10–1.

Institutions as Regulative Systems. Analysts emphasizing the *regulative* features of institutions view institutions as systems of rules or as governance systems. For example, the economic historian, Douglass North, argues that

TABLE 10–1 Three Conceptions of Institutions

	Regulative	*Normative*	*Cultural-Cognitive*
Basis of compliance	Experience	Social obligation	Taken-for-grantedness Shared understanding
Basis of order	Regulative rules	Binding expectations	Constitutive schema
Mechanisms	Coercive	Normative	Mimetic
Logic	Instrumentality	Appropriateness	Orthodoxy
Indicators	Rules Laws Sanctions	Certification Accreditation	Common beliefs Shared logics of action
Basis of legitimacy	Legally sanctioned	Morally governed	Comprehensible Recognizable Culturally supported

Source: Scott (2001a: Table 3–1, p. 52).

[Institutions] are perfectly analogous to the rules of the game in a competitive team sport. That is, they consist of formal written rules as well as typically unwritten codes of conduct that underlie and supplement formal rules . . . The rules and informal codes are sometimes violated and punishments are enacted. Therefore, an essential part of the functioning of institutions is the costliness of ascertaining violations and the severity of punishment. (North, 1990: 4)

North observes that the major source of regulatory rules and enforcement mechanisms in modern society is the nation-state, although a variety of formal and informal regulatory structures exist at the field level—for example, trade associations and widely shared understandings regarding the limits of acceptable competitive practices. In the regulatory view of institutions, it is assumed that the major mechanism by which compliance is effected is coercion. Individuals and groups comply to rules and codes out of expediency—to garner rewards or to avoid sanctions. Behavior is viewed as legitimate to the extent that it conforms to existing rules and laws.

For economic historians, such as North, institutions operate at the level of the wider environment: whether in the relatively uncodified and informal assumptions and understandings underlying some economic markets or through the more direct intervention of governmental regulatory structures. But for a newer generation of institutional economists, including Williamson and others, these wider institutions are viewed as "background conditions" whereas in the foreground are the more specific institutional forms that serve as "governance structures" to manage economic transactions, in particular, organizations (hierarchies) (Williamson, 1994). As described in Chapter 9, transaction cost analysis defines its primary task as explaining why it is that different ("discrete") organizational forms arise to govern various types of economic activity (Williamson, 1991). Because they take a more dyadic approach, these economic institutional arguments were reviewed in the previous chapter.

Institutions as Normative Systems. Most sociologists, from Cooley and Weber to Selznick and Parsons, have viewed institutions primarily as *normative* structures, providing a moral framework for the conduct of social life. Unlike externally enforced rules and laws, norms are internalized by participants; behavior is guided by a sense of what is appropriate, by one's social obligations to others, by a commitment to common values. One of the reasons for the difference in emphasis is that economics and political scientists focus their attention on societal systems—markets and political arenas—in which rational self-interest is viewed as appropriate. Under such conditions, order is achieved by the erection and enforcement of rules. By contrast, sociologists and anthropologists tend to focus on social spheres, such as family and kinship structures and educational and religious systems, in which participants are more likely to embrace other-regarding behaviors, so that much order is built into norms emphasizing mutual obligations.

While most sociologists have emphasized the more widely shared norms and values that give rise to stable social arrangements such as families and communities, sociologists like Selznick, as we have seen (see Chapter 3), emphasized the beliefs and commitments operating at the level of particular organizations which give them a distinctive culture ("character"). This latter approach is also reflected in the work of contemporary students of corporate culture. (See, for example, Martin, 2002; Schein, 1992; Trice and Beyer, 1993).

For social scientists emphasizing the normative pillar of institutions, structures and behaviors are legitimate to the extent that they are consistent with widely shared norms defining appropriate behavior.

Institutions as Cultural-cognitive Systems. The most recent version of institutions—the view associated with "the new institutionalism in organizational analysis" (Powell and DiMaggio, 1991)—emphasizes the role of *cultural-cognitive* processes in social life. We employ the hyphenated concept to emphasize that we are not referring just to individual mental constructs, but also to common symbolic systems and shared meanings. Shared cultural beliefs are external to any given individual but also operate within each providing "the software of the mind" (Hofstede, 1991). Phenomenologists, such as Berger and Luckmann (1967), argue that social life is only possible because and to the extent that individuals in interaction create common cognitive frameworks and understandings that support collective action. The process by which actions are repeated and given similar meaning by self and others is defined as *institutionalization*. It is the process by which social reality is constructed. The distinguished anthropologist Clifford Geertz has developed a very similar conception in his reformulation of culture as "the symbolic dimensions of social action." Geertz amplifies: "The concept of culture I espouse . . . is essentially a semiotic one. Believing, with Max Weber, that man is an animal suspended in webs of significance he himself has spun, I take culture to be those webs" (1973: 5).

It is not necessary to insist that all reality is socially constructed. There exists what Searle (1995) defines as "brute" facts: the world of physical objects and forces obeying natural laws. But there also exists a wide variety of "social facts" that are facts only by virtue of human agreement—language systems, legal institutions, monetary systems, national boundaries, to name only a few. Such constructions are "facts" in that, while dependent on human agreement, they exist independently of your or my attitudes or preferences toward them.

Any fully developed mature institutional framework will include combinations of the three classes of elements: regulative, normative, and cultural-cognitive. The distinctions are analytic and point to different ingredients and processes at work in complex structures. They also are somewhat nested. Cultural-cognitive elements exist at deeper levels. It is not possible to have rules or norms in the absence of categories and distinctions. Cultural-cognitive elements are also the most intransigent, including unconscious beliefs and taken-for-granted assumptions. Regulative elements, which have received the lion's share of attention from institutional scholars, are, by contrast, more visible, more readily designed and altered, but also more superficial than normative and cultural-cognitive elements (Evans, 2004; Roland, 2004).[4]

Institutions and Organizations

These ideas concerning the construction of social reality were first introduced into organizational analysis at the micro or social psychological level by researchers working in the symbolic interactionist and ethnomethodological traditions. Their studies examine the ways in which participants interact to develop shared understandings of their situation—collectively constructing their social reality. Analysts like Bittner (1967), Cicourel (1968), Zimmerman (1970), and Van Mannan (1973) have examined the ways in which organizational participants, such as policemen and welfare workers, forge common meanings through interaction to make sense of their work situations. At the opposite extreme, we have the work of Meyer and colleagues (Drori, Meyer, and Hwang, 2006; Meyer, 1994; Meyer, Boli, and Thomas, 1987; Meyer et al., 1997) and a number of European scholars (Brunsson and Jacobsson, 2000; Djelic and Quack, 2003) who emphasize the role of trans-societal and world-system non-governmental professional associations and organizations that are working to expand the applicability of rational standards to an increasing variety of societal sectors and arenas—from environmental protections to women's rights. The diffusion and adoption of these views and standards importantly shape both the nation-state and organizations.

But the most influential applications of institutional ideas to the analysis of organizations operate at the intermediate level focusing on the effects of societal rules and field-specific norms and beliefs. These socially constructed realities provide a framework for the creation and elaboration of formal organizations in every arena of social life (Meyer and Scott, 1983; Scott and Meyer, 1994).

---

[4]For other general discussions of institutions in relation to organizations, see Campbell (2004), Langlois (1986), March and Olsen (1989), Nee (2005), Peters (1999), and Williamson (1985).

According to Meyer and Rowan, in modern societies these institutions are likely to take the form of "rationalized myths." They are *myths* because they are widely held beliefs whose effects "inhere, not in the fact that individuals believe them, but in the fact that they 'know' everyone else does, and thus that 'for all practical purposes' the myths are true" (Meyer, 1977: 75). They are *rationalized* because they take the form of rules specifying procedures necessary to accomplish a given end. Law provides a good example. How can property legitimately change hands? How can an organization become a corporation? Legal systems—as complexes of rationalized myths—provide solutions to such problems. Meyer and Rowan argue that these institutional belief systems powerfully shape organizational forms:

> Many of the positions, policies, programs, and procedures of modern organizations are enforced by public opinion, by the views of important constituents, by knowledge legitimated through the educational system, by social prestige, by the laws, and by the definitions of negligence and prudence used by the courts. Such elements of formal structure are manifestations of powerful institutional rules which function as highly rationalized myths that are binding on particular organizations. (1977: 343)

Organizations receive support and legitimacy to the extent that they conform to contemporary norms—as determined by professional and scientific authorities—concerning the "appropriate" way to organize. These beliefs are so powerful that organizations that conforming to them receive public support and confidence even in situations where no specific technical advantages are obtained.

The impact of institutional rules and constructs can be pursued at varying levels. In its broadest version, institutional theorists argue that for too long organizations have been thought to somehow be insulated from culture. The received wisdom, as set out by the dominant rational system theorists, has it that organizations—in particular, organizations competing in the marketplace—are technical instruments rationally designed in accord with universal economic laws. It is the other parts of society—families, classes, political parties, churches, schools—that carry the cultural baggage. Organizations (except perhaps for the "soft under-belly" of workers who sometimes abide by collective norms or behave out of sentiment rather than self-interest) are viewed as embodying rational rather than cultural principles.

It is primarily due to the work of Peter Berger and colleagues (Berger and Luckmann, 1967; Berger, Berger, and Kellner, 1973) that institutionalists have slowly begun to advance the argument that the modern conception of rationality is itself a social and cultural construction—a collective, socially realized and enforced agreement emphasizing the value of identifying specific ends and developing explicit, formalized means for pursuing them. We social scientists have been slow to recognize, as Dobbin points out "that rationalized organizational practices are essentially cultural, and are very much at the core of modern culture precisely because modern culture is organized around instrumental rationality" (1994a: 118). Lecturing to contemporary generations of students about norms of rationality is like lecturing to fish about water! From this highly general vantage point, organizations embody the primary values that distinguish modern cultural beliefs from earlier, more traditional or romantic forms. Organizations are the archetypes of modern societal forms. They are, as Zucker argues "the focal defining institution in modern society" (1983: 13). We think it more correct to say that organizations incorporate institutionalized elements. In order to demonstrate that they are serious about achieving some goal or protecting some value, individuals are obliged to create an organization, containing stylized rational elements, in order to symbolize their commitment.

However, most institutional work does not go on at this rarified level—accounting for generic organizational forms and the ubiquity of organizations in the modern world—but rather at the level of organizational populations and fields. We review some of these arguments.

Institutions, Organizational Forms, and Organizational Populations

Models for Organizing. Earlier in this chapter, we described ecological arguments regarding the emergence of new organizational populations. Whereas ecologists have been primarily attentive to the material resources required for constructing and supporting an organizational population, institutionalists have insisted on the equally important role played by cultural materials that provide constitutive models of organizing. Institutions play not only a constraining role via norms and rules, but also a generative one, formulating "particular configurations and forms of actors, and particular opportunities for action" (Dacin, Ventresca, and Beal, 1999: 324). Ideas or schema—about goals, means-ends relations, appropriate forms, and routines—are essential components, interacting with and giving meaning and value to material resources (Campbell, 2004; Sewell, 1992). Suchman (forthcoming) argues that such models provide the basis for crafting an "organizational genetics" to complement extant organizational ecological approaches. Models or templates for organizing arise and diffuse in numerous ways. The most common, termed *filiation,* involves the copying of a pattern as embodied in an existing organization. Filiation reproduces organizations of the same type. New models may arise in at least two ways. One, termed *compilation,* occurs when some type of intermediary—for example, corporation lawyers, venture capitalists, or management consultants—observe variations in forms and practices in a developing community of organizations and codify them as models to be emulated (Suchman and Cahill, 1996). Alternatively, entrepreneurs may combine components from various existing organizations into new combinations, creating by a process, termed *bricolage,* new hybrid forms (Campbell, 1997; 2004; Douglas, 1986). Once developed, models diffuse in a variety of ways: the movement of personnel; the influence of information intermediaries, such as accountants, management consultants, or business media; the actions of trade associations or public regulatory bodies; or the decisions of corporate executives to create branch offices or franchise operations (Strang and Soule, 1998). But, we must also keep in mind that most new models fail to survive or to reproduce.

Population Processes: Density Revisited. As we described earlier in this chapter, in their original version ecological accounts gave primacy to competition for scarce resources as the primary process shaping the dynamics of population growth and decline. But, as institutional arguments became pervasive, ecologists noted their relevance for explaining important aspects of population dynamics. Specifically, Carroll and Hannan (1989) proposed that the gradual growth of a new population could be interpreted as reflecting the growing legitimacy of a new, unfamiliar form which, as the numbers of imitators increased, reflected the increasing acceptance of the form. Hence, the empirical regularities of the density dependence processes long studied by organizational ecologists could be interpreted as reflecting the interaction of two competing pressures—on the one hand, the increasing *legitimacy* of a new form and, on the other, the increasing *competition* among specific carriers of that form for scarce resources. For example, the patterns for union growth and decline exhibited in Figure 10–1 reflect a growing legitimation of union organizing as a recognized and appropriate form, from 1835 to 1960, and, thereafter, increasing competition (and consolidation) among existing union organizations. As the form becomes more widely accepted, the rate of its growth increases up the point where competition among these similar organizations for relevant resources becomes sufficiently intense to end the period of growth and usher in a period of decline, as consolidation occurs and weaker firms are eliminated. Organizational density is depicted as a two-edged sword, having positive (legitimacy) effects on foundings in the early phases of the development of a population and negative (competitive) effects in the later phases. Emphasis is placed here on the cultural-cognitive pillar: "an organizational form is legitimate to the extent that relevant actors regard it as the 'natural' way to organize for some purpose" (Carroll and Hannan, 1989: 525).

Population growth is also influenced by specific normative supports and regulatory systems. Thus, Singh, Tucker, and House (1986) found that formal registration as a charity and listing in community directories reduced failure rates for social services organizations; and Baum and Oliver (1992) report that child-care agencies possessing service agreements with the provincial government or collaborative agreements with existing community-based organizations exhibited lower failure rates than organizations lacking such normative endorsements. Of course, which normative systems are salient varies across settings and over time. For example, Ruef and Scott (1998) showed that in an era dominated by medical professionals, hospitals receiving endorsement from these associations were more likely to survive whereas subsequently, in a time when managerial and market criteria were ascendant, hospitals enjoying the support of medical administrative associations fared better.

Institutional Processes and Strategic Responses

Early theorists examining institutional effects implicitly assumed an overly deterministic causality and an overly unified institutional framework. Much of the theoretical and empirical work during founding decades emphasized the *isomorphic* effects of institutional processes, as organizational fields and populations were asserted to become more alike in structural and procedural features (DiMaggio and Powell, 1983; see Scott 2001a: chap. 7, for a review). For example, Tolbert and Zucker (1983) examined how during a period of about five decades, from 1880 to 1930, a growing number of cities adopted civil service reforms in response to increasing normative pressures. Meyer and colleagues (Meyer et al., 1988) described the spread of systematic bureaucratic administrative forms in U.S. public schools during the middle decades of the twentieth century. And Fligstein (1985) showed that large firms were more like to adopt the M-form structure the more other firms in the same industry had previously adopted it.

But over time, analysts recognized that contradictory logics and frameworks may confront organizations and their participants with conflicting alternatives; and that, rather than presuming conformity to be the dominant response, organizations could and often did respond strategically. Oliver argued the value of combining resource dependence strategies with institutional perspectives to identify a broader range of possible responses available to organizations in response to institutional pressures. Specifically, she suggested that in addition to "acquiescence"—the response presumed to be forthcoming by early institutional theorists—organizations and their participants could seek, variously, to "compromise," engage in "avoidance" tactics, practice "defiance," or attempt to "manipulate" the system (1991: 152). Oliver also developed a testable series of arguments regarding the conditions under which one or another of these strategies might be selected.

Studies by D'Aunno, Sutton, and Price (1991) described the compromises embraced by mental health agencies, which typically embrace one organization template, that decided to incorporate drug abuse programs that embrace a different organizing model; and Abzug and Mezias (1993) detail the range of strategies pursued by organizations responding to court decisions regarding comparative work claims under the Civil Rights Act of 1972. Alexander (1996) describes varying types of compromises made by museum directors and curators who seek funding for their collections and exhibitions from varying sources—wealthy individuals, corporations, foundations, governments—each of whom is likely to hold different, and often, conflicting criteria. Westphal and Zajac (1994) show that during the 1970s–1990s. many U.S. corporations felt under moral pressure to adopt long-term executive compensation plans that would better align shareholder and executive interests, but that some of these same corporations failed to implement them after announcing their adoption. Loose coupling and deception, as well as avoidance and compromise, are among the strategies utilized by organizations in coping with complex and conflicting environments.

These arguments and topics proved to be important in attracting management scholars to institutional theory. For understandable reasons, they had not previously been much drawn to a theory in which managers appeared as passive adopters of externally generated institutional rules and logics. Suddenly, it became clear that here was something else for managers to manage! While recognizing the value of additional challenges and of a more varied portfolio of organizational responses to institutional pressures, it remains important to stress that (1) institutional elements vary in terms of how subject they are to strategic responses—for some kinds of cognitive-cultural systems, a strategic response is literally "unthinkable" (Goodrick and Salancik, 1996); and (2) institutions themselves help to shape the types of strategic reactions which are available to actors in one or another context (Scott, 2001a: chap. 7).

Institutional Systems: Agents and Fields

Institutional Agents. Theorists suggest that, at least in modern societies, the two major types of collective actors who generate institutional rules and frameworks—regulatory policies, normative beliefs, and cultural-cognitive categories—are governmental units and professional groups. DiMaggio and Powell assert that "Bureaucratization and other forms of homogenization [are] effected largely by the state and the professions, which have become the great rationalizers of the second half of the twentieth century" (1983: 147).

Governments. The nation-state is the prime sovereign in the modern world, the major source of legitimate order, the sovereign agent defining, managing, and overseeing the legal framework of society. Earlier accounts of organizations largely overlooked the role of states in shaping the environments of organizations, but contemporary theorists have come to recognize that the nation-state is always a relevant actor, although the ways in which the state acts varies from place to place and time to time (Block, 1994). Although often treated as a monopolistic agency, the state—particularly liberal states such as the United States—is more realistically treated as a highly differentiated, multifaceted, often loosely coupled congeries of organizations. In addition to the three branches of government, within the executive and administrative branch, many semi-independent agencies regulate and fund a wide range of economic and social functions. Federal systems also divide powers between national, state, and local governmental units.

Lindblom has pointed out that "an easy way to acknowledge the special character of government as an organization is simply to say that governments exercise authority over other organizations" (1977: 21). Although Lindblom goes on to caution that governmental authority is sometimes contested, it is nevertheless essential to take account of governments' special powers— including its monopoly over the legitimate use of violence—and of the unique role the nation-state plays as an organization among organizations.

A wide variety of processes and mechanisms operate to link governmental units and their "subjects," whether individuals, organizations, or industries. The lion's share of attention has been accorded by scholars and organizational participants to the allocative and regulative roles of government. Familiar examples of *allocative* powers include taxation, grants-in-aid, subsidies, and various forms of corporate welfare. In addition, governments often act as a direct purchaser of goods and services—for example, military equipment and accounting services—from organizations in the private sector. Indeed, recent years have witnessed an enormous increasing in the contracting out of work by the state to the private sector (Salamon, 2002). Governments also devise *regulative* systems designed to oversee organizational behavior, ensuring that rules protecting competition and employee welfare are observed, and attempting to curb "externalities"—costs such as pollution borne by third parties, including the wider public, that are the byproduct of production (Noll, 1985; Stigler, 1971; Wilson, 1980). Regulative systems are often charged with motivating evasion rather than compliance, but the most successful of them create norms that are internalized—incorporated into the structure of relevant organizations. Thus Edelman (1992) and Dobbin and Sutton (1998) describe the processes by which ambiguous rules intended to advance equal opportunity and diversity in the workplace, even though often weakly enforced, stimulated normative and cognitive changes in personnel and managerial circles to support reforms, often couching their arguments in efficiency terms. And Hoffman (1997) details the growing influence of environmental engineers employed by chemical and petroleum companies in the United States, many of whom worked to advance "green" agendas from within their organizations during the latter decades of the twentieth century.

Less attention has been accorded the *constitutive* powers of the state, although these are arguably the most significant. Working primarily through its legal systems, the state constructs a framework of legal entities, such as corporations and unions, and specifies their attributes, capacities, rights, and responsibilities (Edelman and Suchman, 1997). Of particular importance for economic units are a subset of these rules that define *property rights*—"rules that determine the conditions of ownership and control of the means of production" (Campbell and Lindberg, 1990: 635). For example, the rights accorded to workers and unions by the Wagner Act in 1935 were greatly restricted by the Taft-Hartley Act of 1974.

Another understudied facet of government shifts attention from the state as collective actor to the state as *institutional structure* (Campbell and Lindberg, 1990). In the latter guise, the state presents itself in a variety of organizational configurations—both at the societal and the organizational field levels—providing different means of access, diverse policy determination and implementation processes, and varying forums for conflict resolution (Hult and Walcott, 1990).

But influence processes are not unidirectional. As noted in Chapter 9, organizations, acting both alone and in league with others, exert important effects on state policies and activities (Prechel, 2000). In his historical study of the largest U.S. industrial corporations from the 1920s to the 1980s, Fligstein argues that large firms develop various control strategies "to solve their competitive problems" that vary over time (1990: 12). These strategies emerge out of interactions between leading members of the firm and "through inter-action with the political and legal system in the United States" (p. 296). From the beginning of the republic, organizations have attempted to translate their economic power into political influence. Most of us are aware of the political activities of organizations—petitioning, lobbying, providing data and "expert" testimony—as they attempt to influence governmental programs. A recent example is provided by the ability of corporate interests to persuade most of the fifty states to enact antitakeover legislation during the decade 1980–1990 (Vogus and Davis, 2005). The power of the political action committees (PACs) is only the latest vehicle by which organizations attempt to influence political decisions at the federal level. (See Clawson, Neustadtl, and Weller, 1998; Domhoff, 1998; Mizruchi, 1992).

Professions. More so than other types of collective actors, the professions exercise enormous influence on cultural-cognitive, normative, and regulative systems, collectively creating and warranting these systems of knowledge and control. They have displaced earlier claimants to such wisdom and moral authority—wizards, prophets, seers, sages, intellectuals—currently exercising supremacy in today's secularized and rationalized world. As the dominant contemporary institutional agents, different professions emphasize one or another institutional element in their work (Scott, 2005a).

Some professions operate primarily within the *cultural-cognitive* sphere by creating conceptual systems:

> Their primary weapons are ideas. They exercise control by defining reality—by devising ontological frameworks, proposing distinctions, creating typifications, and fabricating principles or guidelines for action. (Scott and Backman, 1990: 290)

Knowledge systems vary from the periodic table and the laws of physics to medical diagnostic categories and rules of grammar. Some systems are more empirically based, others less so. Exemplary professions stressing cultural-cognitive systems are the various sciences. They exercise control within their own occupational ranks primarily by means of the shared conceptions of problems and approaches they employ (Knorr-Certina, 1999). Externally, these professions exercise "cultural authority" (Starr, 1982): clients and students follow their "orders" to the extent that they accept their knowledge claims.

Others, such as theologians, therapists, and a variety of environmental and human rights specialists, create and promulgate *normative* frameworks. Their professional bodies are increasingly active at national and even transnational levels. As previously discussed, Meyer (1994) argues that such professionals operate at a world-system level, holding conferences, issuing statements, promulgating recipes for reforming and rationalizing one after another sphere of activity—from standards for health and education to procedures for protecting the environment. INGOs organized at the transsocietal level provide important vehicles for these activities (Boli and Thomas, 1999). Brunsson and Jacobsson (2000) point out that these professionals lack coercive power (like states and corporations) or resources to induce compliance but wield substantial influence over the behavior of others by promulgating standards which they invest with moral authority.

Still other professional occupations, such as legal experts, the military, and managerial professionals, exercise substantial influence over *regulatory* bodies ranging from nation-states to state and local governments to private corporations. Such groups draft constitutions and treaties, craft legislation and corporate frameworks, exercise surveillance, and manipulate rewards and sanctions.

And, as discussed above, for our purposes, the most important consequent of all this institutional activity fermented by professionals is the proliferation of organizations in diverse sectors and at multiple levels.

Organizational Fields. Organizational fields have emerged as a vibrant new level of analysis for understanding organizing processes and structures (see Chapter 5). As defined by DiMaggio and Powell (1983), fields are comprised of diverse organizational populations and their supporting (e.g., funding) and constraining (e.g., regulatory/competitive) partners, all of whom operate within an institutionally constructed framework of common meanings. Fields necessarily vary among themselves and over time in their degree of *structuration*—their relational and cultural coherence (DiMaggio and Powell, 1983; Giddens, 1979). DiMaggio, and Powell (1983; DiMaggio, 1983) stress the relational, network features of structuration—for example, extent of isomorphism exhibited by participating structures, flow of information, level of interaction among organizations, degree of defined patterns of coalition and dominance—but it is important to retain the original framing of Gidden's definition that structuration stresses the recursive interdependence of rules and relations, of schemas and resources (see also Sewell, 1992). As structuration increases, meanings become more widely shared: institutional logics—"the practices and symbolic constructions which constitute [a field's] organizing principles" (Friedland and Alford, 1991: 248)—more pervasive. This does not necessarily mean that there is high consensus and ideological unity. Some fields are structured by the issues around which parties contend, as Hoffman (1997) illustrates in his analysis of the rise of environmental issues in the U.S. chemical and petroleum industries during the last decades of the twentieth century. Prior to the 1970s there were few environmentally oriented governmental controls, but with the onset of the environmental movement, activists grew in numbers and influence and were able to obtain passage of a number of laws and the creation of agencies to enforce them. By the 1990s, a "field" of industrial environmentalism had been constructed with industrial, governmental, and social movement actors playing leading roles.

Much has been written and many studies have been conducted to illuminate the dynamics of organizational fields. Much of this work relies and elaborates on the basic argument that fields and organizational forms co-evolve: that field processes produce and reproduce organizations just as organizations both adapt to and transform fields. We review selected studies pertaining to the origins of fields, factors shaping the operation of existing fields, and factors giving rise to the restructuration of fields.

Origins of Fields. The beginning of wisdom for an institutionalist is the recognition that existing institutional structures shape the creation of new fields. Still, studies exist of efforts to create (relatively) new forms in (relatively) unstructured, or understructured, contexts. DiMaggio (1991) relates the history of the creation during the late nineteenth century in America of the "high" culture field of art museums. He posits a contest between two varying models of museums—one more broadly populist (e.g., public libraries), the other more elitist, a connoisseurship model of acquisition and exhibition of fine arts treasures. Differing types or art professionals championed each of these models, but eventually, with the decisive help of the Carnegie Foundation, the latter triumphed.[5] Two important lessons are drawn: (1) fundamental conflicts in institutional logics are more likely to be visible in the early stages of field formation than after a field has become highly structurated; and (2) professional activists operate at two, relatively independent levels—within organizations, as professionals, managers, and trustees jockey for position and, more fatefully, outside organizations at the field level, as logics and frameworks are crafted and contested so that, eventually, one vision of the field is privileged over others.

Morrill (forthcoming) also examines the emergence of a new field—alternative dispute resolution (ADR)—at the "interstices" between the existing fields of law and social work. Tracking the development of this new professional arena, Morrill distinguished three stages, beginning with an innovation phase in which a large and growing number of problem cases not amenable to conventional legal or social work practices began to connect to informal problem-solving methods employed in domestic relations or labor arbitration cases. There followed a mobilization stage in which two models of

---

[5]Also, it is important to note that elite Americans, who on their "grand tour" had visited the great museums of Europe, reflecting the "high culture" tradition. Were anxious to emulate this form (and later to appropriate the associated collections). Thus, the "new" organization form was borrowed from Europe.

dispute resolution competed, a "community mediation" and "multidoor courthouse" approach, each backed by a different professional constituency and associated with a different organizational form. Although none of the parties was able to obtain definitive federal backing for their approach, the field progressed into a phase of increasing structuration as the contenders identified a common body of knowledge, codified normative standards, created new professional organizations, and developed university-based training programs. By the mid 1990s, ADR had successfully carved out "a professional jurisdiction for alternative practices" (p. 29).

Employing an approach that incorporates social movement arguments and market strategies, Lounsbury and colleagues (Lounsbury, 2005; Lounsbury, Ventresca, and Hirsch, 2003) depict the contentious development of a for-profit recycling industry in the United States between 1960 and 2000. With the broad backdrop of increasing salience of environmental concerns, recycling advocates wrestled over issues of technology—waste-to-energy incineration versus recycling—and enterprise form—community-based centers versus for-profit companies. Although activist organizations were able to create a heightened social consciousness, elevating awareness of the importance of environmental issues, they could not successfully compete with corporate interests, which took advantage of regional and national infrastructures allowing them to obtain economics of scale. In this field, during the period of study, a for-profit model drove out the vision of a community-based alternative.

Evolution of Fields. The most characteristic narrative of field structuration stresses the interacting processes of diffusion, imitation, and adaptation, and the resultant community order. A study by Haveman and Rao (1997) details the co-evolution of institutions and organizational forms in their historical analysis of the California thrift industry between 1890 and 1928. Early forms reflected the dominant logics of the virtues of mutual assistance and self-help. Members were shareholders, not depositors, and plans were dissolved when all participants had saved sufficient funds to build or buy they own homes. These do-it-yourself forms were gradually supplanted by a more conventional corporate model, "the Dayton/guarantee-stock plan," in which members were differentiated from managers and depositors from borrowers. A number of hybrid forms also were devised, but in the end, the Dayton model became dominant. Haveman and Rao argue that the earlier mutual forms were consistent with the informal patterns of rural communities while the Dayton model was more congruent with the institutional logics of the Progressive era, "appealing to well-understood rational-bureaucratic procedures and arguing in efficiency terms." (1997: 1641)

A somewhat similar evolutionary process is described by Schneiberg and Soule (2005), who examined the changing forms of rate regulation by the several states in American fire insurance during the first third of the twentieth century. Regulatory policies are depicted as resulting from "contested, multi-level" processes." Whereas groups in northern urban states favored an "associational model" of order in which insurance companies were allowed to work out rate agreements among themselves, other groups, largely in Midwestern and Plains states rejected this "corporate" solution and called for statist antitrust legislation and rate regulation. Between these two extremes, over time a middle way was crafted, involving the creation of an independent inspector to review rates set by companies. These battles and the final institutional settlement are shown to reflect the interaction of three distinct modes of political activity: contests within each state were affected by the size and power of competing interests within the state (e.g., membership in the state Grange or State Farmers Alliance); states monitored activities in neighboring states and "borrowed" reform ideas; and both processes were affected by decisions during this period of the U.S. Supreme Court and by associational activities at the national level.

Field Responses to Challenges. An interesting early study conducted at the field level of analysis is that of Miles (1982), who studied the response of the "Big Six" corporations in the United States tobacco industry to the threat posed by the demonstration of a causal link between smoking and impaired health. Although there was some early warning, the publication of the surgeon general's report linking smoking and cancer and subsequent actions taken by various federal agencies constituted a major "environmental" crisis for these organizations. Although each corporation adopted a variety of individual strategies ranging from product innovation to diversification, they also engaged in collective action. For example, during the first signs of trouble, they created the Tobacco Industry Research Committee to conduct their own studies of the effects of tobacco use. Following the surgeon general's report, they collectively engaged in a wide variety of lobbying efforts, providing cancer-research grants to the American Medical Association and various universities and monitoring closely and attempting to influence legislative and administrative actions affecting their interest.

At the same time that the largest tobacco companies were engaged in these collective actions, however, selective processes were also at work reducing the number of companies in the industry. Population ecologists remind us that it is important not to focus exclusively on the dominant companies in an industry. Turning attention from the Big Six to the entire population of tobacco companies, Hannan and Freeman (1989: 32–33) report that during the period of interest, "of the 78 companies in the U.S. tobacco business in 1956, 49 had left the industry by 1986." Twelve of these companies shifted into other business lines, but thirty-seven firms had closed their doors. Changes in field composition and structure is a joint product of both adaptation and selection processes.

Hoffman (1997), as noted, also examines the response of industry to governmental regulation: the changing nature of the response by the U.S. petroleum and chemical industries to increasing environmental protections, beginning with the Clean Air Act of 1970. Prior to 1970s, there were few governmental controls, and industry participants "displayed an autonomous self-reliance based on technological self-confidence" (p. 12). After the creation of the Environmental Protection Agency (EPA) in 1970, industry members and environmental activists operated largely in separate camps, industry seeking ways to minimally comply with the new federal requirements. When conservatives came to power in 1980, governmental controls were weakened, but environmental groups grew in numbers and influence. After 1990, the power balance between government, the industry, and activists began to equalize. "For the firm, organizational boundaries began to blur, allowing direct influence by these [activist and regulatory] constituents" as "solutions were seen as emerging from the organizational field in its then expanded form" (p. 13). Throughout the entire period, industries were increasingly working to internalize environmental expertise—creating departments of environmental engineering and devoting greater managerial attention to environmental concerns. The story told is not only one of the changing role of governmental agencies and social movements and of changes in organizational and industry structure in response to environmental pressures, but also changes in managerial ideologies—in the "institutional logics" employed by managers to interpret their responsibilities in relation to the environment.

Another study examines changes in field definition and internal structures resulting from changes in the information systems utilized to define the markets served. Anand and Peterson (2000) examined changes in the field of commercial music resulting from alteration of the procedures employed to assess sales of various music genres. Earlier information regimes based their report of record sales on a panel of about 200 reporting sales outlets with the claim that these were a "weighted cross section" of stores selling commercial music records. However, with the introduction of bar codes, it became feasible to track record sales from a much wider range of sales outlets. This new sampling technology revealed that earlier approaches had vastly underestimated sales of country music, whose audiences were more often located in rural areas, patronizing unconventional suppliers—for example, gasoline stations and convenience stores—types of outlets omitted from earlier sampling approaches. This newly available information led to an altered conception of the music industry, in particular, the position of country music within it. And this information also changed the behavior of recording executives, who began to adapt their contracting decisions with recording artists and with distributors to take into account a newly recognized audience.

Organizations that embody existing field logics must also find ways to respond to changing logics—changes in beliefs and norms—that often take the form of changes in market demands. For example, kibbutzim in Israel were initially organized around socialist Zionist principles. A core element of these founding principles was that hired labor was anathema: work was to be performed by the collective (self-labor), not by "wage slaves." Yet, a study by Simons and Ingram (1997) found that those kibbutzim that were more dependent on bank debt employed proportionally more hired labor, indicating that ideology may be trumped by organizational survival. Moreover, as support for socialist logics has waned, all the kibbuzim as a group have moved toward using more hired labor over time, regardless of their founding ideology. In a similar manner, traditional four-year liberal arts colleges in the United States had strong commitments to a particular form of education for decades. But once the Baby Boom generation left college, available students grew scarcer, and those who remained sought more "practical" training in topics like business. Thus, over time, even those colleges most committed to a liberal arts curriculum have begun to offer increasing numbers of business and technical/professional degrees, a survival strategy that has turned out to be quite helpful in staving off bankruptcy (Kraatz and Zajac, 1996).

Field Restructuration. Major changes in organizations can be precipitated by both exogenous and endogenous processes. As we discussed earlier in this chapter, major technological improvements, in particular, those that are "competence destroying," can lead to the replacement of dominant organizational populations by entirely new forms (Tushman and Anderson, 1986). And political and economic crises, such as the fall of communism in the Soviet Union and Eastern Europe, can destabilize existing fields. For example, Stark (2001: 70) proposes that in the aftermath of the upheavals in Eastern Europe in 1989, these countries can be viewed as a genuine social laboratory because individuals are "actively experimenting with new organizational forms"—drawing selected elements from public and private forms and arranging them in new combinations. In a similar manner, and for related reasons, observers report much innovation and variety in today's China (Child, 1994; Lin, 2001; Tsui and Lau, 2002).

Important types of endogenous sources of pressure for change include the ever-present operation of "gaps" or "mismatches" between macromodels and microrealities (Sjöstrand, 1995). General templates must perforce give way over time to the pressure of events on the ground. And, as just noted, market pressures provide impetus for change and reform. For example, pressures for changes in U.S. school organization currently stem from perceived inadequate performance ("failing" test scores compared to systems in comparable countries) or, in the case of health system, escalating costs. Indeed, the organization of health care services in the United States has undergone major transformation in recent decades, as documented by Scott and colleagues (2000).

These researchers studied changes over a fifty-year period in the U.S. health care field. Data were gathered on all organizations comprising five populations of care organizations—hospitals, health maintenance organizations, home health agencies, kidney disease centers, and integrated health care organizations—in one locale, the San Francisco Bay area, during the period 1945–1995. Although the study was restricted to organizational populations in one metropolitan area, changes were assessed in relevant material resource and institutional environments at local, state and national levels. Three periods or eras were identified, based on changes in primary institutional logics and governance structures. *Governance structures* "refer to all those arrangements by which field-level power and authority are exercised involving, variously, formal and informal systems, public and private auspices, regulative and normative mechanisms" (Scott et al., 2000: 173).

At the beginning of the study, professional associations were the primary governance units and physicians exercised uncontested cultural authority over the field (see Starr, 1982). Dominant logics stressed "quality of care" as defined by physicians. However, the growth of specialization, accompanied by the rise of specialist associations, reduced the unity of physicians—an endogenous change—and, partly as a consequence, in 1965 the federal government through the passage of the Medicare and Medicaid acts became a major player, both as purchaser and regulator of health care services. To the controls exercised by professional associations were now added a wide variety of public fiscal and regulatory systems; and to a logic stressing quality was added a more public ideology of improving "equity of access." As health care costs continued to spiral out of control, in 1982 a third era emerged characterized by the increasing use of managerial and market mechanisms to govern the sector. The new logics stressed the importance of "efficiency" (Scott et al., 2000, chap. 6).

In response to these changing governance arrangements and cultural beliefs, as well as changes in local demographic characteristics, organizations delivering health care services underwent important changes. Hospitals and other traditional providers utilized buffering strategies such as leveling and adjusting scale (numbers of beds). Bridging strategies were widely employed as organizational providers increasingly relied on contracts with physician groups, entered into strategic alliances, or were horizontally or vertically integrated into larger health care systems. The most dramatic changes, however, occurred at the population and field levels. Generalist providers (hospitals) failed in large numbers and were increasingly replaced by specialist organizations (for example, home health agencies); public and nonprofit organizations were replaced by for-profit forms. New types of organizations emerged—for example, home health agencies and health maintenance organizations—and the boundaries of existing organizations, such as hospitals, were reconstructed. For example, kidney disease units that originated as subunits of hospitals were "unbundled" and set up as independent units. Even the boundaries of the field of health care itself experienced change. Having been sheltered for decades from the industrializing, bureaucratizing, profit-oriented processes that characterized other industries, health care by the end of the twentieth century looked much less distinctive. Financial market-oriented forces had claimed yet another arena (Scott et al., 2000).

As a final example of institutional-organization restructuring, Rao (2003) combines social movement and institutional arguments to examine the "revolution" occurring in French cuisine as a rebel breed of chefs introduced a new culinary rhetoric, replacing classical with nouvelle cuisine. Rao argues that the two cuisines represent different institutional logics—rules of cooking, types of ingredients, bases for naming dishes—as well as contrasting identities for chefs and waiters. The growing success of the new cuisine was systematically tracked by charting changes over time in the menus of leading restaurants—a random sample of the signature dishes of chefs between the years 1970 and 1997 were coded by category. Increasing adoption of nouvelle cuisine was found to be associated with changes over the period in the number of articles published in culinary magazines favorable to this cuisine, the number of prior chefs adopting this cuisine weighted by the number of stars received from the *Guide Michelin*, a valued measure of culinary excellence, and the proportion of chefs elected to the executive board of the professional society of French chefs. Rao argues that institutional change also entails a "politics of identity" as actors who embrace new social logics must also shift their group allegiance, replacing one role identity with an altered one (p. 835).

As a number of the studies reviewed document, institutional studies of change have been informed by ideas and arguments associated with the study of social movements. The academic study of organizations and movements have developed during roughly the same period, but largely independent of one another (for a review, see McAdam and Scott, 2005). Social movement theorists have long attended to the processes involved in the awakening and empowerment of suppressed groups and interests and to the resulting infusion into a "settled" field of new ideas, of new repertories of action and new forms of organizing (see Clemens, 1997; McAdam, 1999; McAdam, McCarthy, and Zald, 1996a). Whereas numerous social movement theorists have productively imported ideas regarding processes of mobilizing and the value of organization building from organizational scholars (e.g., Zald and McCarthy, 1987), recent years have witnesses the profitable flow of ideas in the other direction— from social movement to organizational scholars (Davis et al., 2005).

Critique

Institutional theory, in its newest guise, burst on the organizational scene in 1977. The early formulations by Meyer and Rowan and by DiMaggio and Powell sketched out a bold argument, insisting that organizational structures, far from reflecting the forces of task demands and competitive/efficiency requirements, were more responsive to a set of social-cultural pressures. Social fitness trumps economic competition as the prime force shaping organizations. Indeed, institutional pressures were seen in many ways as contradictory to rational modes of organizing.

From these early, audacious, and overstated premises, contemporary institutional theorists have reined in and moderated their arguments along several lines (Scott, forthcoming). Early institutional arguments were often inadequately verified. Assertions were made but not empirically tested; cultural forces were described but not measured. In addition, the arguments made were often overly deterministic; the language employed emphasized "institutional effects." More recent work takes a much more interactive view, stressing that (1) institutional frameworks are often contradictory, allowing organizations some discretion in choosing which versions to relate to; (2) the clarity and sanctioning power of institutional agents varies substantially, allowing for organizational latitude in interpretation and conformance; and (3) not only institutional agents, but also organizational participants enjoy latitude and choice in their behavior, so that the latter exercise discretion in determining their response to institutional pressure. More generally, early work gave little attention to agency or power or to mechanisms—Which actors are involved and what are the processes by which observed changes take place? More recent work attends more to agency and to causal mechanisms. At the same time, more attention is given now than previously to the antecedents of institutional change.

Most important, institutionalists increasingly see their arguments not as opposed to but accommodating the concerns of rational/economic theorists. A growing number of institutional theorists (e.g., Hamilton and Biggart, 1988; Powell, 1991; Scott et al., 2000; Whitley, 1992) describe the ways in which wider institutional premises frame the situations within which specific economic agents define and pursue their interests.

SUMMARY

The newly formulated population ecology approach to organizations and the refurbished "new" institutional approaches to organizations both burst on the scene in the late 1970s. Both approaches defocalized attention on a single organization and its immediate environment to examine wider systems—comprised either of similar kinds of organizations (populations) or of organizations operating in the same domain (fields).

Ecologists attend to competitive processes shaping populations of organizations dependent on the same kinds of resources. The dynamics of population processes including founding, growth, and failure rates are examined as these are shaped by demographic, ecological, and environmental factors. Much recent effort has been devoted to examining the entrepreneurial processes and technological factors that give rise to new types of organizations. With the help of institutional theorists, these arguments have been broadened to include political and cultural factors.

Institutional theorists examine the rules, norms, and beliefs that constrain and support social structures and processes, including organizations. While economists and political scientists stress the importance of rules and regulations (both externally in the guise of the state and internally in the form of governance systems), sociologists and organizational theorists have emphasized the role of shared norms and beliefs that provide the cultural foundations of social order. Social order, including organizations in all their forms, is not simply constrained by institutional rules; it is constituted by cultural models. Such models are sometimes conflicting, always contested, giving rise to different kinds of actors, interests, and appropriate actions. The examination of such processes at work within organizational fields has provided valuable insights into the co-evolution of organizational forms and institutional patterns.

CHAPTER 11

Networks In and Around Organizations

[We are] witnessing organisation man's metamorphosis into 'networked person', a species that can now be observed in airport lounges, on fast inter-city trains and at motorway service stations. Networked person is always on the move, juggling with a laptop computer, a mobile phone and a BlackBerry for e-mails, keeping in electronic touch with people he (and increasingly she) no longer regularly bumps into in a corridor. Indeed, there may be no corridor.

THE ECONOMIST (2006)

INTRODUCTION: FROM METAPHOR TO METHOD TO WORLDVIEW

The network has become perhaps the dominant metaphor of our time, used to describe structures from the brain (neural networks) to malevolent social groupings (terrorist networks) to global computer communication systems (the World Wide Web). Defined simply, a network consists of "nodes" and "ties," or relationships among the nodes. Nodes can be actors—such as persons, groups, or organizations—or other entities, such as neurons or abstract ideas. Ties can take on endless forms, from physical linkages to personal relationships. From this definition, it is clear that networks have much in common with the open systems approach described in Chapter 4, where we conceived of organizations as systems of interdependent, loosely coupled parts, among which can flow materials, energy, and information. Just as living systems vary in level from the cell to the organization to the supranational system (Miller, 1978), networks can be used to describe systems at all levels of analysis. Networks are everywhere, from the microscopic cell to the planetary system.

In organizational life, there are interpersonal networks—within and across organizations—that influence who gets a job and who gets promoted as well as interorganizational networks created by exchanges of resources, alliances, and shared directors. Formal organizations are themselves a special case of network: roles (or jobs, or participants) are nodes connected by ties such as authority relations or information exchanges. And network forms of organization link specialists across the value chain into a single quasi firm. Dell Computer's founder Michael Dell describes how "virtual integration" (as opposed to vertical integration) weaves together Dell's suppliers and other customers into an integrated whole that looks and acts like a single organization (Child, 2005: 197). A customer sees "Dell," but behind the scenes are twenty or more firms knit together by an electronic nervous system of information technology.

NETWORK THINKING

Network thinking has a long history in sociology. Many consider Georg Simmel (1955 trans.), a German contemporary of Weber, to be a founder of the sociology of networks with his discussions of the dynamics of triads and the "web of group affiliations." Triads are, of course, small networks, but they have interesting possibilities. A friend of my friend may be a friend, and an enemy of my friend is likely to be an enemy—but there are more interesting possibilities when my friend acts as a broker (keeping the two of us separate and acting as a conduit), an arbitrator (mediating conflicts between us), or a spoiler (fomenting conflicts between us).

Surprisingly, the "sociogram"—the familiar network diagram showing circles (actors) linked by lines (relationships) that we now take for granted—was not invented until the 1930s, when Jacob Moreno (1953) created it as part of a new science of "sociometry." The sociogram, and the sociometric techniques for assessing interpersonal networks pioneered by Moreno and others, provided a basic analytical framework for measuring some of the mathematical properties of networks.[1] C. Wright Mills applied network ideas to analyze the social connections among members of the American "power elite"—"those political, economic, and military circles which, as an intricate set of overlapping cliques, share decisions having . . . national consequences" (Mills, 1956: 18). Mills's work launched a series of empirical studies of power elites in modern societies—all anchored in organizational connections—that continues up to the present time.

During the 1970s and 1980s, advances in network methodology and in computing power allowed the network metaphor to become systematized into a formal method of analysis. New constructs and measures were introduced at a rapid pace, and network methods allowed more rigorous means of testing ideas from theories such as resource dependence and institutional theory. Network theorists also introduced new ways of thinking about organizations, their structures, and their relationships. In this chapter, we provide an

---

[1]In addition to its use as a descriptive and analytic tool, Moreno also regarded his methods as providing an important basis of social improvement and reform, supporting efforts to identify not simply existing, but also preferred social networks.

overview of network concepts and a review of networks in and around organizations that build on theories in the prior chapters to expand the domain of organizational analysis to broader social systems.

Varieties of Networks

A network is a system of relationships among parts. The parts are generally referred to as *nodes*, and the relationships or connections among the parts are *ties*. The underlying premise is that ties are often more influential in affecting behavior than the specific attributes of nodes—for example, demographic or psychological attributes of individuals. In addition, the behavior of a node is influenced not only by the ties in which it is directly involved, but also by the patterning of ties in the wider network structure.

Any organization or other social system can be represented as a network. Indeed, "network" is a general concept applicable at any level of analysis. A few examples of networks will illustrate this. Nodes can be people tied by friendship or acquaintanceship, as in the triads described by Simmel. This is the image that comes most readily to mind when we think of a "social network" or "networking," and a number of Web sites are devoted to mapping and facilitating networks for social (e.g., *Friendster.com*) and business purposes (e.g., *LinkedIn.com*). At a more fine grained level, one can map a conversational network by considering who talks to whom in a group (Gibson, 2005), which can reveal dynamics of power and status. Nodes can be film actors, such as Kevin Bacon and Julia Roberts, who are tied by acting together in the same film.[2]

Nodes can also be at higher levels of analysis. In fifteenth-century Florence, patriarchs of well-bred families routinely married their children off to each other to cement alliances among the families. Padgett and Ansell (1992) have mapped the Florentine family intermarriage network, where nodes are families and ties are marriages, to show the network prominence of Cosimo de Medici and his brood. Boards of directors often share members (or "interlocks"), as we saw in Chapter 8 and will discuss more fully later. These connections create two networks: in one, boards are the nodes connected by shared directors; in the other, directors are the nodes connected by shared board memberships.

Networks need not involve human beings at all. Pages on the World Wide Web can be considered nodes connected by hot links that direct browsers to and from each other. Who eats whom (or what) in an ecosystem, such as a pond, can be mapped as a network (albeit with only one-way connections!). For

---

[2]The "oracle of Bacon" Web site at the University of Virginia Computer Science Department, http://www.cs.virginia.edu/oracle/, documents that Kevin Bacon has acted in films with 1,888 other actors during his career, and those 1,888 actors have appeared in films with another 159,399 actors—that is, more than 160,000 actors are within two degrees of Kevin Bacon. Moreover, of the more than 700,000 actors included in the Internal Movie Database, most are within three degrees of Kevin Bacon, a surprising fact that we explore below.

electric power grids, generators and transformers are odes tied by high-voltage transmission lines (see Watts and Strogatz, 1998 for analyses of these networks). And products bought on-line are nodes "connected" by common purchasers; thus, Valdis Krebs (*http://orgnet.com/divided2.html*) mapped the linkages among political best-sellers purchased on Amazon.com to find that those on the left and right rarely bought the same books during the 2004 election season, a telling sign of political polarization.

Key Concepts and Measures

Networks can be viewed at three analytical levels (see Burt, 1980; Kilduff and Tsai, 2003 for introductions to social network analysis). The first is the *ego network*, consisting of all a node's direct contacts. Although this is the simplest level, it can be quite informative. How many acquaintances do I have? How diverse are they? Do they know each other? Do they like each other? Do I rely on different friends for different things (e.g., playing sports, gossip, job tips)? This conception of network can also be applied at higher levels, for example, to an organization and its direct contacts to other organizations—identical to the concept of organization set.

The second level is the *overall network*, which includes all actors and relationships within a particular domain. If the ego network describes one's immediate social neighborhood, the overall network describes the larger topography of a region. At this level, we can ask how well connected or dense the network is, whether it is highly centralized around a few important actors or balkanized into separate clusters. This is a useful way to analyze networks within a particular organization and fits well with notions of hierarchical versus flat organizations, silos versus matrix organizations, and so on, but it can also be applied at the organizational level, describing the structure of an organizational field. At the third level, if the overall network describes topography, then *network position* identifies an actor's coordinates within that topography. What is my place in the larger system—am I prominent, holding a place at the center of the network, or peripheral, hanging around at the edges? Are my friends well connected, giving me a broad circle of friends of friends? Similarly, at the organizational level, we can ascertain what its location is in the field.

Before describing specific network measures, we note two general caveats. First, the meaning of different network measures depends entirely on the nature of the relationships being mapped, which can include friendship or hatred, corporate alliances or corporate lawsuits. Thus, being central in a network is not necessarily a good thing. Baker and Faulkner (1993) found that those managers who were most central in a famous price-fixing conspiracy network were most likely to be found guilty in court—more central meant more witnesses—and most likely to do jail time! Second, networks are often "multiplex," meaning that different kinds of relationships often overlap. Coworkers can be friends; alliance partners may also share directors; directors on the same board could become romantically involved. It is important when analyzing networks to not lose sight of which specific relationships are being mapped.

Network analysts have developed several useful measures (see also Smith-Doerr and Powell, 2005).

- *Distance.* A basic measure in a network is the length of the shortest path between two actors, known as the "geodesic," or simply "distance." Friends (members of your ego network) are a distance of one, friends of friends are a distance of two, and so on. Imagine that you wanted to get from Bangor, Maine, to Santa Barbara, California, flying on an airline that only flew short hops between adjacent states. The smallest number of hops you could take is the geodesic distance for this trip on this airline. Social networks have a similar property, and distance can be thought of in terms of the question, Who do I know who can introduce me to X, or can introduce me to someone who knows X (say, Kevin Bacon)? A famous experiment by Stanley Milgram (1967) tried to calculate the distance between the average pair of adults in the United States and, along the way, coined the phrase "six degrees of separation." A random set of 160 Nebraskans was given a packet with the instruction to get the envelope to a stranger—specifically, a stockbroker who lived in suburban Boston—by relying on acquaintances who could forward the packet to someone who was likely to be closer to the stockbroker. The acquaintance would do the same thing until the packet eventually reached the target (the Boston broker). Milgram found that, on average, it took six passes between individuals for the packet to reach the broker—that is, people were separated by six degrees of separation. This came to be known as the "small world" phenomenon, after the common experience that, when we meet a stranger, we often find that we have an acquaintance in common—it is, indeed, a small world. The average distance between any two people (or organizations) is an important property of a network—information, fads, and diseases all spread more quickly when average distances are short (Watts, 1999).

- *Centrality.* Centrality describes how important an actor is in a system and is the most common measure of network position. Of course, there are many ways to be "important," and almost as many measures of centrality (Freeman, 1978/79; Wasserman and Faust, 1994: chap. 5). The simplest measure of centrality is *degree*, or how many direct contacts one has. (Put another way: how large is one's ego network?) Relationships can flow both ways and need not be reciprocal—millions of Web sites have links to the site for Adobe Acrobat, but the Acrobat site rarely links back to them. Thus, analysts distinguish between *in-degree* (how many ties flow toward you) and *out-degree* (how many ties flow outward from you). In-degree is often used as a measure of prestige in network analysis: those who are often named by others are particularly likely to be "important." In an important early study of relationships within a federal bureaucratic agency, Blau (1955) found that agents who were more often sought out for consultation on difficult cases enjoyed the highest status within the agency.

  A second measure of centrality is *closeness*, which describes how far (that is, how many degrees of separation on average) are all the other people in the network. A small number here means that one can easily reach friends of friends; thus, a closeness score of two means that the average person in the network is a friend of a friend, while a closeness score of three means the average person is a friend of a friend of a friend. A third centrality measure is *betweenness*. This asks: How often am I on the shortest path between any two other people in a network? An example illustrates this concept. In the Middle

Ages, when roads were relatively undeveloped in Russia, trade goods often moved by river aboard boats (or, during the winter, sleds). Port cities arose at relatively regular points along the rivers as places for trading, getting supplies, and rest. Rivers, of course, form a network, and there are often many possible paths between any two cities. It happens that, when one plots the shortest path between all possible pairs of cities and ranks cities according to how often they were on these shortest paths, Moscow is at the top. That is, boats or sleds traveling by river between any given pair of cities were highly likely to stop in Moscow, making it an important port city—a crossroads, if you will—that ultimately grew in importance to become the national capital in 1328 (Pitts, 1978/79).

Yet another measure of centrality is the *eigenvector* measure. Although the name is almost as unwieldy as the mathematics behind it, the intuition of this measure is straightforward: if degree asks "How many friends do I have?" the eigenvector measure asks, "Do I have many friends who themselves have many friends?" and so on. The search engine Google relies on a measure much like this: a Web page gets a high score to the extent that many other Web pages have links pointing to it, and these pages in turn are pointed to by many others. (Bonacich [1987] gives a more rigorous derivation.)

- *Clustering and structural holes.* In addition to knowing about someone's position in a network—their centrality—we might also want to know how connected or cohesive neighborhoods in a network are. Clustering asks, in short, Are your friends also friendly with each other? Within a family, we might expect that everyone is connected with everyone else, and thus clustering is very high. On the other hand, friends are less likely to be highly clustered. If you were to draw a sociogram of all your friends, with you at the center, then each pair of your friends who did not know each other would form an open triangle, with you in the middle and a gap in between. The fact that you are friends with both suggests that they would like each other if you introduced them, a phenomenon described by Fritz Heider's (1958) balance theory.

Ron Burt (1992b) labeled these gaps in social networks *structural holes* and documented the benefits to those whose ego networks have many structural holes. We mentioned above that Simmel described several possible triads, one of which centered on the broker or "tertius gaudens" ("third who benefits"), acting as a social bridge between people who do not know each other. This situation tends to arise for people who span social boundaries. For example, in Figure 11–1, Lois and Bill both work in design, and each has six friends at work (that is, their degree centrality is six). But while Bill's friends are all in design, and mostly know each other (that is, clustering is high among Bill's friends), Lois joined a cross-functional task force and stayed in touch with the colleagues she met in other departments. As a result, Lois can act as a bridge between these different departments, passing on information, opportunities, and requests—she is, in short, a "broker." The benefits to Lois are that she is likely to learn news faster than Bill and to have friends watching out for her interests at different places in the organization. Burt (1992b) argues that people who have networks rich in structural holes (such as Lois) frequently get better raises, faster promotions, and are in a better position to combine ideas into useful innovations.

Organizations can also benefit from having networks with structural holes within their organization set. For example, while most industrial design firms specialize in a particular industry (e.g., automotive parts), IDEO in Palo Alto, California, and Design Continuum in Boston, instead seek to work with clients in diverse industries because it allows their research staffs to find novel innovations that combine problems and solutions from disconnected domains. For instance, the idea for the Reebok Pump shoe, in which wearers pump up an

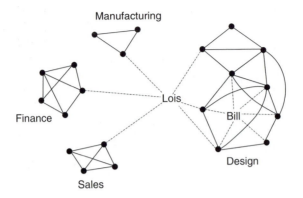

FIGURE 11–1   Networks at Work.
Source: Adapted from Burt (2000) and Baker (2000).

inflatable cuff around their ankle to provide a better fit, came from prior work with a client that made stents for IV bags used in hospitals. Organizations like IDEO and Design Continuum, in short, are like Lois, acting as "knowledge brokers" by maintaining ties to diverse and disconnected industrial clients (see Hargadon and Sutton, 1997, for these and other examples).

- *Equivalence.* Although each of us likes to believe that our situation is unique, network analysis emphasizes that many occupy similar locations in social systems. Two actors are *structurally equivalent* to the extent that they share the same pattern of relationships with other actors in a network. In the Sales Department in Figure 11–1, one person has a tie outside to Lois, while the other three are all tied to each other and to the first person. In network terms, they are equivalent. Note that the equivalent actors are not necessarily connected to each other—they simply have the same set of relationships to others. In practice, this may mean that they are competitors or substitutes. Companies that make disk drives for computers may buy from the same set of suppliers and sell to the same set of buyers—they are competitors, and structurally equivalent, even though they may be unaware of each other's existence. Institutional arguments regarding pressures toward isomorphism frequently apply to networks that are structurally equivalent (DiMaggio, 1986).

- *Density.* While clustering refers to ties among an ego network, density describes the extent to which all actors in an overall network who might be connected really are. More formally, density is the percentage of possible relations in a network that are actually observed. It provides a rough indication of a network's cohesion. Density tends to decrease with size, as the number of possible relationships increases geometrically with the number of nodes, according to the formula $[n^*(n-1)]/2$ (where n is the number of actors in the network). With two people, there is one possible relationship, between A and B. With three people, there are three possible relationships: A-B, B-C, and A-C. With four, there are six: A-B, A-C, A-D, B-C, B-D, and C-D. In a group of fifty, there are $(50^*49)/2$, or 1,225 possible relationships! Thus, if the average actor had five friends, then the density of the network quickly declines as it grows larger.

- *Centralization.* The final network-level measure we describe is centralization, which captures the extent to which some actors in a system are well connected and others are not. If everyone is equally central (by whichever centrality measure is used), then the centralization score is zero; if one person completely dominates the network, then centralization is one.

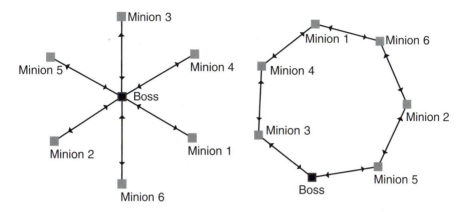

FIGURE 11-2 Centralized versus "Flat" Networks.

Centralization will typically vary with the level of hierarchy on the organization chart. Higher-ups tend to be much more central than lower-downs, and so an organization seeking to flatten its hierarchy should find centralization decreasing.

Networks as Pipes and Prisms

We have described networks in terms of actors and relationships, with the open systems notion that something flows between the actors—materials, energy, or information. Networks in this sense are like pipes, providing a conduit for resources and information to flow through. But Podolny (2001) points out that networks can also serve as prisms, refracting an actor's social position and indicating endorsement, status, or legitimacy—even if nothing in particular flows between the actors in the network. A famous anecdote illustrates this: "At the height of his wealth and success, the financier Baron de Rothschild was petitioned for a loan by an acquaintance. Reputedly, the great man replied, 'I won't give you a loan myself; but I will walk arm-in-arm with you across the floor of the Stock Exchange, and you soon shall have willing lenders to spare'" (Baker, 2000: 32). The prospective borrower's tie to Rothschild was not a pipe—the Baron was not going to provide him a loan— but a prism, a means to burnish his standing in the world. Those who have dealt with the boards of nonprofits, or dissertation committees, will know that similar dynamics play out in these contexts. As we will see later in the chapter, even investors in start-ups are sometimes recruited less for the resources they provide than for the appearance they create in the eyes of outside observers.

INTERORGANIZATIONAL NETWORKS

A large body of work on ties among organizations reflects the types of theories that predominated when network methods were being developed. In particular, resource dependence theory stressed the importance of networks of exchange among organizations and how they create power/dependence relations, as well as the formalized ties such as shared directors and alliances that organizations use to manage their interdependence (Pfeffer and Salancik, 1978). And institutional theorists use network imagery to describe constructs such as the structuration of organizational fields and the "emergence of sharply defined interorganizational structures of domination and patterns of coalition" (DiMaggio and Powell, 1983: 148). Researchers have mapped a large number of interorganizational networks, as we describe next.

Levels of Ties

As we have seen, networks exist within, across, and between organizations. All manner of ties exist among individuals within organizations: information flows, work-flow interdependence, friendship, and authority, among others. A similar range of ties exists between an organization and its exchange partners, competitors, and regulators. Perhaps the most widely studied network at the organization level is the interlocking directorate network created by shared directors on boards. We review these studies below. Another type of tie at the organization level is the alliance, which can range from short-term ties among firms or agencies for particular projects or long-term relationships and joint ventures. Such connections can give rise to new structures of network organizations, as we describe.

Network analysis can also be used as a tool for measuring organizational context. Networks can be created through common affiliations with a third party. For instance, companies can be "tied" through a shared owner. U.S. railroads in the early part of the twentieth century were organized into identifiable (but latent) "communities of interest" that shared both common owners and directors (Roy and Bonacich, 1988). Venture capitalists (VCs) also create implicit "communities" among their portfolio firms, as VCs can facilitate sharing information, best practices, and, potentially, exchanges among the businesses in which they invest. Just as being affiliated with the same owner can connect companies, they can be connected as a result of being covered by the same financial analysts. Zuckerman (1999) used such information to map distances and industry "neighborhoods" among firms based on analyst coverage. Patents that companies file include references much like academic papers; just as intellectual neighborhoods can be identified by patterns of academic citations, technological neighborhoods and distances among patented technologies can be mapped using patent citation data (Podolny and Stuart, 1995). And products bought by the same consumers on Amazon.com are thereby connected, creating "product neighborhood" networks. (To analyze the shortest paths between pairs of products, visit *http://www.baconizer.com/.*)

German firms are connected by relatively short paths via shared owners, and shorter paths between firms often led to mergers (Kogut and Walker, 2001). On the other hand, several hundred large U.S. firms are implicitly connected by having Fidelity as their largest shareholder, but there is no evidence that this translates into shared directors, business ties, or mergers (Davis and Yoo, 2003). But ownership and other dyadic ties often overlap (that is, they are "multiplex"): Fidelity is the largest shareholder in corporate America, but it is also one of the largest providers of employee benefits services (such as running corporate pension plans), which implies that it is frequently in a position of voting on the proposals of boards and managers that it depends on for business (Davis and Kim, 2005).

Finally, when we described dyadic approaches to the environment in Chapter 9, we noted that the entire economy (or polity) can be seen as a giant web of exchange. We briefly review work at the sector and societal level below.

Exchange Networks among Organizations

Exchange is perhaps the most basic tie in a market economy, and the question of why some ties endure and others do not is a central one for businesses. Several scholars have studied how long exchange relationships with professional firms endure, using the same techniques ecologists used to study organizational births and deaths to understand the "births" and "deaths" of relationships. A study of auditors revealed a "liability of adolescence" in the length of time that corporations retained their accounting firms. Following an initial honeymoon period in which auditors were relatively safe, the rate of breakup increased up to a maximum point (perhaps similar to a "seven-year itch") and then declined again with time as, apparently, firms and their auditors became invested in their relationship (Levinthal and Fichman, 1988). (An interesting exception to this general pattern was Arthur Andersen's implosion following Enron, where clients rushed to the exit in a rapid contagion process—see Jensen [2006].) Baker and colleagues (1998) found a similar U-curve pattern for firms' ties to advertising agencies, although the peak year for risk of breakup was much later, at eleven years. Such business ties are evidently overlaid with social ties as well. Broschak (2004) found that ad agencies were more likely to turn over when the managers they dealt with at the client firm exited. And corporations that were issuing bonds were more likely to choose commercial banks as lead underwriter—a relatively new line of business for the banks enabled by financial de-regulation—when the firm had done other types of business with the bank previously (Jensen, 2003).

Beyond specific dyadic ties among firms, researchers have also considered the impact of a firm's portfolio of ties with its organization set. In the New York garment industry, as in other contexts, there are clear advantages to having strong ties with clients—loyalty, trust, and better information—but there are also risks that accompany being overly dependent on a single partner. Thus, Uzzi (1996) found that firms did best—that is, were least likely to fail in a given year—when they had a mix of strong and weak ties. In a subsequent study, he found that corporate law firms charged lower hourly rates to the extent that they had a portfolio of longer-term clients, but higher rates to the extent that its lawyers served on major corporate boards and the firm served high-status clients (Uzzi and Lancaster, 2004).

Interlock Networks

Academic and policy concern with interlocks dates back to Justice Brandeis (1914), who argued that bankers dominated the economy by placing their representatives on corporate boards, and Lenin (1939 trans.), who pointed out that this was the case for most capitalist economies.[3] While the earliest writings reflected anxiety about concentrated economic power (Roe, 1994) and hinted at an almost conspiratorial process centered around banks, subsequent work suggested a more structural interpretation of pervasive interlocks. Mills (1956) argued that connections among elites from the corporate, military, and governmental realms had become increasingly national in character, in part as a result of the mobilization for the Second World War. Because of this increased concentration of power at the national level, it was almost inevitable that elites at the head of the most important institutions would come to know each other, to socialize, and to evolve more-or-less shared opinions. By midcentury, however, banks had become relatively less important to this process as their clients grew to national and international scope. "Not 'Wall Street financiers' or bankers, but large owners and executives in their self-financing corporations hold the keys of economic power" (Mills, 1956: 125).

Debates around banks and the place of interlocks continued through the 1980s. Mizruchi (1982) documented that banks had been central continuously since the days of JP Morgan at the turn of the century. Mintz and Schwartz (1985) analyzed in detail the sources of bank centrality in the 1960s and argued that although bank centrality was economically significant, banks did not "dominate" companies, certainly not through board ties. Rather, banks recruited well-connected executives to serve on their boards to provide high-level intelligence about the operations of the economy, which the bank could then use to guide investment choices. But during the 1980s and 1990s, corporations increasingly turned away from commercial banks for their financing and relied instead on markets for debt, thus removing the primary franchise of the banks. As a result, banks consolidated, shrank their boards, and moved into other lines of business, such as securities underwriting, and by the mid-1990s, they were no longer particularly central in the interlock network (Davis and Mizruchi, 1999).

Antecedents of Interlocks. The consensus view of board interlocks currently is that they are primarily a source of information (or "business scan"— Useem [1984]) rather than a device for interorganizational control. But why do

---

[3]Brandeis's concerns were shared by Congress and encoded into the Clayton Act of 1914, which made sharing directors among competitors illegal.

particular organizations choose to share directors with each other? The most influential view was that organizations used board membership as a form of cooptation—that is, inviting a source of vital resources to serve as an insider on the board in order to gain their favor. Resource dependence theorists documented that shared directorships across industries mapped onto interindustry resource flows, consistent with the idea that companies were inviting executives of troublesome buyers or suppliers to serve on their boards (Burt, 1983; Pfeffer and Salancik, 1978). Shared directors within broad industry sectors were also most likely to be found at intermediate levels of concentration, which was argued to be the situation entailing the most competitive constraint. But the evidence supporting these arguments was at the industry level of analysis, not the firm level. Moreover, the industry level used in most studies was highly aggregated: for example, industry sector 28 ("chemicals") included heavy chemical makers such as Dow and DuPont, drug companies such as Merck and Pfizer, cosmetics firms like Avon and Revlon, and paint makers like Sherwin-Williams. When analyzed at more disaggregated levels, the data showed that interlocks among genuine competitors in the late 1960s were essentially nonexistent (Zajac, 1988).

Similarly, data from the 1990s showed that large corporate boards in the United States only rarely included executives of major buyers or suppliers (Davis, 1996). And when a shared director retired or died, thus severing a tie between a pair of companies, they were replaced with another shared director only about one time in six during the 1960s (Palmer, 1983). The evidence, in short, suggests that board ties among U.S. corporations are not used primarily to manage interorganizational interdependence.

Why do firms recruit the directors they do? For much the same reason that individuals choose particular people to befriend: proximity.[4] Companies located in the same city were more likely to reconstitute broken ties than those in different cities during the 1960s (Palmer, Friedland, and Singh, 1986); businesses in cities with elite social clubs (which provide a place for elites to meet) were more likely to share directors (Kono et al., 1998); companies are more likely to recruit directors from the boards where their current directors already served (Davis, Yoo, and Baker, 2003); and there is a clear geographic clustering by city in the interlock network, particularly in cities with a prior history of interlocking (Marquis, 2003).

To put it another way: boards in general recruit individuals, not "interorganizational ties." What characteristics make a candidate attractive may vary among selectors. Existing board members may want to recruit engaged directors who are likely to get along well with the current board, whereas CEOs might prefer more compliant directors (Zajac and Westphal, 1996). And individuals who are already well connected (e.g., by serving on a

---

[4]We describe below research showing the importance of proximity for choice of friends by individuals.

lot of boards, or by serving on boards whose directors in turn serve on a lot of boards) are more likely to be mentioned as potential candidates (Davis, Yoo, and Baker, 2003). But they are recruited as individuals; the corporate ties they bring appear to be somewhat fortuitous.

Consequences of Interlocks. Fortuitous ties, however, turn out to be consequential. Michel Useem (1984) interviewed dozens of directors in the United States and the United Kingdom and found that a major attraction for serving on a board is "business scan": directors who serve on several boards have access to high-level intelligence from which their own organizations can benefit. For example, CEOs learn about acquisitions from serving on outside boards, particularly if they lack ties to other sources of intelligence, such as business associations (Haunschild and Beckman, 1998). Well-connected CEOs engaged in more acquisitions in the 1960s (Palmer and Barber, 2001) and the 1980s (Haunschild, 1993) than did their less-connected peers. Such board ties are particularly valuable when they connect the firm to diverse sources of information, such as partners who have had a variety of experiences with acquisitions (Beckman and Haunschild, 2002). Board ties to local philanthropic leaders shaped the level of charitable giving by their firms: companies in Minneapolis/St. Paul whose executives had more contact with the philanthropic elite (through serving on the same corporate or nonprofit boards and through membership in the same elite clubs) made greater contributions than those with fewer contacts (Galaskiewicz, 1997).

Because of the dense connections among firms created through shared directors, one might expect that firms are especially susceptible to contagions, just as children in day care are routinely exposed to new viruses. A number of studies have shown that corporate practices and structures diffuse through board ties. This should not be too surprising: companies often face the same problems (e.g., which investment bank to use, what countries to invest in, how to fire the CEO without alarming Wall Street), and shared directors often confront the same problems on several boards. Thus, companies more readily adopted the "poison pill" takeover defense in the mid-1980s to the extent that their directors served on other boards that had done so—a contagion process that led most large U.S. corporations to adopt a pill over a brief period (Davis and Greve, 1997). Similar ties encouraged firms to create an investor relations office to deal with their institutional owners when they heard about it via a shared director (Rao and Sivakumar, 1999). During the 1960s, companies whose outside (nonexecutive) directors had ties to directors of companies with an M-form were more likely to adopt this structure themselves (Palmer, Jennings, and Zhou, 1993). And companies listed on the Nasdaq stock market frequently "defected" to the New York Stock Exchange—Nasdaq's major rival— when companies with which they shared directors had done so, although this effect was dampened among firms sharing directors with other, nondefecting Nasdaq firms (Rao, Davis, and Ward, 2000). Organizations, it seems, can get caught up in contagions (not to say fads) in much the same way as individuals.

Ties among boards have documented effects on decision making and on the spread of information. Surprisingly however, there is virtually no evidence that they influence economic performance, at least in the United States (see Mizruchi, 1996 for a review). Organizations may try to direct their interlocks at sources of constraint, or recruit well-connected directors to impress their investors (à la Baron de Rothschild), but it doesn't seem to help their profitability. Nonetheless, interlocks continue to be widespread in most economies—in 2003, the average large U.S. corporation shared directors with six other large corporations, and there is little sign of decline in their prevalence.

NETWORK FORMS OF ORGANIZATION

After seeing the enormous range of contexts that can be described as "networks," it should come as no surprise that the notion of a "network organization" did not have a consensus meaning, at least initially (see Podolny and Page, 1998 for a review). Baker defined the network organization as "a social network that is *integrated* across formal boundaries. Interpersonal ties are formed without respect to formal groups or categories" (1992: 398). As an illustration he described a commercial real estate firm that had many formal boundaries internally (based on the type of real estate sold, geography, or rank in the organization), but where information flows and social relationships were not substantially constrained by these boundaries. Miles and Snow define network forms as "clusters of firms or specialist units coordinated by market mechanisms instead of chains of command" (1992: 53). These definitions highlight very different aspects of networks: in the first case, *social relations* that cross formal boundaries are the essence of the network, while in the second, the critical characteristic is that *market mechanisms* mediate relationships among formal units. We consider these types of "network organizations" as well as the kinds of networks that arise *inside* organizations and those that arise *among* organizations.

Internal Networks

As we observed in our discussions of organizations as natural systems, the organization chart captures at best a small part of the network of social ties within organizations. The studies of Western Electric's Hawthorne Works during the 1930s, described in Chapter 3, documented the dense pattern of relationships—positive and negative—that arose among co-workers assembling telephone switchboard banks, and how those networks influenced employee productivity. When MIT erected married student housing for returning GIs after World War II, social psychologists seized the opportunity to examine the patterns of social ties that emerged among strangers randomly assigned to be neighbors. They found the predominant determinant of social relationships to be mere proximity—near-by neighbors turned into friends, and the most popular students were those whose apartments were along the most traveled paths (e.g., those housed near the stairways or trash bins). Moreover, the groupings that arose had important influences on the flows of information among neighbors and even the kinds of opinions they held (Festinger, Schachter, and Back, 1950). Subsequent research on R&D labs at MIT documented that the same processes often happened at work—the "Allen curve" describes the inverse relation between how distant any two engineers' offices were and how often they communicated (Allen, 1984). And, as one would expect, the formal structure of the organization (e.g., who is housed in the same department) also influences which relationships form (Baker, 1992).

Whatever their source, social networks at work have an important influence on who gets hired, how well they perform, how much they get paid, and how their careers progress. Many employees find their jobs through tips they hear from personal contacts—usually acquaintances ("weak ties") rather than friends or family (Granovetter, 1973)—and some organizations have sought to harness this process as a low-cost way to recruit new employees. Fernandez and associates (2000) studied employee referrals at a call center within a large national bank, which paid workers a bonus when those they recommended for jobs ended up being hired by the bank. They found that this method was quite cost-effective and resulted in a pool of applicants better suited for these positions. Network properties also matter for career advancement: employees with networks rich in structural holes were promoted faster than colleagues without such networks (Burt, 1992b), although which network was "right" from the employee's perspective differed among men and women, and minority versus majority employees (Ibarra, 1995). Getting things done at work also often requires fitting the right network to the task: bankers consulted their most trusted colleagues within the bank for advice about uncertain transactions, but to get approval for the deal, they were better off relying on more dispersed networks for political reasons (Mizruchi and Stearns, 2001). And employees with networks more like Lois in Figure 11–1 tended to have more innovative ideas than those with networks like Bill. Much as IDEO generates innovation by juxtaposing concepts from diverse contexts, employees come up with better ideas when they are at a "crossroads" that spans different social domains within the organization (Burt, 2004).

External Networks

While the dominant trend among U.S. organizations after World War II was to grow ever larger and more vertically integrated, beginning in the 1980s this tendency reversed course, as outsourcing and focusing on a "core competence" took hold. The organizational outcome was the increasing prevalence of network organizations that combined legally separate firms along a value chain into a loosely integrated whole. We described examples of this, such as the garment industry, in Chapter 9. Miles and Snow (1992) provide a definition and a rationale for these forms. In their account, network organizations entail specialist units that have more-or-less long-term relationships among them that fall somewhere between the "make" or "buy" alternatives also described in Chapter 9. An essential feature of their definition is that the units face a market test—that is, if the price or performance that one of the units offers is not good enough, it can be replaced. For instance, if a computer maker has an internal disk drive unit, it will have a hard time switching to an outside supplier that is cheaper or has higher quality; but if the computer maker buys on the market—even from a long-time supplier—it always has the possibility of switching. This exposes suppliers to competition which, in principle, keeps them more focused and adaptive than they would be as "captive" internal units.[5] From the computer maker's perspective, it has the option to buy components from the best in the world, and this option gives them better information in negotiating with suppliers and in designing future products. Moreover, it allows the lead firm to rapidly scale up production when the market for their goods requires it.

If outsourcing has so many advantages over vertical integration, and (as we saw in Chapter 9) vertical integration is so costly, why did the outsourcing movement take place only recently? We point to two factors. First, recent advances in information and communications technologies (ICTs) have greatly reduced the cost of finding outside suppliers. Consider what would be required to find a supplier for a specialized component and to monitor their performance without e-mail, faxes, or the Internet. ICTs have greatly reduced the transaction costs of outsourcing and accordingly expanded the range of possible organizational forms. (Coase [1937] noted how the invention of the telephone created a regime shift earlier in the opposite direction, enabling the growth of firms with far-flung units by lowering the cost of rapid communication within the organization.)

A second factor encouraging the spread of outsourcing is a generalized rationalization and standardization of organizational practices (Scott, 2004b: 11–12). Common education in business schools, standardized contracts such as franchise agreements, similarity in structural forms, and widely emulated exemplars of "best practices" in business have made organizations more and more alike, a central theme of institutional theory (see Chapter 10). And just as the use of standardized components enabled a huge increase in the production of muskets and other goods during the industrial revolution, standardization at societal and transnational levels has also greatly increased the production of new organizations and organizational forms. "After all, the building blocks for organizations come to be littered around the societal

---

[5]Note, however that profit centers within a single company sometimes set up market arrangements which allow each to decide whether or not they will acquire inputs from another center within the corporation or buy outside (Eccles and White, 1986). See the discussion of internal networks below.

landscape; it takes only a little entrepreneurial energy to assemble them into a structure" (Meyer and Rowan, 1977: 345; see also Brunsson and Jacobson, 2000; Sahlen-Anderssson and Engwall, 2002).

As an example, consider airlines. Dozens of airlines have been started in the United States in the past decade, some aiming for a national scope (e.g., JetBlue) and others serving a few highly specialized routes (e.g., Newark to Fort Lauderdale). Government deregulation aimed at encouraging competition laid the groundwork for this surge of start-ups, but equally important was the availability of contractors that could be hired to perform just about any task a new airline requires, from writing the application required for government certification, to selling the tickets, staffing the gates at airports, catering the food, and even flying the planes. Hundreds of second- and third-hand jets that used to belong to now-defunct airlines sit in the Arizona desert waiting to be sold or leased to new airlines by equipment-leasing units of banks and other firms. Venture capitalists, seeing the rapid revenue growth and low cost structure of some upstart airlines, often provide the seed money for start-up. And some major airlines themselves offer consulting, employee training, reservation services, and aircraft maintenance for their new competitors. In the wake of the terrorist attacks on September 11, 2001, many of the large carriers substantially retrenched, furloughing workers and canceling orders for planes that were already in production. These resources became available to newer and smaller carriers to expand their own operations, which typically faced lower costs than their larger rivals (*Wall Street Journal*, 8/12/04). To paraphrase Meyer and Rowan (1977), the building blocks (and capital) for airlines sit like ready-to-assemble furniture at Ikea so that creating an organization evidently requires only a set of instructions and a little entrepreneurial energy.

Types of Network Organizations

In their discussion of network forms, Miles and Snow describe three main types. In a *stable network,* "a large core firm creates market-based linkages to a limited set of upstream and/or downstream partners" (Miles and Snow, 1992: 64), while these partners also serve firms outside the network, which keeps them competitive. These networks occur mostly in relatively mature industries. Nike, for instances, concentrates its internal resources on R&D and marketing, while almost all production is outsourced to Asian manufacturers, which are allowed and even encouraged to produce for competitors such as Adidas in order to stay competitive (Miles and Snow, 1994: chap. 7).

Ties in a stable network are relatively long-lived. In contrast, in a *dynamic network,* "independent business elements along the value chain form temporary alliances from among a large pool of potential partners" (Miles and Snow, 1992: 64). Dynamic networks are seen in industries with relatively short product cycles. For example, in high-end fashion production, such as in the garment district in New York, a lead firm pulls together a project group of specialist firms for creating each season's line of clothing (Uzzi, 1997). The next product line may or may not draw on the same units; each new line is like a project with a relatively limited duration. Hollywood film production has a similar structure, with actors, producers, directors, and cinematographers coming together to make specific movies; they may or may not work together on subsequent projects (Faulkner and Anderson, 1987). Note that in earlier decades when movies confronted less competition and demand was more stable, movie studios were more vertically integrated: they retained stables of actors, writers, and directors on long-term contracts and often owned the theaters where the movies were exhibited. In fast-moving high-tech industries, Sturgeon (2002) describes modular production networks in which a lead firm (the inaptly named OEM or "original equipment manufacturer") focuses primarily on product design, while other contractors specialize in manufacturing. "Generic" electronics manufacturers such as Flextronics, Solectron, SCI Systems, and Jabil Circuit, formerly known as "box stuffers," have taken on an increasingly important role performing generalized high-tech production. Their existence means that a company with a saleable product design (e.g., for a cell phone or personal digital assistant), but little capital to invest, can rapidly scale up production without owning its own production facilities—and scale down again when, as often happens, their design is superceded.

Finally, in an *internal network*, "organizational units buy and sell goods and services among themselves at prices established in the open market" (Miles and Snow, 1992: 65). This form brings market transactions inside the organization's boundaries; even staff departments, such as human resources, may face competition from external vendors that might provide better service at a lower cost. Taking the example of our computer manufacturer, the internal disk drive unit may offer its products to both its internal "customers" and to external buyers; their corporate siblings, in turn, may turn to external disk drive producers for some or all of their supplies. ABB, for instance, organized in the 1990s as a federation of 1,300 local companies linked into a global matrix, seeking to be both "small" (through the connection of local companies to their domestic and global markets) and "large" at the same time (Miles and Snow, 1994: chap. 7).

One of the most studied network organizations is Dell Computer, famously founded in Michael Dell's college dorm room in the early 1980s and now one of the world's largest producers of personal computers (see Child, 2005: 214–19). In contrast to the value chain in a traditional model of computer production, where manufacturers assemble PCs that are brought by distributors to retailers and sit in inventory until their purchase by a final consumer, Dell pioneered the "Direct from Dell" model in which a customized order from a consumer—initially by phone, now primarily over the Web—set the production process in motion. Dell relays orders for required parts to suppliers, who ship the parts to Dell for final assembly and shipment to customers via a "delivery partner" such as UPS. (Highly trusted suppliers of freestanding components, such as Sony monitors, are shipped directly by the supplier to the customer.) Dell's top suppliers are privy to Supplier Web Pages that give access to real-time data on customer orders in different segments and that facilitate communication and coordination. Dell also works closely with its largest corporate customers, offering services such as preloaded software, or even having Dell staff work on-site for customers such as Boeing. This system, which Dell calls "virtual integration," allow the parts of the network, led by Dell, to coordinate like a single organization, while keeping costly inventory to an absolute minimum and providing customized products to end users.

While our examples of network forms have been drawn primarily from business, many traditional government agencies—the archetype bureaucracy—have also undergone restructuring, moving toward networklike forms. Public agencies have been joined by hybrid forms, such as government corporations and government-sponsored enterprises, which attempt to build in various types of market controls. Moreover, more and more governmental agencies contract out particular tasks to private companies, to both for-profit and nonprofit forms, in the belief that competition among and specialization of such providers will improve the efficiency of governmental services. Public organizations find themselves operating in the world of partnerships and networks (see Brooks, Liebman, and Schelling, 1984; Osborne and Gaebler, 1992; Rosenau, 2000; Salamon, 2002). And nonprofit organizations can also take on sophisticated network structures: Provan and Milward (1995), for instance, analyze the network structures of community mental health systems and the impact of different networks on the quality of patient outcomes.

Whereas Miles and Snow's typology takes the perspective of a particular organization—the lead firm and its organization set, or ego network—Bennett Harrison (1994) proposes a typology emphasizing differences in overall network.

1. *Networks in craft-type industries.* In these forms, work is organized around specific projects and involves the temporary cooperation of varying combinations of skilled workers. Examples include construction projects and artistic productions such as publishing or filmmaking (see Becker, 1982; Hirsch, 1972; Stinchcombe, 1959).

2. *Small firm-led industrial districts.* These network forms include the northern Italian industrial districts, with textile companies such as Benetton (Belussi, 1989), and the semiconductor firms in Silicon Valley (Saxenian, 1994).

3. *Geographically clustered big-firm-led production systems.* These forms include the well-known Asian examples of *keiretsu* ("societies of business") as well as connections that have developed between central assembly firms and multitudes of small suppliers; for example, Volvo of Sweden (Håkansson, 1989) or U.S. automobile companies (Helper, 1991).

4. *Strategic alliances.* Alliances of this type are increasingly found among firms of all sorts, but especially in new knowledge-based industries such as biotechnology

(Barley, Freeman, and Hybels, 1992; Powell, Koput, and Smith-Doerr, 1996) and among large firms attempting to secure competitive advantage in a global environment. The ties may involve equity (subsidiary forms) or be based on contractual agreements (Beamish and Killing, 1997; Kanter, 1994), as we describe below.

Whereas some analysts such as Piore and Sabel (1984) and Perrow (1992) have proclaimed that small-firm networks are the wave of the future and likely to outcompete and outmaneuver larger and presumably less flexible forms, others such as Kanter (1989) and Harrison (1994) argue that large-scale firms have both the power and resources to prevail in the long run by developing strategic alliances under their control. Harrison describes these systems as composed of one lead firm orchestrating the contributions of a "core-ring" set of related, subordinate firms, whether suppliers or merchandizers. At the moment, both forms, which we will generically refer to as industrial districts, are prevalent in different industries.

Industrial districts can be seen as a functional alternative to the vertically integrated firm, and as documented by Piore and Sabel (1984), they thrive in particular industrial and social contexts, although they went largely ignored in the academic literature following their naming by Alfred Marshall. An *industrial district* is "a socioterritorial entity which is characterized by the active presence of both a community of people and a population of firms in one naturally and historically bounded area" (Becattini, 1990: 39). In addition to Silicon Valley, familiar examples include Detroit for cars, Hollywood for movies, and Wall Street for finance. In each case, the city or district came to be a metonym for an industry even after much of the actual work was dispersed to other areas. Hedge funds, for instance, now cluster largely in Greenwich, Connecticut, where taxes are considerably lower than on Wall Street in New York.

Why are there industrial districts—what are the benefits of agglomeration for organizations? Marshall pointed to several: access to information ("The mysteries of the trade become no mysteries, but are as it were in the air" [1890: IV.X.7]), access to relevant labor and other inputs (e.g., iron ore for steelmaking), and increased firm-level specialization. A two-person firm that specializes in sewing pleats on skirts is more likely to find enough work to occupy it in New York's garment district than in Topeka, Kansas. And sociologists have pointed out that physical proximity enables the development of trusting relationships among participants: while Dell may rely on the Internet to manage relations with suppliers, knitwear producers in Modena, Italy, prefer face-to-face contact (Lazerson, 1995).

Yet industrial districts are not without drawbacks—otherwise, one might see all sweaters made in Modena, all cars made in Detroit, all computers made in Austin, Texas. Sorenson and Audia (2000) argue that agglomeration is a mixed blessing—while new firms find it easier to recruit skilled labor, established firms find that their workers get poached by start-ups, and now face competition for customers from their neighbors. Thus, in a study of American shoe manufacturers, they find that the density of local shoe firms increases both birth rates (as one would expect from Marshall and followers) *and* death rates of shoemakers, although this eventually declined with age. And Paniccia (1998) points out that the industrial districts that have received the greatest attention are the unusually successful ones, such as Silicon Valley, which may not be particularly representative of industrial districts overall—an example of "sampling on the dependent variable." Comparing twenty-four small- and medium-sized Italian enterprise districts over forty years revealed that few looked like the idealized settings described in work on Northern Italy or Silicon Valley: performance was sometimes poor, and social connections, rather than always facilitating trust and cooperation, could also enable free-riding, deceit, and opportunism, as one would expect based on Granovetter's (1985) discussion of embeddedness.

Not all business groupings are rooted in geography. Granovetter (2005) points out that groupings based on factors other than geography are far more common than is recognized in the literature—indeed, he argues, they are pervasive in all known economies. As Polanyi (1944) put it in *The Great Transformation*, "Man's economy, as a rule, is submerged in his social relationships." Granovetter defines a business group as "sets of legally separate firms bound together in persistent formal and/or informal ways" (2005: 429) and gives a number of examples: keiretsu in Japan, chaebol in Korea, grupos economicas in Latin America, family-owned pyramids in Europe and Canada—all entail relatively strong ties among members such that understanding a group member requires knowing about its group.

While the reputation of industrial districts has perhaps been unjustifiably positive (Paniccia, 1998), business groups are often derided as "crony capitalism" that allow family ties and favoritism to trump hardheaded business decision making, and even to impede national economic growth. Morck, Stangeland, and Yeung (2000) coined the phrase "Canadian disease" to describe a process by which wealthy elites (e.g., heirs of entrenched business dynasties) use their political power to promote policies that impede entrepreneurship, which they perceive as a threat to their dominance, to the detriment of the larger economy. Modigliani and Perotti (2000) argue that networks are a second-best system for societies that lack the institutional infrastructure to support more efficient and frictionless arm's-length transactions. Yet Evans (1995) points to the central role of chaebol networks in the rapid industrialization of South Korea: through government-directed investment in key industrial sectors, a handful of South Korean chaebols helped turn a peasant economy into a high-tech powerhouse in just two generations following the Korean War.

One way to reconcile these divergent views of the impact of business groups is to link them to a society's stage of economic development. Late industrializers, such as South Korea, had a relatively clear path to industrialization based on the experience of its predecessors: some industries (e.g., steel) are like keystone species in an ecosystem, others (perhaps autos and shipbuilding) are attractive for building export-oriented growth. In each case, businesses could directly emulate the best technologies and practices in the world, bypassing the tortuous path that led there for the earlier industrializers. Business groups with centralized financing, such as the conglomerate chaebols, can benefit from economies of scale in building up such industries. Once an economy has achieved rough parity with other industrials, future growth is driven more by uncertain industries in which placing many bets on independent firms is sensible, which favors more focused firms financed by markets. Kock and Guillén (2001) offer a complementary argument for why different organizational forms are most appropriate at different stages from the entrepreneur's perspective: early on, entrepreneurs build diversified groups (such as the chaebol) because their skills at bringing extant foreign technologies to local markets are broadly applicable across sectors. Eventually, however, such unwieldy forms give way to more focused organizations, although the original ties may linger on, as the keiretsu networks succeeded the zaibatsu in Japan after World War II.

Alliance Networks

Alliances can take many forms and serve many purposes. Child (2005: chap. 10) provides a useful typology of alliances and other interfirm linkages (see Figure 11–3) and describes several rationales for their use: to reduce risk, to attain economies of scale, for technology exchange, to preempt or co-opt competition, to overcome governmental barriers, to facilitate international

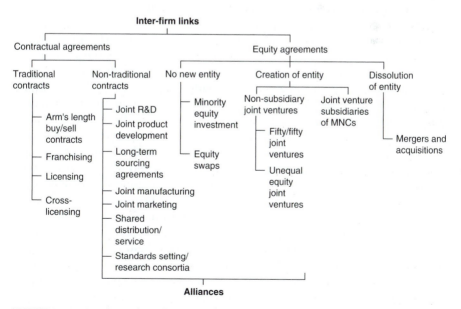

FIGURE 11–3 Typology of Interfirm Linkages.
Source: Child (2005: 224).

expansion; and as a form of vertical quasi integration (see Contractor and Lorange, 1988).

Alliances, or relatively formalized connections among firms that fall short of acquisition, vastly increased in prevalence during the 1980s and 1990s, just as traditional forms of diversification and vertical integration declined in the United States. We have argued that this is driven by a combination of a regime shift in transaction costs and by a generalized organizational rationalization in society, which enables relatively frictionless combinations based on standardized practice. With the flowering of alliance forms has come a wave of research on the causes and consequences of alliances. Much of this work resembles that on interlocks, but research on alliances has also more fully engaged core questions about network origins and evolution. Where connections among firms seem at best a "bonus" that comes with recruiting a particular director, alliances entail genuine relationships among organizations, and in that sense they are analogous to friendship and other social networks.

Antecedents of Alliances. We have described several strategic reasons that organizations undertake alliances. But the choice of which particular partner to work with requires a more social explanation. First, some organizations are simply more attractive as alliance partners. Semiconductor firms with more widely cited patents formed more alliances than those with less influential patents (Stuart, 1998). In the biotechnology industry, firms with more R&D alliances were able subsequently to gain more alliances of other types, and the greater their centrality in these networks, the greater their rate of growth and the greater their likelihood of going public (Powell, Koput, and Smith-Doerr, 1996). In investment banking, firms may prefer to ally with those of a similar status, particularly when entering an uncertain market such as junk bonds (Podolny, 1994).

Second, the propensity to form alliances can depend on the joint characteristics of a potential pair—such as their prior history of alliances, or having partners in common—and on their broader surroundings. In a study of alliances among European, Japanese, and American firms in the new materials, industrial automation, and automotive industries from 1981 to 1989, Gulati (1995) found that the likelihood of two firms forming an alliance during a given year was greater when they had previously engaged in alliances with each other, when they had alliance partners in common, and when their geodesic in the alliance network was short. Of course, alliances cannot always depend on prior alliances—new firms have to start somewhere. Rosenkopf and colleagues (2001) found that alliances among firms in the cellphone industry were more common when engineers and managers from the firms had worked together on technical committees—which allowed them to scope out potential partners—but this effect declined when the firms had prior alliances—which presumably gave sufficient information about their suitability as partners. A follow-up paper to Gulati (1995) found that alliances were more likely among partners that were both jointly central (using the eigenvector measure described above), and when the larger alliance network in the industry was itself centralized (again, by our prior definition). Moreover, interdependence between potential partners increased the likelihood of alliance, but this effect became weaker as the overall network became more centralized, while the effect of the potential partners' joint centrality increased as the network became more centralized (Gulati and Gargiulo, 1999). This study suggests a complex dynamic in which the likelihood of firms forming a tie depends on their individual characteristics, their ego networks and network positions, their character as a dyad, and the shape of the broader network in which they are embedded. Finally, while differences in partners' centrality or status may reduce the propensity to form alliances, differences in technological capabilities enhance it—up to a point. Firms receive little benefit from allying with those that overlap with them substantially in their technological resources (after all, such firms are likely to be direct competitors), but those with no overlap might be too distant to be comprehensible. Drawing on patents and patent citation patterns to track technological overlap and distance among firms, Mowery and colleagues (1996) report evidence consistent with this argument.

Consequences of Alliances. Unlike interlocks, alliances appear to influence organizational performance, both in terms of innovation and speed. Biotech firms with diverse portfolios of alliances tend to become more central, and thus to grow faster (Powell, Koput, and Smith-Doerr, 1996), and such firms were faster to go public (through an initial public offering, or IPO) when they had prominent equity investors (i.e., firms that themselves held well-cited patents and had many alliances), particularly in the case of firms that were younger and therefore harder to assess (Stuart, Hoang, and Hybels, 1999). More broadly, affiliations with prominent outsiders generally bring the greatest benefit as a form of endorsement when uncertainty is high and the quality of an organization's work is difficult for outsiders to evaluate—for example, in investment banking (Podolny, 1993). Finally, although we have described the potential benefits of structural holes for innovation, not all evidence supports this contention—specifically, in a study of the international chemical industry, Ahuja (2000) finds that while direct collaborative ties increase firms' rates of patenting, structural holes had no positive impact, and perhaps a negative influence. This study reminds us that the meaning of different network measures and concepts, such as structural holes, depends on the kind of relationship being mapped: effective collaboration may require a different ego network than profitable brokerage.

SECTORAL AND SOCIETAL NETWORKS

We have described the causes and consequences of dyadic ties, networks among organizations and their organization set, and network forms of organization. We turn now to examine more macrolevels, including industry exchange networks and the character of the overall economy.

Industry and Sector Structure

In network terminology, an organization's relationships with suppliers contribute to its in-degree, and its ties to sellers define its out-degree. At an industry level, an input-output matrix in which the row-industry buys the amount in the cell from the column-industry can describe this web of exchanges. (These data can be downloaded from the Bureau of Economic Affairs at *http://www.bea.doc.gov/bea/dn2/i-o.htm.*) Ron Burt combined these data with information about how concentrated industries were (using the four-firm concentration ratio, which is the proportion of the industry's output accounted for by the four largest producers) to analyze an industry participant's structural autonomy, defined as the "ability to pursue and realize interests without constraint from other actors in the system" (Burt, 1982: 265). In essence, firms have high structural autonomy to the extent that their own industries are concentrated (they have few competitors/substitutes) and the industries of their buyers and suppliers are dispersed (that is, they have many competitors/substitutes). Organizations located in industries fitting this description have characteristically experienced higher profitability. For example, Sealed Air Corporation, maker of bubble wrap packaging materials, occupied such a spot in the late 1980s: its major supplies came from the commodity chemical industry (which, as the name implies, was quite competitive), its buyers included nearly every home and business in America that shipped fragile items (also a disconnected group posing little constraint on pricing), and its patents protected it from significant competition by firms within its industry. As a result, its margins (the difference between how much it cost to make its products and how much it could charge for them) were very, very high—on the order of 50 percent. Burt (1988) found the network structures of interindustry transactions to be highly stable over several decades, at least for aggregated industry sectors.

Network analysis can also be used to characterize relations among organizations and agencies attempting to influence policy decisions in the public sector. Laumann and Knoke (1987) compare the networks of "players" in the energy and the health care domains during the late 1970s and the types of issues that activated their involvement. Rather than seeing "the state" as a singular entity, potentially subject to elite rule, they conceive of the state as a collection of policy arenas in which private actors (such as businesses) that have strong, continuing interests interact with public agencies to shape policy. "Events" are triggered when concrete proposals for action come into the arena. Laumann and Knoke find that, at least in energy and health, no single issues were so central as to draw in all organizations within the field into the arena—organizations tended to participate in issues that affected them directly. There appeared to be few issues that mobilized everyone's interests. Rather, "issue publics" were identified, consisting of organizations concerned about the same sets of issues (although possibly with opposing interests).

Policy systems differ in the nature and extent of their order. Laumann and Knoke's study suggests that public agencies were more influential in the health policy than the energy networks in the United States. Moreover, "consensus about who matters appears to be much more systematically—indeed, almost institutionally—organized in the health domain" (Laumann and Knoke 1987: 188). Energy was a relatively newer focus for national policy in the United States in the 1970s, and stable patterns of interaction and influence among organizational interests, both private and public, had not emerged at the time of the study.

This approach brings together both organization theory and network analysis in a useful synthesis for understanding how policy is made and how political interests are served. It also suggests an avenue for comparative research that examines the structural properties of policy networks. Thus, Song (2003) used network methods to contrast the relations among organizations and groups determining reading curricula across eight American states. Her study revealed quite divergent patterns of policy influence for varying actors, suggesting how it might happen that evolution is taught in almost all—but not quite all—states.

The Network Structure of the Economy

One can examine the network structure of an economy over time and compare it to the network structures of other economies, using comparable measures such as those described at the beginning of this chapter. Work of this sort is currently underway, but it requires a fairly massive scale of effort. In the meantime, we can sketch what is currently known.

The United States is undoubtedly the most studied economy among network researchers, and as we have described, both interlock and ownership networks have received considerable attention. The transformation of the American economy from an entrepreneurial to a corporate one at the end of the nineteenth century was accompanied by the elaboration of an interindustry interlock network, with the railroad, coal, and telegraph industries forming an early and enduring core among industrials. Ties across industries became increasingly dense but maintained a spoked wheel pattern, with core industries tightly interlinked and "periphery" industries tied to the core but not to each other (Roy, 1983). By the turn of the century, railroads were organized into relatively balkanized communities of interest linked by shared owners and directors (Roy and Bonacich, 1988). By the time the Clayton Act ruled out interlocks among competitors in 1914, banks—particularly so-called "money center" banks headquartered in major cities that cater to corporate clients—had become the dominant actors in the network, a position they held until the 1980s. Brandeis (1914) pointed out at the time that executives of three large New York banks—JP Morgan, National City (predecessor of Citibank), and First National (another Citibank predecessor that merged with National City in 1955)—held dozens of directorships on outside boards (seventy-two for JP Morgan, forty-nine for First National, forty-eight for National City). Remarkably, the same companies remained at the center of

TABLE 11–1   Ten Most Central Firms in the Interlock Network, 1962–2001

1962	1982	2001
JP Morgan [56]	*AT&T [43]*	*JP Morgan Chase [28]*
Chemical Bank [51]	*JP Morgan [48]*	Pfizer [26]
Chase Manhattan [50]	*Chase Manhattan [43]*	Sara Lee [28]
First National City Bank [47]	*Citicorp [43]*	Georgia Pacific [29]
Manufacturers Hanover [43]	IBM [38]	AMR [25]
Southern Pacific RR [38]	General Foods [31]	Dell Computer [19]
Ford Motor Co [34]	*Chemical NY [38]*	Verizon [28]
AT&T [31]	*Bankers Trust [39]*	3M [25]
Chrysler [28]	*Manufacturers Hanover [36]*	Allstate [24]
Bankers Trust [41]	Mobil [28]	Bellsouth [22]

Rankings are based on Bonacich's (1987) eigenvector measure of point centrality, in which a node is more central if the nodes it is connected to are also central. Banks are in italics.
Source: Davis, Yoo, and Baker (2003).

the network for seven decades, in spite of depression, bank regulation, and war (see Mintz and Schwartz, 1985; Mizruchi, 1982). Table 11–1 documents the surprising stability of the most central firms in the network between 1962 and 1982, and the relative upheaval in the subsequent two decades as the fortunes of commercial banks declined (Davis and Mizruchi, 1999).

In Japan, keiretsu networks describe groupings of firms that can be both horizontal (in particular, the Big Six keiretsu of large firms reciprocally connected by cross-shareholdings) and vertical (organized around dominant lead firms, either banks or large industrials; Lincoln, Gerlach, and Takahashi [1992]). Group membership influences performance in surprising ways: while one might expect that group members are more profitable as a result of advantageous relationships with other group members, empirically group membership seems to make the average firm worse off. Lincoln and colleagues (1996) explain this by examining the dynamic performance effects of group membership: members that perform poorly subsequently return to normal levels of profitability more quickly than nonmembers, perhaps due to assistance from other group members, but unusually profitable firms also subsequently return to normal levels more quickly, a sort of group tax on performance.

In France, unlike the United States, the process for joining the economic elite has traditionally been fairly standardized, partly as a result of a long tradition of state ownership for the most substantial enterprises. Attendance at either the Ecole Nationale d'Administration (ENA) or perhaps the Ecole Polytechnique is virtually mandatory, as is a stint working in the Treasury Department. Optional, but highly recommended, is residence in the Sixteenth Arrondissement in Paris (Kadushin, 1995). The result of these preferential old school ties is a tightly centralized network (see Figure 11–4).

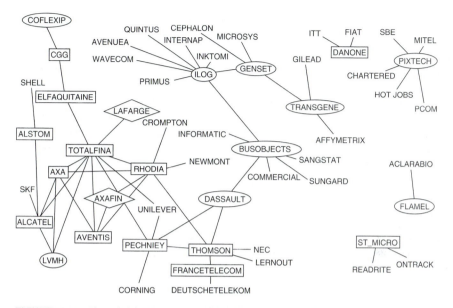

FIGURE 11–4 Shared Directors among French Firms Listed on U.S. Stock Markets. Rectangles are French firms listed on NYSE; ovals are French Nasdaq firms; diamonds are U.S. subsidiaries of French parents. *Source:* Davis and Marquis (2005a).

In Germany, the three largest banks (Deutsche Bank, Dresdner Bank, and Commerzbank) traditionally held large ownership positions in major corporations, sometimes sufficient for control. The ownership of these three, as well as ownership of midsized firms by regional entities, traditionally knit the economy into relatively coherent groups. This situation, however, began to break down during the late 1990s, although ownership networks still reveal a relatively close-knit industrial economy relative to the United States (Kogut and Walker, 2001).

The economic importance of networks is revealed particularly starkly in situations of major transition, as in the case of post-socialist economies. Stark (1996) argues that in post-socialist Eastern Europe, "organizations and institutions [are rebuilt] not *on the ruins* but *with the ruins* of communism as they redeploy available resources in response to their immediate practical dilemmas." That is, rather than discarding all old institutions and starting anew, or mimicking the institutional structure of Western capitalist economies, Hungarian businesspeople recombined old and new elements into an emerging "East European capitalism" that did not belong squarely in either camp. Using data on the largest 220 firms in Hungary in 1993–1994 and fieldwork in a half-dozen enterprises, Stark found unexpected patterns in the transition. Semiautonomous firms were linked by keiretsu-like cross-ownership ties with hard-to-decode assets and liabilities; and government agencies continued to hold most shares of many firms.

As a final example, in China, the state actively encouraged the formation of groups like the chaebol in Korea and keiretsu in Japan in the 1980s in order to stimulate rapid, directed economic growth. In contrast to Japan, group membership enhanced organizational performance (Keister, 1998), and this effect grew stronger over time, as preferences for exchange with fellow group members (those they had worked with before) often trumped price in contracting relations (Keister, 2001). And in a provocative test of transaction cost analysis in a distinctive setting, Zhou and colleagues (2003) found that state-owned firms in China relied on social ties less than nonstate firms to find exchange partners, while riskier transactions induced more social interaction among contracting firms. This latter finding contrasts with prior work which suggested that social networks *enable* contracting; instead, it appears that in some instances contracting *induces* social networks.

Business Networks and Political Power

Political sociologists have long viewed networks, particularly among business elites, as providing an indicator of cohesion and potential political power (e.g., Mills, 1956). A long-standing debate between pluralists and elite theorists ran like this: elite theorists argued that the capitalist class (or the corporate elite, depending on the formulation) was able to act as a relatively coherent group when it came to politics, while pluralists argued that the issues that divided businesspeople were at least as great as those uniting them, so political outcomes were determined on an issue-by-issue basis according to different coalitions. Pluralists might point to issues like, say, steel tariffs (domestic steel manufacturers favor them; automakers who use steel oppose them), or environmental regulation (businesses with "clean" technologies favor it, particularly when it would be costly for their less-clean competitors, who oppose it). Elite theorists argue that on the big issues, business is relatively united, aided by common backgrounds (education at the same elite schools; membership in social clubs) and common organizations such as the Business Roundtable (an organization of roughly 200 CEOs that meets about policy matters).

The debate between pluralists and elitists is precisely the sort of "glass half full" topic that academics love: it is hard to imagine evidence that would actually sway either side, but many researchers have spent careers trying. Mills's intellectual heirs documented institutions thought to promote elite cohesion, such as secretive clubs (e.g., the Bohemian Grove, an all-male summer camp attended by California elites and the worthies they invite as guests, such as Ronald Reagan and Henry Kissinger) and shared board memberships (Domhoff, 1971). A primary piece of evidence for oligarchy, as Mills pointed out, was that the elites all seem to know each other—for those in positions of power, if not for the rest of us, it's a small world. On the other hand, analyses of the average geodesic in the corporate interlock network from 1982 to 1999 showed that this "small world" phenomenon (the fact that elites all seem to have friends in common) was unaffected by the declining fortunes of the banking industry and to turnover in the majority of the corporations that the elites oversee, suggesting that it is an intrinsic property of the elite network *as* a network, rather than the result of conspiracy (Davis, Yoo, and Baker, 2003).

Useem (1984) argued that service on multiple boards across different industries promoted a more cosmopolitan political worldview able to reconcile the divergent interests pointed to by pluralists, and he documented that such multiple directors (dubbed the "inner circle") were particularly likely to be involved with public policy organizations. Whether individual directors end up in the inner circle by design or by chance, it still has an influence on their outlook and on their access to power. Thus, Clawson and Neustadtl (1989) found that more central firms (those whose boards contain more multiple directors) made more PAC (political action committees) contributions to incumbents and fewer to conservatives in the 1980 elections, but they were more likely to be involved with conservative policy organizations, suggesting that PAC contributions are used to further corporate interests, but that policy organizations are used to pursue collective interests. And Vogus and Davis (2005) found that states whose corporations were overseen by densely connected elites were quicker to pass antitakeover laws favored by those corporations than less-connected states, indicating that a more cohesive state-level corporate elite is better able to get the laws it wants.

The seemingly irresolvable debate among pluralists and elitists experienced a sensible call for a cease-fire from Mark Mizruchi (1992). He argued that the appropriate question was not "Is the elite fragmented or unified?" but "*Under what conditions* are businesses unified?" His answer, drawing on organizational theory, found a number of mechanisms that led pairs of organizations to be more similar in their political activities (measured by the similarity of their portfolio of PAC contributions to candidates for office, testifying on the same side in hearings, and others). He found that interindustry constraint (described above in the discussion of Burt [1983]) increased the degree of similarity of PAC contributions made by firms in those industries, and that indirect interlocking through financial institutions (that is, having executives who served on the same bank boards) as well as common ownership by financials increased the similarity of PAC contributions. Whether these contributions influence policy in any direct way is still a matter for debate, as the profusion of subsequent studies on PAC contributions attests (Clawson, Neustadtl, and Weller, 1998; Mizruchi, 1992).

SUMMARY

Network analysis provides a way to visualize and analyze patterns of relationships among parts or "nodes," including flows of information, resources, energy, and authority. Organizations are characterized by formal and informal networks among members and units. Networks can describe ties among participants and ties among organizations. Social network analysts have developed an array of measures to quantify the position or importance of individual actors within networks and the shapes of the networks themselves. Network analysis can also be used to characterize technological, industry, and product space.

Researchers have studied several types of ties among organizations: who exchanges with whom, who shares members of the board of directors with whom, and who forms alliances with whom. In each case, one can examine why organizations choose particular partners, how long the relationship lasts, and what leads it to end. Examinations of board interlocks, created when organizations appoint as directors members of other boards, date back nearly a century to political concerns about the power of banks. Although banks had particularly well-connected boards for many decades, their position declined beginning in the 1980s. Companies generally recruit board members because of their expected qualities as directors and their accessibility, not as representatives of outside organizations; however, once on board, their external ties provide conduits useful for "business scan."

Alliances take many forms and have grown immensely in prevalence in recent years. Organizations form alliances for a variety of strategic reasons and in some cases alliances have proven to be a robust alternative to vertical integration. Alliance formation is linked to prior alliances: prior partners and "friends of friends" are more likely to be chosen than strangers. Research suggests that organizations that are well connected via alliances subsequently grew faster, formed more alliances, and were more likely to go public. For both interlock and alliance ties, the benefits to focal organizations often come as much from the appearance that these affiliations create as from the access to information and resources that they provide.

Networks are also used to describe a form of organization distinct from the functional, divisional, or matrix form. One typology defines network forms in terms of hybrid ties among organizational units—that is, relationships that stand between the arm's-length tie of buying an input on the market and the complete integration of making it internally. In a stable network, a lead firm maintains relatively long-term ties to outside partners upstream or downstream (e.g., shoe manufacturers in Asia, or retail distribution channels in the United States). Such forms are most common in mature industries with relatively long product cycles. In industries with short cycles, such as as fashion, movies, or high-technology manufacturing, a dynamic network is most common. This form consists of relatively temporary alliances of partners along a value chain formed for particular temporary productions (e.g., a movie, a product line, a construction project). Dynamic networks are often sited in industrial districts, that is, particular geographic areas with a high concentration of industry participants, such as Silicon Valley, Hollywood, or New York's garment district. Participants in dynamic networks often work with the same partners over and over again. A third type of network organization, the internal network, introduces marketlike interfaces into large organizations by encouraging units to buy and sell to each other at market prices and to look outside the organization for alternatives. As with the other forms, the intention is to keep each participant nimble by exposing it to market tests, while reaping the information and trust benefits of relatively close ties.

Societies can be analyzed in terms of the network structures of their economies and polities. Economies can be described by interindustry flows of goods and services, by ownership and other ties linking firms, and by linkages among banks and other organizations through shared directors. Analysts have also drawn on these tools to analyze political relations among businesses and governments. Cross-cultural comparisons of such networks are a particularly promising area of future research.

CHAPTER 12

Strategy, Structure, and Performance: The Sociology of Organizational Strategy

> There is no such thing as a "good organization" in any absolute sense. Always it is relative; and an organization that is good in one context or under one criterion may be bad under another.
>
> W. Ross Ashby (1968)

The study of organizational strategy seeks to answer the question, "Why do some organizations perform better than others?" by whatever meaning of "performance" is relevant. For academic scholars of corporate strategy, the general answer has three parts. First, some industries are structured in ways that are more conductive to better performance. This might entail having abundant sources of supplies, few competitors, and customers willing to pay high prices. Of course, this combination of conditions does not normally hold for very long—price-insensitive customers are likely to attract competitors, who denude the abundant sources of supply. Second, managers can implement strategies that put their organizations in better positions with respect to their competitors, for instance, by offering their products or services for lower prices, or making them particularly attractive or valuable to particular kinds of customers in ways that are hard for competitors to match. Third, some organizational structures work better than others in some contexts. Performance, then, follows from locating an attractive industry or industry segment and choosing an appropriate combination of business strategy and supporting organizational structure to compete in that industry—and doing so in a way that can be defended against actual or potential rivals who might want to do the same thing.

In contrast to strategists, organization theorists in general are more interested in why firms choose the strategies and structures they do, and how industries come to be structured as they are, rather than the performance consequences of these processes. This creates a characteristically different approach to questions of strategy. As Dobbin and Baum put it, strategists "observe the winners and look for what makes them win. The most basic method in economic sociology [and organization theory] is to observe large numbers of firms and look for what explains differences in their behavior . . . the new strategies they choose are shaped by public policy, imitation, network position, power, and historical happenstance" (2000: 2). As a result, studies of the interaction among strategy, structure, and performance have become comparatively rare in organization theory.

The Triumph of Antimanagerial Theory?

Some lament this neglect of performance as an egregious wrong turn by American scholars beginning somewhere in the mid-1970s, a departure from the promising open systems/contingency theory consensus. Donaldson (1995) summarizes the various strains of contingency theory in terms of the SARFIT (structural-adaptation-to-regain-fit) model. In an open systems world, environments create requirements for organizations that their managers address in part by adopting strategies. These strategies in turn create contingencies—size, technology, level of diversification, or others—for which some organizational structures are better suited than others. When managers of an organization find themselves with a structure that does not match its contingencies (e.g., because these contingencies have changed), their organization's performance suffers, and they endeavor to change its structure to one with a better fit, to improve performance. In short, fit affects performance; a change in the contingency variable (technology, diversification, etc.) causes misfit; misfit leads to structural change; and change in structure leads to new fit, which restores performance. Yet just as structural contingency theorists had arrived at a plausible model of how organizations interact with their environments, with useful implications for managers (e.g., Burns and Stalker, 1961; Lawrence and Lorsch, 1967; Thompson, 1967), Donaldson and similar critics were dismayed to see American "antimanagement" theorists respond with paradigms viewing managers as Machiavellian (Pfeffer and Salancik, 1978), lemminglike (DiMaggio and Powell, 1983), perverse (Meyer and Rowan, 1977), or unable to overcome inertia in order to make sensible organizational changes (Hannan and Freeman, 1977). These critics suggested that delight in novelty had apparently overcome a commitment to cumulative knowledge building founded on the sold rock of contingency theory (Donaldson, 1995).

For better or worse, organizational researchers in the past two decades have focused primarily on the third link in the SARFIT chain—that is, the antecedents of structural change (whether "misfit" or something else). There are exceptions, of course, for example, Siggelkow's (2002) study of how the Vanguard Fund's organization evolved over time toward fit, or Nickerson and Silverman's (2003) study of transaction cost reducing contract structures in the trucking industry. But this chapter focuses more on *why* organizations come to have the strategies and structures that they do, rather than on their performance consequences.

Pitfalls in Performance Studies

While this emphasis may reflect the field's preference for novelty over cumulation, it also represents methodological concerns with studies of strategy, structure, and performance. In the arcane terms of research design, studies of performance effects in general represent quasi experiments with endogenous assignment to treatment conditions—which, in plain English, is bad.[1] Consider an analogy: you would like to determine the effect of ginseng on human health. The gold standard in drug research is the double-blind study, where neither the researchers nor the study participants know whether any particular participant has received the real ginseng or a placebo. If those who received ginseng are assessed by "blind" researchers to have performed better in terms of their health than those who received a placebo, then one can, with reasonable confidence, attribute this to the ginseng. But suppose instead that the sample that received ginseng consisted of people who sought the supplement out at a health food store, while your control group is a matched sample of people of the same age and sex recruited from a shopping mall. If the ginseng eaters are healthier, you could reasonably suspect that they might be different in other important ways: perhaps the kinds of people who buy ginseng at health food stores are nonsmoking vegetarians who bicycle to work and take breaks for yoga. Most likely the new ginseng eaters are different from the "control" group in a large number of unknowable ways that might make them healthier on average, regardless of the benefits of ginseng. Conversely, they might have been unhealthier than the control group, which led them to seek out nutritional supplements.

Studies of organizational performance are plagued by this problem. Does having a multidivisional (M-form) structure improve the performance of large firms? In the ideal case, researchers would assign a sample of large firms to two conditions, M-form and placebo. Neither the researchers nor employees in the firms would know which condition they were assigned to. After two years, their performance would be assessed, and the envelope revealing which firms had the M-form and which the placebo would be opened. Practically speaking, researchers are likely to end up comparing a set of M-form adopters and nonadopters, and the adopters (like other firms making major changes) may have simultaneously gotten a new CEO, changed compensation systems, made a few acquisitions and divestitures to balance their portfolio, retained a consulting firm specializing in effective organizational change—and encouraged top management to begin taking

---

[1]Cook and Campbell (1979) provide the classic analysis of valid and invalid study designs for nonlaboratory settings. Achen (1986: chaps. 1–2) analyzes the limitations of statistical "fixes" for quasi experiments.

ginseng supplements. In the worst case, researchers "in search of excellence" don't even bother to find a comparison group; rather, they take a sample of "successful" firms to see what they all have in common (a research strategy known as "sampling on the dependent variable"). Such analysts are likely to find that, in all successful firms, the CEO wears a wristwatch and talks on the telephone, which will then be described as "key success factors" (see Vedder [1992] for an accessible discussion of the logical flaws of this approach).

In the absence of experimental control, the problem of determining which strategies and structures improve organizational performance is a thorny one. The common practice of including a large group of control variables in statistical models of performance can often make the problem of inference worse rather than better, as Achen (1986) points out. We are, in short, skeptical of performance studies. One approach that avoids the inferential problem of nonexperimental performance studies is to use computer simulations of structure, performance, and change (e.g., Ethiraj and Levinthal, 2004; Levitt et al., 1994), which can prove quite informative. But such studies are relatively few in number. In this chapter, we focus on an organizational approach to strategy that regards strategies and structures primarily as dependent variables, as consequences of rather than causes of performance. We document how organization theorists have drawn on the theoretical tools described in prior chapters to address questions of organizational strategy, as well as how performance enters into the equation.

WHY ARE ORGANIZATIONS IN SOME INDUSTRIES MORE PROFITABLE THAN THOSE IN OTHERS?

Forces Shaping Industry Competition

Industrial organization economists have long studied the industry conditions that undermine competition and promote oligopoly or monopoly, with an interest in informing public policies to prevent monopoly power (e.g., Scherer, 1980). From an organization's point of view, of course, having a monopoly is perhaps the surest path to superior financial performance. Thus, scholars of corporate strategy provide tools for the structural analysis of industries that can identify industries with higher potential for profits. Porter (1980: chap. 1) codifies this in terms of five forces shaping industry competition:

1. *Threat of entry by new competitors*—factors that impede or encourage companies to enter an industry. Barriers to entry by new competitors include things like economies of scale (i.e., big firms have lower costs), loyalty or switching costs on the part of current customers, and proprietary technology or patents held by incumbents—all of which make it more difficult for new competitors to enter, to the benefit of incumbents.

2. *Intensity of rivalry among existing competitors*—results from a low rate of growth, low switching costs for customers, high fixed costs, and having unpredictable or equally powered competitors.

3. *Pressure from substitute products*—products that are in a different industry but can serve the same function (e.g., coffee and caffeinated energy drinks, or compact discs and music downloads).

4. *Bargaining power of buyers*—such power is high to the extent that buyers are few in number, the industry's product is relatively standardized and unimportant to the buyer's quality, and buyers can credibly threaten to make the product themselves.

5. *bargaining power of suppliers*—the obverse of buyer bargaining power: suppliers are powerful as a group to the degree that they are concentrated, have few substitutes, sell to many industries, and are not particularly dependent for sales on the focal industry.

The structural analysis framework argues that the profit potential of an industry is determined by the collective strength of these five factors. A firm with dispersed and weak suppliers and buyers, buyers who depend on its products, few competitors or substitutes, and high barriers to entry is in a position to be particularly profitable—for instance, Sealed Air Corporation, maker of bubble wrap, enjoyed this situation in the late 1980s, as we saw in Chapter 11.[2] Porter states that, "All five competitive forces jointly determine the intensity of industry competition and profitability, and the strongest force or forces are governing and become crucial from the point of view of strategy formulation" (1980: 6). Thus, organizations face two kinds of strategic choices: whether and when to enter a particular industry, and how to compete in that context once it has entered. We discuss each in turn.

What Makes Industries Attractive?

Industries vary in their attractiveness and the prospects for entry over time, and the choice of when and how to enter turns out to be critical. Industries can be conceived as a set of niches defined by technologies and consumers, and these niches in turn create "peer groups" of organizations that attend to each other's action for cues as to prices, quantities, and quality (White, 1981). One way to locate niches within industries is through technological overlap; for example, firms with patents on the same kinds of technologies, and whose patents cite the same kinds of other patents, are likely to be competitors in the same niche (Podolny, Stuart, and Hannan, 1996). Moreover, technological change within niches appears to follow a particular tempo. As described in Chapter 10, Tushman and Anderson (1986) argue that some technological innovations are *competence-enhancing*, building on pre-existing organizational knowledge, skills, and routines and thus bolstering the position of incumbents while increasing the barriers to new entrants.

---

[2]Recall also that Burt (1983) demonstrates a network-based analysis of industries similar to Porter's, using industry input-output data and information about levels of industry concentration.

In situations of radically new technologies, on the other hand, space opens to new entrants not trapped by sunk costs and by skills tied to older technologies—such innovations are *competence-destroying* from the perspective of incumbents. For reasons discussed by both ecologists and institutionalists, (Chapter 10), incumbent firms are often relatively inert and limited in their ability to adapt to radical change. In these contexts, new entrants are better placed to exploit the new technologies than incumbents, and indeed in the airline, cement, and minicomputer industries, new entrants were more likely than incumbents to have generated or adopted radical technological breakthroughs (Tushman and Anderson, 1986). The introduction of radical new technologies, in short, is often followed by the decline of incumbent firms and by a spurt of new entrants, often bearing new organizational forms. This rhythm of industrial development—termed by Schumpeter (1961 ed.) "gales of creative destruction"—bears some resemblance to the pattern of punctuated equilibrium in biological evolution (Gould and Eldredge, 1977), in which a period of technological ferment (revolution/paradigm shift) is followed by gradual change and refinement (evolution/normal science).

Technological change can also erode industry boundaries or create competition from substitutes, requiring responses from incumbents. Information technology undermined much of the raison d'être for commercial banks during the 1970s and 1980s, as the kind of credit information formerly hoarded by banks became more widely available, and credit-worthy corporate borrowers found they were able to turn to money markets or securities issuance for lower-cost sources of debt. At the same time, depositors (such as individual households) found that they could receive superior returns by depositing their savings in money market accounts rather than bank savings accounts (Davis and Mizruchi, 1999). John Reed, CEO of Citibank, predicted in 1996 that banking would eventually become "a little bit of application code in a smart network" (quoted in Mayer, 1997). As their traditional business eroded at both ends, commercial banks sought out other lines of business, such as overseas lending and investment banking. Health care evolved from a relatively simple system of general practitioners in private practice and nonprofit community hospitals in the period just after World War II, to a field of technologically sophisticated for-profit insurance/hospital hybrids (HMOs), free-standing clinics for kidney dialysis and plastic surgery, specialized urgent care clinics to provide one-off emergency services, and franchise-style medical offices organized on mass production principles (Scott et al., 2000). Many traditional community hospitals in rural areas responded to their new competition by turning into drug-treatment centers, nursing homes, or outpatient clinics (D'Aunno, Succi, and Alexander, 2000). And for firms in many industries, the advent of the World Wide Web in the mid-1990s created access to new markets, unexpected competitors and substitutes, and entirely new industries such as "Web design" that drew on participants and business models from publishing, advertising, engineering, computers, and retail, among others (see, e.g., Robbins, 2002).

The attractiveness of industries to new entrants can also change due to nontechnological factors, such as the degree of industry concentration. As discussed in Chapter 10, Carroll (1985) describes a process of *resource partitioning* in which increasing concentration encourages new, specialized providers to enter. The cases of mainstream newspapers providing space for specialist publications and of generalist national beer companies giving rise to specialist local microbrewers illustrate these processes.

In addition to such technological and ecological factors, political and institutional forces also shape the prospects for new entrants. The generation of electric power for utilities exemplifies many of the conditions for high barriers to entry: generators can be enormously costly to construct (e.g., consider what is required to open a nuclear power plant); there is normally only one buyer in a particular geographic location capable of distributing the product, and that buyer usually owns the existing power generation facilities; and the industry is highly regulated. But in 1978 the federal government implicitly encouraged the development of an independent power production industry by requiring electric utilities to purchase output from independent producers—although it left it to the states to determine the prices that would be paid. States in which the independent producers had formed an industry association, and those with clearly defined terms of exchange between independents and the utilities, negotiated greater rates for new entrants (Russo, 2001). In short, political factors at the federal level made the industry possible, while state-level politics shaped how attractive it was to new entrants. But what the state gives, the state can take away: prior to federal laws prohibiting the sale of alcohol, some states enacted their own alcohol prohibition laws, which eliminated domestic industries in those states but often benefited alcohol producers in bordering states without prohibition (Wade, Swaminathan, and Saxon, 1998).

The boundaries around industries, and thus who counts as competitors, are also shaped by regulation. In the United States, commercial banking (taking deposits and lending money to companies) and investment banking (underwriting securities like stocks and bonds) were strictly separated for six decades following the Glass-Steagall Act of 1933, and commercial banks were largely limited to owning branches within a single state or region until the early 1990s. But the Riegle-Neal Act of 1994 effectively eliminated barriers to interstate banking, and Glass-Steagall was repealed in 1999; thus, commercial banks faced new competitors from other states and enjoyed new opportunities in investment banking, such as underwriting bonds for their old lending clients (Jensen, 2003).

Industries typically morph out of prior industries, drawing on elements such as what to call jobs, how to organize work, and so on—auto production, for instance, drew on carriage production. But the recycling industry can, with only modest exaggeration, date its founding to Earth Day 1970, when pressures from the environmental movement spontaneously created demand for a solution to the solid waste problem. Lounsbury (2001) tracked the development of this industry in the subsequent three decades, focusing initially on how colleges and universities elected to handle demands to implement recycling programs (which essentially all have done). Some added new responsibilities to their existing waste management departments and their administrators; some created entirely new jobs for recycling managers, often young activists who went about their responsibilities rather differently than did regular waste managers. Much of this difference is explained by networks: a national student activist organization acted as a disseminator of activist tactics and approaches to recycling, and the schools that added new jobs for recycling were typically those whose students were tied to the social movement organization. Once in place, the activist recyclers evolved into a self-organized profession, creating a national professional organization that helped members deal with the various pressures they faced (e.g., they were on average younger and more likely to be female than the existing maintenance staff). Moreover, once they were defined as a profession, they could generate best practices, spread standardized tools and techniques, and advocate for new "solutions" within their respective organizations. In spite of such localized successes within colleges, activists, who succeeded in raising consciousness and initiating reforms, lost the battle within communities, where for-profit recycling companies have largely replaced nonprofit and volunteer programs (Lounsbury, 2005; Lounsbury, Ventresca, and Hirsch 2003).

How Are Strategies and Structures Chosen?

Once its managers have chosen an industry, what does an organization do in order to be successful? Chandler defines *strategy* as "the determination of the basic long-range goals and objectives of an enterprise, and the adoption of courses of action and the allocation of resources necessary for carrying out these goals" (1962: 13). This widely accepted definition identifies several distinctive features of strategy.

First, the primary focus is on external concerns: the linkage of the organization to its environment. Second, two types of goals are differentiated: (1) selection of domain—"What business or businesses shall we be in?—affected by the factors just described; and (2) selection of competitive stance—"How shall we compete in each business?" (Chaffee, 1985). Porter (1980) has identified a number of "generic" competitive strategies among which firms may choose:

- *Overall cost leadership*—producing in high volume and holding costs low relative to competitors or budgets
- *Differentiation*—creating a product or service that is perceived industrywide as being unique, such as a design or brand image
- *Focus*—emphasizing a particular buyer group, clientele, segment of the product or service line, or geographic market

An alternative formulation is provided by Miles and Snow (1978; 1994), who identify three types of firms in terms of their dominant strategy:

- *Prospectors*—firms that anticipate and shape the development of the market through their own research and development efforts, focusing on innovative products and services
- *Defenders*—firms that wait until technologies and product designs have stabilized and focus on the development of process efficiencies
- *Analyzers*—firms that combine the prospector and defender strategies, creating a base of established products to which they add selected new products and services (1994: 12–14)

Third, as emphasized by natural system analysts, treatments of strategy—like all discussions of goals—often confuse intentions with actions, official with operational goals. To avoid this difficulty, Mintzberg (1987) suggests that distinctions be made between "intended" strategy (plans), "emergent" strategy (unplanned patterns of behavior), and "realized" strategy (actual behavior, whether planned or unplanned). Intended strategies may or may not be realized; realized strategies may be intended or emergent.

Fourth, many discussions presume that strategic decisions are made exclusively by executives high up in the organization. Indeed, as described in Chapter 9, Chandler and Williamson stress the value of segregating operational and strategic decisions and reserving the latter for top officials. By contrast, analysts such as Burgelman and Sayles (1986) propose a more incremental, bottom-up account, pointing out that innovations, including new products and processes, typically develop deep down in the research and production units of companies, acquire support from (are selected by) middle managers, and, after the fact, become recognized and legitimated by top executives. They insist that

> [Middle managers'] initiatives, when successful, change the direction(s) and the strategic plans of the corporation. . . . Thus, relatively autonomous, unplanned initiatives from the operational and middle levels of the organization help to shape corporate strategy. (1986: 144)

Eccles and Crane (1988) make similar arguments with respect to investment banking, referring to a "grassroots" process of strategy formulation as individual investment bankers—"those closest to the markets"—make decisions which, within broad management constraints, determine business strategy (p. 49).

Finally, institutional scholars remind us that, like structures, the choice of a strategy is constrained by institutional forces (Scott, 2001a). There will exist a range of possible, recognizable, legitimate ways of competing that vary by society, sector, and time. How an organization selects its strategy is substantially affected by existing cultural-cognitive models, normative standards, and regulatory rules.

Analysts of public organizations, both political and administrative, tend to substitute the term *policy* for strategy. Like strategy, the concept of policy is employed in many ways, each of which is related but somewhat distinct. Paralleling Mintzberg's (1987) discussion of strategies, policies sometimes refer to a

- *Plan*—a consciously intended course of action
- *Ploy*—a maneuver intended to mislead others
- *Pattern*—a consistent cluster of actions, whether or not intended
- *Position*—a location or niche that specifies the domain of action
- *Perspective*—a way of perceiving the world

And, like strategies, while it is widely presumed that policies are determined by political leaders and high-ranking officials, a vast body of research on implementation suggests that a variety of factors—poorly specified or conflicting objectives, inadequate budgets, weakness of authority, misdirected incentives, existing work routines of operational personnel—transform policies so that the actions of "street-level bureaucrats" differ markedly from the intentions of those who designed the programs but establish the meaning of the policies (see Elmore, 1978; Lipsky, 1980; Pressman and Wildavsky, 1973).

Founding Conditions

One of the most influential accounts of the origins of strategies and structures is Stinchcombe's (1965) discussion of time stamping or "imprinting." Stinchcombe observed that organizational foundings tend to occur in spurts, perhaps driven by technological shifts or by societal events such as wars or political upheavals. Moreover, there was a correlation between the time in history an organization was founded and its organizational structure, even decades later. That is, organizations founded just after the Civil War tended to look similar to each other, and unlike those organizations founded at the turn of the twentieth century, which in turn were unlike those founded in the 1950s. Organizations in society are like the fossils appearing at different strata in the walls of the Grand Canyon. Yet the SARFIT model described at the beginning of this chapter suggests that when contingencies change, organizational performance suffers, and thus their structures ought to change to match their new contingencies. The idea of time stamping seems to fly in the face of this common-sense expectation. How are we to account for this?

The time-stamping argument has two parts: Why do organizations founded at a particular time tend to look similar to each other? and Why do they retain their birthmarks over time? First, "The organizations formed at a given time must obtain the resources essential to their purpose by the devices developed at the time. Since these devices differ, the structures of organizations differ" (Stinchcombe, 1965: 164). To quote Meyer and Rowan again, "[T]he building blocks for organizations come to be littered around the societal landscape; it takes only a little entrepreneurial energy to assemble them into a structure" (1977: 345). The building blocks available in the 1850s differed from those available in 1900 or 1950, and the shape of the structures assembled will reflect the character of the available building blocks. We expect medieval churches to be built from locally quarried stone, cabins in the woods to be constructed out of logs from local trees, pueblos on the plains to be built of adobe, and contemporary art museums to be clad in local titanium. By the same token, organizations are built from existing technologies, locally available qualified labor, contracting structures (which vary by legal jurisdiction), information technology, financing arrangements, norms governing business practice, and so on. In short, organizations construct strategies and structures from available materials that allow them to recruit capital and labor, drawing from the available repertoire of organization structure designs. Of course, the appropriate structures vary across societies and over time: a business named "Amazon.com" would find few investors in 1895, while a business named "The Pennsylvania Railroad" would have a hard time in 1995.

Once in place, why do founding structures persist? There are three possible explanations: (1) the structure is still the most efficient form for its purpose; (2) the organization is not in a competitive situation in which it has to be better than alternatives to survive; or (3) traditionalizing forces, vested interests, and/or outside ideologies support it (Stinchcombe, 1965: 169). The first and second are readily understandable from a rational system perspective. The third describes a natural system process of institutionalization—as Selznick put it, organizations come to be "infused with value" above and beyond their utility as instrumental tools, and participants become vested in them and the values they represent (1957: 17). Nearly all historically black colleges, for instance, continue to enroll primarily African American students even though their potential "market" would be greatly enlarged by recruiting outside this population—the colleges represent a distinctive set of values that their constituents do not want to compromise (Wooten, 2006; see also Clark, 1970).

To the extent that time stamping describes strategy, a critical question becomes where the original strategy came from. There are several possibilities. The composition of the organization's founding team shapes strategies and structures. Founders often draw on models from their experience in prior organizations, and new organizations are very often created by "migrants" from existing organizations—either those hoping to replicate the parent company's success, or those seeking to avoid the mistakes of the parent. Fairchild Semiconductor is regarded as the parent (and grandparent, and great-grandparent) of Silicon Valley because so many firms, including Intel and its rival Advanced Micro Devices, were founded by expatriates from Fairchild.[3] Boeker (1988) found that the initial strategy chosen by fifty-one semiconductor start-ups from among four broad strategy types reflected both the founder's functional background—that is, the specialized function they worked in previously, such as R&D or engineering—and the period in which the organization was founded, consistent with the imprinting idea. More recent executive migrants also brought their prior experiences to bear on

---

[3]These firms, inevitably, are referred to as "Fairchildren," and the Fairchild family tree is displayed in offices across Silicon Valley (Saxenian, 1994).

strategies for entry into new product markets (Boeker, 1997). Elsewhere in Silicon Valley, new law firms are often created by the migration of lawyers from parent firms. Progeny firms started by "name" partners of the parent firm (those whose names are part of the firm's name, such as Martin Lipton at Wachtell Lipton) had the greatest chance of success, but their "defection" increased the chances of failure of their former parent firm (Phillips, 2002).

In addition to where they come from, who they are—the background and demography of the founders, and the mix of employees at start-up—can have enduring effects on organizations. Founders often draw on those who are demographically similar—"birds of a feather"—and those with strong social bonds when starting new organizations (Ruef, Aldrich, and Carter, 2003). Local norms can also influence how new companies staff their boards of directors, as start-ups emulate their geographic peers when they go public, leading to community-level imprinting in local networks (Marquis, 2003). And the composition of founding teams can have a lasting influence on how organizations are managed. Silicon Valley firms that started with proportionally more women subsequently had lower administrative intensity—that is, relatively fewer full-time managers and administrators—than predominantly male firms, and the founder's mental model of the appropriate way to structure employment (how to select employees; the best way to coordinate and control work; and the basis of employee attachment to the firm) also shaped the growth of the administrative component, as firms whose founders had a commitment-based model later grew less in administrative intensity (Baron, Hannan, and Burton, 1999). Finally, in a study of top management teams in the thirty largest firms in the computer and branded food industries during the mid-1980s, Geletkanycz and Hambrick (1997) found that ties inside the industry (through holding offices in trade associations) promoted strategic conformity while ties outside the industry (through managers' prior employment in other industries or through outside directors on the firm's board) promoted divergence.

If building an organization is like building a house, then consultants and law firms are like architects who can help draw up blueprints prior to construction. That is, organizational strategies and structures need not arise spontaneously according to the background or whims of the founders. As discussed in Chapter 10, Silicon Valley law firms (and venture capitalists), for instance, act as "compilers" for new organizations, drawing on their prior experience to generate "pre-tested" organizational strategies and structures for the start-ups they work with (Suchman, 1995a; Suchman and Cahill, 1996). Venture capitalists are particularly likely to understand what types of corporate governance structures (such as boards of directors) will appeal to investors—after all, they reap the benefit of their investment only when the portfolio firm has gone public or been sold to another company, so they have strong incentives to understand what buyers want. Thus, IPO firms funded by venture capitalists tended to have boards of directors that looked more alike than IPO firms without VC funding, while there was no such effect on management teams—in other words, VCs appeared to promote isomorphism among boards, but not among management structure, indicating that VCs believe investors to be more attentive to board composition (Weber, 2000). Biotech firms and others appear to conform to the expectations of investors by recruiting high-profile directors and investors prior to going public, inducing a kind of Potemkin Village conformity (Stuart, Hoang, and Hybels, 1999). It is possible that these latter two findings are particularly characteristic of the stock market bubble era of the 1990s—one might imagine that investors eventually catch on to corporate window dressing! But the more general point is that new organizations structure themselves in ways to ensure access to resources—although *how* they do so varies by time and place. Thus, as payment schemes for home health agencies created a munificent context for new organizational foundings, nonprofit and for-profit organizations in the home health sector came to look almost indistinguishable in terms of staffing, clients served, and funding, which Clarke and Estes (1992) refer to as "accommodative isomorphism." For small nonprofit health agencies and for high-tech IPO firms alike, the funding environment when they are born is an important driver of their strategies and structures.

Law and Public Policy

Choices of strategy take place against a background of law and public policy that allow and encourage some choices, and limit or prevent others. Thus, the kinds of industry structures and strategies observed often vary widely across national economies around the world. Dobbin (1994b) analyzed how the growth and industrial organization of railroads—the first national-scale industries—varied among France, Britain, and the United States in the nineteenth century, observing that each nation had a characteristic style of regulation that drew on its political culture and subsequently extended to the regulation of other industries. France organized its railroads from a political center, and its style of centralized regulation extended to other industries as they arose in France. Britain's system reflected values of individual autonomy, and thus its characteristic mode of regulation was a relatively unregulated free-for-all. The United States valued local autonomy, and thus state and local political control predominated over a central federal policy. By contrast, in France, large industries, starting with railroads, were typically state-owned and centrally controlled, whereas in the United States industry was almost always privately owned, and one might observe competing entrepreneurs building two adjacent railroads running between the same two cities! Indeed, local autonomy also meant that many of the early independently constructed railroads did not connect to one another.

Even in the United States, however, the nation-state did begin to intervene to influence strategy, most notably through antitrust legislation. The Sherman Act of 1890 prohibited cartels or "trusts" within industries and thus inadvertently encouraged a massive merger wave producing the first manufacturing behemoths, including US Steel and General Electric. The Clayton Act of 1914 limited collusion and thereby induced competitors to vertically integrate. The Celler-Kevauver Act of 1950 limited vertical and horizontal mergers and thus unexpectedly produced the growth of highly diversified conglomerates during the 1960s (see Fligstein [1990] for a history of the interplay between antitrust and organizational strategies). State-level laws and regulations also shape competition in some industries in the United States, and therefore multiple levels of jurisdiction may come into play (Scott and Meyer, 1983). As we described above, state-level prohibition created favorable conditions for new breweries to be founded just over the border in neighboring states (Wade, Swaminathan, and Saxon, 1998). Founding and merger rates of railroads in Massachusetts from 1825–1922 reflected different competitive dynamics according to the regulatory regime in place in the state (Dobbin and Dowd, 1997; 2000). And states in some cases are much more responsive to grass-roots politics than federal governments: the founding rates of insurance mutuals, dairy cooperatives, and grain elevators—all cooperatively owned alternatives to corporations—were greatest in states with strong agrarian anticorporate movements in place in the early twentieth century, which tended to be those states in the upper Midwestern United States (Schneiberg, 2006; Schneiberg and Soule, 2005).

Public policy can alter what counts as "competitive" organizational strategies and structures. Diversification was the predominant corporate strategy in the United States in the 1970s, and the conglomerate was perhaps the modal form. By 1980, for instance, Beatrice Corporation operated in branded foods (La Choy Chinese foods); audio equipment (Harman-Kardon); recreational vehicles (Airstream); plumbing equipment (Culligan); luggage (Samsonite); and other industries. Financial analysts documented that for such conglomerates, the whole was often less than the sum of the parts—specifically, the stock market value of the conglomerate as a whole was less than the expected value of all the parts if they were free-standing, "focused" companies. In the natural world, predators would take down such sloths. But a combination of state corporate laws limiting takeovers of local companies and Justice Department antitrust regulations meant that financial predation—hostile takeover, in which outsiders ("raiders") take control through buying the stock of a company against the will of its managers—was difficult or impossible for many conglomerates during the 1970s. In the early 1980s, however, new Justice Department rules easing horizontal mergers, coupled with the 1982 Supreme Court *Edgar* v. *MITE* decision striking down state-level antitakeover laws, enabled a wave of hostile takeovers, many directed at conglomerates that were bought and "busted up" (i.e., the components were sold to buyers in related industries). Financial firms essentially enabled raiders to purchase conglomerates on credit, based on the expected disaggregated value of individual components. One-third of the largest U.S. manufacturers were absorbed through mergers during this decade, and the ones that remained shunned the strategy of diversification and typically began to sell off unrelated parts to focus on a "core competence." By the end of the decade, the average U.S. corporation was far more focused than at the beginning, and the industrial conglomerate had all but disappeared (Davis, Diekmann, and Tinsley, 1994).

Of course, organizations are not completely hapless in the face of threats from public policy. As noted in Chapter 10, organizations react to institutional demands not only by compliance, but also by defiance, or other, intermediate postures. After the takeover wave began in earnest, corporations sought ways to protect themselves, both individually and collectively, by lobbying state legislatures. Legislatures experimented with alternative ways of structuring antitakeover statutes that would conform to the Supreme Court's 1982 decision, and once the right formula was found, these statues spread widely among the states. The states that were quickest to enact such legislation were those that were particularly well connected to local business elites: to the extent that individuals running local corporations knew each other, they were better able to press business-friendly legislators for quick passage of laws to protect them from raiders (Vogus and Davis, 2005). Similarly, Ingram and Rao (2004) document how local merchants effectively pressed for state laws limiting chain stores, and how the chain stores and their allies joined forces at the national level to overcome these state laws.

In addition to facilitating or frustrating the growth of industries, public policy can also create industries and shape their subsequent evolution. Independent power production dates its birth to 1978 (Russo, 2001), as we saw, while the diversity of types of technology introduced into the sector in California and New York was enhanced by media coverage and public awareness but decreased by the existence of state-level trade associations (Sine, Haveman, and Tolbert, 2005). And cross-national variation in policy can also influence the variety of organizational forms observed across nations, as demonstrated by Eastern Europe's and China's transition from communism (Guthrie, 1997; Stark, 2001).

Emulation

Although contingency and transaction costs theorists sometimes appear to assume that organizational change is readily accomplished, from the point of view of those running an organization, changing strategies or structures is a highly fraught endeavor. As James March points out: "Organizations change in response to their environments, but they rarely change in a way that fulfills the intentions of a particular group of actors" (1988: 168). Dumb luck might have blessed the organization with a set of founders whose prior experiences, functional backgrounds, and social connections gave the organization an endowment to see it through the early years, when most organizations fail. But the world does not stand still, and neither can organizations. What to do when critical contingencies change?

Boundedly rational individuals muddle through as best they can, and they often turn to their peers for cues as to appropriate next steps. This is an important theme in institutional and organization learning theory: it is possible, although difficult, for organizations to learn both from their own and others' experiences. Visitors looking for a good restaurant in a new town are likely to choose the one with the line of customers waiting in front rather than the one across the street sitting empty. Presumably, those lining up know something about the comparative quality of the two restaurants. Similarly, large firms adopted the M-form when their competitors were doing so, whether or not they were themselves diversified (Fligstein, 1985). Emulation is particularly powerful when actors have direct contact. Those considering a change or other innovation can gather from prior adopters "important data concerning costs, problems, political risks, likelihood of opposition from interest groups, efficacy of the innovation when initiated, and so forth—a kind of information only available from peers who have already adopted" an innovation (Becker, 1970: 269). Thus, firms whose corporate directors served with other M-form adopters during the 1960s were subsequently more likely to adopt the structure themselves (Palmer, Jennings, and Zhou, 1993).

Evidence for both direct and indirect emulation of strategies is substantial. Channels for direct communication with prior adopters include links like shared directors and buyer-supplier relations. Thus, companies whose CEOs served as outside directors on the boards of acquisitive firms were more likely to make acquisitions of the same types themselves (Haunschild, 1993), and in Chapter 11 we described a number of other instances of emulation through interlocks, including takeover defenses, investor relations offices, and stock market listings. Ties with buyers or suppliers can also influence broad aspects of strategy, such as locational choice. For example, Japanese auto component makers tended to follow their actual or potential buyers when choosing whether to open their first North American plants (Martin, Swaminathan, and Mitchell, 1998).

Organizations also look to their competitors in choosing among specific strategies. California-based savings and loan institutions—banklike organizations whose primary purpose was to fund home mortgages with the savings of their depositors—emulated successful competitors in entering new types of market segments traditionally served by commercial banks, such as nonresidential mortgages and mortgage-backed securities (Havemen, 1993). Ontario nursing home chains followed the locational choices of their competitors when making acquisitions (Baum, Li, and Usher, 2000). And in choosing the locations for new plants overseas, Japanese multinationals followed the leads of their predecessors in overseas expansion (Henisz and Delios, 2001).

Prudent emulation can also shade into faddishness, as businesses seem prone to taking on practices like building a corporate culture, quality circles, TQM, re-engineering, downsizing, or e-commerce in waves of adoption and abandonment. The business press encourages this trendiness by featuring vivid success stories and revealing their "secrets" to an anxious audience seeking an edge in a competitive world (see Abrahamson and Fairchild [1999] on the role of "management-knowledge entrepreneurs" in the rise and fall of quality circles). Management consultants are anxious to help organizations adopt the next new thing (Sahlen-Andersson and Engwall, 2002). Top managers, hearing success stories about TQM from colleagues or the press, sent subordinates out to investigate, and if the subordinates came back impressed, they often got the task of implementing the program. These middle managers might have had little success in implementing TQM—the core elements, such as statistical process control, are hard, and often fell by the wayside, while more cosmetic elements like brainstorming received wide use. But the middle managers prudently edited the feedback they provided to top management by highlighting successes and deleting failures, and the top managers, who now had their own success stories to retail, duly passed them on to more colleagues (Zbaracki, 1998). Strang and Macy (2001) use an agent-based computer simulation to analyze which types of trends in business have staying power and which will turn out to be mere fads. By simultaneously modeling adoption (rooted in observation of "success stories") and abandonment (rooted in direct experience with trendy innovations), they are able to show the fragility of organizational innovations within populations. This result helps address one of the puzzles arising out of institutional theory, namely, why all those S-shaped adoption curves do not imply that every practice that comes down the pike becomes an "institution": many of them turn out not to work as advertised! Nevertheless, as Cole (1999) reminds us, the adoption of the latest fad is not necessarily inconsistent with organizational learning.

ORGANIZATIONAL PERFORMANCE

Multiple Criteria and Indicators

To the novice, defining and measuring the performance of an organization must seem a relatively straightforward affair: to inquire into performance is to ask how well an organization is doing, relative to some kind of standard. This is not wrong, but by this time we experts in organizational analysis know that the pursuit of this simple question leads us to confront complex and controversial issues. A flurry of interest in organizational performance or organizational effectiveness erupted during the 1970s, calling attention to the diverse range of potential measures. Steers (1977), Campbell (1977) and Cameron and Whetten (1983) among others assembled lengthy lists of criteria that had been used by one or another analyst. Campbell, for example, listed thirty different criteria, ranging from productivity and profits to growth, turnover, stability and cohesion.

In attempting to understand why so many and varied criteria have been proposed, we do not need to search very far beyond the thesis of this volume: quite diverse conceptions of organizations are held by various analysts, and associated with each of these conceptions are somewhat distinctive sets of criteria for evaluating the performance of an organization. Proponents of rational, natural, and open system models privilege differing indicators of effectiveness (Scott, 1977).

For example, rational system theorists early focused on the number and quality of outputs and on the economies realized in transforming inputs into outputs. Natural system theorists insist on the importance of factors contributing to the survival and viability of the organization, for example, sufficient incentives to induce continuing contributions from participants and morale. Open system theorists point to the importance of criteria such as "the ability of the organization . . . to exploit its environment in the acquisition of scarce and valued resources" (Yuchtman and Seashore, 1967: 898) and its adaptability/flexibility. These and other criteria point to the complexity of the processes involved in simultaneously carrying on complex work, sustaining the enterprise, and managing relations with the environment.

In addition to issues regarding the choice of criteria, there can be disagreement over the types of indicators employed to assess performance. Three general types of indicators point to important distinctions regarding what is being assessed (Donabedian, 1966; Scott, 1977).

- *outcomes*—focus on the specific characteristics of materials or objects on which the organization has performed, for example, reliability of product functioning, sales, changes in the health status of patients.

While typically regarded as the quintessential indicators of effectiveness, they can present serious problems of interpretation. Outcomes do not just reflect the care and accuracy with which work activities are conducted, but also differences in the input or output environment of the organization. For example, schools in impoverished neighborhoods are unlikely to attract students who will perform well on standardized exams; sales may decline because of an economic downturn. For these and other reasons, outcome data are often adjusted or standardized so that more accurate inferences can be made about the actual performance of the unit (see Flood and Scott, 1987). Customers and clients prefer to focus on outcome measures.

- *Processes*—focus on the quantity or quality of activities carried on by the organization, for example, numbers of cars produced per day, accuracy and completeness of the medical history taken.

Process measures emphasize "an assessment of input or energy regardless of output. It is intended to address the questions 'What did you do?' and "How well did you do it?'" (Suchman, 1967: 61). In general, performers prefer that process measures of performance be utilized since they are typically in a better position to control processes rather than outcomes in connection with work. Data on process are also more readily collected and easier to interpret. The drawback is that process measures often correlate weakly with outcomes.

Critics such as Illich (1972; 1976) claim that the substitution of process for outcome measures is one of the great shell games perpetrated by modern institutions against individuals, claiming that contemporary individuals are trained

> to confuse process and substance. Once these become blurred, a new logic is assumed: the more treatment there, the better are the results . . . The pupil is thereby "schooled" to confuse teaching with learning, grade advancement with education, a diploma with competence, and fluency with the ability to says something new. His imagination is "schooled" to accept service in place of value. Medical treatment is mistaken for health care, social work for the improvement of community life, police protection for safety, military poise for national security, the rat race for productive work. (1972: 1)

- *structure*—assess the capacity of the organization for effective performance, for example, the skill level of workers, the proportion of faculty with doctoral degrees.

If process measures are once removed from outcomes, then structural indicators are twice remote, for these measures index not the work performed by personnel or systems, but their capacity to perform work. Economists warn us that quality of outputs should not be confused with quality (or cost) in inputs, although many measures of productivity make precisely this association (see Panel to Review Productivity Statistics, 1979).

The manner in which the standards used in performance assessment are established is also a complex affair, which we address later in our discussion of internal assessment of performance. The general lesson, however, is that there is a politics to performance measures. Choice of criteria, indicators, and standards are not neutral, technical issues: power and preference play a role in their selection.

The Rise of Shareholder Value

While organization theorists have attended to a variety of criteria for evaluating performance, in recent years the business community has converged around a single, primary criterion: shareholder value as measured by financial markets. For the publicly traded corporation, financial markets currently exercise unmatched influence over the fate of the organization. The stock market provides a minute-by-minute evaluation of how well a company is doing and how well it is expected to do in the future, and through price changes it renders almost instant judgments on corporate strategies and structures.

It was not always this way. The relentless focus on shareholder value resulted in part from the hostile takeover wave of conglomerates in the 1980s and the subsequent advent of shareholder activism, led by institutional investors such as pension funds (Davis and Thompson, 1994; Useem, 1996). But by the end of the 1990s, when the compensation of top executives had come to depend overwhelmingly on their company's share price, shareholder value had become the consensus measure by which businesses were judged. Even the very purpose of the organization had been retrofitted to this evaluation. Coca Cola's mission statement in 1999 read, "*We exist to create value for our share owners* on a long-term basis by building a business that enhances The Coca-Cola Company's trademarks," while Sara Lee's stated, "Sara Lee Corporation's mission is to build leadership brands in consumer packaged goods markets around the world. *Our primary purpose is to create long-term stockholder value*" (emphasis added).

Why is shareholder value the ultimate performance measure? Davis (2005b: 147) explains:

> The answer is the efficient market hypothesis (EMH), the claim that financial markets are "informationally efficient"—that is, that they value capital assets (such as shares of stock) according to all available public information about their expected future ability to generate value . . . According to Jensen (1988: 26), "no proposition in any of the sciences is better documented" than the EMH. Because financial markets are future oriented—they value expected income rather than current or past performance—they are a useful augur of the consequences of present-day actions. Stock market reactions thus provide indications of the wisdom of corporate strategies and structures much more quickly than product market reactions (which may have long lags and, in any case, are well predicted by financial market reactions), and "a firm whose managers feel the necessity to respond to capital market signals will move quicker and will adapt more rapidly to a changing competitive environment." (Gordon, 1997: 1486)

With shareholder value ensconced as the True North of organizational performance, corporations came to structure themselves and convey their strategies in ways designed to influence this measure (Useem, 1996). Zuckerman (1999; 2000) documented both that financial analysts discounted firms whose portfolio of products could not be readily classified, and that U.S. corporations frequently deleted parts of their portfolios that did not fit with the industry boundaries recognized by these arbiters of value. And when corporate leaders announced restructurings, they almost inevitably alluded to the stock market when explaining their rationale—and anxiously watched the market's reaction to their announcement later in the day. ITT's CEO Rand Araskog explained his plan to divide the company into free-standing firms in insurance, industrial products, and hotels and casinos: "We just think that having these three companies acting and operating and being evaluated in their own business environments will provide investors, [financial] analysts and those who deploy debt a simpler, more clear way to evaluate us." When Ford spun off its Associates financial unit, CEO Alex Trotman explained, "We believe the market value of The Associates is neither fully nor consistently reflected in Ford's stock price. Because the market views Ford as an automotive company, it has not fully recognized or rewarded us for our diversification in nonautomotive financial services businesses." And when Sara Lee

Corporation, which produced goods ranging from Ball Park Franks and lunch meats to Champion sweatshirts and Wonderbras, announced a plan to sell off most of its manufacturing capability to focus on marketing, CEO John Bryan stated, "Wall Street can wipe you out. They are the rule-setters. They do have their fads, but to a large extent there is an evolution in how they judge companies, and they have decided to give premiums to companies that harbor the most profits for the least assets."

Financial market evaluations have had an enormous impact on the kinds of structures seen as legitimate and have even induced entirely new structures and professions. Investor relations offices for dealing with the "investment community" (in particular, institutional investors and financial analysts) went from being a novelty to an essential element of the public corporation (Rao and Sivakumar, 1999). The job "chief financial officer" was also a relative rarity, used primarily by conglomerates to manage their acquisitions, until regulatory changes and the shareholder value movement helped push it to nearly universal adoption between the early 1980s and the late 1990s (Zorn, 2004).

As institutional theorists would anticipate, some practices and structures adopted to impress outside evaluators, such as financial markets, were often decoupled from the inner workings of the firm. Young firms that recruited impressive-looking directors to serve on their board were quicker to go public (Stuart, Hoang, and Hybeis, 1999), and established firms that added well-connected directors improved their standing in the eyes of analysts and executives—but their organizations did not perform better by any operational measures of performance (Davis and Robbins, 2005). Moreover, some firms found that they got an uptick in share price for announcing stock buybacks (where the company uses excess cash to buy its own shares and thus increase the proportional stake of those that remain)—even when they never actually followed through! (see Westphal and Zajac, 2001). Companies, it seems, are fairly savvy about playing to their external evaluators.

Shareholders and Other Stakeholders

Most organization theorists continue to insist that organizations confront not one but many evaluators or "stakeholders": persons having an interest in the organization. As noted in Chapter 8, "*Stakeholders* are the social actors (meaning groups of individuals or other organizations) who play a role in the survival and success of the organization and who are affected by the organization's activities" (Ancona et al., 1996: module 9, p. 11).[4] Major categories of stakeholders include employees, customers, suppliers, and members of the community in which the organization operates. Each of these groups is

---

[4]The term "stakeholder" appears to be a rather egalitarian concept that may not diffuse easily. The *Wall Street Journal* in December 2005 reported that U.S. State Department officials discovered that the Chinese language had no corollary for this term so that Chinese officials and academics were baffled by its meaning.

in a position to make claims on the organization although, of course, their ability to enforce these claims varies greatly over time and place.

The stakeholder view is (a) descriptive—describing what the corporation is; (2) instrumental—establishing a framework for examining the connections between organizations and their many constituencies; and (3) normative—asserting that the interests of all stakeholders merit consideration (Donaldson and Preston, 1995). The stakeholder model holds that all persons or groups with legitimate interests deserve consideration, and that "there is no prima facie priority of one set of interests and benefits over another" (p. 68).

Some economists strongly dispute the idea that "stakeholders" who are not investors in the firm should receive special attention. The title of Milton Friedman's famous 1970 article in the *New York Times Magazine* conveys its conclusion bluntly: "The social responsibility of business is to increase its profits." Friedman states that those who talk about broader social responsibilities for business are "preaching pure and unadulterated socialism. Businessmen who talk this way are unwitting puppets of the intellectual forces that have been undermining the basis of a free society these past decades." Businesses are run for the profit of their owners, and if executives channel those profits to uses that do not benefit the business—without the consent of the owners—then they are imposing an unjust tax.

Organizational scholars responded by seeking to document a positive relation between corporate social performance—the extent to which firms engage in "socially responsible" actions, defined in a variety of ways—and corporate financial performance, arguing that companies can do well by doing good. Margolis and Walsh (2003) reviewed 127 such studies published between 1972 and 2002 and found that research tends to find a modest positive relation (although not always), but that methodological difficulties were widespread. What counts as "socially responsible behavior"? How does one measure on the same scale such diverse initiatives as employee volunteer programs, dollars donated to support public television, or in-kind donations of water and logistic support for flood victims? And how does one disentangle cause and effect? A company that donates 5 percent of its profits to charity will, of course, have a perfect correlation between profits and social responsibility as measured by charitable donations (assuming its profits are greater than zero). Moreover, Margolis and Walsh (2003) point out that executives frequently justify their social responsibility not on bottom-line grounds, but because it is the "right" thing to do; thus, the question should not be, Does business benefit from being socially responsible? but, Why do they do what they do, and how does it help its intended beneficiaries (if at all)?

Jensen (2002) argues that the stakeholder model is either blandly unobjectionable—yes, businesses should take account of those affected by its operations, because it is unlikely to succeed otherwise—or a recipe for paralysis. Those running organizations need some way to make trade-offs and to recognize better and worse. "Any theory of action must tell the actors, in this case managers and boards of directors, how to choose among multiple competing and inconsistent constituent interests" (Jensen, 2002: 241), but it is precisely this issue that stakeholder theories avoid. By asserting that no group's interests come first, it gives no guidance for how to make choices among competing "goods." Managing for profitability, on the other hand, gives clear guidance; furthermore, Jensen states,

> 200 years' worth of work in economics and finance indicate that social welfare is maximized when all firms in an economy maximize total firm value. The intuition behind this criterion is simply that (social) value is created when a firm produces an output or set of outputs that are valued by its customers at more than the value of the inputs it consumes (as valued by their suppliers) in such a production. Firm value [roughly proxied by share price] is simply the long-term market value of this stream of benefits. (2002: 239).

Suppliers and employees agree to sell their contribution at a particular wage (which is presumably the best price they could get), firms combine the inputs to produce a good or service, and customers voluntarily pay a price for this output. Assuming no externalities or monopoly power, everyone has voluntarily agreed to these exchanges, and profit—the difference between what customers paid and what it cost to produce the output—measures the net value created for society.

This argument suggests that firms should maximize shareholder value not because shareholders are specially privileged, but because profit over the long term is the best measure of a firm's contribution to social welfare, and share price is the best measure of expected long-term profit. As Gilson (1981) memorably concludes, "[I]f the statute did not provide for shareholders, we would have to invent them." Shareholders, or their share price-motivated agents, are "residual claimants," meaning that they only get paid *after* all the other participants ("fixed claimants") are satisfied—suppliers, employees, those that provided debt and, of course, customers. Shareholders thus bear the greatest financial risk. By hypothesis, this gives them the right incentives to make sure that all these other stakeholders are well taken care of.

Yet this story is also oversimplified. Blair (1995: chap. 6) points out that shareholders in general are highly diversified—most stock is held by institutional investors such as mutual funds, which hold stakes in dozens or, in some cases, thousands of companies, and who are thus relatively risk-neutral. If a company in their portfolio declines, they can always sell their stake and move the funds elsewhere. Employees, on the other hand, often have large specialized investments in their employer that they cannot redeploy elsewhere (see Chapter 10 on transaction costs and asset specificity). If the company fails, or if they lose their job, they suffer a much greater loss that cannot be easily diversified—especially if they own company stock as well, as did large numbers of Enron employees. And employees are often residual claimants too: both employment risk and compensation tied to firm performance leave them in a situation much like that of shareholders and, Blair argues, in a legitimate position to demand some influence in corporate governance. She redefines stakeholders as analogous to shareholders thus: "all parties who have contributed inputs to the enterprise and who, as a result, have at risk investments that are highly specialized to the enterprise" (Blair, 1995: 239). This definition narrows the problem of conflicting interests described by Jensen (2002), but unfortunately does not eliminate it. On the other hand, Blair, echoing Cyert and March (1963), points out that organizations have been balancing conflicting objectives for some time, and it does not appear to be quite as paralyzing as advertised.

Walsh (2005) points out a troubling aspect of stakeholder theory: based on the definitions of "stakeholders" described above, businesses often have no responsibility to those with the greatest need. Kofi Annan visited the U.S. Chamber of Commerce in 2001 to encourage America's business leaders to join the international fight against the AIDS pandemic. AIDS is perhaps the greatest public health crisis in history and had already killed 24 million children when Annan spoke, primarily in sub-Saharan Africa where the disease has had its greatest impact. Millions of AIDS sufferers live in impoverished nations run by corrupt or failed states, and even when the public health system is functioning, drug therapies are often beyond the reach of most of those who need them. Yet Walsh points out that, according to any standard definition of "stakeholder," most businesses have no particular obligation to answer Annan's call: after all, children with AIDS in Africa are not their stakeholders. Clearly, something is missing from a theory that yields this result.

While the business community appropriately focuses attention on for-profit enterprise, organizational theorists rightfully emphasize the full range of organizational forms. An early typology of organizations proposed by Blau and Scott (1962) devised a classification system based on the question: *Cui bono?* Who benefits? They pointed out that while business concerns exist primarily to serve the interests of their owners, other organizations, such as voluntary associations, operate to serve their members, and still other, primarily public and nonprofit organizations, the public at large.

Internal Assessments of Performance

A simple but extremely powerful model of how performance and strategic decisions interact comes from the behavioral theory of the firm (Cyert and March, 1963). The behavioral theory was created to provide an approach to the business firm that took into account three important ideas absent from the traditional economic theory of the firm. First, actors are boundedly rational, constrained by limits in their access to information and their ability to process it, which leads them to satisfy rather than maximize, to economize on what they attend to, and to follow standard operating procedures where possible. Second, organizational practices and structures need not perfectly match their environment and may be slow to change, so understanding how they got to where they are is useful. Third, participants bring different interests to organizations, and conflicts among them are frequently unresolved, leading to continuous renegotiation of goals among participants. The resulting theory is both behaviorally plausible—the people in it look like the people we know, not the characters in economics—and simply enough to be represented in a flow chart (see Figure 12–1).

In the behavioral theory, organizations set goals which include standards or, in Cyert and March's terms, *aspiration levels*. For example, "Increase profits by 15% next year" would count as an aspiration level. "Performance" is defined relative to these aspiration levels. Aspiration levels, in turn, depend on the organization's prior goals, its past performance, and the past performance of its peers. It is, therefore, adaptive—when one's own performance was recently very good, or the performance of one's competitors was good, aspiration levels are likely to go up. But when actual performance is short of the aspiration level, organizations engage in problemistic search—that is, "search that is stimulated by a problem (usually a rather specific one) and is directed toward finding a solution to that problem" (Cyert and March, 1963: 169). (An alternative would be "opportunistic search," enabled by an excess of resources rather than driven by problems.) Problemistic search is *motivated* (it continues until the problem is perceived to be solved), *simpleminded* (search is in the neighborhood of the problem symptom and in the neighborhood of the current alternative solution), and *biased* (reflecting the backgrounds and interactions of the participants).

From this perspective, to understand how an organization interprets its own performance, we need to know what its own past performance has been, the backgrounds of its goal setters, and who they consider to be "peers" against which the organization's performance should be benchmarked. Peer groups turn out to be susceptible to their own form of "local search." Porac and associates (1995), for example, found that Scottish knitwear producers had extremely local definitions of their peers/competitors, highly differentiated and rooted in local knowledge. On the store shelves, of course, their "real" competitors might well be in Italy, or China, but locally transmitted traditions had an enduring effect on collective cognitive maps of the industry. In deciding whom to emulate on consequential decisions, corporations tend to look both to geographic neighbors (Marquis, 2003) and those in the same broad industry or those perceived to be of similar size and status (Davis and Greve, 1997). PC manufacturers were quicker to adopt the "Pentium Pro" processor to the extent that direct competitors—those that sold the same kinds of computers (e.g., notebooks vs. desktops) in the same countries through the same distribution channels (e.g., direct to customer vs. retail stores) had done so (Bothner, 2003).

On the other hand, when firms seek to justify their performance to outside evaluators, they may choose a different group of peers—"choosing the right pond" to enhance the appearance of their own relative performance. A 1992 rule by the Securities and Exchange Commission required public corporations

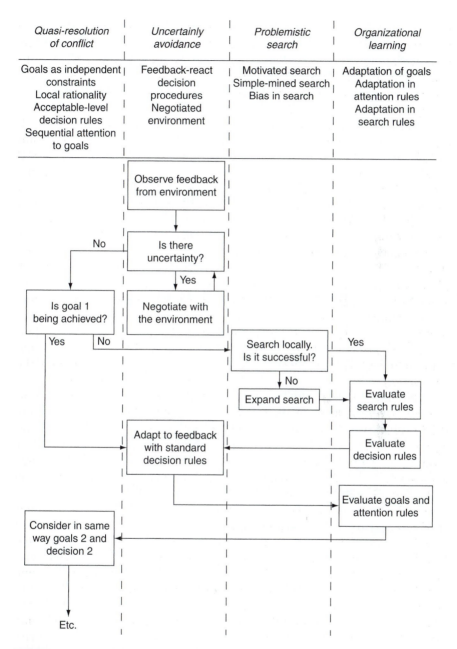

FIGURE 12-1 Organizational Decision Process in Abstract Form.

to display a diagram in their annual proxy statement comparing their five-year stock market performance with that of their "peers" but left it to the companies to decide who counted as peers (within broad limits). Porac, Wade, and Pollock (1999) examined who companies chose as peers, finding that for the most part they were industry competitors, but that poorer performers and companies that paid their CEOs particularly well tended to include firms outside the industry among their comparison group in order to enhance the appearance of their relative performance.

The behavioral theory implies that, once a firm has identified peers and checked its own performance, it is in a position to compare it to aspiration levels. How do firms respond to gaps in performance? First, as the theory predicts, poor performance (falling short of aspirations) prompts problemistic search; for instance, radio broadcasters whose performance was poor were likely to make significant changes in their format—say, shifting from classical to country and western music formats (Greve, 1998). And when poor performers change formats, their market share tends to improve, while when successful radio stations change formats, it is likely to harm their market share (Greve, 1999). On the other hand, good prior performance can promote "competence traps" in which organizations that have previously experienced success respond to performance difficulties by doing what they are already good at doing—only more so (e.g., Miller and Chen, [1994] on airlines; Starbuck [1983] on a Swedish office equipment maker).

One surprising finding from performance studies is that organizations can limp along for years in spite of terrible performance. Meyer and Zucker (1989) refer to these as "permanently failing organizations" and describe the array of forces that can keep organizations on life support long after their performance should have shuttered them—support from the community, sentimental value, barriers to exit, and others. An underappreciated dimension here is the aspiration level of the entrepreneur running the organization: some individuals run organizations that barely break even, or even consistently lose money (if one takes opportunity costs into account), because they enjoy being their own boss, or simply have relatively lower performance targets for themselves (Gimeno et al., 1997).

External Assessment of Performance

The world would be much simpler for organizational participants if there were not external players making demands on them and holding independent aspirations regarding what the organization could or should be doing. For private firms, the market—representing the scale of demand and the availability of alternative products and suppliers—is a prime focus of external assessments; for public organizations, various client groups and special publics, lacking an "exit" option, exercise "voice"—through letters to the editors, political organizing, and the ballot box (Hirschman, 1970).

One of the important changes in organizational environments over time is the extent to which organizations confront not disaggregated customers, clients, or citizens, but other organizations: consumer groups, coalitions of buyers, political action committees (PACs), professionally staffed advocacy groups, and think tanks. Moreover, these organizations of consumers and political interests are increasingly served by a wide range of intermediary organizations and associations functioning to provide improved information and expertise on suppliers of goods and services. Ranging from consumer rating agencies—attempting to assess the quality of products—to certifying agencies providing information on process and structural measures of performance—these organizations contribute importantly to the governance and structuration of organizational fields (see Chapter 10).

Sometimes the information provided by an intermediary agency is simply more accurate information on consumer tastes. For example, as described in Chapter 10, Anand and Peterson (2000) report how changes in the ways in which sales data on music records were collected resulted in a redefinition of the commercial music field. And consider the ways in which the decision processes of college admissions departments were affected by the development of standardized aptitude and achievement tests, as provided by Educational Testing Services in the United States (Lemann, 1999). In subsequent developments, the structure and behavior of colleges and universities have themselves been greatly affected by the crafting and marketing of college and school rating systems, such as those promulgated in *U.S. News and World Report* and *Business Week*. We have previously described the role played by security analysts in informing and influencing the decisions of investors and corporate officials (Zuckerman, 1999; 2000). Rao (1998) provides a detailed account of the emergence of nonprofit consumer research organizations during the first part of the twentieth century in the United States. Precursor organizations, such as professional and trade associations, conducted testing and established standards, but nonprofits differentiated themselves from these industry groups to align themselves with consumer interests. Competition existed among forms oriented to serving "rational" consumer interests using impartial testing methods and those pursuing a broader and more radical agenda of attending to the interests of both consumers and workers. Opposition from conservative media and political bodies resulted in the eventual triumph of the more conservative, scientific form.

Other intermediaries provide data not on outcomes, but on procedures and structural indicators of performance. A wide range of professional associations provides certification (of practitioners) and accreditation (of organizations) after gathering appropriate information on qualifications, structures, and procedures. Such bodies are particularly influential in those professional arenas that are more complex and arcane, for example, medicine or law. Ruef and Scott (1998) examined the accreditation procedures conducted by a range of professional associations involved in evaluating the quality and standards of U.S. hospitals. Employing factor analysis, they report that the hospital reviews could be subdivided into two clusters (factors), one reflecting technical (medical) qualifications, the other, managerial. During the period up to the early 1980s, technical ratings were associated with improved hospital survival, but after the 1980s, ratings of managerial quality were more strongly associated with hospital survival. The salience of differing modes of accreditation (normative legitimation) vary according to prevailing institutional logics.

One of the most widespread and successful systems for rating the quality of management systems is that devised by the International Organization for Standardization (ISO), which introduced their ISO 9000 rating systems in 1987. In 1992, these standards were incorporated in the European Union's (EU) trade directives (ISO, 1992). This approach is rather novel in that "they offer accreditation regimes for organizational actors—or 'soft standards'—as opposed to conventional product or technical requirements. Such systems tend to standardize procedures, rights, and roles rather than goals or outcomes" (Mendel, 2002: 408). Mendel examined the global diffusion of these standards during the period 1992–1998, and while there were some differences by industry, the coercive mechanisms employed by the EU in requiring adoption have resulted in huge variations across world regions. Firms outside of the EU have adopted these standards primarily in response to market and customer pressure rather than government regulation.

SUMMARY

Organizational performance results from a combination of industry or environmental conditions, the strategy that an organization's decision makers choose (or back into), and the structure in place to support the strategy. Industries vary in their potential for profitability according to several factors governing their competitiveness, including the power of buyers and suppliers and the existence of barriers to entry by potential competitors. The attractiveness of industries for new entrants varies over time according to technological factors—new technologies often create advantages for new entrants having few sunk costs—and regulatory factors that enable or discourage competitors, as well as by the degree of market concentration.

Strategies and structures often reflect conditions at the time of the organization's founding. Founders draw on materials such as available labor, information and other technology, and contracting laws to create organizations, and in order to survive these organizations must be structured in ways that allow them to recruit labor and capital in their particular time and locale. Founding teams often use models seen in other organizations, either through direct experience or by third parties such as law firms or investment firms that compile blueprints of successful organizations. Law and public policy sets the ground rules for possible organizational strategies and structures, and regulatory changes can both eliminate existing forms and enable new ones. Organizations often emulate peers or competitors in making changes in strategies and structures, leading to occasional waves of adoption and abandonment.

Performance can be measured by many yardsticks, according to which constituency is doing the measuring. In American business, shareholder value as measured by the stock market has become the predominant metric of organizational performance. Supporters of shareholder value argue that other stakeholders' interests are taken into account by organizations that maximize shareholder value, and that profit-maximizing firms thereby maximize social welfare. Business executives have adopted an array of structures and practices in an effort to raise their share price; some of these structures and practices are evidently decoupled from actual operating performance.

Internal assessments of performance can be described in terms of aspiration levels. Aspiration levels reflect an organization's prior aspiration levels, whether its prior performance fell short or exceeded its prior aspiration levels, and how well its peers are doing. Gaps between aspirations and performance prompt organizations to change strategies and structures, although the effectiveness of these changes can be contentious. External assessments of performance have becoming increasingly organized by outside organizations such as standard-setting bodies and ratings agencies.

CHAPTER 13

The Rise and Transformation of the Corporate Form

Organizational forms and types have a history, and this history determines some aspects of the present structure of organizations of that type. The organizational inventions that can be made at a particular time depend on the social technology available at the time.

ARTHUR L. STINCHCOMBE (1965)

The twentieth century was a time when formal organizations came to be the dominant structures in society. As Perrow put it, "organizations are the key to society because *large organizations have absorbed society*. They have vacuumed up a good part of what we have always thought of as society, and made organizations, once a part of society, into a surrogate of society" (1991: 726). Nearly half the U.S. labor force was spread among almost six million farms in 1900, and even the largest industrial employers were relatively small. Yet by the early years of the twenty-first century, Wal-Mart Stores had as many paid employees as all farms in the United States combined. The kinds of organizations we have, and particularly the ones we work in, shape the kinds of lives we live—what our careers and compensation look like, whether we have health insurance or child care, how much we pay for goods, who our friends are, and even whether we are safe. According to commentators such as Presthus (1978), Perrow and Ritzer (1993), social class structure, the development of technology, and even religion and family life came to be shaped by the requirements of large employing organizations in the twentieth century, and nearly all significant organizations—hospitals, schools, prisons, foundations, universities, government agencies—adopted the kinds of organizational structures and rationalized processes pioneered by corporations. Moreover, this transformation happened over a relatively brief period—a few decades—in historical terms.

By the close of the twentieth century, however, many of the trends toward increasing concentration identified by commentators from Berle and Means

(1932) to Perrow (1991) had begun to reverse, as information technology, competitive pressures, and globalization increasingly "unbundled" business enterprises. AT&T, the largest American industrial employer in 1980 with almost 850,000 workers, was split into a long-distance provider and seven "baby Bell" regional companies in 1984, and, after a long decline in business, ended up employing fewer than 50,000 in 2005, when it was bought by SBC (one of its former "babies"). General Motors and Ford, the second- and third-largest industrial employers in 1980 (with 746,000 and 426,700 employees, respectively), spun off their parts divisions as Delphi and Visteon in the 1990s, and by 2004 each employed roughly 325,000 workers—together, less than GM alone in 1980. Theorists argued that the corporation was nothing but a "nexus of contracts" (Jensen and Meckling, 1976) and that, far from absorbing the lives of their workers, companies had no stronger tie to their employees than a customer does to a grocer (Alchian and Demsetz, 1972)—a statement that came to seem increasingly prophetic with the rise of temporary and contract employment. It appears that rather than absorbing society, organizations are themselves being increasingly absorbed by society (Scott and Meyer 1994: 4) as well as by wider global processes.

From River Rouge to Linux

Organization theorists have attempted to identify the most consequential organizations of the time to understand core aspects of society. Business historian Alfred Chandler (1977) viewed the railroads of the late nineteenth century as the quintessential professional managerial firms, providing the engine of modernization for an industrializing society. For Weber, writing at the beginning of the twentieth century, the Prussian state provided a model of the rational organization—one with which he was quite familiar since his father was a bureaucrat in Berlin and subsequently a member of parliament. In the mid-twentieth century, General Motors served as a model of the multidivisional structure (Chandler, 1962; Drucker, 1946; Williamson, 1975) and competent management in general (e.g., Alfred P. Sloan's 1963 memoir *My Years with General Motors*). Indeed, judging by the literature on transaction costs reviewed in Chapter 9, a cynic might call organization theory the "science of General Motors"! Today, Wal-Mart Stores may well stand as the prototypical large American organization. Overall employment in manufacturing firms such as GM fell below retail employment in the United States beginning in 1990, and Wal-Mart surpassed GM as the largest private employer in 1996—a telling indicator of the shift from a manufacturing to a service economy. By 2005, Wal-Mart employed over 1.7 million people (1.3 million in the United States)—more than the number of paid employees in the entire U.S. agriculture sector, at 1.2 million.[1] The story of successive generations of organizations is the story of our time, a natural history of the changing building blocks of society.

[1]Another million agricultural workers were self-employed or unpaid family members according to the U.S. Bureau of Labor Statistics.

By unpacking the operations of different kinds of organizations and how they change over time, organization theory seeks to provide an understanding of the intersection of biography and history in social structure, as C. Wright Mills (1959) put it in *The Sociological Imagination*—how our lives play out at particular points in the flow of history through the social structures we live in. When societies look like landmasses colonized by large organizations, with occasionally shifting borders between them—and a few disputed territories—then organization theory can provide the tools to understand how individuals make their way through this geography (see Simon, 1991). Regularities in how organizations function—what kinds of people get to the top, patterns of growth and decline, how structures arise and change internally—can help make sense of the biographies of their participants. In a quite literal sense, the history of the development of modern society is also a history of the development of special-purpose organizations. Organizations were both created by and helped to produce these changes.

Yet the natural history analogy cautions us against inferring that the organizations we happen to study—railroads, the Prussian bureaucracy, GM, or Wal-Mart—will tell us about how things inevitably must be. On the verge of its one hundredth birthday, General Motors, for decades the world's largest manufacturer, teeters on the edge of bankruptcy while Google, a seven-year old company that employs 4,000 people and which first sold shares to the public in August 2004, has a stock market value ten times higher than GM. As we have moved from an industrial to a post-industrial society, the idea of any particular organization providing *the* model for organizing seems increasingly suspect.

In this chapter, we document how the predominant kinds of organizations that we know today emerged in the nineteenth century and evolved over the twentieth. This history traces an evolution from rational systems, organized for the efficient production of goods, to natural systems that increasingly enveloped their members, to open systems in which "goods" and "members" are often virtual. The bookends of this process could be the Ford River Rouge plant at one end, and Linux at the other. The River Rouge plant (named after the Rouge River where it is sited) was built over a ten-year period beginning in 1917 to apply the assembly line principles Ford perfected in building the Model T on a grand scale, within a single integrated facility. The River Rouge plant made its own steel from iron ore and coal transported by Ford-owned railroads and shiped from Ford-owned mines; it used rubber from Ford-owned plantations in Brazil and made its own glass and cement. When the first Model A rolled out of the factory in 1927, the River Rouge plant employed 75,000 people—and grew from there, becoming part of the "arsenal of democracy" during the Second World War. The River Rouge represented the apex of rational systems, and Ford Motor Company was nearly a total institution for employees, many of whom lived in Ford-built houses in Dearborn, Michigan, effectively Ford's company town.

In many ways, Linux represents the inverse of the River Rouge plant. Linux is a computer operating system that many regard as the primary alternative to Microsoft Windows, and it is used on millions of servers and personal computers around the world. Unlike Windows, however, Linux is legally available free to anyone (you can download it right now—visit *www.linux.org*) and was written by thousands of globally dispersed, unpaid volunteer programmers as part of an "open source" software development. (Open source means the source code—the text that programmers write, which is then compiled into a computer-useable program—is open for everyone to read, evaluate, and modify for their own or others' use.) The project evolved out of a program that Linus Torvalds, a student at the University of Helsinki, wrote in 1991. A small team of developers, including Torvalds, is responsible for reviewing and approving the standard version of Linux, but there are dozens of nonstandard variants available, often for free. And the licensing for the product guarantees that it remains free—that no one "owns" Linux (although Torvalds owns the trademark for the name). In other words, Linux has hundreds of thousands of users and contributors, but almost no bosses, employees, ownership, or physical presence. Moreover, interdependence among components of the program is organized for "modular isolation," limiting potential side effects among parts, in stark contrast to the vertically integrated Rouge plant. (Axelrod and Cohen [1999: 52–58] provide an enlightening discussion of how Linux works.)

Between the River Rouge plant and Linux—from a tightly bounded rational system par excellence to a loosely coupled open system that stretches the boundary of the concept "organization"—organizations have traveled a long distance during the twentieth century, with theorists often moving a step or two behind. In this chapter, we chart this journey; in the next and last, we survey the path ahead.

CHANGING FORMS OF ORGANIZATIONS

From Corps to Corporation

When we speak of the emergence of organizations, we do not mean to imply that previous societal arrangements exhibited disorganization. Indeed, in important ways some of the pre-existing social systems exhibited higher degrees of order. Feudal systems, for example, were highly organized, stable structures (Bloch, 1964). The proper contrast, then, is between different types of ordered social arrangements. The principal ways in which modern social structures differ from earlier, traditional forms are (1) in the relation of individual actors to corporate actors and (2) in the relation of corporate actors to one another.

James Coleman's (1974; 1990: 531–52) analysis of these developments is most illuminating. Examining the corporate bodies of the Middle Ages, he observes that the basic units—manor, guild, village—wholly contained their members and possessed full authority over them. What rights and interests individuals possessed were acquired from membership in these units. (Note that these bodies are the patrimonial systems described by Weber, as discussed in Chapter 2.) The very term *corporation* (which applied to all these formally recognized collectives) derived from the word *corps*, or body. Sewell described the metaphysics of this system:

> All bodies were composed of a variety of organs and members, which were hierarchically arranged and were placed under the command of the head. Each body was distinct from every other, with its own will, its own interests, its own internal order, and its own esprit de corps. Each body was made of a single internally differentiated but interconnected substance, and harm inflicted on any member was felt by the whole . . . Indeed, one might argue that the entire French kingdom was composed of a hierarchy of such units—from corporations, seigneuries, and parishes at the bottom, through cities, provinces, and the three estates of the realm at an intermediate level, to the monarchy at the top. (1981: 36–37)

Guilds—trade corporations typically given a monopoly by the monarch on a particular kind of trade in a particular location, such as winemaking in the city of Caen, or goldsmithing in Nantes—were the most important form of business organization during much of the Middle Ages and a precursor to the business corporation we know today. Trade corporations were granted *privilege*—literally, "private law," which gave particular rights and obligations to a particular person (singular or collective) and thereby gave them immunity from the common law. Rights were often specified in minute detail—winemakers might be forbidden from making vinegar, which was the exclusive domain of the vinegar makers, and knife makers might not be able to use gold in decorating their wares because this was the province of the goldsmiths (Sewell, 1981: 26). Apprentices and journeymen lived with their masters and ate at their table, and they were in turn under "the domestic authority of the masters" without separate legal standing, much like children or farm animals (p. 31). Upon becoming a master and entering the trade, an artisan spoke a solemn religious oath—literally, a *profession*—signifying a lifetime commitment to the corporation "until death do us part," when the master's colleagues lowered him into his grave. Masters were also typically entitled to *charites* from the corporation, such as "corporate funerals, widows' pensions, and aid in sickness or disaster" (p. 31)—not unlike the benefits provided by some employers today.

Over time, these relations were altered. Individuals were able to acquire rights and recognized to have interests, and corporate actors were allowed to acquire rights and to pursue interests that were not simply aggregates of the interests of their members. In France, the transition from a "corporate society" to a society of individual citizens equal before the law happened abruptly with the French Revolution, which abolished the corporations—although they continued in practice in various forms. Under these altered conditions, corporate actors no longer contained their individual members but only the specific resources invested in them by persons acting as owners or investors; and they no longer fully controlled their members but only the specific behaviors contracted for by persons who agreed to function as their participants or agents. Individuals were only *partially involved* in these new organizations. These organizations were no longer arranged in a concentric, hierarchical pattern but began to function somewhat independently of one another, competing for the loyalties and resources of individuals.

Coleman (1979) emphasizes the impact of individualism on the development of special-purpose organizations. Durkheim and Simmel stress the reverse effect. In his influential analysis of the changes in social structure associated with the industrial revolution, Durkheim (1949 trans.) argued that, because of an increasing division of labor, the "mechanical" solidarity that characterized traditional societies had been replaced by an "organic" solidarity based on functional interdependence of the parts. In mechanical societies, parts are interchangeable: "the individual does not appear"; whereas in organic societies, individualism is highly developed: "the unity of the organism is as great as the individuation of the parts is more marked" (1949 trans.: 130–31). Simmel (1955 trans.) comes to the same conclusion but emphasizes the network effects of overlapping versus concentric groupings. When social arrangements consist of layers of concentrically related systems, the social spaces created tend to produce homogeneous individuals. Batches of individuals are likely to share the same social location and perceive themselves as holding the same social identity. However, as social arrangements shift to contain overlapping and intersecting systems, a vastly increased variety of social spaces is created, and no two individuals are likely to share the same social location or exhibit the same social identity. As Simmel explains,

> The groups with which the individual is affiliated constitute a system of coordinates, as it were, such that each new group with which he becomes affiliated circumscribes him more exactly and more unambiguously. To belong to any one of these groups leaves the individual considerable leeway. But the larger the number of groups to which an individual belongs, the more improbable is it that other persons will exhibit the same combination of group-affiliations, that these particular groups will "intersect" once again in a second individual.
>
> . . . As individuals, we form the personality out of particular elements of life, each of which has arisen from, or is interwoven with, society. This personality is subjectivity par excellence in the sense that it combines the elements of culture in an individual manner. . . . As the person becomes affiliated with a social group, he surrenders himself to it. A synthesis of such subjective affiliations creates a group in an objective sense. But the person also regains his individuality, because his pattern of participation is unique; hence the fact of multiple group-participation creates in turn a new subjective element. (1955 trans.: 140–41)

The idea of identity being framed by the intersection of one's "web of affiliations" is one we take up again in the context of corporations and nationalities later in the chapter.

In addition to guilds, a second important transitional form were the trading or "'chartered companies' that bore the names of almost every part of the known world ('East India,' 'Muscovy,' 'Hudson's Bay,' 'Africa,' 'Levant,' 'Virginia,' 'Massachusetts')" (Micklethwait and Wooldridge, 2003: 25). Beginning roughly in the middle of the sixteenth century, these companies were chartered by the king, receiving exclusive rights to trade in a particular part of the world, and were supported by shares that could be sold on the open market. These companies collectively experienced an exotic, dangerous, often ruthless existence, causing Micklethwait and Wooldridge to note that, in spite of today's peccadilloes and scandals, the company's past has been "more dramatic than its present" (p. 8).

The emergence of the modern idea of the corporation appears in retrospect as a distinct break with prior ways of organizing, yet the corporation evolved fitfully out of prior collective bodies. Corporations as we know them today are typically distinguished by three features: (1) a *separate legal personality* (that is, the corporation is not the aggregate of its "members,"), and thus the ability to make contracts and own property; (2) *unlimited life*, meaning that its continued existence under the law is not dependent on particular persons and it can carry on indefinitely; and (3) *limited liability*, which implies that the people who own it are not liable for debts taken on by the corporation—that is, the corporation's creditors cannot demand that its owners or trustees repay them out of their own funds. Carruthers notes that the earliest English joint-stock companies "inherited a number of features from guilds, a much older form of corporate organization. Early companies, including the East India Company, were considered to be a kind of brotherhood. Shareholders were also members, and as such had to take an oath upon entry into the company . . ." (1996: 132–33).

Like the guilds, corporations are legal entities, created by states. Initially, every new corporation required a separate act of the monarch (or parliament, or legislature), as their creators had to document that the corporation served a public purpose worthy of such a grant. The earliest business corporations in the United States were often quasi-public agencies, granted corporate status to build canals or roads—public projects—that were too costly for individuals to fund. In the United States, state governments, not the federal government, are responsible for corporate law, including the act of incorporation. As a result, it originally took a separate act of a state legislature to grant incorporation, although over time this gave way to general incorporation statutes that allowed the creation of a corporation simply by filling out the relevant paperwork, beginning with New York in 1811. The process of incorporation had become institutionalized.

In the nineteenth century, states varied substantially in their approach to the corporation. Ohio, which had come close to bankruptcy through its public subsidization of canals and railroads earlier in the century, enacted highly restrictive corporate laws, while New Jersey, with limited corporate experience, had the most permissive corporate laws (Roy, 1997). Because companies in the United States can incorporate in any state, regardless of where they operate, New Jersey—with its permissive corporate law—became the most common state of incorporation at the end of the 1800s. By enacting general incorporation statutes, states found that they could raise substantial revenues by being in the incorporation business, and over the twentieth century, tiny Delaware won the race to provide the laws most attractive to businesses. Today, 60 percent of the 1,000 largest U.S. businesses are incorporated in Delaware, while less than 2 percent are incorporated in California, the most populous state. Delaware gets almost one-fifth of its budget from corporate franchise fees, and the state's lawyers do a thriving business servicing Delaware corporations (Romano, 1985). Creighton (1990) has shown that competition among states fueled the expansion of corporations in the United States.

Since creating corporations had become a routined and trivial matter, governments outside the United States discovered that incorporation was a moneymaker: consulting firm Accenture and conglomerate Tyco are incorporated in Bermuda, Hong Kong-based Tommy Hilfiger is incorporated in the British Virgin Islands, and Royal Caribbean Cruises is incorporated in Liberia. (One can incorporate in Liberia online at *www.liscr.com* for $713.50 plus a $450 annual fee; major credit cards are accepted.)

Over time, corporations shifted from being relatively rare entities, created for the explicit purpose of serving the public interest, to being the characteristic structural economic unit of the contemporary world, explicitly serving the interests of their shareholders. Throughout this process, the law of corporations has reflected an antinomy in society: Are corporations merely legal fictions holding a place in a web of contracts (the "contractarian" view), or are they bodylike entities with members and social responsibilities, as in old regime France (the "social entity" view; see Bradley et al., 1999; see also Chapter 14)? William Allen, long-serving chancellor of Delaware's Chancery Court—the major forum for questions of corporate law—discusses this contrast in an article entitled "Our Schizophrenic Conception of the Corporation" and concludes that there is no permanent resolution to the question, only pendulum swings among opposing visions (Allen, 1992).

Railroads: Origins of the Managerial Firm

While law provided the skeleton, businesses created the flesh of the corporation. Alfred Chandler (1977) provides the canonical account of the emergence of the large, professionally managed enterprise in the United States. The period just after the Civil War was a time of rapid expansion and resource accumulation. This was the age of the larger-than-life entrepreneurs who expanded their organizations, most often through vertical integration. In the subsequent phase, a new generation of professional managers, differentiated from the owners or the founding entrepreneurs, developed "methods for managing rationally the larger agglomerations of men, money, and materials" (Chandler, 1962: 388). Attention was concentrated on the reduction of unit costs and the coordination of diverse functional activities. As Frederick Taylor (1911) observed, this constituted a "mental revolution" for managers, who had been largely engaged in ongoing face-to-face supervision, to begin to focus their attention on broader issues of organizational design and long-range planning.

Defining Features. The first two phases are best exemplified in the United States by the development of the railroads. Chandler points out that,

> The safe, reliable movement of goods and passengers, as well as the continuing maintenance and repair of locomotives, rolling stock, and track, roadbed, stations, roundhouses, and other equipment, required the creation of a sizable administrative organization. It meant the employment of a set of managers to supervise these functional activities over an extensive geographical area; and the appointment of an administrative command of middle and top executives to monitor, evaluate, and coordinate the work of the managers responsible for the day-to-day operations. It meant, too, the formulation of brand new types of internal administrative procedures and accounting and statistical controls. Hence, the operational requirements of the railroads demanded the creation of the first administrative hierarchies in American business. (1977: 87)

Railroads were hence associated with the development of the *functional, unitary* or *U-form*, the now conventional structure composed of a central management unit and several functionally organized departments. This structure was the great organizational achievement of the nineteenth century when, as scale and complexity increased, individual entrepreneurial forms gave way to those that relied on technical expertise, specialization, and salaried managers: a full-fledged corporate bureaucracy.

Associated Developments. Railroads were also responsible for a set of developments that continue to shape the organizational landscape today. The emergence of the railways in the nineteenth century forced the question of the appropriate role for governments in an industrial market economy. How, exactly, should states and the nation-state deal with the growing business sector? Railroads were the first big businesses, and they enabled trade on a scale previously unthinkable (e.g., selling flour made from wheat grown in Kansas to bakers in Paris). Should they be run by a national government, like an army, or should they be operated by private businesses and encouraged by enabling laws, or should their growth and tendencies toward concentration be curtailed? Dobbin (1994b) compares the development of economic policies in France, Britain, and the United States during the railway era and argues that culture and precedent had a decisive influence on how these three countries ended up with their divergent railway systems in the nineteenth century.

Political structures that were originally created to achieve social order or military glory were retrofitted to the new problem of promoting economic expansion, initially through the railroads, but later with other industries. Britain saw individual sovereignty as the source of political order; too much concentration as a problem for economies; and thus encouraged a proliferation of competing private railways. France saw sovereignty of a strong central state as a source of political order; too little concentration as a problem; and ended up with a centrally organized national rail system. In the United States, local autonomy and self-rule were seen as the source of political order, and the organization of railroads varied by state. Moreover, Dobbin argues that the policy paradigms that eventually evolved to regulate railroads—the first major national industry—subsequently became templates for other national economic policies. As new industries emerged, governments applied the lessons learned from experiences with the railroads—lessons that varied widely among the three countries—to new industries, creating recurring national templates that still echo in divergent patterns and policies today.

A second ramification of the development of railroads was the widespread use of stock markets to fund business. Prior to the railroads, stock exchanges primarily traded in government debt. But the scale of railroads required comparably vast amounts of capital, outstripping the capacity of wealthy families or individual banks. Indeed, U.S. railroads were funded to a very large extent by foreign—particularly British—investors, and ". . . the railways' voracious requirements for capital did more than anything else to create the modern New York Stock Exchange . . . From the end of the Civil War until the 1890s, Wall Street existed almost exclusively to finance the railroads," and "it was the railways that spawned an investor culture" (Mickelthwait and Wooldridge, 2003: 65). A stock exchange with rigorous quality standards was essential for enticing foreign investors to take a risk on a distant, wild-and-woolly emerging market—the United States—and these standards in turn set the stage for the development of the American system of corporate governance (Coffee, 2001).

Equally important, the railroads created a class of "robber barons," such as Jay Gould, Cornelius Vanderbilt, and Leland Stanford, and financial elites, like Edward H. Harriman and J. P. Morgan, who raised funds for these ventures and continued to hold influential positions on their boards (Chandler, 1977). Major railroads were organized into keiretsu-like "communities of interest"—the Morgan group, the Vanderbilt group, the Gould-Rockefeller group, and so on—that shared directors and common ownership ties (Roy and Bonacich, 1988). Moreover, through their board positions and control of loan capital, according to critics, bankers became a financial oligarchy, a "Money Trust" that "joined forces to control the business of the country, and 'divide the spoils'" (Brandeis, 1914: 27).

Railroads thus set a tone for the interaction of business elites and governments. The federal government in the United States was relatively small and weak prior to the Progressive era: the Pennsylvania Railroad employed 2.5 times as many people as the Army, Navy, and Marine Corps combined in 1891 (Mickelthwait and Wooldridge, 2003: 66). Furthermore, railroads and the wealthy elites who built them had the wherewithal to have significant influence on state and local governments, where the most significant laws governing corporations were made (Perrow, 2002). The business-friendly corporation statutes in New Jersey owed at least some of their character to the railroad barons' influence on New Jersey's legislators (Roy, 1997: 14).

The final legacy of the railroads was their opening of vast markets for agricultural export, in which the United States became a major power in the late nineteenth century, and for enabling broad distribution of products across a continent-wide consumer market. In contrast to Europe, the United States provided a single, integrated, relatively homogeneous market for mass retailers like Sears Roebuck and Montgomery Ward, whose catalogues reached millions of homes. "In the second part of the nineteenth century the American domestic market was the largest and, what is more important, the fastest growing market in the world" (Chandler, 1977: 498). As a result, businesses in America could grow to enormous size before reaching the optimum economies of scale. Railroads thereby made mass production—and huge manufacturing firms—economically practical.

Roy summarizes the nineteenth-century development of the corporate form:

> From a quasi-public device used by governments to create and administer public services such as turnpikes and canals, the corporation germinated within a system of stock markets, brokerage houses, and investment banks. With railroads it shed its public accountability, then redefined its legal underpinning to redefine the nature of property, and then only when fully mature, flowered at the turn of this century into the realm of manufacturing, when many of the same giants that still dominate the American landscape were created". (1997: 6–7)

It is to this turn-of-the-century movement—the "corporate revolution"—that we now turn.

The Corporation in the Twentieth Century

If General Motors is the prototypical twentieth-century corporation, then the *Fortune* 500 is its tribe. Commentators such as Fligstein (1990) often portray the *Fortune* 500 as the defining organizational population in the U.S. economy, the "institutional field" of big business. This group is comprised of the U.S.-based businesses with the largest revenues (sales) and, until 1995, was exclusively made up of manufacturers.[2] These firms were often vertically

---

[2] In 1995 *Fortune* magazine added service firms, which were previously counted in a different set of lists, to the Fortune 500 in recognition of the incresingly fuzzy boundary between manufacutring and service.

integrated, organized into multidivisional forms, run by professional managers with no particular ties to the founders, and owned by dispersed and relatively powerless shareholders. Moreover, they controlled the bulk of the assets of the U.S. economy and much of the employment of the U.S. workforce. Thus, while some might quibble that a mere 500 firms are not statistically representative of the millions of organizations in America (e.g., Aldrich, 1999; Carroll and Hannan, 2000), this is somewhat like arguing that the president, Congress, and Supreme Court (a mere 548 people) are not statistically representative of the 2.5 million employees of the U.S. federal government—true, but beside the point. The ten largest manufacturers alone employed over 5 percent of the private workforce in 1980, and the hundred largest employed 14 percent.

Yet large manufacturing corporations traded on stock markets are a comparatively recent phenomenon. The largest manufacturer in the world in 1890 was Carnegie Steel in Pittsburgh, which was organized as a partnership and effectively dominated by its majority partner, Andrew Carnegie. Outside the United States and the United Kingdom, mass production initially took hold in relatively few places, and dispersed ownership in almost none (Davis and Useem, 2002; Piore and Sabel, 1984). Moreover, there was nothing inevitable about the rise of the large industrial corporation in the United States: things could have been different. It was the corporate revolution, particularly during the years 1898–1903, that saw the birth of the archetypical American corporation, and the subsequent five decades that witnessed the growing dominance of a particular form of corporate capitalism, first in the United States and later abroad.

As we have seen, corporations were comparatively rare in the United States until late in the nineteenth century, and manufacturers particularly so. There were fewer than ten manufacturers traded on the New York Stock Exchange in 1890, and their net worth was trivial. Mergers among electric companies created General Electric in 1891, and in 1901 J.P. Morgan and others created the first billion-dollar corporation by combining almost all major producers of steel, iron, and coke into a single corporation: U.S. Steel (Roy, 1997: 3). By 1904, 72 percent of the value-added in manufacturing came from corporations, and the value of the stocks and bonds of manufacturers totalled $7 billion. The turn of the twentieth century was very much the birth of the American corporate economy, "a major change from one economic system to another, a new corporate order" (Roy, 1997: 5). As Roy documents, manufacturers built on the institutional precedent of the railroads—and the guiding hand of Wall Street—in selling shares to the public to raise capital. The Sherman Antitrust Act of 1890 prevented firms from forming cartels to stabilize prices at high levels. Thus, encouraged by economies of scale in mass production and mass distribution, and enabled by Wall Street, firms consolidated in industry after industry—cotton oil, paper, sugar, tobacco, culminating with the creation of U.S. Steel. According to Chandler, "In those industries where administrative coordination of mass production and mass distribution was profitable, a few large vertically integrated firms [the U-form] quickly dominated. Concentration and oligopoly appeared as a consequence of the need and the profitability of administrative coordination" (1977: 489).[3]

Although financiers had a major role in creating the manufacturing corporations via mergers, and their presence on corporate boards continued to arouse political concerns about the Money Trust (e.g., Brandeis, 1914), their influence quickly waned in the early years of the twentieth century, as manufacturers relied on retained earnings for capital and ownership grew increasingly dispersed, while the bankers had no particular expertise to guide the operations of the new industrial behemoths they had helped create (Chandler, 1977: 491). The large corporation that we know today, run by professional managers, had come into its own, and its influence on economic and social life spread quickly. "By the outbreak of the First World War, the big company had become a defining institution in American society: the motor of one of the most rapid periods of economic growth in history; a dominating figure in political life; and a decisive actor in transforming America from a society of 'island communities' into a homogeneous national community" (Mickelthwait and Wooldridge, 2003: 102).

Diversification: The M-form. As we have described, the U-form was pioneered by the railroads and adopted and adapted by large industrial firms and retailers. From the turn of the twentieth century to the First World War, these firms continued to expand and fill out existing product lines (Chandler, 1977). In order to ensure the continuing and efficient use of their resources, they began to diversify by expanding their range of products and services, moving into related fields that would capitalize on their technical skills and marketing contacts. Following the war, a few major companies that had diversified and were struggling to manage multiple related product lines found it useful to restructure in order to ensure the efficient deployment of their resources. In this manner, a novel form first appeared in this country during the early 1920s, having been developed at about the same time by a number of major companies, including du Pont, General Motors, Standard Oil of New Jersey, and Sears Roebuck (Chandler, 1962).

The new form that emerged was the *multidivisional* or *M-form* structure, which consisted of a general corporate office and several product-based or regional divisions, each of which contained functionally differentiated departments.[4] This form was well suited for firms operating in diverse markets; put another way, according to Chandler, firms that failed to support a strategy of diversification with an appropriate multidivisional structure suffered for it:

> Unless structure follows strategy, inefficiency results. This certainly appears to be the lesson to be learned from the experience of our four companies [du Pont,

---

[3]Roy (1997) and Perrow (2002), naturally, dissent from the this efficiency-oriented interpretation of the causes of consolidation, but not with the description of the effects in creating oligopolies.

[4]We previously described the M-form and its features in Chapter 6.

General Motors, Standard Oil, and Sears Roebuck]. Volume expansion, geographical dispersion, vertical integration, product diversification, and continued growth by any of these basic strategies laid an increasingly heavy load of entrepreneurial decision making on the senior executives. If they failed to reform the lines of authority and communication and to develop information necessary for administration, the executives throughout the organization were drawn deeper and deeper into operational activities and often were working at cross purposes to and in conflict with one another. (Chandler, 1962: 314–15)

Thus, a key feature of the M-form is the emergence of a new hierarchical level—the general corporate office, responsible for overall strategy and the allocation of resources among divisions—that is differentiated from the divisional level, responsible for coordinating the production of particular goods and services. Chandler argues that, given a diversified strategy, the M-form is superior to the U-form because it frees selected officials from the tyranny of daily operational decisions and allows them to concentrate on positioning the organization in its environment and determining the proper mix of product lines and markets and thereby the allocation of resources among divisions.[5] The M-form is also particularly well suited to supporting a multinational strategy, in which numerous divisions offering the same general product lines are situated to take advantage of multiple national markets (see Bartlett and Ghoshal, 1989; Tsurumi, 1977; Vaupel and Curhan, 1969).

Rumelt (1986) examined changes in the strategy and structure of a random sample of 100 of the 500 largest U.S. corporations in 1949, 1959, and 1969 and found broad support for Chandler's account.[6] Rumelt devised a set of categories to characterize company strategy: single business, dominate business, related businesses, and unrelated businesses. During the period of study the number of diversified corporations more than doubled, the percent of firms expanding their scope to include related or unrelated business strategies growing from 30 percent to 65 percent. With respect to structural change, during the same period, the percent of firms employing a product-division (M-form) structure increased from 20 percent to 76 percent, and diversification strategies were strong predictors of structural form. Fligstein (1985) extended this sample and time period to cover 216 large U.S. nonfinancial firms spanning the period 1919 to 1979, finding that whereas less than 2 percent of these corporations had

---

[5]Based on a detailed analysis of the workings of General Motors—one of Chandler's principal exemplar companies—during the period 1924–1958, Freeland (1996; 2001) argues that there is little evidence that the M-form produced a clear distinction between strategic and tactical planning. Rather, the lines between corporate and divisional decision making were both blurred and contested, and the resulting participative decentralization was better suited to generating consent among middle managers than to simplifying information processing.

[6]Rumelt (1986:149), in addition, found support for institutional arguments that "structure follows fashion." Firms imitated the practices of other firms in their industry, regardless of their own level of diversification.

adopted the M-form structure before 1929, over 84 percent had done so by 1979. The M-form's spread was consistent with Chandler's account:

> Industries where product-related strategies dominated, like machine, chemical and transportation industries, adopted the MDF [M-form] in large numbers relatively early; while industries that were more likely to be vertically integrated, like mining, metalmaking, lumber and paper, and petroleum, adopted the MDF later and to a lesser extent. (Fligstein, 1985: 386)

As the managers of large U.S. corporations were changing their organization's internal structures, they were also finding themselves increasingly freed from the demands of the firms' owners. In their highly influential 1932 book *The Modern Corporation and Private Property,* Adolph Berle and Gardiner Means argued that as corporations grew large, ownership grew increasingly dispersed among disconnected (and therefore powerless) shareholders, while managerial control grew increasingly consolidated. Ownership, as they put it, was centrifugal, while control by management was centripetal. They dubbed this situation the "separation of ownership and control" and argued that it characterized most of the largest U.S. corporations. This separation—later dubbed "managerialism"—allowed professional managers to pursue objectives different from those their owners might want, such as growing the firm too large at the expense of profitability, staffing the board of directors with their cronies, and ensuring that the management group was well paid and lavished with perquisites. Thus, three decades after the corporate revolution, the shareholders had been thrown out of the palace, and professional management was firmly in charge, a situation that would last another five decades until the hostile takeover wave of the 1980s.

American Exceptionalism? It is worth noting that the developments described here were essentially unique to the United States. No other economy came to be dominated by vertically integrated M-forms with dispersed ownership, operating in oligopoly industries—at least for a few decades. A distinct combination of factors enabled this particular path in the United States. Continent-wide markets and consumers with relatively homogeneous tastes enabled profitable mass production, while the Sherman Act of 1890 in effect banned cartels and thereby inadvertently encouraged industries to consolidate into oligopolies (Chandler, 1977: 1990). Germany, in contrast, actively encouraged cartels with an eye toward dominating export markets, thus preserving smaller firms. In the United States, expansive financial markets that developed by funding privately owned railroads, along with the preferences of financiers for joint-stock corporations, encouraged those consolidating firms to sell shares to the public (Roy, 1997). In France, on the other hand, large firms were commonly owned by the state and staffed with veterans of the government bureaucracy. Long-standing mistrust of concentrated economic power by Americans led to laws that kept commercial banks local—they could operate branches only within a single state—and relatively weak, preventing them from becoming powerful corporate owners, as they were in Germany and Japan (Roe, 1994). A combination of diffuse owners and retained oligopoly profits meant that corporate managers were often unconstrained by capital (Chandler, 1977). And the dispersal of political power among the states, coupled with a relatively weak federal government early on, allowed business elites to have a significant influence over how the rules of the game were written (Perrow, 2002). In other industrial nations, governments grew up before business; in the United States the opposite was the case. "Not until the late 'thirties did the annual revenues of the federal government rival those of the assets of the largest industrial corporation. . . . In the United States the professionally managed, oligopolistic, multidivisional firm literally exists for a generation without the modern equivalent of the state" (Vogel, 1978: 58–59). Thus was the United States the "seedbed of managerial capitalism" (Chandler, 1977).

Ironically, a growing federal government also stimulated the further growth of big business. The mobilization for World War II further expanded the scale and bureaucratization of the corporation. The number of people employed in manufacturing increased from 9.9 million in 1939 to 17.9 million in 1944—representing 49 percent of the nongovernmental labor force. And the conditions of their employment grew increasingly rationalized due to federal intervention encouraging particular employment practices, including the establishment of departments of personnel administration, as described in Chapter 7. The trend toward increasing size, scope, and concentration that the war exacerbated continued for decades after the war: the share of assets owned by 200 largest industrials increased from 47.2 percent in 1947 to 60.9 percent in 1968.

By the 1950s, the managerialist firm held a secure place as the predominant organization in the United States. As Chandler puts it, ". . . by the 1950s the managerial firm had become the standard form of modern business enterprise in major sectors of the American economy. In those sectors where modern multiunit enterprise had come to dominate, managerial capitalism had gained ascendancy over family and financial capitalism" (1977: 493). Moreover, they had become increasingly multinational, accounting for 49 percent of accumulated foreign direct investment around the world by 1960 (compared with 16 percent for Great Britain, the next largest foreign investor).

After a few decades of managerial control, large corporations had come to look rather different from the soulless, profit-maximizing abstractions of economics. Economist Carl Kaysen described this new entity as "the soulful corporation" and its professional managers as a new breed, more akin to public-spirited civil servants than rapacious robber barons. "No longer the agent of proprietorship seeking to maximize return on investment, management sees itself as responsible to stockholders, employees, customers, the general public, and, perhaps most important, the firm itself as an institution" (1957: 313–414). The benevolent employment practices implemented by the war-era personnel departments had grown even more encompassing, as "the whole labor force of the modern corporation is, insofar as possible, turned into a corps of lifetime employees, with great emphasis on stability of employment" (p. 312). As a result, "Increasingly, membership in the modern corporation becomes the single strongest social force shaping its career members . . ." (p. 318), which was a situation much like membership within a guild during the Middle Ages.

Although the United States, with its distinctive institutional ecosystem, may have germinated this corporate model, it subsequently diffused widely among the industrial economies. Like Buddhism, the model spread via trade (and occasional coercion) and was adapted to local conditions. Guillén (1994) compares the changing managerial models utilized by managers in the United States, Germany, Spain, and Great Britain during the twentieth century, arguing that while a succession of similar general models can be discerned across these rather diverse societies, there is considerable variance in when one or another model was ascendant. The models examined—scientific management, human relations, and structural analysis (contingency theory)—penetrated managerial thought and practice in each country, but the patterns of adoption were seen to vary by stage of industrial development, nation-state industrial policies, and the actions of professional groups such as engineers. And Djelic (1998) has examined the extent to which the "American model" of corporate enterprise has diffused in Europe following World War II. Her study contrasts the response of three countries—Germany, France, and Italy—noting that the penetration of the American model varied substantially not only because of background political and industrial differences among these countries but also because of their differing connections with the United States. For example, the Marshall Plan—a postwar recovery program provided by the United States to European countries—was not readily embraced by the Italian government, so that the American and other international economic models were slower to take hold in Italy than in France and Germany. And American and Japanese manufacturing plants using similar technologies showed characteristic differences, with Japanese firms exhibiting less specialization and taller hierarchies than the American firms (Lincoln, Hanada, and McBride, 1986).

Convergence and Divergence: Alternative Pathways? In some respects, there has been convergence. "Regardless of country, by the early 1990s, the typical large industrial firm in Western Europe was diversified and divisionalized. France, Germany and the United Kingdom now all follow the Harvard model discovered two or three decades ago by Chandler (1962) and Rumelt (1986) in the United States" (Mayer and Whittington, 1999: 951). In other ways—particularly in corporate governance—divergence persists. Stock exchanges opened in new nations around the world during the 1980s and 1990s, even in nominally communist countries such as China and Vietnam, while hundreds of foreign firms began selling shares on the New York Stock Exchange and Nasdaq. By 2005, all but two of the world's twenty-five largest corporations were traded on U.S. stock markets, and thus subject to American securities laws such as Sarbanes-Oxley. In spite of this, the structures of corporate boards, and the extent of ownership dispersion, continued to retain distinct national differences through the end of the twentieth century (Davis and Marquis, 2005a).

Moreover, important aspects of the American system itself have changed since the 1980s, as we saw in Chapter 9. One-third of the largest industrial firms disappeared during the 1980s merger wave, and diversified conglomerates were busted up, either voluntarily or through hostile takeover. Institutional investors became increasingly organized to influence company strategies, and attention to shareholder value decisively challenged managerialism (Useem, 1996). U.S. firms became increasingly global, both in where they produced their products and where they sold them: the average *Fortune* 500 firm derived nearly one-third of its sales outside the United States by the turn of the twenty-first century. And the share of the private labor force employed by the 500 largest firms shrank from 21 percent to 16 percent between 1980 and 2000, in spite of the two largest mergers waves in U.S. history during the 1980s and the 1990s (White, 2001).

Scholars after Chandler have increasingly emphasized two themes. First, while Chandler implies that the large-scale managerialist corporation was inevitable, others have emphasized the critical turning points where things might have gone otherwise. Piore and Sabel (1984) suggest that small-firm networks with a craft orientation might have been an alternative developmental path. Schneiberg and colleagues (Berk and Schneiberg, 2005; Schneiberg, 2002) report that a variety of noncorporate associational forms emphasizing mutualism flourished in the Midwestern United States early in the twentieth century, providing alternative solutions in arenas ranging from commercial printing to electrical utilities to mutual companies in fire insurance. And Roy (1997) argues that large-scale businesses had existed in the United States in noncorporate forms—for example, Carnegie Steel, the world's largest manufacturer, was a partnership—but such forms were discouraged after the 1890s, when investment bankers would only fund corporations. If banks and corporate law had come under federal rather than state jurisdiction, or if William Jennings Bryan had become president, things might have turned out differently. This insight has encouraged scholars to study branching points—particular periods when decisions were made that critically shaped subsequent organizational history, such as the birth of the railways, or the corporate revolution.

Second, the United States is idiosyncratic. Piore and Sabel (1984) and Perrow's (1991) vision of small firm networks in fact survived and prospered in industrial districts around the world, in places such as northern Italy, which provide a functional alternative to vertically integrated firms. Moreover, such districts have seen a resurgence in recent decades, as indicated by the success of Silicon Valley, a vertically disaggregated industrial district that is lauded for its flexibility relative to the slow-moving integrated firms of Boston (Saxenian, 1994; see Chapter 11).

Cross-national evidence shows that there are many paths to economic development that bear little resemblance to the approach in the United States. Japanese industrialists, with the help of consultants like W. Edwards Deming (ignored in the United States, his home country) and state support, reenvisioned manufacturing by inventing "lean production" techniques that led them to quickly gain on and then to overtake Detroit in market share for automobiles as well as other kinds of consumer products (Womack, Jones, and Roos, 1990). South Korea transformed itself from a war-devastated agricultural society to the world's eleventh largest economy in just two generations thanks to state-led industrialization accomplished by a handful of large, family-dominated *chaebol* conglomerates (Evans, 1995). China has drawn from this lesson in encouraging the creation of chaebollike business groups, whose members share directors and preferentially exchange with each other and which typically have superior performance relative to their ungrouped competitors (Keister, 1998). The U.S. corporation has often been treated as a model, a blueprint for success. Yet violators of this model—such as the Korean chaebol—can thrive, while emulators often fail. Media conglomerate Vivendi, one of France's largest corporations, whose CEO was so taken with American shareholder capitalism that he moved his family to New York, verged near bankruptcy in 2002 after a series of acquisitions and an ill-advised share buyback program depleted its resources. It was only saved by the intervention of the French old boy's network, the business elites who typically attend the Ecole Nationale d'Administration together and move up through the Treasury as a cohort (Kadushin, 1995). Moreover, the cultural and legal differences between the United States and other nations are far too large to permit substantial convergence (see Guillén, 2001; Whitley, 1999). The ability to sustain a substantial stock market, for instance, is heavily dependent on a nation's legal system having derived from English common law: nations that inherited French code law have systematically smaller financial markets and more highly concentrated corporate ownership because of the comparatively weaker property rights they offer small shareholders (LaPorta et al., 1998). The American system is not only idiosyncratic; it may also be nontransferable (Davis and Useem, 2002).

Variation and Continuity. That said, predictions about the future of economic institutions like the corporation often turn out badly because of capitalism's built-in quest for novelty and innovation. Geographer David Harvey argues that capitalism's

> developmental trajectory is not in any ordinary sense predictable, precisely because it has always been based on speculation—on new products, new technologies, new spaces and locations, new labor processes and the like . . . There are laws of process at work under capitalism capable of generating a seemingly infinite range of outcomes out of the slightest variation in initial conditions or of human activity and imagination. (1990: 343)

The histories of individual companies bear this out. Westinghouse Electric, founded in Pittsburgh 1886 to sell electric power generating equipment, grew to be GE's major competitor in the power generation business as well as a diversified manufacturer of locomotives, appliances, and broadcasting equipment. By the early 1980s, it employed nearly 150,000 people and was a prototypical managerialist firm: the five largest owners combined owned less than 15 percent of the shares, the company was integrated and diversified, and its disparate divisions sold products around the world. But facing pressures to enhance shareholder value, it began a program of divestitures in the late 1980s and early 1990s, and by 1995 it had shrunk to 84,000 employees. That year a new CEO, Michael Jordan—whose prior history was primarily with Pepsi—bought broadcaster CBS. Two years later, Westinghouse put its remaining industrial businesses on the sales block, changed its name to CBS, and moved its headquarters to New York, further shrinking to 29,000 employees. It was acquired by Viacom in 2000, then split off again as a free-standing company in early 2006. Westinghouse's transformation— from Pittsburgh-based industrial conglomerate, to New York-based broadcaster CBS, to media conglomerate Viacom, and back again into CBS—vividly demonstrates how organizational boundaries, location, industry, and employees are surprisingly labile (Davis and Marquis, 2005b).

While there may be no timeless features of organizations, there are recurring themes and, perhaps, "laws of process," as Harvey suggests. One of these might be called the "institutional conservation of energy." Our survey suggests that genuine institutional novelty is rather rare: humans are like magpies, building new structures from the materials we have handy. Just as peasants in the Middle Ages incorporated bricks from Roman city walls into the dwellings they built, medieval jurists drew on Roman law in theorizing collective entities such as guilds. As already discussed, Stark (1996) has described the ways in which Hungarian entrepreneurs are combining aspects of public and private forms, by bricolage, in Hungary's transition from communism to capitalism.

By analogy, bricolage, and outright copying, actors create institutions and organizations, engendering family resemblances that persist over time. Government policies evolved to promote order in society are applied to promote order in the economy—first with the railways and later by analogy with other industries, creating characteristic economic "styles" that vary by nation (Dobbin, 1994b). The proper analogy may not always be obvious. In the United States, the advent of radio saw competing analogies with different regulatory implications: was radio a natural monopoly, like a utility (or the post office, or public schools), best operated by the government? Or was it like a "magazine of the air," analogous to a free press, and thus best operated by private companies with a constitutionally-protected role? In the end, the winning analogy conceived of the radio spectrum as a public waterway, and regulation and appropriate property rights followed accordingly (Leblebici et al., 1991: 340–41). The Internet spawned its own competing analogies—information superhighway, marketplace, cyberspace.

Search "engine" company Google styled itself as an information provider with a public-service obligation like that of newspapers, and accordingly when it first sold shares to the public it followed a practice common among newspapers and other media, but relatively rare in other industries (such as technology): creating two classes of stock, one for the public (with one vote per share) and one for Google founders, directors, and employees (with ten votes per share).

Institutions created for one purpose, such as markets for trading government debt, can be adapted for other purposes, such as selling shares of company stock (see Carruthers, 1996). The idea of incorporation for essentially "private" purposes, which was pioneered by the railroads, proved quite useful for consolidation by manufacturing corporations (Roy, 1997). And the organizational structures created to operate these new corporations, adapted by the railways from the military and by manufacturers from the railways, spread to nonbusiness organizations such as hospitals, colleges, and government agencies, as we have described.

Barred from some outlets, institutional entrepreneurs often invent or import new modes of organizing from other fields. Thus, Clemens (1993; 1997) described how at the beginning of the twentieth century, womens' groups, barred from the franchise, adopted and appropriated more direct avenues for influencing the political process from then-disreputable interest groups, including monitoring the legislative and budgeting processes, intervening in the drafting of bills, mobilizing public opinion and protest groups, and lobbying activities. These formerly questionable tactics now provide the traditional repertory of contemporary political interest and advocacy groups in the United States.

Institutions also spread through direct copying. Companies reveal the terms of their "golden parachute" executive severance contracts in their annual proxy statement, from which they may be copied verbatim in the contracts provided by other corporations the next year (Davis and Greve, 1997). Organizational structures that prove sufficient to ward off legal challenge for one organization are quickly imported by other organizations (Dobbin et al., 1988; Edelman, 1992). By the same token, state legislatures emulate the laws of their peers that have survived the scrutiny of federal courts, sometimes evidently crafting legislation with the help of a copying machine (Vogus and Davis, 2005).

Laws against plagiarism evidently do not apply to institutions, where sampling, mixing, and "re-purposing" are the norm and novelty the exception. While economically minded historians often imply that there is one best path, and that deviators are quickly selected out, the evidence suggests something else. The late evolutionary biologist Steven Jay Gould (1997) put it aptly: "If we want a biological metaphor for cultural change, we should probably invoke infection rather than evolution." We would amend this by pointing out that actors are not just recipients of these "infections," but active participants in their construction and transmission.

We next turn to recent challenges to how organization theorists think about this process.

ARE ORGANIZATIONS STILL THE DEFINING STRUCTURES OF SOCIETY?

Class versus Organizations

We opened this chapter alluding to Mills's description of the task of the social scientist as locating the intersection of biography and history in social structure. Theorists vary in what they construe as the most consequential social structures—that is, where they look for this intersection. Westhues asserts "In sociology, it is safe to say that paradigms are shaped to a great extent by what the sociologist regards as the most critical decision-making unit in a society" (1976: 41). Organization theorists have followed Weber in viewing the organization as the most critical structure of society. Class theorists, following Marx, have seen social classes as defining the essential divisions in society.

This distinction between class and organization provides an illuminating contrast for how social scientists have told history. In this chapter we have examined the natural history of the business corporation as it has evolved from the guild to the railways to the contemporary multinational. We have described how its characteristic features have been altered as more facets and features of the work process were rationalized, formalized, and internalized. But Marx famously opened the first chapter of the *Communist Manifesto* by stating that "The history of all hitherto existing society is the history of class struggles." Class conflict, not increasing rationalization, was the "law of motion" of society, particularly in modern capitalist society. Along the way, there have been attempts at synthesis among class and organization theories. Writing in 1959, Ralf Dahrendorf argued that capitalist society was a specific type of a more comprehensive category, "industrial society," which was defined by "mechanized commodity production in factories and enterprises" (Dahrendorf, 1959: 40). Dahrendorf pointed out that Marx had theorized prior to the "second industrial revolution" at the end of the nineteenth century, which witnessed the growth of massive industrial bureaucracies, and the separation of ownership and control in the early part of the twentieth century, which introduced managerialism. Thus, he described a basis for class conflict that was no longer relevant. "A theory of class based on the division of society into owners and nonowners of means of production loses its analytical value as soon as legal ownership and factual control are separated" (p. 136), a situation Dahrendorf (along with other commentators at that time) claimed had come true. We instead lived in a "postcapitalist" industrial society.

Yet class conflict has not disappeared; rather, to a large extent it has been encompassed within organizations, where class is now defined by the distribution of authority within large enterprises, with executives and managers at the top and blue- and white-collar workers, in diminishing numbers in the middle, and temp and part-time workers primarily on the bottom. Thus, "the participants, issues, and patterns of conflict have changed, and the pleasing simplicity of Marx's view of society has become a nonsensical construction" (Dahrendorf, 1959: 57). It has also been dampened by the ideology, if not the full reality, of social mobility whereby yesterday's lower and working classes could, through education and achievement, move into today's middle and upper classes. Although such hopes and aspirations continue to burn brightly for many, there is also evidence of a widening gap between rich and poor, and a dampening of the extent of intra- and intergenerational mobility (DiPrete and Grusky, 1990).

Organizations and States

Similarities, Competition. Is there an alternative to classes? In a different formulation, John Meyer and associates (Meyer, 1994; Meyer, Drori, and Hwang 2006) propose that, beginning during the Enlightenment, three central types of social actors have evolved as the major foci of agentic power into the modern period: the nation-state, organizations, and individuals. Although each of these types of actors lays claims to and celebrates its own capacities for self-determination and unique agency, all are constituted by the wider environment, by cultural rules that determine their features and modes of action. Over time, cultural forces shape each category—nation-states, organizations, and individuals—as they are pressured to adhere to prescribed models and to act in appropriate ways. Nation-states are under much pressure to exhibit the same structures and programs, even when large differences in economic development and human resources often prevent more than superficial conformity (Meyer et al., 1997). In a parallel manner, organizations have become more alike over time (Pedersen and Dobbin, 1997). The corporate form and managerial structures have largely triumphed over competing alternatives.

And there are surprising similarities between states and corporations in recent years. Corporations in the United States provide many of the social welfare benefits that states provide elsewhere: health care, child care, and old age pensions, although this is less the case in the United States today than in the past. Organizations increasingly have adopted and adapted a wide range of legal functions and procedures, including the widespread use of private security and surveillance services, in-house legal counsel, internal dispute resolution procedures, and disciplinary hearings and grievance procedures, much like law courts (Edelman and Suchman, 1999). Corporations are patrons of the arts in their local communities (Galaskiewicz, 1997), support the construction of low-cost housing (Guthrie and McQuarrie, 2005), subsidize medicines to those with low incomes, and make higher education affordable for their employees (Marquis, Glynn, and Davis, 2006). Some of them are as large as nation-states—Wal-Mart employs six times as many people as the population of Iceland, for instance. Indeed, from some perspectives, the "socially responsible" global corporation looks more like a European welfare state than does the U.S. federal government! And with operations spread around the world, they often require a foreign policy and a diplomatic corps to deal with other governments. The "soulful corporation" described by Kaysen (1957) has grown ever more expansive in its orientation.

At the same time, states are becoming more like corporations in their operations and rhetoric. The imagery of governments as service providers to their citizen-consumers has a long history. Charles Thiebout in 1956 proposed "A pure theory of local expenditures" to argue that—in contrast to those who saw no market forces inducing governments to spend "appropriately" on public goods—in fact municipal governments do compete to attract resident-taxpayers through their packages of tax rates and amenities (schools, police protection, golf courses, etc.). His stylized case was a city dweller choosing which suburb to move to, with suburban governments competing for his residence, but the idea applies more generally to businesses.

As we have seen, states compete for incorporation revenues through the bodies of corporate law they provide. Law and economics scholars argue that such competition is a positive feature. Roberta Romano (1993) refers to its federal structure as "the genius of American corporate law," which enables the establishment of ever-wiser law from the perspective of the economy. The reason is that financial markets provide an external monitor that rewards firms that choose the right laws (e.g., Delaware's) and punishes those that do not. Thus, when states pass "bad" laws (laws that are perceived as harmful to shareholder interests), firms incorporated in those states decline in value: when the Pennsylvania state legislature passed its strict law regulating hostile takeovers in 1990 (a law that institutional investors fought against vigorously), Pennsylvania corporations reportedly lost over $4 billion in stock market value.[7]

Business executives are aware of this dynamic, and because of the many institutions that ensure their devotion to shareholder value, they make their incorporation choices accordingly. And legislators are aware of this dynamic as well, recognizing that laws must be somehow aligned with shareholder value if they are to avoid a corporate out-migration. Occasionally there is ad hoc legislation to please particular business clients, as when Michigan's legislature quickly acted on a law in 2003 protecting the locally headquartered and incorporated Taubman shopping mall empire from a hostile bid by rival Simon Properties of Indiana. But in general, in the domain of corporate law the dynamic of state regulation is not the "capture" of state policy by elites, but a regulatory shopping mall. Instead of state legislatures being the tailors of bespoke suits for their corporate masters, they compete by providing ready-to-wear bodies of law and hoping to attract buyers.

---

[7]These arguments assume that financial markets are accurate instruments for measuring economic rationality. Competition among states for industries by, for example, eliminating pollution controls, may result in long-term economic and social costs.

Not all the competition among vendor-states is friendly. Thus, while "Toys R Us" the organization was headquartered in Wayne, New Jersey in 2002, "Toys R Us" the trademark resided in Delaware, where it collected millions of dollars in annual licensing fees from Toys R Us stores for the use of the brand, thereby reducing earnings that would otherwise be subject to state income taxes. Delaware does not collect income taxes on out-of-state companies, and dozens of retailers and other firms (including Home Depot, Kmart, Gap, Burger King, Radio Shack, and Staples) established Delaware subsidiaries to house their intellectual property (trademarks, patents, and copyrights) for the evident purpose of shielding income from state income taxes in the states where they actually operate.[8] Bermuda is the preferred locale for intellectual property subsidiaries aimed at avoiding federal taxes, and more than two dozen software, biotech, and pharmaceutical firms have established such "tax efficient" entities in the past few years. And while wholesale re-incorporation in Bermuda became markedly less popular after September 11, 2001 and the scandals at Tyco, there appear to be valuable tax advantages for housing intellectual property in Bermuda.

In the law and economics view, competition among states as vendors is unproblematic. Corporations have no intrinsic nationality, and they do not carry a passport (although they have First Amendment rights, and perhaps Second Amendment rights in the case of Halliburton)—they are legal fictions that serve as useful devices for raising financing. Just as teenagers are not citizens of Tommy Hilfiger, corporations are not citizens of the states whose labels they wear. Moreover, governments have learned from companies about the importance of branding. Britain in search of tourist dollars has rebranded itself as "Cool Britannia," and marketing companies now provide their advice to many other nation-state clients.

Some states advertising the benefits of their legal frameworks have sought to be the low-cost provider (one of the three primary corporate strategies described by Porter [1980]). This is particularly evident in the case of so-called "flags of convenience." Ships at sea are subject to the laws of the nation where they are registered, which is signified by whose flag they are flying. Through the end of the nineteenth century and into the twentieth, it was customary for ships to fly the flags of nations where they had a significant attachment. But there were advantages to registering elsewhere; American shipowners, for instance, began to register ships in Panama, which put them outside the reach of alcohol prohibition laws. In spite of resistance from unions, shipowners could avoid American shipping regulations, and hire non-U.S. crews, by registering elsewhere. After World War II, American oil companies created a ship registry for

---

[8]Delaware Corporate Management, Inc. services some of these entities by providing Potemkin Village offices to establish the appearance of local residency, including an address (1105 North Market Street in Wilmington), phone answering, mail forwarding, and a staff of temps to serve as officers, auditors, and corporate directors. Several states, such as Maryland, Iowa, and Massachusetts, launched legal cases against these devices, which are evidently legal under a 1992 Supreme Court ruling. (See *Wall Street Journal*, 8/9/02.)

Liberia for their oil tankers, and by the 1980s a number of nations began to compete for registry revenues as the volume of international shipping exploded with globalization.

At this point, Panama has the largest number of registered ships, followed by Liberia—but even landlocked Bolivia earned $1 million per year for registering about 300 ships in 2002, and its Web site promised "immediate registration, total tax exemption, no restrictions in respect to size and age of the vessel and no restrictions as to nationality of ship owner or crew" (*Wall Street Journal*, 10/23/02). Any sovereign nation can register ships, and there is no binding international oversight; moreover, the doctrine of "innocent passage" means that foreign ships can sail unhindered through territorial waters as long as they are not an immediate threat to the adjacent state. Ships may change name and nationality while *en route*, and some registries make this relatively easy. Liberia's registry has been outsourced to a company in a nondescript suburban office park in Vienna, Virginia, and while written documentation for registering a ship is preferred, apparently a fax or e-mail may be sufficient in a pinch.[9]

In Martin Wolf's apt paraphrase of Stalin, "The interests of a transnational company are not the same as those of the country from which it originates or of the workers it has historically employed. It has become, to coin a phrase, a 'rootless cosmopolitan.'" (2004: 243–44)—and has largely jettisoned the mantle of the "soulful corporation." Through shopping for jurisdictions among competing states, corporations find themselves with a "web of affiliations" much like that described by Simmel earlier in this chapter. Just as multinationals are skilled in their choices among suppliers located in nations with low labor costs, they are able to optimize their legal jurisdictions with respect to corporate, securities, and tax regulations. In 2005 Tommy Hilfiger Corporation, for instance, had its headquarters in Hong Kong, was incorporated in the British Virgin Islands, listed its shares on the New York Stock Exchange (of which 40 percent were owned by five U.S. institutional investors), held its annual meeting in Bermuda, sourced production to manufacturers in Mexico and Asia, licensed its trademark to producers globally, and retailed its "classic American clothing" in Europe and North America.

The vacation cruise industry draws on interstate competition for both ship registries and incorporations. With revenues of $4.6 billion in 2004 and a market capitalization of $8.2 billion, Royal Caribbean Cruises would be well into the list of the *Fortune* 500 if it were an American corporation. Although Royal Caribbean is headquartered in Miami and traded on the New York Stock Exchange, its twenty-eight ships are registered in the Bahamas, Ecuador,

---

[9]William Langewiesche's *The Outlaw Sea* describes the consequences of the nautical "race to the top": "By shopping globally, [shipowners] found that they could choose the laws that were applied to them, rather than haplessly submitting to the jurisdictions of their native countries . . . What's more, because of the registration fees the shipowners could offer to cash-strapped governments and corrupt officials, the various flags competed for business, and the deals kept getting better," making global shipping both incredibly cheap and dangerous for the labor force that staffs the ships (2004).

and Norway, while the firm itself is incorporated in Liberia (along with a half-dozen other cruise and shipping companies that trade in the United States). Its two primary owners are a Norwegian family corporation and a Bahamian partnership owned by trusts of the Pritzker family of Chicago and the Ofer family of Israel. Why incorporate in Liberia? Royal Caribbean notes that Liberia lacks the substantial body of legal precedent that more popular business jurisdictions such as Delaware have, and "our public shareholders may have more difficulty in protecting their interests in the face of actions by the management, directors or controlling shareholders than would shareholders of a corporation incorporated in a U.S. jurisdiction." Furthermore, Liberia's 2004 GDP, at $2.9 billion, is substantially less than Royal Caribbean's annual revenues, and the quality of Liberian jurisprudence is somewhat uncertain. There are, however, offsetting advantages: although most cruise passengers are American and pay in U.S. dollars, income "derived from . . . the international operation of a ship or ships" (i.e., vacation cruises) is exempt from U.S. income taxes, according to the firm's legal counsel. Note that if you are an unhappy shareholder, you can sue the company—but while incorporation may be handled in an office park in Virginia, using Liberia's courts requires a trip to Monrovia.

We might go further and state that, if the railroad was the keystone industry of industrialization and represented many of the central themes of the modern corporation, shipping is the keystone industry of globalized postindustrialism and the postmodern corporation. Railroads generally crossed lands with clear territorial boundaries and jurisdictions, governed by particular states that were able to regulate their corporate structures and labor practices. In the United States, the railroads unified a single continent-wide society and enabled the construction of a mass-production industrial economy. Shipping has made postindustrialism possible. More than half the retail goods sold in the United States arrive by ship (*Wall Street Journal*, 8/22/05), and ships carry 90 percent of total global exports (*The Economist*, 8/18/05). The roughly 40,000 vessels that carry this trade are effectively stateless, able to change name and nationality virtually at will around the world.

Challenges and Changes. We believe it incontestable that the two most fundamental forms of collective organization throughout the twentieth century were the organization, in particular the corporation, and the nation-state. But, as the foregoing discussion suggests, these two types of collective actors are themselves both challenged and changing. We now confront a world that might be called hypercapitalist postindustrial society, in which even such basic units as organizations and states are called into question as defining institutions in society. In his American Sociological Association presidential address, Michael Burawoy (2005) stated, "Globalization is wreaking havoc with sociology's basic unit of analysis—the nation-state." The same might be said for the basic unit of organizational scholars. Both are experiencing the "creative destruction" processes of intense competition and globalization.

To a large extent, theory about organizations has not yet caught up with these developments. Our conceptions of organizations are largely rooted in a backwards-looking view and leave us straining to make sense of contemporary developments. This perhaps reflects the time period in which the most central organizational paradigms that we have described were developed. If organization theorists, following the advice of writing teachers everywhere, chose to "write what you know," then we have inherited a legacy of theory that, like the strata of the Grand Canyon, trace forms that often no longer exist (Davis and Marquis, 2005b). General Motors was not much like the Prussian state, and Wal-Mart is not much like GM.

What are we to do? Chapter 14 does not provide the answers but, we hope, provides some guidelines for pursuing promising directions for change.

SUMMARY

The business corporation came to dominance during the twentieth century and served as a model for organizations and rationalization in other domains. Predecessors to the corporation include the guild in the Middle Ages and chartered companies that held monopolies on trade during the age of empire. Corporations are distinguished by having a separate legal personality, unlimited life, and limited liability; in combination, these features enabled corporations to grow to vast size and influence.

Railroads incubated the private, professionally managed corporation in the second half of the nineteenth century, and mass-production manufacturers established the characteristic features of the contemporary corporation. These include a multidivisional structure, professional management, and ownership by dispersed shareholders. These features were initially distinctive to American corporations, but aspects of them spread broadly, particularly after the Second World War. Although often portrayed as an inevitable development, cross-cultural comparisons show robust alternatives to the American managerialist firm.

Globalization, information technology, and competitive pressures have reversed prior trends toward increasing scale and scope in many industries, and contemporary multinationals challenge many of the categories and assumptions of modernist organization theory. Corporations have come to look more like states in the range of their activities, while states have come to look more like business corporations, as both compete for each others' business.

CHAPTER 14

Changing Contours of Organizations and Organization Theory

> As every past generation has had to disenthrall itself from an inheritance of truism and stereotypes, so in our own time we must move on from the reassuring repetition of stale phrases to a new, difficult, but essential confrontation with reality. For the great enemy of the truth is very often not the lie—deliberate, contrived, and dishonest—but the myth—persistent, persuasive, and unrealistic. Too often we hold fast to the clichés of our forebears.
>
> JOHN F. KENNEDY (1962)

The kinds of changes that organizations have undergone over the years, described in Chapter 13 as well as elsewhere in this volume, suggest the need to consider the ways in which organizational theories are challenged by changes in the nature of the object we study. Our discussion of these forces in this chapter is governed by two overriding assumptions: (1) we embrace a "postpositivist" view of science; and (2) we recognize the power of the past to shape and inform our own efforts.

Postpositivist Persuasion

We subscribe to Jeffrey Alexander's (1983, vol. 1) depiction of science as a "two-directional continuum," stretching between the metaphysical and the empirical environment. At the far end of the metaphysical pole are the general presuppositions and models—the theoretical paradigms—that anchor our understanding and interpretations. At the opposite empirical pole are the observations we make and the data we collect. In between these poles lies a continuum that includes concepts, definitions, and classifications (closer to the metaphysical pole) and propositions, metrics and correlations (closer to the empirical pole). The points along the continuum are not independent, but interdependent. Alexander observes:

> Even the most metaphysical theory of society, which explicitly focuses upon and elaborates only the most general properties, is influenced by implicit though

underdeveloped notions of models, propositions, and empirical correlations. Similarly, even for the most self-consciously neutral and precise scientific exercise, 'empirical observations' represents only an explicit focus. Generalized presuppositions, definitions, classifications, and models—all levels influenced by more metaphysically oriented concerns—still affect such specific statements, even though their influence remains completely implicit. (1983: vol. 1, p. 4)

Several basic scientific postulates follow from this formulation:

- *All scientific data are theoretical informed.*
- *Empirical commitments are not based solely on experimental evidence.*
- *General theoretical elaboration is not guided solely by evidence.*
- *"Fundamental shifts in scientific belief occur only when empirical changes are matched by the availability of alternative theoretical commitments"* (Alexander 1983: vol. 1, pp. 30–32).

Given this view, we address questions in this chapter both about how changes in the empirical world of organizations have led to changes in organizational theory, and how theories change the observed world of organizations.

The Power of the Past

Our second guiding assumption is rooted in the institutional perspective and reminds us that we do not begin today, or any day, with a blank slate. While, as Kennedy reminds us, we must be mindful of the sometimes faulty assumptions and blind spots that we inherit from our predecessors, we also benefit by drawing on their insights, models, and methods. It is for this reason that we began the journey of this book with considerable attention devoted to reviewing the work of founding mothers and fathers of our field. In Stark's (1996) metaphor, we build not just "*on* but *with* the ruins" left by our predecessors. This suggests that as we attempt to identify directions and trends that will craft future scholarship, we do not mean to imply that our suggestions are novel or without precedent but rather that, among the many strands of work that make up the tapestry of organizational studies, these seem to be to us the more promising to pursue.

We identify five major trends to which we would lend our support. All of them are currently underway and deserve, we believe, to be nurtured and advanced if organization studies is to remain a vigorous and relevant enterprise into the twenty-first century.

FROM UNITARY TO MULTIPARADIGM

One of us has argued that the field of organization studies emerged from the "cleft rock" provided by the scientific management and the human relations schools (Scott, 2004b: 2–3). This dualistic perspective, enshrined in the rational and natural system perspectives, remains with us up to the present time. But, as we have seen, perspectives on organizations—particularly macrotheory—have become vastly more complex and differentiated during the second half of the twentieth century. Indeed, this is the first "master trend" depicted in our book. From the 1960s to the 1990s, a wide range of competing models or paradigms for studying organizations were proposed, elaborated, and, to varying degrees, tested. We have reviewed theory and research associated with the bounded rationality perspective, contingency theory, transaction costs, resource dependence, sociotechnical systems, organizational ecology, institutional theory, and network approaches, to name only the main contenders (see Table 5–1).

One of the characteristics of much of this work is that analysts often employ language sufficiently general to imply that the ideas are applicable to all types of organizations and to all or most conditions. Grandori (1987), among others, has challenged this assumption, pointing out that some theories are much more applicable to some types of organizations, or situations within or aspects of organizations, than are others. There is also an unfortunate tendency for theorists to overstate both the novelty and scope of their arguments, in part because, as within any science, new ideas are highly prized and rewards are heaped on their creators (Donaldson, 1995).

There is no doubt that the current profusion of multiple competing theoretical perspectives poses difficult problems for all field participants—from beginning students to seasoned scholars. Using our own jargon, one might suggest that we occupy a field with low consensus on field logics—an important sign of low field structuration (see Chapter 10). Using more direct language, Aldrich (1992) labeled the period up to the 1990s as one characterized by "paradigm wars" in which camps of scholars cultivate and advance their own models, attacking the claims and diminishing the contributions of rival camps. There has, indeed, been some of that in our field.

Sources of Multiplicity

Why the proliferation of models in organization studies? Open system theorists assert that systems reflect the complexity of their environments. So, for example, organizations in more complex environments map the complexity of the environment into their own structures. In an analogous way, our mental models reflect the complexity of our social structures. Consider organization studies in this regard. Organizations have been studied from the perspectives of sociology, psychology, political science, economics, history, and anthropology, as well as disciplines outside the social sciences. Scholars bring their disciplinary habits with them to their object of study; thus, political scientists such as March and Simon (1958) focus on institutional design and questions of collective decision making; sociologists such as Blau and Scott (1962) examine authority structures and the distribution of benefits; psychologists such as Katz and Kahn (1978) highlight individual well-being and inter-group relations; and economists like Williamson (1975) orient toward least cost contracting in a competitive environment. Organization studies is thus like a cosmopolitan port city, where traders from diverse lands mingle, haggle, and make exchanges. (Of course, one might also see it as an alloy, made stronger by a deft mixture of components, or a mongrel, containing a random mix of attributes from its ancestors!) As McKinley, Mone, and Moon (1999) point out, our field "is subject to the larger development processes in those disciplines" on which it draws (see also Pfeffer, 1993). Developments in sociology or political science make their way into the study of organizations, and vice versa. Of course, differences *within* these disciplines can also be quite pronounced. One of the most profound differences running through all the social sciences is the epistemological division between objectivists and subjectivists (see Burrell and Morgan, 1979; Baum and Dobbin, 2000).

Organization studies also stands between academia and the world of practice, in business, government, and elsewhere. Academics look to the world outside for problems meriting study, and practitioners look to scholars of organizations for insights into how to do their work more effectively. Some of the most important contributors to organization studies—Warren Bennis, Peter Drucker, Rosabeth Kanter, Henry Mintzberg, Michael Porter, among many others—spent much of their time consulting with businesses and other organizations but established their reputations by contributing to generalized knowledge within organization theory. Professional schools such as schools of business, education, public administration, and engineering provide ready homes for organizational scholars (see Augier, March, and Sullivan, 2005). To reach for another metaphor, professional schools are like the estuaries (not to say swamps) that stand between river and ocean—where practical and theoretical concerns mingle. The major professional association for scholars of organization and management within professional schools, the 16,000-member Academy of Management, now encompasses twenty-four different divisions and interest groups, ranging from Business Policy and Strategy, through International Management, to Organizational Behavior. Organization and Management Theory (OMT), the primary home of "macro" organization theory, includes 3,500 members from dozens of different countries.

Given these diverse locations, backgrounds, and interests, can it be any surprise that we organization scholars inhabit a multiparadigm world?

Proposed Solutions

Given the complexity of the problem posed by multiple paradigms, it is not surprising that the solutions proposed cover a similarly wide range. We do not attempt to consider them all, but comment on major directions for seeking remedy.

At one extreme, an influential contributor to organization studies, Jeffrey Pfeffer, points to all the liabilities associated with a multi- or low-paradigm field and enumerates all the advantages to be obtained from paradigm consensus.

His "success" stories are drawn from economics and from "reforms" underway in political science, as rational choice theorists assume dominance. These fields exhibit and benefit from higher consensus on basic premises. Pfeffer notes that low-paradigm fields suffer, as a consequence, low power and low status in relation to other fields: there is lack of consensus on who should be hired, what articles should be published, what research should be funded. In scientific arenas, such dissensus undercuts competition for support. Pfeffer's solution comes out of his power perspective. Believing that "unity of perspective and the ability to take collective action with ease provides an important source of power" (Pfeffer, 1993: 617), he observes that "consensus is, at least to some degree, created and imposed in those fields or subspecialties in which it exists" (p. 613). His not-quite-explicit recommendation seems to be that some (unnamed) subgroup should settle ongoing disputes and impose unity on our field.

At the opposite extreme, many scholars celebrate paradigm diversity, citing the benefits of multiple perspectives, diverse methodologies, and openness to new ideas. Thus, Canella and Paetzold take issue with Pfeffer's position—both diagnosis and prescription:

> In sharp contrast to Pfeffer, we conclude that a high degree of consensus, however, achieved, suggests that the evolution of knowledge has been slowed, not facilitated . . . we argue that the evolution of knowledge requires fuzzy boundaries and a tolerance of (if not acceptance of) a plurality of paradigms. (1994: 332)

They cite with approval Jevon's (1965 trans.) comment on employing power to increase consensus in scientific matters:

> In matters of philosophy and science authority has ever been the great opponent of truth. A despotic calm is usually the triumph of error. In the republic of the sciences sedition and even anarchy are beneficial in the long run to the greatest happiness of the greatest number. (1965 trans.: 275–76)

A skeptic might point out that ant colonies have the same level of consensus and conformity as certain high-paradigm subfields, not because the queen imposes order from above, but because the constitents hold a highly simplified "worldview" that entails only a handful of extremely simple decision rules. Organizations are acknowledged to be varied and complex systems. Why would one want to suppress this variety, which can be fruitfully explored from differing models, by imposing some kind of arbitrary consensus? Scholars ranging from Burrell and Morgan (1979) to Astley and Van de Ven (1983) to Scott (1981–2003) in the varying editions of his predecessor text on organizations, have defended the value of a multiparadigm approach.

Still, these and other scholars have also seen value in seeking integration and synthesis whenever possible. Lewis and Grimes (1999) catalog some of the ways in which organizational scholars have crafted multiparadigm approaches. We adapt and augment their discussion to suggest the following modes:

- *Multiparadigm bracketing*—attempts to distinguish among and lay bare the assumptions underlying existing approaches. Chapters 2–5 of the current volume illustrates this approach.
- *Parallel studies*—"preserve theoretical conflicts by depicting the organizational voices, images, and interests magnified by opposing lenses" (1999: 675). This *Rashomon*-like strategy was used to good effect by Allison (1971) in his celebrated attempt to explain the Cuban Missile Crisis from three differing perspectives: rational actor, organizational process, and governmental politics.
- *Sequential studies*—in which the "outputs of one paradigm-specific study provide inputs for a subsequent study" (p. 675). For example, Staw's discussion of escalation of commitment to a course of action blends models of bounded rationality together with institutional arguments of commitment to norms for consistency into a process model in which differing phases of the process are reinforced by different arguments (1976; 2005).
- *Interplay studies*—in which differing paradigms are combined, perhaps by nesting or by blending. An example of *nesting* is provided by one of the author's proposals that it would be fruitful to view the field of medical services from a complex multilevel model utilizing institutional arguments at the field level, population ecology arguments at the population level, and strategic management and resource dependence arguments at the health care organization level (Scott, 1993). This synthesis of arguments guided the design of a subsequent study of longitudinal change in health care systems (Scott et al., 2000).[1] We have described numerous instances in researchers' *blending* paradigms in the preceding chapters. For example, Hannan and Carroll's combination of ecological and institutional arguments in the processes underlying density dependence (see Chapter 10); or Oliver's arguments combining resource dependence and institutional arguments to consider strategic responses to institutional pressures (Chapter 10). Chapter 11 describes some of the many ways in which network theory arguments have been blended with resource dependence, transaction costs, ecological, and institutional arguments.

Another, somewhat different alternative to solve the problem of multiple paradigms was proposed by Donald Campbell (1969a), an approach that might be termed *juxtaposition*. Campbell's own label is somewhat more colorful:

> A fish-scale model of omni-science represents the solution . . . [the] slogan is collective comprehensiveness through overlapping patterns of unique narrownesses. Each narrowness is in this analogy a 'fish scale' . . . Our only hope of a comprehensive social science, or other multi-science, lies in a continuous texture of narrow specialties which overlap with other narrow specialties. (1969: 328)

However, as McKelvey and Baum (1999) remind us, such a multiscience only works when each of its 'fish-scales' has scientific credibility in its own right.

---

[1]For additional examples of multilevel theory building, see Klein, Tosi, and Cannella (1999).

More generally, Baum and Dobbin suggest that effective integration of such fragments requires "an epistemology capable of unifying diverse, even seemingly contradictory, approaches," deciding which to discard and which to integrate by juxtaposition (2000: 392). This is not the place nor are we the people, to will provide such an epistemology, but we do add our voices to those calling for the integration, not the suppression, of diversity in organizational paradigms and theories.

FROM MONOCULTURAL TO MULTICULTURAL STUDIES

Our Myopic View

Throughout this volume, with the aid of institutional theorists, we have insisted on the importance of the cultural (and associated cognitive) dimension of organizational life. Our social experience is filtered through cultural lenses. Here we modify the emphasis a bit to focus on the importance of cultural understandings rooted in national systems. Although there exists great variance of cultural experience and expression within most societies, on the one hand, and societies are struggling to maintain relevance in a globalizing world, on the other, nation-states and their associated cultural systems continue to be significant and influential social contexts for organizations.

As Augier and colleagues point out, although organization studies has its roots in social theory spawned primarily in Western Europe in the nineteenth century, the contemporary field is "primarily a creation of a shorter and more parochial history created in the last half of the twentieth century in Anglophone North America" (Augier, March, and Sullivan, 2005: 85). Our knowledge is culturally circumscribed, largely resulting from the work of American scholars with input from Canadian and English colleagues. Moreover, and as a direct consequence, the great bulk of our knowledge rests on the study of contemporary American organizations. (We deal with the implications and limitations of a contemporary focus in the next section.) American organizations have certainly been innovative and influential, often serving as models for organizing around the world, and American organizational scholars have their good points. But do we truly believe that the creation of a well-grounded field of organization studies can be based on such a biased sample of the world's scholars and organizational forms?

Signs of Progress

Fortunately, in recent years, this myopic situation is changing. Surveying progress in organization studies during the last half of the twentieth century, Hickson (1996) reports that for him the event of "most import" was the appearance of genuinely multicultural studies in the early 1980s with the work of scholars such as Hofstede (1984) and Ouchi (1980; 1981). Both researchers were well versed in American scholarship but able to point to important differences in organizing associated with cultural differences. Interestingly, Hofstede, whose catalog of cultural dimensions had been developed in studies of multinational organizations operating primarily in the Western world, was obliged to add a new dimension when the range of informants was expanded to include non-Western organizational participants (Hofstede and Bond, 1988; Hofstede, 1991).[2] With the rise of the Asian Tigers and China to rival Japan, much recent attention has been accorded to organizational forms in East Asia. We have learned in the past few decades how idiosyncratic American corporate forms are. Davis points out:

> Around the world, sovereign and autonomous organizations appeared rare, while long-standing networks and business groups were both common and influential—to understand a given large corporation in most industrial nations required knowing its group membership. (2005a: 481)

Other parts of the world—Latin America, India, the mid-East, and Africa—remain understudied relative to North America, although this is beginning to change (for example, see Khanna and Palepu [2000] on Chilean business groups; Simons and Ingram [1997] on Israeli kibbutzim; Evans [1995] on information technology businesses in Brazil, India, and Korea). As Hickson concludes: in spite of recent positive developments to increase the representativeness of studies, "the geographic flow of research remains predominantly west to east, north to south" (1996: 222).

There are other important indicators of change. Starbuck (1999) reports that although U.S. membership in the Academy of Management, the leading professional association of management and organization scholars, remains a decided majority, since 1980 non-U.S. membership has been increasing at a faster rate than has that of the United States. As of 2006, 35 percent of the Academy of Management's members—44 percent within the Organization and Management Theory division—were at institutions outside the United States. Yet much of the increase is fostered by the spread of U.S.-modeled management schools in foreign locations (see Sahlen-Andersson and Engwall, 2002). Such trends may represent the spread of rationality and enlightenment to the far corners of our globe, but in our opinion, more accurately signals the triumph of a form of cultural "monocropping" based on the "premise that idealized versions of Anglo-American institutions are optimal developmental instruments, regardless of level of development or position in the global economy" (Evans, 2004: 33).

However, in spite of these concerns, we are encouraged by the ascendance of international research attending to diversity at all levels—from the broad range of scholarship devoted to the development of transnational institutions (e.g., Boli and Thomas, 1999; Brunsson and Jacobsson,

---

[2]Based on research using Hofstede's instruments, Bond proposed the addition of a new dimension: Confucian dynamism or, more generally, long-term/short-term orientation.

2000; Djelic and Quack, 2003; Muldoon, 2004), to studies of broad political-economic differences in organizational contexts related to differing world regions (e.g., Garrett, 1998; Hall and Soskice, 2001), to studies of different "recipes" for organizing in particular societies or regional areas (Orrù, Biggart, and Hamilton, 1997; Whitley, 1999), to studies of the density dependence processes in populations of organizations operating across national boundaries (Hannan et al., 1995), to studies of the ways in which institutional factors in local contexts shape structures and strategies for responding to global economic pressures (e.g., Biggart and Guillén, 1999; Guillén, 2001), to studies of how leadership strategies must adapt to differing cultural contexts (e.g., House et al., 2004). As Dacin, Ventresca, and Beal point out:

> Central principles of economic rationality vary dramatically across countries and time. Comparative/institutional studies of economic organization give evidence of how political, cultural, and social institutions organize features of competitive markets (i.e., property rights, institutional and legal elements, economic actors, network forms and governance, and control mechanisms. (1999: 323)

All of this work represents, in a larger sense, ways in which organizational scholars are moving in the direction of "a more contextualized approach to the study of organizations and management" (Dacin, Ventresca, and Beal, 1999: 318). Our field increasingly attends to the embeddedness of organizational structures and processes in their local as well as wider contexts, the ways in which they are affected by differences in space and time—and it is to the latter that we now turn.

FROM PRESENT-CENTERED TO LONGITUDINAL AND HISTORICAL ANALYSIS

It's About Time

It continues to be the case that up to the present, the great bulk of scholarship on organizations rests on research conducting on existing organizations examined cross-sectionally or over a brief period of time. Although political scientist Paul Pierson (2004) addresses his challenge to economists and political scientists, his concerns apply with equal force to students of organizations. Pierson observed:

> Especially in economics and political science, the time horizons of most analysts have become increasingly restricted. Both in what we seek to explain and in our search for explanations, we focus on the immediate—we look for causes and outcomes that are both temporally contiguous and rapidly unfolding. In the process, we miss a lot. There are important things that we do not see at all, and what we do see we often misunderstand. (2004: 79)

Pierson points out that many important causal processes exhibit a "long time horizon" either in the time it takes for pressures for change to build up or in the time it takes for effects to be observable. To attend to such processes is not to treat history as simply "a study of the past."

Still, even in this more limited sense, there is much to be learned from studying the past. We have tried to illustrate throughout this volume, but particularly in the previous chapter, that organizations have changed dramatically over time. The ingredients for making organizations vary over time, as do the uses to which they are put. We have learned much from the relatively small set of business historians, social historians, historical sociologists—Chandler (1977), Heilbroner (1977), Jacoby (1985), Roy (1997), Micklethwait and Wooldridge (2003), and Thompson (1968), among others—about how organizations and organizational life were conducted in different eras. Moreover, as we have pointed out, many of the pre- and early-industrial forms are still scattered across the landscape, bearing their birthmarks and retaining many of their original forms and ways. There could usefully be a parallel field of organizational archeology to put alongside the existing field of industrial archeology.

Pierson again: "The best case for connecting history to the social sciences is neither empirical nor methodological, but theoretical. We turn to an examination of history because social life unfolds over time. Real social processes have distinctly temporal dimensions" (2004: 5). Recognition of this truth has led to the increasing use of "process" over "variance" approaches in the social sciences generally and organizational studies, specifically, in recent years. In 1982, Mohr usefully differentiated between variance and process theories. *Variance theories* focus attention on characteristics of actors or situations, treating them as abstract variables and examining the extent of their interdependence. *Process theories* deal with "a series of occurrences of events rather that a set of relations among variables" (1982: 54). While variance questions focus on *why* things happen—what factors were associated with the observed characteristics of the phenomena of interest, process theories address the question of *how* the observed effects happened. The latter approach "assumes that 'history matters,' that how things occur influences what things happen" (Scott, 2001a: 93). As our field has matured, a growing number of studies utilize historical or longitudinal data sets that emphasize the unfolding of events over time; and many scholars supplement their cross-sectional data with case studies or interviews with informants to shed light on how the results were produced.

The previous chapter highlighted another reason to attend to history: understanding the turns taken at particular points help us explain where we are today, and why organizations look the way they do. This need not be true. If strong environmental pressures select out organizations and institutions that are not fit, then the failed forms that litter the path that got us here are of little interest. But as we have seen, there are critical periods in which choices are made that shape subsequent history, and the outcomes vary by society. How a society organized the railroad industry laid the tracks for the development of markets and the organization of subsequent industries (Chandler, 1977; Dobbin, 1994b). Whether major enterprises were initially funded by banks or by stock markets laid the groundwork for the subsequent development of the nation's system of corporate governance (Roe, 1994; Roy, 1997). When a city grew up—before or after the advent of automotive and air transport—shaped the norms of local corporate structures that continue to influence start-ups today (Marquis, 2003). And "The conditions under which a nation industrializes leave a permanent legacy to its political and economic institutions and to the relation between them" (Vogel, 1978). Some of the most engaging recent work has examined just such turning points in organizational history, and we are encouraged to see more.

Social Mechanisms

In the past few years, there has been a flurry of interest in the study of "social mechanisms." For many sociologists, an interest in mechanisms can be traced back to the writing of Robert K. Merton, who discussed mechanisms in terms of the structures and processes that meet functional requirements of system maintenance (e.g., Merton, 1957: 341–53). Later theorists have dropped the functionalist assumptions. Thus, Coleman argued that social mechanisms are "sometime true theories" that provide "an intermediary level of analysis in-between pure description and story-telling, on the one hand, and universal social laws, on the other" (1964: 516). Somewhat later, Stinchcombe (1991) suggested that mechanisms be treated as tracing the connections between more general entities, such as organizations, and the subprocesses that account for their features. More generally and graphically, Elster (1987) regarded them as the "nuts and bolts" of social processes, which Hernes later amends to the "cogs and wheels . . . the wheelwork or agency by which an effect is produced" (1998: 74).

These notions have found much resonance with recent theorists, in particular, institutional scholars. Emphasizing attention to mechanisms has been particularly salutary for this group who, in their early work emphasizing macro-institutional pressures, tended to neglect questions of agency—who is exerting pressure—and mechanisms—how are these pressures being transmitted (see DiMaggio, 1988; Clemens, 1993; Scott, 1987; Schneiberg and Clemens, forthcoming). The developing productive connections between institutional-organizational theorists and social movement theorists have help to fuel these interests (Davis et al., 2005). In their iconoclastic argument that attempts to move social movement theory away from (their own previous) relatively static polity-protest group models to focus more on dynamic processes, McAdam, Tarrow, and Tilly reinforce the need to attend to mechanisms—"a delimited class of events that alter relations among specified sets of elements in identical or closely similar ways over a variety of situations"—to processes—"regular sequences of such mechanisms that produce similar . . . transformations of those elements"—and to "episodes"—collections of two more processes that together define a situation of interest to the analyst (2001: 24–32). They propose a rough typology:

- *Environmental mechanisms*—external, contextual influences, for example, changes in the political opportunity structure
- *Cognitive mechanisms*—processes of conceptualization and interpretation, for example, framing processes, diffusion and translation of ideas
- *Relational mechanisms*—that affect the connections among individuals, groups and organizations, for example, network cultivation, brokerage

These and similar mechanisms are discussed and illustrated in Campbell (2004: chap. 2; 2005); Hedstrom and Swedberg (1998); McAdam, Tarrow, and Tilly (2001); and Stinchcombe (2002). Davis and Marquis (2005b) assert that "mechanism-based" theorizing is particularly appropriate for understanding the world of organizations in rapidly changing times, such as we are now experiencing.

As in any scientific field, there is a tension between grand theorizing and "bench science" in organization studies. The rewards often seem to go to those who generate novel theory (Donaldson, 1995) or manage to coin a felicitous phrase that catches on widely. But grand unifying theories about organizations cannot precede the accumulation of diverse observations. "Perhaps sociology is not yet ready for its Einstein because it has not yet found its Kepler—to say nothing of its Newton, Laplace, Gibbs, Maxwell or Planck" (Merton, 1968: 47). Again, following Merton, "sociology will advance insofar as its major (but not exclusive) concern is with developing theories of the middle range, and it will be retarded if its primary attention is focussed on developing total sociological systems" (1968: 50–51). Thus, small-t theory about middle-range organizational phenomena provide the best path forward—and the world obliges us with new puzzles almost daily.

Longitudinal Studies

Recent decades have witnessed an upsurge within organization studies of the use of longitudinal studies of over-time data. Both theoretical and methodological advances have fueled interest in such approaches. Foremost on the theory side are the emergence of ecological/evolutionary models of organizations, in particular population ecology and institutional theories. In their formative early studies, from the mid-1970s, population ecologists assembled data sets to study the development (growth and decline) of particular populations of organizations (see Chapter 10). Almost from the beginning, ecological theorists criticized the approach of most students of organization, who concentrated their research attention on the largest and longest lived organizations, thereby ignoring "the full range of variation along these dimensions" (Hannan and Freeman, 1989: 154; see also, Aldrich, 1999).

To correct the bias inherent in studying only the largest and most successful players, they searched out data that would allow them an overview of the history of an entire organizational population—all organizations of a kind that had ever existed—from the creation of the form to the present. Incomplete or truncated data sets bias findings regarding the dynamics of population processes (see Carroll and Hannan, 1989).

To broaden the purview to consider the full range of organizations of a given type provided clear advantages. However, although ecologists collected data over time regarding their populations (for example, changes in population density), too often these data registered only the passing of time, neglecting the relevance of "historical time"—exogenous conditions obtaining in the environment at differing points of time that could affect the population processes of interest (Zucker, 1989). Some ecologists, notably, Baum (e.g., Baum and Oliver, 1991), Carroll (Delacroix and Carroll, 1983), and Haveman (Haveman and Rao, 1997) have attended to the effects of historical events in their analyses, but this has not been the norm in ecological research.

Although institutional theorists studying organizations focused, in the early stages of their work, on "institutional effects"—the impact of institutional environmental conditions on organizational forms at a particular point in time—the agenda was gradually reframed to examine "institutional processes"—the ways in which changing institutional conditions interact with changing organizational structures and responses (Scott, 2001a). This time-sensitive approach had its beginning in the early diffusion studies, for example, Tolbert and Zucker (1983) comparing differences between early and late adopters of reform, but gradually turned to larger patterns of change. These efforts began in the 1990s with the work of scholars such as DiMaggio (1991) and Dezaley and Garth (1996), who examined the construction of new institutional forms and their organizational implications, and has continued up to the present with a growing number of studies of institutional change (e.g., Barley, 1986; Greenwood and Hinings, 1993; Haveman and Rao, 1997), institutional conflict (e.g., Hoffman, 1997; Scott et al., 2000), and institutional decline (Greve, 1995; Sine and Tolbert, 2006). (See also Chapter 10.)

On the methodological side, many important advances in the analysis of dynamic processes have come to the fore. These include, but are not limited to, the use of event-history models and the development of sequence analysis techniques (Abbott, 2001; Petersen, 1993; Tuma and Hannan, 1984). These and related statistical tools have been productively employed in organizational research. More generally, in a valuable contribution, Ventresca and Mohr differentiate between three approaches to longitudinal studies:

- *Historiographic approaches*—the employment of historical materials to examine the "rich details of organizational life," including studies of individual organizations or organizational practices.
- *Ecological approaches*—the employment of "small amounts of information gleaned from the life history of large numbers of organizations," to examine the dynamics of organizational environments, organizational fields, or organizational

populations. This approach has been fruitfully employed by population ecologists as well as by institutional theorists.

- *New archival approaches*—employment of formal analytic methodologies to directly examine organizational relations and processes, including "measuring the shared forms of meaning" that underlie them (2002: 807–10).

The new methods attend more to process than structure, and to relations rather than objects. A strong example of these "new" approaches is provided by the study by Mohr and Guerra-Pearson (forthcoming) who examined the emergence of differentiated types of welfare organizations at the turn of the nineteenth century employing archival data on types of client needs served, solution repertoires offered, and the status or "merit" of their clients. Conflicts and negotiations among competing, more generalist forms, resulted in the emergence of more differentiated and specialized forms. A second example of the imaginative use of new archivalist approaches has already been described in Chapter 10: Rao's (2003) analysis of changes in the menus of leading restaurants as an indicator of "revolutionary" change in French gastronomy—for example, the displacement of classical with nouvelle cuisine.

Again, we conclude that a desirable shift from synchronic to diachronic approaches to the study of organizations is well underway.

FROM MICRO- TO MACRO UNITS AND LEVELS OF ANALYSIS

This inclination should come as no surprise to the readers of preceding chapters. One of the overriding trends—the second of two "master trends"— that characterizes developments in organizational studies during the past half century is the relentless move by organizations to more macrounits and by theorists to more macrolevels of analysis.

Levels of Units

Throughout this volume, but especially in Chapter 13, we have taken note of changes in the levels at which organizations operate. From an earlier, simpler time when all organizations (like politics) were local, situated in specific geographically delimited contexts, we now find ourselves in a world in which the reach of many organizations is worldwide. While there are still many—probably most—organizations that operate in a single, restricted locale, they now share space with different types operating in wider arenas— state, region, national, transnational, and global. Moreover, an increasing number of organizations situated in our local communities, are connected— as branches, franchises, local offices—to larger corporate systems. Astute analysts of changes in the American community, such as Warren (1972) noted long ago a shift in the structure of community relations from a predominantly "horizontal pattern," involving connections with other organizations that exist at the same (local) level, to the ascendance of a "vertical pattern," involving relations between localized units and nonlocal actors who, because they exercise ownership or control, take precedence over local connections. He concludes that American communities have undergone a "great change" that entails the "increasing orientation of local community units toward extra-community systems of which they are a part, with a corresponding decline in community cohesion and autonomy" (1972: 53).

This development is not entirely new. One pair of commentators described a familiar pattern of globalization:

> All old established national industries have been destroyed or are daily being destroyed. They are dislodged by new industries, whose introduction becomes a life and death question for all civilised nations, by industries that no longer work up indigenous raw material, but raw material drawn from the remotest zones; industries whose products are consumed, not only at home, but in every quarter of the globe. In place of the old wants, satisfied by the productions of the country, we find new wants, requiring for their satisfaction the products of distant lands and climes.

This was, of course, Marx and Engels, writing in 1848!

As local connections are in decline, developments at higher levels have accelerated. As Chandler and others have chronicled the rise of industrial firms with a national reach (see Chapter 13), political analysts, such as Berry (1989) have observed the remarkable rise in the number and influence of interest groups and trade associations that operate primarily at the national level. And, as discussed elsewhere (Chapter 10), rapid growth has occurred in the number of organizations and associations operating at the international level (Boli and Thomas, 1999; Smith, 2005). Industrial and multinational concerns, with their agenda of development and modernization, are increasingly confronted by social and political movements effectively mobilized at the international level (Khagram, 2004; Smith, 2005). Organizational units are now effectively represented at international, national, state, and local levels.

Levels of Analysis

We have been even more attentive in this volume to the shift over time in the level of analysis at which organizational systems and processes are framed. We described in Chapter 5, the emergence of such constructs as organization "sets," "populations," and "fields." More generally, as open system conceptions took hold, we have emphasized the shift from "dyadic" models privileging a focal actor's immediate organizational environment to broader conceptions linked to ecological, institutional, or network conceptions addressing the increasing extent to which the environment of organizations is itself organized.

Throughout many of the previous chapters of this volume, we have emphasized the value of studies conducted at the organization field level. The major reason for this elevation in level of analysis is the simple fact that the boundaries of today's organizations are no longer stable or fixed, but transitory and flexible, and that they no longer circumscribe all of the actors and processes of interest. This is true not just for individual organizations but for organizational populations, whose forms over time are recognized to erode, expand, and merge with related forms. Population ecologists have had to acknowledge that "the clarity of a set of boundaries is not a permanent property of a set of classifications"—that over time the boundaries delimiting organizational forms shift as a consequence of both segregating and blending processes, as new forms arise, undergo random drift, recombination, and deinstitutionalization (Hannan and Freeman, 1989: 57–58). Scott (2004a: 297) points out that only the field level allows an investigator to consider changes over time in the boundaries of individual organizations, in relations among diverse organizations, in the nature, variety, and distribution of organizational forms (populations)—including the emergence of new forms—in social logics, in governance systems unpinning field structure, and in the boundaries of the field itself.

Yes, not only the components but also the boundaries of fields and industries also undergo change. Davis describes some of the processes at work:

> Boundaries around industries similarly became more difficult to locate, as deregulation and new technologies encouraged permeability. Telecommunications, information technology, computers, software, and media blurred into an amorphous metaindustry; insurance, commercial banking, and investment banking morphed into 'financial services.' New industries drew on models and personnel from old while engaging in distinctively new forms of activity (e.g., in biotech and web design). And even determining whether a company was engaged in "manufacturing" or "service" proved increasingly difficult . . . . (2005a: 480)

In order to accommodate these sorts of challenges, organization-institutional theorists have adjusted and broadened the original conception of field (see Chapter 10) in various ways. For example, Hoffman has proposed that for some analytic purposes, instead of treating fields as formed around a common product or market, fields are often

> formed around the issues that become important to the interests and objectives of a specific collection of organizations. Issues define what the field is, making links that may not have previously been present. . . . Conceptualizing a field as centered around issues rather than networks reveals great complexity in field formation and evolution. (1999: 352)

Hoffman utilized this conception is his analysis of the shifting fields involving relations between environmental groups, regulatory and judicial agencies and U.S. petroleum and chemical industries (1997; see also Chapter 10). Hoffman's use of the field concept is resonant with Bourdieu's conception of field as "a space in which a game takes place, a field of objective relations between individuals or institutions who are competing for the same stake" (Bourdieu and Wacquant, 1992: 97). A second example of an altered field conception is provided by Fligstein's (1990) analysis of the transformation of large corporate forms in the United States during the twentieth century, described in Chapter 13. As corporations during this period began to diversity, shifting from a grounding in a single industry to participation in multiple fields and markets, instead of orienting themselves to other firms in one or another product line, large corporations began to construct a new field around organizations like themselves—large, multidivisional corporations. These firms provided both the major source of competition as well as models to emulate—providing "firms with evidence of appropriate strategies and structures and define acceptable courses of action" (1990:19).

In dealing with the related, but even more complex, problems posed by multinational corporations—operating in multiple fields and countries—Westney proposes a solution similar to that adopted by Fligstein. She observes:

> If a single organization straddles two or more organizational fields, the research can focus on how the organization copes with different and potentially contradictory isomorphic pulls. But when a number of organizations cross the same organizational fields, do not the boundaries of the field begin to change?
>
> . . . Institutional theory gives us reason to expect that global industries constitute organizational fields whose boundaries have come to transcend national borders. (1993: 61–63)

Westney goes on to speculate that there is increasing evidence to suggest that "global industries *in toto* constitute a single organizational field" (p. 63), as they engage in competitive benchmarking and lobby for similar types of trade agreements.

While the concept of organization field may not be the last word in our ongoing attempts to circumscribe the relevant system for study, to date it has proved a valuable and malleable instrument in our analytic toolkit.

FROM STRUCTURE TO PROCESS

Open systems imagery does not simply loosen the more conventional views of the structural features of organizations, as discussed in Chapter 4: it substitutes process for structure. Whether viewed at the more abstract level through concepts such as enacting, selecting, and retaining processes, or at the more concrete level with concepts such as input, throughput, and output production flows and feedback-control loops, the emphasis is on organizing as against organization. Maintaining these flows and preserving these processes are viewed as problematic. As Weick insists, "processes are repetitive only if this repetitiveness is continuously accomplished" (1969: 36). Both morphostatic and morphogenetic processes are of interest: many processes are reproductive; others are not recurrent cycles, but actions that change existing routines and arrangements.

Changing Conceptions of Structure

A process view is taken not only of the internal operations of the organization, but of the organization itself as a system persisting over time. Much of the work rests on an evolutionary theory foundation. The organization as an arrangement of roles and relationships is not the same today as it was yesterday or will be tomorrow: to survive is to adapt, and to adapt is to change. As Leavitt, Dill, and Eyring conclude:

> The complex organization is more like a modern weapons system than like old-fashioned fixed fortifications, more like a mobile than a static sculpture, more like a computer than an adding machine. In short, the organization is a dynamic system. (1973: 4)

This kind of view has been slow to develop. All of the definitions underlying the modern field of organization studies emphasized organizations as bounded social entities capable of autonomous action (see rational and natural systems definitions reviewed in Chapter 1). A major body of empirical research during the 1960s and early 1970s was devoted to the comparative analysis of structure examining either similar of diverse organizational forms (see Blau and Schoenherr, 1971; Pugh and Hickson, 1976). Reflecting on this period, Hickson notes that it was not until the next decade, the 1980s, that a concentration on form and structure began to transmute into an examination of " 'survival strategies' for the structured entity" (1996: 219).

A set of distinctions proposed by Mustafa Emirbayer (1997) for describing general changes in conceptions of social structure helps illuminate parallel changes occurring in the more specialized area of organization studies (see also, Scott, 2001a). Emirbayer differentiates between substantialist and relational definitions, noting two subtypes of the former.

- *Substantialist self-action definitions*—As applied to organizations, such conceptions emphasize the independence of organizations, stressing those features that distinguish organizations from other types of social organizations. As noted, such conceptions, including those of Weber, March, and Simon, and Blau and Scott, provided the founding definitions of our field.
- *Substantialist interaction definitions*—These are the conceptions that emerged soon after the introduction of open system models. Organizations are treated as discrete units but recognized to possess attributes that vary in response to changing circumstances, whether technical, political, transactional, or institutional.

Systems design, contingency theorists, transaction cost economists, and resource dependence scholars continue to embrace a substantialist conception of organizations but shift from the "self-action" to a more *interactional conception* viewing organizations as "fixed entities having variable attributes" that interact to create diverse outcomes (Emirbayer, 1997: 286). These theories provided a halfway house within which many early open system theorists gathered—and many are still there. Reflecting on these interactive models,

Bidwell and Kasarda argue that such theorists did not fully embrace open system models, but were rather "control" theorists, an intermediate category between open and closed. They assert that although such theories

> purport to be open-system formulations of structuring in organizations . . . they retain certain assumptions akin to those of close-system theory, namely that (1) organizations are strongly bounded, (2) stability is essential within this boundary, and (3) organizational form is primarily a consequence of managerial decision making. (1985: 1–2)

In a similar vein, as noted in Chapter 4, Pondy and Mitroff observed that too many "open-system" models took the position that organizations must defend themselves against environmental complexity, failing to recognize that "it is precisely throughput of nonuniformity that preserves the differential structure of an open organization" (1979: 7). These critiques seem basically correct to us.

- *Relational or process definitions*—recognize that organizations are "inseparable from the transactional contexts in which they are embedded" (Emirbayer 1997: 287).

Relational conceptions began to emerge in organizations relatively soon after the open system revolution and have gradually increased in variety and numbers over time. To our knowledge, the earliest scholar to adopt a process view was social psychologist, Karl Weick (1969/1979; see also Chapter 4), who, following Bateson's (1972) lead urged his colleagues to "stamp out nouns!" (Weick, 1974: 358). Weick continues:

> The word, organization, is a noun, and it is also a myth. If one looks for an organization one will not find it. What will be found is that there are events, linked together, that transpire within concrete walls and these sequences, their pathways, their timing, are the forms we erroneously make into substances when we talk about an organization. (1974: 358)

Rather than focusing on organizations and their structural features, Weick proposes:

> Instead, assume that there are processes which create, maintain, and dissolve social collectivities, that these processes constitute the work of organizing, and the ways in which these processes are continuously executed *are* the organization. (1969: 1)

At about the same time, Silverman (1971), in the United Kingdom proposed an interpretive framework, suggesting that the dominant "system" view of organizations should be replaced with an "action" based model. And soon thereafter, Burrell and Morgan (1979), also scholars in the United Kingdom distinguished between dominant organizational paradigms that stressed stability and order versus those focusing on change.

These somewhat isolated and distant voices from England got a substantial assist from the work of their compatriot Anthony Giddens, one of the most prominent and productive social theorists of our time. As discussed at several points in this volume, Giddens's (1979; 1984) proposal to replace a focus on structures with attention to *structuration* processes has been hugely influential in organization studies, particularly among institutional scholars. For Giddens, structures exist only to the extent that they are continually reproduced by the repetitive actions of participants. Working to overcome the gap between structuralists and theorists emphasizing the agency of actors, Giddens emphasized the "duality" of structure—as both "outcome" of and "context" for ongoing behaviors which work to both maintain and change existing patterns of action.

Recent decades have witnessed a proliferation of process approaches to organizations, ranging from behavioral economists to phenomenologists. Prominent examples include

- organizations as shifting coalitions of participants (Cyert and March, 1963)
- organizations as shifting relational networks (Burt, 1982; Nohria and Eccles, 1992)
- organizations as a "nexus of contracts" (Jensen and Meckling, 1976)
- organizations as a fluid "network of treaties" (Powell, 2001)
- organizations as "portfolios of financial assets" (Fligstein, 1990; Davis, Diekmann, and Tinsley, 1994)
- organizations as ongoing narratives of conversations among participants (Czarniawska, 1997)

In sum, relational approaches applied to organizations

> celebrate process over structure, becoming over being. What is being processed varies greatly. In some versions it is symbols and words, in others, relationships or contracts, in still others, assets. But in relational approaches, if structures exist it is because they are continually being created and recreated, and if the world has meaning, it is because actors are constructing and reconstructing intensions and accounts, and thereby, their own and others' identities. (Scott, 2001b: 10913)

Having reviewed, and taken a position on, major trends now underway in organizational studies, let us conclude with a comment on two "outstanding" issues in our field: (1) the problem of organizational boundaries, and (2) the relative priority of theory and empirical events in shaping our work. These are two matters on which your co-authors have taken differing positions.

The Boundary Problem

From the very beginning of our field, many theorists have emphasized the vital role played by organization boundaries. One of us (the sober grey-beard) has argued that "all collectivities—including informal groups, communities, organizations, and entire societies—possess, by definition, boundaries that distinguish them from other systems" (Scott, 2003: 186). To which the other (the brash young Turk) responds: "In many contexts—particularly in high-technology and cultural production industries—seeking to distinguish separate organizations [is] like trying to separate out distinct lumps in a bowl of oatmeal" (Davis, 2005a: 480).

There is no question but that the world of organizations circa 2000 is vastly different from that of 1950 or 1900. We have tried to chronicle the many changes that differentiate the past from the present and future of organizations and organizing processes, with an emphasis on boundary setting and spanning processes. These include

- Replacement of internalization with externalization strategies (see Chapter 7)
- The increased mobility of the labor force and its more contingent connection between worker and employer (see Chapter 7)
- The replacement of structures designed to insure independence with those designed to manage interdependence (see Chapter 6)
- The increasing mobility of organizations, so that they increasingly select the environments in which they operate (see Chapter 13)
- The replacement of earlier communication modes (simultaneous, face-to-face) by new ICT developments (asynchronous, distant) (see Chapter 7)
- The gradual breakdown of the public/private–profit/nonprofit distinctions (see Chapter 11)

This represents a lot of change to apprehend and accommodate as we modify our view of organizations/organizing in the present world.

But what do all of these changes say about the central concept of "boundaries"? It surely is the case, as we have argued throughout, that we must modify earlier ideas of strong and fixed boundaries to allow for much more flexibility. But, as noted, as the physical and territorial markers for delimiting boundaries have relaxed or disappeared, other indicators— normative, cognitive (e.g., shared beliefs, identities)—may still be serviceable and become more salient. Moreover, in an instructive response to organizational theorists Powell, Stark, and Westney, who describe the volatile world of networked organizations (in DiMaggio, 2001), Kraakman suggests that under such conditions legal boundaries become all the more important:

> On the level of legal forms, there is no evidence that the firm—the corporate form—is in any danger of being displaced. Indeed, the network structures explored by the principal contributors to this volume overwhelmingly depend on the legal attributes of the corporate form . . .
> . . . corporations are essential as hitching posts in larger networks of supply contracts and joint ventures. As the 'nexus of contracts' metaphor suggests, one of the most important functions of the corporation is precisely to provide a durable point of legal attachment for the wider network of participants behind every firm." (2001: 158, 159)

The boundary debate will no doubt continue into the foreseeable future, but it does seem premature at this point to announce the arrival of the "boundaryless" organization.

The Rhythm of Field Development

No scientific field develops in a predictable or orderly manner. After all, if, as Merton suggested, science is a system of "organized skepticism," then how could it be otherwise? All of the uncertain and shifting processes that characterize organizational field development also apply to any scientific field: we would expect to see periods of quiescence and tranquility followed by periods of "destructive creation" and spurts of "punctuated equilibrium." In addition, given our postpositivist persuasion, we would also expect to see periods in which theoretical frameworks and models dominate and drive progress in the field followed by periods in which empirical events are in the saddle. As noted at the outset of this chapter, theoretical models and empirical facts are inexorably "joined at the hip," but that does not preclude the possibility that in some periods one or another emphasis exerts more leverage on the direction of our work.

Davis and Marquis (2005b) suggest that during the last decade, organization studies have shifted from "paradigm-driven" to "problem-driven" work. While there is merit in this observation, it is also incumbent on us—particularly at the end of a lengthy book—to take a longer perspective. If one reviews the history of organization studies throughout the twentieth century, one can discern a rhythm, an ebb and flow, in which our field seems to move back and forth between more theory-driven and more problem-driven periods. We know that we enjoyed a highly fertile period of theoretical growth in the early 1900s, with the work of Weber, Michels, Simmel, and Taylor, among others. From the 1930s to the 1950s, the field seems to have been more empirically driven with attention to field studies of workers, work groups, and managerial activities, for example, the work of Mayo, Roethlisberger, and others. The 1950s saw the rise of structural sociology at Columbia and the seminal contributions of Simon and the Carnegie School; and, of course, the 1970s witnessed the highly productive period when many of the paradigms central to our field were developed. It does not seem surprising, then, that we find ourselves today in a period of consolidation and stocktaking, with more attention being given to empirical developments or "problems."

In a thoughtful, but neglected, discussion of trends over time in U.S. policy and political processes, Brown (1983) discusses the pattern traced by periods of liberal regimes in which "breakthrough" policies abound and governmental programs grow followed by periods of more conservative regimes in which "rationalizing" policies are pursued and previous programs are retrenched or reformed. The policies at time one and their associated programs provide the agenda for time two. And only when new kinds of problems emerge do we witness another period of innovation and breakthrough. Brown's observations provide, we believe, a helpful analogy for viewing developments in our own field. Having recently experienced a time of remarkable theoretical growth, it should not be surprising that we find ourselves today in a period of consolidation and stocktaking, or that much current theoretical work addresses problems or limitations in previous theory.

To conclude on a postpositivist note, even work that is problem-driven is, nevertheless, theory-ridden. The world we observe is watched through theory-tinted lenses. Hopefully, the lenses we use will improve our focus, not distort our subject.

References

Abbott, Andrew (1988). *The System of Professions: An Essay on the Division of Expert Labor.* Chicago: University of Chicago Press.

——— (2001). *Time Matters: On Theory and Method.* Chicago: University of Chicago Press.

Abegglen, James C. (1958). *The Japanese Factory: Aspects of Its Social Organization.* Glencoe, IL.: Free Press.

Abrahamson, Eric, and Gregory Fairchild (1999). "Management Fashion: Lifecycles, Triggers, and Collective Learning Processes," *Administrative Science Quarterly* 44:708–40.

Abrahamson, Eric, and Charles J. Fombrun (1994). "Macro-cultures: Determinants and Consequences," *Academy of Management Review,* 19:728–55.

Abzug, Rikki, and Stephen J. Mezias (1993). "The Fragmented State and Due Process Protections in Organizations: The Case of Comparable Worth," *Organization Science* 4:433–53.

Achen, Christopher H. (1986). *The Statistical Analysis of Quasi-Experiments.* Berkeley: University of California Press.

Acker, Joan (1990). "Hierarchies, Jobs, Bodies: A Theory of Gendered Organizations," *Gender & Society,* 4:139–58.

Adler, Paul S. (1990). "Managing High-tech Processes: The Challenge of CAD/CAM," in *Managing Complexity in High-Technology Industries, Systems and People,* ed. M. A. Von Glinow and S. A. Mohrman. Oxford: Oxford University Press.

Agger, Ben (1991). "Critical Theory, Poststructuralism, Postmodernism: Their Sociological Relevance," *Annual Review of Sociology,* 17:105–31.

Ahmadjian, Christina L., and Patricia Robinson (2001). "Safety in Numbers: Downsizing and the Deinstitutionalization of Permanent Employment in Japan," *Administrative Science Quarterly,* 46:622–54.

Ahuja, Gautam (2000). "Collaboration Networks, Structural Holes, and Innovation: A Longitudinal Study," *Administrative Science Quarterly,* 45:425–55.

Albert, Stuart, and David A. Whetten (1985). "Organizational Identity," in *Research in Organizational Behavior,* 14:263–95, ed. L. L. Cummings and Barry Staw. Greenwich, CT: JAI Press.

Albrow, Martin (1970). *Bureaucracy.* New York: Praeger.

Alchian, Armen R., and Harold Demsetz (1972). "Production, Information Costs, and Economic Organization," *American Economic Review,* 62:777–95.

Aldrich, Howard E. (1979). *Organizations and Environments.* Upper Saddle River, NJ: Prentice Hall.

——— (1992). "Incommensurable Paradigms? Vital Signs from Three Perspectives," in *Rethinking Organization: New Directions in Organization Theory and Analysis,* 17–45, ed. Michael Reed and Michael Hughes. Newbury Park, CA: Sage.

——— (1999). *Organizations Evolving.* Thousand Oaks, CA: Sage.

———— 2005. "Entrepreneurship," in *The Handbook of Economic Sociology* (2nd ed.), 451–77, ed. Neil J. Smelser and Richard Swedberg. Princeton and New York: Princeton University Press and Russell Sage Foundation.

Aldrich, Howard E., and S. Mueller (1982). "The Evolution of Organizational Forms: Technology, Coordination, and Control," in *Research in Organizational Behavior* 4:33–87, ed. Barry M. Staw and L. L. Cummings. Greenwich, CT: JAI Press.

Aldrich, Howard E., and Jeffrey Pfeffer (1976). "Environments of Organizations," *Annual Review of Sociology*, 2:79–105.

Aldrich, Howard E., and Martin Ruef (2006). *Organizations Evolving*. (2nd ed.). Thousand Oaks, CA: Sage.

Alexander, Jeffrey C. (1983). *Theoretical Logic in Sociology*, vols. 1–4. Berkeley: University of California Press.

Alexander, Victoria D. (1996). "Pictures at an Exhibition: Conflicting Pressures in Museums and the Display of Art," *American Journal of Sociology*, 101:797–839.

Allen, Thomas J. (1984). *Managing the Flow of Technology: Technology Transfer and the Dissemination of Technological Information within the R&D Organization*. Cambridge MA: MIT Press.

Allen, William T. (1992). "Our Schizophrenic Conception of the Business Corporation," *Cardozo Law Review* 14:261–281.

Allison, Graham T. (1971). *Essence of Decision: Explaining the Cuban Missile Crisis*. Boston: Little, Brown.

Althauser, Robert P. (1989). "Internal Labor Markets," *Annual Review of Sociology*, 15:143–61.

Alvesson, Mats (1987). *Organization Theory and Technocratic Consciousness: Rationality, Ideology, and Quality of Work*. New York: de Gruyter.

Alvesson, Mats, and Stanley Deetz (1996). "Critical Theory and Postmodernism Approaches to Organizational Studies," in *Handbook of Organization Studies*, 191–217, ed. Stewart R. Clegg, Cynthia Hardy, and Walter R. Nord. Thousand Oaks, CA: Sage.

Anand, N., and Richard A. Peterson (2000). "When Market Information Constitutes Fields: Sensemaking of Markets in the Commercial Music Industry," *Organization Science*, 11:260–84.

Ancona, Deborah, Thomas Kochan, Maureen Scully, John Van Maanen, and D. Eleanor Westney (1996). *Managing for the Future: Organizational Behavior and Processes*. Cincinnati, OH: South-Western College Publishing.

Anderson, Bo, Joseph Berger, Bernard P. Cohen, and Morris Zelditch, Jr. (1966). "Status Classes in Organizations," *Administrative Science Quarterly*, 11:264–83.

Appelbaum, Eileen, and Rosemary Batt (1994). *The New American Workplace: Transforming Work Systems in the United States*. Ithaca, NY: ILR Press of Cornell University Press.

Arendt, Hannah (1963). *Eichmann in Jerusalem*. New York: Viking.

Argyris, Chris (1957). *Personality and Organization*. New York: Harper.

———— (1973). "Personality and Organization Theory Revisited," *Administrative Science Quarterly*, 18:141–67.

———— (1982). *Reasoning, Learning and Action: Individual and Organizational*. San Francisco: Jossey-Bass.

Armour, Henry Ogden, and David J. Teece (1978). "Organizational Structure and Economic Performance: A Test of the Multidivisional Hypothesis," *Bell Journal of Economics*, 9:106–22.

Arrow, Kenneth J. (1974). *The Limits of Organization*. New York: W. W. Norton.

Arthur, Michael B., and Denise M. Rousseau, eds. (1996). *The Boundaryless Career: A New Employment Principle for a New Organizational Era*. New York: Oxford University Press.

Ashby, W. Ross (1952). *A Design for a Brain*. New York: John Wiley.

———— (1956). "The Effect of Experience on a Determinant System," *Behavioral Science*, 1:35–42.

———— (1968). "Principles of the Self-Organizing System," in *Modern Systems Research for the Behavioral Scientist*, 108–18, ed. Walter Buckley. Chicago: Aldine.

Ashkanasy, Neal M., Celeste P. M. Wilderom, and Marak F. Peterson, ed. (2000). *Handbook of Organizational Culture and Climate*. Thousand Oaks, CA: Sage.

Astley, W. Graham (1985). "The Two Ecologies: Population and Community Perspectives on Organizational Evolution," *Administrative Science Quarterly*, 30:224–41.

Astley, W. Graham, and Andrew H. Van de Ven (1983). "Central Perspectives and Debates in Organization Theory," *Administrative Science Quarterly*, 28:245–73.

Augier, Mie, James G. March, and Bilian Ni Sullivan (2005). "Notes on the Evolution of a Research Community: Organization Studies in Anglophone North America, 1945–2000," *Organization Science*, 16:85–95.

Averitt, Richard T. (1968). *The Dual Economy: The Dynamics of American Industry Structure.* New York: W. W. Norton.

Axelrod, Robert, and Michael D. Cohen (1999). *Harnessing Complexity: Organizational Implications of a Scientific Frontier.* New York: Free Press.

Baker, Wayne E. (1990). "Market Networks and Corporate Behavior," *American Journal of Sociology*, 96:589–625.

———— (1992). "The Network Organization in Theory and Practice," in *Networks and Organizations: Structure, Form, and Action*, 397–429, ed. Nitin Nohria and Robert G. Eccles. Boston: Harvard Business School Press.

———— (2000). *Achieving Success Through Social Capital.* San Francisco: Jossey-Bass.

Baker, Wayne E., and Robert R. Faulkner (1991). "Role as Resource in the Hollywood Film Industry," *American Journal of Sociology*, 97:279–309.

———— (1993). "The Social Organization of Conspiracy: Illegal Networks in the Heavy Electrical Equipment Industry," *American Sociological Review*, 58:837–60.

Baker, Wayne E., Robert R. Faulkner, and Gene A. Fisher (1998). "Hazards of the Market: The Continuity and Dissolution of Interorganizational Market Relationships," *American Sociological Review*, 63:147–77.

Bales, Robert F. (1952). "Some Uniformities of Behavior in Small Social Systems," in *Readings in Social Psychology*, 2nd ed., 146–59, ed. Guy E. Swanson, Theodor M. Newcomb, and Eugene L. Hartley. New York: Holt, Rinehart & Winston.

———— (1953). "The Equilibrium Problem in Small Groups," in *Working Papers in the Theory of Action*, 111–61, by Talcott Parsons, Robert F. Bales, and Edward A. Shils. Glencoe, IL: Free Press.

Bales, Robert F., and Philip E. Slater (1955). "Role Differentiation in Small Decision-Making Groups," in *Family, Socialization and Interaction Process*, 259–306, ed. Talcott Parsons and Robert F. Bales. New York: Free Press.

Bamberger, Peter A., and William J. Sonnenstuhl, eds. (1998). *Deviance in and of Organizations*, vol. 15 in *Research in the Sociology of Organizations*, ed. Samuel B. Bacharach. Stamford, CT: JAI Press.

Barley, Stephen R. (1986). "Technology as an Occasion for Structuring: Evidence from Observations of CT Scanners and the Social Order of Radiology Departments," *Administrative Science Quarterly*, 31:78–108.

Barley, Stephen R., John Freeman, and Ralph C. Hybels (1992). "Strategic Alliances in Commercial Biotechnology," in *Networks and Organizations: Structure, Form, and Action*, 311–47, ed. Nitin Nohria and Robert G. Eccles. Boston: Harvard Business School Press.

Barley, Stephen R., and Gideon Kunda (2001). "Bringing Work Back In," *Organization Science*, 12:76–95.

———— (2004). *Gurus, Hired Guns and Warm Bodies: Itinerant Experts in a Knowledge Economy.* Princeton, NJ: Princeton University Press.

Barnard, Chester I. (1938). *The Functions of the Executive.* Cambridge, MA.: Harvard University Press.

Baron, James N. (1984). "Organizational Perspectives on Stratification," *Annual Review of Sociology*, 10:37–69.

Baron, James N., and William T. Bielby (1980). "Bringing the Firms Back In: Stratification, Segmentation, and the Organization of Work," *American Sociological Review*, 45:737–65.

Baron, James N., Frank R. Dobbin, and P. Deveraux Jennings (1986). "War and Peace: The Evolution of Modern Personnel Administration in U.S. Industry," *American Journal of Sociology*, 92:350–83.

Baron, James N, Michael T. Hannan, and M. Diane Burton (1999). "Building the Iron Cage: Determinants of Managerial Intensity in the Early Years of Organizations," *American Sociological Review*, 64:527–47.

Barron, David N. (1999). "The Structuring of Organizational Populations," *American Sociological Review* 64:421–45.

Barron, David N., Elizabeth West, and Michael T. Hannan (1994). "A Time to Grow and a Time to Die: Growth and Mortality of Credit Unions in New York City, 1914–1990," *American Journal of Sociology*, 100:381–421.

Bartlett, C. A., and Sumantra Ghoshal (1989). *Managing Across Borders: The Transnational Solution*. Boston: Harvard Business School Press.

Bartley, Tim (2003). "Certifying Forests and Factories: States, Social Movements, and the Rise of Private Regulation in the Apparel and Forest Products Fields," *Politics & Society*, 3:433–64.

Bateson, Gregory (1972). *Steps to an Ecology of Mind*. New York: Ballantine.

Baum, Joel A. C. (1996). "Organizational Ecology," in *Handbook of Organization Studies*, 77–114, ed. Stewart R. Clegg, Cynthia Hardy, and Walter Nord. Thousand Oaks, CA: Sage.

——— ed. (1998). *Disciplinary Roots of Strategic Management*, vol. 15 of *Advances in Strategic Management*. Greenwich, CT: JAI Press.

Baum, Joel A. C., and Terry L. Amburgey (2002). "Organizational Ecology," in *The Blackwell Companion to Organizations*, 304–326, ed. Joel A. C. Baum. Oxford: Blackwell.

Baum, Joel A. C., and Frank Dobbin (2000). "Doing Interdisciplinary Research in Strategic Management—Without a Paradigm War," in *Advances in Strategic Management* 17:389–410, ed. Joel A. C. Baum and Frank Dobbin. Stamford, CT: JAI Press.

Baum, Joel A. C. and Stephen J. Mezias (1992). "Localized Competition and Organizational Failure in the Manhattan Hotel Industry, 1898–1990," *Administrative Science Quarterly*, 37:580–604.

Baum, Joel A. C., and Christine Oliver (1991). "Institutional Linkages and Organizational Mortality," *Administrative Science Quarterly*, 36:187–218.

——— (1992). "Institutional Embeddedness and the Dynamics of Organizational Populations," *American Sociological Review* 57:540–59.

Baum, Joel A. C., and Jitendra V. Singh (1994). "Organizational Niches and the Dynamics of Organizational Mortality," *American Journal of Sociology*, 100:346–80.

Baum, Joel A. C., Stan Xiao Li, and John M. Usher (2000). "Making the Next Move: How Experiential and Vicarious Learning Shape the Locations of Chains' Acquisition," *Administrative Science Quarterly*, 45:766–801.

Baumol, William J., Alan S. Blinder, and Edward N. Wolff (2003). *Downsizing in America: Reality, Causes, and Consequences*. New York: Russell Sage Foundation.

Bazerman, Max H. (2002). *Judgment in Managerial Decision Making* (5th ed.). New York: John Wiley.

Beamish, P. W., and J. P. Killing, eds. (1997). *Cooperative Strategies: North American Perspectives, European Perspectives, Asian Pacific Perspectives*, 3 vols. San Francisco: New Lexington Press.

Bean, Frank D., and Gillian Stevens (2003). *America's Newcomers and the Dynamics of Diversity*. New York: Russell Sage Foundation.

Becattini, Giacomo (1990). "The Marshallian Industrial District as a Socio-Economic Notion," in *Industrial Districts and Inter-Firm Co-operation in Italy*, 37–51. ed. Frank Pyke, Giacomo Becattini, and Werger Sengenberger. Geneva: International Institute for Labor Studies.

Becker, Howard S. (1982). *Art Worlds*. Berkeley: University of California Press.

Becker, Howard S., Blanch Geer, Everett C. Hughes, and Anselm Strauss (1961). *Boys in White*. Chicago: University of Chicago Press.

Becker, Marshall H. (1970). "Sociometric Location and Innovativeness: Reformulation and Extension of the Diffusion Model," *American Sociological Review*, 35:267–82.

Beckman, Christine M., and Pamela R. Haunschild (2002). "Network Learning: The Effects of Partners' Heterogeneity of Experience on Corporate Acquisitions," *Administrative Science Quarterly*, 47:92–124.

Beer, Stafford (1964). *Cybernetics and Management*. New York: John Wiley.

Bell, Daniel (1960). "Work and Its Discontents: The Cult of Efficiency in America," in *The End of Ideology*, 222–62, by Daniel Bell. Glencoe, IL: Free Press.

——— (1973). *The Coming of Post-Industrial Society*. New York: Basic Books.

Bellah, Robert N., Richard Madsen, William M. Sullivan, Ann Swidler, and Steven M. Tipton (1991). *The Good Society*. New York: Knopf.

Belussi, Fiorenza (1989). "Benneton Italy: Beyond Fordism and Flexible Specialization to the Evolution of the Network Firm Model," in *Information Technology and Women's Employment: The Case of the European Clothing Industry*, ed. S. Mitter. Berlin: Springer Verlag.

Bendix, Reinhard (1956; 2001). *Work and Authority in Industry: Managerial Ideologies in the Course of Industrialization*. New York: John Wiley [1956]; New Brunswick, NJ: Transaction Publishers [2001].

——— (1960). *Max Weber. An Intellectual Portrait*. Garden City, NY: Doubleday, 1960.

Bendix, Reinhard, and Lloyd H. Fisher (1949). "The Perspectives of Elton Mayo," *Review of Economics and Statistics*, 31:312–19.

Bendor, Johnathan, Terry M. Moe, and Kenneth W. Shotts (2001). "Recycling the Garbage Can: An Assessment of the Research Program," *American Political Science Review*, 95:169–90.

Beniger, James R. (1986). *The Control Revolution: Technological and Economic Origins of the Information Society*. Cambridge, MA: Harvard University Press.

Bennis, Warren G. (1959). "Leadership Theory and Administrative Behavior," *Administrative Science Quarterly*, 4:259–301.

Berger Peter L., Brigitte Berger, and Hansfried Kellner (1973). *The Homeless Mind: Modernization and Consciousness*. New York: Random House, Vintage Books.

Berger, Peter L., and Thomas Luckmann (1967). *The Social Construction of Reality*. New York: Doubleday.

Berger, Suzanne, ed. (1981). *Organizing Interest in Western Europe: Pluralism, Corporatism and the Transformation of Politics*. New York: Cambridge University Press.

Berk, Gerald, and Marc Schneiberg (2005). "Varieties *in* Capitalism, Varieties *of* Association: Collaborative Learning in American Industry, 1900–1925," *Politics & Society*, 33:1–43.

Berle, Adolf A., and Gardiner C. Means (1932). *The Modern Corporation and Private Property*. New York: Macmillan.

Berman, Harold J. (1983). *Law and Revolution: The Formation of the Western Legal Tradition*. Cambridge, MA: Harvard University Press.

Berry, Jeffrey M. (1989). *The Interest Group Society.* (2nd ed.). Glenview, IL: Scott, Foresman.

Bertalanffy, Ludwig von (1956). "General System Theory," in *General Systems: Yearbook of the Society for the Advancement of General Systems Theory*, vol. 1, 1–10, ed. Ludwig von Bertalanffy and Anatol Rapoport. Ann Arbor, MI: The Society.

——— (1962). "General System Theory: A Critical Review," in *General Systems: Yearbook of the Society for General Systems Research*, vol. 7, 1–20, ed. Ludwig von Bertalanffy and Anatol Rapoport. Ann Arbor, MI: The Society.

Bidwell, Charles E. (1965). "The School as a Formal Organization," in *Handbook of Organizations*, 972–1022, ed. James G. March. Chicago: Rand McNally.

Bidwell, Charles E., and John D. Kasarda (1985). *The Organization and Its Ecosystem: A Theory of Structuring in Organizations*. Greenwich, CT: JAI Press.

Bielby, William T., and James N. Baron (1986). "Men and Women at Work: Sex Segregation and Statistical Discrimination," *American Journal of Sociology*, 91:759–99.

Biggart, Nicole Woolsey (1989). *Charismatic Capitalism: Direct Selling Organizations in America*. Chicago: University of Chicago Press.

Biggart, Nicole Woolsey, and Mauro F. Guillén (1999). "Developing Difference: Social Organization and the Rise of the Auto Industries of South Korea, Taiwan, Spain, and Argentina," *American Sociological Review*, 64:722–47.

Bittner, Egon (1967). "The Police on Skid Row: A Study of Peace Keeping," *American Sociological Review*, 32:699–715.

Black, Bernard S. (1992). "The Value of Institutional Investor Monitoring: The Empirical Evidence," *UCLA Law Review*, 39:895–939.

Blair, Margaret M. (1995). *Ownership and Control: Rethinking Corporate Governance for the Twenty-First Century*. Washington DC: Brookings Institution.

Blair, Margaret M., and Thomas A. Kochan, eds. (2000). *The New Relationship: Human Capital in the American Corporation*. Washington, DC: Brookings Institution.

Blake, R. R., and J. S. Mouton (1964). *The Managerial Grid*. Houston: Gulf.

Blau, Peter M. (1955). *The Dynamics of Bureaucracy*. Chicago: University of Chicago Press (rev. 1963).

———— (1956). *Bureaucracy in Modern Society*. New York: Random House.

———— (1957). "Formal Organization: Dimensions of Analysis," *American Journal of Sociology*, 63:58–69.

———— (1964). *Exchange and Power in Social Life*. New York: John Wiley.

———— (1970). "A Formal Theory of Differentiation in Organizations," *American Sociological Review*, 35:201–18.

Blau, Peter M., and Richard A. Schoenherr (1971). *The Structure of Organizations*. New York: Basic Books.

Blau, Peter M., and W. Richard Scott (1962; 2003). *Formal Organizations: A Comparative Approach*. San Francisco: Chandler Publications (1962): Stanford University Press (2003).

Blauner, Robert (1964). *Alienation and Freedom*. Chicago: University of Chicago Press.

Bloch, Marc (1964). *Feudal Society*, vols. 1–2. Chicago: University of Chicago Press.

Block, Fred (1994). "The Roles of the State in the Economy," in *The Handbook of Economic Sociology*, 691–710, ed. Neil J. Smelser and Richard Swedberg. Princeton, NJ: Princeton University Press and the Russell Sage Foundation.

Bluestone, Barry, and Irving Bluestone (1992). *Negotiating the Future: A Labor Perspective on American Business*. New York: Basic Books.

Blumberg, Paul (1968). *Industrial Democracy: The Sociology of Participation*. New York: Schocken Books.

Boeker, Warren P. (1988). "Organizational Origins: Entrepreneurial and Environmental Imprinting at the Time of Founding," in *Ecological Models of Organizations*, ed. Glenn R. Carroll. Cambridge, MA: Ballinger.

———— (1997). "Executive Migration and Strategic Change: The Effect of Top Manager Movement on Product-Market Entry," *Administrative Science Quarterly*, 42:213–36.

Boguslaw, Robert (1965). *The New Utopians: A Study of System Design and Social Change*. Upper Saddle River, NJ: Prentice Hall.

Boli, John, and George M. Thomas (1997). "World Culture in the World Polity: A Century of International Non-Governmental Organization," *American Sociological Review*, 62:171–90.

———— ed. (1999). *Constructing World Culture: International Nongovernmental Organizations since 1875*. Stanford, CA: Stanford University Press.

Bonacich, Phillip (1987). "Power and Centrality: A Family of Measures," *American Journal of Sociology*, 92:1170–82.

Bose, Christine, Roslyn Feldberg, and Natalie Sokoloff, ed. (1987). *Hidden Aspects of Women's Work*. New York: Praeger.

Bothner, Matthew S. (2003). "Competition and Social Influence: The Diffusion of the Sixth-Generation Processor in the Global Computer Industry," *American Journal of Sociology*, 108:1175–1210.

Boulding, Kenneth E. (1956). "General Systems Theory: The Skeleton of Science," *Management Science*, 2:197–208.

Bourdieu, Pierre (1986). "The Forms of Capital," in *Handbook of Theory and Research for the Sociology of Education*, 241–58, ed. John G. Richardson. Westport, CT: Greenwood Press.

Bourdieu, Pierre, and Jean-Claude Passeron (1977). *Reproduction in Education, Society and Culture*, trans. Richard Nice. Beverly Hills, CA: Sage.

Bourdieu, Pierre, and Loic J. D. Wacquant (1992). *An Invitation to Reflexive Sociology*. Chicago: University of Chicago Press.

Bowles, Samuel, and Herbert Gintis (1977). *Schooling in Capitalist America: Educational Reform and the Contradictions of Economic Life*. New York: Basic Books.

Bradley, Michael, Cindy A. Schipani, Anant K. Sundaram, and James P. Walsh. (1999). "The Purposes and Accountability of the Corporation in Contemporary Society: Corporate Governance at a Crossroads," *Law and Contemporary Problems*, 62(3): 9–85.

Brandeis, Louis D. (1914). *Other People's Money: And How the Bankers Use It*. New York: Frederick A. Stokes Company.

Brass, Daniel J. (2002). "Intraorganizational power and dependence," in *The Blackwell Companion to Organizations*, 138–57, ed. Joel A. C. Baum. Oxford, UK: Blackwell Publications.

Bratton, William W. (2003). "Enron, Sarbanes-Oxley and Accounting: Rules versus Principles versus Rents," *Law Review*, 48:1023–55. University of Villanova School of Law.

Braverman, Harry (1974). *Labor and Monopoly Capital: The Degradation of Work in the Twentieth Century*. New York: Monthly Review Press.

Brayfield, Arthur H., and Walter H. Crockett (1955). "Employee Attitudes and Employee Performance," *Psychological Bulletin*, 52:396–424.

Brock, David, Michael Powell, and C. R. Hinings, ed. (1999). *Restructuring the Professional Organization: Accounting, Health Care and Law*. London: Routledge.

Brooks, Harvey (1984). "Seeking Equity and Efficiency: Public and Private Roles," in *Public–Private Partnership: New Opportunities for Meeting Social Needs*, 3–29, ed. Harvey Brooks, Lance Liebman, and Corinne S. Schelling. Cambridge, MA: Ballinger.

Brooks, Harvey, Lance Liebman, and Corinne S. Schelling, eds. (1984). *Public-Private Partnership: New Opportunities for Meeting Social Needs*. Cambridge, MA: Ballinger.

Broom, Leonard, and Philip Selznick (1955). *Sociology* (2nd ed.). Evanston, IL: Row, Peterson.

Broschak, Joseph P. (2004). "Managers' Mobility and Market Interface: The Effect of Managers' Career Mobility on the Dissolution of Market Ties," *Administrative Science Quarterly*, 49:608–40.

Brown, John Seely, and Paul Duguid (1998). "Organizing Knowledge," *California Management Review*, 40:90–111.

Brown, Lawrence D. (1983). *New Policies, New Politics: Government's Response to Government's Growth*. Washington DC: The Brookings Institution.

Bruderl, Josef, Peter Preisendorfer, and Rolf Ziegler (1992). "Survival Chances of Newly Founded Business Organizations," *American Sociological Review*, 57:227–42.

Brunsson, Nils (1985). *The Irrational Organization*. New York: John Wiley.

——— (1989). *The Organization of Hypocrisy: Talk, Decisions and Actions in Organizations*. New York: John Wiley.

Brunsson, Nils, and Bengt Jacobsson, ed. (2000). *A World of Standards*. Oxford: Oxford University Press.

Brusco, Sebastiano (1982). "The Emilian Model: Productive Decentralisation and Social Integration," *Cambridge Journal of Economics*, 6:167–84.

Buckley, Walter (1967). *Sociology and Modern Systems Theory*. Upper Saddle River, NJ: Prentice Hall.

Burawoy, Michael (1979). *Manufacturing Consent: Changes in the Labor Process under Monopoly Capitalism*. Chicago: University of Chicago Press.

Burawoy, Michael (1982). "Introduction: The Resurgence of Marxism in American Sociology," in *Marxist Inquiries: Studies of Labor, Class, and States*. Supplement to *American Journal of Sociology*, 88, S1–S30, ed. Michael Burawoy and Theda Skocpol. Chicago: University of Chicago Press.

——— (1985). *The Politics of Production*. London: Verso.

——— (2005). "For Public Sociology," *American Sociological Review*, 70:4–28.

Burgelman, Robert A., and Leonard R. Sayles (1986). *Inside Corporate Innovation: Strategy, Structure, and Managerial Skills*. New York: Free Press.

Burgess, John William (1902). *Political Science and Comparative Constitutional Law*. Boston: Ginn.

Burns, Tom, and George M. Stalker (1961). *The Management of Innovation*. London: Tavistock.

Burrell, Gibson, and Gareth Morgan (1979). *Sociological Paradigms and Organizational Analysis*. London: Heinemann.

Burt, Ronald S. (1980). "Models of Network Structure," *Annual Review of Sociology*, 6:79–141.

——— (1982). *Toward a Structural Theory of Action: Network Models of Social Structure, Perception, and Action*. New York: Academic Press.

——— (1983). *Corporate Profits and Cooptation*. New York: Academic Press.

——— (1988). "The Stability of American Markets," *American Journal of Sociology*, 94:356–95.

——— (1990). "Kinds of Relations in American Discussion Networks," in *Structures of Power and Constraint: Papers in Honor of Peter M. Blau*, 411–51, ed. Craig Calhoun, Marshall W. Meyer, and W. Richard Scott. Cambridge: Cambridge University Press.

———— (1992a). "The Social Structure of Competition," in *Networks and Organizations: Structure, Form, and Action*, 57–91, ed. Nitin Nohria and Robert G. Eccles. Boston: Harvard Business School Press.

———— (1992b). *Structural Holes*. Cambridge, MA: Harvard University Press.

———— (2000). "The Network Structure of Social Capital," *Research in Organizational Behavior*, 22:345–423.

———— (2004). "Structural Holes and Good Ideas," *American Journal of Sociology* 110:349–99.

Burton, Richard M., and Børge Obel (2004). *Strategic Organizational Diagnosis and Design: The Dynamics of Fit*. (3rd ed.). Boston: Kluwer Academic Publishers.

Callahan, R. E. (1962). *Education and the Cult of Efficiency*. Chicago: University of Chicago Press.

Calvert, Monte A. (1967). *The Mechanical Engineer in America, 1830–1910: Professional Cultures in Conflict*. Baltimore: Johns Hopkins University Press.

Cameron, Kim S., and David A. Whetten, eds. (1983). *Organizational Effectiveness: A Comparison of Multiple Models*. New York: Academic Press.

Cameron, Kim S., and Robert E. Quinn (1996). *Diagnosing and Changing Organizational Culture*. San Francisco: Jossey-Bass.

Campbell, Donald T. (1969a). "Ethnocentrism of Disciplines and the Fish-scale Model of Omniscience," in *Interdisciplinary Relationships in the Social Sciences*, 328–48, ed. Muzafer Sherif and Caroline W. Sherif. Chicago: Aldine.

———— (1969b). "Variation and Selective Retention in Socio-Cultural Evolution," in *General Systems: Yearbook of the Society for General Systems Research*, 16:69–85. Ann Arbor MI: The Society.

Campbell, John L. (1997). "Mechanisms of Evolutionary Change in Economic Governance: Interaction, Interpretation, and Bricolage," in *Evolutionary Economics and Path Dependence*, 10–31, ed. Lars Magnusson and Jan Ottosson. Cheltenham, UK: Edward Elgar.

———— (2004). *Institutional Change and Globalization*. Princeton: Princeton University Press.

———— (2005). "Where Do We Stand? Common mechanisms in organizations and social movements research," in *Social Movements and Organization Theory*, 41–68, ed. Gerald F. Davis, Doug McAdam, W. Richard Scott, and Mayer N. Zald. New York: Cambridge University Press.

Campbell, John L., and Leon N. Lindberg (1990). "Property Rights and the Organization of Economic Activities by the State," *American Sociological Review*, 55:634–47.

Campbell, John L., J. Rogers Hollingsworth, and Leon N. Lindberg, eds. (1991). *Governance of the American Economy*. Cambridge: Cambridge University Press.

Campbell, John P. (1977). "On the Nature of Organizational Effectiveness," in *New Perspectives on Organizational Effectiveness*, 13–55, ed. Paul S. Goodman and Johannes M. Pennings. San Francisco: Jossey-Bass.

Canella, Albert A., Jr., and Romona L. Paetzold (1994). "Pfeffer's Barriers to the Advance of Organizational Science: A Rejoinder," *Academy of Management Review* 19:331–41.

Cappelli, Peter (1999). *The New Deal at Work: Managing the Market-Driven Workforce*. Boston: Harvard Business School Press.

———— (2000). "Market-Mediated Employment: The Historical Context," in *The New Relationship: Human Capital in the American Corporation*, 66–101, ed. Margaret M. Blair and Thomas A Kochan. Washington, DC: Brookings Institution.

———— (2001). "Assessing the Decline of Internal Labor Markets," in *Sourcebook of Labor Markets*, ed. Ivar Berg and Arne Kalleberg. New York: Kluwer Academic Press.

Carey, Alex (1967). "The Hawthorne Studies: A Radical Criticism," *American Sociological Review*, 32:403–16.

Carré, Françoise, Marianne A. Ferber, Lonnie Golden, and Stephen A. Herzenberg (2000). *Nonstandard Work: The Nature and Challenges of Emerging Employment Arrangements*. Ithaca, NY: Cornell University Press (IRRA Research Volume).

Carroll, Glenn R. (1983). "A Stochastic Model of Organizational Mortality: Review and Reanalysis," *Social Science Research*, 12:303–29.

———— (1984). "Organizational Ecology," *Annual Review of Sociology*, 10:71–93.

———— (1985). "Concentration and Specialization: Dynamics of Niche Width in Populations of Organizations," *American Journal of Sociology*, 90:1262–83.

———— (1987). *Publish and Perish: The Organizational Ecology of Newspaper Industries.* Greenwich, CT: JAI Press.

Carroll, Glenn R., and Jacques Delacroix (1982). "Organizational Mortality in the Newspaper Industries of Argentina and Ireland: An Ecological Approach," *Administrative Science Quarterly*, 27:169–98.

Carroll, Glenn R., Jacques Delacroix, and Jerry Goodstein (1988). "The Political Environments of Organizations: An Ecological View," *Research in Organizational Behavior*, vol. 10: 359–92, ed. Barry Staw and L. L. Cummings. Greenwich, CT: JAI Press.

Carroll, Glenn R., and Michael T. Hannan (1989). "Density Dependence in the Evolution of Populations of Newspaper Organizations," *American Sociological Review*, 54:524–48.

———— (2000). *The Demography of Corporations and Industries.* Princeton, NJ: Princeton University Press.

Carroll, Glenn R., and J. Richard Harrison (1994). "On the Historical Efficiency of Competition Between Organizational Populations," *American Journal of Sociology*, 100:720–49.

Carroll, Glenn R., and Anand Swaminathan (2000). "Why the Microbrewery Movement? Organizational Dynamics of Resource Partitioning in the U.S. Brewing Industry," *American Journal of Sociology*, 106:715–62.

Carroll, W. K. (1986). *Corporate Power and Canadian Capitalism.* Vancouver: University of British Columbia Press.

Carruthers, Bruce G. (1996). *City of Capital: Politics and Markets in the English Financial Revolution.* Princeton: Princeton University Press.

Carter, Launor, William Haythorn, Beatrice Shriver, and John Lanzetta (1953). "The Behavior of Leaders and Other Group Members," in *Group Dynamics*, 551–60, ed. Dorwin Cartwright and Alvin Zander. Evanston, IL: Row, Peterson.

Cartwright, Dorwin (1965). "Influence, Leadership, Control," in *Handbook of Organizations*, 1–47, ed. James G. March. Chicago: Rand McNally.

Carzo, Rocco, Jr, and John N. Yanouzas (1967). *Formal Organization: A Systems Approach.* Homewood, IL: Richard D. Irwin, Dorsey.

Chaffee, Ellen Earle (1985). "Three Models of Strategy," *Academy of Management Review*, 10:89–98.

Chandler, Alfred D., Jr. (1962). *Strategy and Structure: Chapters in the History of the American Industrial Enterprise.* Cambridge, MA: MIT Press.

———— (1977). *The Visible Hand: The Managerial Revolution in American Business.* Cambridge, MA: Belknap Press of Harvard University Press.

———— with the assistance of Takashi Hikino (1990). *Scale and Scope: The Dynamics of Industrial Capitalism.* Cambridge, MA: Belknap Press of Harvard University Press.

Chandler, Alfred D., Jr., and Herman Daems, eds. (1980). *Managerial Hierarchies: Comparative Perspectives on the Rise of the Modern Industrial Enterprise.* Cambridge, MA: Harvard University Press.

Chase, Richard B., and David A. Tansik (1983). "The Customer Contact Model for Organization Design," *Management Science*, 29:1037–50.

Child, John (1972). "Organizational Structure, Environment and Performance: The Role of Strategic Choice," *Sociology*, 6:1–22.

———— (1994). *Management in China During the Age of Reform.* Cambridge: Cambridge University Press.

———— (2005). *Organization: Contemporary Principles and Practice.* Oxford: Blackwell Publishing.

Child, John, and Roger Mansfield (1972). "Technology, Size and Organization Structure," *Sociology* 6:369–93.

Christensen, Clayton M., and Joseph J. Bower (1996). "Customer Power, Strategic Investment, and the Failure of Leading Firms," *Strategic Management Journal*, 17:197–218.

Cialdini, Robert B. (2001). *Influence: Science and Practice.* (4th ed.). Boston: Allyn & Bacon.

Cicourel, Aaron (1968). *The Social Organization of Juvenile Justice.* New York: John Wiley.

Clark, Burton R. (1956). *Adult Education in Transition.* Berkeley: University of California Press.

———— (1963). "Faculty Organization and Authority," in *The Study of Academic Administration*, 37–51, ed. Terry F. Lunsford. Boulder, CO: Western Interstate Commission for Higher Education.

——— (1970). *The Distinctive College: Antioch, Reed and Swarthmore*. Chicago: Aldine.

——— (1972). "The Organizational Saga in Higher Education," *Administrative Science Quarterly*, 17:178–83.

Clark, Peter M., and James Q. Wilson (1961). "Incentive Systems: A Theory of Organizations," *Administrative Science Quarterly*, 6:129–66.

Clarke, D. C. (2003). "How Do We Know When an Enterprise Exists? Unanswerable Questions and Legal Polycentricity in China." Working paper, University of Washington School of Law.

Clarke, Lee, and Carroll L. Estes (1992). "Sociological and Economic Theories of Markets and Nonprofits: Evidence from Home Health Organizations," *American Journal of Sociology* 97:945–69.

Clawson, Dan, and Alan Neustadtl (1989). "Interlocks, PACs, and Corporate Conservatism," *American Journal of Sociology* 94:749–73.

Clawson, Dan, Alan Neustadtl, and Mark Weller (1998). *Dollars and Votes*. Philadelphia: Temple University Press.

Clegg, Stewart R. (1990). *Modern Organizations: Organization Studies in the Postmodern World*. London: Sage.

Clegg, Stewart R., and D. Dunkerley (1977). *Critical Issues in Organizations*. London: Routledge & Kegan Paul.

Clemens, Elisabeth S. (1993). "Organizational Repertoires and Institutional Change: Women's Groups and the Transformation of U.S. Politics, 1890–1920," *American Journal of Sociology*, 98:755–98.

——— (1997). *The People's Lobby: Organizational Innovation and the Rise of Interest Group Politics in the United States, 1890–1925*. Chicago: University of Chicago Press.

Clemmer, Donald (1940). *The Prison Community*. Boston: Christopher.

Clinard, Marshall B. (1990). *Corporate Corruption*. New York: Praeger.

Clinard, Marshall B., and R. Quinney (1973). *Criminal Behavior Systems: A Typology*. New York: Holt, Rinehart & Winston.

CNN Web site (2005). http://money.cnn.com/2005/01/05/news/economy/jobs_challenger/

Coase, R. H. (1937). "The Nature of the Firm," *Economica*, 4:386–405.

Coch, L., and J. R. P. French, Jr. (1948). "Overcoming Resistance to Change," *Human Relations*, 1:512–32.

Coffee, John C., Jr. (2001). "The Rise of Dispersed Ownership: The Roles of Law and the State in the Separation of Ownership and Control," *Yale Law Journal* 111:1–82.

Cohen, Bernard P. (1972). "On the Construction of Sociological Explanations," *Synthese*, 24:401–9.

Cohen, Michael D., and James G. March (1974). *Leadership and Ambiguity: The American College President*. New York: McGraw-Hill.

——— (1976). "Decisions, Presidents, and Status," in *Ambiguity and Choice in Organizations*, 174–205, ed. James G. March and Johan P. Olsen. Bergen, Norway: Universitetsforlaget.

——— (1976). "People, Problems, Solutions and the Ambiguity of Relevance," in *Ambiguity and Choice in Organizations*, 24–37, ed. James G. March and Johan P. Olsen. Bergen, Norway: Universitetsforlaget.

Cohen, Michael D., James G. March, and Johan P. Olsen (1972). "A Garbage Can Model of Organizational Choice," *Administrative Science Quarterly*, 17:1–25.

——— (1976). "People, Problems, Solutions and the Ambiguity of Relevance," in *Ambiguity and Choice in Organizations*. 24–37, ed. James G. March and Johan P. Olsen, Bergen, Norway: Universitetsforlaget.

Cole, Robert E. (1979). *Work, Mobility, and Participation*. Berkeley: University of California Press.

——— (1989). *Strategies for Learning: Small Group Activities in American, Japanese, and Swedish Industry*. Berkeley: University of California Press.

——— (1994). "Different Quality Paradigms and their Implications for Organizational Learning," in *The Japanese Firm: Sources of Competitive Strength*, 66–83, ed. Masahiko Aoki and Ronald S. Dore. Oxford: Clarendon Press.

——— (1999). *Managing Quality Fads: How American Business Learned to Play the Quality Game*. New York: Oxford University Press.

Cole, Robert E., and W. Richard Scott, eds. (2000). *The Quality Movement & Organization Theory*. Thousand Oaks, CA: Sage.

Coleman, James S. (1964). *Introduction to Mathematical Sociology*. New York: Free Press.

——— (1974). *Power and the Structure of Society*. New York: W. W. Norton.

——— (1975). "Social Structure and a Theory of Action," in *Approaches to the Study of Social Structure*, 76–93, ed. Peter M. Blau. New York: Free Press.

——— (1990). *Foundations of Social Theory*. Cambridge, MA: Belknap Press of Harvard University Press.

Colignon, Richard A. (1996). *Power Plays: Critical Events in the Institutionalization of the TVA*. Albany: State University of New York Press.

Collins, Orvis (1946). "Ethnic Behavior in Industry: Sponsorship and Rejection in a New England Factory," *American Journal of Sociology*, 21:293–98.

Collins, Randall (1975). *Conflict Sociology: Toward an Explanatory Science*. New York: Academic Press.

——— (1986). *Weberian Sociological Theory*. Cambridge: Cambridge University Press.

Commons, John R. (1924). *Legal Foundations of Capitalism*. New York: Macmillan.

Comstock, Donald E., and W. Richard Scott (1977). "Technology and the Structure of Subunits: Distinguishing Individual and Workgroup Effects," *Administrative Science Quarterly*, 22:177–202.

Contractor, Farok J., and Peter Lorange (1988). "Why Should Firms Cooperate? The Strategy and Economics Basis for Cooperative Ventures." in *Cooperative Strategies in International Business*, 3–29. ed. Farok J. Contractor and Peter Lorange. New York: Lexington Books.

Cook, Thomas D., and Donald T. Campbell (1979). *Quasi-Experimentation: Design & Analysis Issues for Field Settings*. Chicago: Rand-McNally.

Cooley, Charles Horton (1956 ed.). *Social Organization*. Glencoe, IL: Free Press (first published in 1902).

Cooper, Robert, and Gibson Burrell (1988). "Modernism, Postmodernism and Organizational Analysis: An Introduction," *Organization Studies*, 9:91–112.

Cornfield, Daniel B., Karen Campbell, and Holly McCammon (2001). *Working in Restructured Workplaces: Challenges and New Directions for the Sociology of Work*. Thousand Oaks, CA: Sage.

Coser, Lewis (1956). *The Functions of Social Conflict*. Glencoe, IL: Free Press.

Cotton, J. L. (1993). *Employee Involvement: Methods for Improving Performance and Work Attitudes*. Newbury Park, CA: Sage.

Cox, Taylor, Jr., Stella M. Nkomo, and Julia Welch (2000). "Research on Race and Ethnicity: An Update and Analysis," *Handbook of Organizational Behavior*, ed. Robert T. Golembiewski. New York: Marcel Dekker.

Creighton, Andrew L. (1990). "The Emergence of Incorporation as a Legal Form for Organizations." Unpublished Ph.D. Dissertation, Department of Sociology, Stanford University.

Cressey, Donald R. (1969). *Theft of a Nation: The Structure and Operations of Organized Crime in America*. New York: Harper & Row.

Crozier, Michel (1964). *The Bureaucratic Phenomenon*. Chicago: University of Chicago Press.

Cyert, Richard M., and James G. March (1963). *A Behavioral Theory of the Firm*. Upper Saddle River, NJ: Prentice Hall.

Czarniawska, Barbara (1997). *Narrating the Organization: Dramas of Institutional Identity*. Chicago: University of Chicago Press.

Dacin, M. Tina, Jerry Goodstein, and W. Richard Scott (2002). "Institutional Theory and Institutional Change," *Academy of Management Journal*, 45:45–56.

Dacin, M. Tina, Marc J. Ventresca, and Brent D. Beal (1999). "The Embeddedness of Organizations: Dialogue & Directions," *Journal of Management*, 25:317–56.

Daft, Richard L. (1980). "The Evolution of Organization Analysis in *ASQ*, 1959–1979," *Administrative Science Quarterly*, 25:623–36.

Dahrendorf, Ralf (1959). *Class and Class Conflict in Industrial Society*. Stanford, CA: Stanford University Press.

Dalton, Melville (1950). "Conflicts between Staff and Line Managerial Officers," *American Sociological Review*, 15:342–51.

———— (1959). *Men Who Manage.* New York: John Wiley.

D'Aunno, Thomas, Melissa Succi, and Jeffrey A. Alexander (2000). "The Role of Institutional and Market Forces in Divergent Organizational Change," *Administrative Science Quarterly*, 45:679–703.

D'Aunno, Thomas, Robert I. Sutton, and Richard H. Price (1991). "Isomorphism and External Support in Conflicting Institutional Environments: A Study of Drug Abuse Treatment Units," *Academy of Management Journal*, 14:636–61.

David, Robert J., and Shin-Kap Han (2004). "A Systematic Assessment of the Empirical Support for Transaction Cost Economics," *Strategic Management Journal*, 25:39–58.

Davis, Gerald F. (1990). "Agents Without Principles? The Spread of the Poison Pill Through the Intercorporate Network." *Administrative Science Quarterly*, 36:583–613.

———— (1994). "The Corporate Elite and the Politics of Corporate Control," in *Current Perspectives in Social Theory*, Supplement 1, *Recent Developments in the Theory of Social Structure*, vol. 14, 215–38, ed. J. David Knottnerus and Christopher Prendergast. Greenwich, CT: JAI Press.

———— (1996). "The Significance of Board Interlocks for Corporate Governance," *Corporate Governance*, 4:154–59.

———— (2005a). "Firms and Environments," in *Handbook of Economic Sociology*, 478–502, ed. Neil J. Smelser and Richard Swedberg. Princeton and New York: Princeton University Press and Russell Sage Foundation.

———— (2005b). "New Directions in Corporate Governance," *Annual Review of Sociology*, 31:143–62.

Davis, Gerald F., Kristina A. Diekmann, and Catherine H. Tinsley (1994). "The Decline and Fall of the Conglomerate Firm in the 1980s: The Deinstitutionalization of an Organizational Form," *American Sociological Review*, 59:547–70.

Davis, Gerald F., and Henrich R. Greve (1997). "Corporate Elite Networks and Governance Changes in the 1980s," *American Journal of Sociology*, 103:1–37.

Davis, Gerald F., Robert L. Kahn, and Mayer N. Zald (1990). "Contracts, Treaties, and Joint Ventures," in *Organizations and Nation-States: New Perspectives on Conflict and Cooperation*, 19–54, ed. Robert L. Kahn and Mayer N. Zald. San Francisco: Jossey-Bass.

Davis, Gerald F., and E. Han Kim (2005). "Business Ties and Proxy Voting by Mutual Funds," *Journal of Financial Economics*.

Davis, Gerald F., and Christopher Marquis (2005a). "The Globalization of Stock Markets and Convergence in Corporate Governance," in *The Economic Sociology of Capitalism*, 352–90, ed. Victor Nee and Richard Swedberg. Princeton: Princeton University Press.

Davis, Gerald F., and Christopher Marquis (2005b). "Prospects for Organization Theory in the Early 21st Century: Institutional Fields and Mechanisms," *Organization Science*, 16: 332–43.

Davis, Gerald F., Doug McAdam, W. Richard Scott, and Mayer N. Zald, eds. (2005). *Social Movements and Organization Theory*. New York: Cambridge University Press.

Davis, Gerald F., and Mark S. Mizruchi (1999). "The Money Center Cannot Hold: Commercial Banks in the U.S. System of Corporate Governance," *Administrative Science Quarterly*, 44:215–39.

Davis, Gerald F., and Walter W. Powell (1992). "Organization-Environment Relations," in *Handbook of Industrial and Organizational Psychology* (2nd ed.), vol. 3, 315–75, ed. Marvin Dunnette. Palo Alto, CA: Consulting Psychologists Press.

Davis, Gerald F., and Gregory E. Robbins (2005). "Nothing but Net? Networks and Status in Corporate Governance." in *The Sociology of Financial Markets*, 290–311, ed. Karin Knorr-Cetina and Alex Preda. Oxford: Oxford University Press.

Davis, Gerald F. and Tracy A. Thompson (1994). "A Social Movement Perspective on Corporate Control," *Administrative Science Quarterly*, 39:141–73.

Davis, Gerald F., and Michael Useem (2002). "Top Management, Company Directors, and Corporate Control," in *Handbook of Strategy and Management*, 233–50, ed. Andrew Pettigrew, Howard Thomas, and Richard Whittington. London: Sage.

Davis, Gerald F., and Mina Yoo (2003). "Le Monde Toujours Plus Petit des Grandes Entreprises Americaines: Partipationes Communes et Liens dans les Conseils d'Administration (1990–2001)," *Gerer et Comprendre*, 74:51–62.

Davis, Gerald F., Mina Yoo, and Wayne E. Baker (2003). "The Small World of the American Corporate Elite, 1982–2001," *Strategic Organization*, 1:301–26.

Davis, Kingsley (1949). *Human Society*. New York: Macmillan.

Davis, Stanley M., and Paul R. Lawrence (1977). *Matrix*. Reading, MA: Addison-Wesley.

Deal, Terrence E., and Allan A. Kennedy (1982). *Corporate Cultures*. Reading, MA: Addison-Wesley.

Delacroix, Jacques and Glenn R. Carroll (1983). "Organizational Foundings: An Ecological Study of the Newspaper Industries of Argentina and Ireland," *Administrative Science Quarterly*, 28:274–91.

Derrida, J. (1976). *Speech and Phenomenon*. Evanston, IL: Northwestern University Press.

Dezalay, Yves, and Bryant G. Garth (1996). *Dealing in Virtue: International Commercial Arbitration and the Construction of a Transnational Legal Order*. Chicago: University of Chicago Press.

Dibble, Vernon K. (1965). "The Organization of Traditional Authority: English County Government, 1558 to 1640," in *Handbook of Organizations*, 879–909, ed. James G. March. Chicago: Rand McNally.

DiMaggio, Paul J. (1983). "State Expansion and Organizational Fields," in *Organizational Theory and Public Policy*, 147–61, ed. Richard H. Hall and Robert E. Quinn. Beverly Hills, CA: Sage.

——— (1986). "Structural Analysis of Organizational Fields: A Blockmodel Approach," in *Research in Organizational Behavior*, vol. 8, 355–70, ed. Barry M. Staw and L. L. Cummings. Greenwich, CT: JAI Press.

——— (1988). "Interest and Agency in Institutional Theory," in *Institutional Patterns and Organizations: Culture and Environment*, 3–21, ed. Lynne G. Zucker. Cambridge, MA: Ballinger.

——— (1991). "Constructing an Organizational Field as a Professional Project: U.S. Art Museums, 1920–1940," in *The New Institutionalism in Organizational Analysis*, 267–92, ed. Walter W. Powell and Paul J. DiMaggio. Chicago: University of Chicago Press.

——— ed. (2001). *The Twenty-First-Century Firm: Changing Economic Organization in International Perspective*. Princeton: Princeton University Press.

DiMaggio, Paul J., and Walter W. Powell (1983). "The Iron Cage Revisited: Institutional Iso-morphism and Collective Rationality in Organizational Fields," *American Sociological Review*, 48:147–60.

——— (1991). "Introduction," in *The New Institutionalism in Organizational Analysis*," 1–38, ed. Walter W. Powell and Paul J. DiMaggio. Chicago: University of Chicago Press.

DiPrete, Thomas A. (1989). *The Bureaucratic Labor Market: The Case of the Federal Civil Service*. New York: Plenum.

DiPrete, Thomas A., and David B. Grusky (1990). "Structure and Trend in the Process of Stratification for American Men and Women," *American Journal of Sociology*, 96:107–43.

Djelic, Marie-Laure (1998). *Exporting the American Model: The Postwar Transformation of European Business*. New York: Oxford University Press.

Djelic, Marie-Laure, and Sigrid Quack, ed. (2003). *Globalization and Institutions: Redefining the Rules of the Economic Game*. Cheltenham, UK: Edward Elgar.

Dobbin, Frank R. (1994a). "Cultural Models of Organization: The Social Construction of Rational Organizing Principles," in *The Sociology of Culture: Emerging Theoretical Perspectives*, 117–53, ed. Diana Crane. Cambridge, MA: Basil Blackwell.

——— (1994b). *Forging Industrial Policy: The United States, Britain, and France in the Railway Age*. New York: Cambridge University Press.

Dobbin, Frank R., and Joel A. C. Baum (2000). "Introduction: Economics Meets Sociology in Strategic Management," in *Economics Meets Sociology in Strategic Management, Advances in Strategic Management*, vol. 17, 1–26, ed. Joel A. C. Baum and Frank Dobbin. Stamford, CT: JAI Press.

Dobbin, Frank, and Timothy J. Dowd (1997). "How Policy Shapes Competition: Early Railroad Foundings in Massachusetts," *Administrative Science Quarterly*, 42:501–29.

——— (2000). "The Market that Antitrust Built: Public Policy, Private Coercion, and Railroad Acquisition, 1825 to 1922," *American Sociological Review*, 65:631–57.

Dobbin, Frank R., Lauren Edelman, John W. Meyer, W. Richard Scott, and Ann Swidler (1988). "The Expansion of Due Process in Organizations," in *Institutional Patterns and Organizations: Culture and Environment*, 71–98, ed. Lynne G. Zucker. Cambridge, MA: Ballinger.

Dobbin, Frank R., and John R. Sutton (1998). "The Strength of a Weak State: The Rights Revolution and the Rise of Human Resources Management Divisions," *American Journal of Sociology*, 104:441–76.

Dobbin, Frank R., John R. Sutton, John W. Meyer, and W. Richard Scott (1993). "Equal Opportunity Law and the Construction of Internal Labor Markets," *American Journal of Sociology*, 99:396–427.

Doeringer, Peter B., and Michael J. Piore (1971). *Internal Labor Markets and Manpower Analysis*. Lexington, MA: Heath.

Domhoff, G. William (1971). *The Higher Circles: The Governing Class in America*. New York: Viking.

———— (1998). *Who Rules America?* (3rd ed.). Mountain View, CA; Mayfield.

Donabedian, Avedis (1966). "Evaluating the Quality of Medical Care," *Milbank Memorial Fund Quarterly*, 44:(part 2)166–206.

Donaldson, Lex (1985). *In Defence of Organization Theory: A Reply to the Critics*. Cambridge: Cambridge University Press.

———— (1995). *American Anti-Management Theories of Organization: A Critique of Paradigm Proliferation*. Cambridge: Cambridge University Press.

———— (1996). "The Normal Science of Structural Contingency Theory," in *Handbook of Organization Studies*, 57–76, ed. Stewart R. Clegg, Cynthia Hardy, and Walter R. Nord. Thousand Oaks, CA: Sage.

———— (2001). *The Contingency Theory of Organizations*. Thousand Oaks, CA: Sage.

Donaldson, Thomas, and Lee E. Preston (1995). "The Stakeholder Theory of the Corporation: Concepts, Evidence and Implications," *Academy of Management Review*, 20:65–91.

Dore, Ronald (1973). *British Factory—Japanese Factory*. Berkeley: University of California Press.

Dornbusch, Sanford M., and W. Richard Scott, with the assistance of Bruce C. Busching and James D. Laing (1975). *Evaluation and the Exercise of Authority*. San Francisco: Jossey-Bass.

Douglas, Mary (1986). *How Institutions Think*. Syracuse, NY: Syracuse University Press.

Drori, Gili S., John W. Meyer, and Hokyu Hwang, ed. (2006). *Globalization and Organization: World Society and Organizational Change*. New York: Oxford University Press.

Drucker, Peter F. (1946). *The Concept of the Corporation*. New York: John Day.

———— (1976). "What Results Should You Expect? A User's Guide to MBO," *Public Administration Review*, 36:1–45.

Durkheim, Emile (1949 trans.). *Division of Labor in Society*. Glencoe, IL: Free Press (first published in 1893).

———— (1961 trans.). *The Elementary Forms of Religious Life*. New York: Collier (first published in 1912).

Dutton, Jane E., and Janet M. Dukerich (1991). "Keeping an Eye on the Mirror: Image and Identity in Organizational Adaptation," *Administrative Science Quarterly*, 34:517–54.

Eccles, Robert G., and Dwight B. Crane (1988). *Doing Deals: Investment Banks at Work*. Boston: Harvard Business chool Press.

Eccles, Robert G., and Harrison C. White (1986). "Firm and Market Interfaces of Profit Center Control," in *Approaches to Social Theory*, 203–20, ed. Siegwart Lindenberg, James S. Coleman, and Stefan Nowak. New York: Russell Sage Foundation.

———— (1988). "Price and Authority in Inter-Profit Center Transactions," *American Journal of Sociology*, 94(Supplement):S17–S51.

Edelman, Lauren B. (1992). "Legal Ambiguity and Symbolic Structures: Organizational Mediation of Civil Rights Law," *American Journal of Sociology*, 97:1531–76.

Edelman, Lauren B., and Mark C. Suchman (1997). "The Legal Environment of Organizations," *Annual Review of Sociology*, 23:479–515.

———— (1999). "When the 'Haves' Hold Court: Speculations on the Organizational Internalization of Law," *Law and Society Review*, 33:941–92.

Edwards, Richard (1979). *Contested Terrain: The Transformation of the Workplace in the Twentieth Century*. New York: Basic Books.

Eisenberg, Daniel (2001). "Paying to Keep Your Job," *Time* (October 15), 80–83.

Ellul, Jacques (1964 trans.). *The Technological Society*. New York: Knopf (first published in 1954).

Elmore, Richard F. (1978). "Organizational Models of Social Program Implementation," *Public Policy*, 26(Spring):185–228.

Elster, Jon (1983). *Explaining Technical Change: A Case Study in the Philosophy of Science*. Cambridge: Cambridge University Press.

——— (1987). *Nuts and Bolts for the Social Sciences*. Chicago: University of Chicago Press.

Emerson, Richard M. (1962). "Power-Dependence Relations," *American Sociological Review*, 27:31–40.

Emery, Fred E., and E. L. Trist (1965). "The Causal Texture of Organizational Environments," *Human Relations*, 18:21–32.

Emirbayer, Musifer (1997). "Manifesto for a Relational Sociology," *American Journal of Sociology*, 103:281–317.

England, Paula (1992). *Comparable Worth: Theories and Evidence*. New York: Aldine de Gruyter.

England, Paula, and Nancy Folbre (2005). "Gender and Economic Sociology," in *Handbook of Economic Sociology*, 627–49, ed. Neil J. Smelser and Richard Swedberg. Princeton and New York: Princeton University Press and Russell Sage Foundation.

Ermann, M. David, and Richard J. Lundman (1982). *Corporate Deviance*. New York: Holt, Rinehart & Winston.

Esping-Andersen, Gøsta (1985). *The Three Worlds of Welfare Capitalism*. Princeton: Princeton University Press.

Ethiraj, Sendil K., and Daniel Levinthal (2004). "Bounded Rationality and the Search for Organizational Architecture: An Evolutionary Perspective on the Design of Organizations and Their Evolvability," *Administrative Science Quarterly*, 49:404–37.

Etzioni, Amitai (1961). *A Comparative Analysis of Complex Organizations*. New York: Free Press of Glencoe (rev. 1975).

——— (1964). *Modern Organizations*. Upper Saddle River, NJ: Prentice Hall.

——— ed. (1969). *The Semi-Professions and Their Organization*. New York: Free Press.

Evan, William M. (1966). "The Organization Set: Toward a Theory of Interorganizational Relations," in *Approaches to Organizational Design*, 173–88, ed. James D. Thompson. Pittsburgh, PA: University of Pittsburgh Press.

Evans, Peter B. (1981). "Recent Research on Multinational Corporations," *Annual Review of Sociology*, 7:199–223.

——— (1995). *Embedded Autonomy: States and Industrial Transformation*. Princeton: Princeton University Press.

——— (2004). "Development as Institutional Change: The Pitfalls of Monocropping and the Potentials of Deliberation," *Studies in Comparative International Development*, 38(4): 30–52.

Farley, Reynolds (1984). *Blacks and Whites: Narrowing the Gap?* Cambridge, MA: Harvard University Press.

——— (1996). *The New American Reality: Who We Are, How We Got Here, Where We are Going*. New York: Russell Sage Foundation.

Faulkner, Robert R., and Andy B. Anderson (1987). "Short-Term Projects and Emergent Careers: Evidence from Hollywood," *American Journal of Sociology*, 92:879–909.

Faunce, William A. (1968). *Problems of an Industrial Society*. New York: McGraw-Hill.

Fayol, Henri (1949 trans.). *General and Industrial Management*. London: Pitman (first published in 1919).

Featherman, David L., and Robert M. Hauser (1978). *Opportunity and Change*. New York: Academic Press.

Ferber, Marianne A., Brigid O'Farrell, with La Rue Allen, ed. (1991). *Work and Family: Policies for a Changing Work Force*. Washington, DC: National Academy Press.

Fernandez, Roberto M., Emilio J. Castilla, and Paul Moore (2000). "Social Capital at Work: Networks and Employment at a Phone Center," *American Journal of Sociology*, 105:1288–1356.

Festinger, Leon (1957). *A Theory of Cognitive Dissonance*. Evanston, IL: Row, Peterson.

Festinger, Leon, Stanley Schachter, and Kurt Back (1950). *Social Pressures in Informal Groups: A Study of Human Factors in Housing.* Stanford, CA: Stanford University Press.

Fichman, Mark, and Daniel A. Levinthal (1991). "Honeymoons and the Liability of Adolescence: A New Perspective on Duration Dependence in Social and Organizational Relationships," *Academy of Management Review,* 16:442–68.

Fiedler, Fred E. (1964). "A Contingency Model of Leadership Effectiveness," in *Advances in Experimental Social Psychology,* 149–90, ed. Leonard Berkowitz. New York: Academic Press.

——— (1971). "Validation and Extension of the Contingency Model of Leadership Effectiveness: A Review of Empirical Findings," *Psychological Bulletin,* 76:128–48.

Fine, Gary Alan, and Lori J. Ducharme (1995). "The Ethnographic Present: Images of Institutional Control in Second-school Research," in *A Second Chicago School? The Development of a Postwar American Sociology,* 108–35. Chicago: University of Chicago Press.

Finegold, David, Alex Levenson, and Mark Van Buren (2003). "A Temporary Route to Advancement? The Career Opportunities for Low-skilled Workers in Temporary Employment," in *Low-Wage America: How Employers Are Reshaping Opportunity in the Workplace,* ed., Eileen Appelbaum, Annette Berhardt and Richard Murnam. New York: Russell Sage Foundation.

Fineman, Stephen, ed. (2000). *Emotion in Organizations* (2nd ed.). Thousand Oaks, CA: Sage.

Finkelstein, Sydney (1997). "Interindustry Merger Patterns and Resource Dependence: A Replication and Extension of Pfeffer (1972)," *Strategic Management Journal,* 18:787–810.

Fligstein, Neil (1985). "The Spread of the Multidivisional Form among Large Firms, 1919–1979," *American Sociological Review,* 50:377–91.

——— (1987). "The Intraorganizational Power Struggle: The Rise of Finance Presidents in Large Corporations," *American Sociological Review,* 52:44–58.

——— (1990). *The Transformation of Corporate Control.* Cambridge, MA: Harvard University Press.

Flood, Ann Barry, and W. Richard Scott (1987). *Hospital Structure and Performance.* Baltimore: Johns Hopkins University Press.

Follett, Mary Parker (1941). *Dynamic Administration: The Collected Papers of Mary Parker Follett,* ed. Mary C. Metcalf and L. Urwick. New York: Harper.

Foucault, Michel (1977). *Discipline and Punish.* New York: Pantheon.

Franke, Richard Herbert, and James D. Kaul (1978). "The Hawthorne Experiments: First Statistical Interpretation," *American Sociological Review,* 43:623–43.

Freeland, Robert F. (1996). "The Myth of the M-Form? Governance, Consent, and Organizational Change," *American Journal of Sociology,* 102:483–526.

——— (2000). "Creating Holdup through Vertical Integration: Fisher Body Revisited," *Journal of Law and Economics* 43:33–66.

——— (2001). *The Struggle for Control of the Modern Corporation: Organizational Change at General Motors, 1924–70.* New York: Cambridge University Press.

Freeman, John H. (1978). "The Unit of Analysis in Organizational Research," in *Environments and Organizations,* 335–51, ed. Marshall W. Meyer. San Francisco: Jossey-Bass.

——— (1990). "Ecological Analysis of Semi-conductor Firm Mortality," in *Organizational Evolution: New Directions,* 53–77, ed. Jitendra V. Singh. Newbury Park, CA: Sage.

Freeman, John H., and Michael T. Hannan (1983). "Niche Width and the Dynamics of Organizational Populations," *American Journal of Sociology,* 88:1116–45.

Freeman, Linton C. (1978/79). "Centrality in Social Networks: I. Conceptual Clarification," *Social Networks,* 1:215–39.

Freidson, Eliot (1970). *Profession of Medicine.* New York: Dodd, Mead.

——— (1975). *Doctoring Together: A Study of Professional Social Control.* New York: Elsevier.

Friedland, Roger, and Robert R. Alford (1991). "Bringing Society Back In: Symbols, Practices, and Institutional Contradictions," in *The New Institutionalism in Organizational Analysis,* 232–63, ed. Walter W. Powell and Paul J. DiMaggio. Chicago: University of Chicago Press.

Friedman, Milton (1970). "The Social Responsibility of Business is to Increase its Profits," *New York Times Magazine.*

Frost, Peter J., Larry F. Moore, Meryl Reis Louis, Craig C. Lundberg, and Joanne Martin, eds. (1985). *Organizational Culture.* Beverly Hills, CA: Sage.

Galanter, Mark, and T. Palay (1991). *Tournament of Lawyers.* Chicago: University of Chicago Press.

Galaskiewicz, Joseph (1985). *Social Organization of an Urban Grants Economy: A Study of Business Philanthropy and Nonprofit Organizations.* Orlando, FL: Academic Press.

——— (1997). "An Urban Grants Economy Revisited: Corporate Charitable Contributions in the Twin Cities, 1979–81, 1987–89," *Administrative Science Quarterly,* 42:445–71.

Galaskiewicz, Joseph, and Wolfgang Bielefeld (1998). *Nonprofit Organizations in an Age of Uncertainty: A Study of Organizational Change.* New York: Aldine de Gruyter.

Galbraith, Jay R. (1973). *Designing Complex Organizations.* Reading, MA: Addison-Wesley.

——— (1977). *Organization Design.* Reading, MA: Addison-Wesley.

Galbraith, John Kenneth (1967). *The New Industrial State.* Boston: Houghton Mifflin.

Gall, John (1978). *Systematics.* New York: Simon and Schuster, Pocket Books.

Garrett, G. (1998). *Partisan Politics in the Global Economy.* New York: Cambridge University Press.

Geertz, Glifford (1973). *The Interpretation of Cultures.* New York: Basic Books.

Geletkanycz, Marta A., and Donald C. Hambrick (1997). "The External Ties of Top Executives: Implications for Strategic Choice and Performance," *Administrative Science Quarterly,* 42:654–81.

Georgopoulos, Basil S. (1972). "The Hospital as an Organization and Problem-Solving System," in *Organization Research on Health Institutions,* 9–48, ed. Basil S. Georgopoulos. Ann Arbor: Institute for Social Research, University of Michigan.

Gerlach, Michael L., and James R. Lincoln (1992). "The Organization of Business Networks in the United States and Japan," in *Networks and Organizations: Structure, Form, and Action,* 471–90, ed. Nitin Nohria and Robert G. Eccles. Boston: Harvard Business School Press.

Gerstel, N., and Gross, H. E., eds. (1987). *Families and Work.* Philadelphia: Temple University Press.

Ghoshal, Sumantra, and Peter Moran (1996). "Bad for Practice: A Critique of the Transaction Cost Theory," *Academy of Management Review,* 21:13–47.

Ghoshal, Sumantra, and D. Eleanor Westney, eds. (1993). *Organization Theory and the Multinational Corporation.* New York: St. Martin's Press.

Gibson, David (2005). "Taking Turns and Talking Ties: Networks and Conversational Interaction," *American Journal of Sociology,* 110:1561–97.

Gibson, David V., and Everett M. Rogers (1988). "The MCC Comes to Texas," in *Measuring the Information Society: The Texas Studies,* ed. F. Williams. New York: Sage.

Giddens, Anthony (1979). *Central Problems in Social Theory.* Berkeley: University of California Press, 1979.

——— (1983). *Profiles and Critiques in Social Theory.* Berkeley: University of California Press.

——— (1984). *The Constitution of Society.* Berkeley: University of California Press.

——— (2000). *Runaway World: How Globalization is Reshaping Our Lives.* New York: Routledge.

Gilbreth, F. B., and L. M. Gilbreth (1917). *Applied Motion Study.* New York: Van Nostrand.

Gilson, Ronald C. (1981). "A Structural Approach to Corporations: The Case Against Defensive Tactics in Tender Offers," *Stanford Law Review,* 33: 819–91.

Gimeno, Javier, Timothy B. Folta, Arnold C. Cooper, and Carolyn Y. Woo (1997). "Survival of the Fittest? Entrepreneurial Human Capital and the Persistence of Underperforming Firms," *Administrative Science Quarterly,* 42:750–83.

Glassman, Robert (1973). "Persistence and Loose Coupling in Living Systems," *Behavioral Science,* 18:83–98.

Goffman, Erving (1961). *Asylums.* Garden City, NY: Doubleday, Anchor Books.

Goldberg, Victor P. (1980). "Bridges over Contested Terrain: Exploring the Radical Account of the Employment Relation," *Journal of Economic Behavior and Organization* 1:249–74.

Goldner, Fred H. (1970). "The Division of Labor: Process and Power," in *Power in Organizations,* 97–143, ed. Mayer N. Zald. Nashville, TN: Vanderbilt University Press.

Goodman, Paul (1968). *People or Personnel* and *Like a Conquered Province.* New York: Random House, Vintage Books.

Goodrick, Elizabeth, and Gerald R. Salancik (1996). "Organizational Discretion in Responding to Institutional Practices: Hospitals and Cesarean Births," *Administrative Science Quarterly,* 41:1–28.

Gordon, David M., Richard Edwards, and Michael Reich (1982). *Segmented Work, Divided Workers.* Cambridge: Cambridge University Press.

Gordon, Jeffrey N. (1997). "The Shaping Force of Corporate Law in the New Economic Order," *University of Richmond Law Review,* 31:1473–99.

Gosnell, Harold F. (1937). *Machine Politics: Chicago Model.* Chicago: University of Chicago Press.

Gould, Steven Jay. (1997). "Evolution: The Pleasures of Pluralism," *New York Review of Books,* 26:47–52.

Gould, Steven Jay, and N. Eldredge (1977). "Punctuated Equilibria: The Tempo and Mode of Evolution Reconsidered," *Paleobiology,* 3:115–51.

Gouldner, Alvin W. (1954). *Patterns of Industrial Bureaucracy.* Glencoe, IL: Free Press.

Gouldner, Alvin W. (1959). "Organizational Analysis," in *Sociology Today,* 400–28, ed. Robert K. Merton, Leonard Broom, and Leonard S. Cottrell, Jr. New York: Basic Books.

Gowing, Marilyn K., John D. Kraft, and James Campbell Quick, eds. (1998). *The New Organizational Reality: Downsizing, Restructuring and Revitalization.* Washington, DC: American Psychological Association.

Grandori, Anna (1987). *Perspectives on Organization Theory.* Cambridge, MA: Ballinger.

Granovetter, Mark (1973). "The Strength of Weak Ties," *American Journal of Sociology,* 78:1360–80.

——— (1985). "Economic Action and Social Structure: The Problem of Embeddedness," *American Journal of Sociology,* 91:481–510.

——— (1994). "Business Groups," in *The Handbook of Economic Sociology,* 453–75, ed. Neil J. Smelser and Richard Swedberg. Princeton and New York: Princeton University Press and Russell Sage Foundation.

——— (2005). "Business Groups and Social Organization." in *Handbook of Economic Sociology,* (2nd ed.), 429–50, ed., eil J. Smelser and Richard Swedberg. Princeton and New York: Princeton University Press and Russell Sage Foundation.

Granovetter, Mark, and Charles Tilly (1988). "Inequality and Labor Processes," in *Handbook of Sociology,* 175–221, ed. Neil J. Smelser. Newbury Park, CA: Sage.

Green, Pauline, ed. (1995). *Mary Parker Follett: Prophet of Management.* Boston: Harvard Business School Press.

Greenwood, Royston, and C. R. Hinings (1993). "Understanding Strategic Change: The Contribution of Archetypes," *Academy of Management Journal,* 36:1022–54.

——— (1996). "Understanding Radical Organizational Change: Bringing Together the Old and the New Institutionalism," *Academy of Management Review,* 21:1022–54.

Greve, Henrich R. (1995). "Jumping Ship: The Diffusion of Strategy Abandonment," *Administrative Science Quarterly,* 40:444–73.

——— (1998). "Performance, Aspirations, and Risky Organizational Change," *Administrative Science Quarterly,* 43:58–86.

——— (1999). "The Effect of Core Change on Performance: Inertia and Regression Toward the Mean," *Administrative Science Quarterly,* 44:590–614.

Gross, Edward (1953). "Some Functional Consequences of Primary Controls in Formal Work Organizations," *American Sociological Review,* 18:368–73.

——— (1968). "Universities as Organizations: A Research Approach," *American Sociological Review,* 33:518–44.

Guillén, Mauro F. (1994). *Models of Management: Work, Authority, and Organization in Comparative Perspective.* Chicago: University of Chicago Press.

——— (2001). *The Limits of Convergence: Globalization and Organizational Change in Argentina, South Korea, and Spain.* Princeton: Princeton University Press.

Gulati, Ranjay (1995). "Social Structure and Alliance Formation Patterns: A Longitudinal Analysis," *Administrative Science Quarterly,* 40:619–52.

Gulati, Ranjay, and Martin Gargiulo (1999). "Where Do Interorganizational Networks Come From?" *American Journal of Sociology,* 104:1439–93.

Guler, Isin, Mauro E. Guillén, and Hohn Muir MacPherson (2002). "Global Competition, Institutions and the Diffusion of Organizational Practices: The International Spread of ISO 9000 Quality Certificates," *Administrative Science Quarterly,* 47:207–32.

Gulick, Luther, and L. Urwick, eds. (1937). *Papers on the Science of Administration*. New York: Institute of Public Administration, Columbia University.

Gusfield, Joseph R. (1968). "The Study of Social Movements," in *International Encyclopedia of the Social Sciences*, vol. 14, 445–52. New York: Macmillan.

Guthrie, Douglas (1997). "Between Markets and Politics: Organizational Responses to Reform in China," *American Journal of Sociology*, 102:1258–1304.

Guthrie, Douglas, and Michael McQuarrie (2005). "Privatization and the Social Contract: Corporate Welfare and Low-Income Housing in the United States Since 1986," *Research in Political Sociology*, 14:15–51.

Gyllenhammar, P. G. (1977). *People at Work*. Reading, MA: Addison-Wesley.

Habermas, Jurgen (1984/1987). *The Theory of Communicative Action*, vol. 1: *Reason and the Rationalization of Society*; vol. 2: *Lifeworld and System*, trans. T. McCarthy. Boston: Beacon Press.

Haberstroh, Chadwick J. (1965). "Organization Design and Systems Analysis," in *Handbook of Organizations*, 1171–1211, ed. James G. March. Chicago: Rand McNally.

Hackman, J. Richard (1987). "The Design of Work Teams," in *Handbook of Organizational Behavior*, 315–42, ed. Jay W. Lorsch. Upper Saddle River, NJ: Prentice Hall.

——— ed. (1990). *Groups that Work (and Those That Don't): Creating Conditions for Effective Teamwork*. San Francisco: Jossey-Bass.

Hackman, J. Richard, and Greg R. Oldham (1980). *Work Redesign*. Reading, MA: Addison-Wesley.

Hackman, J. Richard, and Ruth Wageman (1995). "Total Quality Management: Empirical, Conceptual and Practical Issues," *Administrative Science Quarterly*, 40:309–42.

Håkansson, Hakon (1989). *Corporate Technological Behavior: Cooperation and Networks*. London: Routledge.

Hall, A. D., and R. E. Fagen (1956). "Definition of System," *General Systems: The Yearbook of the Society for the Advancement of General Systems Theory*, vol. 1, 18–28. Ann Arbor, MI: The Society.

Hall, Douglas T. (1996). "Protean Careers of the 21st Century," *Academy of Management Executive*, 10:(4) 8–16.

Hall, Peter, and David Soskice, eds. (2001). *Varieties of Capitalism*. New York: Oxford University Press.

Hall, Richard H. (1999). (7th ed.). *Organizations: Structures, Processes, and Outcomes*. Upper Saddle River, NJ: Prentice-Hall.

Hamilton, Gary G., and Nicole Woolsey Biggart (1984). *Govenor Reagan, Governor Brown: A Sociology of Executive Power*. New York: Columbia University Press.

——— (1988). "Market, Culture, and Authority: A Comparative Analysis of Management and Organization in the Far East," *American Journal of Sociology*, 94:S52–S94.

Hannan, Michael T., and Glenn R. Carroll (1995). "An Introduction to Organizational Ecology," in *Organizations in Industry: Strategy, Structure and Selection*, 17–31, ed. Glenn R. Carroll and Michael T. Hannan. New York: Oxford University Press.

Hannan, Michael T., Glenn R. Carroll, Elizabeth A. Dundon, and John Charles Torres (1995). "Organizational Evolution in a Multinational Context: Entries of Automobile Manufacturers in Belgium, Britain, France, Germany, and Italy," *American Sociological Review*, 60:509–28.

Hannan, Michael T., and John Freeman (1977). "The Population Ecology of Organizations," *American Journal of Sociology*, 82:929–64.

——— (1984). "Structural Inertia and Organizational Change," *American Sociological Review*, 49:149–64.

——— (1987). "The Ecology of Organizational Founding: American Labor Unions, 1836–1985," *American Journal of Sociology*, 92:910–43.

——— (1989). *Organizational Ecology*. Cambridge, MA: Harvard University Press.

Hardy, Cynthia, and Stewart R. Clegg (1996). "Some Dare Call It Power," in *Handbook of Organizational Studies*, 622–41, ed. Stewart R. Clegg, Cynthia Hardy, and Walter R. Nord. Thousand Oaks, CA: Sage.

Hargadon, Andrew, and Robert I. Sutton (1997). "Technology Brokering and Innovation in a Product Development Firm," *Administrative Science Quarterly*, 42:716–49.

Harris, Douglas H., ed. (1994). *Organizational Linkages: Understanding the Productivity Paradox.* Washington, DC: National Academy Press.

Harrison, Bennett (1994). *Lean and Mean: The Changing Landscape of Corporate Power in the Age of Flexibility.* New York: Basic Books.

Harvey, David (1989). *The Condition of Postmodernity: An Enquiry into the Origins of Cultural Change.* Oxford: Blackwell.

———— (1990). *The Condition of Postmodernity: An Enquiry into the Origins of Cultural Change.* Cambridge: Blackwell.

Haunschild, Pamela R. (1993). "Interorganizational Imitation: The Impact of Interlocks on Corporate Acquisition Activity," *Administrative Science Quarterly*, 38:564–92.

Haunschild, Pamela R., and Christine M. Beckman (1998). "When Do Interlocks Matter?: Alternate Sources of Information and Interlock Influence," *Administrative Science Quarterly*, 43:815–44.

Haveman, Heather A. (1993). "Follow the Leader: Mimetic Isomorphism and Entry into New Markers," *Administrative Science Quarterly*, 38:593–627.

Haveman, Heather A., and Hayagreeva Rao (1997). "Structuring a Theory of Moral Sentiments: Institutional and Organizational Coevolution in the Early Thrift Industry," *American Journal of Sociology*, 102:1606–51.

Hawley, Amos (1950). *Human Ecology.* New York: Ronald Press.

Heclo, Hugh (1977). *A Government of Strangers: Executive Politics in Washington.* Washington, DC: Brookings Institution.

Hedberg, Bo (1981). "How Organizations Learn and Unlearn," in *Handbook of Organizational Design*, vol. 1, 3–27, ed. Paul C. Nystrom and William H. Starbuck. Oxford: Oxford University Press.

Hedberg, Bo, Paul C. Nystrom, and William H. Starbuck (1976). "Camping on Seesaws: Prescriptions for a Self-Designing Organization," *Administrative Science Quarterly*, 21:41–65.

Hedstrom, Peter, and Richard Swedberg, eds. (1998). *Social Mechanisms: An Analytical Approach to Social Theory.* New York: Cambridge University Press.

Heider, Fritz (1958). *The Psychology of Interpersonal Relations.* New York: Wiley.

Heilbroner, Robert L. (1977). *The Economic Transformation of America.* New York: Harcourt Brace Jovanovich.

———— (1980). *An Inquiry into the Human Prospect* (rev. ed.). New York: W. W. Norton.

Heinz, John P., and Edward O. Laumann (1982). *Chicago Lawyers: The Social Structure of the Bar.* New York: Russell Sage Foundation and American Bar Association.

Helper, Susan (1991). "How Much Has Really Changed between U.S. Automakers and Their Suppliers?" *Sloan Management Review*, 32 (Summer):15–28.

Henisz, Witold J., and Andrew Delios (2001). "Uncertainty, Imitation, and Plant Location: Japanese Multinational Corporations, 1990–1996," *Administrative Science Quarterly*, 46:443–75.

Herman, Edward S. (1981). *Corporate Control, Corporate Power.* New York: Cambridge University Press.

Hernes. G. (1998). "Real Virtuality," in *Social Mechanisms: An Analytic Approach to the Social Sciences*, 74–101, ed., Peter Hedstrom and Richard Swedberg. New York: Cambridge University Press.

Herzberg, Frederick (1966). *Work and the Nature of Man.* Cleveland: World Publishing.

Hickson, David J. (1996). "The *ASQ* Years Then and Now Through the Eyes of a Euro-Brit," *Administrative Science Quarterly*, 41:217–28.

Hickson, David J., C. R. Hinings, C. A. Lee, R. E. Schneck, and J. M. Pennings (1971). "A Strategic Contingencies' Theory of Intraorganizational Power," *Administrative Science Quarterly*, 16:216–29.

Hill, Raynard E., and Bernard J. White (1979). *Matrix Organization and Project Management.* Ann Arbor: University of Michigan Press.

Hillery, George A., Jr. (1968). *Communal Organization: A Study of Local Societies.* Chicago: University of Chicago Press.

Hinings, C. R., D. J. Hickson, J. M. Pennings, and R. E. Schneck (1974). "Structural Conditions of Intraorganizational Power," *Administrative Science Quarterly*, 19:22–44.

Hirsch, Paul M. (1972). "Processing Fads and Fashions: An Organization-Set Analysis of Cultural Industry Systems," *American Journal of Sociology*, 77:639–59.

—— (1985). "The Study of Industries," in *Research in the Sociology of Organizations*, vol. 4, 271–309, ed. Samuel B. Bacharach and Stephen M. Mitchell. Greenwich, CT: JAI Press.

Hirschman, Albert O. (1970). *Exit, Voice, and Loyalty*. Cambridge, MA: Harvard University Press.

Hobsbawn, Eric, and Terence Ranger, eds. (1983). *The Invention of Tradition*. Cambridge: Cambridge University Press.

Hochschild, Arlie Russell (1983). *The Managed Heart: Commercialization of Human Feeling*. Berkeley: University of California Press.

—— (1989). *The Second Shift: Working Parents and the Revolution at Home*. New York: Viking.

Hodson, R. D. (1996). "Dignity in the Workplace Under Participative Management: Alienation and Freedom Revisited," *American Sociological Review*, 61:719–38.

Hoffman, Andrew J. (1997). *From Heresy to Dogma: An Institutional History of Corporate Environmentalism*. San Francisco: New Lexington Press.

—— (1999). "Institutional Evolution and Change: Environmental and the U.S. Chemical Industry," *Academy of Management Journal*, 42:351–71.

Hoffman, Andrew J., and Marc J. Ventresca, eds. (2002). *Organizations, Policy and the Natural Environment: Institutional and Strategic Perspectives*. Stanford, CA: Stanford University Press.

Hofstadter, Richard (1945). *Social Darwinism in American Thought, 1860–1915*. Philadelphia: University of Pennsylvania Press.

Hofstede, Geert (1984). *Culture's Consequences: International Differences in Work-Related Values* (abridged ed.). Beverly Hills, CA: Sage.

—— (1991). *Cultures and Organizations: Software of the Mind*. New York: McGraw-Hill.

Hofstede, Geert, and Michael Harris Bond (1988). "The Confucius Connection: From Cultural Roots to Economic Growth," *Organizational Dynamics*, 16:4–21.

Hofstede, Geert, and M. S. Kassem, eds. (1976). *European Contributions to Organization Theory*. Assen, The Netherlands: Van Gorcum.

Hollander, Edwin P., and James W. Julian (1969). "Contemporary Trends in the Analysis of Leadership Processes," *Psychological Bulletin*, 71:387–97.

Homans, George C. (1950). *The Human Group*. New York: Harcourt.

—— (1961). *Social Behavior: Its Elementary Forms*. New York: Harcourt, Brace & World.

House, Robert J., Paul J. Hanges, Mansour Javidan, Peter W. Dorfman, and Vipin Gupta, eds. (2004). *Culture, Leadership, and Organizations: The GLOBE Study of 62 Societies*. Thousand Oaks, CA: Sage.

Huber, George P. (1990). "A Theory of the Effects of Advanced Information Technologies on Organizational Design, Intelligence, and Decision Making," *Academy of Management Review*, 15:47–71.

Huber, George P., and William H. Glick (1993). *Organizational Change and Redesign: Ideas and Insights for Improving Performance*. New York: Oxford University Press.

Hughes, Everett C. (1958). *Men and Their Work*. Glencoe, IL: Free Press.

Hulin, Charles L., and Milton R. Blood (1968). "Job Enlargement, Individual Differences, and Worker Responses," *Psychological Bulletin*, 69:41–55.

Hulin, Charles L., and M. Roznowski (1985). "Organizational Technologies: Effects on Organizations' Characteristics and Individuals' Responses," in *Research in Organizational Behavior*, vol. 7, 39–85, ed. L. L. Cummings and Barry M. Staw. Greenwich, CT: JAI Press.

Hult, Karen M., and Charles Walcott (1990). *Governing Public Organizations: Politics, Structures, and Institutional Design*. Pacific Grove, CA: Brooks/Cole.

Ibarra, Herminia (1995). "Race, Opportunity, and Diversity of Social Circles in Managerial Networks," *Academy of Management Journal*, 38:673–703.

Illich, Ivan (1972). *Deschooling Society*. New York: Harper & Row.

—— (1976). *Medical Nemesis*. New York: Random House.

Ingram, Paul, and Joel A. C. Baum (1997). "Chain Affiliation and the Failure of Manhattan Hotels, 1898–1980," *Administrative Science Quarterly*, 42:68–102.

Ingram, Paul, and Crist Inman (1996). "Institutions, Intergroup Competition, and the Evolution of Hotel Populations Around Niagara Falls," *Administrative Science Quarterly*, 41:629–58.

Ingram, Paul, and Hayagreeva Rao (2004). "Store Wars: The Enactment and Repeal of Anti-Chain-Store Legislation in America," *American Journal of Sociology*, 110:446–87.

Inkeles, Alex, and Daniel J. Levinson (1969). "National Character: The Study of Modal Personality and Sociocultural Systems," in *The Handbook of Social Psychology* (2nd ed.), vol. 4, 418–506, ed. Gardner Lindzey and Elliot Aronson. Reading, MA: Addison-Wesley.

ISO (International Organization for Standardization) (1992). *International Standards for Quality Management—Compendium.* (2nd ed.). Geneva: ISO 9000 Central Secretariat.

Israel, Joachim (1971). *Alienation: From Marx to Modern Sociology.* Boston: Allyn & Bacon.

Jacoby, Sanford M. (1985). *Employing Bureaucracy: Managers, Unions, and the Transformation of Work in American Industry, 1900–1945.* New York: Columbia University Press.

James, Henry (1907). Preface to *Roderick Hudson.* New York: Scribner's.

Jaques, Elliott (1951). *The Changing Culture of a Factory.* London: Tavistock.

Jelinek, Mariann, Linda Smircich, and Paul M. Hirsch, eds. (1983). "Organizational Culture," *Administrative Science Quarterly*, 28(September), entire issue.

Jensen, Michael (2003). "The Role of Network Resources in Market Entry: Commercial Banks' Entry into Investment Banking, 1991–1997," *Administrative Science Quarterly*, 48:466–97.

——— (2006). "Should We Stay or Should We Go? Accountability, Status Anxiety, and Client Defections," *Administrative Science Quarterly*, 51:97–128.

Jensen, Michael C. (1988). "Takeovers: Their Causes and Consequences," *Journal of Economic Perspectives*, 2:21–48.

——— (2002). "Value Maximization, Stakeholder Theory, and the Corporate Objective Function," *Business Ethics Quarterly*, 12:235–56.

Jensen, Michael C., and William H. Meckling (1976). "Theory of the Firm: Managerial Behavior, Agency Costs, and Ownership Structure," *Journal of Financial Economics*, 3:305–60.

Jensen, Michael C., and Kevin J. Murphy (1990). "It Not How Much You Pay, But How," *Harvard Business Review*, 90(3):128–53.

Jevon, W. S. (1965 trans.). *The Theory of Political Economy.* New York: Kelley (first published in 1871).

Jones, Stephen R. G. (1990). "Worker Interdependence and Output: The Hawthorne Studies Reevaluated," *American Sociological Review*, 55:176–90.

——— (1992). "Was There a Hawthorne Effect?" *American Journal of Sociology*, 98:451–68.

Kadushin, Charles (1995). "Friendship among the French Financial Elite," *American Sociological Review*, 60:202–21.

Kahn, Robert L. (1990). "Organizational Theory and International Relations: Mutually Informing Paradigms," in *Organizations and Nation-States: New Perspectives on Conflict and Cooperation*, 1–15, ed. Robert L. Kahn and Mayer N. Zald. San Francisco: Jossey-Bass.

Kahneman, Daniel, P. Slovic, and Amos Tversky (1982). *Judgment under Uncertainty: Heuristics and Biases.* Cambridge: Cambridge University Press.

Kalberg, Stephen (1980). "Max Weber's Types of Rationality: Cornerstones for the Analysis of Rationalization Processes in History," *American Journal of Sociology*, 85:1145–79.

Kalleberg, Arne L., David Knoke, Peter V. Marsden, and Joe L. Spaeth (1996). *Organizations in America: Analyzing Their Structures and Human Resource Practices.* Thousand Oaks, CA: Sage.

Kanigel, Robert (1997). *The One Best Way: Frederick Winslow Taylor and the Enigma of Efficiency.* New York: Viking.

Kanter, Rosabeth Moss (1977a). *Men and Women of the Corporation.* New York: Basic Books.

——— (1977b). *Work and Family in the United States: A Critical Review and Agenda for Research and Policy.* New York: Russell Sage Foundation.

——— (1989). *When Giants Learn to Dance: Mastering the Challenges of Strategy, Management and Careers in the 1990s.* New York: Simon and Schuster.

——— (1994). "Collaborative Advantage: The Art of Alliances," *Harvard Business Review*, 72 (July–August):96–108.

Katz, Daniel, and Robert L. Kahn (1952). "Some Recent Findings in Human Relations Research in Industry," in *Readings in Social Psychology* (2nd ed.), 650–65, ed. Guy E. Swanson, Theodor M. Newcomb, and Eugene L. Hartley. New York: Holt.

———— (1966). *The Social Psychology of Organizations.* New York: John Wiley.

———— (1978). *The Social Psychology of Organizations* (2nd ed.). New York: John Wiley (first ed. published in 1966).

Katz, Daniel, Nathan Maccoby, and Nancy Morse (1950). *Productivity, Supervision and Morale in an Office Situation.* Ann Arbor, Ml: Insitute for Social Research.

Kaysen, Carl (1957). "The Social Significance of the Modern Corporation," *American Economic Review* (Papers and Proceedings), 47:311–19.

Keister, Lisa A. (1998). "Engineering Growth: Business Group Structure and Firm Performance in China's Transition Economy," *American Journal of Sociology*, 104:404–40.

———— (2001). "Exchange Structures in Transition: Lending and Trade Relations in Chinese Business Groups," *American Sociological Review*, 66:336–60.

Kelman, Herbert C., and V. Lee Hamilton (1989). *Crimes of Obedience: Toward a Social Psychology of Authority and Responsibility.* New Haven: Yale University Press.

Kennedy, John F. (1962). "Commencement Address at Yale University, June 11, 1962" in *Public Papers of the Presidents*, 470–475. Washington, DC: U.S. Government Printing Office.

Kennedy, Robert F. (1969). *Thirteen Days: A Memoir of the Cuban Missile Crisis.* New York: W. W. Norton.

Kerr, Clark, John T. Dunlop, Frederick Harbison, and Charles A. Myers (1964). *Industrialism and Industrial Man* (2nd ed.). New York: Oxford University Press.

Khagram, Sanjeev (2004). *Dams and Development: Transnational Struggles for Water and Power.* Ithaca, NY: Cornell University Press.

Khandwalla, Pradip N. (1974). "Mass Output Orientation of Operations Technology and Organizational Structure," *Administrative Science Quarterly*, 19:74–97.

Khandwalla, Pradip N. (1977). *The Design of Organizations.* New York: Harcourt Brace Jovanovich.

Khanna, Tarun, and Krishna Palepu (2000). "The Future of Business Groups in Emerging Markets: Long-Run Evidence from Chile," *Academy of Management Journal*, 43:268–85.

Khurana, Rakesh (2002). *Searching for a Corporate Savior: The Irrational Quest for Charismatic CEOs.* Prince, NJ: Princeton University Press.

Kilduff, Martin, and Wenpin Tsai (2003). *Social Networks and Organizations.* Thousand Oaks, CA: Sage.

Klein, Benjamin, Robert G. Crawford, and Armen A. Alchian (1978). "Vertical Integration, Appropriable Rents, and the Competitive Contracting Process," *Journal of Law and Economics*, 21:297–326.

Klein, Katherine, Henry Tosi, and Albert A. Cannella, Jr., eds. (1999). "Special Topic Forum on Multilevel Theory Building," *Academy of Management Review*, 24:243–343.

Klitgaard, Robert (1991). *Controlling Corruption.* Berkeley: University of California Press.

Knoke, David (2001). *Changing Organizations: Business Networks in the New Political Economy.* Boulder, CO: Westview Press.

Knorr-Cetina, Karin (1999). *Epistemic Cultures: How the Sciences Make Knowledge.* Cambridge, MA: Harvard University Press.

Kochan, Thomas A., Harry C. Katz, and Robert B. McKersie (1994). *The Transformation of American Industrial Relations* (2nd ed.). New York: Basic Books.

Kock, Carl J., and Mauro F. Guillén (2001). "Strategy and Structure in Developing Countries: Business Groups as an Evolutionary Response to Opportunities for Unrelated Diversification," *Industrial and Corporate Change*, 10:77–113.

Kogut, Bruce, and Gordon Walker (2001). "The Small World of Germany and the Durability of National Networks," *American Sociological Review*, 66:317–35.

Kohn, Melvin L., and Carmi Schooler (1983). *Work and Personality: An Inquiry into the Impact of Social Stratification.* Norwood, NJ: Ablex.

Kono, Clifford, Donald Palmer, Roger Friedland, and Matthew Zafonte (1998). "Lost in Space: The Geography of Corporate Interlocking Directorates," *American Journal of Sociology*, 103:863–911.

Kornhauser, William (1962). *Scientists in Industry: Conflict and Accommodation.* Berkeley: University of California Press.

Korten, David C. (2001). *When Corporations Rule the World* (2nd ed.). San Francisco: Berrett-Koehler.

Kotter, John P. (1995). *The New Rules: How to Succeed in Today's Post-Corporate World*. New York: Free Press.

Kraakman, Reinier (2001). "The Durability of the Corporate Form," in *The Twenty-First-Century Firm: Changing Economic Organization in International Perspective*, 147–60, ed. Paul J. DiMaggio. Princeton: Princeton University Press.

Kraatz, Matthew S., and Edward J. Zajac (1996). "Exploring the Limits of the New Institutionalism: The Causes and Consequences of Illegitimate Organizational Change," *American Sociological Review*, 61:812–36.

Kreps, Gary L. (1986). *Organizational Communication: Theory and Practice*. New York: Longman.

Krupp, Sherman (1961). *Pattern in Organizational Analysis*. Philadelphia: Chilton.

Kuhn, Thomas S. (1962). *The Structure of Scientific Revolutions*. Chicago: University of Chicago Press.

Kunda, Gideon (1992). *Engineering Culture: Control and Commitment in a High-Tech Corporation*. Philadelphia: Temple University Press.

Lambsdorff, Johann Graf (1999a). "Corruption in Empirical Research—A Review," *Transparency International Working Paper*.

——— (1999b). "The transparency international corruption perceptions index," Framework document.

Lammers, Cornelis J., and David J. Hickson, eds. (1979). *Organizations Alike and Unlike: International and Interinstitutional Studies in the Sociology of Organizations*. London: Routledge & Kegan Paul.

Landsberger, Henry A. (1958). *Hawthorne Revisited*. Ithaca, NY: Cornell University Press.

——— (1961). "Parsons' Theory of Organizations," in *Social Theories of Talcott Parsons*, 214–49, ed. Max Black. Upper Saddle River, NJ: Prentice Hall.

Langewiesche, William (2004). *The Outlaw Sea: A World of Freedom, Chaos, and Crime*. New York: North Point Press.

Langlois, Richard N., ed. (1986). *Economics as a Process: Essays in the New Institutional Economics*. New York: Cambridge University Press.

Lant, Theresa A., and Joel A. C. Baum (1995). "Cognitive Sources of Socially Constructed Competitive Groups," in *The Institutional Construction of Organizations: International and Longtudinal Studies*, 15–38, ed. W. Richard Scott and Søren Christensen. Thousand Oaks, CA: Sage.

LaPorta, Rafael, Florencio Lopez-de-Silanes, Andrei Shleifer, and Robert W. Vishny (1998). "Law and Finance," *Journal of Political Economy*, 106:1113–55.

LaPorte, Todd R. (1982). "On the Design and Management of Nearly Error-Free Organizational Control Systems," in *Accident at Three Mile Island: The Human Dimensions*, 185–200, ed. David L. Sills, C. P. Wolf, and Vivian B. Shelanski. Boulder, CO: Westview Press.

Larson, Andrea (1992). "Network Dyads in Entrepreneurial Settings: A Study of the Governance of Exchange Relationships," *Administrative Science Quarterly*, 37:76–104.

Larson, Erik W., and David H. Gobeli (1987). "Matrix Management: Contradictions and Insight," *California Management Review*, 29:126–38.

Larson, Magali Sarfatti (1977). *The Rise of Professionalism*. Berkeley: University of California Press.

Lash, S. (1988). "Postmodernism as a Regime of Signification," *Theory, Culture and Society*, 5:311–36.

Laumann, Edward O., and David Knoke (1987). *The Organizational State: Social Choice in National Policy Domains*. Madison: University of Wisconsin Press.

Laumann, Edward O., Peter V. Marsden, and David Prensky (1983). "The Boundary Specification Problem in Network Analysis," in *Applied Network Analysis*, 18–34, ed. Ronald S. Burt and Michael J. Minor. Beverly Hills, CA: Sage.

Lawrence, Paul R. (1993). "The Contingency Approach to Organization Design," in *Handbook of Organizational Behavior*, 9–18, ed. Robert T. Golembiewski. New York: Marcel Dekker.

Lawrence, Paul R., and Jay W. Lorsch (1967). *Organization and Environment: Managing Differentiation and Integration*. Boston: Graduate School of Business Administration, Harvard University.

———— (1967a). "Differentiation and Integration in Complex Organizations," *Administrative Science Quarterly*, 12:1–47.

Lazerson, Mark (1995). "A New Phoenix?: Modern Putting-Out in the Modena Knitwear Industry," *Administrative Science Quarterly*, 40:34–59.

Leavitt, Harold J., William R. Dill, and Henry B. Eyring (1973). *The Organizational World*. New York: Harcourt Brace Jovanovich.

Leblebici, Husayin, Gerald R. Salancik, Anne Copay, and Tom King (1991). "Institutional Change and the Transformation of Interorganizational Fields: An Organizational History of the U.S. Radio Broadcasting Industry," *Administrative Science Quarterly*, 36:333–63.

Leicht, Kevin T., and Mary L. Fennell (2001). *Professional Work: A Sociological Approach*. Malden, MA: Basil Blackwell.

Lemann, N. (1999). *The Big Test*. New York: Farrar, Straus & Giroux.

Lenin, V. I. (1939). *Imperialism: The Highest Stage of Capitalism*. New York: International Publishers (originally published, 1916).

Levine, Sol, and Paul E. White (1961). "Exchange as a Conceptual Framework for the Study of Interorganizational Relationships," *Aministrative Science Quarterly*, 5:583–601.

Levinthal, Daniel A., and Mark Fichman (1988). "Dynamics of Interorganizational Attachments: Auditor-Client Relationships," *Administrative Science Quarterly*, 33:345–69.

Levitt, Barbara, and James G. March (1988). "Organizational Learning," *Annual Review of Sociology*, 14:319–40.

Levitt, Ray E., J. Thomson, T. R. Christiansen, John C. Kunz, and Yan Jin (1994). "Virtual Design Team: Simulating How Organizational Structure and Information Processing Tools Affect Team Performance," in *Computational Organization Theory*, ed. Kathleen M. Carley and M. J. Prietula. Hillsdale, NJ: Lawrence Erbaum Associates.

Levy, David (1994). "Chaos Theory and Strategy: Theory, Applications, and Managerial Implications," *Strategic Management Journal*, 15:167–78.

Lewin, Kurt (1948). *Resolving Social Conflicts*. New York: Harper.

Lewis, Marianne W., and Andrew J. Grimes (1999). "Metatriangulation: Building Theory from Multiple Paradigms," *Academy of Management Review*, 24: 672–90.

Likert, Rensis (1961). *New Patterns of Management*. New York: McGraw-Hill.

Lilienthal, David E. (1944). *TVA: Democracy on the March*. New York: Harper & Brothers.

Lin, Yi-min (2001). *Between Politics and Markets: Firms, Competition, and Institutional Change in Post-Mao China*. New York: Cambridge University Press.

Lincoln, James R., Michael L. Gerlach, and Christina L. Ahmadjian (1996). "Keiretsu Networks and Corporate Performance in Japan," *American Sociological Review*, 61:67–88.

Lincoln, James R., Michael L. Gerlach, and Peggy Takahashi (1992). "Keiretsu Networks in the Japanese Economy: A Dyad Analysis of Intercorporate Ties," *American Sociological Review*, 57:561–85.

Lincoln, James R., Mitsuyo Hanada, and Kerry McBride (1986). "Organizational Structures in Japanese and U.S. Manufacturing," *Administrative Science Quarterly*, 31:338–64.

Lincoln, James R., and Arne L. Kalleberg (1990). *Culture, Control and Commitment: A Study of Work Organization and Work Attitudes in the United States and Japan*. New York: Cambridge University Press.

Lindblom, Charles E. (1977). *Politics and Markets*. New York: Basic Books.

Lipset, Seymour Martin (1986). "North American Labor Movements: A Comparative Perspective," in *Unions in Transition: Entering the Second Century*, 421–77, ed. Seymour Martin Lipset. San Francisco: Institute for Contemporary Studies.

Lipset, Seymour Martin, Martin A. Trow, and James S. Coleman (1956). *Union Democracy*. Glencoe, IL: Free Press.

Lipsky, Michael (1980). *Street-Level Bureaucracy*. New York: Russell Sage Foundation.

Littman, Mark S., ed. (1998). *A Statistical Portrait of the United States: Social Conditions and Trends*. Lanham, MD: Bernan Press.

Litwak, Eugene (1961). "Models of Bureaucracy Which Permit Conflict," *American Journal of Sociology*, 67:177–84.

Litwak, Eugene, and Henry J. Meyer (1966). "A Balance Theory of Coordination between Bureaucratic Organizations and Community Primary Groups," *Administrative Science Quarterly*, 11:3–58.

Lomi, Alessandro (1995). "The Population Ecology of Organizational Founding: Location Dependence and Unobserved Heterogeneity," *Administrative Science Quarterly*, 40:111–44.

Lounsbury, Michael (2001). "Institutional Sources of Practice Variation: Staffing College and University Recycling Programs," *Administrative Science Quarterly*, 46:29–56.

―――― (2005). "Institutional Variation in the Evolution of Social Movements: Competing Logics and the Spread of Recycling Advocacy Groups," in *Social Movements and Organization Theory*, 73–95, ed. Gerald F. Davis, Doug McAdam, W. Richard Scott, and Mayer N. Zald. New York: Cambridge University Press.

Lounsbury, Michael, Marc J. Ventresca, and Paul M. Hirsch (2003). "Social Movements, Field Frames, and Industry Emergence: A Cultural-political Perspective," *Socio-Economic Review*, 1:70–104.

Lowin, Aaron, and James R. Craig (1968). "The Influence of Level of Performance on Managerial Style: An Experimental Object-Lesson in the Ambiguity of Correlational Data," *Organizational Behavior and Human Performance*, 3:440–58.

Lowther, Nicola J. (1997). "Organized Crime and Extortion in Russia: Implications for Foreign Companies," *Transnational Organized Crime*, 3(1):23–38.

Lyden, F. J. (1975). "Using Parsons' Functional Analysis in the Study of Public Organizations," *Administrative Science Quarterly*, 20:59–70.

Lyotard, J. F. (1984). *The Postmodern Condition: A Report on Knowledge*. Minneapolis: University of Minnesota Press.

MacIver, Robert M. (1947). *The Web of Government*. New York: Macmillan.

Mannheim, Karl (1950 trans.). *Man and Society in an Age of Reconstruction*, trans. Edward Shils. New York: Harcourt Brace Jovanovich (first published in 1935).

March, James G., ed. (1965). *Handbook of Organizations*. Chicago: Rand McNally.

―――― (1981). "Decisions in Organizations and Theories of Choice," in *Perspectives on Organization Design and Behavior*, 205–44, ed. Andrew H. Van de Ven and William F. Joyce. New York: John Wiley, Wiley-Interscience.

―――― (1988). *Decisions and Organizations*. Oxford: Basil Blackwell.

―――― (1991). "Exploration and Exploitation in Organizational Learning," *Organization Science*, 2:71–87.

―――― (1994). *A Primer on Decision Making: How Decisions Happen*. New York: Free Press.

March, James G., and Herbert A. Simon (1958). *Organizations*. New York: John Wiley.

March, James G., and Johan P. Olsen (1976). *Ambiguity and Choice in Organizations*. Bergen, Norway: Universitetsforlaget.

―――― (1989). *Rediscovering Institutions: The Organizational Basis of Politics*. New York: Free Press.

Marglin, Stephen (1974). "What Do Bosses Do?: The Origins and Functions of Hierarchy in Capitalist Production," *Review of Radical Political Economics*, 6(Summer):60–112.

Margolis, Joshua D., and James P. Walsh (2003). "Misery Loves Companies: Rethinking Social Iniatives by Business," *Administrative Science Quarterly*, 48:268–305.

Marini, Margaret Mooney (1989). "Sex Differences in Earnings in the United States," *Annual Review of Sociology*, 15:343–80.

Marion, Russ (1999). *The Edge of Organization: Chaos and Complexity Theories of Formal Social Systems*. Thousand Oaks, CA: Sage.

Marquis, Christopher (2003). "The Pressure of the Past: Network Imprinting in Intercorporate Communities," *Administrative Science Quarterly*, 48:655–89.

Marquis, Christopher, MaryAnn Glynn, and Gerald F. Davis (2006). "Community Isomorphism and Corporate Social Action," *Academy of Management Review*.

Marsden, Peter M. (1990). "Network Data and Measurement," *Annual Review of Sociology*, 16:435–63.

Marshall, Alfred (1890). *Principles of Economics*. London: Macmillan.

Martin, Joanne (1990). "Deconstructing Organizational Taboos: The Suppression of Gender Conflict in Organizations," *Organization Science*, 1:339–59.

―――― (1992). *Cultures in Organizations: Three Perspectives*. New York: Oxford University Press.

―――― (2002). *Organizational Culture: Mapping the Terrain*. Thousand Oaks, CA: Sage.

Martin, Joanne, and Kathy Knopoff (1997). "The Gendered Implications of Apparently Gender-Neutral Organizational Theory: Re-reading Weber," in *Ruffin Lectures Series*, vol. 3,

Business Ethics and Women's Studies, 30–49, ed. A. Larson and E. Freeman. Oxford: Oxford University Press.

Martin, Xavier, Anand Swaminathan, and Will Mitchell (1998). "Organizational Evolution in the Interorganizational Environment: Incentives and Constraints on International Expansion Strategy," *Administrative Science Quarterly*, 43:566–601.

Marx, Karl (1954 trans.). *Capital.* Moscow: Foreign Languages Publishing House (first published in 1867).

—— (1963 trans.). *Karl Marx: Early Writings*, trans. and ed. T. B. Bottomore. London: C. A. Watts (first published as *Economic and Philosophical Manuscripts* in 1844).

—— (1972 trans.). "Economic and Philosophic Manuscripts of 1844: Selections," in *The Marx-Engels Reader*, ed. Robert C. Tucker. New York: W. W. Norton.

—— (1973 trans.). *Grundrisse: Foundations of the Critique of Political Economy.* Harmondsworth, England: Penguin (first published in 1839–1841).

Marx, Karl, and Frederick Engels (1955 trans.). *Manifesto of the Communist Party.* Moscow: Foreign Languages Publishing House (first published in 1848).

Maslow, Abraham (1954). *Motivation and Personality.* New York: Harper.

Massie, Joseph L. (1965). "Management Theory," in *Handbook of Organizations*, 387–422, ed. James G. March. Chicago: Rand McNally.

Masten, Scott E. (1984). "The Organization of Production: Evidence from the Aerospace Industry," *Journal of Law and Economics*, 27:403–17.

Maurice, Marc (1979). "For a Study of 'The Societal Effect': Universality and Specificity in Organization Research," in *Organizations Alike and Unlike: Inter-Institutional Studies in the Sociology of Organizations*, 42–60, ed. Cornelis J. Lammers and David J. Hickson. London: Routledge & Kegan Paul.

Maurice, Marc, Arndt Sorge, and Malcolm Warner (1980). "Societal Differences in Organizing Manufacturing Units: A Comparison of France, West Germany, and Great Britain," *Organizational Studies*, 1:59–86.

Mayer, Martin (1997). *The Bankers: The Next Generation.* New York: Truman Talley.

Mayer, Michael C. J., and Richard Whittington (1999). "Strategy, Structure and 'Systemness': National Institutions and Corporate Change in France, Germany and the UK, 1950–1993," *Organization Studies*, 20:933–59.

Mayo, Elton (1945). *The Social Problems of an Industrial Civilization.* Boston: Graduate School of Business Administration, Harvard University.

McAdam, Doug (1999). *Political Process and the Development of Black Insurgency, 1930–1970* (2nd ed.). Chicago: University of Chicago Press (first edition published in 1982).

McAdam, Doug, John D. McCarthy, and Mayer N. Zald, eds. (1996a). *Comparative Perspectives on Social Movements: Political Opportunities, Mobilizing Structures and Cultural Framings.* New York: Cambridge University Press.

McAdam, Doug, John D. McCarthy, and Mayer N. Zald (1996b). "Introduction: Opportunities, Mobilizing Structures, and Framing Processes—Toward a Synthetic, Comparative Perspective on Social Movements," in *Comparative Perspectives on Social Movements: Political Opportunities, Mobilizing Structures and Cultural Meanings*, 1–40, ed. Doug McAdam, John D. McCarthy, and Mayer D. Zald. Cambridge: Cambridge University Press.

McAdam, Doug, and W. Richard Scott (2005). "Organizations and Movements." in *Social Movements and Organizational Theory*, ed. Davies, Gerald F., Doug Mc Adam, W. Richard Scott, and Mayer N. Zald. New York: Cambridge University Press.

McAdam, Doug, Sidney Tarrow, and Charles Tilly (2001). *Dynamics of Contention.* New York: Cambridge University Press.

McClelland, Douglas C. (1961). *The Achieving Society.* New York: D. Van Nostrand.

McEwen, C. A. (1980). "Continuities in the Study of Total and Nontotal Institutions," *Annual Review of Sociology*, 6:143–85.

McGregor, Douglas (1960). *The Human Side of Enterprise.* New York: McGraw-Hill.

McKelvey, Bill (1982). *Organizational Systematics.* Berkeley: University of California Press.

McKelvey, Bill, and Joel A. C. Baum (1999). "Donald T. Campbell's Evolving Influence in Organization Science," in *Variations in Organization Science: In Honor of Donald T. Campbell*, 383–411. Thousand Oaks, CA: Sage.

McKinley, William, Mark A. Mone, and Gyewan Moon (1999). "Determinants and Development of Schools in Organization Theory," *Academy of Management Review*, 24: 634–48.

McLean, Bethany, and Peter Elkind (2003). *The Smartest Guys in the Room: The Amazing Rise and Scandalous Fall of Enron.* New York: Portfolio.

McLuhan, Marshall (1964). *Understanding Media: The Extensions of Man.* New York: Signet.

McNeil, Kenneth (1978). "Understanding Organizational Power: Building on the Weberian Legacy," *Administrative Science Quarterly*, 23:65–90.

McPherson, J. Miller (1983). "An Ecology of Affiliation," *American Sociological Review*, 48:519–35.

Mechanic, David (1962). "Sources of Power of Lower Participants in Complex Organizations," *Administrative Science Quarterly*, 7:349–62.

Mendel, Peter J. (2002). "International Standardization and Global Governance: The Spread of Quality and Environmental Management Standards, in *Organizations, Policy, and the Natural Environment: Institutional and Strategic Perspectives*, 407–31, ed. Andrew J. Hoffman and Marc J. Ventresca. Stanford, CA: Stanford University Press.

Merton, Robert K. (1957). *Social Theory and Social Structure* (2nd ed.). Glencoe, IL: Free Press.

——— (1968). "On Sociological Theories of the Middle Range." in *Social Theory and Social Structure* (3rd ed.), 39–72. New York: Free Press.

Merton, Robert K., Ailsa P. Gray, Barbara Hockey, and Hanan C. Selvin, eds. (1952). *Reader in Bureaucracy.* Glencoe, IL: Free Press.

Meyer, John W. (1977). "The Effects of Education as an Institution," *American Journal of Sociology*, 83:55–77.

——— (1978). "Strategies for Further Research: Varieties of Environmental Variation," in *Environments and Organizations*, 352–68, ed. Marshall W. Meyer. San Francisco: Jossey-Bass.

——— (1983). "Institutionalization and the Rationality of Formal Organizational Structure," in *Organizational Environments: Ritual and Rationality*, 261–82, by John W. Meyer and W. Richard Scott. Beverly Hills, CA: Sage.

——— (1994). "Rationalized Environments," in *Institutional Environments and Organizations: Structural Complexity and Individualism*, 28–54, ed. W. Richard Scott and John W. Meyer. Thousand Oaks, CA: Sage.

Meyer, John W., John Boli, and George M. Thomas (1987). "Ontology and Rationalization in the Western Cultural Account," in *Institutional Structure: Constituting State, Society, and the Individual*, 12–37, ed. George M. Thomas, John W. Meyer, Francisco O. Ramirez, and John Boli. Newbury Park, CA: Sage.

Meyer, John W., John Boli, George M. Thomas, and Francisco O. Ramirez (1997). "World Society and the Nation State," *American Journal of Sociology*, 103:144–81.

Meyer, John W., Gili S. Drori, and Hokhu Hwang (2006). "World Society and the Proliferation of Formal Organization," in *Globalization and Organization: World Society and Organizational Change*," 25–49, ed., Gili S. Drori, John W. Meyer and Hokyu Hwang. New York: Oxford University Press.

Meyer, John W., and Ronald L. Jepperson (2000). "The 'Actors' of Modern Society: The Cultural Construction of Social Agency," *Sociological Theory*, 18:100–20.

Meyer, John W., and Brian Rowan (1977). "Institutionalized Organizations: Formal Structure as Myth and Ceremony," *American Journal of Sociology*, 83:340–63.

——— (1978). "The Structure of Educational Organizations," in *Environments and Organizations*, 78–109, ed. Marshall W. Meyer. San Francisco: Jossey-Bass.

Meyer, John W., and W. Richard Scott, with the assistance of Brian Rowan and Terrence E. Deal (1983). *Organizational Environments: Ritual and Rationality.* Beverly Hills, CA: Sage.

Meyer, John W., W. Richard Scott, and David Strang (1987). "Centralization, Fragmentation, and School District Complexity," *Administrative Science Quarterly*, 32:186–201.

Meyer, John W., W. Richard Scott, David Strang, and Andrew L. Creighton (1988). "Bureaucratization without Centralization: Changes in the Organizational System of U.S. Public Education, 1940–80," in *Institutional Patterns and Organizations: Culture and Environment*, 139–68, ed. Lynne G. Zucker. Cambridge, MA: Ballinger.

Meyer, Marshall W. (1990). "The Weberian Tradition in Organizational Research," in *Structures of Power and Constraint: Papers in Honor of Peter M. Blau*, 191–215, ed. Craig Calhoun, Marshall W. Meyer, and W. Richard Scott. Cambridge: Cambridge University Press.

Meyer, Marshall W., and Lynne G. Zucker (1989). *Permanently Failing Organizations.* Newbury Park, CA: Sage.

Meyerson, Debra (2001). *Tempered Radicals: How People Use Difference to Inspire Change at Work.* Boston: Harvard Business School Press.

Michels, Robert (1949 trans.). *Political Parties*, trans. Eden and Cedar Paul. Glencoe, IL: Free Press (first published in 915).

Micklethwait, John, and Adrian Woolridge (2003). *The Company: A Short History of a Revolutionary Idea.* London: Phoenix.

Miles, Raymond E., and Charles C. Snow (1978). *Organizational Strategy, Structure, and Process.* New York: McGraw-Hill.

Miles, Raymond E., and Charles C. Snow (1992). "Causes of Failure in Network Organizations," *California Management Review*, 34:53–72.

——— (1994). *Fit, Failure, and the Hall of Fame: How Companies Succeed or Fail.* New York: Free Press.

Miles, Robert H. (1982). *Coffin Nails and Corporate Strategies.* Upper Saddle River, NJ: Prentice Hall.

Milgram, Stanley (1967). "The Small World Problem," *Psychology Today*, 22:61–67.

Miller, George A. (1953). "What Is Information Measurement?" *American Psychologist*, 8:3–12.

Miller, J. (1986). *Pathways in the Workplace: The Effects of Gender and Race on Access to Organizational Resources.* Cambridge: Cambridge University Press.

Miller, James Grier (1978). *Living Systems.* New York: McGraw-Hill.

Miller, E. J., and A. K. Rice (1967). *Systems of Organizations.* London Tavistock.

Miller, Danny and Ming-Jer Chen (1994). "Sources and Consequences of Competitive Inertia: A Study of the U.S. Airline Industry," *Administrative Science Quarterly*, 39:1–23.

Mills, C. Wright (1956). *The Power Elite.* New York: Oxford University Press.

——— (1959). *The Sociological Imagination.* New York: Oxford University Press.

Miner, Anne S. (1994). "Seeking Adaptive Advantage: Evolutionary Theory and Managerial Action," in *Evolutionary Dynamics in Organizations*, 76–89, ed. Joel A. C. Baum and Jitendra V. Singh. New York: Oxford University Press.

Miner, Anne S., and Pamela R. Haunschild (1995). "Population Level Learning," in *Research in Organizational Behavior*, vol. 17, 115–66, ed. L. L. Cummings and Barry M. Staw. Greenwich, CT: JAI Press.

Mintz, Beth, and Michael Schwartz (1985). *The Power Structure of American Business.* Chicago: University of Chicago Press.

Mintzberg, Henry (1973). *The Nature of Managerial Work.* New York: Harper & Row.

——— (1979). *The Structure of Organizations.* Upper Saddle River, NJ.: Prentice Hall.

——— (1983). *Power in and around Organizations.* Upper Saddle River, NJ: Prentice Hall.

——— (1987). "The Strategy Concept I: Five Ps for Strategy," in *Organizational Approaches to Strategy*, 7–20, ed. Glenn R. Carroll and David Vogel. Cambridge, MA: Ballinger.

Mintzberg, Henry, and Alexandra McHugh (1985). "Strategy Formation in an Adhocracy," *Administrative Science Quarterly*, 30:160–97.

Mintzberg, Henry, and Ludo Van der Heyden (1999). "Organigraphs: Drawing How Companies Actually Work," *Harvard Business Review*, 77(5):87–94.

Mises, Ludwig von (1944). *Bureaucracy.* New Haven: Yale University Press.

Mishel, Lawrence, Jared Bernstein, and John Schmitt (1999). *The State of Working America, 1998–99.* Ithaca, NY: ILR Press of Cornell University Press.

Mishel, Lawrence, Jared Bernstein, and Sylvia Allegretto (2005). *The State of Working America 2004/2005.* Ithaca, NY: Cornell University Press.

Mizruchi, Mark S. (1982). *The American Corporate Network, 1904–1974.* Beverly Hills, CA: Sage.

——— (1992). *The Structure of Corporate Political Action.* Cambridge, MA: Harvard University Press.

——— (1996). "What Do Interlocks Do? An Analysis, Critique, and Assessment of Research on Interlocking Directorates," *Annual Review of Sociology*, 22:271–98.

Mizruchi, Mark S, and Linda Brewster Stearns (2001). "Getting Deals Done: The Use of Social Networks in Bank Decision-Making," *American Sociological Review*, 66:647–71.

Modigliani, Franco, and Enrico Perotti (2000). "Security Markets versus Bank Finance: Legal Enforcement and Investor Protection," *International Review of Finance*, 1:81–96.

Mohr, John W., and Francesca Guerra-Pearson (Forthcoming). "The Differentiation of Institutional Space: Organizational Forms in the New York Social Welfare Sector, 1888–1917" in *How Institutions Change*, ed., Walter W. Powell and Daniel L. Jones. Chicago: University of Chicago Press.

Mohr, Lawrence B. (1982). *Explaining Organizational Behavior*. San Francisco: Jossey-Bass.

Moi, T. (1985). *Sexual/Texual Politics: Feminist Literary Theory*. New York: Methuen.

Monteverde, Kirk, and David J. Teece (1982). "Supplier Switching Costs and Vertical Integration in the Automobile Industry," *Bell Journal of Economics*, 12:206–13.

Mooney, James D. (1937). "The Principles of Organization," in *Papers on the Science of Administration*, 89–98, ed. Luther Gulick and L. Urwick. New York: Institute of Public Administration, Columbia University.

Mooney, James D., and Allan C. Reiley (1939). *The Principles of Organization*. New York: Harper.

Morck, Randall K., Andrei Shleifer, and Robert W. Vishny (1990). "Do Managerial Objectives Drive Bad Acquisitions?" *Journal of Finance*, 45:31–48.

Morck, Randall K., David A. Stangeland, and Bernard Yeung (2000). "Inherited Wealth, Corporate Control, and Economic Growth: The Canadian Disease?" in *Concentrated Corporate Ownership*, ed. Randall K. Morck. Chicago: University of Chicago Press.

Moreno, Jacob L. (1953). *Who Shall Survive?* Beacon, NY: Beacon House, rev. ed.

Morgan, Gareth (1980). "Paradigms, Metaphors, and Puzzle Solving in Organization Theory," *Administrative Science Quarterly*, 25:605–22.

Morgan, Gareth (1986). *Images of Organization*. Beverly Hills, CA: Sage.

Morrill, Calvin (Forthcoming). "Institutional Change Through Interstitial Emergence: The Growth of Alternative Dispute Resolution in American Law, 1965–1995," in *How Institutions Change*, ed. Walter W. Powell and Daniel L. Jones. Chicago: University of Chicago Press.

Morton, Michael S. Scott, ed. (1991). *The Corporation of the 1990s: Information Technology and Organizational Transformation*. New York: Oxford University Press.

——— (1992). "The Effects of Information Technology on Management and Organization," in *Transforming Organizations*, 261–79, ed. Thomas A. Kochan and Michael Useem. New York: Oxford University Press.

Mowery, David C., Joanne E. Oxley, and Brian S. Silverman (1996). "Strategic Alliances and Interfirm Knowledge Transfer," *Strategic Management Journal*, 17:77–91.

Muldoon, James P., Jr. (2004). *The Architecture of Global Governance: An Introduction to the Study of International Organizations*. Boulder, CO: Westview Press.

Nadler, David, and Michael L. Tushman (1988). *Strategic Organization Design: Concepts, Tools, and Processes*. Glenview, IL: Scott-Foresman.

——— (1997). *Competing by Design: The Power of Organizational Architecture*. New York: Oxford University Press.

National Commission on Terrorist Attacks Upon the United States (2003). *The 9/11 Commission Report*. New York: W.W. Norton.

National Training Laboratories (1953). *Explorations in Human Relations Training*. Washington, DC: National Training Laboratories.

Nee, Victor. (2005). "The New Institutionalisms in Economics and Sociology," in *The Handbook of Economic Sociology* (2nd ed.), 49–74, ed., Neil J. Smelser and Richard Swedberg. Princeton and New York: Princeton University Press and Russell Sage Foundation.

Nelson, Daniel (1975). *Managers and Workers: Origins of the New Factory System in the United States, 1880–1920*. Madison: University of Wisconsin Press.

Nelson, Richard R., and Sidney G. Winter (1982). *An Evolutionary Theory of Economic Change*. Cambridge, MA: Belknap Press of Harvard University Press.

Newton, Kenneth (1975). "Voluntary Associations in a British City," *Journal of Voluntary Action Research*, 4:43–62.

Nickerson, Jack A., and Brian S. Silverman (2003). "Why Firms Want to Organize Efficiently and What Keeps Them from Doing So: Inappropriate Governance, Performance, and Adaptation in a Deregulated Industry," *Administrative Science Quarterly*, 48:433–65.

Nisbett, Richard, and Lee Ross (1980). *Human Inference: Strategies and Shortcomings of Social Judgment*. Upper Saddle River, NJ: Prentice Hall.

Nissen, Mark E. (2006). *Harnessing Knowledge Dynamics: Principled Organizational Knowing and Learning*. Hershey, PA: IRM Press.

Noble, David F. (1977). *America by Design: Science, Technology and the Rise of Corporate Capitalism*. New York: Oxford University Press.

———— (1984). *Forces of Production: A Social History of Industrial Automation*. New York: Oxford University Press.

Nohria, Nitin, and Robert G. Eccles, ed. (1992). *Networks and Organizations: Structure, Form and Action*. Boston: Harvard Business School Press.

Noll, Roger G., ed. (1985). *Regulatory Policy and the Social Sciences*. Berkeley: University of California Press.

Nonaka, Ikujiro, and Hirotaka Takeuchi (1995). *The Knowledge-Creating Company*. New York: Oxford University Press.

North, Douglass C. (1990). *Institutions, Institutional Change and Economic Performance*. Cambridge: Cambridge University Press.

O'Reilly, Charles A., and Jennifer A. Chapman (1996). "Culture as Social Control: Corporations, Cults, and Commitment," in *Research in Organizational Behavior*, vol. 18, 157–200, ed. Barry M. Staw and L. L. Cummings. Greenwich, CT: JAI Press.

O'Toole, J., ed. (1972). *Work in America: A Report to the Secretary of State for Health, Education and Welfare*. Cambridge, MA: MIT Press.

Oberschall, Anthony (1973). *Social Conflict and Social Movements*. Upper Saddle River, NJ: Prentice Hall.

Oberschall, Anthony, and Eric M. Leifer (1986). "Efficiency and Social Institutions: Uses and Misuses of Economic Reasoning in Sociology," *Annual Review of Sociology*, 12:233–53.

Odione, George S. (1965). *Management by Objective*. New York: Pitman.

Oliver, Christine (1991). "Strategic Responses to Institutional Processes," *Academy of Management Review*, 16:145–79.

Olsen, Johan P. (2001). "Garbage Cans, New Institutionalism and the Study of Politics." *American Political Science Review*, 95: 191–98.

Orlikowski, Wanda J. (1992). "The Duality of Technology: Rethinking the Concept of Technology in Organizations," *Organization Science*, 3:398–427.

Orrù, Marco, Nicole Woolsey Biggart, and Gary G. Hamilton (1997). *The Economic Organization of East Asian Capitalism*. Thousand Oaks, CA: Sage.

Orton, J. Douglas, and Karl E. Weick (1990). "Loosely Coupled Systems: A Reconceptualization," *Academy of Management Review*, 15:203–23.

Osborne, David, and Ted Gaebler (1992). *Reinventing Government*. Reading, MA: Addison-Wesley.

Osterman, Paul (1999). *Securing Prosperity: The American Labor Market: How It Has Changed and What to Do about It*. Princeton: Princeton University Press.

Ouchi, William G. (1979). "Markets, Bureaucracies and Clans." Unpublished paper, Graduate School of Management, University of California, Los Angeles.

———— (1980). "Markets, Bureaucracies and Clans," *Administrative Science Quarterly*, 25:129–41.

———— (1981). *Theory Z*. Reading, MA: Addison-Wesley.

Padavic, Irene, and Barbara Reskin (2002). *Women and Men at Work*. Thousand Oaks, CA: Sage.

Padgett, John F., and Christopher K. Ansell (1992). "Robust action and the rise of the Medici, 1400–1434," *American Journal of Sociology*, 101:993–1028.

Palmer, Donald A. (1983). "Broken Ties: Interlocking Directorates and Intercorporate Coordination," *Administrative Science Quarterly*, 28:40–55.

Palmer, Donald A., and Brad M. Barber (2001). "Challengers, Elites, and Owning Families: A Social Class Theory of Corporate Acquisitions in the 1960s," *Administrative Science Quarterly*, 46:87–120.

Palmer, Donald A., Roger Friedland, and Jitendra V. Singh (1986). "The Ties that Bind: Organizational and Class Bases of Stability in a Corporate Interlock Network," *American Sociological Review*, 51:781–96.

Palmer, Donald A., P. Devereaux Jennings, and Xueguang Zhou (1993). "Late Adoption of the Multidivisional Form by Large U.S. Corporations: Institutional, Political, and Economic Accounts," *Administrative Science Quarterly*, 38:100–31.

Panel to Review Productivity Statistics (1979). *Measures and Interpretation of Productivity.* Washington, DC: National Academy of Sciences.

Paniccia, Ivana (1998). "One, a Hundred, Thousands of Industrial Districts: Organizational Variety in Local Networks of Small and Medium-sized Enterprises," *Organization Studies*, 19:667–99.

Parcel, Toby L., ed. (1999). "Work and Family," in *Research in the Sociology of Work*, vol. 7, ed. Randy Hodson. Stamford, CT: JAI Press.

Parkinson, C. Northcote (1957). *Parkinson's Law and Other Studies in Administration.* Boston: Houghton Mifflin.

Parsons, Talcott (1947). Introduction to *The Theory of Social and Economic Organization*, 3–86, by Max Weber. Glencoe, IL: Free Press.

——— (1951). *The Social System.* Glencoe, IL: Free Press.

——— (1953). "A Revised Analytical Approach to the Theory of Social Stratification," in *Class, Status and Power: A Reader in Social Stratification*, 92–129, ed. Reinhard Bendix and Seymour Martin Lipset. Glencoe, IL: Free Press.

——— (1960). *Structure and Process in Modern Societies.* Glencoe, IL: Free Press.

——— (1966). *Societies: Evolutionary and Comparative Perspectives.* Upper Saddle River, NJ: Prentice Hall.

Parsons, Talcott, Robert F. Bales, and Edward A. Shils (1953). *Working Papers in the Theory of Action.* Glencoe, IL: Free Press.

Pedersen, Jesper Strandgaard, and Frank Dobbin (1997). "The Social Invention of Collective Actors: On the Rise of the Organization," *American Behavioral Scientist*, 40:431–43.

Pelz, Donald C. (1952). "Influence: A Key to Effective Leadership in the First-Line Supervisor," *Personnel*, 29:209–17.

Pennings, Johannes M. (1973). "Measures of Organizational Structure: A Methodological Note," *American Journal of Sociology*, 79:686–704.

Penrose, Edith T. (1959). *Theory of the Growth of the Firm.* Oxford: Blackwell.

Perrow, Charles (1961). "The Analysis of Goals in Complex Organizations," *American Sociological Review*, 26:854–66.

——— (1967). "A Framework for the Comparative Analysis of Organizations," *American Sociological Review*, 32:194–208.

——— (1970). *Organizational Analysis: A Sociological View.* Belmont, CA: Wadsworth.

——— (1973). "The Short and Glorious History of Organizational Theory," *Organizational Dynamics*, 2(Summer):2–15.

——— (1982). "Three Mile Island: A Normal Accident," in *The International Yearbook of Organizational Studies 1981*, 1–25, ed. David Dunkerley and Graeme Salaman. London: Routledge & Kegan Paul.

——— (1984). *Normal Accidents: Living with High-Risk Technologies.* New York: Basic Books.

——— (1986). *Complex Organizations: A Critical Essay* (3rd ed.). New York: Random House.

——— (1991). "A Society of Organizations," *Theory and Society*, 20:725–62.

——— (1992). "Small-Firm Networks," in *Networks and Organizations*, 445–70, ed., Nitin Nohria and Robert G. Eccles. Boston: Harvard Business School Press.

——— (2002). *Organizing America: Wealth, Power, and the Origins of Corporate Capitalism.* Princeton: Princeton University Press.

Peters, B. Guy (1999). *Institutional Theory in Political Science: The "New Institutionalism."* London: Pinter.

Peters, Thomas J. (1992). *Liberation Management: Necessary Disorganization for the Nanosecond Nineties.* New York: Knopf.

Peters, Thomas J., and N. Austin (1985). *A Passion for Excellence.* New York: Random House.

Peters, Thomas J., and Robert H. Waterman Jr. (1982). *In Search of Excellence.* New York: Harper & Row.

Petersen, Trond (1993). "Recent Advances in Longitudinal Methodology," *Annual Review of Sociology*, 19:425–54.

Pfeffer, Jeffrey (1981). *Power in Organizations.* Marshfield, MA: Pitman.

——— (1982). *Organizations and Organization Theory.* Boston: Pitman.

——— (1987). "A Resource Dependence Perspective on Intercorporate Relations," in *Intercorporate Relations: The Structural Analysis of Business*, 25–55, ed., Mark S. Mizruchi and Michael Schwartz. New York: Cambridge University Press.

——— (1992). *Managing with Power: Politics and Influence in Organizations.* Boston: Harvard Business School Press.

——— (1993). "Barriers to the Advance of Organizational Science: Paradigm Development as a Dependent Variable," *Academy of Management Review*, 19:599–620.

——— (1994). *Comparative Advantage Through People: Unleashing the Power of the Workforce.* Boston: Harvard Business School Press.

——— (1997). *New Directions for Organization Theory: Problems and Prospects.* New York: Oxford University Press.

——— (2003). "Introduction to the Classic Edition." In *The External Control of Orgaqnizations: A Resource Dependence Perspective, Classic Edition.* Stanford, CA: Stanford University Press.

Pfeffer, Jeffrey, and James N. Baron (1988). "Taking the Workers Back Out: Recent Trends in the Structuring of Employment," in *Research in Organizational Behavior*, vol. 10, 257–303, ed. Barry M. Staw and L. L. Cummings. Greenwich, CT: JAI Press.

Pfeffer, Jeffrey, and Yinon Cohen (1984). "Determinants of Internal Labor Markets in Organizations," *Administrative Science Quarterly*, 29:550–72.

Pfeffer, Jeffrey, and Gerald R. Salancik (1974). "Organizational Decision Making as a Political Process: The Case of a University Budget," *Administrative Science Quarterly*, 19:135–51.

——— (1978; 2003). *The External Control of Organizations: A Resource Dependence Perspective.* New York: Harper & Row (1978); Standard, CA: Standford University Press (2003).

Pfeffer, Jeffrey, and Robert I. Sutton (2000). *The Knowing–Doing Gap: How Smart Companies Turn Knowledge into Action.* Boston: Harvard Business School Press.

Phillips, Damon J. (2002). "A Genealogical Approach to Organizational Life Chances: The Parent-Progeny Transfer among Silicon Valley Law Firms, 1946–1996," *Administrative Science Quarterly*, 47:474–506.

Pierson, Paul (2004). *Politics in Time: History, Institutions and Social Analysis.* Princeton: Princeton University Press.

Pinch, Trevor J., and W. E. Bijker (1987). "The Social Construction of Facts and Artifacts," in *The Social Construction of Technological Systems*, 17–50, ed. W. E. Bijker, Thomas P. Hughes, and Trevor J. Pinch. Cambridge, MA: MIT Press.

Piore, Michael J., and Charles F. Sabel (1984). *The Second Industrial Divide: Possibilities for Prosperity.* New York: Basic Books.

Pitts, Forrest R. (1978/79). "The Medieval River Trade Network of Russia Revisited," *Social Networks*, 1:285–92.

Podolny, Joel M. (1993). "A Status-Based Model of Market Competition," *American Journal of Sociology*, 98:829–72.

——— (1994). "Market Uncertainty and the Social Character of Economic Exchange," *Administrative Science Quarterly*, 39:458–83.

——— (2001). "Networks as the Pipes and Prisms of the Market," *American Journal of Sociology*, 107:33–60.

Podolny, Joel M., and Karen L. Page (1998). "Network Forms of Organization," *Annual Review of Sociology*, 24:57–76.

Podolny, Joel M., and Toby E. Stuart (1995). "A Role-Based Ecology of Technological Change," *American Journal of Sociology*, 100:1224–60.

Podolny, Joel M., Toby E. Stuart, and Michael T. Hannan (1996). "Networks, Knowledge, and Niches: Competition in the Worldwide Semiconductor Industry, 1984–1991," *American Journal of Sociology*, 102:659–89.

Polanyi, Karl (1944). *The Great Transformation.* New York: Holt.

Polanyi, Michael (1967). *The Tacit Dimension.* Garden City, NY: Doubleday Anchor.

Pondy, Louis R., and Ian I. Mitroff (1979). "Beyond Open System Models of Organization," in *Research in Organizational Behavior,* vol. 1, 3–39, ed. Barry M. Staw. Greenwich, CT: JAI Press.

Porac, Joseph. F., Howard Thomas, and C. Badden-Fuller (1989). "Competitive Groups as Cognitive Communities: The Case of the Scottish Knitwear Manufacturers," *Journal of Management Studies,* 26:397–415.

Porac, Joseph F., Howard Thomas, Fiona Wilson, Douglas Paton, and Alaina Kanfer (1995). "Rivalry and the Industry Model of Scottish Knitwear Producers," *Administrative Science Quarterly,* 40:203–27.

Porac, Joseph F., James B. Wade, and Timothy G. Pollock (1999). "Industry Categories and the Politics of the Comparable Firm in CEO Compensation," *Administrative Science Quarterly,* 44:112–44.

Porter, Lyman W., and Edward E. Lawler III (1968). *Managerial Attitudes and Performance.* Homewood, IL: Richard D. Irwin.

Porter, Michael E. (1980). *Competitive Strategy.* New York: Free Press.

———— ed. (1986). *Competition in Global Industries.* Boston: Harvard Business School Press.

———— (1987). "From Competitive Advantage to Corporate Strategy," *Harvard Business Review,* 65:43–59.

———— (1990). *The Competitive Advantage of Nations.* New York: Free Press.

Powell, Walter W. (1990). "Neither Market nor Hierarchy: Network Forms of Organizations," in *Research in Organizational Behavior,* vol. 12, 295–336, ed. Barry M. Staw and Larry L. Cummings. Greenwich, CT: JAI Press.

———— (1991). "Expanding the Scope of Institutional Analysis," in *The New Institutionalism in Organizational Analysis,* 183–203, ed. Walter W. Powell and Paul J. DiMaggio. Chicago: University of Chicago Press.

———— (2001). "The Capitalist Firm in the 21st Century," in *The Twenty-First-Century Firm: Changing Economic Organization in International Perspective,* ed. Paul J. DiMaggio. Princeton: Princeton University Press.

Powell, Walter W., and Paul DiMaggio, eds. (1991). *The New Institutionalism in Organizational Analysis.* Chicago: University of Chicago Press.

Powell, Walter W., Kenneth W. Koput, and Laurel Smith-Doerr (1996). "Interorganizational Collaboration and the Locus of Innovation: Networks of Learning in Biotechnology," *Administrative Science Quarterly,* 41:116–45.

Pralahad, C. K., and Gary Hamel (1990). "The Core Competence of the Organization," *Harvard Business Review,* 90(3):79–91.

Pratt, John W., and Richard J. Zeckhauser (1985). "Principals and Agents: An Overview," in *Principals and Agents: The Structure of Business,* 1–25, ed. John W. Pratt and Richard J. Zeckhauser. Boston: Harvard Business School Press.

Prechel, Harland (2000). *Big Business and the State: Historical Transitions and Corporate Transformation, 1880s–1900s.* Albany: State University of New York Press.

Presser, Harriet B. (2003). *Working in a 24/7 Economy.* New York: Russell Sage Foundation.

Pressman, Jeffrey L., and Aaron B. Wildavsky (1973). *Implementation.* Berkeley: University of California Press.

Presthus, Robert (1978). *The Organizational Society.* New York: St. Martin's Press, rev. ed.

Provan, Keith G., and H. Brinton Milward (1995). "A Preliminary Theory of Interorganizational Network Effectiveness: A Comparative Study of Four Community Mental Health Systems," *Administrative Science Quarterly,* 40:1–33.

Przeworski, Adam, and Henry Teune (1970). *The Logic of Comparative Social Inquiry.* New York: John Wiley.

Pugh, D. S., and D. J. Hickson (1976). *Organizational Structure in Its Context: The Aston Programme I.* Lexington, MA: Heath, Lexington Books.

———— eds. (1996). *Writers on Organizations* (5th ed.). Thousand Oaks, CA: Sage.

Pugh, D. S., D. J. Hickson, and C. R. Hinings (1969). "An Empirical Taxonomy of Structures of Work Organizations," *Administrative Science Quarterly,* 14:115–26.

———— (1985). *Writers on Organizations* (3rd. ed.). Beverly Hills, CA: Sage Publications.

Pugh, D. S., D. J. Hickson, C. R. Hinings, and C. Turner (1968). "Dimensions of Organization Structure," *Administrative Science Quarterly*, 13:65–91.

Putnam, Robert D. (1993). "The Prosperous Community: Social Capital and Public Life," *The American Prospect*, 13(Spring):35–42.

——— (2000). *Bowling Alone: The Collapse and Revival of American Community*. New York: Touchstone.

Rabinow, Paul, and William M. Sullivan (1987). "The Interpretive Turn: A Second Look," in *Interpretive Social Science: A Second Look*, 1–30, ed. Paul Rabinow and William M. Sullivan. Berkeley: University of California Press.

Rafaeli, Anat, and Robert I. Sutton (1991). "Emotional Contrast Strategies as Social Influence Tools: Lessons from Bill Collectors and Criminal Interrogators," *Academy of Management Journal*, 34:749–75.

Ranger-Moore, James, Jane Banaszak-Holl, and Michael T. Hannan (1991). "Density-Dependent Dynamics in Regulated Industries: Founding Rates of Banks and Life Insurance Companies," *Administrative Science Quarterly*, 36:36–65.

Rao, Hayagreeva (1998). "Caveat Emptor: The Construction of Nonprofit Consumer Watchdog Organizations," *American Journal of Sociology*, 103:912–61.

——— (2003). "Institutional Change in Toque Ville: Novelle Cuisine as an Identity Movement in French Gastronomy," *American Journal of Sociology*, 108:795–843.

Rao, Hayagreeva, Gerald F. Davis, and Andrew Ward (2000). "Embeddedness, Social Identity and Mobility: Why Firms Leave the NASDAQ and Join the New York Stock Exchange," *Administrative Science Quarterly*, 45:268–92.

Rao, Hayagreeva, and Kumar Sivakumar (1999). "Institutional Sources of Boundary-Spanning Structures: The Establishment of Investor Relations Departments in the Fortune 500 Industrials," *Organization Science*, 10:27–42.

Reynolds, Paul D., and Sammis B. White (1997). *The Entrepreneurial Process: Economic Growth, Men, Women, and Minorities*. Westport, CT: Quorum Books.

Ritzer, George (1993). *The McDonaldization of Society: An Investigation into the Changing Character of Contemporary Social Life*. Thousand Oaks, CA: Pine Forge Press.

——— (2005). "Paradigm," in *Encyclopedia of Social Theory*, 543–44, ed. George Ritzer. Thousand Oaks, CA: Sage.

Rivoli, Pietra (2005). *The Travels of a T-Shirt in the Global Economy: An Economist Examines the Markets, Power, and Politics of World Trade*. Hoboken NJ: John Wiley & Sons.

Robbins, Gregory E. (2002). "Titles and Tasks: New Jobs for New Media in Silicon Alley?" in Graduate School of Business. New York: Columbia University.

Roberts, Karlene H. (1990). "Some Characteristics of One Type of High Reliability Organization," *Organization Science*, 1:160–76.

Robinson, James C. (1999). *The Corporate Practice of Medicine: Competition and Innovation in Health Care*. Berkeley: University of California Press.

Robinson, William S. (1950). "Ecological Correlations and the Behavior of Individuals," *American Sociological Review*, 15:351–57.

Roe, Mark J. (1994). *Strong Managers, Weak Owners: The Political Roots of American Corporate Finance*. Princeton: Princeton University Press.

Roethlisberger, F. J., and William J. Dickson (1939). *Management and the Worker*. Cambridge, MA: Harvard University Press.

Roland, G. (2004). "Understanding Institutional Change: Fast-moving and Slow-moving Institutions," *Studies in Comparative International Development*, 38:109–31.

Roman, Paul M., and Terry C. Blum (2000). "Work–Family Role Conflict and Employer Responsibility: An Organizational Analysis of Workplace Responses to a Social Problem," *Handbook of Organizational Behavior*, ed. Robert T. Golembiewski. New York: Marcel Dekker.

Romanelli, Elaine (1991). "The Evolution of New Organizational Forms," *Annual Review of Sociology*, 17:79–103.

Romano, Roberta (1985). "Law as Product: Some Pieces of the Incorporation Puzzle," *Journal of Law, Economics, and Organization*, 1:225–83.

——— (1993). *The Genius of American Corporate Law*. Washington, DC: American Enterprise Institute.

Rose, Michael (1985). "Universalism, Culturalism, and the Aix Group: Promise and Problems of a Societal Approach to Economic Institutions," *European Sociological Review*, 1:65–83.

Rose-Ackerman, S. (1999). *Corruption and Government Causes: Consequences and Reform*. Cambridge: Cambridge University Press.

Rosenau, Pauline Marie (1992). *Post-Modernism and the Social Sciences: Insights, Inroads, and Intrusions*. Princeton: Princeton University Press.

Rosenau, Pauline Vaillancourt, ed. (2000). *Public–Private Policy Partnerships*. Cambridge, MA: MIT Press.

Rosenberg, Hans (1958). *Bureaucracy, Aristocracy and Autocracy: The Prussian Experience 1660–1815*. Cambridge, MA: Harvard University Press.

Rosenberg, Nathan, and L. E. Birdzell, Jr. (1986). *How the West Grew Rich: The Economic Transformation of the Industrial World*. New York: Basic Books.

Rosenkopf, Lori, Anca Metiu, and Varghese P. George (2001). "From the Bottom Up? Technical Committee Activity and Alliance Formation," *Administrative Science Quarterly*, 46:748–72.

Rousseau, Denise M. (1977). "Technological Differences in Job Characteristics, Employee Satisfaction, and Motivation: A Synthesis of Job Design Research and Sociotechnical Theory," *Organizational Behavior and Human Performance*, 19:18–42.

Roy, Donald (1952). "Quota Restriction and Goldbricking in a Machine Shop," *American Journal of Sociology*, 57:427–42.

Roy, William G. (1983). "The Unfolding of the Interlocking Directorate Structure of the United States," *American Sociological Review*, 48:248–57.

——— (1997). *Socializing Capital: The Rise of the Large Industrial Corporation in America*. Princeton: Princeton University Press.

Roy, William G., and Phillip Bonacich (1988). "Interlocking Directorates and Communities of Interest among American Railroad Companies, 1905," *American Sociological Review*, 53:368–79.

Rubinstein, Saul A., and Thomas A. Kochan (2001). *Learning from Saturn: Possibilities for Corporate Governance and Employee Relations*. Ithaca, NY: ILR Press of Cornell University Press.

Ruef, Martin, and W. Richard Scott (1998). "A Multidimensional Model of Organizational Legitimacy: Hospital Survival in Changing Institutional Environments," *Administrative Science Quarterly*, 43:877–904.

Ruef, Martin, Howard E. Aldrich, and Nancy M. Carter (2003). "The Structure of Organizational Founding Teams: Homophily, Strong Ties and Isolation among U.S. Entrepreneurs," *American Sociological Review*, 68: 195–200.

Rumelt, Richard (1986). *Strategy, Structure, and Economic Performance*. Boston: Harvard Business School Press (first published in 1974).

Russell, Bertrand (1938). *Power: A New Social Analysis*. New York: W.W. Norton.

Russo, Michael V. (2001). "Institutions, Exchange Relations, and the Emergence of New Fields: Regulatory Policies and Independent Power Producing in America, 1978–1922," *Administrative Science Quarterly*, 46:57–86.

Sabel, Charles F. (1982). *Work and Politics: The Division of Labor in Industry*. Cambridge: Cambridge University Press.

Sagan, Scott D. (1993). *The Limits of Safety: Organizations, Accidents, and Nuclear Weapons*. Princeton: Princeton University Press.

Sahlen-Andersson, Kerstin, and Lars Engwall eds. (2002). *The Expansion of Management Knowledge: Carriers, Flows and Sources*. Stanford, CA: Stanford University Press.

Saint-Simon, Henri Comte de (1952 trans.). *Selected Writings*, trans. F. M. H. Markham. New York: Macmillan (first published in 1859).

Salamon, Lester M. (2002). "The Resilient Sector: The State of Nonprofit America," in *The State of Nonprofit America*, 3–61, ed. Lester M. Salamon. Washington, DC: Brookings Institution Press.

Salmon, J. Warren, ed. (1994). *The Corporate Transformation of Health Care: Perspectives and Implications*. Amityville, NY: Baywood.

Santos, Filipe M. (2003). "The Role of Information Technologies for Knowledge Management in Firms," *International Journal of Technology Policy and Management*, 3:194–203.

Saxenian, Annalee (1994). *Regional Advantage: Culture and Competition in Silicon Valley and Route 128*. Cambridge, MA: Harvard University Press.

Sayles, Leonard R. (1958). *Behavior of Industrial Work Groups*. New York: John Wiley.

―――― (1976). "Matrix Organization: The Structure with a Future," *Organizational Dynamics*, (Autumn):2–17.

Schein, Edgar H. (1992). *Organizational Culture and Leadership* (2nd ed.). San Francisco: Jossey-Bass.

Scherer, Frederic M. (1980). *Industrial Market Structure and Economic Performance* (2nd ed.). Chicago: Rand-McNally.

Schilling, Melissa A. (2002). "Intraorganizational Technology," in *The Blackwell Companion to Organizations*, 158–80, ed. Joel A. C. Baum. Oxford: Blackwell.

Schlosser, Eric (2001). *Fast Food Nation: The Dark Side of the All-American Meal*. Boston: Houghton Mifflin.

Schneiberg, Marc (2002). "Organizational Heterogeneity and the Production of New Forms: Politics, Social Movements and Mutual Companies in American Fire Insurance, 1900–1930," *Social Structure and Organizations, Revisited*, vol. 19, 39–89, ed. Michael Lounsbury and Marc J. Ventresca. Boston: JAI, Elsevier Science.

―――― (2006). "Social Movements and Organizational Form: Cooperative Alternatives to Corporations in Three American Industries." Unpublished, Reed College.

Schneiberg, Marc, and Elisabeth S. Clemens (Forthcoming). "The Typical Tools for the Job: Research Strategies in Institutional Analysis," in *How Institutions Change*, ed. Walter W. Powell and Dan L. Jones. Chicago: University of Chicago Press.

Schneiberg, Mark, and Sarah A. Soule (2005). "Institutionalization as a Contested, Multilevel Process," in *Social Movements and Organization Theory*, 122–60, ed. Gerald F. Davis, Doug McAdam, W. Richard Scott, and Mayer N. Zald. New York: Cambridge University Press.

Schoonhoven, Claudia Bird (1981). "Problems with Contingency Theory: Testing Assumptions Hidden within the Language of Contingency Theory," *Administrative Science Quarterly*, 26:349–77.

Schoonhoven, Claudia Bird, and Elaine Romanelli, eds. (2001). *The Entrepreneurship Dynamic: Origins of Entrepreneurship and the Evolution of Industries*. Stanford, CA: Stanford University Press.

Schrödinger, Erwin (1945). *What is Life?* Cambridge: Cambridge University Press.

Schumpeter, Joseph A. (1947). *Capitalism, Socialism and Democracy* (2nd ed.). New York: Harper & Row.

―――― (1961). *The Theory of Economic Development*. New York: Oxford University Press (first published in 1926).

Schwab, Donald P., and Larry L. Cummings (1970). "Theories of Performance and Satisfaction: A Review," *Industrial Relations*, 9:408–30.

Schwab, J. J. (1960). "What Do Scientists Do?" *Behavioral Science*, 5(January):1–27.

Scott, James C. (1985). *Weapons of the Weak*. New Haven: Yale University Press.

Scott, Marvin B., and Stanford M. Lyman (1968). "Accounts," *American Sociological Review*, 33:46–62.

Scott, W. Richard (1965). "Reactions to Supervision in a Heteronomous Professional Organization," *Administrative Science Quarterly*, 10:65–81.

―――― (1966). "Professionals in Bureaucracies—Areas of Conflict," in *Professionalization*, 265–75, ed. Howard M. Vollmer and Donald L. Mills. Upper Saddle River, NJ: Prentice Hall

―――― (1970). *Social Processes and Social Structures: An Introduction to Sociology*. New York: Holt, Rinehart & Winston.

―――― (1975). "Organizational Structure," *Annual Review of Sociology*, 1:1–20.

―――― (1977). "Effectiveness of Organizational Effectiveness Studies," in *New Perspectives on Organizational Effectiveness*, 63–95, ed. Paul S. Goodman and Johannes M. Pennings. San Francisco: Jossey-Bass.

―――― (1978). "Theoretical perspectives," in *Environments and Organizations*, 21–28, ed. Marshall W. Meyer. San Francisco: Jossey-Bass.

―――― (1981). *Organizations: Rational, Natural and Open Systems* (1st ed.). Upper Saddle River, NJ: Prentice Hall.

———— (1982). "Managing Professional Work: Three Models of Control for Health Organizations," *Health Services Research*, 17:213–40.

———— (1986). "The Sociology of Organizations," in *Sociology: From Crisis to Science?* vol. 2, *The Social Reproduction of Organization and Culture*, 38–58, ed. Ulf Himmelstrand. Beverly Hills, CA: Sage.

———— (1987). "The Adolescence of Institutional Theory," *Administrative Science Quarterly*, 32:493–511.

———— (1990). "Symbols and Organizations: From Barnard to the Institutionalists," in *Organization Theory: From Chester Barnard to the Present and Beyond*, 38–55, ed. Oliver E. Williamson. New York: Oxford University Press.

———— (1992). *Organizations: Rational, Natural and Open Systems* (3rd ed.). Upper Saddle River, NJ: Prentice Hall.

———— (1993). "The Organization of Medical Care Services: Toward an Integrated Theoretical Model," *Medical Care Review*, 50:271–303.

———— (1994). "Conceptualizing Organizational Fields: Linking Organizations and Societal Systems," in *Systemrationalitat und Partial Interesse [System Rationality and Partial Interests]*, 203–21, ed. Hans-Ulrich Derlien, Uta Gerhardt, and Fritz W. Scharpf. Baden-Baden, Germany: Nomos Verlagsgesellschaft.

———— (1995). *Institutions and Organizations*. Thousand Oaks, CA: Sage.

———— (1998). *Organizations: Rational, Natural and Open Systems* (4th ed.). Upper Saddle River, NJ: Prentice Hall.

———— (2001a). *Institutions and Organizations* (2nd ed.). Thousand Oaks, CA: Sage.

———— (2001b). "Organizations, Overview," in *International Encyclopedia of the Social and Behavioral Sciences*, 16:10910–17, ed. Neil J. Smelser and Paul B. Baltes. Amsterdam: Pergamon, Elsevier Science.

———— (2003). *Organizations: Rational, Natural and Open Systems* (5th ed.). Upper Saddle River, NJ: Prentice-Hall.

———— (2004a). "Competing Logics in Health Care: Professional, State and Managerial," in *The Sociology of the Economy*, 205–315, ed. Frank Dobbin. New York: Russell Sage Foundation.

———— (2004b). "Reflections on a Half-century of Organizational Sociology," *Annual Review of Sociology*, 39:1–20.

———— (2005a). "Evolving Professions: An Institutional Field Approach," in *Organisation und Profession*, 119–41, ed. Thomas Klatetzki and Veronika Tacke. Weisbaden, Germany: Verlag für Sozialwissenschaften.

———— (2005b). "Institutional theory: Contributing to a Theoretical Research Program." in *Great Minds in Management: The Process of Theory Development*, 460–84, ed. Ken G. Smith and Michael A. Hitt. Oxford: Oxford University Press.

———— (Forthcoming). "Approaching Adulthood: The Maturing of Institutional Theory," *Theory and Society*.

Scott, W. Richard, and Elaine V. Backman (1990). "Institutional Theory and the Medical Care Sector," in *Innovations in Health Care Delivery: Insights for Organization Theory*, 20–52, ed. Stephen S. Mick. San Francisco: Jossey-Bass.

Scott, W. Richard, and Søren Christensen (1995a). "Crafting a Wider Lens," in *The Institutional Construction of Organizations: International and Comparative Studies*, 302–13, ed. W. Richard Scott and Søren Christensen. Thousand Oaks, CA: Sage.

———— eds. (1995b). *The Institutional Construction of Organizations: International and Longitudinal Studies*. Thousand Oaks, CA: Sage.

Scott, W. Richard, and John Meyer (1983). "The Organization of Societal Sectors." in *Organizational Environments: Ritual and Rationality*, 129–53, ed. W. Richard Scott and John Meyer. Beverly Hills: Sage.

———— (1988). "Environmental Linkages and Organizational Complexity: Public and Private Schools," in *Comparing Public and Private Schools*, vol. 1, 128–60, ed. Thomas James and Henry M. Levin. New York: Falmer Press.

———— (1991a). "The Organization of Societal Sectors: Propositions and Early Evidence," in *The New Institutionalism in Organizational Analysis*, 108–40, ed. Walter W. Powell and Paul DiMaggio. Chicago: University of Chicago Press.

———— (1991b). "The Rise of Training Programs in Firms and Agencies: An Institutional Perspective," in *Research in Organizational Behavior*, vol. 13, 297–326, ed. L. L. Cummings and Barry Staw. Greenwich CT: JAI Press.

———— eds. (1994). *Institutional Environments and Organizations: Structural Complexity and Individualism*. Thousand Oaks, CA: Sage.

Scott, W. Richard, Martin Ruef, Peter J. Mendel, and Carol A. Caronna (2000). *Institutional Change and Healthcare Organization: From Professional Dominance to Managed Care*. Chicago: University of Chicago Press.

Scott, William G. (1992). *Chester I. Barnard and the Guardians of the Managerial State*. Lawrence: University of Kansas Press.

Searle, John R. (1995). *The Construction of Social Reality*. New York: Free Press.

Seashore, Stanley E. (1954). *Group Cohesiveness in the Industrial Work Group*. Ann Arbor: Institute for Social Research, University of Michigan.

Seeman, Melvin (1959). "On the Meaning of Alienation," *American Sociological Review*, 24:783–91.

———— (1975). "Alienation Studies," *Annual Review of Sociology*, 1:91–123.

Seibold, David R., and B. Christine Shea (2001). "Participation and Decision Making," in *The New Handbook of Organizational Communication: Advances in Theory, Research, and Methods*, 664–703, ed. Fredric M. Jablin and Linda L. Putnam. Thousand Oaks, CA: Sage.

Selznick, Philip (1948). "Foundations of the Theory of Organization," *American Sociological Review*, 13:25–35.

———— (1949). *TVA and the Grass Roots*. Berkeley: University of California Press.

———— (1952). *The Organizational Weapon*. New York: McGraw-Hill.

———— (1957). *Leadership in Administration*. New York: Harper & Row.

———— (1996). "Institutionalism 'Old' and 'New,'" *Administrative Science Quarterly*, 41:270–77.

Sewell, William H., Jr. (1981). *Work and Revolution in France: The Language of Labor from the Old Regime to 1848*. New York: Cambridge University Press.

———— (1992). "A Theory of Structure: Duality, Agency, and Transformation," *American Journal of Sociology*, 98:1–29.

Shannon, Claude E., and Warren Weaver (1963). *The Mathematical Theory of Communication*. Urbana: University of Illinois Press.

Shelanski, Howard A., and Peter G. Klein (1995). "Empirical Research in Transaction Cost Economics: A Review and Assessment," *Journal of Law, Economics, & Organization*, 7:335–61.

Shenhav, Yehouda (1995). "From Chaos to Systems: The Engineering Foundations of Organization Theory, 1879–1932," *Administrative Science Quarterly*, 40:557–85.

———— (1999). *Manufacturing Rationality: The Engineering Foundations of the Managerial Revolution*. Oxford: Oxford University Press.

Sherif, Muzafer, and Caroline W. Sherif (1953). *Groups in Harmony and Tension*. New York: Harper & Row.

Shulman, Beth (2003). *The Betrayal of Work: How Low-Wage Jobs Fail 30 Million Americans*. New York: New Press.

Siggelkow, Nicolaj (2002). "Evolution toward Fit," *Administrative Science Quarterly*, 47:125–59.

Sills, David L. (1957). *The Volunteers*. New York: Free Press.

Silverman, David (1971). *The Theory of Organizations*. New York: Basic Books.

Simmel, Georg (1955 trans.). *Conflict and The Web of Group-Affiliations*. Glencoe, IL: Free Press. (The first essay was first published in 1908, the second in 1922.)

Simon, Herbert A. (1962). "The Architecture of Complexity," *Proceedings of the American Philosophical Society*, 106:467–82.

———— (1964). "On the Concept of Organizational Goal," *Administrative Science Quarterly*, 9:1–22.

———— (1991). "Organizations and Markets," *Journal of Economic Perspectives*, 5:25–44.

———— (1997). *Administrative Behavior: A Study of Decision-Making Processes in Administrative Organizations* (4th ed.). New York: Free Press (first edition published in 1945).

Simons, Tal, and Paul Ingram (1997). "Organization and Ideology: Kibbutzim and Hired Labor, 1951–1965," *Administrative Science Quarterly*, 42:784–813.

Sine, Wesley, Heather A. Haveman, and Pamela Tolbert (2005). "Risky Business? Entrepreneurship in the New Independent-Power Sector." *Administrative Science Quarterly*, 50:200–32.

Sine, Wesley D., and Pamela S. Tolbert (2006). "Institutions in Action: Tenure Systems and Faculty Employment in Colleges and Universities." Unpublished Paper, Johnson Graduate School of Management, Cornell University.

Singh, Jitendra V., and Charles J. Lumsden (1990). "Theory and Research in Organizational Ecology," *Annual Review of Sociology*, 16:161–95.

Singh, Jitendra V., David J. Tucker, and Robert J. House (1986). "Organizational Legitimacy and the Liability of Newness," *Administrative Science Quarterly*, 31:171–93.

Sjöstrand, Sven-Erik (1995). "Toward a Theory of Institutional Change," in *On Economic Institutions: Theory and Applications*, 19–44, ed., John Groenewegen, Chistos Pitelis, and Sven-Eric Sjöstrand. Aldershot, UK; Edward Elgar.

Skocpol, Theda (1985). "Bringing the State Back In: Strategies of Analysis in Current Research," in *Bringing the State Back In*, 3–37, ed. Peter B. Evans, Dietrich Rueschemeyer, and Theda Skocpol. Cambridge: Cambridge University Press.

Slater, Philip E. (1955). "Role Differentiation in Small Groups," *American Sociological Review*, 20:300–10.

Sloan, Alfred P. (1963). *My Years at General Motors*. Garden City, NY: Doubleday.

Smelser, Neil J., and Richard Swedberg, ed. (2005). *The Handbook of Economic Sociology* (2nd ed.). Princeton and New York: Princeton University Press and Russell Sage Foundation,

Smigel, Erwin O. (1964). *The Wall Street Lawyer: Professional Organization Man?* New York: Free Press.

Smircich, Linda (1983). "Concepts of Culture and Organizational Analysis," *Administrative Science Quarterly*, 28:39–58.

——— (1985). "Is the Concept of Culture a Paradigm for Understanding Organizations and Ourselves?" in *Organizational Culture*, 55–72, ed. Peter J. Frost, Larry F. Moore, Meryl Reis Louis, Craig C. Lundberg, and Joanne Martin. Beverly Hills, CA: Sage.

Smircich, Linda, and Marta B. Calás (1987). "Organization Culture: A Critical Assessment," in *Handbook of Organizational Communication*, 228–63, ed. Fredric M. Jablin, Linda L. Putnam, Karlene H. Roberts, and Lyman W. Porter. Newbury Park, CA: Sage.

Smith, Adam (1957). *Selections from the Wealth of Nations*, ed. George J. Stigler. New York: Appleton Century Crofts (first published in 1776).

Smith, Jackie (2005). "Globalization and Transnational Social Movement Organizations," in *Social Movements and Organization Theory*, 226–49, ed. Gerald F. Davis, Doug McAdam, W. Richard Scott, and Mayer N. Zald. New York: Cambridge University Press.

Smith, Thomas Spence, and R. Danforth Ross (1978). "Cultural Controls on the Demography of Hierarchy: A Time-Series Analysis of Warfare and the Growth of the United States Army, 1960–68." Unpublished paper, University of Rochester.

Smith-Doerr, Laurel, and Walter W. Powell (2005). "Networks and Economic life," in *The Handbook of Economic Sociology* (2nd ed.), 379–402, ed. Neil J. Smelser and Richard Swedberg. Princeton and New York: Princeton University Press and Russell Sage Foundation.

Song, Mengli (2003). "Influence in the Reading Policy Domain: A Cross-State Social Network Analysis," School of Education. Ann Arbor, Michigan: University of Michigan.

Sorenson, Olav, and Pino G. Audia (2000). "The Social Structure of Entrepreneurial Activity: Geographic Concentration of Footwear Production in the United States, 1940–1989," *American Journal of Sociology*, 106:424–62.

Spangler, E., M. A. Gordon, and R. M. Pipkin (1978). "Token Women: An Empirical Test of Kanter's Hypothesis," *American Journal of Sociology*, 84:160–70.

Special Task Force to the Secretary of Health, Education and Welfare (1973). *Work in America*. Cambridge, MA: MIT Press.

Spenner, Kenneth I. (1988). "Social Stratification, Work, and Personality," *Annual Review of Sociology*, 14:69–97.

Sproull, Lee S., and Paul S. Goodman (1990). "Technology and Organizations: Integration and Opportunities," in *Technology and Organizations*, 254–65, ed. Paul S. Goodman and Lee S. Sproull. San Francisco: Jossey-Bass.

Staber, Udo, and Howard Aldrich (1983). "Trade Association Stability and Public Policy," in *Organizational Theory and Public Policy*, 163–78, ed. Richard H. Hall and Robert E. Quinn. Beverly Hills, CA: Sage.

Starbuck, William H. (1983). "Organizations as Action Generators," *American Sociological Review*, 48:91–102.

———— (1999). "Our Shrinking Earth" [1998 Presidential address], *Academy of Management Review*, 24:187–90.

Starbuck, William H., and F. J. Milliken (1988). "Challenger: Fine-Tuning the Odds until Something Breaks," *Journal of Management Studies*, 25(4):319–40.

Stark, David (1980). "Class Struggle and the Transformation of the Labour Process: A Relational Approach," *Theory and Society*, 9:89–130.

———— (1996). "Recombinant Property in East European Capitalism," *American Journal of Sociology*, 101:993–1027.

———— (2001). "Ambiguous Assets for Uncertain Environments: Heterarchy in Postsocialist firms," in *The Twenty-First-Century Firm: Changing Economic Organization in International Perspective*, 69–104, ed. Paul DiMaggio. Princeton: Princeton University Press.

Starr, Paul (1982). *The Social Transformation of American Medicine*. New York: Basic Books.

Staw, Barry M. (1976). "Knee-deep in the Big Muddy: A Study of Escalating Commitment to a Chosen Course of Action," *Organization Behavior and Human Performance*, 16:27–44.

———— (1980). "Rationality and Justification in Organizational Life," in *Research in Organizational Behavior*, vol. 2, 45–80, ed. Barry M. Staw and L. L. Cummings. Greenwich, CT: JAI Press.

———— (2005). "The Escalation of Commitment: Steps Toward an Organizational Theory," in *Great Minds in Management: The Process of Theory Development*, 215–38, ed. Ken G. Smith and Michael A. Hitt. New York: Oxford University Press.

Stawser, Cornelia, ed. (2005). *Business Statistics of the United States*. Lanham, MD: Bernan Press.

Stearns, Linda Brewster, and Mark S. Mizruchi (1986). "Broken Tie Reconstitution and the Functions of Interorganizational Interlocks: A Reexamination," *Administrative Science Quarterly*, 31:522–38.

Steers, Richard M. (1977). *Organizational Effectiveness: A Behavioral View*. Pacific Palisades, CA: Goodyear.

Steinbruner, John D. (1974) *The Cybernetic Theory of Decision*. Princeton: Princeton University Press.

Sternman, John D. (1994). "Learning In and About Complex Systems," *System Dynamics Review*, 10:291–330.

Stigler, George J. (1971). "The Theory of Economic Regulation," *Bell Journal of Economics and Management Science*, 2(Spring):3–21.

Stinchcombe, Arthur L. (1959). "Bureaucratic and Craft Administration of Production: A Comparative Study," *Administrative Science Quarterly*, 4:168–87.

———— (1965). "Social Structure and Organizations," in *Handbook of Organizations*, 142–93, ed. James G. March. Chicago: Rand McNally.

———— (1968). *Constructing Social Theories*. Chicago: University of Chicago Press.

———— (1983). *Economic Sociology*. New York: Academic Press.

———— (1985). "Contracts as Hierarchical Documents," in *Organization Theory and Project Management*, by Arthur Stinchcombe and Carol Heimer. Bergen, Norway: Universitetsforlaget.

———— (1990). *Information and Organizations*. Berkeley: University of California Press.

———— (2001). *When Formality Works: Authority and Abstraction in Law and Organization*. Chicago: University of Chicago Press.

———— (2002). "New Sociological Microfoundations for Organizational Theory: A Postscript," in *Social Structure and Organizations Revisited: Research in the Sociology of Organizations*, vol. 19; 415–33, ed. Michael Lounsbury and Marc J. Ventresca. Amsterdam: JAI.

Stogdill, R. M., and A. E. Coons, eds. (1957). *Leader Behavior: Its Description and Measurement.* Research Monograph 88. Columbus: Bureau of Business Research, Ohio State University.

Stokes, Donald E. (1997). *Pasteur's Quadrant: Basic Science and Technological Innovation.* Washington DC: Brookings Institution Press.

Strang, David, and Michael W. Macy (2001). "In Search of Excellence: Fads, Success Stories, and Adaptive Emulation," *American Journal of Sociology,* 107:147–82.

Strang, David, and Sarah A. Soule (1998). "Diffusion in Organizations and Social Movements: From Hybrid Corn to Poison Pills," *Annual Review of Sociology,* 24:265–90.

Streeck, Wolfgang (1991). "On the Institutional Conditions of Diversified Quality Production," in *Beyond Keynesianism: The Socio-Economics of Production and Full Employment,* 21–61, ed. Egon Matzner and Wolfgand Steeck. Brookefield, VT: Edward Elgar.

Streeck, Wolfgang, and Philippe C. Schmitter, eds. (1985). *Private Interest Government: Beyond Market and State.* Beverly Hills, CA: Sage.

Stuart, Toby E. (1998). "Network Positions and Propensities to Collaborate: An Investigation of Strategic Alliance Formation in a High-Technology Industry," *Administrative Science Quarterly,* 43:668–98.

Stuart, Toby E., Ha Hoang, and Ralph C. Hybels (1999). "Interorganizational Endorsements and the Performance of Entrepreneurial Ventures," *Administrative Science Quarterly,* 44:315–49.

Sturgeon, Timothy J. (2002). "Modular Production Networks: A New American Model of Industrial Organization," *Industrial and Corporate Change,* 11:451–96.

Suchman, Edward A. (1967). *Evaluative Research.* New York: Russell Sage Foundation.

Suchman, Mark C. (1995a). "Localism and Globalism in Institutional Analysis: The Emergence of Contractual Norms in Venture Finance," in *The Institutional Construction of Organizations: International and Longitudinal Studies,* 39–63, ed. W. Richard Scott and Søren Christensen. Thousand Oaks, CA: Sage.

——— (1995b). "Managing Legitimacy: Strategic and Institutional Approaches," *Academy of Management Review,* 20:571–610.

——— (Forthcoming). "Constructed Ecologies: Reproduction and Structuration in Emerging Organizational Communities," in *How Institutions Change,* ed. Walter W. Powell and Daniel L. Jones. Chicago: University of Chicago Press.

Suchman, Mark C., and Mia L. Cahill (1996). "The Hired-Gun as Facilitator: The Case of Lawyers in Silicon Valley," *Law and Social Inquiry,* 21:837–74.

Susman, Gerald I., and Richard B. Chase (1986). "A Sociotechnical Analysis of the Integrated Factory," *Journal of Applied Behavioral Science,* 22:257–70.

Sutherland, Edwin H. (1949). *White-Collar Crime.* New York: Dryden Press.

Sutton, John R., and Frank Dobbin (1996). "The Two Faces of Governance: Responses to Legal Uncertainty in U.S. Firms, 1955 to 1985," *American Sociological Review,* 61:794–811.

Sutton, John, Frank Dobbin, John W. Meyer, and W. Richard Scott (1994). "Legalization of the Workplace," *American Journal of Sociology,* 99:944–71.

Swanson, Guy E. (1976). "The Tasks of Sociology," *Science,* 192:665–67.

Swedberg, Richard (1998). *Max Weber and the Idea of Economic Sociology.* Princeton: Princeton University Press.

Swinth, Robert L. (1974). *Organizational Systems for Management: Designing, Planning and Implementation.* Columbus, OH: Grid.

Tannenbaum, Arnold S. (1968). *Control in Organizations.* New York: McGraw-Hill.

Tannenbaum, Arnold S., Bogdan Kavcic, Menachem Rosner, Mino Vianello, and Georg Wieser (1974). *Hierarchy in Organizations.* San Francisco: Jossey-Bass.

Taylor, Donald W. (1965). "Decision Making and Problem Solving," in *Handbook of Organizations,* 48–86, ed. James G. March. Chicago: Rand McNally.

Taylor, Frederick W. (1911). *The Principles of Scientific Management.* New York: Harper.

——— (1947). *Scientific Management.* New York: Harper & Brothers.

Teece, David J. (1998). "Capturing Value from Knowledge Assets: The New Economy, Markets for Know-How, and Intangible Assets," *California Management Review,* 40:55–79.

Teece, David J., and G. Pisano (1994). "The Dynamic Capabilities of Firms: An Introduction," in *Industrial and Corporate Change,* 3:537–56.

Terreberry, Shirley (1968). "The Evolution of Organizational Environments," *Administrative Science Quarterly*, 12:590–613.

Thiebout, Charles M. (1956). "A Pure Theory of Local Expenditures," *Journal of Political Economy*, 64.

Thibaut, John W., and Harold H. Kelley (1959). *The Social Psychology of Groups*. New York: John Wiley.

Thietart, R. A., and B. Forgues (1995). "Chaos Theory and Organization," *Organization Science*, 6:19–31.

Thomas, Robert J. (1994). *What Machines Can't Do: Politics and Technology in the Industrial Enterprise*. Berkeley: University of California Press.

Thompson, E. P. (1967). "Time, Work Discipline and Industrial Capitalism," *Past and Present*, 38:56–97.

——— (1968). *The Making of the English Working Class*. Harmondsworth, UK: Penguin, Pelican Books.

Thompson, James D. (1967; 2003). *Organizations in Action: Social Science Bases of Administrative Theory*. New York: McGraw-Hill (1967); New Brunswick, NJ: Transaction Publishers (2003).

Thompson, James D., and Frederick L. Bates (1957). "Technology, Organization, and Administration," *Administrative Science Quarterly*, 2:325–42.

Thompson, James D., and Arthur Tuden (1959). "Strategies, Structures, and Processes of Organizational Decision," in *Comparative Studies in Administration*, 195–216, ed. James D. Thompson. Pittsburgh, PA: University of Pittsburgh Press.

Thompson, Kenneth (1980). "The Organizational Society," in *Control and Ideology in Organizations*, 3–23, ed. Graeme Salaman and Kenneth Thompson. Cambridge, MA: MIT Press.

Thompson, Victor A. (1961). *Modern Organization*. New York: Knopf.

Thornton, Patricia H. (1999). "The Sociology of Entrepreneurship," *Annual Review of Sociology*, 25:19–46.

Thornton, Patricia H., and William Ocasio (1999). "Institutional Logics and the Historical Contingency of Power in Organizations: Executive Succession in the Higher Education Publishing Industry, 1958–1990," *American Journal of Sociology*, 105:801–43.

Tilly, Chris, and Charles Tilly (1998). *Work Under Capitalism*. Boulder, CO: Westview Press.

Tolbert, Pamela S., and Lynne G. Zucker (1983). "Institutional Sources of Change in the Formal Structure of Organizations: The Diffusion of Civil Service Reform, 1880–1935," *Administrative Science Quarterly*, 28:22–39.

Tonn, Joan C. (2003). *Creating Democracy, Transforming Management*. New Haven: Yale University Press.

Trahair, R. C. S. (1984). *The Humanist Temper: The Life and Work of Elton Mayo*. New Brunswick, NJ: Transaction Books.

Trice, Harrison M., and Janice M. Beyer (1993). *The Cultures of Work Organizations*. Upper Saddle River, NJ: Prentice Hall.

Triesmann, J. S., A. R. Dennis, G. B. Northcraft, and J. W. Nieme, Jr. (2000). "Serving Multiple Constituencies in Business Schools: MBA Program versus Research Performance," *Academy of Management Journal*, 43:1130.

Trist, Eric L. (1981). "The Evolution of Sociotechnical Systems as a Conceptual Framework and as an Action Research Program." in *Perspectives on Organization Design and Behavior*, 19–75, ed. Andrew H. Van de Ven and William F. Joyce. New York: John Wiley, Wiley-Interscience.

Trist, Eric L., and K. W. Bamforth (1951). "Social and Psychological Consequences of the Longwall Method of Coal-Getting," *Human Relations*, 4:3–28.

Tsui, Anne S., and Chung-Ming Lau, eds. (2002). *The Management of Enterprises in the People's Republic of China*. Boston: Kluwer Academic Publishers.

Tsurumi, Y. (1977). *Multinational Management*. Cambridge, MA: Ballinger.

Tuma, Nancy B., and Michael T. Hannan (1984). *Social Dynamics: Models and Methods*. Orlando, FL: Academic.

Turner, Arthur N., and Paul R. Lawrence (1965). *Industrial Jobs and the Worker*. Boston: Harvard Graduate School of Business Administration.

Tushman, Michael L., and Philip Anderson (1986). "Technological Discontinuities and Organizational Environments," *Administrative Science Quarterly*, 31:439–65.

Tyler, Tom R. (1993). "The Social Psychology of Authority," in *Social Psychology in Organizations: Advances in Theory and Research*, 141–60, ed. J. Keith Murnighan. Upper Saddle River, NJ: Prentice Hall

U.S. Bureau of Labor Statistics (2004). "Employee Tenure in 2004" September. http://www.bls.gov/news.release/pdf/tenure.pdf.

U.S. Bureau of Labor Statistics (2005). www.bis.gov/CPS.

U.S. Office of the Federal Register, General Service Administration (2006). *The United States Government Manual.* Washington DC: Government Printing Office.

Udy, Stanley H., Jr. (1959). *Organization of Work.* New Haven: Human Relations Area Files Press.

——— (1962). "Administrative Rationality, Social Setting, and Organizational Development," *American Journal of Sociology*, 68:299–308.

——— (1970). *Work in Traditional and Modern Society.* Upper Saddle River, NJ: Prentice Hall.

Useem, Michael (1984). *The Inner Circle.* New York: Oxford University Press.

——— (1993). *Executive Defense: Shareholder Power and Corporate Reorganization.* Cambridge, MA: Harvard University Press.

——— (1996). *Investor Capitalism: How Money Managers Are Changing the Face of Corporate America.* New York: Basic Books.

Uzzi, Brian (1996). "The Sources and Consequences of Embeddedness for the Economic Performance of Organizations: The Network Effect," *American Sociological Review*, 61:674–98.

——— (1997). "Social Structure and Competition in Interfirm Networks: The Paradox of Embeddedness," *Administrative Science Quarterly*, 42:35–67.

Uzzi, Brian, and Ryon Lancaster (2004). "Embeddedness and Price Formation in the Corporate Law Market," *American Sociological Review*, 69:319–44.

Van de Ven, Andrew H., A. L. Delbecq, and R. Koenig, Jr. (1976). "Determinants of Coordination Modes within Organizations, *American Sociological Review*, 41: 322–38.

Van de Ven, Andrew H., and Diane L. Ferry (1980). *Measuring and Assessing Organizations.* New York: John Wiley, Wiley-Interscience.

Van de Ven, Andrew H., Douglas E. Polley, Raghu Garud, and Sankaran Venkataraman (1999). *The Innovation Journey.* New York: Oxford University Press.

Van Mannen, John (1973). "Observations on the Making of Policemen," *Human Organization*, 32:407–17.

——— (1991). "The Smile Factory: Work at Disneyland," in *Reframing Organizational Culture*, ed. Peter J. Frost, Larry Moore, Meryl Reis Louis, Craig C. Lundberg, and Joanne Martin. Thousand Oaks, CA: Sage.

Vaughan, Diane (1983). *Controlling Unlawful Organizational Behavior: Social Structure and Corporate Misconduct.* Chicago: University of Chicago Press.

——— (1996). *The Challenger Launch Decision: Risky Technology, Culture and Deviance at NASA.* Chicago: University of Chicago Press.

Vaupel, James W., and Joan P. Curhan (1969). *The Making of Multinational Enterprise.* Cambridge, MA: Harvard University Press.

Veblen, Thorstein (1904). *The Theory of Business Enterprise.* New York: Scribner's.

Vedder, James N. (1992). "How Much Can We Learn from Success?" *Academy of Management Executive*, 6:56–65.

Ventresca, Marc J., and John W. Mohr (2002). "Archival Research Methods," in *The Blackwell Companion to Organizations*, 805–28, ed. Joel A. C. Baum. Oxford: Blackwell Business.

Verba, Sidney (1961). *Small Groups and Political Behavior.* Princeton: Princeton University Press.

Vogel, David (1978). "Why Businessmen Distrust their State: The Political Consciousness of American Corporate Executives," *British Journal of Political Science*, 8:45–78.

Vogus, Timothy J., and Gerald F. Davis (2005). "Elite Mobilizations for Antitakeover Legislation," in *Social Movements and Organization Theory*, 96–121, ed. Gerald F. Davis, Doug McAdam, W. Richard Scott, and Mayer N. Zald. New York: Cambridge University Press.

Wade, James B., Anand Swaminathan, and Michael Scott Saxon (1998). "Normative and Resource Flow Consequences of Local Regulations in the American Brewing Industry, 1845–1918," *Administrative Science Quarterly*, 43:905–35.

Walder, Andrew G. (1986). *Communist Neo-Traditionalism: Work and Authority in Chinese Industry*. Berkeley: University of California Press.

Walker, Charles R., and Robert H. Guest (1952). *The Man on the Assembly Line*. Cambridge, MA: Harvard University Press.

Walker, Gordon, and David Weber (1984). "A Transaction Cost Approach to Make-or-Buy Decisions," *Administrative Science Quarterly*, 29:373–91.

Walker, Gordon, and Laura Poppo (1991). "Profit Centers, Single-Source Suppliers, and Transaction Costs," *Administrative Science Quarterly*, 36:66–87.

Wallace, Walter L. (1975). "Structure and Action in the Theories of Coleman and Parsons," in *Approaches to the Study of Social Structure*, 121–34, ed. Peter M. Blau. New York: Free Press.

Walsh, James P. (2005). "Taking Stock of Stakeholder Management," *Academy of Management Review*, 30:426–52.

Ward, John William (1964). "The Ideal of Individualism and the Reality of Organization," in *The Business Establishment*, 37–76, ed. Earl F. Cheit. New York: John Wiley.

Waring, Stephen P. (1991). *Taylorism Transformed: Scientific Management Theory Since 1945*. Chapel Hill: University of North Carolina Press.

Warner, W. Lloyd, and J. O. Low (1947). *The Social System of the Modern Factory*. New Haven: Yale University Press.

Warren, Roland L. (1963). *The Community in America*. Chicago: Rand McNally (rev. ed., 1972).

——— (1967). "The Interorganizational Field as a Focus for Investigation," *Administrative Science Quarterly*, 12:396–419.

——— (1972). *The Community in America* (2nd ed.). Chicago: Rand McNally.

Wasserman, Stanley, and Katherine Faust (1994). *Social Network Analysis: Methods and Applications*. New York: Cambridge University Press.

Watts, Duncan J. (1999). "Networks, Dynamics, and the Small-World Phenomenon," *American Journal of Sociology*, 105:493–507.

——— (2004). "The 'New' Science of Networks," *Annual Review of Sociology*, 30:243–70.

Watts, Duncan J., and Stephen Strogatz (1998). "Collective Dynamics of 'Small World' Networks," *Science*, 393:440–42.

Weber, Klaus (2000). "The Influence of Venture Capital Funding on the Organization of IPO Firms: Isomorphism or Diversity?" Ann Arbor: University of Michigan Business School.

Weber, Marianne (1975 trans.). *Max Weber: A Biography*, trans. and ed. Harry Zohn. New York: John Wiley (first published in 1926).

Weber, Max (1946 trans.). *From Max Weber: Essays in Sociology*, ed. Hans H. Gerth and C. Wright Mills. New York: Oxford University Press (first published in 1906–1924).

——— (1947 trans.). *The Theory of Social and Economic Organization*, ed. A. H. Henderson and Talcott Parsons, Glencoe, IL: Free Press (first published in 1924).

——— (1958 trans.). *The Protestant Ethic and the Spirit of Capitalism*, trans. Talcott Parsons. New York: Scribner's (first published in 1904–1905).

——— (1968 trans.). *Economy and Society: An Interpretive Sociology*, 2 vols., ed. Guenther Roth and Claus Wittich. New York: Bedminister Press, (first published in 1924).

Weick, Karl E. (1969). *The Social Psychology of Organizing*. Reading, MA: Addison-Wesley.

——— (1974). "Middle Range Theories of Social Systems," *Behavioral Science*, 19:357–67.

——— (1976). "Educational Organizations as Loosely Coupled Systems," *Administrative Science Quarterly*, 21:1–19.

——— (1979). *The Social Psychology of Organizing* (2nd ed.). Reading, MA: Addison-Wesley.

——— (1987). "Organizational Culture as a Source of High Reliability," *California Management Review*, 29(Winter):116–36.

——— (1990). "Technology as Equivoque: Sensemaking in New Technologies," in *Technology and Organizations*, 1–44, ed. Paul S. Goodman and Lee S. Sproull. San Francisco: Jossey-Bass.

——— (1995). *Sensemaking in Organizations.* Thousand Oaks, CA: Sage.

Weick, Karl E., Kathleen M. Sutcliffe, and David Obstfeld (1999). "Organizing for High Reliability: Processes of Collective Mindfulness," in *Research in Organization Behavior,* 81–124, ed. Robert I. Sutton and Barry M. Staw. Stamford, CT: JAI Press.

Westhues, Kenneth (1976). "Class and Organization as Paradigms in Social Science," *American Sociologist,* 11:38–49.

Westney, D. Eleanor (1987). *Imitation and Innovation: The Transfer of Western Organizational Patterns to Meiji Japan.* Cambridge, MA: Harvard University Press.

——— (1993). "Institutional Theory and the Multinational Corporation," in *Organization Theory and the Multinational Corporation,*" 53–76, ed. Sumantra Ghoshal and D. Eleanor Westney. New York: St. Martin's Press.

Westphal, James D., and Edward J. Zajac (1994). "Substance and Symbolism in CEO's Long-Term Incentive Plans," *Administrative Science Quarterly,* 39:367–90.

——— (2001). "Decoupling Policy from Practice: The Case of Stock Repurchase Programs," *Administrative Science Quarterly,* 46:202–28.

Whetten, David A., and Paul C. Godfrey, eds. (1998). *Identity in Organizations: Building Theory Through Conversations.* Thousand Oaks, CA: Sage.

White, Harrison C. (1981). "Where Do Markets Come From?" *American Journal of Sociology,* 87:517–47.

White, Lawrence J. (2001). "What's Been Happening to Aggregate Concentration in the United States? (And Should We Care?)," New York: Department of Economics, New York University.

White, Ralph, and Ronald Lippitt (1953). "Leader Behavior and Member Reaction in Three 'Social Climates,'" in *Group Dynamics,* 586–611, ed. Dorwin Cartwright and Alvin Zander. Evanston, IL: Row, Peterson.

Whitehead, Alfred North (1925). *Science and the Modern World.* New York: Macmillan.

Whitley, Richard (1992). "The Social Construction of Organizations and Markets: The Comparative Analysis of Business Recipes," in *Rethinking Organizations: New Directions in Organization Theory and Analysis,* 120–43, ed., Michael Reed and Michael Hughes. Newbury Park, CA: Sage.

——— (1999). *Divergent Capitalisms: The Social Structuring and Change of Business Systems.* Oxford: Oxford University Press.

Whyte, William Foote (1948). *Human Relations in the Restaurant Industry.* New York: McGraw-Hill.

——— (1951). "Small Groups and Large Organizations," in *Social Psychology at the Crossroads,* 297–312, ed. John H. Rohrer and Muzafer Sherif. New York: Harper.

——— (1959). *Man and Organization.* Homewood, IL: Richard D. Irwin.

———, ed. (1946). *Industry and Society.* New York: McGraw-Hill.

Whyte, William H., Jr. (1956). *The Organization Man.* New York: Simon and Schuster.

Wieland, George F., and Robert A. Ullrich (1976). *Organizations: Behavior, Design, and Change.* Homewood, IL: Richard D. Irwin.

Wiener, Norbert (1954). *The Human Use of Human Beings: Cybernetics and Society.* Garden City, NY: Doubleday Anchor.

——— (1956). *I Am a Mathematician.* New York: Doubleday.

Wildavsky, Aaron B. (1979). *Speaking Truth to Power: The Art and Craft of Policy Analysis.* Boston: Little, Brown.

——— (1988). *The New Politics of the Budgetary Process.* Glenview, IL: Scott, Foresman.

Williamson, Oliver E. (1975). *Markets and Hierarchies: Analysis and Antitrust Implications.* New York: Free Press.

——— (1981). "The Economics of Organization: The Transaction Cost Approach," *American Journal of Sociology,* 87:548–77.

——— (1985). *The Economic Institutions of Capitalism.* New York: Free Press.

———, ed. (1990). *Organization Theory: From Chester Barnard to the Present and Beyond.* New York: Oxford University Press.

——— (1991). "Comparative Economic Organization: The Analysis of Discrete Structural Alternatives," *Administrative Science Quarterly,* 36:269–96.

———— (1994). "Transaction Cost Economics and Organization Theory," in *The Handbook of Economic Sociology*, 77–107, ed. Neil J. Smelser and Richard Swedberg. Princeton: Princeton University Press and Russell Sage Foundation.

Williamson, Oliver E., and William G. Ouchi (1981). "The Markets and Hierarchies and Visible Hand Perspectives," in *Perspectives on Organization Design and Behavior*, 347–70, ed. Andrew H. Van de Ven and William E. Joyce. New York: John Wiley.

Wilson, Edward O. (1998). *Consilience: The Unity of Knowledge*. New York: Knopf.

Wilson, James Q., ed. (1980). *The Politics of Regulation*. New York: Basic Books.

Wilson, James Q. (1989). *Bureaucracy: What Government Agencies Do and Why They Do It*. New York: Basic Books.

Winter, Sidney G. (1990). "Organizing for Continuous Improvement: Evolutionary Theory Meets the Quality Revolution," in *Evolutionary Dynamics of Organizations*, 90–108, ed., Joel A. C. Baum and Jitendra V. Singh. New York: Oxford University Press.

Wolf, Martin (2004). *Why Globalization Works*. New Haven: Yale University Press.

Wolin, Sheldon S. (1960). *Politics and Vision: Continuity and Innovation in Western Political Thought*. Boston: Little, Brown.

Womack, James P., Daniel T. Jones, and Daniel Roos (1990). *The Machine That Changed the World: The Story of Lean Production*. New York: Macmillan.

———— (1991). *The Machine That Changed the World: The Story of Lean Production*. New York: Harper Perennial.

Woodward, Joan (1958). *Management and Technology*. London: H.M.S.O.

———— (1965). *Industrial Organization: Theory and Practice*. New York: Oxford University Press.

Wooten, Melissa (2006). "The Development of the Field of Black Higher Education," Ross School of Business. Ann Arbor: University of Michigan.

Wu, Xun (2005). "Corporate Governance and Corruption: A Cross-Country Analysis," *Governance: An International Journal of Policy, Administration, and Institutions*, 18(2): 151–70.

Yin, Y.-M. (2004). *Between Politics and Markets: Firms, Competition, and Institutional Change in Post-Mao China*. Cambridge: Cambridge University Press.

Yuchtman, Ephraim, and Stanley E. Seashore (1967). "A System Resource Approach to Organizational Effectiveness," *American Sociological Review*, 32:891–903.

Zajac, Edward J. (1988). "Interlocking Directorates as an Interorganizational Strategy: A Test of Critical Assumptions," *Academy of Management Journal*, 31:428–38.

Zajac, Edward J., and James D. Westphal (1995). "Accounting for the Explanations of CEO Compensation: Substance and Symbolism," *Administrative Science Quarterly*, 40:283–308.

———— (1996). "Director Reputation, CEO-Board Power, and the Dynamics of Board Interlocks," *Administrative Science Quarterly*, 41:507–29.

Zald, Mayer N. (1970). "Political Economy: A Framework for Comparative Analysis," in *Power in Organizations*, 221–61, ed. Mayer N. Zald. Nashville, TN: Vanderbilt University Press.

————, ed., (1970). *Power and Organizations*. Nashville, TN: Vanderbilt University Press

Zald, Mayer N., and Patricia Denton (1963). "From Evangelism to General Service: The Transformation of the YMCA," *Administrative Science Quarterly*, 8:214–34.

Zald, Mayer N., and John D. McCarthy, eds. (1987). *Social Movements in an Organizational Society*. New Brunswick, NJ: Transaction Books.

Zammuto, Raymond F. (1982). *Assessing Organizational Effectiveness*. Albany: State University of New York Press.

Zbaracki, Mark J. (1998). "The Rhetoric and Reality of Total Quality Management," *Administrative Science Quarterly*, 43:602–36.

Zelditch, Morris, Jr., and Henry A. Walker (1984). "Legitimacy and the Stability of Authority," in *Advances in Group Processes: Theory and Research*, vol. 1, 1–25, ed. Edward J. Lawler. Greenwich, CT: JAI Press.

Zey, Mary (1993). *Banking on Fraud: Drexel, Junk Bonds, and Buyouts*. New York: Aldine de Gruyter.

———— (1998). "Embeddedness of Interorganizational Corporate Crime in the 1980s: Securities Fraud of Banks and Investment Banks," in *Deviance in and of Organizations*, 111–59, ed. Peter A. Bamberger and William J. Sonnenstuhl. Stamford, CT: JAI Press.

Zey-Ferrell, Mary, and Michael Aiken, eds. (1981). *Complex Organizations: Critical Perspectives.* Glenview, IL: Scott, Foresman.

Zhou, Xueguang, Wei Zhao, Qiang Li, and He Cai (2003). "Embeddedness and Contractual Relationships in China's Transitional Economy," *American Sociological Review*, 68:75–102.

Zimmerman, Don H. (1970). "The Practicalities of Rule Use," in *Understanding Everyday Life*, ed. J. D. Douglas. Chicago: Aldine.

Zorn, Dirk M. (2004). "Here a Chief, There a Chief: The Rise of the CFO in the American Firm," *American Sociological Review*, 69:345–64.

Zuboff, Shoshana (1985). "Technologies that Informate: Implications for Human Resource Management in the Computerized Industrial Workplace," in *Human Resources Management Trends and Challenges*, 103–39, ed. Richard E. Walton and Paul R. Lawrence. Boston: Harvard Business School Press.

——— (1988). *In the Age of the Smart Machine.* New York: Basic Books.

Zucker, Lynne G. (1977). "The Role of Institutionalization in Cultural Persistence," *American Sociological Review*, 42:726–43.

——— (1983). "Organizations as Institutions," in *Research in the Sociology of Organizations*, vol. 2, 1–47, ed. Samuel B. Bacharach. Greenwich, CT: JAI Press.

———, ed. (1988). *Institutional Patterns and Organizations: Culture and Environment.* Cambridge, MA: Ballinger.

——— (1989). "Combining Institutional Theory and Population Ecology: No Legitimacy, No History," *American Sociological Review*, 54:542–45.

Zuckerman, Ezra W. (1999). "The Categorical Imperative: Securities Analysts and the Illegitimacy Discount," *American Journal of Sociology*, 104:1398–438.

——— (2000). "Focusing the Corporate Product: Securities Analysts and De-Diversification," *Administrative Science Quarterly*, 45:591–619.

Name Index

Subject Index